H . L . MENCKEN

H. L. MENCKEN

PREJUDICES:
FOURTH, FIFTH, AND SIXTH SERIES

THE LIBRARY OF AMERICA

Library of Congress Control Number: 2010924447
ISBN 978-1-59853-075-9

———

First Printing
The Library of America—207

MARION ELIZABETH RODGERS
WROTE THE CHRONOLOGY AND NOTES FOR THIS VOLUME

Contents

PREJUDICES
FOURTH SERIES

I.
The American Tradition

Ever since Dr. William Crary Brownell, *de l'Académie Américaine*, published his little volume, "Standards," in 1917, a vast hullabaloo has been going on among the native, white, Protestant *Gelehrte* of the Republic, particularly in the great open spaces of the South and Middle West, in favor of what they call the American tradition in letters. Perhaps I libel Brownell, a worthy if somewhat gummy man, by hinting that he started this whooping; it may be that its actual generator was George Creel, the Rev. Dr. Newell Dwight Hillis, the Hon. James M. Beck, the Hon. A. Mitchell Palmer or some other such master-mind of that patriotic and intelligent era. Whatever its parentage, it was at least born in the holiest of wedlock, and to the applause of all right-thinking men; and if I now presume to pull its ear I surely hope that no one will suspect that I thereby question its legitimacy. It is, in fact, absolutely and irrefragably American from snout to *os calcis*, not only in outward seeming and demeanor, but also in inner essence, and anyone who flouts it also flouts everything that is most sacred in the spirit of Americanism. To that business I herewith address myself briefly.

What, then, is the spirit of Americanism? I precipitate it conveniently into the doctrine that the way to ascertain the truth about anything, whether in the realms of exact knowledge, in the purple zone of the fine arts or in the empyrean reaches of metaphysics, is to take a vote upon it, and that the way to propagate that truth, once it has been ascertained and proclaimed by lawful authority, is with a club. This doctrine, it seems to me, explains almost everything that is indubitably American, and particularly everything American that is most puzzling to men of older and less inspired cultures, from American politics to American learning, and from the lush and unprecedented American code of morals to the amazing and almost fabulous American code of honor. At one end it explains the

3

archetypical buffooneries of the Ku Klux Klan, the American Legion, the Anti-Saloon League, the Department of Justice and all other such great engines of cultural propaganda, and at the other end it explains the amusing theory that the limits of the nation's æsthetic adventures are to be fixed by a vague and self-appointed camorra of rustic Ph.D.'s, and that any artist, indigenous or imported, who dares to pass them is not only a sinner against the beautiful but also a traitor to the flag, and that he ought, shall and must be throttled by the secular arm. Patriotism thus gathers in æsthetics and gives it suck, as it has already given suck to ethics. There are artists who are worthy of the boon of freedom, and there are artists who are criminal and must be put down, as anarchists and polygamists are put down. The fancies of the poet in his velvet coat, the vast soarings and grapplings of the metaphysician in his damp cell, the writhings of the logician chained to his rock, become either right or wrong, and whatever is right in them is American and whatever is wrong is not American.

How far this last notion goes under the Constitution is best shown, not in the relatively *pianissimo* pronunciamentoes of such suave and cautious dons as Brownell, who are themselves often sadly polluted by foreign ideas, despite their heroic struggle to remember Valley Forge and San Juan Hill, but in the far more frank and passionate bulls of their followers in the seminaries of the cow States, where every male of *Homo sapiens* has copious *vibrissæ* on his chest and Nordic blue eyes in his head, and is a red-blooded, go-getting, up-and-coming he-man. I introduce at once a perfect specimen, Doughty of Texas —a savant but little known in the diabetic East, but for long a favorite expert in comparative morals in the university at Austin—not a professor, alas, for he lacks the Ph.D., but *amicus curiæ* to the other professors, as befits his trade of jurisconsult, and a frequent author of critical papers. Doughty has passion but he also has diligence: a combination not too common. Unlike the lean and slippered Beers, of Yale, who once boasted that he had read none of the books he was denouncing, Doughty is at pains to look into even the most subversive, as a dutiful Censor Librorum looks into even "Science and Health" and the works of Dr. Marie C. Stopes. Some time ago, determined to get at and expose the worst, he plowed magnificently through a whole library—through all the new poetry from Carl Sandburg to "The Spoon River Anthology," and all the new novels from Dreiser to Waldo Frank, and all the vast mass of immoral criticism accompanying them, from that in the *Dial* and the *Nation* to that in the *Little Review*, *S4N* and the Chicago *Literary Times*. "For many months now," he reported when he emerged at last, "there has passed before me the whole ghastly array. . . . I have read the 'books'; the 'fiction' and the 'verse'; the 'drama,' the 'articles' and 'essays'; the 'sketches' and the 'criticisms,' and whatever else is squeaked and gibbered by these unburied and not-to-be-handled dead. . . . It is this unnamable by-product of congenital deficiency, perverted dissipation and adulterated narcotics . . . which I refer to as 'modern [American] literature.'"

And what is the Texas Taine's verdict upon this modern American literature? The verdict, in brief, of all other right-thinking, forward-looking he-men, North, East, South, West —the verdict of every American who truly loves the flag, and knows congenitally what is right and what is wrong. He not only finds that it is, in itself, nothing but "swept-up rottenness and garbage—the dilute sewage of the sordid mental slums of New York and Chicago"; he also finds that the ladies and gentlemen who compose it are no more than "a horde of chancre-laden rats," that they constitute a "devil's crew of perverted drug-addicts," that they are engaged unanimously upon a "flabby and feeble assault . . . upon that ancient decency that for unnumbered generations of the white Northern races of mankind, at least, has grown and strengthened as a seed cast upon kindly soil," and, finally, that "no one of the 'writers' of this unhappy array was in the service of the United States in the Great War"—in brief, that the whole movement is no more than a foul conspiracy to tear down the flag, uproot the Republic and exterminate the Nordic Blond, and that, in consequence, it is the duty of every American who is a member "of a white Nordic race, save the Teutonic," to come sliding down the pole, grab the tarpot, and go galloping to the alarm. So concluding and stating in rich Texan phrases, the Doughty proceeds to rend specifically a typical book by one of these immigrant foes to "the heritage of American and English men." . . . The one he chooses is "Jurgen," by James Branch Cabell, of Virginia!

2

This long-horned policeman of letters, I admit, is more exuberant than most. There are no soothing elms on the campus at Austin; instead there is only the cindered *plaza de toros* of the Ku Klux Klan. Patriotism, down there, runs wilder than elsewhere. Men have large hands and loud voices. The sight of the flag makes their blood leap and boil; when it is affronted they cannot control themselves. Nevertheless, the doctrine thus stated in harsh terms by the dreadful Doughty, is, in its essence, precisely the doctrine of his more urbane colleagues—of Brownell *de l'Académie Américaine*, of Brander Matthews *de l'Académie Américaine*, of Sherman *de l'Académie Américaine*, of Erskine *de l'Institut National*, of Boynton, of old Beers, of all the rest. It is a doctrine, as I have said, that is thoroughly American—as American, indeed, as Prohibition, correspondence schools, the Knights of Pythias or chewing-gum. But by the same token it is a doctrine that has no more fundamental sense or dignity than the politics of a Coolidge or the theology of a Billy Sunday. It is, to come to the bald fact at once, mere drivel—an endless series of false assumptions and *nonsequiturs*—bad logic piled recklessly upon unsound facts. It is the product of men who, drilled beyond their capacity for taking in ideas and harrowed from infancy by harsh and unyielding concepts of duty, have borrowed the patriotic philosophy of surburban pastors and country schoolmarms, and now seek to apply it to the consideration of phenomena that are essentially beyond their comprehension, as honor is beyond the comprehension of a politician. It is rural Fundamentalism in the black gown and disarming whiskers of *Wissenschaft*; its inevitable fruit is what Ernest Boyd has aptly called Ku Klux Kriticism.

The simple truth, of course, is that the standards and traditions these sublimated Prohibition enforcement officers argue for so eloquently have no actual existence in the first-line literature of the American people—that what they demand is not a

lofty fidelity to a genuine ideal, but only an artificial and absurd subservience to notions that were regarded with contempt by every American of the civilized minority even when
they prevailed. In other words, what they argue for is not a
tradition that would take in Poe, Hawthorne, Emerson, Whitman and Mark Twain, but a tradition that would pass over all
these men to embrace Cooper, Bryant, Donald G. Mitchell,
N. P. Willis, J. G. Holland, Charles Dudley Warner, Mrs. Sigourney and the Sweet Singer of Michigan. Even Longfellow, I
daresay, must be left out, for didn't he drink of green and terrible waters in Paris as a youth and didn't Poe accuse him of
stealing from the Spanish and the German? Certainly even
Longfellow, to go back to Doughty's interdict, "simmered in
the devil's cauldron of central Europe" and was "spewed out
of Italy and France." Could Bryant himself qualify? Didn't he
trifle with strange tongues and admire enemy aliens? And what
of Lowell? His Dante studies surely had a sinister smack; one
can't imagine a Texas Grand Goblin approving them. Bayard
Taylor I refrain from mentioning at all. His translation of
"Faust" came to a just judgment at last when it was hurled
from the shelves of every American university patronized by
the issue of 100 per cent. Americans. Its incineration on a hundred far-flung campuses, indeed, was the second great patriotic event of the *annus mirabilis* which saw the launching of
Brownell's "Standards" and the entrance of the Ku Klux Klan
into literary criticism.

How little the patriot-pedagogues know of the verist elements of American literary history was shown very amusingly
some time ago when one of them, a specialist in the Emerson
tradition, got himself into a lather denouncing some Greenwich Village Brandes for arguing that beauty was independent
of morals and its own sufficient justification—only to be confronted by the disconcerting fact that Emerson himself had argued the same thing. Can it be that even pedagogues are
unaware that Emerson came to fame by advocating a general
deliverance from the stupid and flabby tradition his name is
now evoked to support, that his whole system of ideas was an
unqualified protest against hampering traditions of every sort,
that if he were alive today he would not be with the professors
but unalterably against them? And Emerson was surely not

alone. Go through the list of genuinely first-rate men: Poe, Hawthorne, Whitman, Mark Twain. One and all they stood outside the so-called tradition of their time; one and all, they remained outside the tradition that pedants try so vainly to impose upon a literature in active being today. Poe's poems and tales not only seemed strange to the respectable dolts of his time; they seemed downright horrible. His criticism, which tells us even more about him, was still worse: it impinged upon such dull fellows as Griswold exactly as "Jennie Gerhardt" impinged upon the appalled tutors in the alfalfa colleges. And what of Hawthorne? Hawthorne's onslaught upon the Puritan ethic was the most formidable and effective ever delivered, save only Emerson's. And Whitman? Whitman so staggered the professors that it is only within the last few years that they have begun to teach him at all; those who flourished in 1870 avoided all mention of him as carefully as their successors of today avoid mention of Dreiser or Cabell. And Mark Twain? I put a professor on the stand, to wit, my Christian friend, Phelps of Yale. Go to Phelps' "Essays on Modern Novelists," and you will find a long and humorous account of the efforts of unintelligent pedagogues to read Mark out of the national letters altogether—and go to Van Wyck Brooks' "The Ordeal of Mark Twain" and you will discover what great damage that imbecility did to the man himself. Phelps printed his book in 1910. It was the first book by a doctor of beautiful letters to admit categorically that Mark was an artist at all! All the other professors, even in 1910, were still teaching that Washington Irving was a great humorist and Mark a mere clown, just as they are teaching now that the criticism of Howells and Lowell was superior to the criticism of Huneker, and that Henry van Dyke is a great artist and Cabell a bad one.

Historically, there is thus nothing but folly and ignorance in all the current prattle about a restoration of the ancient American tradition. The ancient American tradition, in so far as it was vital and productive and civilized, was obviously a tradition of individualism and revolt, not of herd-morality and conformity. If one argues otherwise, one must inevitably argue that the great men of the Golden Age were not Emerson, Hawthorne, Poe and Whitman, but Cooper, Irving, Longfellow and Whittier. This nonsense, no doubt, is actually ar-

gued in the prairie seminaries; it even has its prophets, perhaps, in backwaters of the East; certainly one finds little in
controversion of it in the prevailing text-books. But it remains
nonsense all the same. The fact that it has been accepted for
years explains the three great disgraces of American letters: the
long neglect of Whitman, Melville and Mark Twain. And the
fact that it is now challenged actively—that practically all
young Americans of any appreciable intelligence now rebel
against it—that the most significant sign of the times, in many
ways, is the open revolt of the new generation against the
teaching of their elders—this fact explains the new vigor that
has got into American literature, and its consequent running
amok. That running amok, to be sure, is leading to excesses—
but so did the running amok of Whitman lead to excesses; so
did the timorous running amok of Mark Twain. In order to
get the rest of "Leaves of Grass" we must somehow manage to
survive "A Woman Waits for Me"; in order to get "Huckleberry Finn" we must swallow the buffooneries of "The Inno-
cents Abroad." In brief, we must be willing to pay a price for
freedom, for no price that is ever asked for it is half the cost of
doing without it.

3

It so happens that many of the men and women who have
sought to exercise this freedom in our time have been of stocks
other than the so-called Anglo-Saxon, either wholly or in part
—that they have represented the newer stocks which threaten,
not only in the fine arts but in practically all departments of
human activity, including even business, to oust the Anglo-
Saxon from his old hegemony. The fact, in a day of increasing
racial consciousness, has greatly colored the whole controversy
and made it extraordinarily bitter. The doctrine gradually set
up between 1914 and 1917, and given the full force of law in the
latter year, that a citizen of German blood, or suspected of
German blood, stood on a plane inferior to that occupied by a
citizen of British blood, and had a less valid claim to the equal
protection of the Constitution and the laws—this doctrine was
extended, in the post-war years of terror, to all Americans not
specifically Anglo-Saxon. How seriously it has been taken in

the more remote parts of the Republic is well displayed by the strophes that I have quoted from good Doughty—a gentleman who seems quite as content to take his anthropology from Madison Grant and Gertrude Atherton as he is to take his manners from the cattle-herders of his native steppes. Even more ludicrous attempts to set up Ku Klux criteria in letters might be dredged from the writings of more urbane, and, in theory, more intelligent and civilized critics—for example, Brander Matthews. The rancorous animosity that has pursued such men as Dreiser is certainly not wholly æsthetic, or even moral; it is, to a very large extent, racial. The man is obviously not an Anglo-Saxon; *ergo*, there is something sinister about him, and he must be put down. The more solid becomes his position as a man of letters, the more offensive he becomes to the colonial mind. His crime, indeed, is that he has made headway—that a new American tradition, differing radically from the old one that pedagogues preach, tends to grow up around him—that in European eyes, and even in English eyes, he becomes more typical of America than any of the literary Knights of Pythias who are pitted against him. It thus becomes a matter of self-preservation to dispose of him, and when it turns out to be difficult to do so by logical means then there is a quick and easy recourse to evangelistic means.

The effects of this holy war, alas, have differed greatly from those intended. Far from alarming and stampeding the non-Anglo-Saxons upon whom it has been waged, it has actually forced them, despite their differences, into a certain common action, and so made them far more formidable than they were when it began. And far from establishing any superiority in the Anglo-Saxon, it has only spread the suspicion that, for all his pretensions, he must be a very inferior fellow at bottom, else he would not be so eager to call in the mob to help him in a purely literary feud. As one who has stood on the battlements for years, and smelt the powder of every salvo, I can only report that I have come to believe in this inferiority thoroughly, and that it seems to me to be most obvious in those who most vociferously uphold the so-called American tradition. They are, in the main, extremely stupid men, and their onslaughts are seldom supported by any formidable weight of metal. What they ask the rest of us to do, in brief, is simply to come down voluntarily and irrationally to their own cultural level—the level of a class that easily dominated the country when it was a series of frontier settlements, but that has gradually lost leadership as civilization has crept in. The rest of us naturally refuse, and they thereupon try to make acquiescence a patriotic matter, and to alarm the refractory with all sorts of fantastic penalties. But it must be obvious that they fail far more often than they succeed—and their failure is a melancholy proof of their intrinsic inferiority. The current of thought in the United States, at least among the relatively civilized minority, is not actually toward the abject colonialism that they advocate; it is against that colonialism. We are further from sweetness and light today than we ever were before, and we are further from cultural slavery to the harassed and care-worn Motherland. With overwhelming numbers on their side, and every form of external authority, and all the prevailing shibboleths, the spokesmen of Anglo-Saxon domination come to grief every time they tackle the minority, or even any minority within the minority, and at no time do they come to grief more dramatically than when they prepare for battle, in the traditional Anglo-Saxon manner, by first trying to tie their opponents' hands.

When I speak of Anglo-Saxons, of course, I speak inexactly and in the common phrase. Even within the bounds of that phrase the American of the prevailing stock is Anglo-Saxon only partially, for there is probably just as much Celtic blood in his veins as Germanic, and his norm is to be found, not South of the Tyne and west of the Severn, but on the bleak Scotch hills. Among the first English colonists there were unquestionably many men of purely Teutonic stock from the East and South of England, and their influence is yet visible in many characteristic American folkways, in certain traditional American ideas—some of them now surviving only in national hyprocrisies—, and, above all, in the fundamental peculiarities of the American dialect of English. But their Teutonic blood was early diluted by Celtic strains from Scotland, from the North of Ireland and from the West of England, and today those Americans who are regarded as being most thoroughly Anglo-Saxons—for example, the mountaineers of the Appalachian slopes from Vermont to Georgia—are obviously far more

Celtic than Teutonic, not only physically but also mentally. They are leaner and taller than the true English, and far more given to moral obsessions and religious fanaticism. A Methodist revival is not an English phenomenon; it is Scotch. So, fundamentally, is Prohibition. So is the American tendency, marked by every foreign student of our history, to turn all political combats into moral crusades. The English themselves, of course, have been greatly polluted by Scotch, Irish and Welsh blood during the past three centuries, and for years past their government has been largely in the hands of Celts, but though this fact, by making them more like Americans, has tended to conceal the difference that I am discussing, it has certainly not sufficed to obliterate it altogether. Such a man as Lloyd George, in all his ways of thinking, is almost precisely like an American—but the English notion of humor remains different from the American notion, and so does the English view of personal liberty, and on the same level of primary ideas there are many other obvious differences.

But though I am thus convinced that the American Anglo-Saxon wears a false label, and grossly libels both of the great races from which he claims descent, I can imagine no good coming of trying to change it. Let him call himself whatever he pleases. Whatever he calls himself, it must be plain that the term he uses designates a genuinely distinct and differentiated race—that he is separated definitely, in character and habits of thought, from the men of all other recognizable strains—that he represents, among the peoples of the earth, almost a special species, and that he runs true to type. There is, indeed, very little tendency to variation in him—that is, in the mass. The traits that he developed when the first mixture of races took place in colonial days are the traits that he still shows; despite the vast changes in his material environment, he is almost precisely the same, in the way he thinks and acts, as his forefathers were. Some of the other great races of men, during the past two centuries, have changed very noticeably—for example, think of the complete dying out of adventurousness in the Spaniards and its sudden appearance in the Germans—but the American Anglo-Saxon has stuck to his hereditary guns. Moreover, he tends to show much less variation than other races between man and man. It is an axiom that, when five Russians or Germans meet, there are four parties in conflict, but it is equally an axiom that, among a hundred Americans, at least ninety-five will be found to hold exactly the same views upon all subjects that they can grasp at all, and may be trusted to react exactly alike to all ordinary stimuli. No other race, save it be the Chinese, is so thoroughly solid, or so firmly unresponsive to ideas from without.

4

The good qualities of this so-called Anglo-Saxon are many, and I am certainly not disposed to question them, but I here pass them over without apology, for he devotes practically the whole of his literature and fully a half of his oral discourse to celebrating them himself, and so there is no danger that they will ever be disregarded. No other known man, indeed, is so violently the blowhard, save it be his English kinsman; even the Frenchman, by comparison, is relatively modest and reticent. In this fact lies the first cause of the ridiculous figure he commonly cuts in the eyes of other people: he brags and blusters so incessantly that, if he actually had the combined virtues of Socrates, the Cid and the Twelve Apostles, he would still go beyond the facts, and so appear a mere Bombastes Furioso. This habit, I believe, is fundamentally English, but it has been exaggerated in the Americano by his larger admixture of Celtic blood. In late years in America it has taken on an almost pathological character, and is to be explained, perhaps, only in terms of the Freudian necromancy. Braggadocio, in the 100 per cent American—"we won the war," "it is our duty to lead the world," "the land of the free and the home of the brave," the "Americanization" movement, and so on—is probably no more than a protective mechanism erected to conceal an inescapable sense of inferiority.

That this inferiority is real must be obvious to any impartial observer. Whenever the Anglo-Saxon, whether of the English or of the American variety, comes into sharp conflict with men of other stocks, he tends to be worsted, or, at best, to be forced back upon extraneous and irrelevant aids to assist him in the struggle. Here in the United States his defeat is so palpable that it has filled him with vast alarms, and reduced him to seeking succor in grotesque and extravagant devices. In the fine arts, in the sciences and even in the more complex sorts of business the children of the later immigrants are running away from the descendants of the early settlers. To call the roll of Americans eminent in almost any field of human endeavor beyond that of mere dull money-grubbing is to call a list of strange and often outlandish names; even the panel of Congress presents a startling example. Of the Americans who have come into notice during the past fifty years as poets, as novelists, as critics, as painters, as sculptors and in the minor arts, less than half bear Anglo-Saxon names, and in this minority there are few of pure Anglo-Saxon blood. So in the sciences. So in the higher reaches of engineering and technology. So in philosophy and its branches. So even in industry and agriculture. In those areas where the competition between the new and the old blood-streams is most sharp and clear-cut, say in New York, in seaboard New England and in the farming States of the upper Middle West, the defeat of the Anglo-Saxon is overwhelming and unmistakable. Once his predominance everywhere was actual and undisputed; today, even where he remains heavily superior numerically, it is largely sentimental and illusory.

The descendants of the later immigrants tend generally to move upward; the descendants of the first settlers, I believe, tend plainly to move downward, mentally, spiritually and even physically. Civilization is at its lowest mark in the United States precisely in those areas where the Anglo-Saxon still presumes to rule. He runs the whole South—and in the whole South there are not as many first-rate men as in many a single city of the mongrel North. Wherever he is still firmly in the saddle, there Ku Kluxery flourishes and Fundamentalism, and lynching, and Prohibition, and all the other stupid and anti-social crazes of inferior men. It is not in the big cities, with their mixed population, that the death-rate is highest, and politics most corrupt, and religion nearest to voodooism, and every decent human aspiration suspect; it is in the areas that the recent immigrations have not penetrated, where "the purest Anglo-Saxon blood in the world" still flows. I could pile up evidences, but they are not necessary. The fact is too plain to be challenged. One testimony will be sufficient: it comes from two inquirers who made an exhaustive survey of a region in Southeastern Ohio, where "the people are more purely Americans than in the rest of the State":

Here gross superstition exercises strong control over the thought and action of a large proportion of the people. Syphilitic and other venereal diseases are common and increasing over whole counties, while in some communities nearly every family is afflicted with inherited or infectious disease. Many cases of incest are known; inbreeding is rife. Imbeciles, feeble-minded, and delinquents are numerous, politics is corrupt, and selling of votes is common, petty crimes abound, the schools have been badly managed and poorly attended. Cases of rape, assault, and robbery are of almost weekly occurrence within five minutes walk of the corporation limits of one of the county seats, while in another county political control is held by a self-confessed criminal. Alcoholic intemperance is excessive. Gross immorality and its evil results are by no means confined to the hill districts, but are extreme also in the towns.

As I say, the American of the old stock is not unaware of this steady, and, of late, somewhat rapid degeneration—this gradual loss of his old mastery in the land his ancestors wrung from the Indian and the wild cat. He senses it, indeed, very painfully, and, as if in despair of arresting it in fact, makes desperate efforts to dispose of it by denial and concealment. These efforts often take grotesque and extravagant forms. Laws are passed to hobble and cage the citizen of newer stocks in a hundred fantastic ways. It is made difficult and socially dangerous for him to teach his children the speech of his fathers, or to maintain the cultural attitudes that he has inherited from them. Every divergence from the norm of the low-cast Anglo-Saxon is treated as an *attentat* against the commonwealth, and punished with eager ferocity. On the level of the country Ku Kluxers the thing goes to the length of downright assault; a man in Arkansas or Mississippi who ventured to speak a foreign language, or to concern himself publicly with such of the fine arts as country Methodists cannot comprehend, or to let it be known that he was a member of the Roman Catholic Church would run some risk of being tarred and feathered by his neighbors or of having his house burned down over his head. Worse, there is scarcely less pressure in the higher reaches of the so-called intellect. The demand for a restoration of what is called the American tradition in letters is nothing more or less, at bottom, than a demand for a supine and nonsensical conformity—a demand that every American, regardless of his racial character and his natural way of thinking, force all his thoughts into the low-caste Anglo-Saxon mold. It is bound to fail of effect, of course, and in that very fact lies the best of imaginable proofs of the mental poverty of those who voice it. It is not brought forward in an effort at persuasion; it is issued as an order, raucously and absurdly—and every time it is flouted the Anglo-Saxon slips another inch down the hill. He cannot prevail in fair competition, and, for all his bellicose flourishes, he cannot prevail by force and intimidation. There remains for him the rôle of martyr, and in this he already begins to display himself affectingly. The music of Americans, we are told gravely, is barred out of our concert halls and opera houses because their managers and conductors are all accursed foreigners. American painters and sculptors have to struggle against a dense tide of immigrants. American criticism has become so anti-American that poets and novelists of the old stock are on a sort of blacklist, and cannot get justice. Only in the colleges does the Anglo-Saxon intellectual hold his own, and even there he is now menaced by swarms of Jews, and must devise means of putting them down or perish with his brothers of the fine arts.

5

It so happens that I am myself an Anglo-Saxon—one of far purer blood, indeed, than any of the half-bleached Celts who pass under the name in the United States and England. I am Angle and I am Saxon, and I am very little else, and that little is all safely white, Nordic, Protestant and blond. Thus I feel free, without risk of venturing into bad taste, to regard frankly the *soi-disant* Anglo-Saxon of this incomparable Republic and his rather less dubious cousin of the Motherland. How do the two appear to me, after a quarter of a century spent largely in accumulating their disfavor? What are the characters that I discern most clearly in the so-called Anglo-Saxon type of man? I may answer at once that two stick out above all others. One is his curious and apparently incurable incompetence—his congenital inability to do any difficult thing easily and well, whether it be isolating a bacillus or writing a sonata. The other is his astounding susceptibility to fears and alarms—in short, his hereditary cowardice.

To accuse so enterprising and successful a race of cowardice, of course, is to risk immediate derision; nevertheless, I believe that a fair-minded examination of its history will bear me out. Nine-tenths of the great feats of derring-do that its sucklings are taught to venerate in school—that is, its feats as a race, not the isolated exploits of its extraordinary individuals, most of them at least partly of other stocks—have been wholly lacking in even the most elementary gallantry. Consider, for example, the events attending the extension of the two great empires, English and American. Did either movement evoke any genuine courage and resolution? The answer is plainly no. Both empires were built up primarily by swindling and butchering unarmed savages, and after that by robbing weak and friendless nations: Mexico, Spain, the Boer republics. Neither produced a hero above the average run of those in the movies; neither exposed the folks at home to the slightest danger of reprisal. The battles of Omdurman and Manila Bay were typical of these great swarmings of the Anglo-Saxon—the first a bald massacre, and the second a combat at odds of at least fifty to one. They produced highly typical Anglo-Saxon heroes— Kitchener, an Irishman, and Dewey, largely French. Almost always, indeed, mercenaries have done the Anglo-Saxon's fighting for him—a high testimony to his common sense, but scarcely flattering, I fear, to the truculence he boasts of. The British empire was won mainly by Irishmen, Scotchmen and native allies, and the American empire, at least in large part, by Frenchmen and Spaniards. Moreover, neither great enterprise cost any appreciable amount of blood; neither presented grave and dreadful risks; neither exposed the conqueror to the slightest danger of being made the conquered. The British won most of their vast dominions without having to stand up in a single battle against a civilized and formidable foe, and the Americanos won their continent at the expense of a few dozen puerile skirmishes with savages. All the Indian wars in American history, from the days of John Smith to those of Custer, did not bring down as many men as the single battle of

Tannenberg. The total cost of conquering the whole area from Plymouth Rock to the Golden Gate and from Lake George to the Everglades, including even the cost of driving out the French, Dutch, English and Spaniards, was less than the cost of defending Verdun.

So far as I can make out there is no record in history of any Anglo-Saxon nation entering upon any great war without allies, nor upon any war at all when there was the slightest danger of getting beaten, or even of suffering serious damage. The French have done it, the Dutch have done it, the Germans have done it, the Japs have done it, and even such inferior nations as the Danes, the Spaniards, the Boers and the Greeks have done it, but never the English or Americans. Can you imagine the English taking such a chance as the Germans took in 1914, or as the Turks took in 1922, or as the French prepare to take today? Can you imagine the United States resolutely facing a war in which the odds against it were as huge as they were against Spain in 1898? It seems to me that the facts of history are wholly against any such fancy. The Anglo-Saxon always tries to take a gang with him when he goes to war, and even when he has it behind him he is very uneasy, and prone to fall into panic at the first threat of genuine danger. Here I put an unimpeachably Anglo-Saxon witness on the stand, to wit, Dr. Charles W. Eliot, of Harvard. I find him saying, in an article quoted with approbation by the *Congressional Record*, that during the Revolutionary War the colonists now hymned so eloquently in the school-books "fell into a condition of despondency from which nothing but the steadfastness of Washington and the Continental army *and the aid from France* saved them," and that "when the War of 1812 brought grave losses a considerable portion of the population experienced a moral collapse, from which they were rescued only by the exertions of a few thoroughly patriotic statesmen and the exploits of three or four American frigates on the seas"—to say nothing of an enterprising Corsican gentleman, Bonaparte by name. In both these wars the Americans had enormous and obvious advantages, in terrain, in allies and in men; nevertheless, they fought, in the main, very badly, and from the first shot to the last a majority of them stood in favor of making peace on almost any terms. The Mexican and Spanish Wars I pass over as perhaps too obscenely ungallant to be discussed at all; of the former, General U. S. Grant, who fought in it, said that it was "the most unjust war ever waged by a stronger against a weaker nation." Who remembers that, during the Spanish War, the whole Atlantic Coast trembled in fear of the Spaniards' feeble fleet—that all New England had hysterics every time a strange coal-barge was sighted on the sky-line, that the safe-deposit boxes of Boston were emptied and their contents transferred to Worcester, and that the Navy had to organize a patrol to save the coast towns from depopulation? Perhaps those Reds, atheists and pro-Germans remember it who also remember that during the World War the entire country went wild with fear of an enemy who, without the aid of divine intervention, obviously could not strike it a blow at all—and that the great moral victory was gained at last with the assistance of twenty-one allies at odds of eight to one.

But the American Civil War remains? Does it, indeed? The almost unanimous opinion of the North, in 1861, was that it would be over after a few small battles; the first soldiers were actually enlisted for but three months. When, later on, it turned unexpectedly into a severe struggle, recruits had to be driven to the front by force, and the only Northerners remaining in favor of going on were Abraham Lincoln, a few ambitious generals and the profiteers. I turn to Dr. Eliot again. "In the closing year of the war," he says, "large portions of the Democratic party in the North *and of the Republican party* advocated surrender to the Confederacy, *so down-hearted were they.*" Down-hearted at odds of two to one! The South was plainly more gallant, but even the gallantry of the South was largely illusory. The Confederate leaders, when the war began, adopted at once the traditional Anglo-Saxon device of seeking allies. They tried and expected to get the aid of England, and they actually came very near succeeding. When hopes in that direction began to fade (*i.e.*, when England concluded that tackling the North would be dangerous), the common people of the Confederacy, the progenitors of the chivalric Ku Kluxers of today, threw up the sponge, and so the catastrophe, when it came at last, was mainly internal. The South failed to bring the quaking North to a standstill because, to borrow a phrase that Dr. Eliot uses in another connection, it "experienced a moral collapse of unprecedented depth and duration." The folks at home failed to support the troops in the field, and the troops in the field began to desert. Even so early as Shiloh, indeed, many Confederate regiments were already refusing to fight.

This reluctance for desperate chances and hard odds, so obvious in the military record of the English-speaking nations, is also conspicuous in times of peace. What a man of another and superior stock almost always notices, living among so-called Anglo-Saxons, is (*a*) their incapacity for prevailing in fair rivalry, either in trade, in the fine arts or in what is called learning —in brief, their general incompetence, and (*b*) their invariable effort to make up for this incapacity by putting some inequitable burden upon their rivals, usually by force. The Frenchman, I believe, is the worst of chauvinists, but once he admits a foreigner to his country he at least treats that foreigner fairly, and does not try to penalize him absurdly for his mere foreignness. The Anglo-Saxon American is always trying to do it; his history is a history of recurrent outbreaks of blind rage against peoples who have begun to worst him; hence Know Nothingism, Ku Kluxery, American Legionism, and all the rest of it. Such movements would be inconceivable in an efficient and genuinely self-confident people, wholly assured of their superiority, as a Frenchman is of his or a German of his, and they would be equally inconceivable in a truly gallant and courageous people, disdaining unfair advantages and overwhelming odds. Theoretically launched against some imaginary inferiority in the non-Anglo-Saxon man, either as patriot, as democrat or as Christian, they are actually launched at his general superiority, his greater fitness to survive in the national environment. The effort is always to penalize him for winning in fair fight, to handicap him in such a manner that he will sink to the general level of the Anglo-Saxon population, and, if possible, even below it. Such devices, of course, never have the countenance of the Anglo-Saxon minority that is authentically superior, and hence self-confident and tolerant. Of that minority I do not speak here. It is serene in peace as it is brave in war. But in the United States, at least, it is pathetically small, and it tends steadily to grow smaller and feebler. The communal laws and the communal *mores* are made by the folk, and they offer all the proof that is necessary, not only of its general inferiority, but also of its alarmed awareness of that inferiority. The normal American of the "pure-blooded" majority goes to rest every night with an uneasy feeling that there is a burglar under the bed, and he gets up every morning with a sickening fear that his underwear has been stolen.

6

It is difficult, I submit, to admire such a people unreservedly, despite the good qualities that I have passed over. They lack the ease and tolerance, the fine adventurousness and love of hazard which go with a sense of firm security—in other words, with a sense of genuine superiority. The Anglo-Saxon of the great herd is, in many important respects, the least civilized of men and the least capable of true civilization. His political ideas are crude and shallow. He is almost wholly devoid of æsthetic feeling; he does not even make folk-lore or walk in the woods. The most elementary facts about the visible universe alarm him, and incite him to put them down. Educate him, make a professor of him, teach him how to express his soul, and he still remains palpably third-rate. He fears ideas almost more cravenly than he fears men. His blood, I believe, is running thin; perhaps it was not much to boast of at the start; in order that he may exercise any functions above those of a trader, a pedagogue or a mob orator, it needs the stimulus of other and less exhausted strains. Poe, Whitman, Mark Twain— these were typical products of such crosses. The fact that they increase is the best hope of the intellect in America. They shake the old race out of its spiritual lethargy, and introduce it to disquiet and experiment. They make for a free play of ideas. In opposing the process, whether in politics, in letters or in the ages-long struggle toward the truth, the prophets of Anglo-Saxon purity and tradition only make themselves ridiculous. Under the absurd *Kultur* that they advocate Agassiz would have been deported and Whitman would have been hanged, and the most eminent literati flourishing in the Republic today would be Edgar Guest and Dr. Frank Crane.

The success of these so-called Anglo-Saxons in the world, I am convinced, has been due, not so much to their merits but to their defects—and especially to their high capacity for being alarmed and their aversion to what may be called romance—in other words, to their harshly practical minds, their disdain of intellectual enterprise, their dull common sense. They have saved their hides and their money while better sportsmen were taking chances. But the bitter must go with the sweet. Such qualities belong to *Lumbricus terrestris* rather than to *Homo sapiens*. They may be valuable, but they are not pretty. Today, at the height of his triumph in the world, the Anglo-Saxon somehow looks shabby—England trembling before one-legged and bankrupt France, the United States engaged in a grotesque *pogrom* against the wop, the coon, the kike, the papist, the Jap, the what-not—worse, engaged in an even more grotesque effort to put down ideas as well as men—to repeal learning by statute, regiment the arts by lynch-law, and give the puerile ethical and theological notions of lonely farmers and corner grocers the force and dignity of constitutional axioms. As I stand on the side-lines, observing the show, I find it very hard to admire. But, save when ethyl alcohol in dilute aqueous solution has dulled my native pity, I find it even harder to laugh.

II.

The Husbandman

A READER for years of the *Congressional Record*, I have encountered in its dense and pregnant columns denuncia-
tions of almost every human act or idea that is imaginable to
political pathology, from adultery to Zionism, and of all classes
of men whose crimes the legislative mind can grasp, from atheists to Zoroastrians, but never once, so far as I can recall, has
that great journal shown the slightest insolence, direct or indi-
rect, to the humble husbandman, the lonely companion of *Bos
taurus*, the sweating and persecuted farmer. He is, on the contrary, the pet above all other pets, the enchantment and delight, the saint and archangel of all the unearthly Sganarelles
and Scaramouches who roar in the two houses of Congress.
He is more to them day in and day out, than whole herds of
Honest Workingmen, Gallant Jack Tars and Heroic Miners; he
is more, even, than a platoon of Unknown Soldiers. There are
days when one or another of these totems of the statesman is
bathed with such devotion that it would make the Gracchi
blush, but there is never a day that the farmer, too, doesn't get
his share, and there is many a day when he gets ten times his
share—when, indeed, he is completely submerged in rhetorical
vaseline, so that it is hard to tell which end of him is made in
the image of God and which is mere hoof. No session ever
begins without a grand assault at all arms upon his hereditary
foes, from the boll-weevil and the San José scale to Wall Street
and the Interstate Commerce Commission. And no session
comes to an end without a huge grist of new laws to save him
from them—laws embodying the most subtle statecraft of the
most daring and ingenious body of lawmakers ever assembled
under one roof on the habitable globe. One might almost argue that the chief, and perhaps even only aim of legislation in
These States is to succor and secure the farmer. If, while the
bombs of goose-grease and rockets of pomade are going off in
the two Chambers, certain evil men meet in the basement and
hook *banderillas* into him—say, by inserting jokers into the

chemical schedule of a new tariff bill, or by getting the long-haul rules changed, or by manipulating the loans of the Federal Reserve Banks,—then the crime is not against him alone; it is against the whole American people, the common decency of Christendom, and the Holy Ghost. Horn a farmer, and you stand in contumacy to the platforms of all known parties, to the devout faith of all known statesmen, and to God. *Laborantem agricolam oportet primum de fructibus percipere.*

Paul wrote to the Bishop of Ephesus, at the latest, in the year 65 A.D.; the doctrine that I have thus ascribed to the Mesmers and Grimaldis of our politics is therefore not a novelty of their contrivance. Nor is it, indeed, their monopoly, for it seems to be shared by all Americans who are articulate and devote themselves to political metaphysics and good works. The farmer is praised by all who mention him at all, from archbishops to zoölogists, day in and day out. He is praised for his industry, his frugality, his patriotism, his altruistic passion. He is praised for staying on the farm, for laboriously wringing our bread and meat from the reluctant soil, for renouncing Babylon to guard the horned cattle on the hills. He is praised for his patient fidelity to the oldest of learned professions, and the most honorable, and the most necessary to all of us. He takes on, in political speeches and newspaper editorials, a sort of mystical character. He is no longer a mundane laborer, scratching for the dollar, full of staphylococci, smelling heavily of sweat and dung; he is a high priest in a rustic temple, pouring out his heart's blood upon the altar of Ceres. The farmer, thus depicted, grows heroic, lyrical, pathetic, affecting. To murmur against him becomes a sort of sacrilege, like murmuring against the Constitution, Human Freedom, the Cause of Democracy. . . . Nevertheless, being already doomed, I herewith and hereby presume to do it. More, my murmur is scored in the manner of Berlioz, for ten thousand trombones *fortissimo*, with harsh, cacophonous chords for bombardons and ophicleides in the bass clef. Let the farmer, so far as I am concerned, be damned forevermore! To hell with him, and bad luck to him! He is, unless I err, no hero at all, and no priest, and no altruist, but simply a tedious fraud and ignoramus, a cheap rogue and hypocrite, the eternal Jack of the human pack. He deserves all that he suffers under our economic system, and more. Any city man, not insane, who sheds tears for him is shedding tears of the crocodile.

No more grasping, selfish and dishonest mammal, indeed, is known to students of the Anthropoidea. When the going is good for him he robs the rest of us up to the extreme limit of our endurance; when the going is bad he comes bawling for help out of the public till. Has anyone ever heard of a farmer making any sacrifice of his own interests, however slight, to the common good? Has anyone ever heard of a farmer practising or advocating any political idea that was not absolutely self-seeking—that was not, in fact, deliberately designed to loot the rest of us to his gain? Greenbackism, free silver, government guarantee of prices, all the complex fiscal imbecilities of the cow State John Baptists—these are the contributions of the virtuous husbandmen to American political theory. There has never been a time, in good seasons or bad, when his hands were not itching for more; there has never been a time when he was not ready to support any charlatan, however grotesque, who promised to get it for him. Why, indeed, are politicians so polite to him—before election, so romantically amorous? For the plain and simple reason that only one issue ever interests or fetches him, and that is the issue of his own profit. He must be promised something definite and valuable, to be paid to him alone, or he is off after some other mountebank. He simply cannot imagine himself as a citizen of a commonwealth, in duty bound to give as well as take; he can imagine himself only as getting all and giving nothing.

Yet we are asked to venerate this prehensile moron as the *Ur*-burgher, the citizen *par excellence*, the foundation-stone of the state! And why? Because he produces something that all of us must have—that we must get somehow on penalty of death. And how do we get it from him? By submitting helplessly to his unconscionable blackmailing—by paying him, not under any rule of reason, but in proportion to his roguery and incompetence, and hence to the direness of our need. I doubt that the human race, as a whole, would submit to that sort of high-jacking, year in and year out, from any other necessary class of men. When the American railroad workman attempted it, in 1916, there was instant indignation; when a certain small squad of the *Polizei* tried it, a few years later, there was such

universal horror that a politician who denounced the crime became President of the United States. But the farmers do it over
and over again, without challenge or reprisal, and the only
thing that keeps them from reducing us, at intervals, to actual
famine is their own imbecile knavery. They are all willing and
eager to pillage us by starving us, but they can't do it because
they can't resist attempts to swindle each other. Recall, for example, the case of the cotton-growers in the South. They
agreed among themselves to cut down the cotton acreage in
order to inflate the price—and instantly every party to the
agreement began planting *more* cotton in order to profit by
the abstinence of his neighbors. That abstinence being wholly
imaginary, the price of cotton fell instead of going up—and
then the entire pack of scoundrels began demanding assistance
from the national treasury—in brief, began demanding that
the rest of us indemnify them for the failure of their plot to
blackmail us!

The same demand is made almost annually by the wheat
farmers of the Middle West. It is the theory of the zanies who
perform at Washington that a grower of wheat devotes himself
to that banal art in a philanthropic and patriotic spirit—that he
plants and harvests his crop in order that the folks of the cities
may not go without bread. It is the plain fact that he raises
wheat because it takes less labor than any other crop—because
it enables him, after working sixty days a year, to loaf the rest
of the twelve months. If wheat-raising could be taken out of
the hands of such lazy *fellahin* and organized as the production
of iron or cement is organized, the price might be reduced by
a half, and still leave a large profit for *entrepreneurs*. It vacil-
lates dangerously today, not because speculators manipulate it,
but because the crop is irregular and undependable—that is to
say, because those who make it are incompetent. The worst
speculators, as everyone knows, are the farmers themselves.
They hold their wheat as long as they can, borrowing our
money from the country banks and hoping prayerfully for a
rise. If it goes up, then we pay them an extra and unearned
profit. If it goes down, then they demand legislation to prevent it going down next time. Sixty days a year they work; the
rest of the time they gamble with our bellies. It is probably the
safest gambling ever heard of. Now and then, true enough, a

yokel who plunges too heavily comes to grief, and is ingested by the county-town mortgage-shark; now and then a whole county, or State or even larger area goes bankrupt, and the financial dominoes begin falling down all along the line from Saleratus Center to New York. But such catastrophes are rare, and they leave no scars. When a speculator goes broke in Wall Street it is a scandalous matter, and if he happens to have rooked anybody of importance he is railroaded to jail. But when a speculator goes broke in the great open spaces, there is a great rush of political leucocytes to the scene, and presently it is made known that the sin was not the speculator's at all, but his projected victims', and that it is the prime duty of the latter, by lawful order upon the Treasurer of the United States, to reimburse him his losses and set him up for a new trial.

The notion that wheat would be much cheaper and the supply far more dependable if it were grown, not by a motley horde of such puerile loafers and gamblers, but by competent men intelligently organized is not mine; I borrow it from Henry Ford, a busted seer. Since he betrayed them to Dr. Coolidge for a mess of pottage, the poor Liberals, once so enamored of his sagacity, denounce Ford as an idiot and a villain; nevertheless, the fact remains that his discussion of the wastefulness of our present system of wheat-growing, in the autobiography which he didn't write, is full of a powerful plausibility. Ford was born and brought up on a farm—and it was a farm, as farms go, that was very competently managed. But he knows very well that even the most competent farmer is but seldom more adept than a chimpanzee playing the violin. The Liberals, indeed, cannot controvert his judgment; they have been thrown back upon belaboring his political morals. What he proposes, they argue, is simply the enslavement of the present farmer, now so gloriously free. With capitalism gradually absorbing his fields, he would have to go to work as a wage-slave. Well, why not? For one, I surely offer no objection. All the rubber we use today is raised by slave labor; so is all the morphine consumed at Hollywood. Our children are taught in school by slaves; our newspapers are edited by slaves. Wheat raised by slave labor would be just as nutritious as wheat raised by men earning $10,000 a year, and a great deal cheaper. If the business showed a good profit, the political clowns at

Washington would launch schemes to confiscate it, as they now launch schemes to make good the losses of the farmers. In any case, why bother about the fate of the farmer? If wheat went to $10 a bushel tomorrow, and all the workmen of the cities became slaves in name as well as in fact, no farmer in this grand land of freedom would consent voluntarily to a reduction of as much as ⅛ of a cent a bushel. "The greatest wolves," say E. W. Howe, another graduate of the farm, "are the farmers who bring produce to town to sell." Wolves? Let us not insult *Canis lupus*. I move the substitution of *Hyæna hyæna*.

Meanwhile, how much truth is in the common theory that the husbandman is harassed and looted by our economic system, that the men of the cities prey upon him—specifically, that he is the chronic victim of such devices as the tariff, railroad regulation, and the banking system? So far as I can make out, there is none whatever. The net effect of our present banking system, as I have already said, is that the money accumulated by the cities is used to finance the farmers, and that they employ it to blackmail the cities. As for the tariff, is it a fact that it damages the farmer, or benefits him? Let us turn for light to the worst Tariff Act ever heard of in human history: that of 1922. It put a duty of 30 cents a bushel on wheat, and so barred out Canadian wheat, and gave the American farmer a vast and unfair advantage. For months running the difference in the price of wheat on the two sides of the American-Canadian border—wheat raised on farms not a mile apart—ran from 25 to 30 cents a bushel. Danish butter was barred out by a duty of 8 cents a pound—and the American farmer pocketed the 8 cents. Potatoes carried a duty of 50 cents a hundredweight—and the potato growers of Maine, eager, as the phrase has it, to mop up, raised such an enormous crop that the market was glutted, and they went bankrupt, and began bawling for government aid. High duties were put, too, upon meats, upon cheese, upon wool—in brief, upon practically everything that the farmer produced. But his profits were taken from him by even higher duties upon manufactured goods, and by high freight rates? Were they, indeed? There was, in fact, no duty at all upon many of the things he consumed. There was no duty, for example, upon shoes. The duty upon woolen goods gave a smaller advantage to the manufacturer than the duty on wool gave to the farmer. So with the duty on cotton goods. Automobiles were cheaper in the United States than anywhere else on earth. So were all agricultural implements. So were groceries. So were fertilizers.

But here I come to the brink of an abyss of statistics, and had better haul up. The enlightened reader is invited to investigate them for himself; they will bring him, I believe, some surprises, particularly if he has been reading the *Congressional Record* and accepting it gravely. They by no means exhaust the case against the consecrated husbandman. I have said that the only political idea he can grasp is one which promises him a direct profit. It is, alas, not quite true: he can also grasp one which has the sole effect of annoying and damaging his enemy, the city man. The same mountebanks who get to Washington by promising to augment his gains and make good his losses devote whatever time is left over from that enterprise to saddling the rest of us with oppressive and idiotic laws, all hatched on the farm. There, where the cows low through the still night, and the jug of Peruna stands behind the stove, and bathing begins, as at Biarritz, with the vernal equinox—there is the reservoir of all the nonsensical legislation which now makes the United States a buffoon among the great nations. It was among country Methodists, practitioners of a theology degraded almost to the level of voodooism, that Prohibition was invented, and it was by country Methodists, nine-tenths of them actual followers of the plow, that it was fastened upon the rest of us, to the damage of our bank accounts, our dignity and our ease. What lies under it, and under all the other crazy enactments of its category, is no more and no less than the yokel's congenital and incurable hatred of the city man—his simian rage against everyone who, as he sees it, is having a better time than he is.

That this malice is at the bottom of Prohibition, and not any altruistic yearning to put down the evils of drink, is shown clearly by the fact that most of the State enforcement acts—and even the Volstead Act, as it is interpreted at Washington—permit the farmer himself to make cider as in the past, and that every effort to deprive him of that astounding immunity has met with the opposition of his representatives. In other words, the thing he is against is not the use of alcohol *per se*, but simply the use of alcohol in its more charming and romantic forms. Prohibition, as everyone knows, has not materially diminished the consumption of alcohol in the cities, but it has obviously forced the city man to drink decoctions that he would have spurned in the old days—that is, it has forced him to drink such dreadful stuff as the farmer has always drunk. The farmer is thus content with it: it brings his enemy down to his own level. The same animus is visible in innumerable other moral statutes, all ardently supported by the peasantry. For example, the Mann Act. The aim of this amazing law, of course, is not to put down adultery; it is simply to put down that variety of adultery which is most agreeable. What got it upon the books was simply the constant gabble in the rural newspapers about the byzantine debaucheries of urban Antinomians—rich stockbrokers who frequented Atlantic City from Friday to Monday, vaudeville actors who traveled about the country with beautiful mistresses, and so on. Such aphrodisiacal tales, read beside the kitchen-stove by hinds condemned to monogamous misery with stupid, unclean and ill-natured wives, naturally aroused in them a vast detestation of errant cockneys, and this detestation eventually rolled up enough force to attract the attention of the quacks who make laws at Washington. The result was the Mann Act. Since then a number of the cow States have passed Mann Acts of their own, usually forbidding the use of automobiles "for immoral purposes." But there is nowhere a law forbidding the use of barns, cow-stables, hay-ricks and other such familiar rustic ateliers of sin. That is to say, there is nowhere a law forbidding yokels to drag virgins into infamy by the technic practised since Tertiary times on the farms; there are only laws forbidding city youths to do it according to the technic of the great municipalities.

Here we come to the limits of bucolic moral endeavor. It never prohibits acts that are common on the farms; it only prohibits acts that are common in the cities. In many of the Middle Western States there are statutes forbidding the smoking of cigarettes, for cigarette-smoking, to the louts of those wastes, bears the aspect of a citified and levantine vice, and if they attempted it themselves they would be derided by their fellows and perhaps divorced by their wives, just as they would be derided and divorced if they bathed every day, or dressed for dinner, or attempted to play the piano. But chewing tobacco, whether in public or in private, is nowhere forbidden by law, for the plain reason that nine-tenths of all husbandmen practise it, as they practice the drinking of raw corn liquor. The act not only lies within their tastes; it also lies within their means, and hence within their *mores*. As a consequence the inhabitants of the towns in those remote marches are free to chew tobacco all they please, even at divine service, but are clapped into jail the instant they light cigarettes. The same consideration gets into comstockery, which is chiefly supported, like Prohibition, by farmers and chiefly aimed at city men. The Comstock Act is very seldom invoked against newspapers, for the matter printed in newspapers lies within the comprehension of the peasantry, and hence within their sphere of enjoyment. Nor is it often invoked against cheap books of a frankly pornographic character—such things as "Night Life in Chicago," "Adventures on a Pullman Sleeper" and "The Confessions of an ex-Nun"—for when yokels read at all, it is commonly such garbage that they prefer. But they are hot against the infinitely less gross naughtiness of serious books, including the so-called classics, for these books they simply cannot read. In consequence the force of comstockery is chiefly directed against such literature. For one actually vile book that it suppresses it attempts to suppress at least a dozen good ones.

Now the pious husbandman shows signs of an itch to proceed further. Not content with assaulting us with his degraded and abominable ethics, he begins trying to force upon us his still worse theology. On the steppes Methodism has got itself all the estate and dignity of a State religion; it becomes a criminal offense to teach any doctrine in contempt of it. No civilized man, to be sure, is yet actually in jail for the crime; civilized men simply keep out of such bleak parking spaces for human Fords, as they keep out of Congress and Franz Josef Land. But the long arm of the Wesleyan revelation now begins to stretch forth toward Nineveh. The mountebank, Bryan, after years of preying upon the rustics on the promise that he would show them how to loot the cities by wholesale and *à outrance*, now reverses his collar and proposes to lead them in a *jehad* against what remains of American intelligence, already beleaguered in a few walled towns. We are not only to abandon the social customs of civilization at the behest of a rabble of peasants who sleep in their underclothes; we are now to give up all the basic ideas of civilization and adopt the gross superstitions of the same mob. Is this fanciful? Is the menace remote, and to be disregarded? My apologies for suggesting that perhaps you are one of the multitude who thought that way about Prohibition, and only half a dozen years ago. Bryan is a protean harlequin, and more favored by God than is commonly assumed. He lost with free silver but he won with Prohibition. The chances, if my mathematics do not fail, are thus 1 to 1 that he will win, if he keeps his health, with Fundamentalism—in his own phrase, that God will be put into the Constitution. If he does, then *Eoanthrophus* will triumph finally over *Homo sapiens*. If he does, then the humble swineherd will drive us all into his pen.

Not much gift for Vision is needed to imagine the main outlines of the ensuing *Kultur*. The city man, as now, will bear nine-tenths of the tax burden; the rural total immersionist will make all the laws. With Genesis firmly lodged in the Testament of the Fathers he will be ten times as potent as he is now and a hundred times as assiduous. No constitutional impediment will remain to cripple his moral fancy. The Wesleyan code of Kansas and Mississippi, Vermont and Minnesota will be forced upon all of us by the full military and naval power of the United States. Civilization will gradually become felonious everywhere in the Republic, as it already is in Arkansas. What I sing, I suppose, is a sort of Utopia. But it is not the Utopia of bawdy poets and metaphysicians; it is not the familiar Utopia of the books. It is a Utopia dreamed by simpler and more virtuous men—by seven millions of Christian bumpkins, far-flung in forty-eight sovereign States. They dream it on their long journeys down the twelve billion furrows of their seven million farms, up hill and down dale in the heat of the day. They dream it behind the egg-stove on Winter nights, their boots off and their socks scorching, Holy Writ in their hands. They dream it as they commune with *Bos taurus*, *Sus scrofa*, *Mephitis mephitis*, the Methodist pastor, the Ford agent. It floats before their eyes as they scan the Sears-Roebuck catalogue for horse liniment, porous plasters and Bordeaux mixture; it rises before them when they assemble in their Little

Bethels to be instructed in the word of God, the plots of the Pope, the crimes of the atheists and Jews; it transfigures the chautauquan who looms before them with his Great Message. This Utopia haunts and tortures them; they long to make it real. They have tried prayer, and it has failed; now they turn to the secular arm. The dung-fork glitters in the sun as the host prepares to march. . . .

Well, these are the sweet-smelling and altruistic agronomists whose sorrows are the *leitmotif* of our politics, whose votes keep us supplied with Bryans and Bleases, whose welfare is alleged to be the chief end of democratic statecraft, whose patriotism is the so-called bulwark of this so-called Republic!

III.
High and Ghostly Matters

The Cosmic Secretariat

T HE argument by design, once the bulwark of Christian apologetics, is so full of holes that it is no wonder that it has had to be abandoned. The more, indeed, the theologian seeks to prove the wisdom and omnipotence of God by His works, the more he is dashed by evidences of divine incompetence and stupidity. The world is not actually well run; it is very badly run, and no Huxley was needed to labor the obvious fact. The human body, very adeptly designed in some details, is cruelly and senselessly bungled in other details, and every reflective first-year medical student must notice a hundred ways to improve it. How are we to reconcile this mixture of finesse and blundering with the concept of a single omnipotent Designer, to whom all problems are equally easy? If He could contrive so efficient and durable a machine as the human hand, then how did He come to make such botches as the tonsils, the gall-bladder, the uterus and the prostate gland? If He could perfect the hip joint and the ear, then why did He boggle the teeth?

Having never encountered a satisfactory—or even a remotely plausible—answer to such questions, I have had to go to the trouble of devising one myself. It is, at all events, quite simple, and in strict accord with all the known facts. In brief, it is this: that the theory that the universe is run by a single God must be abandoned, and that in place of it we must set up the theory that it is actually run by a board of gods, all of equal puissance and authority. Once this concept is grasped all the difficulties that have vexed theologians vanish, and human experience instantly lights up the whole dark scene. We observe in everyday life what happens when authority is divided, and great decisions are reached by consultation and compromise. We know that the effects at times, particularly when one of the consultants runs away with the others, are very good, but we also know that they are usually extremely bad. Such a mixture, precisely, is on display in the cosmos. It presents a series of brilliant successes in the midst of an infinity of failures.

I contend that my theory is the only one ever put forward that completely accounts for the clinical picture. Every other theory, facing such facts as sin, disease and disaster, is forced to admit the supposition that Omnipotence, after all, may not be omnipotent—a plain absurdity. I need toy with no such non-sense. I may assume that every god belonging to the council which rules the universe is infinitely wise and infinitely power-ful, and yet not evade the plain fact that most of the acts of that council are ignorant and foolish. In truth, my assumption that a council exists is tantamount to an *a priori* assump-tion that its acts are ignorant and foolish, for no act of any conceivable council can be otherwise. Is the human hand per-fect, or, at all events, practical and praiseworthy? Then I ac-count for it on the ground that it was designed by some single member of the council—that the business was handed over to him by inadvertence or as a result of an irreconcilable difference of opinion among the others. Had more than one member participated actively in its design it would have been measura-bly less meritorious than it is, for the sketch offered by the original designer would have been forced to run the gauntlet criticisms and suggestions from all the other councillors, and human experience teaches us that most of these criticisms and suggestions would have been inferior to the original idea— that many of them, in fact, would have had nothing in them save a petty desire to maul and spoil the original idea.

But do I here accuse the high gods of harboring discred-itable human weaknesses? If I do, then my excuse is that it is impossible to imagine them doing the work universally as-cribed to them without admitting their possession of such weaknesses. One cannot imagine a god spending weeks and months, and maybe whole geological epochs, laboring over the design of the human kidney without assuming him to have been moved by a powerful impulse to express himself vividly, to marshal and publish his ideas, to win public credit among his fellows—in brief, without assuming him to be egoistic. And one cannot assume him to be egoistic without assuming him to prefer the adoption of his own ideas to the adoption of any other god's. I defy anyone to make the contrary assumption without plunging instantly into clouds of mysticism. Ruling it out, one comes inevitably to the conclusion that the inept management of the universe must be ascribed to clashes of egos, *i.e.*, to petty spites and revenges, among the gods, for any one of them alone, since we must assume him to be infinitely wise and powerful, could run it perfectly. We suffer from bad stomachs simply because the god who first proposed making a stomach aroused thereby the ill-nature of those who had not thought of it, and because they proceeded instantly to wreak that ill-nature upon him by improving, *i.e.*, botching, his work. We must reproduce our species in the familiar arduous, uneconomic, embarrassing and almost pathological manner because the god who devised the excellent process prevailing among the protozoa had to be put in his place when he proposed to extend it to the Primates.

2
The Nature of Faith

Many years ago, when I was more enterprising intellectually than I am to-day, I proposed the application of Haeckel's celebrated biogenetic law—to wit, that the history of the individual rehearses the history of the species—to the domain of human ideas. So applied, it leads to some superficially startling but probably quite sound conclusions, for example, that an adult poet is simply an individual in a state of arrested development —in brief, a sort of moron. Just as all of us, *in utero*, pass through a stage in which we are tadpoles, and almost indistinguishable from the tadpoles which afterward become frogs, so all of us pass through a stage, in our nonage, when we are poets. A youth of seventeen who is not a poet is simply an ass: his development has been arrested even anterior to the stage of the intellectual tadpole. But a man of fifty who still writes poetry is either an unfortunate who has never developed, intellectually, beyond his teens, or a conscious buffoon who pretends to be something that he isn't—something far younger and juicier than he actually is—, just as the late Richard Mansfield, in Schiller's play, pretended, by the use of a falsetto voice and a girlish skip, to be the eighteen-year-old Don Carlos.

Something else, of course, may enter into it. The buffoonery may be partly conscious and deliberate, and partly Freudian. Many an aging man keeps on writing poetry simply because it gives him the illusion that he is still young. For the same reason, perhaps, he plays tennis, wears green cravats, and tries to convince himself that he is in love.

It is my conviction that no normal man ever fell in love, within the ordinary meaning of the term, after the age of thirty. He may, at forty, pursue the female of his species with great assiduity, and he may, at fifty, sixty or even seventy, "woo" and marry a more or less fair one in due form of law, but the impulse that moves him to these follies at such ages is never the complex of illusions and hallucinations that poets describe as love. This complex is quite natural to all males between adolescence and the age of, say, twenty-five, when the kidneys begin to disintegrate. For a youth to reach twenty-one without having fallen in love in an abject and preposterous manner would be for doubts to be raised as to his normalcy. But if he does it after his wisdom teeth are cut, it is no more than a sign that they have been cut in vain—that he is still in his teens, whatever his biological and legal age. Love, so-called, is based upon a view of women that is impossible to any man who has had any experience of them. Such a man may, to the end of his life, enjoy their society vastly, and even respect them and admire them, but, however much he respects and admires them, he nevertheless sees them more or less clearly, and seeing them clearly is fatal to the true romance. Find a man of forty who heaves and moans over a woman in the manner of a poet and you will behold either a man who ceased to develop intellectually at twenty-four or thereabout, or a fraud who has his eye on the lands, tenements and hereditaments of the lady's deceased first husband. Or upon her talents as nurse, cook, amanuensis and audience. This, no doubt, is what George Bernard Shaw meant when he said that every man over forty is a scoundrel.

As I say, my suggestion has not been adopted by psychologists, who, in the main, are a very conservative and unimaginative body of men. If they applied the biogenetic law in the field of religion they might make some interesting observations. The chances are, indeed, that religion belongs exclusively to an extremely early stage of human development, and that its rapid decay in the world since the Reformation is evidence of a very genuine progress. Reduced to its logical essence, every religion now advocated in Christendom is simply the doctrine that there are higher powers, infinitely wise and virtuous, which take an active interest in the sordid everyday affairs of men, and not infrequently intervene in them. This doctrine is not purely romantic and *a priori*; it is based upon what is regarded by its subscribers as objective evidence. But it must be plain that that evidence tends to go to pieces as human knowledge widens—that it appears massive and impressive in direct proportion as the individual impressed is ignorant. A few hundred years ago practically every phenomenon of nature was ascribed to superhuman intervention. The plague, for example, was caused by God's anger. So was war. So was lightning. Today no enlightened man believes anything of the kind. All these phenomena are seen to be but links in an endless chain of amoral causation, and it is known that, given a certain quite intelligible and usually inevitable combination of causes, they will appear infallibly as effects. Thus religion gradually loses its old objective authority, and becomes more and more a mere sentimentality. An enlightened man's view of it is almost indistinguishable from his view of the Spirit of 1776, the Henty books, and the rosewood casket containing his grandmother's false teeth.

Such a man is not "dead" to religion. He was not born with a congenital inaptitude for it. He has simply outgrown it, as he has outgrown poetry, Socialism and love. At adolescence practically all individuals have attacks of piety, but that is only saying that their powers of perception, at that age, outrun their knowledge. They observe the phenomenon, but cannot account for it. Later on, unless their development is arrested, they gradually emerge from that romantic and spookish fog, just as they emerge from the hallucinations of secular romance. I speak here, of course, of individuals genuinely capable of education—always a small minority. If, as the Army tests of conscripts showed, nearly 50 per cent. of American adult males never get beyond the mental development of a twelve-year-old child, then it must be obvious that a much smaller number get beyond the mental development of a youth at the end of his teens. I put that number, at a venture, at 5 per cent. The remaining 95 per cent. never quite free themselves from religious superstitions. They may no longer believe it is an act of God every time an individual catches a cold, or sprains his ankle, or cuts himself shaving, but they are pretty sure to see some trace of divine intervention in it if he is struck by lightning, or hanged, or afflicted with leprosy or syphilis. That God causes wars has been believed by all the Presidents of the United States, save Grover Cleveland, since Jefferson's time. During the late war the then President actually set aside a day for praying to God to stop what He had started as soon as possible, and on terms favorable to American investments. This was not done, remember, by a voodoo man in the Congo forest, but by a sound Presbyterian, a Ph.D. of Johns Hopkins University, and the best-dressed professor ever seen at Princeton.

I have said that all modern religions are based, at least on their logical side, on this notion that there are higher powers which observe all the doings of man, and constantly take a hand in them. It should be added that a corollary is almost always appended, to the effect that these higher powers also pronounce ethical judgments upon such human acts as happen to be performed without this intervention, and are themselves animated by a lofty and impeccable morality. Most religions, of course, also embrace a concept of higher powers that are not benign, but malignant—that is, they posit the existence of demons as well as of gods. But there are very few in which the demons are regarded as superior to the gods, or even as their full equals. The great majority of creeds, East and West, savage and so-called civilized, put the gods far above the demons, and teach that the gods always wish the good of man, and that man's virtue and happiness run in direct ratio to his obedience to their desires. That is, they are all based upon the doctrine of what is called the goodness of God. This is true pre-eminently of the chief oriental faiths: Buddhism, Brahminism and Confucianism. It is true even of Christianity, despite its luxuriant demonology. No true Christian can believe that God ever deliberately and wantonly injures him, or could conceivably wish him ill. The slings and arrows of God, he believes, are brought down upon him by his own ignorance and contumacy. He believes that if he could be like God he would be perfect.

This doctrine of the goodness of God, it seems to me, is no more, at bottom, than an evidence of arrested intellectual development. It does not fit into what we know of the nature and operations of the cosmos today; it is a survival from a day of universal ignorance. That it is still given credit in the Far East is not surprising, for the intellectual development of the Far East, despite all the nonsense that is talked about Indian and Chinese "philosophy," is really no further advanced than that of Europe was in the time of St. Louis. The most profound Hindoo or Chinese "philosopher" believes, as objective facts, things that would make even a Georgia Fundamentalist snicker, and so his "philosophy" is chiefly worthless, as was that of the Greeks. The Greeks sometimes guessed right, just as the swamis and yogis of Los Angeles sometimes guess right, but in the main their speculations, being based upon false observations, were valueless, and no one would pay any attention to them today if it were not for the advertising they get from theologians, who find them to their taste, and professional "philosophers," who make a living trying to teach them to sophomores. But if the belief in the goodness of God is natural to misinformed orientals, as it was natural to the singularly ignorant Greeks, it is certainly *not* natural to the enlightened races of the West today, for all their science is simply a great massing of proofs that God, if He exists, is neither good nor bad, but simply indifferent—an infinite Force carrying on the operation of unintelligible processes without the slightest regard, either one way or the other, for the comfort, safety and happiness of man.

Why, then, does this belief survive? Largely, I am convinced, because it is supported by another hoary relic from the adolescence of the race, to wit, the weakness for poetry. The Jews fastened their religion upon the Western world, not because it was more reasonable than the religions of their contemporaries —as a matter of fact, it was vastly less reasonable than many of them—, but because it was far more poetical. The poetry in it was what fetched the decaying Romans, and after them the barbarians of the North; not the so-called Christian evidences. For the Jews were poets of a truly colossal eloquence, and they put their fundamental superstitions into dithyrambs of such compelling loveliness that they disarmed the common sense

even of skeptical Romans, and so knocked out all other contemporary religions, many of which were in far closer accord
with what was then known of the true operations of the universe. To this day no better poetry has ever been written. It is
so powerful in its effects that even men who reject its content
in toto are more or less susceptible to it. One hesitates to flout
it on purely æsthetic grounds; however dubious it may be in
doctrine, it is nevertheless almost perfect in form, and so even
the most violent atheist tends to respect it, just as he respects a
beautiful but deadly toadstool. For no man, of course, ever
quite gets over poetry. He may seem to have recovered from it,
just as he may seem to have recovered from the measles of his
school-days, but exact observation teaches us that no such recovery is ever quite perfect; there always remains a scar, a
weakness and a memory.

Now, there is reason for maintaining that the taste for poetry,
in the process of human development, marks a stage measurably later than the stage of religion. Savages so little cultured
that they know no more of poetry than a cow have elaborate
and often very ingenious theologies. If this be true, then it follows that the individual, as he rehearses the life of the species,
is apt to carry his taste for poetry further along than he carries
his religion—that if his development is arrested at any stage
before complete intellectual maturity that arrest is far more
likely to leave him with poetical hallucinations than it is to
leave him with theological hallucinations. Thus, taking men in
the mass, there are many more natural victims of the former
than of the latter—and here is where the talent of the ancient
Jews does its execution. It holds countless thousands to the
faith who are actually against the faith, and the weakness with
which it holds them is their weakness for poetry, i.e., for the
beautiful but untrue. Put into plain, harsh words most of the
articles they are asked to believe would revolt them, but put
into sonorous dithyrambs the same articles fascinate and over-
whelm them. It is not the logical substance of the Old Testament that continues to hold the mind of modern man, for that
logical substance must often revolt him, even when he is of
sub-normal intelligence; it is the sonorous strophes of the
ancient bards and prophets. And it is not the epistemology, or
the natural history, or the ethical scheme, or the system of

jurisprudence of the New Testament that melts his heart and wets his eyes; it is simply the poetical magic of the Sermon on the Mount, the exquisite parables, and the incomparable story of the Child in the Manger.

This persistence of the weakness for poetry, no doubt, explains the great growth of ritualism in an age of skepticism. Almost every day theology gets another blow from science. So badly has it been battered during the past century, indeed, that educated men now give it little more credence than they give to sorcery, its ancient ally. But squeezing out the logical nonsense does no damage to the poetry; on the contrary, it frees, and, in a sense, dignifies the poetry. Paul's chief doctrines, clearly stated, offend the intelligence intolerably, but clothed and concealed by the gorgeous vestments of the mass they separate themselves from logic entirely and take on something of the witchery of beauty. Thus there is a constant movement of Christians, and particularly of newly-intellectual Christians, from the more literal varieties of Christian faith to the more poetical varieties. The normal Babbitt, in the United States, is born a Methodist or a Baptist, but when he begins to lay by money he and his wife tend to go over to the American branch of the Church of England, which is not only more fashionable but also less revolting to the higher cerebral centers. His daughter, when she emerges from the finishing-school, is very High Church; his grand-daughter, if the family keeps its securities, will probably go over to Rome.

In view of all this, I am convinced that the Christian church, as a going concern, is quite safe from danger, despite the rapid growth of agnosticism. The theology it merchants is full of childish and disgusting absurdities; practically all the other religions of civilized and semi-civilized man are more plausible. But all of these religions, including even Moslemism, contain the fatal defect that they appeal primarily to the reason. Christianity will survive not only Modernism but also Fundamentalism, a much more difficult business. It will survive because it makes its first and foremost appeal to that moony sense of the poetic which is in all men—to that elemental sentimentality which, in men of arrested mental development, which is to say, in the average men of Christendom, passes for the passion to seek and know beauty.

3
The Devotee

If religion is thus charming to the more enlightened modern Christian only in proportion as it is poetical, *i.e.*, as it is regarded as not literally true, it is charming to the enlightened
spectator only when it is formal and hence more or less insin-
cere. A devotee on her knees in some abysmal and mysterious
cathedral, the while solemn music sounds, and clouds of incense come down the wind, and priests in luxurious, levantine
costumes busy themselves with stately ceremonials in a dead
and not too respectable language—this is unquestionably
beautiful, particularly if the devotee herself be sightly. But the
same devotee aroused to hysterical protestations of faith by the
shrieks and contortions of a Methodist dervish in the costume
of a Southern member of Congress, her knees trembling with
the fear of God, her hands clenched as if to do combat with
Beelzebub, her lips discharging hosannas and hallelujahs—this
is merely obscene.

4
The Restoration of Beauty

I have said that the poetry which safeguards Christianity
from destruction today was borrowed from the ancient Jews,
authors of the two Testaments. But there was a long period
during which it was overshadowed by purely logical ideas,
many of them of a sort that would be called bolshevistic today.
The principal Christians of the apostolic age were almost exactly like the modern Calvinists and Wesleyans—men quite
without taste or imagination, whoopers and shouters, low vul-
garians, cads. So far as is known, their public worship was
wholly devoid of the sense of beauty; their sole concern was
with the salvation of their so-called souls. Thus they left us
nothing worth preserving—not a single church, or liturgy, or
even hymn. The objects of art exhumed from the Catacombs
are inferior to the drawings and statuettes of Crô-Magnon
man. All the moving beauty that adorns the corpse of Christianity today came into being long after the Fathers had perished. The faith was centuries old before Christians began to

build cathedrals, and nearly a thousand years old before they learned how to build good ones. It was twelve hundred years old before they invented mariolatry—the prime cause of the appearance of a purely Christian poetry. We think of Christmas as the typical Christian festival, and no doubt it is; none other is so generally kept by Christian sects, or so rich in charm and beauty. Well, Christmas, as we now have it, was almost unknown in Christendom until the Eleventh Century, when the relics of St. Nicholas of Myra, originally the patron of pawnbrokers, were brought from the East to Italy. At this time the Universal Church was already torn by controversies and menaced by schisms, and the shadow of the Reformation was plainly discernible in the West. Religions, in fact, like castles, sunsets and women, never reach their maximum of beauty until they are touched by decay.

5
End-Product

Christendom may be defined briefly as that part of the world in which, if any man stands up in public and solemnly swears that he is a Christian, all his auditors will laugh.

6
Another

At the end of one millennium and nine centuries of Christianity, it remains an unshakable assumption of the law in all Christian countries and of the moral judgment of Christians everywhere that if a man and a woman, entering a room together, close the door behind them, the man will come out sadder and the woman wiser.

7
Holy Clerks

Around no class of men do more false assumptions cluster than around the rev. clergy, our lawful commissioners at the Throne of Grace. I proceed at once to a crass example: the assumption that clergymen are necessarily religious. Obviously, it is widely cherished, even by clergymen themselves. The most ribald of us, in presence of a holy clerk, is a bit self-conscious, reticent and awed. I am myself given to criticizing Divine Providence somewhat freely, but in the company of the rector of my parish, even at the *Biertisch*, I tone down my animadversions to a level of feeble and polite remonstrance. I know the fellow too well, of course, to have any actual belief in his piety. He is, in fact, rather less pious than the average right-thinking Americano, and I doubt gravely that the sorceries he engages in professionally every day awaken in him any emotion more lofty than boredom. I have heard him pray for Coolidge, for the heathen and for rain, but I have never heard him pray for himself. Nevertheless, the public assumption that he is highly devout, though I dispute it, colors all my intercourse with him, and deprives him of hearing some of my most searching and intelligent observations.

All that is needed to expose the hollowness of this ancient delusion is to consider the chain of causes which brings a young man to taking holy orders. Is it, in point of fact, an irresistible religious impulse that sets him to studying exegetics, homiletics and the dog-Greek of the New Testament, and an irresistible religious impulse only, or is it something quite different? I believe that it is something quite different, and that that something may be described briefly as a desire to shine in the world without too much effort. The young theologue, in brief, is commonly an ambitious but somewhat lazy and incompetent fellow, and he studies theology instead of medicine or law because it offers a quicker and easier route to an assured job and public respect. The sacred sciences may be nonsensical bores, but they at least have the vast virtue of short-circuiting, so to speak, the climb up the ladder of security. The young doctor, for a number of years after he graduates, either has to work for nothing or to content himself with the dregs of practise, and the young lawyer, unless he has unusual influence or complete atrophy of the conscience, often teeters on the edge of actual starvation. But the young divine is a safe and distinguished man the moment he is ordained; indeed, his popularity, especially among the faithful who are fair, is often greater at that moment than it ever is afterward. His livelihood is assured instantly. At one stroke, he becomes a person of dignity and importance, eminent in his community, deferred to even by those who question his magic, and vaguely and pleasantly feared by those who credit it.

These facts, you may be sure, are not concealed from ambitious young men of the sort I have mentioned. Such young men have eyes, and even a certain capacity for ratiocination. They observe the nine sons of the police sergeant: one a priest at twenty-five, with a fine house to live in, invitations to all christenings and birthday parties for miles around, and plenty of time to go to the ball-game on Summer afternoons; the others struggling desperately to make their livings as piano-movers, tin-roofers, motormen or bootleggers. They observe the young Methodist dominie in his Ford sedan, flitting about among the women while their husbands labor down in the yards district, a clean collar around his neck, a solid meal of fried chicken in his gizzard, and his name in the local paper every day. They observe the Baptist dervish in his white neck-tie, raiding saloons, touring the bawdy-houses and raising hell generally, his tabernacle packed every Sunday night, a noble clink of silver in his collection-plates, and a fat purse for him now and then from the Ladies' Aid or the Ku Klux Klan. Only crazy women ever fall in love with young doctors or lawyers, but every young clergyman, if he is so inclined, may have a whole harem, and with infinitely less danger than a struggling lawyer, a bootlegger or a bank clerk runs every day. Even if he is celibate, the gals bathe him in their smiles; in truth, the more celibate he is, the more attention he gets from them. No wonder his high privileges and immunities propagate the sin of envy! No wonder there are still candidates for the holy shroud, despite the vast growth of atheism among us!

It seems to me that the majority of the young men who are thus sucked into holy orders are not actually pious at all, but rather somewhat excessively realistic—that genuine piety is far more apt to keep a youth out of the pulpit than to take him into it. The true devotee, frequenting the sacred edifice constantly, becomes too familiar with the daily duties of a clergyman to see any religious satisfaction in them. In the main, they have nothing to do with religion at all, but are basically social or commercial. In so far as a clergyman works at all, he works as the general manager of a corporation, and only too often it is in financial difficulties and rent by factions among the stock-holders. His specifically religious duties are of a routine and monotonous nature, and must needs depress him mightily, as a surgeon is depressed by the endless snaring of tonsils and excision of appendices. He debases spiritual exaltation by reducing it to a hollow and meaningless formality, as a politician debases patriotism and a lady of joy debases love. He becomes, in the end, quite anæsthetic to religion, and even hostile to it. The fact is made distressingly visible by the right rev. the bench of bishops. For a bishop to fall on his knees spontaneously and begin to pray to God would make almost as great a scandal as if he mounted his throne in a bathing-suit. The piety of the ecclesiastic, on such high levels, becomes wholly formal and theoretical. The servant of God has been lifted so near to the saints and become so familiar with the inner workings of the divine machinery that the sense of awe and wonder has oozed out of him. He can no more undergo a genuine religious experience than a veteran scene-shifter can laugh at the wheezes of the First Gravedigger. It is, perhaps, well that this is so. If the higher clergy were actually religious some of their own sermons and pastoral epistles would scare them to death.

IV.

Justice Under Democracy

I

PERHAPS the chief victims of Prohibition in the Republic, in the long run, will turn out to be the Federal judges. I do not argue here, of course, that drinking bootleg liquors will kill them bodily; I merely suggest that enforcing the unjust and insane provisions of the Volstead Act will rob them of all their old dignity. A dozen years ago a Federal judge was perhaps the most dignified and respected official yet flourishing under our democracy. The plain people, many years before that, had lost all respect for lawmakers, whether Federal, State or municipal, and save for the President himself, they had very little respect left for the gentlemen of the executive arm, high or low. More, they had begun to view the judiciary of the States very biliously, and showed no sign of surprise when a member of it was taken in judicial adultery. But for the Federal judges they still continued to have a high veneration, and for plain reasons. *Imprimis*, the Federal judges sat for life, and thus did not have to climb down from their benches at intervals and clamor obscenely for votes. Secondly, the laws that they were told off to enforce, and especially the criminal laws, were few in number, simple in character, and thoroughly in accord with almost universal ideas of right and wrong. No citizen in his right mind had much sympathy for the felons who were shipped to Atlanta each morning by the marshals of the Federal courts—chiefly counterfeiters, fraudulent bankrupts, adulterators of food and drugs, get-rich-quick swindlers, thieving letter-carriers, crooked army officers, and so on. Public sentiment was almost unanimously behind the punishment of such rogues, and it rejoiced that that punishment was in the hands of men who carried on the business in an austere and elevated manner, without fear and without favor. It was, in those days, almost unheard of for a petit jury in a Federal court to acquit a prisoner whose guilt was plain; the percentage of convictions in some jurisdictions ran beyond ninety per cent. For

48

guilt of the kind then dealt with by those courts met with the reprehension of practically all men not professional criminals themselves—and Federal juries, petit and grand, were picked with some care, as Federal judges themselves were picked.

I describe a Golden Age, now lamentably closed. The Uplift in its various lovely forms has completely changed the character of the work done by a Federal judge. Once the dispenser of varieties of law that only scoundrels questioned, he is now the harassed and ludicrous dispenser of varieties of law that only idiots approve. It was the Espionage Act, I suppose, that brought him to this new and dreadful office, but it is Prohibition—whether of wine-bibbing, of drug-taking, of interstate week-ending, or of what not—that has carried him beyond the bounds of what, to most normal men, is common decency. His typical job today, as a majority of the plain people see it, especially in the big cities, is simply to punish men who have refused or been unable to pay the bribes demanded by Prohibition enforcement officers. In other words, he is now chiefly apprehended by the public, not as a scourge of rascals, but as an agent of rascals and a scourge of peaceable men. He gets a great deal more publicity than he used to get in his palmy days, but it is publicity of a sort that rapidly undermines his dignity. Unfortunately for him, but perhaps very fortunately for what remains of civilized government among us, the plain people have never been able to grasp the difference between law and justice. To them the two things are one—or ought to be. So the fact that the judge is bound by law to enforce all the intolerable provisions of the Volstead Act, including even its implicit provision that men wearing its badges shall get a fair percentage upon every transaction in bootlegging—this fact does not relieve the judge himself of responsibility for the ensuing injustice. All that the vulgar observe is that justice has departed from his courtroom. Once the equal of an archbishop, he is now the equal of a police captain; once respected, he is now distrusted and disliked.

If this were all, of course, it might be possible to dismiss the whole matter on the ground that the public is an ass. That men of the highest worth are not always respected, even when they wear official robes, is a commonplace. But in the present case there is more to it than merely that. Not a few of the Federal judges have begun to show signs that the noisome work that has been forced upon them has begun to achieve its inevitable subjective effects; in other words, not a few begin to attack their sneaking sense of its lack of dignity and good repute by bedizening it with moral indignation. The judicial servant of the Anti-Saloon League thus takes on some of the neo-Christian character of the League's own dervishes and sorcerers. He is not content to send some poor yokel to jail for an artificial crime that, in the view of at least eighty per cent. of all even half-civilized Americans, is no crime at all; he must also denounce the culprit from the bench in terms fit for a man accused of arson or mayhem. Here the Freudians, perhaps, may have something to say; the great masses of the innocent and sinful, knowing nothing of Freud, observe only that the learned jurist is silly as well as unjust. There issues from that observation a generally bilious view of his office and his person. He slides slowly down a fatal chute. His day of arctic and envied eminence passes. A few sensitive judges quietly retire from the bench. But the legal mind is usually tougher than that. It can almost always find justification for doing, as agent of the law, what would be inconceivable privately to a man of honor.

2

The truth is, indeed, that the decline in dignity from which the Federal judges now suffer is not wholly due to the external fact of Prohibition; it is due quite as much to their own growing pliancy and lack of professional self-respect. All that Prohibition does to them is to make brilliantly plain, even to the meanest understanding, their lamentable departure from that high integrity of purpose, that assiduous concern for justice, that jealous watchfulness over the rights of man which simple men, at all times and everywhere, like to find in the judges set over them, and which the simple men of the United States, not so long ago, saw or thought they saw in the learned ornaments of the Federal bench. Before ever Volstead emerged from the Christian Endeavor belt with his preposterous Act, confidence had begun to shake. The country had seen Federal judges who were unmistakably mountebanks; it had seen some who were, to the naked eye, indistinguishable from rascals. It had seen one step down from the highest court in the land to engage in an undignified stumping-tour, soliciting the votes of the rabble. It had seen another diligently insinuate himself into the headlines of the yellow press, in competition with Jack Dempsey and Babe Ruth. It had seen others abuse their powers of equity in the frank interest of capital, and deny the commonest justice to poor men in their clutches. And during the war it had grown accustomed to seeing the Federal bench converted into a sort of rival to the rostrum of Liberty Loan orators, with judges hurling pious objurgations at citizens accused of nothing worse than speaking their minds freely, and all pretense to fair hearings and just punishments abandoned.

Of late the multiplication of such Dogberries has gone on apace as the best of the old-time judges have retired from the bench. These new jurisconsults, rejecting justice openly and altogether, have even begun to reject the Constitution and the law. A judicial process before them is indistinguishable from a bull-fight, with the accused, if he is unpopular enough, as the bull. It is their theory, apparently, that the sole function of a judge is to fill the jails. If the accused happens to be guilty or to be reasonably suspected of guilt, well and good. But if, as in the Chicago Socialist trials, he is obviously innocent, to hell with him anyhow. True enough, a majority of the Federal judges, high and low, still stand clear of such buffooneries. Even in the midst of the worst hysteria of the war there were plenty who refused to be run amok by Palmer, Burleson and company; I need cite only Hand, J., and Rose, J., as admirable examples of a number of judges who preserved their dignity 'mid the rockets' red glare. But the headlines in the newspapers had nothing to say about such judges; their blackest ink was reserved for the other kind. That other kind gradually established a view of the Federal bench that still persists, and that is growing more and more fixed as the farce of Prohibition enforcement unrolls. It is a view which, in brief, holds that the Federal bench is no longer the most exalted and faithful protector of the liberties of the citizen, but the most relentless and inordinate foe of them—that its main purpose is not to dispense justice at all, but to get men into jail, guilty or not guilty, by fair means or foul—that to this end it is willing to lend itself to the execution of any law, however extravagant, and to support that execution with a variety of casuistry that is flatly against every ordinary conception of common sense and common decency. The Espionage Act cases, the labor injunction cases, the deportation cases, the Postal Act cases, the Mann Act cases, and now the Prohibition cases—all of these, impinging in rapid succession upon a people brought up to regard the Bill of Rights as a reality and liberty as a precious thing, have bred suspicion of the Federal courts, including especially the Supreme Court, and, on the heels of that suspicion, a positive and apparently ineradicable distrust. I doubt that the Radical fanatics who dodge about the land have ever converted any substantial body of Americans to their crazy doctrines; certainly there is not the slightest sign today of the Revolution that they were predicting for last year, and the year before. But when they have denounced the Federal courts and produced the overwhelming evidence, their shots have gone home.

Now and then a judge has argued, defending himself against some manifestation of popular discontent, that he is helpless—that he is the agent, not of justice, but of law. Even in the heyday of the Espionage Act a few were moved to make that apology from the bench, including, if I remember rightly, the judge who sentenced Debs. The distinction thus set up is one that seems clear to lawyers, but, as I have said, it seldom gets a hospitable hearing from plain men. If the latter believe anything at all it is that law without justice is an evil thing—that such law, indeed, leads inevitably to a contradiction in terms—that the highest duty of the judiciary is not to enforce it pedantically, but to evade it, vitiate it, and, if possible, destroy it. The plain man sees plenty of other sorts of law destroyed by the courts; he can't help wondering why the process is so seldom applied to statutes that violate, not merely legal apothegms, but the baldest of common sense. Thus when he beholds a Federal judge fining a man, under a constitutional amendment prohibiting the sale of intoxicating beverages, for selling a beverage that is admittedly not intoxicating, or jailing another man who has got before the bar, as everyone knows, not because he ran a still but because he refused to pay the bribe demanded by the Prohibition enforcement officer, or issuing against a third an injunction whose sole and undisguised purpose is to deprive him, by a legal swindle, of his constitutional right to a trial by jury of his peers—when he observes such monkey-shines going on in the name of the law, is it any wonder that he concludes dismally that the law is an ass, and its agent another? In ordinary life men cannot engage in such lunatic oppressions of their fellow-men without paying a penalty for it; even a policeman must be measurably more plausible and discreet. If a judge is bound by his oath to engage in them, then so much the worse for the judge. He can no more hope to be respected than a hangman can hope to be respected.

The truth is, of course, that the judges are by no means under the compulsion that is alleged. The injunction clause of the Volstead Act actually has no constitutional mandate behind it; the only constitutional mandate that I can find, bearing upon it at all, is against it. That is to be found in the Fifth and Sixth Amendments. The first of these amendments provides that "no person shall be held to answer for a capital or otherwise infamous crime unless on a presentment or indictment of a grand jury"; the second requires that "in all criminal prosecutions the accused shall enjoy the right to a speedy and public trial by an impartial jury of the State and district wherein the crime shall have been committed." It must be obvious to everyone that the aim of the injunction clause is simply and solely to deprive the accused of these safeguards— to rob him of his clear right to a trial by a jury of his peers. The history of the clause reveals the fact clearly. It was first heard of in Iowa in the early years of the century, and it was invented there, not by Prohibitionists, but by the frantic vice-crusaders who then raged and roared in the hinterland, inflaming the pious with gaudy yarns about white slave traders, seducers armed with hypodermic syringes, and other such phantasms. In Iowa these vice-crusaders specialized in the harassing of the sort of poor women who keep cheap lodging-houses. When such a woman, by ignorance or inadvertance, admitted a lady no longer a lady to her establishment, they raided her, dragged her to jail, and charged her with keeping a bawdy-house. This was good sport, and the rev. pastors urged it on every Sunday. But after the first uproar, it began to develop defects, and the chief of these defects was that juries refused to convict. Now and then a man of sense and self-respect got upon the panel and spoiled the show. Perhaps he found it impossible to believe the sworn testimony of the vice-crusaders. Perhaps he concluded that the accused, though guilty, had been punished enough by the raid. Whatever his motive, he hung the jury and killed the hunting.

It was then that Christian lawyers came to the rescue of pious and baffled men. They did it by the simple process of throwing the whole responsibility upon the judge. Juries were hard to intimidate; there was always apt to be at least one juror who didn't care a hoot what was said against him from the sacred desk—some hell-cat who positively rejoiced in the indignation of the knock-'em-down-and-drag-'em-out clergy. But judges were tenderer. Some of them were candidates for reelection to the bench; all of them were solicitous about their dignity, and did not care to face ecclesiastical curses, pious whispers, suggestive winks. So the Iowa lawyers amended the law by inventing and inserting the injunction clause. This clause flatly abolished the right of trial by jury. When the vice-crusaders found a likely victim they simply got a friendly judge to issue an injunction against her, restraining her from using her premises for immoral purposes. Then they watched her closely. The moment they detected a dubious female entering her door they raided her again, dragged her before the same judge—and he jailed her for contempt of court, an offense punishable summarily and without a jury trial. Nine times out of ten, perhaps, a jury would have acquitted her, but the judge was already safely against her.

This scheme gave the vice-crusaders a new lease of life and greatly increased their takings in the Sunday-schools. Naturally enough, the Prohibitionists, who were, in most cases, none other than the vice-crusaders themselves, instantly borrowed it, and so it got into the Prohibition acts of all the dry States. Volstead, as a country State's attorney on the Minnesota steppes, employed it diligently and to vast effect. He put it into the Volstead Act as a matter of course. There it stands today, a dishonest and disgraceful blemish upon American law. Its deliberate aim is to take away from the citizen accused of crime his constitutional right to a jury trial; no imaginable argument in favor of it can dodge that plain fact. When it is invoked, as under the Volstead Act, against a man who has been found guilty of one violation of the act, it not only punishes him doubly for that violation; it also punishes him in advance for a second offense that he has admittedly not committed, and deprives him of his constitutional means of defense in case he is subsequently accused. He is, in brief, put absolutely at the mercy of the judge—and the judge is already obviously suspicious of him, and may be a senile sadist or Prohibitionist demagogue to boot. The constitutional provision that a man accused of crime may throw himself upon a jury of plain men like himself, sworn to regard only the evidence actually before them—that if he is able to convince only one of the twelve that he is innocent, or not proved guilty beyond a doubt, he shall go free—this fundamental guarantee of the citizen, this most sacred of all human rights under Anglo-Saxon jurisprudence, is specifically nullified and made a mock of in order to satisfy the frenzy of a minority of fanatics!

That contempt of court should be an offense standing outside the purview of the Fifth and Sixth Amendments—that a judge should have the power to punish summarily all deliberate floutings of his dignity—this may be reasonably argued, though there are many sound considerations against it. But that it should be lawful to convert some other and wholly unrelated offense into contempt of court by a legal fiction, and so get around the Fifth and Sixth Amendments by a swindle—this is surely more than any sensible man would soberly maintain. When it is maintained, it is only by persons who are trying to put men into jail by processes that any average jury would revolt against—mill owners eager to get rid of annoying labor leaders, coal operators bent upon making slaves of their miners, Prohibitionists lusting for the punishment of their opponents. The injunction in strike cases has been a stench for years; it is, indeed, so bad that a large number of Federal judges refuse absolutely to employ it. It is a worse stench in Prohibition cases, for here it is becoming a formidable and favorite weapon, not merely in the hands of property-owners who want to put down strikes, but in the hands of criminal Prohibition agents who seek to wring blackmail from their victims. In brief, it has become a dishonest means of oppression for men who are even more dishonest than it is. Certainly it is idle to talk of respect for the laws when such devices have legislative and judicial sanction. No reasonable man, save he be ignorant of their nature and purpose, can conceivably respect them. If, on the ground that whatever is in the law should be given full faith and credit, he maintains that they should not be resisted, then he maintains that the Bill of Rights is no more than a string of empty phrases, and that any shyster who invents a way to evade and abrogate it is a jurist as dignified as John Marshall.

3

Is a judge bound to lend himself to such gross and dishonest attacks upon the common rights of the citizen? I am no lawyer, but I presume to doubt it. There were judges in 1918 who did not think themselves obliged to sacrifice the Bill of Rights to the Espionage Act, and who resolutely refused to do so, and yet, so far as I know, nothing happened to them; at least one of them, to my knowledge, has been since promoted to a circuit. Why should any judge enforce the injunction clause of the Volstead Act? Its enforcement is surely not an automatic act; it involves deliberation and decision by the judge; he may refuse his injunction without offering any explanation to anyone. What would follow if he arose one day in his high pulpit, and announced simply that his court was purged of all such oblique and dishonest enactments henceforth—that he had resolved to refuse to lend himself to the schemes of blackmailers with badges, or to harass and punish free citizens in violation of their fundamental constitutional rights and their plain dignity as human beings, or, in brief, to engage in any other enterprise as a judge that he would shrink from engaging in as a good citizen and a man of honor? Would the result be impeachment? I should like to meet a Congressman insane enough to move the impeachment of such a judge! Would it be a storm of public indignation? . . . Or would it be a vociferous yell of delight?

It seems to me, indeed, that the first judge who rises to such a rebellion will be the first judge ever to become a popular hero in the Republic—that he will be elevated to the Supreme Court by a sort of acclamation, even if it is necessary to get rid of one of the sitting justices by setting fire to his gown. But even imagining him so elevated, the remaining eight justices will still function, and all of us know what they think of the Bill of Rights. Wouldn't such a rebel judge succumb to the system of which he was a discreet particle? Couldn't the other eight judges nullify and make a mock of his heroic defiance? Could they, indeed? Then how? If a judge, high or low, actually called in justice to rescue a citizen from the law, what precisely could the Supreme Court do about it? I know of no appeal by the District Attorney in criminal cases, once the accused has been put in jeopardy; I know only of impeachment for judges who forget the lines of the solemn farce to which they are sworn. But try to imagine the impeachment of a judge charged with punching a hole in the Volstead Act, and letting in some common justice and common decency!

So far, no such rambunctious and unprecedented judge has been heard of,—none, that is, has objected to the injunction clause in toto and head on—nor do I specifically predict his advent. He may come, but probably he won't. The law is a curse to all of us, but it is a curse of special virulence to lawyers. It becomes for them a sort of discreditable vice, a stealthy and degrading superstition. It robs them of all balance, of all capacity for clear thought, of all imagination. Judges tend to show this decay of the faculties in an exaggerated form; they become mere automata, bound by arbitrary rules, precedents, the accumulated imbecilities of generations of bad logic; to their primary lack of sense as lawyers they add the bombastic manner of bureaucrats. It is thus too much to hope for a judge showing any originality or courage; one Holmes in an era of Hardings and Coolidges is probably more than a fair allotment. But while the judges of the District Courts go on driving wild teams of jackasses through the Bill of Rights, and the rev. seniors of the Supreme Court give their approval to the business in solemn form, sometimes but not always with Holmes, J., and Brandeis, J., dissenting—while all this is going on, there are black clouds rolling up from the hinterland, where the Constitution is still taught in the schools and even Methodists are bred to reverence Patrick Henry. The files of Congress already show the way the wind is blowing—constitutional amendments to drag down and denaturize the Supreme Court, simple acts to the same end, other acts providing for the election of Federal judges, yet others even more revolutionary. I know of no such proposal that has any apparent merit. Even the best of them, hamstringing the courts, would only augment the power of a Congress that is ten times worse. But so long as judges pursue fatuously the evil business of converting every citizen into a subject, demagogues will come forward with their dubious remedies, and, soon or late, unless the bench pulls up, some of these demagogues will get themselves heard.

V.

Reflections on Human Monogamy

I
The Eternal Farce

As every attentive patron of the drama is well aware, it is difficult for even the most skillful actors to keep Ibsen's "Hedda Gabler" from degenerating to farce in the performance. The reason is certainly not occult. It lies in the plain fact that such transactions as the dramatist here deals with—a neurotic woman's effort to be heavily romantic, her horror when romance is followed by pregnancy, the manœuvres of a satanic and idiotic lover, the cuckolding of a husband wearing whiskers—are intrinsically and incurably farcical. *All* love affairs, in truth, are farcical—that is, to the spectators. When one hears that some old friend has succumbed to the blandishments of a sweet one, however virtuous and beautiful she may be, one does not gasp and roll one's eyes; one simply laughs. When one hears, a year or two later, that they are quarreling, one laughs again. When one hears that the bride is seeking consolation from the curate of the parish, one laughs a third time. When one hears that the bridegroom, in revenge, is sneaking his stenographer to dinner at an Italian restaurant, one laughs a fourth time. And so on. But when one goes to the theatre, the dramatist often asks one to wear a solemn frown when he displays the same puerile and ludicrous phenomena— that is, while he depicts a fat actress as going crazy when she discovers that her husband, an actor with a face like the abdomen of a ten-pin, has run off to Asbury Park, N.J., with another actress who pronounces all French words in the manner of the Texas Christian University.

The best dramatists, of course, make no such mistake. In Shakespeare love is always depicted as comedy—sometimes light and charming, as in "Twelfth Night," but usually rough and buffoonish, as in "The Taming of the Shrew." This comic attitude is plainly visible even in such plays as "Hamlet" and "Romeo and Juliet." In its main outlines, I suppose, "Hamlet"

is properly looked upon as a tragedy, but if you believe that the
love passages are intended to be tragic then all I ask is that you
give a sober reading to the colloquies between Hamlet and
Ophelia. They are not only farcical; they are downright obscene; Shakespeare, through the mouth of Hamlet, derides the
whole business with almost intolerable ribaldry. As for "Romeo
and Juliet," what is it but a penetrating burlesque upon the
love guff that was fashionable in the poet's time? True enough,
his head buzzed with such loveliness that he could not write
even burlesque without making it beautiful—compare "Much
Ado About Nothing" and "Othello"—but nevertheless it is
quite absurd to say that he was serious when he wrote this tale
of calf-love. Imagine such a man taking seriously the spasms
and hallucinations of a *Backfisch* of fourteen, the tinpot heroics
of a boy of eighteen! Shakespeare remembered very well the
nature of his own amorous fancies at eighteen. It was the year
of his seduction by Ann Hathaway, whose brothers later made
him marry her, much to his damage and dismay. He wrote the
play at forty-five. Tell it to the Marines!

I have a suspicion that even Ibsen, though he seldom permitted himself overt humor, indulged in some quiet spoofing
when he wrote "A Doll's House," "Hedda Gabler," "The
Lady From the Sea" and "Little Eyolf." The whole last act of
"Hedda Gabler" could be converted into burlesque by changing ten words; as I have said, it is almost always burlesque as
bad actors play it. In the cases of "Ghosts" and "The Master-
Builder" there can be no doubt whatever. The former is a
piece of buffoonery designed to make fun of the fools who
were outraged by "A Doll's House"; the latter is a comic piece
founded upon personal experience. At the age of sixty Ibsen
amused himself with a flirtation with a girl of sixteen. Following the custom of her sex, she took his casual winks and cheek-
pinchings quite seriously, and began hinting to the whole
neighborhood that the old boy was hopelessly gone on her,
and that he intended to divorce Fru Ibsen and run off with her
to Italy. All this gave entertainment to Ibsen, who was a sardonic man, and he began speculating as to what would happen
to a man of his age who actually yielded to the gross provocations of such a wench. The result was "The Master-Builder."
But think of the plot! He makes the master-builder climb a

church-steeple, and then jump off! Imagine him regarding such slap-stick farce seriously!

The world has very little sense of humor. It is always wagging its ears solemnly over elaborate jocosities. For 600 years it has gurgled over the "Divine Comedy" of Dante, despite the plain fact that the work is a flaming satire upon the whole Christian hocus-pocus of heaven, purgatory and hell. To have tackled such nonsense head-on, in Dante's time, would have been to flout the hangman; hence the poet clothed his attack in an irony so delicate that the ecclesiastical police were baffled. Why is the poem called a comedy? I have read at least a dozen discussions of the question by modern pedants, all of them labored and unconvincing. The same problem obviously engaged the scholars of the poet's own time. He called the thing simply "comedy"; they added the adjective "divine" in order to ameliorate what seemed to them to be an intolerable ribaldry. Well, here is a "comedy" in which human beings are torn limb from limb, boiled in sulphur, cut up with red-hot knives, and filled with molten lead! Can one imagine a man capable of such a poem regarding such fiendish imbecilities seriously? Certainly not. They appeared just as idiotic to him as they appear to you or me. But the Federal judiciary of the day made it impossible to say so in plain language, so he said so behind a smoke-screen of gaudy poetry. How Dante would have roared if he could have known that six hundred years later an illiterate President of the United States, a good Baptist with money in the bank, married happily to a divorcée—would take the whole thing with utter seriousness, and deliver a nonsensical harangue upon the lessons in it for American Christians!

The case of Wagner's "Parsifal" is still more remarkable. Even Nietzsche was deceived by it. Like the most maudlin German fat woman at Baireuth, he mistook the composer's elaborate and outrageous burlesque of Christianity for a tribute to Christianity, and so denounced him as a jackass and refused to speak to him thereafter. To this day "Parsifal" is given with all the trappings of a religious ceremonial, and pious folks go to hear it who would instantly shut their ears if the band began playing "Tristan und Isolde." It has become, in fact, a sort of "'Way Down East" or "Ben Hur" of music drama—a bait for luring patrons who are never seen in the opera-house otherwise. But try to imagine such a thumping atheist as Wagner writing a religious opera seriously! And if, by any chance, you succeed in imagining it, then turn to the Char-Freitag music, and play it on your victrola. Here is the central scene of the piece, the moment of most austere solemnity—and to it Wagner fits music that is so luscious and so fleshly—indeed, so downright lascivious and indecent—that even I, who am almost anæsthetic to such provocations, blush every time I hear it. The Flower Maidens do not raise my blood-pressure a single ohm; I have actually snored through the whole second act of "Tristan." But when I hear that Char-Freitag music all of my Freudian suppressions begin groaning and stretching their legs in the dungeons of my unconscious. And what does Char-Freitag mean? Char-Freitag means Good Friday!

2
Venus at the Domestic Hearth

One inclines to the notion that women—and especially homely women—greatly overestimate the importance of physical beauty in their eternal conspiracy against the liberty of men. It is a powerful lure, to be sure, but it is certainly not the only one that fetches the game, nor even, perhaps, the most effective one. The satisfaction that a man gets out of conquering—which is to say, out of succumbing to—a woman of noticeable pulchritude is chiefly the rather banal one of parading her before other men. He likes to show her off as he likes to show his expensive automobile or his big door-knob factory. It is her apparent costliness that is her principal charm. Her beauty sets up the assumption that she was sought eagerly by other men, some of them wealthy, and that it thus took a lot of money or a lot of skill to obtain the monopoly of her.

But very few men are so idiotic that they are blind to the hollowness of such satisfactions. A husband, after all, spends relatively few hours of his life parading his wife, or even contemplating her beauty. What engages him far more often is the unromantic business of living with her—of listening to her conversation, of trying to fathom and satisfy her whims, of detecting and counteracting her plots against his ego, of facing with her the dull hazards and boredoms of everyday life. In the discharge of this business personal beauty is certainly not necessarily a help; on the contrary, it may be a downright hindrance, if only because it makes for the hollowest and least intelligent of all forms of vanity. Of infinitely more value is a quality that women too often neglect, to wit, the quality of simple amiability. The most steadily charming of all human beings, male or female, is the one who is tolerant, unprovocative, good-humored, kind. A man wants a show only intermittently, but he wants peace and comfort every day. And to get them, if he is sagacious, he is quite willing to sacrifice scenery.

3
The Rat-trap

Much of the discontent with modern marriage centers in the fact that the laws which condition it and safeguard it all assume that its purpose is the founding of a family. This was unquestionably its purpose when those laws were devised, say three thousand years ago, but that purpose, at least among the civilized minority, is now almost forgotten. Very few educated men of today, it seems to me, have any notion of founding a family in mind when they marry. Their vanity takes different forms; moreover, they have rejected the old doctrine that they have any duty in the premises; the *Stammhalter* has pretty well disappeared from their visions. Most of them, it is probable, marry without any intelligible purpose whatever. Women flatter them, mark them down and lure them to the holy altar: everything else is afterthought. Many an American man finds himself on the brink of marriage without ever having given any sober thought even to so important a matter as the probable charm of his bride-elect as mistress. This explains many connubial calamities.

As things stand, the only legal relief from uncomfortable marriages is afforded by divorce. Every other workable device is frowned upon, and most of them are punished. The chief purpose of legal divorce, of course, is to protect the children of the marriage, *i.e.*, to safeguard the family. But the scheme is clumsy, expensive and cruel. To employ it is to cut off a leg in order to cure what may be, after all, merely a barked shin—worse, what may be no injury at all. Suppose there *are* no children? Suppose the marriage is entered upon with the clear understanding that there *shall* be no children? In the latter case it is obviously insane to surround it with safeguards for the family that will never exist. As well insure a pile of bricks against fire. What is needed is legal recognition of such marriages—recognition that will establish decorum and fair play within their actual limits, but that will not seek to burden them with conditions that look quite outside their limits. Human inertia and sentimentality, of course, will be a long while countenancing any such change. Until quite recently a marriage without children was utterly impossible, save as an act of God, and so the inevitable, by a familiar process, was converted into the creditable. This nonsense survives, despite the disappearance of the excuse for it. It is still believed, by the great majority of human beings, that there is something mysteriously laudable about achieving viable offspring. I have searched the sacred and profane scriptures for many years, but have yet to find any logical ground for this notion. To have a child is no more creditable than to have rheumatism—and no more discreditable. Ethically, it is absolutely meaningless. And practically, it is mainly a matter of chance.

4

The Love Chase

The notion that man is the aggressor in love is frequently supported by old-fashioned psychologists by pointing to the example of the lower animals. The lion, it appears, stalks the lioness to her shame and undoing; the amorous cock pursues the reluctant and virtuous hen. Granted. But all that this proves, giving the analogy all the value asked for it, is that man is the aggressor as *lover*, pure and simple, *i.e.*, as seducer. Is he also the aggressor as suitor and husband? To ask the question is almost to answer it. . . . Well, it is precisely his rôle of husband that differentiates man from lion and cock. And once he is thus differentiated, all his previous likeness disappears. . . . In civilized societies, there is a double stalking: for mistresses and for husbands. The fact that the majority of women retain their virtue to the altar and that the majority of men, soon or late, are married—this offers a capital indication of the relative enthusiasm and pertinacity with which the two varieties of aggression are carried on.

5
Women as Realpolitiker

Women in general are far too intelligent to have any respect for so-called ideas. One seldom hears of them suffering and dying for any of the bogus Great Truths that men believe in. When a woman is on good terms with her husband she is quite willing to accept his idiotic theorizings on any subject that happens to engage him, whether theological, economic, epistemological or political. When one hears of a Republican man who has a Democratic wife, or *vice versa*, it is always safe to assume that she has her eye on a handsomer, richer or more docile fellow, and is thinking of calling up a lawyer.

6
Footnote for Suffragettes

The double standard of morality will survive in this world so long as a woman whose husband has been debauched is favored with the sympathetic tears of other women, and a man whose wife has run away with an actor is laughed at by other men.

7
The Helpmate

The notion that a true and loving (and, let us hope, amiable and beautiful) wife inspires a man to high endeavor is largely illusory. Every sane woman knows instinctively, as a matter of fact, that the highest aspirations of her husband are fundamentally inimical to her, and that their realization is apt to cost her her possession of him. What she dreams of is not an infinitely brilliant husband, but an infinitely "solid" one, which is to say, one bound irretrievably by the chains of normalcy. It would delight her to see him get to the White House, for a man in the White House is as relentlessly policed as an archbishop.

But it would give her a great deal of disquiet to see him develop into a Goethe or a Wagner.

I have known in my time a good many men of the first talent, as talent is reckoned in America, and most of them have been married. I can't recall one whose wife appeared to view his achievements with perfect ease of mind. In every case the lady was full of a palpable fear—the product of feminine intuition, *i.e.*, of hard realism and common sense—that his rise shook her hold upon him, that he became a worse husband in proportion as he became a better man. In the logic I can discern no flaw. The ideal husband is surely not a man of active and daring mind; he is the man of placid and conforming mind. Here the good business man obviously beats the artist and adventurer. His rewards are all easily translated into domestic comfort and happiness. He is not wobbled by the admiration of other women, none of whom, however much they may esteem his virtues as a husband, are under any illusion as to his virtues as a lover. Above all, his mind is not analytical, and hence he is not likely to attempt any anatomizing of his marriage—the starting point for the worst sort of domestic infelicity. No man, examining his marriage intelligently, can fail to observe that it is compounded, at least in part, of slavery, and that he is the slave. Happy the woman whose husband is so stupid that he never launches into that coroner's inquest!

8

The Mime

The fundamental objection to actors, stripping the business of all mere sophistry and snobbery, is that they give away the idiotic vanity of the whole male sex. An actor is simply a man who, by word and strut, says aloud of *him*self what all normal men think of *them*selves. Thus he exposes, in a highly indiscreet and disconcerting manner, the full force of masculine vanity. But I doubt that he exaggerates it. No healthy male is ever actually modest. No healthy male ever really thinks or talks of anything save himself. His conversation is one endless boast—often covert, but always undiluted. His politics is a mere sneering at what he conceives to be inferiors; his philosophy is simply an exposure of asses; he cannot imagine himself save as superior, dominating, the center of situations. Even his theology is seldom more than a stealthy comparison of himself and God, to the disadvantage of God. . . . The youngest flapper knows all this. Feminine strategy, in the duel of sex, consists almost wholly of an adroit feeding of this vanity. Man makes love by braggadocio. Woman makes love by listening. . . . Once a woman passes a certain point in intelligence she finds it almost impossible to get a husband: she simply cannot go on listening without snickering.

9
Cavia Cobaya

I find the following in Theodore Dreiser's "Hey-Rub-a-Dub-Dub";

Does the average strong, successful man confine himself to one woman? Has he ever?

The first question sets a insoluble problem. How are we, in such intimate matters, to say what is the average and what is not the average? But the second question is easily answered, and the answer is, He has. Here Dreiser's curious sexual obsession simply leads him into absurdity. His view of the traffic of the sexes remains the naïve one of an ex-Baptist nymph in Greenwich Village. Does he argue that Otto von Bismarck was not a "strong, successful man"? If not, then let him remember that Bismarck was a strict monogamist—a man full of sin, but always faithful to his Johanna. Again, there was Thomas Henry Huxley. Again, there was William Ewart Gladstone. Again, there was Robert Edward Lee. Yet again, there were Robert Schumann, Felix Mendelssohn, Johann Sebastian Bach, Ulysses S. Grant, Andrew Jackson, Louis Pasteur, Martin Luther, Helmuth von Moltke, Stonewall Jackson, Lyof Tolstoi, Robert Browning, Henrik Ibsen, William T. Sherman, Carl Schurz, old Sam Adams, . . . I could extend the list to pages. . . . Perhaps I am unfair to Dreiser. His notion of a "strong, successful man" may be, not such a genuinely superior fellow as Bismarck or Bach, but such a mere brigand as Shonts, Yerkes or Jim Fisk. If so, he is still wrong. If so, he still runs aground on John D. Rockefeller.

10
The Survivor

Around every bachelor of more than thirty-five legends tend to congregate, chiefly about the causes of his celibacy. If it is not whispered that he is damaged goods, and hence debarred from marriage by a lofty concept of Service to the unborn, it is told under the breath that he was insanely in love at the age of twenty-six with a beautiful creature who jilted him for an insurance underwriter and so broke his heart beyond repair. Such tales are nearly always moonshine. The reason why the average bachelor of thirty-five remains a bachelor is really very simple. It is, in brief, that no ordinarily attractive and intelligent woman has ever made a serious and undivided effort to marry him.

11
The Veteran's Disaster

The tragedy of experience is that a man no longer believes it when a woman shows all the orthodox signs of having been flustered by him. In youth it gives him immense delight to discover that he has made a mash, but when he gets into the middle years the thing merely annoys him. He is irritated that yet another female Cagliostro should try to floor him with the immemorial mumbo-jumbo, and so make a fool of him. The girl he succumbs to is the one who tells him frankly that her heart is buried in France, but that she admires him tremendously and would esteem it a singular honor to be the wife of so meritorious a fellow. This helps to explain, perhaps, why aging men so often succumb to flappers.

12
Moral Indignation

The ill-fame of the Turks in the English-speaking world is not due to their political medievalism, as is usually alleged, but to their practise of polygamy. That practise inevitably excites the erotic imagination of men doomed to monogamy, and particularly of men doomed to monogamy with despotic, prudish and unappetizing wives, which is to say, the normal, typical men of England and the United States. They envy the Turk his larger and more charming joys, and hence hate him. Every time Reuter reports him dragging a fresh herd of dark-eyed, voluptuous Georgian or American women into his seraglio, they hate him the more. The way to arouse a Puritan to his highest pitch of moral indignation is not to burn down an orphan-asylum; the way to do it is to grab a pretty girl around the waist and launch with her into the lascivious measures of a Wiener Walz. Men always hate most what they envy most.

13
The Man and His Shadow

Every man, whatever his actual qualities, is credited with and judged by certain general qualities that are supposed to appertain to his sex, particularly by women. Thus man the individual is related to Man the species, often to his damage and dismay. Consider my own case. I am by nature one of the most orderly of mortals. I have a place for every article of my personal property, whether a Bible or a cocktail-shaker, an undershirt or an eye-dropper, and I always keep it where it belongs. I never drop cigar-ashes on the floor. I never upset a wastebasket. I am never late for trains. I never run short of collars. I never go out with a purple necktie on a blue shirt. I never fail to appear in time for dinner without telephoning or telegraphing. Yet the women who are cursed by God with the care of me maintain and cherish the fiction that I am an extremely careless and even hoggish fellow—that I have to be elaborately nursed, supervised and policed—that the slightest relaxation of vigilance over my everyday conduct would reduce me to a state of helplessness and chaos, with all my clothes mislaid, half my books in the ash-can, my mail unanswered, my face unshaven, and my office not unlike an I.W.W. headquarters after a raid by the *Polizei*. It is their firm theory that, unaided by superior suggestion, I'd wear one shirt six weeks, and a straw hat until Christmas. They never speak of my workroom save in terms of horror, though it is actually the most orderly room in my house. Weekly I am accused of having lost all my socks and handkerchiefs, though they are in my clothes-press all the while. At least once a month formal plans are discussed for re-organizing my whole mode of life, that I may not sink into ir-remediable carelessness, inefficiency and barbarism.

I note that many other men lie under the same benign espi-onage and misrepresentation—in fact, nearly all men. But it is my firm belief that very few men are really disorderly. The business of the world is managed by getting order into it, and the feeling for discipline thus engendered is carried over into domestic life. I know of very few men who ever drop ashes on the dining-room rug, or store their collars in their cigar-box, or put on brown socks with their dress-clothes, or forget to turn off the water after they have bathed, or neglect to keep dinner engagements—and most of these few, I am firmly con-vinced, do it because their women-folk expect it of them, because it would cause astonishment and dismay if they re-frained. I myself, more than once, have deliberately hung my hat on an electrolier, or clomped over the parquetry with muddy shoes, or gone out in a snowstorm without an over-coat, or come down to dinner in a ragged collar, or filled my shirt-box with old copies of the *Congressional Record*, or upset a bottle of green ink, or used Old Dutch Cleanser for shaving, or put olives into Jack Rose cocktails, or gone without a hair-cut for three or four weeks, or dropped an expensive beer *Sei-del* upon the hard concrete of my cellar floor in order to give a certain necessary color to the superstition of my oafishness. If I failed to do such things now and then I'd become unpopular, and very justly so, for nothing is more obnoxious than a human being who is always challenging and correcting the prevailing view of him. Even now I make no protest; I merely record the facts. On my death-bed, I daresay, I shall carry on the masquerade. That is to say, I shall swallow a clinical ther-mometer or two, upset my clam-broth over my counterpane, keep an ouija board and a set of dice under my pillow, and maybe, at the end, fall clumsily out of bed.

14
The Balance-Sheet

Marriage, as everyone knows, is chiefly an economic matter. But too often it is assumed that economics concerns only the wife's hats; it also concerns, and perhaps more importantly, the husband's cigars. No man is genuinely happy, married, who has to drink worse gin than he used to drink when he was single.

15
Yearning

Ah, that the eugenists would breed a woman as capable of laughter as the girl of twenty and as adept at knowing when not to laugh as the woman of thirty-five!

VI.

The Politician

HALF the sorrows of the world, I suppose, are caused by making false assumptions. If the truth were only easier to ascertain the remedy for them would consist simply of ascertaining it and accepting it. This business, alas, is usually impossible, but fortunately not always: now and then, by some occult process, half rational and half instinctive, the truth gets itself found out and an ancient false assumption goes overboard. I point, in the field of the social relations, to one which afflicted the human race for millenniums: that one, to wit, which credited the rev. clergy with a mysterious wisdom and awful powers. Obviously, it has ceased to trouble all the superior varieties of men. It may survive in those remote marches where human beings go to bed with the cows, but certainly it has vanished from the cities. Asphalt and the apostolic succession, indeed, seem to be irreconcilable enemies. I can think of no clergyman in any great American city today whose public dignity and influence are much above those of an ordinary Class I Babbitt. It is hard for even the most diligent and passionate of the ancient order to get upon the first pages of the newspapers; he must make a clown-show, discreditable to his fraying cloth, or he must blush unseen. When bishops begin launching thunderbolts against heretics, the towns do not tremble; they laugh. When elders denounce sin, sin only grows more popular. Imagine a city man getting a notice from the ordinary of his diocese that he had been excommunicated. It would trouble him far less, I venture, than his morning *Katzenjammer*.

The reason for all this is not hard to find. All the superior varieties of men—and even the lowest varieties of city workmen are at least superior to peasants—have simply rid themselves of their old belief in devils. Hell no longer affrights and palsies them, and so the magic of those who profess to save them from it no longer impresses them. That profession, I believe, was bogus, and its acceptance was therefore a false assumption.

Being so, it made men unhappy; getting rid of it has delivered them. They are no longer susceptible to ecclesiastical alarms and extortions; *ergo*, they sleep and eat better. Think of what life must have been under such princes of damnation as Cotton Mather and Jonathan Edwards, with even bartenders and metaphysicians believing in them! And then compare it to life under Bishop Manning and the Rev. Dr. John Roach Straton, with only a few half-wits believing in them! Or turn to the backwoods of the Republic, where the devil is still feared, and with him his professional exterminators. In the country towns the clergy are still almost as influential as they were in Mather's day, and there, as everyone knows, they remain public nuisances, and civilized life is almost impossible. In such Neolithic regions nothing can go on without their consent, on penalty of anathema and hell-fire; as a result, nothing goes on that is worth recording. It is this survival of sacerdotal authority, I begin to believe, and not hookworm, malaria or the event of April 9, 1865, that is chiefly responsible for the cultural paralysis of the late Confederate States. The South lacks big cities; it is run by its country towns—and in every country town there is some Baptist *mullah* who rules by scaring the peasantry. The false assumption that his pretensions are sound, that he can actually bind and loose, that contumacy to him is a variety of cursing God—this false assumption is what makes the yokels so uneasy, so nervous, and hence so unhappy. If they could throw it off they would burn fewer Aframericans and sing more songs. If they could be purged of it they would be purged of Ku Kluxry too.

The cities got rid of that false assumption half a century ago, and have been making cultural progress ever since. Somewhat later they got rid of its brother, to wit, respect for government, and, in particular, respect for its visible agents, the police. That respect—traditional, and hence irrational—had been, for years, in increasingly unpleasant collision with a great body of obvious facts. The police, by assumption austere and almost sacrosanct, were gradually discovered to be, in reality, a pack of rogues and but little removed, save by superior impudence and enterprise, from the cut-throats and purse-snatchers they were set to catch. When, a few decades ago, the American people, at least in the big cities, began to accept them frankly for what they were—when the old false assumption of their integrity and public usefulness was quietly abandoned and a new and more accurate assumption of their roguery was adopted in its place—when this change was effected there was a measurable increase, I believe, in the public happiness. It no longer astonished anyone when policemen were taken in evildoing; indignation therefore abated, and with it its pains. If, before that time, the corps of Prohibition enforcement officers—*i.e.*, a corps of undisguised scoundrels with badges—had been launched upon the populace, there would have been a great roar of wrath, and much anguished gnashing of teeth. People would have felt themselves put upon, injured, insulted. But with the old false assumption about policemen removed from their minds, they met the new onslaught calmly and even smilingly. Today no one is indignant over the fact that the extortions of these new *Polizei* increase the cost of potable alcohol. The false assumption that the police are altruistic agents of a benevolent state has been replaced by the sound assumption that they are gentlemen engaged assiduously, like the rest of us, in finding meat and raiment for their families and in laying up funds to buy Liberty Bonds in the next war to end war. This is human progress, for it increases human happiness.

So much for the evidence. The deduction I propose to make from it is simply this: that a like increase would follow if the American people could only rid themselves of another and worse false assumption that still rides them—one that corrupts all their thinking about the great business of politics, and vastly augments their discontent and unhappiness—the assumption, that is, that politicians are divided into two classes, and that one of those classes is made up of good ones. I need not argue, I hope, that this assumption is almost universally held among us. Our whole politics, indeed, is based upon it, and has been based upon it since the earliest days. What is any political campaign save a concerted effort to turn out a set of politicians who are admittedly bad and put in a set who are thought to be better? The former assumption, I believe, is always sound; the latter is just as certainly false. For if experience teaches us anything at all it teaches us this: that a good politician, under democracy, is quite as unthinkable as an honest burglar. His very existence, indeed, is a standing subversion of the public good in every rational sense. He is not one who serves the common weal; he is simply one who preys upon the commonwealth. It is to the interest of all the rest of us to hold down his powers to an irreducible minimum, and to reduce his compensation to nothing; it is to his interest to augment his powers at all hazards, and to make his compensation all the traffic will bear. To argue that these aims are identical is to argue palpable nonsense. The politician, at his ideal best, never even remotely approximated in practise, is a necessary evil; at his worst he is an almost intolerable nuisance.

What I contend is simply that he would be measurably less a nuisance if we got rid of our old false assumption about him, and regarded him in the cold light of fact. At once, I believe, two-thirds of his obnoxiousness would vanish. He would remain a nuisance, but he would cease to be a swindler; the injury of having to pay freight on him would cease to be complicated by the insult of being rooked. It is the insult and not the injury that makes the deeper wounds, and causes the greater permanent damage to the national psyche. All of us have been trained, since infancy, in putting up with necessary evils, plainly recognized *as* evils. We know, for example, that the young of the human species commonly smell badly; that garbage men, bootblacks and messenger boys commonly smell worse. These facts are not agreeable, but they remain tolerable because they are universally assumed—because there is no sense of having been tricked and cozened in their perennial discovery. But try to imagine how distressing fatherhood would become if prospective fathers were all taught that the human infant radiates an aroma like the rose—if the truth came constantly as a surprise! Each fresh victim of the deception would feel that he had been basely swindled—that his own child was somehow bogus. Not infrequently, I suppose, he would be tempted to make away with it in some quiet manner, and have another—only to be shocked again. That procedure would be idiotic, admittedly, yet it is exactly the one we follow in politics. At each election we vote in a new set of politicians, insanely assuming that they are better than the set turned out. And at each election we are, as they say in the Motherland, done in.

Of late the fraud has become so gross that the plain people

begin to show a great restlessness under it. Like animals in a cage, they trot from one corner to another endlessly seeking a way out. If the Democrats win one year, it is a pretty sure sign that they will lose the next year. State after State becomes doubtful, pivotal, skittish; even the solid South begins to break. In the cities it is still worse. An evil circle is formed. First the poor taxpayers, robbed by the politicians of one great party and then by those of the other, turn to a group of free-lance rogues in the middle ground—non-partisan candidates, Liberals, reformers or what not: the name is unimportant. Then, flayed and pillaged by these gentry as they never were by the old-time professionals, they go back in despair to the latter, and are flayed and pillaged again. Back to Bach! Back to Tammany! Tammany reigns in New York because the Mitchel outfit was found to be intolerable—in other words, because the reformers were found to be even worse than the professionals. Is the fact surprising? Why should it be? Reformers and professionals are alike politicians in search of jobs; both are trying to bilk the taxpayers. Neither ever has any other motive. If any genuinely honest and altruistic politician had come to the surface in America in my time I'd have heard of him, for I have always frequented newspaper offices, and in a newspaper office the news of such a marvel would cause a dreadful tumult. I can recall no such tumult. The unanimous opinion of all the journalists that I know, excluding a few Liberals who are obviously somewhat balmy—they all believed, for example, that the late war would end war,—is that, since the days of the national Thors and Wotans, no politician who was not out for himself, and for himself alone, has ever drawn the breath of life in the United States.

The gradual disintegration of Liberalism among us, in fact, offers an excellent proof of the truth of my thesis. The Liberals have come to grief by fooling their customers, not merely once too often, but a hundred times too often. Over and over again they have trotted out some new hero, usually from the great open spaces, only to see him taken in the immemorial malprac-tises within ten days. Their graveyard, indeed, is filled with cracked and upset headstones, many covered with ribald pen-cilings. Every time there is a scandal in the grand manner the Liberals lose almost as many general officers as either the

Democrats or Republicans. Of late, racked beyond endurance by such catastrophes at home, they have gone abroad for their principal heroes; losing humor as well as hope, they now ask us to venerate such astounding paladins as the Hon. Bela Kun, a gentleman who, in any American State, would not only be in the calaboose, but actually in the death-house. But this absurdity is only an offshoot of a deeper one. Their primary error lies in making the false assumption that some politicians are better than others. This error they share with the whole American people.

I propose that it be renounced, and contend that its renunciation would greatly rationalize and improve our politics. I do not argue that there would be any improvement in our politicians; on the contrary, I believe that they would remain substantially as they are today, and perhaps grow even worse. But what I do argue is that recognizing them frankly for what they are would instantly and automatically dissipate the indignation caused by their present abominations, and that the disappearance of this indignation would promote the public contentment and happiness. Under my scheme there would be no more false assumptions and no more false hopes, and hence no more painful surprises, no more bitter resentment of fraud, no more despair. Politicians, in so far as they remained necessary, would be kept at work—but not with any insane notion that they were archangels. Their rascality would be assumed and discounted, as the rascality of the police is now assumed and discounted. Machinery would be gradually developed to limit it and counteract it. In the end, it might be utilized in some publicly profitable manner, as the insensitiveness to filth of garbage men is now utilized, as the reverence of the clergy for capitalism is now utilized. The result, perhaps, would be a world no better than the present one, but it would at least be a world more intelligent.

In all this I sincerely hope that no one will mistake me for one who shares the indignation I have spoken of—that is, for one who believes that politicians can be made good, and cherishes a fond scheme for making them so. I believe nothing of the sort. On the contrary, I am convinced that the art and mystery they practise is essentially and incurably anti-social— that they must remain irreconcilable enemies of the common

weal until the end of time. But I maintain that this fact, in itself, is not a bar to their employment. There are, under Christian civilization, many necessary offices that demand the
possession of anti-social talents. A professional soldier, regarded realistically, is much worse than a professional politician, for he is a professional murderer and kidnaper, whereas
the politician is only a professional sharper and sneak-thief. A
clergyman, too, begins to shrink and shrivel on analysis; the
work he does in the world is basically almost indistinguishable
from that of an astrologer, a witch-doctor or a fortune-teller.
He pretends falsely that he can get sinners out of hell, and col-
lects money from them on that promise, tacit or express. If he
had to go before a jury with that pretension it would probably
go hard with him. But we do not send him before a jury; we
grant him his hocus-pocus on the ground that it is necessary to
his office, and that his office is necessary to civilization, so-
called. I pass over the journalist delicately; the time has not
come to turn State's evidence. Suffice it to say that he, too,
would probably wither under a stiff cross-examination. If he is
no murderer, like the soldier, then he is at least a sharper and
swindler, like the politician.

What I plead for, if I may borrow a term in disrepute, is simply *Realpolitik*, *i.e.*, realism in politics. I can imagine a political
campaign purged of all the current false assumptions and false
pretenses—a campaign in which, on election day, the voters
went to the polls clearly informed that the choice between
them was not between an angel and a devil, a good man and a
bad man, an altruist and a go-getter, but between two frank
go-getters, the one, perhaps, excelling at beautiful and nonsensical words and the other at silent and prehensile deeds—
the one a chautauqua orator and the other a porch-climber.
There would be, in that choice, something candid, free and
exhilarating. Buncombe would be adjourned. The voter would
make his selection in the full knowledge of all the facts, as he
makes his selection between two heads of cabbage, or two
evening papers, or two brands of chewing tobacco. Today he
chooses his rulers as he buys bootleg whiskey, never knowing
precisely what he is getting, only certain that it is not what it
pretends to be. The Scotch may turn out to be wood alcohol
or it may turn out to be gasoline; in either case it is not Scotch.

How much better if it were plainly labelled, for wood alcohol and gasoline both have their uses—higher uses, indeed, than Scotch. The danger is that the swindled and poisoned consumer, despairing of ever avoiding them when he doesn't want them, may prohibit them even when he does want them, and actually enforce his own prohibition. The danger is that the hopeless voter, forever victimized by his false assumption about politicians, may in the end gather such ferocious indignation that he will abolish them teetotally and at one insane swoop, and so cause government by the people, for the people and with the people to perish from this earth.

VII.

From a Critic's Notebook

Progress

THE most important change that has come over American literature in my time is this: that American satire, which once aimed all of its shafts at the relatively civilized minority, now aims most of them at the imbecile majority. If a satirist of today undertook to poke fun at the paintings of Titian and the music of Richard Wagner, he would be dismissed at once as a clown strayed in from the barber-shop weeklies and the chautauquas. Yet Mark Twain did both, and to great applause. To Mark, for all his humor, there was little that was ridiculous in such American go-getters as George F. Babbitt. He looked upon one of them, Henry H. Rogers, as his best friend, and he made another the hero of "A Connecticut Yankee." What amused Mark most profoundly was precisely whatever was most worthy of sober admiration—sound art, good manners, the aristocratic ideal. And he was typical of his age. The satirists of the present age, though they may be less accomplished workmen, are at all events more civilized men. What they make fun of is not what is dignified, or noble, or beautiful, but what is shoddy, and ignoble, and ugly.

2

The Iconoclast

Of a piece with the absurd pedagogical demand for so-called constructive criticism is the doctrine that an iconoclast is a hollow and evil fellow unless he can prove his case. Why, indeed, should he prove it? Doesn't he prove enough when he proves by his blasphemy that this or that idol is defectively convincing —that at least *one* visitor to the shrine is left full of doubts? The fact is enormously significant; it indicates that instinct has somehow risen superior to the shallowness of logic, the refuge of fools. The pedant and the priest have always been the most expert of logicians—and the most diligent disseminators of nonsense and worse. The liberation of the human mind has never been furthered by such learned dunderheads; it has been furthered by gay fellows who heaved dead cats into sanctuaries and then went roistering down the highways of the world, proving to all men that doubt, after all, was safe—that the god in the sanctuary was finite in his power, and hence a fraud. One horse-laugh is worth ten thousand syllogisms. It is not only more effective; it is also vastly more intelligent.

3
The Artists' Model

The doctrine that art is an imitation of nature is full of folly. Nine-tenths of all the art that one encounters in this world is actually an imitation of other art. Fully a half of it is an imitation twice, thrice or ten times removed. The artist, in fact, is seldom an accurate observer of nature; he leaves that gross and often revolting exploration to geologists, engineers and anatomists. The last thing he wants to see is a beautiful woman in the bright, pitiless sunlight.

4
The Good Citizen as Artist

Again, there is the bad author who defends his manufacture of magazine serials and movie scenarios on the ground that he has a wife, and is in honor bound to support her. I have seen a few such wives. I dispute the obligation. . . . As for the biological by-products of this fidelity, I rate them even lower. Show me 100 head of ordinary children who are worth one "Heart of Darkness," and I'll subside. As for "Lord Jim," I would not swap it for all the children born in Trenton, N. J., since the Spanish War.

5
Definitive Judgments

The doctrine that every critic worth reading is primarily an artist—that his fundamental aim is not to ascertain the truth, or to mete out justice, or to defend the maxims of Aristotle, or the Ten Commandments, or the statutes of the Harvard Corporation, or the Harrison Anti-Narcotic Act, or the Mann Act—this doctrine seems to give a great deal of offense to pedagogues, and every time one of them mentions it he mourns. Always he makes the accusation that it relieves the critic of his most important duty, to wit, the duty of telling his readers what the thing he criticizes is, and how far it carries out its pretension, and how it relates itself to other things in the same category, or presumably in the same category. The answer here, of course, is that no such duty exists. Its existence, indeed, is no more than a delusion of pedagogues, who invariably labor under the notion that they have said something about this or that when they have given it a name. That delusion is responsible for all of the so-called "criticism" that pedagogues write—the heavy, soggy essays upon Matthew Arnold, Poe as a poet, Browning as a philosopher, the Pre-Raphaelites, Henley, Schiller, Ibsen, Whitman, Milton, Herrick, Molière —in brief, all the blowsy efforts to reach "definite judgments" that such tedious wind-jammers delight in. What is accomplished by such "definitive judgments"? Absolutely nothing. A hedge Lowell's elaborate treatise upon Joaquin Miller will never convince any intelligent man that Miller was an important writer, nor will the same professor's effort to fit Ralph Waldo Emerson into the Methodist æsthetic and gnosiology ever stop any intelligent man from reading Emerson for himself, and enjoying him more or less. Such "criticism" invariably fails of its ostensible purpose. In so far as it has any validity and significance at all, it is not as jurisprudence but as work of art. In brief, the pedagogue, when he essays criticism, becomes an artist in spite of himself. As a moral man, of course, he avoids the sin of being a good artist, but nevertheless he is, within the limits set by his superstitions, an artist.

What separates good critics from bad ones is simply the fact that the former are sound enough artists to make the matter they discuss seem charming. It is by this route that they induce their readers to look into it further, and so achieve their function. This function is not to be confused with the pedagogical. It is infinitely more urbane and expansive. Dryden was surely no schoolmaster, even *in petto*, but when he set down his views about Shakespeare in his beautiful and ingratiating prose he interested more readers in the Bard than a whole herd of pedagogues could have mustered, and so, despite the chill that often got into his enthusiasm, he probably did more than any other man to rescue the greatest of English poets from his Restoration days' neglect. What a palpable artist finds interesting is very apt to seem interesting to all persons of taste and education; what a mere birchman advocates is apt to arouse their instinctive aversion. They do not want to be told precisely what to think about the thing discussed; all they want to be told is that it is worth examining. Every effort to lay down immutable conclusions, to state impeccable principles, to instruct them in their moral and æsthetic duties—in other words, every effort to think for them, as a college tutor thinks for a sophomore, and a professor for a tutor, and a university president for a professor, and a board of trustees for a president —is bound to annoy them and chase them away. Despite all the "definitive judgments" that pedants have pronounced upon Walt Whitman, almost always unfavorably, he continues to live and to grow. And despite all their herculean efforts to hold up Howells, he is dead.

VIII.

Totentanz

I CAN think of no great city of this world (putting aside Rio
de Janeiro, Sydney and San Francisco) that is set amid
scenes of greater natural beauty than New York, by which I
mean, of course, Manhattan. Recall Berlin on its dismal plain,
Paris and London on their toy rivers, Madrid on its desert,
Copenhagen on its swamp, Rome on its ancient sewer and its
absurd little hills, and then glance at Manhattan on its narrow
and rock-ribbed island, with deep rivers to either side and
the wide bay before it. No wonder its early visitors, however
much they denounced the Dutch, always paused to praise the
scene! Before it grew up, indeed, New York must have been
strangely beautiful. But it was the beauty of freshness and
unsophistication—in brief, of youth—and now it is no more.
The town today, I think, is quite the ugliest in the world—
uglier, even, than Liverpool, Chicago or Berlin. If it were actually beautiful, as London, say, is beautiful, or Munich, or
Charleston, or Florence, or even parts of Paris and Washington, then New Yorkers would not be so childishly appreciative
of the few so-called beauty spots that it has—for example,
Washington Square, Gramercy Park, Fifth avenue and Riverside drive. Washington Square, save for one short row of old
houses on the North side, is actually very shabby and ugly—a
blot rather than a beauty spot. The trees, year in and year out,
have a mangy and sclerotic air; the grass is like stable litter; the
tall tower on the South side is ungraceful and preposterous;
the memorial arch is dirty and undignified; the whole place
looks dingy, frowsy and forlorn. Compare it to Mt. Vernon
Square in Baltimore: the difference is that between a char-
woman and a grand lady. As for Gramercy Park, it is celebrated
only because it is in New York; if it were in Washington or
London it would not attract a glance. Fifth avenue, to me,
seems to be showy rather than beautiful. What gives it its distinction is simply its spick and span appearance of wealth; it is
the only New York street that ever looks well-fed and clean.

Riverside drive lacks even so much; it is second-rate from end to end, and especially where it is gaudiest. What absurd and hideous houses, with their brummagem Frenchiness, their pathetic effort to look aristocratic! What bad landscaping! What grotesque monuments! From its heights the rich look down upon the foul scars of the Palisades, as the rich of Fifth avenue and Central Park West look down upon the anemic grass, bare rocks and blowing newspapers of Central Park. Alone among the great cities of the East, New York has never developed a domestic architecture of any charm, or, indeed, of any character at all. There are neighborhoods in Boston, in Philadelphia, in Baltimore and in many lesser cities that have all the dignity and beauty of London, but in New York the brownstone mania of the Nineteenth Century brought down the whole town to one level of depressing ugliness, and since brownstone has gone out there has been no development whatever of indigenous design, but only a naïve copying of models—the skyscraper from Chicago and the dwelling-house from Paris. Along Fifth avenue, from the Fifty-ninth street corner to the upper end of Central Park, there is not a single house that looks reposeful and habitable. Along Park avenue—but Park avenue, for all its flash of creamy brick, is surely one of the most hideous streets in all the world!

But the life of the city, it must be confessed, is as interesting as its physical aspect is dull. It is, even more than London or Paris, the modern Babylon, and since 1914 it has entered upon a period of luxuriousness that far surpasses anything seen on earth since the fall of the Eastern Empire. During many a single week, I daresay, more money is spent in New York upon useless and evil things than would suffice to run the kingdom of Denmark for a year. All the colossal accumulated wealth of the United States, the greatest robber nation in history, tends to force itself at least once a year through the narrow neck of the Manhattan funnel. To that harsh island come all the thieves of the Republic with their loot—bankers from the fat lands of the Middle West, lumbermen from the Northwestern coasts, mine owners from the mountains, oil speculators from Texas and Oklahoma, cotton-mill sweaters from the South, steel magnates and manufacturers from the Black Country, blacklegs and exploiters without end—all laden with cash, all

eager to spend it, all easy marks for the town rogues and pan-
ders. The result is a social organization that ought to be far
more attractive to novelists than it is—a society founded upon
the prodigious wealth of Monte Cristo and upon the tastes
of sailors home from a long voyage. At no time and place in
modern times has harlotry reached so delicate and yet so effu-
sive a development; it becomes, in one form or another, one of
the leading industries of the town. New York, indeed, is the
heaven of every variety of man with something useless and expensive to sell. There come the merchants with their bales, of
Persian prayer-rugs, of silk pajamas, of yellow girls, of strange
jugs and carboys, of hand-painted oil-paintings, of old books,
of gim-cracks and tinsel from all the four corners of the world,
and there they find customers waiting in swarms, their check-
books open and ready. What town in Christendom has ever
supported so many houses of entertainment, so many mimes
and mountebanks, so many sharpers and coney-catchers, so
many bawds and pimps, so many hat-holders and door-openers,
so many miscellaneous servants to idleness and debauchery?
The bootlegging industry takes on proportions that are almost
unbelievable; there are thousands of New Yorkers, resident
and transient, who pay more for alcohol every year than they
pay for anything else save women. I have heard of a single
party at which the guests drank 100 cases of champagne in an
evening—100 cases at $100 a case—and it was, as entertain-
ments go in New York today, a quiet and decorous affair. It is
astonishing that no Zola has arisen to describe this engrossing
and incomparable dance of death. Upton Sinclair once attempted it, in "The Metropolis," but Sinclair, of course, was
too indignant for the job. Moreover, the era he dealt was mild
and amateurish; today the pursuit of sensation has been
brought to a far higher degree of perfection. One must go
back to the oriental capitals of antiquity to find anything even
remotely resembling it. Compared to the revels that go on in
New York every night, the carnalities of the West End of Berlin
are trivial and childish, and those of Paris and the Côte
d'Azure take on the harmless aspect of a Sunday-school picnic.

What will be the end of the carnival? If historical precedent
counts for anything, it will go on to catastrophe. But what sort
of catastrophe? I hesitate to venture upon a prophecy. Manhat-

tan Island, with deep rivers all around it, seems an almost ideal
scene for a great city revolution, but I doubt very much that
there is any revolutionary spirit in its proletariat. Some mysterious enchantment holds its workers to their extraordinarily
uncomfortable life; they apparently get a vague sort of delight
out of the great spectacle that they are no part of. The New
York workman patronizes fellow workmen from the provinces
even more heavily than the Wall Street magnate patronizes
country mortgage-sharks. He is excessively proud of his citizenship in the great metropolis, though all it brings him is an
upper berth in a dog kennel. Riding along the elevated on the
East Side and gaping into the windows of the so-called human
habitations that stretch on either hand, I often wonder what
process of reasoning impels, say, a bricklayer or a truckdriver to
spend his days in such vile hutches. True enough, he is paid a
few dollars more a week in New York than he would receive
anywhere else, but he gets little more use out of them than an
honest bank teller. In almost any other large American city he
would have a much better house to live in, and better food; in
the smaller towns his advantage would be very considerable.
Moreover, his chance of lifting himself out of slavery to some
measure of economic independence and autonomy would be
greater anywhere else; if it is hard for the American workman
everywhere to establish a business of his own, it is triply hard
in New York, where rents are killingly high and so much capital is required to launch a business that only Jews can raise it.
Nevertheless, the poor idiot hangs on to his coop, dazzled by
the wealth and splendor on display all around him. His susceptibility to this lure makes me question his capacity for revolution. He is too stupid and poltroonish for it, and he has too
much respect for money. It is this respect for money in the
proletariat, in fact, that chiefly safeguards and buttresses capitalism in America. It is secure among us because Americans
venerate it too much to attack it.

What will finish New York in the end, I suppose, will be an
onslaught from without, not from within. The city is the least
defensible of great capitals. Give an enemy command of the
sea, and he will be able to take it almost as easily as he could
take Copenhagen. It has never been attacked in the past, indeed, without being taken. The strategists of the General Staff

at Washington seem to be well aware of this fact, for their preparations to defend the city from a foe afloat have always been half-hearted and lacking in confidence. Captain Stuart Godfrey, U.S.A., who contributes the note on the fortifications of the port to Fremont Rider's "New York City: A Guide to Travelers," is at pains to warn his lay readers that the existing forts protect only the narrow spaces in front of them—that "they cannot be expected to prevent the enemy from landing elsewhere," *e.g.*, anywhere along the long reaches of the Long Island coast. Once such a landing were effected, the fact that the city stands upon an island, with deep water behind it, would be a handicap rather than a benefit. If it could not be taken and held, it could at least be battered to pieces, and so made untenable. The guns of its own forts, indeed, might be turned upon it, once those forts were open to attack from the rear. After that, the best the defenders could do would be to retire to the natural bombproofs in the cellars of the Union Hill, N.J., breweries, and there wait for God to deliver them. They might, of course, be able to throw down enough metal from the Jersey heights to prevent the enemy occupying the city and reopening its theatres and bordellos, but the more successful they were in this enterprise the more cruelly Manhattan would be used. Altogether, an assault from the sea promises to give the New Yorkers something to think about.

That it will be attempted before many years have come and gone seems to me to be very likely and I have a sneaking fear that it may succeed. As a veteran of five wars and a life-long student of homicidal science, I am often made uneasy, indeed, by the almost universal American assumption that no conceivable enemy could inflict serious wounds upon the Republic—that the Atlantic Ocean alone, not to mention the stupendous prowess of *Homo americanus*, makes it eternally safe from aggression. This notion has just enough truth in it to make it dangerous. That the *whole* country could not be conquered and occupied I grant you, but no intelligent enemy would think for a moment of trying to conquer it. All that would be necessary to bring even the most intransigeant patriots to terms would be to take and hold a small part of it—say the part lying to the East and North of the general line of the Potomac river. Early in the late war, when efforts were under way to scare the American *booboisie* with the German bugaboo, one of the Allied propagandists printed a book setting forth plans alleged to have been made by the German General Staff to land an army at the Virginia capes, march on Pittsburgh, and so separate the head of the country from its liver, kidneys, gizzard, heart, spleen, bladder, lungs and other lights. The plan was persuasive, but I doubt that it originated in Potsdam; there was a smell of Whitehall upon it. One of the things most essential to its execution, in fact, was left out as it was set forth, to wit, a thrust southward from Canada to meet and support the thrust northwestward. But even this is not necessary. Any invader who emptied New York and took the line of the Hudson would have Uncle Sam by the tail, and could enter upon peace negotiations with every prospect of getting very polite attention. The American people, of course, could go on living without New York, but they could not go on living as a great and puissant nation. Steadily, year by year, they have made New York more and more essential to the orderly functioning of the American state. If it were cut off from the rest of the country the United States would be in the hopeless position of a man relieved of his medulla oblongata—that is to say, of a man without even enough equipment left to be a father, a patriot and a Christian.

Nevertheless, it is highly probable that the predestined enemy, when he comes at last, will direct his first and hardest efforts to cutting off New York, and then make some attempt to keep it detached afterward. This, in fact, is an essential part of the new higher strategy, which is based upon economic considerations, as the old strategy was based upon dynastic considerations. In the Middle Ages, the object of war was to capture and hamstring a king; at present it is to dismember a great state, and so make it impotent. The Germans, had they won, would have broken up the British Empire, and probably detached important territories from France, Italy and Russia, beside gobbling Belgium *in toto.* The French, tantalized by a precarious and incomplete victory, attempted to break up Germany, as they broke up Austria. The chances are that an enemy capable of taking and holding New York would never give it back wholly—that is, would never consent to its restoration to the Union on the old terms. What would be proposed, I venture, would be its conversion into a sort of free state—a new Dantzig, perhaps functioning, as now, as the financial and commercial capital of the country, but nevertheless lying outside the bounds politically. This would solve the problem of the city's subsistence, and still enable the conqueror to keep his hold upon it. It is my belief that the New Yorkers, after the first blush of horror, would agree to the new arrangement and even welcome it. Their patriotism, as things stand, is next to nothing. I have never heard, indeed, of a single honest patriot in the whole town; every last man who even pretends to kiss the flag is simply a swindler with something to sell. This indifference to the great heart-throbs of the hinterland is not to be dismissed as mere criminality; it is founded upon the plain and harsh fact that New York is alien to the rest of the country, not only in blood and tastes, but also in fundamental interests— that the sort of life that New Yorkers lead differs radically from the sort of life that the rest of the American people lead, and that their deepest instincts vary with it. The city, in truth, already constitutes an independent free state in all save the name. The ordinary American law does not run there, save when it has been specifically ratified, and the ordinary American *mores* are quite unknown there. What passes as virtue in Kansas is regarded as intolerable vice in New York, and *vice versa*. The town is already powerful enough to swing the whole country when it wants to, as it did on the war issue in 1917, but the country is quite impotent to swing the town. Every great wave of popular passion that rolls up on the prairies is dashed to spray when it strikes the hard rocks of Manhattan.

As a free state, licensed to prey upon the hinterland but unharassed by its Crô-Magnon prejudices and delusions, New York would probably rise to heights of very genuine greatness, and perhaps become the most splendid city known to history. For one thing, it would be able, once it had cut the painter, to erect barriers and conditions around the privilege of citizenship, and so save itself from the double flood that now swamps it—first, of broken-down peasants from Europe, and secondly and more important, of fugitive rogues from all the land West and South of the Hudson. Citizenship in New York is now worth no more than citizenship in Arkansas, for it is open to any applicant from the marshes of Bessarabia, and, still worse, to any applicant from Arkansas. The great city-states of history have been far more fastidious. Venice, Antwerp, London, the Hansa towns, Carthage, Tyre, Cnossus, Alexandria—they were all very sniffish. Rome began to wobble when the Roman franchise was extended to immigrants from the Italian hill country, *i.e.*, the Arkansas of that time. The Hansa towns, under the democracy that has been forced upon them, are rapidly sinking to the level of Chicago and Philadelphia. New York, free to put an end to this invasion, and to drive out thousands of the gorillas who now infest it—more, free from the eternal blackmail of laws made at Albany and the Methodist tyranny of laws made at Washington—could face the future with resolution and security, and in the course of a few generations it might conceivably become genuinely civilized. It would still stand as toll-taker on the chief highway of American commerce; it would still remain the premier banker and usurer of the Republic. But it would be loosed from the bonds which now tend so strenuously to drag it down to the level of the rest of the country. Free at last, it could cease to be the auction-room and bawdy-house that it is now, and so devote its brains and energy to the building up of a civilization.

IX.

Meditations in the Methodist Desert

I

The New Galahad

MY agents in attendance upon the so-called moving pictures tell me that persons who frequent such shows begin to tire of Western films—that they are no longer roused to clapper-clawing by the spectacle of actors in patent-leather jack-boots murdering Indians and Mexicans. Several of the astute Ashkenazim in charge of the movie industry, noting that slackening of taste, have sought to find a new hero to replace the scout and cowboy, but so far without success. The children of today, young and old, seem to take no interest in pirates, nor are they stirred by train-robbers, safe-blowers and other such illicit adventurers. It can't be that the movie censorship is to blame, for the same thing is visible in the field of *belles lettres*. The dime novel, once so prosperous, is practically dead. The great deeds of the James brothers, known to every literate boy in my youth, are now forgotten. And so are the great deeds of Nick Carter and Old Sleuth: the detective has fallen with his prey.

What is needed, obviously, is a new hero for the infantry of the land, for if one is not quickly supplied there is some danger that the boys will begin admiring Y.M.C.A. secretaries, crooked members of the Cabinet and lecturers on sex hygiene. In this emergency I nominate the bootlegger—not, of course, the abject scoundrel who peddles bogus Scotch in clubs and office buildings, but the dashing, romantic, defiant fellow who brings the stuff up from the Spanish Main. He is, indeed, almost an ideal hero. He is the true heir, not only of the old-time Indian fighters and train-robbers, but also of the tough and barnacled deep-water sailors, now no more. He faces the perils of the high seas in a puny shallop, and navigates the worst coast in the world in contempt of wind and storm.

Think of him lying out there on wild nights in Winter, with the waves piling mountain-high and the gale standing his crazy little craft on her beam! Think of him creeping in in his motor-boat on Christmas Eve, risking his life that the greatest of Christian festivals may be celebrated in a Christian and re-spectable manner! Think of him soaked and freezing, facing his exile and its hardships uncomplainingly, saving his money that his old mother may escape the poor-farm, that his wife may have her operation for gall-stones, that his little children may be decently fed and clad, and go to school regularly, and learn the principles of Americanism!

This brave lad is not only the heir of Jesse James and Ned Buntline; he is also the heir of John Hancock and of all the other heroes who throttled the accursed Hun in 1776. All the most gallant among them were smugglers, and in their fragile craft they brought in, not only rum, but also liberty. The Revolu-tion was not only against the person of the Potsdam tyrant, George III; it was also, and especially, against harsh and intol-erable laws—the worst of them the abhorrent Stamp Act. But was the Stamp Act worse than Prohibition? I leave it to any fair man. Prohibition, in fact, is a hundred times as foul, false, op-pressive and tyrannical. If the Stamp Act was worth a Revolu-tion, the Prohibition is worth a massacre and an earthquake. Well, it has already bred its Hancocks, and soon or late, no doubt, it will breed its Molly Pitchers, Paul Reveres and Mad Anthony Waynes. Liberty, driven from the land by the Methodist White Terror, has been given a refuge by the hardy boys of the Rum Fleet. In their bleak and lonely exile they cherish her and keep her alive. Some day, let us hope, they will storm the coast, slit the gullets of her enemies, and restore her to her dominion, The lubbers of the land have limber necks; their blood runs pale and yellow. But on the roaring deep there are still men who are colossally he, and when the bugle calls they will not fail.

2

Optimist vs. Optimist

If these heroes *do* fail, alas, alas, then all will be lost, includ-ing honor. For there is not the slightest sign of revolt among the craven hordes who cling to the land, ignominiously dependent for their very existence as Christians upon the gallant fellows beyond the twelve-mile limit. They simply go on hoping against hope. Each successive Congress is to relieve them, rescue them, restore the liberties bequeathed to them by the Fathers. And each successive Congress does nothing of the kind. Nor, I believe, will any one coming hereafter. Congress is made up eternally of petty scoundrels, pusillanimous poltroons, highly vulnerable and cowardly men: they will never risk provoking the full fire of the Anti-Saloon League. The notion that such degraded fellows will ever rise up and put down Prohibition, so fondly cherished by the wets, is thus a snare and a mocking, and so is the notion that they will presently find a way to enforce it, cherished by the drys. Optimist eat optimist! As for me, can find no reason whatever for believing that, within the lifetime of men now living, the voluptuous consumption of alcohol will be countenanced by law in the Republic, and neither do I see any reason for believing that it will ever be stopped, nor, indeed, any reason for believing that any serious effort will be made to stop it.

It is commonly argued by the more impatient and worthy opponents of the Methodist millennium that the Eighteenth Amendment was slipped through Congress and the State legislatures against the wishes of the majority of American freemen —that the thing was accomplished by a sort of trick, partly political and partly magical. It is further argued that, had the soldiers who were then abroad, fighting for human liberty, been at home and voting, they would have piled up such majorities for wet candidates that both Houses of Congress would have been made proof against the Anti-Saloon League. It seems to me that both contentions are unsound. The Eighteenth Amendment, when it was passed, actually had a majority behind it, and I incline to think that that majority was a very substantial one. What made it so large was simply the war hysteria of the time. *Homo boobiens* was scientifically rowelled and run amok with the news that all the German brewers of the country were against the amendment; he observed himself that all German sympathizers, whether actual Germans or not, were bitter opponents of it. His nights made dreadful by dreams of German spies, he was willing to do anything to put them down, and one of the things he was willing to do was to swallow Prohibition. When he recovered from his terror, it was too late; the first article of the Methodist Book of Discipline had been read into the Constitution, and there it remains today, an unpleasant fly in imperishable amber. The soldiers, had they been at home, would have gone the way of their lay brothers. They were, if anything, even more in terror of Germans than the latter, and even more eager to floor them and so get rid of them. In every camp and cantonment Y.M.C.A. secretaries addressed the conscripts daily, instructing them in the moral nature of the crusade they were engaged in. The effects are visible today in the familiar swineries of the American Legion; its members are still down with the war psychosis. Moreover, it is not to be forgotten that large numbers of soldiers could not have voted, even if they had been at home. For example, those who were minors. Again, the Southern Negroes. Yet again, the enormous number of aliens who were rushed to the trenches by the draft boards to relieve native patriots—in New York City alone, fully 25,000, most of them Russian Jews. Finally, it is to be recalled that there was no plebiscite on Prohibition—that the men who put it into the Constitution were all safely in office at the time the test suddenly confronted them.

But what of the state of public opinion today? Isn't it a fact that hundreds of thousands of persons who were in favor of Prohibition in 1919 are now so disgusted by its colossal failure that they have turned violently against it? I doubt it. I know of no such person. I know of a great many persons who, though they voted for Prohibition when they had the chance, or, at all events, favored it, now guzzle like actors or policemen, but I believe that substantially all of them, if the thing were put up to them tomorrow, would be for it again. Whoever believes that they have changed heart is a very poor student of the Puritan psyche. What a Puritan advocates and what he does have no necessary connection. The late Anthony Comstock was a diligent collector of dirty books, and used to entertain favored callers by exhibiting his worst specimens to them. Nevertheless, Comstock was honestly in favor of suppressing such books, and would have gone to the extreme length of giving up his own recreation if he had ever been convinced that it would have helped the cause. To the Puritan, indeed, moral obligation is something quite outside personal conduct, and has very little contact with it. He may be, in private, an extremely gross and porcine fellow, and he frequently is, but that fact doesn't diminish his veneration for his ethical ideal in the slightest. Brought to the mark, he always sticks to that ideal, however absurdly his conduct clashes with it. As everyone knows, he is rather more prone than most other men to commit fornication, particularly in its more sordid and degrading forms; nevertheless, it is impossible to imagine him advocating any relaxation of the prevailing sexual taboos, however beneficial it would be. Again, as everyone also knows, he is very apt, when he drinks at all, to make a hog of himself, for the amiable drinking customs of civilized men are beyond him; nevertheless, it is impossible to imagine him admitting specifically that any man has a right to drink at all. This last fact explains something that often puzzles foreign observers: the relative smallness and impotence of anti-Prohibition organizations in America, despite the great amount of gabbling against Prohibition that goes on. It is due to the Puritan's fear of appearing on the side of the devil. He will drink in private, but he will not defend the practise in public.

It thus seems to me that so long as Puritanism remains the dominant philosophy in America—and certainly it shows no sign of relaxing its hold upon the low-caste Anglo-Saxon majority—it will be quite hopeless to look for an abandonment of Prohibition, or even for any relaxation of its extravagant and probably unconstitutional excesses. But for precisely the same reason it seems to me to be very unlikely that Prohibition will ever be enforced, or, indeed, that any honest effort will ever be made to enforce it. For the Puritan's enthusiasm for the moral law is always grounded, at least in large part, upon a keen realization that it is, after all, only an ideal—that it may be evaded whenever the temptation grows strong enough—that he himself may evade it, readily and safely. Like every other man, he likes to kick up now and then, and forget his holiest principles. He achieves this kicking up by sinning. When drinking was perfectly lawful, he got no pleasure out of it and so tried to put it down, but now that it is against the law he delights in it, and so long as he delights in it he will keep on doing it. If the Seventh Commandment were repealed tomorrow, military marriages would decrease 95 per cent. in rural America, and the great hotels at Atlantic City would be given over to the bats and owls. Let us, therefore, neither delude ourselves nor get into sweats of Puritan-like fear. Prohibition officers will continue to beat the land for stills and bribes until you and I are long gone and forgotten, and bootleggers will continue to elude them. No genuinely wet President will be elected, save by accident, in our time, and no President will ever be able to enforce Prohibition. Respect for the Constitution will be heard of in every campaign, and then it will be forgotten for four years more. It will give candidates something to talk about, but it will not give the rest of us anything to worry about.

3
Caveat for the Defense

The wets, I often think, are worse frauds than the drys. For example, consider their great current eagerness to assure everyone that they are absolutely against the saloon—that they would not revive it for an instant, even if they could. All of their spokesmen stop short dramatically after demanding the restoration of light wines and beer; they are virtuously opposed, it would appear, to all forms of hard liquor, as they are opposed to the saloon. In this position I can detect nothing respectable. Either the advocates of it are hypocrites trying to fool the Prohibitionists with pious protestations, or they have been themselves corrupted by Methodist superstitions. The plain fact is, of course, that the saloon, at its worst, was a great deal better than any of the substitutes that have grown up under Prohibition—nay, that it was a great deal better than the ideal substitutes imagined by the Prohibitionists: for example the Y.M.C.A. And it must be equally plain that light wines and beer would not always satisfy the yearning of the normal man for alcoholic refreshment—that there are times when his system, if he is sound in body, craves far stronger stuff. To say that such a normal man, at five o'clock in the afternoon, wants to drink a *Humpen* of beer, or that, on a cold Winter morning, his inner urge would be met by half a bottle of Pontet Canet is to say something so absurd that the mere statement of it is sufficient refutation. The fact is, of course, that the last chance to exile hard liquors for light wines and beer went glimmering when the Eighteenth Amendment was ratified. In 1918, perhaps, the scheme had a certain plausibility, for the American consumption of spirits had been declining for years, and very good beer, imported from Germany and Bohemia, was everywhere obtainable at low prices, and the use of wine, chiefly because of the influence of Italian restaurants and the propaganda of the California vinegrowers, was rapidly increasing. But the years of Prohibition have reconverted Americans into a nation of whiskey and gin drinkers, as they were before the Germans brought in lager beer in the fifties of the last century. Light wines and beer, I believe, would not satisfy them now, even at meals; there would be just as much bootlegging under a modified Volstead Act as there is today. Prohibition has restored the hard guzzling of Daniel Webster's day.

As for the saloon, the case against it, as voiced by both Prohibitionists and anti-Probibitionists, is chiefly based upon a recollection of what the thing was at its lowest and worst, which is just as sensible as arguing against Christianity on the ground that a certain minority of the rev. clergy are notorious swine. The utterly vicious saloons were always relatively rare, even along the waterfront, and an honest execution of the laws in force before Prohibition would have exterminated them in ten days. Their existence was a proof, not that the saloon itself was inherently evil, but simply that it could be made evil by corrupt government. To blame it for that fact would be like blaming the Constitution for the fact that Federal judges habitually violate it. The normal saloon, I am convinced, was not an evil influence in its vicinage, but a good one. It not only enabled the poor man to effect that occasional escape from wife and children which every man must make if he would remain sane; it also threw him into a society palpably better than that of his home or his workshop, and accustomed him to refinements which unquestionably improved him. The conversation of a precinct leader or of a brewery collector would make but little impression, I daresay, in the Century Club, on the Harvard campus or in the cloakrooms of the United States Senate, but in the average saloon of a poor neighborhood it took on an unmistakable dignity and authority. This collector (or *Todsäufer*, as he was called) had fresh news; he was a man of comparatively large affairs; he had an air about him of the great world; most important of all, he was professionally communicative and affable. The influence of such a man upon the customers of the place, all of whom were bidden to drink and permitted to converse with him, was necessarily for the good. He was, in every sense comprehensible to them, a better man than they were. He had the use of more money; he dressed better; he knew more; he couched his ideas in subtler and more graceful terms; he was better bathed and had better table manners. The effect of his visits, though perhaps not as massive, was comparable to the effect that would have been worked by visits by, say, Bishop Manning or Dr. Nicholas Murray Butler. In his presence discussion took on a higher tone, and he left behind him, in many a simple heart, an aspiration toward nobler things.

But it was not only the *Todsäufer* who was a missionary of light and a pattern of the amenities; so also was the saloon itself. It represented the only concept of beauty and dignity that ever entered into the lives of many of its customers. Surrounded all day by the inconceivable hideousness of the American workshop, and confronted on their return from work by the depressing ugliness of homes outfitted out of departmentstores and on the instalment plan, with slatternly women and filthy children as the fauna of the scene, they found themselves, in the saloon, in a markedly superior milieu. Here some regard was given to æsthetics. Here was relatively pretentious architecture. Here were polished hardwoods, resplendent mirrors, comfortable chairs, glittering glassware and metals, innumerable small luxuries. Here, above all, was an attempt at genuine cleanliness. The poor saloons of the by-streets were not to be compared, of course, to the superb drinking-rooms of the great hotels, but they were at least much cleaner than any of the homes or factories surrounding them, and they were at least more beautiful than the adjacent livery-stables, cigarstores, barber-shops and Methodist Little Bethels. Furthermore, they set forth an example of life upon a more urbane and charming scale. Men had to be more polite in saloons than they were at home; if they were not, they ran risks of colliding with the fists of their fellow patrons and with the bartender's Excaliburs, the bung-starter and ice-pick. The braggart and bully here met his quick doom; the unsocial fellow felt the weight of public disapproval; the ignoramus learned the bitter taste of sniffs and sneers. Life was more spacious spiritually and more luxurious physically. Instead of the nicked chinaware of his home the customer encountered shining glass; instead of spitting out of the window or on the floor he discharged himself into magnificent brass spittoons or into the brook that ran under the bar-rail; instead of the ghastly fried beefsteaks and leathery delicatessen of his wife's cuisine, he ate appetizing herring, delicate *Wienerwürste*, well-devised *Kartoffelsalat*, celery, olives, and even such exotic titbits as *Blutwurst*, *Pumpernickel*, *Bohnensalat* and caviare.

To argue that such luxuries and amenities had no effect is to argue utter nonsense. I believe fully that the rise of the latter-day saloon (a product of the financing of saloonkeepers by wealthy brewers, so much denounced by superficial sociologists) had a very benign effect upon American manners. It purged the city workmen of their old boorishness and pugnacity; it taught them the difference between mere fodder and civilized food; it shamed them into a certain cleanliness; it gave them some dim comprehension of design and ornamentation. In more than one American city the influence of the saloon is visible today in ecclesiastical architecture, and everywhere it is visible in theatre architecture. I name one thing specifically: the use of polished hardwoods. The first parquetry ever seen in America was in saloons. And so was the first tile-work. And so was the first plate-glass. Where the saloon reached its highest development there American life became richest and most expansive. The clatter against it is ignorant, unfair, philistine and disingenuous.

4

Portrait of an Ideal World

That alcohol in dilute aqueous solution, when taken into the human organism, acts as a depressant, not as a stimulant, is now so much a commonplace of knowledge that even the more advanced varieties of physiologists are beginning to be aware of it. The intelligent layman no longer resorts to the jug when he has important business before him, whether intellectual or manual; he resorts to it after his business is done, and he desires to release his taut nerves and reduce the steam-pressure in his spleen. Alcohol, so to speak, unwinds us. It raises the threshold of sensation and makes us less sensitive to external stimuli, and particularly to those that are unpleasant. It reduces and simplifies the emotions. Putting a brake upon all the qualities which enable us to get on in the world and shine before our fellows—for example, combativeness, shrewd-ness, diligence, ambition,—it releases the qualities which mellow us and make our fellows love us—for example, amiability, generosity, toleration, humor, sympathy. A man who has taken aboard two or three cocktails is less competent than he was before to steer a battleship down the Ambrose Channel, or to cut off a leg, or to draw up a deed of trust, or to conduct Bach's B minor mass, but he is immensely more competent to entertain a dinner party, or to admire a pretty girl, or to *hear* Bach's B minor mass. The harsh, useful things of the world, from pulling teeth to digging potatoes, are best done by men who are as starkly sober as so many convicts in the death-house, but the lovely and useless things, the charming and ex-hilarating things, are best done by men with, as the phrase is, a few sheets in the wind. *Pithecanthropus erectus* was a teetotaler, but the angels, you may be sure, know what is proper at 5 P.M.

All this is so obvious that I marvel that no utopian has ever proposed to abolish all the sorrows of the world by the simple device of getting and keeping the whole human race gently stewed. I do not say drunk, remember; I say simply gently stewed —and apologize, as in duty bound, for not knowing how to describe the state in a more seemly phrase. The man who is in it is a man who has put all of his best qualities into his show-case. He is not only immensely more amiable than the cold sober man; he is immeasurably more decent. He reacts to all situations in an expansive, generous and humane manner. He has become more liberal, more tolerant, more kind. He is a better citizen, husband, father, friend. The enterprises that make human life on this earth uncomfortable and unsafe are never launched by such men. They are not makers of wars; they do not rob and oppress anyone; they invent no such plagues as high tariffs, 100 per cent. Americanism and Prohibition. All the great villainies of history, from the murder of Abel to the

Treaty of Versailles, have been perpetrated by sober men, and chiefly by teetotalers. But all the charming and beautiful things, from the Song of Songs to terrapin *à la* Maryland, and from the nine Beethoven symphonies to the Martini cocktail, have been given to humanity by men who, when the hour came, turned from well water to something with color to it, and more in it than mere oxygen and hydrogen.

I am well aware, of course, that getting the whole human race stewed and keeping it stewed, year in and year out, would present formidable technical difficulties. It would be hard to make the daily dose of each individual conform exactly to his private needs, and hard to get it to him at precisely the right time. On the one hand there would be the constant danger that large minorities might occasionally become cold sober, and so start wars, theological disputes, moral, reforms, and other such unpleasantnesses. On the other hand, there would be danger that other minorities might proceed to actual intoxication, and so annoy us all with their fatuous bawling or maudlin tears. But such technical obstacles, of course, are by no means insurmountable. Perhaps they might be got around by abandoning the administration of alcohol *per ora*, and distributing it instead by impregnating the air with it. I throw out the suggestion, and pass on. Such questions are for men skilled in therapeutics, government and business efficiency. They exist today and their enterprises often show a high ingenuity, but, being chiefly sober, they devote too much of their time to harassing the rest of us. Half-stewed, they would be ten times as humane, and perhaps at least half as efficient. Thousands of them, relieved of their present anti-social duties, would be idle, and eager for occupation. I trust to them in this small matter. If they didn't succeed completely, they would at least succeed partially.

The objection remains that even small doses of alcohol, if each followed upon the heels of its predecessor before the effects of the latter had worm off, would have a deleterious effect upon the physical health of the race—that the death-rate would increase, and whole categories of human beings would be exterminated. The answer here is that what I propose is not lengthening the span of life, but augmenting its joys. Suppose we assume its duration is reduced 20 per cent. My reply is that its delights will be increased at least 100 per cent. Misled by statisticians, we fall only too often into the error of worshiping mere figures. To say that A will live to be eighty and B will die at forty is certainly not to argue plausibly that A is more to be envied than B. A, in point of fact, may have to spend all of his eighty years in Kansas or Arkansas, with nothing to eat save corn and hog-meat and nothing to drink save polluted river water, whereas B may put in his twenty years of discretion upon the Côte d'Azure, *wie Gott im Frankreich*. It is my contention that the world I picture, even assuming the average duration of human life to be cut down 50 per cent., would be an infinitely happier and more charming world than that we live in today—that no intelligent human being, having once tasted its peace and joy, would go back voluntarily to the harsh brutalities and stupidities that we now suffer, and idiotically strive to prolong. If intelligent Americans, in these depressing days, still cling to life and try to stretch it out longer and longer, it is surely not logically, but only atavistically. It is the primeval brute in them that hangs on, not the man. The man knows only too well that ten years in a genuinely civilized and happy country would be infinitely better than a geological epoch under the curses he must face and endure every day.

Moreover, there is no need to admit that the moderate alcoholization of the whole race would materially reduce the duration of life. A great many of us are moderately alcoholized already, and yet manage to survive quite as long as the bluenoses. As for the blue-noses themselves, who would repine if breathing alcohol-laden air brought them down with delirium tremens and so sterilized and exterminated them? The advantage to the race in general would be obvious and incalculable. All the worst strains—which now not only persist, but even prosper—would be stamped out in a few generations, and so the average human being would move appreciably away from, say, the norm of a Baptist clergyman in Georgia and toward the norm of Shakespeare, Mozart and Goethe. It would take aeons, of course, to go all the way, but there would be progress with every generation, slow but sure. Today, it must be manifest, we make no progress at all; instead we slip steadily backward. That the average civilized man of today is inferior to the average civilized man of two or three generations ago is too plain to need arguing. He has less enterprise and courage; he is less resourceful and various; he is more like a rabbit and less like a lion. Harsh oppressions have made him what he is. He is the victim of tyrants. . . . Well, no man with two or three cocktails in him is a tyrant. He may be foolish but he is not cruel. He may be noisy, but he is also genial, tolerant, generous and kind. My proposal would restore Christianity to the world. It would rescue mankind from moralists, pedants and brutes.

X.

Essay in Constructive Criticism

I

ONE of the defects in the American system of government, if so superb a confection of the human mind and heart may be said, without indecency, to have any defects at all, lies in the fact that it fails to provide swift and condign punishment for the special crimes of public officials. Even when their wrong-doings take the form of offenses against the ordinary criminal statutes of the realm—as, for example, embezzlement, conversion, blackmail, armed entry, kidnaping or common assault—it seems to be very difficult to bring them under the lash of justice; they enjoy, as it were, an unwritten immunity to criminal process, running with the constitutional immunity of United States Senators, who cannot be taken by the *gendarmerie*, even for adultery or bootlegging, while the Senate is in session. The thugs and perjurers of the so-called Department of Justice, during the reign of the Martyr Wilson, committed nearly all the crimes of fraud and violence on the books, and yet, so far as I know, not one of them was ever punished, or, indeed, so much as prosecuted. Several Federal district attorneys, toward the end of that festival of oppression and worse, protested against it publicly, and there were bitter yells from specialists in human liberty and from the relatives, lodge-brothers and creditors of some of the victims, but no Federal grand jury indicted any of the criminals, and no Federal judge condemned them to the hulks. To this day, if my agents are to be believed, the same thing is going on, though perhaps on a more modest scale. Prohibition enforcement officers in all parts of the country are breaking into houses without warrants, destroying property without due process of law, engaging in blackmail in a wholesale manner, and assaulting and murdering citizens almost at their will, and yet one seldom hears of them going to jail for it, and I know of none who has been hanged.

When it comes to crimes that are peculiar to public officials and that arise out of the nature of their legal status, as bigamy and wife-beating arise out of the nature of a married man's, the case is even worse. I allude here to such special offenses as dissipating the public funds, loading the public rolls with useless and pediculous job-holders, letting contracts and franchises to political and private friends, converting public property to private uses, condoning crimes against the government, and administering the laws in a partial and dishonest manner—all of them impossible to the mere citizen and taxpayer, as default in alimony is impossible to the bachelor. Here the ordinary criminal statutes are obviously ineffective, and of special statutes there are almost none. What was the late Mr. Fall guilty of? His accusers, it appears, had to fall back upon the vague charge of conspiracy, which was not unlike accusing a burglar of trespass. With the general run of official delinquents it is impossible to go even so far. Their crimes have no names, and no adequate punishments. Certain high dignitaries, when taken in gross malfeasances, may be impeached, and most lesser ones, though not all, may be cashiered. But neither punishment is harsh enough to be a deterrent, and neither is swift and sure. Since the first days of the Republic but eight Federal job-holders have been brought before the bar of the Senate on impeachment by the House of Representatives, and of these but two have been found guilty and removed from office. Both of the latter were judges; one was convicted of drunkenness on the bench and the other of corrupt dealings with litigants. Is it argued seriously by anyone that, during all those years, but two Federal judges have been guilty of such offenses? Is it argued, indeed, that the bench is wholly guiltless of them, and of all other crimes, today?

Many of the sitting Federal judges, as a matter of fact, are obviously unfit for the duties they have to perform. Some of them owe their jobs to litigants who are habitually before them, and others are admittedly beholden to such corrupt agencies as the Anti-Saloon League. Is it maintained that such dubious fellows make competent and respectable judges, or that the clumsy and enormously costly process of impeachment offers a practicable means of dealing with their frequent and flagrant peccadillos? Plainly not. Even when their obscenities upon the bench become publicly scandalous they are protected by the fact that impeachment is essentially a political, not a judicial process, and that in consequence it is excessively slow and uncertain—in other words, by the fact that it lacks the very characters which legal punishment fundamentally needs. It is, as a matter of practise, almost as safe for a Federal judge to take care of his fellow-golfers and scofflaws as it is for a Prohibition officer to blackmail a bootlegger or for an agent of the Department of Justice to manufacture perjury against so-called Reds. If he belongs to the party in control of Congress he cannot be impeached for any crime short of highway robbery or piracy on the high seas, and even if he belongs to the minority party the citizen who complains of him must be extremely influential to be heard at all, and extremely rich to meet the heavy costs of prosecuting him. In brief, the remedy against him that is offered by the Constitution and the laws is, in substance, no remedy at all. No matter how grossly he violates his oath and the decencies, he commonly remains upon the bench until some grateful litigant or syndicate of litigants offers him a better job.

Moreover, it must be plain that the punishment of impeachment and removal from office, or of removal by executive order, without impeachment, is usually grossly inadequate. When job-holders become so unbearably corrupt or incompetent that they are actually separated from their jobs, they commonly deserve hanging, or, at least, long confinement in the hoosegow. Simply to turn them out, leaving them free to aspire to other offices, is as absurd as it would be to limit a burglar's punishment to kicking him out of the house. The case of the late Denby, Secretary of the Navy, is in point. I have no opinion as to the guilt or innocence of the gentleman; I merely recall the fact that he was accused of the very grave offense of dissipating the national property and imperilling the national defense. It would be difficult to imagine anything more flagrantly anti-social, more thoroughly vicious, more damaging to the common weal; put beside it, such ordinary crimes as arson and larceny seemed relatively harmless. Nevertheless, the worst punishment that could be inflicted upon Denby was the banal one of depriving him of his office. It was impossible, for political reasons, to impeach him or even to attempt to impeach him, and he was simply turned out, with a file of high

naval dignitaries saluting him as he left and a great crowd
cheering him as he got home. Here cause and effect took on a
disproportion that was truly colossal; it was almost as if Czolgosz had been fined $10 for dispatching McKinley. If Denby
was innocent, he deserved the salute and the cheers without
the loss of his job. And if he was guilty, if only of negligence,
he plainly merited at least a geological epoch on Devil's Island.

2

In the effete monarchies of the continent of Europe, now
happily abolished by God's will, there was, in the old days of
sin, a far more intelligent and effective way of dealing with
delinquent officials. Not only were they subject, when taken in
downright corruption, to the ordinary processes of the criminal laws; in addition, they were liable to prosecution in special
courts for such offenses as were peculiar to their offices. In this
business the abominable Prussian state, though founded by
Satan, took the lead. It maintained a tribunal in Berlin that devoted itself wholly to the trial of officials accused of malfeasance, corruption, tyranny and incompetence, and any citizen
was free to lodge a complaint with the learned judges. The
trial was public and in accordance with rules fixed by law. An
official found guilty could be punished summarily and in a
dozen different ways. He could be reprimanded, reduced in
rank, suspended from office for a definite period, transferred
to a less desirable job, removed from the rolls altogether,
fined, or sent to jail. If he was removed from office he could be
deprived of his right to a pension in addition, or fined or jailed
in addition. He could be made to pay damages to any citizen
he had injured, or to apologize publicly. All this, remember,
was in addition to his liability under the ordinary law, and the
statutes specifically provided that he could be punished twice
for the same offense, once in the ordinary courts and once in
the administrative court. Thus, a Prussian official who, imitating the daily routine of the agents of our own Treasury or Department of Justice, assaulted a citizen, invaded his house
without a warrant, and seized his property without process of
law, could be deprived of his office and fined heavily by the administrative court, sent to jail by an ordinary court, and forced

to pay damages to his victim by either or both. Our Federal judges, as a matter of everyday practise, issue thousands of injunctions depriving citizens of their right to a jury trial, to the sanctity of domicile and to lawful assemblage, all guaranteed by the Bill of Rights. Had a Prussian judge, overcome by *kaiserliche* passion, undertaken anything of the sort in those far-off days of despotism, any aggrieved citizen might have haled him before the administrative court and recovered heavy damages from him, beside enjoying the felicity of seeing him transferred to some dismal swamp in East Prussia, to listen all day to the unintelligible perjury of Poles. The law specifically provided that responsible officials should be punished, not more leniently than ordinary offenders, but more severely. If a corrupt policeman got six months a corrupt chief of police got two years. More, these statutes were enforced with Prussian barbarity, and the jails were constantly full of errant officials.

I do not propose, of course, that such medieval laws be set up in the United States. We have, indeed, gone far enough in imitating the Prussian system already; if we go much further the moral and enlightened nations of the world will have to unite in a new crusade to put us down. Hints to that effect are not lacking even now; they are heard in England every time the Department of State revives the question of the Bahaman rum trade, and in France every time there is mention of the war debt. As a matter of fact, the Prussian scheme would probably prove ineffective in the Republic, if only because it involved setting up one gang of job-holders to judge and punish another gang. This worked very well in Prussia before the country was civilized by force of arms because, as everyone knows, a Prussian judge was trained in ferocity from infancy, and regarded every man arraigned before him as guilty *ipso facto*; in fact, any thought of a prisoner's possible innocence was abhorrent to him as a reflection upon the *Polizei*, and, hence, by inference, upon the Throne, the whole monarchic idea, and God. But in America, even if they had no other sentiment in common, which would be rarely, judge and prisoner would often be fellow-Democrats or fellow-Republicans, and hence jointly interested in protecting their party against scandal and its members against the loss of their jobs. The operations of the Department of Justice under Mr. Daugherty showed how this community of interest impedes the flow of justice even to-day; it would be far more obstructive, obviously, if job-holders had to execute the laws against other job-holders, and not merely against the friends of other job-holders. Moreover, the Prussian system has another plain defect: the punishments it provides are, in the main, platitudinous and banal. They lack dramatic quality, and they lack ingenuity and appropriateness. To punish a judge taken in judicial crim. con. by fining him or sending him to jail is a bit too facile and obvious. What is needed is a system (*a*) that does not depend for its execution upon the good-will of job-holders, and (*b*) that provides swift, certain and unpedantic punishments, each fitted neatly to its crime. Such a system, after due prayer, I have devised. It is sim-ple, it is unhackneyed, and I believe that it would work. It is divided into two halves. The first half takes the detection and punishment of the crimes of job-holders away from courts of impeachment, congressional smelling committees, and other such agencies—*i.e.*, away from other job-holders—and vests it in the whole body of free citizens, male and female. The sec-ond half provides that any member of that body, having looked into the acts of a job-holder and found him delinquent, may punish him instantly and on the spot, and in any manner that seems appropriate and convenient—and that in case this pun-ishment involves physical damage to the job-holder, the ensu-ing inquiry by the grand jury or coroner shall confine itself strictly to the question whether the job-holder deserved what he got. In other words, I propose that it shall be no longer *malum in se* for a citizen to pummel, cow-hide, kick, gouge, cut, wound, bruise, maim, burn, club, bastinado, flay or even lynch a job-holder, and that it shall be *malum prohibitum* only to the extent that that the punishment exceeds the job-holder's deserts. The amount of this excess, if any, may be de-termined very conveniently by a petit jury, as other questions of guilt are now determined. The flogged judge, or Congress-man, or Prohibition officer, or other job-holder, on being dis-charged from hospital—or his chief heir, in case he has perished —goes before a grand jury and makes complaint, and, if a true bill is found, a petit jury is empanelled and all the evidence is put before it. If it decides that the job-holder deserved the punishment inflicted upon him, the citizen who inflicted it is acquitted with honor. If, on the contrary, it decides that this punishment was excessive, then the citizen is adjudged guilty of assault, mayhem, murder, or whatever it is, in a degree apportioned to the difference between what the job-holder deserved and what he got, and punishment for that excess follows in the usual course.

3

The advantages of this plan, I believe, are too patent to need argument. At one stroke it removes all the legal impediments which now make the punishment of a recreant job-holder so hopeless a process and enormously widens the range of possible penalties. They are now stiff and, in large measure, illogical; under the system I propose they could be made to fit the crime precisely. Say a citizen today becomes convinced that a certain judge is a jackass—that his legal learning is defective, his sense of justice atrophied, and his conduct of cases before him tyrannical and against decency. As things stand, it is entirely impossible to do anything about it. A judge could not be impeached on the mere ground that he is a jackass; the process is far too costly and cumbersome, and there are too many judges liable to the charge. Nor is anything to be gained by denouncing him publicly and urging all good citizens to vote against him when he comes up for re-election, for his term may have ten or fifteen years to run, and even if it expires tomorrow and he is defeated the chances are good that his successor will be quite as bad, and maybe even worse. Moreover, if he is a Federal judge he never comes up for re-election at all; once he has been appointed by the President of the United States, at the advice of his more influential clients and with the consent of their agents in the Senate, he is safe until he is so far gone in senility that he has to be propped on the bench with pillows. But now imagine any citizen free to approach him in open court and pull his nose! Or even, in aggravated cases, to cut off his ears, throw him out of the window, or knock him in the head with an ax! How vastly more attentive he would be to his duties! How diligently he would apply himself to the study of the law! How careful he would be about the rights of litigants before him! How polite and even suave he would become! For judges, like all the rest of us, are vain fellows: they do not enjoy having their noses pulled. Do not forget here that the ignominy resident in the operation would not be abated by the subsequent trial of the puller, even if he should be convicted and jailed. The fact would still be brilliantly remembered that at least one citizen had deemed the judge sufficiently a malefactor to punish him publicly, and to risk going to jail for it. A dozen such episodes, and the career of any judge would be ruined, even though the jails bulged with his critics. He could not maintain his dignity on the bench; even his own catchpolls would snicker at him behind their hands, especially if he showed a cauliflower ear, a black eye or a scar over his bald head. Moreover, soon or late some citizen who had at him would be acquitted by a petit jury, and then, obviously, he would have to retire. It might be provided by law, indeed, that he should be compelled to retire in that case—that an acquittal would automatically vacate the office of the complaining job-holder.

The present system, as I have said, has in late years eloquently demonstrated its ineffectiveness on a colossal scale in the great city of Washington, the seat of the First Chief of the Republic and of a hundred thousand job-holders of gradually lessening puissance, from members of the Cabinet down to janitors, messengers and bookkeepers. All efforts to impeach Daugherty failed; when he was got rid of at last it was by a blow below the belt; in the case of Denby, his fellow-Republicans of Detroit actually treated his dismissal as a martyrdom, and received him when he got home with a band of music and public prayers. If these eminent men were actually guilty of malfeasance in office they obviously deserved far more rigorous punishment; if they were guilty merely of carelessness and neglect they deserved a severe handling as public nuisances. Under the existing system they got what was virtually no punishment at all; under my system, at the most moderate guess, some bored and impatient citizen, during the long months when they were desperately hanging on to their jobs, would have at least ventured to duck them in the Potomac or set their shirt-tails afire. I doubt that any jury would have convicted him of excess, even had he held them under while he counted 100,000. The plain people could not make out just what they had done that was immoral, if anything; but there was an almost universal feeling that they were nuisances, and ought to be got rid of. Even if the citizen who, under my system, had laid hands upon them had been convicted subsequently and sent to jail, the weary newspaper readers of the land would have given three cheers for him, and he would have become a formidable candidate for the presidency on the completion of his term. Even Dr. Coolidge, I daresay, would have had a very friendly feeling for him, and perhaps might have sent him a box of cigars or some White House pies while he was in jail.

I present my system formally to the consideration of the Congress, and offer to explain it in greater detail before a joint session of both Houses at any time not in conflict with my literary engagements. I am no lawyer, to be sure. I once studied law for a space, but forgot it on closing the books. But I retain enough technic to be convinced that my scheme presents no constitutional difficulties. It violates no constitutional right that I am aware of; on the contrary, it specifically reaffirms the right to a trial by jury, now denied in a wholesale and shameless manner by the Federal courts. It sets up no new corps of corrupt and oppressive enforcement officers; it establishes no new jobs; it does not augment the already excessive powers of the police. If there is any lingering taint of injustice in it, then that injustice would be suffered by job-holders, nine-tenths of whom now rob and persecute the rest of us incessantly, and are fast habilitating the doctrine that we are *feræ naturæ* and have no rights that they are bound to respect. It is a system of criminal law that is democratic in the widest and loftiest sense. It augments the dignity and responsibility of the citizen, and tends to increase his concern with problems of government. It sets higher standards of conduct for public officers than prevail now, and makes corruption and incompetence dangerous. Above all, it breaks down the rigid and unintelligent formalism of our scheme of punishments, and makes it infinitely more pliant, appropriate and various. We have been tending for years to reduce all punishments to two: fine and imprisonment, the first usually no punishment at all, but a mere bribe to escape punishment, and the second often cruel and almost always ineffective. That this tendency is widely regarded as evil is shown by the extra-legal efforts to combat it that are made constantly by the Ku Klux Klan, the American Legion and other such agents of lynch law. My scheme would take over the rich ingenuities of these agents and give them formal legal sanction; it would restore to the art of putting down crime something of the fine bounce and gusto that it had in the Middle Ages, when tort and penalty were united by logical, and even, indeed, æsthetic bonds, and a judge who was imaginative and original was esteemed. The certainty of punishment would daunt the offender, and the uncertainty of its nature would fill him with dread. Once proceeded against, he would become enormously cautious and conscientious. A Congressman with his ears cut off, you may be sure, would not do it again. A judge, after two or three rocket flights through his court-room window, would be forced, by an irresistible psychological process, to give heed thereafter to the Constitution, the statutes, and the common rights of man. Even a police captain or a United States Senator, once floored with a bung-starter or rolled in a barrel, would begin to think.

I dedicate my plan to my country.

XI.

On the Nature of Man

The Animal That Thinks

THAT the great majority of human beings, even under our perfected Christian civilization, are still almost as incapable of rational thought as so many diamond-back terrapin—this is a fact to which we have all been made privy of late by the babbling of eminent psychologists. Granted. But let us not rashly assume that this infirmity is confined strictly to the nether herd—that, above the level where thinking may be said genuinely to begin, it goes on, level by level, to greater and greater heights of clarity and acumen. Nothing, indeed, of the sort. The curve goes upward for a while, but then it begins to flatten, and finally it dips very sharply. Thinking, indeed, is so recent an accomplishment phylogenetically that man is capable of it only in a narrow area, as he is capable of sight and hearing only in narrow areas. To one side lie the instinctive tropisms and intellectual peristaltic motions of the simple, rational only by a sort of pious license; to the other side lie the more complex but even more nonsensical speculations of metaphysicians. The difference between the two is vastly less than is commonly assumed; we are all misled by the sombre, portentous manner of the metaphysicians. The truth is that between a speech by a Salvation Army convert, a Southern Congressman or a Grand Goblin of the Rotary Club and a philosophical treatise by an American Neo-Realist there is no more to choose than between the puling of an infant and the puling of a veteran of the Civil War. Both show the human cerebrum loaded far beyond its Plimsoll mark; both, strictly speaking, are idiotic.

2
Veritas Odium Parit

An old human delusion, largely fostered by theologians, is
the one to the effect that truth has a mysterious medicinal
power—that its propagation makes the world better and man
happier . . . *et cognoscetis veritatem, et veritas liberabit vos.*
But is this so-called truth about truth true? It is not. The
truth, nine times out of ten, is extremely disturbing and uncomfortable; if it is not grossly discreditable to someone it is
apt to be painfully amazing to everyone. The masses of men
are thus wise to hold it in suspicion, as they are wise to suspect
that other delusion, liberty. Let us turn to an example. The
most rational religious ideas held in modern times, at least
among Christians, are probably those of the Unitarians; the
most nonsensical are those of the Christian Scientists. Yet it
must be obvious to every observer that the average Unitarian,
even when he is quite healthy, which is not often, is a sour,
conscience-striken and unhappy fellow, whereas, the average
Christian Scientist, even when he is down with gall-stones, is
full of a childish and enviable peace. The one is disquieted by
his apprehension of damning facts about God and the universe; the other is lulled by his magnificent imbecilities. I have
had the honor of knowing, in my time, a number of eminent
philosophers, some of them intelligent. The happiest among
the latter, in his moments of greatest joy, used to entertain himself by drawing up wills leaving his body to a medical college.

3
The Eternal Cripple

Man, at his best, remains a sort of one-lunged animal, never
completely rounded and perfect, as a bacillus, say, is perfect. If
he shows one valuable quality, it is almost unheard of for him
to show any other. Give him a head, and he lacks a heart. Give
him a heart of a gallon capacity, and his head holds scarcely a
pint. The artist, nine times out of ten, is a dead-beat and given
to the debauching of virgins, so-called. The patriot is a bigot,
and, more often than not, a cad and a coward. The man of

physical bravery is often on a level, intellectually, with a Baptist clergyman. The intellectual giant has bad kidneys and cannot thread a needle. In all my years of search in this world, from the Golden Gate in the West to the Vistula in the East, and from the Orkney Islands in the North to the Spanish Main in the South, I have never met a thoroughly moral man who was honorable.

4
The Test

Don't ask what delusion he entertains regarding God, or what mountebank he follows in politics, or what he springs from, or what he submits to from his wife. Simply ask how he makes his living. It is the safest and surest of all known tests. A man who gets his board and lodging on this ball in an ignominious way is inevitably an ignominious man.

5
National Characters

The character of a nation, like its mind, is always determined, not by the masses of its citizens, but by a small minority of resolute and influential men. Nothing, for example, could be more absurd than the common notion that the French, as a people, are gallant, courageous and fond of hazard. The truth is that they are mainly dull shopkeepers and peace-loving peasants, and have been driven into all their wars of conquest by their masters, who are extraordinarily prehensile and audacious. The French plain people bitterly disapproved the military enterprises of Bonaparte, and resisted his conscriptions by every means within their power. In the late war they abandoned themselves to a melodramatic despair after the first few months, frequently broke and ran under pressure, and were kept in the fight only by heroic devices. The apparent resolution of France was largely external. That is to say, it was supplied by England. Internally, it was confined to a small group of leaders, most of them professional adventurers, and many of them, such as Marshal Foch, of enemy blood. The French masses, despite the enormous military advantages on their side, were ready to quit after every losing battle, and after not a few—for example, the Verdun operations—they did quit.

The character of the Germans, as it was displayed during the war, was also foreign to the great majority of the German people. The Germans are not pugnacious by nature, nor have they any talent for organization; on the contrary, they are incurable particularists, and never meet without quarrelling. Their political history is a history of endless squabbles in the face of the enemy. Fully a half of them believed in Napoleon I at the time he was ravaging their country; in the late war millions of them were deceived by the late Woodrow's hypocritical Fourteen Points—a deliberate and successful device to divide and conquer them. The gigantic skill and resolution visible on the German side during the war were supplied by less than one per cent. of the German people, and so were the harsh, realistic theories which underlaid them. The average German was and is quite incapable of any such theories; they horrify him almost as much as they would horrify a member of the Lake Mohonk Conference. Once the one per cent. of dominating Germans had been disposed of by their heavy losses on the field, the rest of the nation turned out to be a mob of moony sentimentalists, hot for all the democratic fallacies ever heard of, and eager to put down every surviving man of genuine courage and enterprise. That mob will continue to pursue these chimeras until a new race of rulers arises—and then the world will once more mistake the ideas of those rulers for the ideas of the average German.

The English are judged just as inaccurately, and in the same way. There is, for example, the common notion that all Englishmen are good sportsmen, resolute in battle, generous in victory and calm in defeat. It would be difficult to imagine anything more ridiculous. The English masses are probably the worst sportsmen in the world, save only, perhaps, the American masses. During the war their hysterical whoops and yells deafened the universe, and after it was over the so-called khaki election brilliantly displayed the true color of their generosity. To this day, like their brethren of the Republic, they believe it to be quite honorable to pick a German's pocket or rob a German corpse. But there is in England a small minority

of men, chiefly Celtic in blood, who practise good sportsmanship as a sort of substitute for religion, and these men are still
influential enough to give the hue of their own character to
what appears to be the general English character. Once they
succumb to democracy, not even American Anglomaniacs will
ever mention English sportsmanship again.

6
The Goal

The central aim of civilization, it must be plain, is simply to
defy and correct the obvious intent of God, *e.g.*, that five per
cent. of the people of Christendom shall die of smallpox every
year, that the issue of every love affair shall be a succession of
little strangers, that cows shall devote themselves wholly to
nursing their calves, that it shall take longer to convey a message from New York to Chicago than it takes to convey one
from New York to Newark, that the wicked shall be miserable
and the virtuous happy. Has civilization a motto? Then certainly it must be "Not *Thy* will, O Lord, but *ours*, be done!"

7
Psychology at 5 A.M.

It is in the throes of sober second thought, of spiritual
Katzenjammer, that men reveal their true souls. The Puritan
always swears a bloody oath that he will never do it again. The
civilized man simply resolves to be a bit more careful next
time.

8
The Reward

The cadence at the end is always in the crystalline and sardonic key of C major. . . The heroic sweatings and strivings
of the Knights Templar, for a whole age the marvel of Christendom, are now embalmed in a single essay by James Anthony Froude, M.A., LL.D., an historian of charming style but
dubious accuracy. If it were not for that single essay, it would
be difficult, if not impossible, for an inquirer of English speech

to find out what their finish was, and why they perished from the earth. Their old stronghold in London is now—what? An office-building for lawyers, a roost for such rogues as they would have put to the sword at sight. And Palestine, for which they died by the thousand, is now given over to *Schnorrer* and *Meshulachim* from Grand street and the Mile End road.

9
The Altruist

A large part of altruism, even when it is perfectly honest, is grounded upon the fact that it is uncomfortable to have unhappy people about one.

This is especially true in family life. A man makes sacrifices to his wife's desires, not because he greatly enjoys giving up what he wants himself, but because he would enjoy it even less to see her cutting a sour face across the dinner table.

10
The Man of Honor

The difference between a moral man and a man of honor is that the latter regrets a discreditable act, even when it has worked and he has not been caught.

XII.

Bugaboo

ALL of the Great Thinkers of the world, East, West, North and South, have been alarming their customers, for two or three years past, with the same bugaboo. According to the New York *Times* and the Department of State, there must be a complete restoration of the capitalistic system in Russia and Mexico, or our sweet Christian civilization will go to pot. According to the masterminds of France, the Germans must first lose all their trade and then pay 10,000 cents on the dollar, or our sweet Christian civilization will go to pot. According to H. G. Wells, the Treaty of Versailles must be denounced by all parties to it, or our sweet Christian civilization will go to pot. And so on, and so on. On the main point the propagandists of all schools are unanimously agreed: that the civilization of the West teeters on the edge of an abyss, and that a few more wobbles will send it over. The barbarians once more thunder upon the gates of Rome. Let the turmoils within go on for a brief while longer, and they will burst in with their hellish cries, and every great boon and usufruct that men have sweated and died for since the days of Charlemagne, from the cathedral at Rheims to the pneumatic automobile tire, and from fiddle music to diphtheria antitoxin, and from the inferiority complex to the bichloride tablet, will vanish in one universal catastrophe. Blood drips from the moon; another general war impends. This war, according to Will H. Irwin, a soothsayer employed by the *Saturday Evening Post*, will be so colossal a butchery that there will be no survivors save a few undertakers and profiteers, and no material salvage save a few stone quarries and a couple of million bales of worthless bonds.

Personally, I should be glad to see such a war, for it seems to me that the human race has run on long enough—that the high gods would show unaccustomed sense if they dropped it into hell and so ended the farce. I know of no existing nation that deserves to live, and I know of very few individuals. But despite the fact that my wishes are thus on the side of Dr.

Irwin's thought, I find it quite impossible to follow him. In brief, I see absolutely no sign of a general *débâcle*. On the contrary, it seems to me that the thing we call civilization was never more secure than it is today, either in Europe or in America. More bloodshed, of course, is pretty certain to come; the French, to name only one people, are obviously headed for another shambles. But that is a small matter, almost a private matter. Even the complete destruction of France would not materially damage civilization, save, perhaps, in the eyes of touring American Puritans, a-search for a moral oasis. I also incline to think that England and the United States will be by the ears before many years have come and gone, and that one or the other of them, probably the United States, will get a severe beating. But they have fought before, and civilization was scarcely aware of it. Either could be wiped out utterly, and it would still be possible to buy Ford parts, Bibles, oil stocks, canned salmon, union suits, First Folio Shakespeares, hair tonics, books on sex hygiene, diamonds, coffins, dice, dog soap, glass eyes, and all the other great blessings of our Christian *Kultur*. Both could be destroyed, wholly and horribly, and men in Italy would continue to grow excellent wine, and men in Germany would continue to pursue the colloids and the cocci, and men in Scandinavia would continue to shiver and curse God through their long, grisly Winter nights, and so keep the world supplied with its normal doses of theology, metaphysics and political theory. Moreover, there are the Chinese. If the entire population of Christendom were disposed of by some cosmic delousing operation the Chinese would have a chance —a chance denied to them today, in free competition, by their superior dignity, decency and sense of honor.

The interdependence of nations, indeed, is much overestimated by sentimentalists, chiefly of the economic faculty. They permit the gyrations of foreign exchange to alarm them. But what is it to a man in Kansas, or Uruguay, or Saskatchewan, expressed in hard figures, that a million Poles have been slaughtered, or that the Turks have again ravaged Armenia, or that the British and Dutch are at odds over human liberty and the oil-wells of Mesopotamia, or that Belgrade has fallen, or that the French refuse to go back to work but propose to live hereafter by highway robbery? It is, at most, a matter of ten per cent. This is all he feels, and this is all he cares. If he shows any excitement or even any interest it is because some drive manager has played upon his credulities, as Dr. Wells seeks to play upon the credulities of all of us. For one I refuse to be alarmed. If Paris were burned tomorrow, I'd scarcely know it on my estates in Maryland, feeding upon my razor-back hams, listening to Caruso's ghost, and reading the state papers of Thomas Jefferson. Even if I tired of that idyllic life and went abroad, I'd admire the ruins quite as much as have ever admired the Trocadero or the Eiffel tower. Both, perhaps, would escape the fire—and no doubt the incendiaries would make off with the best things in the Luxembourg and the Louvre. Nor am I greatly alarmed by the current doctrine that the late war stamped out the best strains of all the contesting nations, and that they are rapidly sinking to the level of their lower classes. This alarm is raised in an inflammatory book called "Is America Safe for Democracy?" by one William McDougall, a Scotchman imported to civilize the sophomores at Harvard. The McDougall also raises and parades another hobgoblin, once a favorite of the immortal zany, Major-General Roosevelt. That is the bugaboo of race suicide, especially among the upper classes. The wops in the ditch and the Slovaks in the mining towns, it appears, breed up to the limit of human endurance, but bank presidents seldom have more than four or five legitimate children, and the great majority of poets, metaphysicians, Oxford dons, lady Ph.D.s, assyriologists and moving-picture actors are childless, and perhaps even sterile. At the present rate of reproduction, says Prof. McDougall, 1000 Harvard graduates of today will have but 50 descendants 200 years hence, whereas 1000 Rumanians will have 100,000.

But what of it? On the one hand this gay professor assumes far too readily that Harvard graduates, taking one with another, deserve to be ranked as first-rate men, and on the other hand he greatly overestimates the number of first-rate men needed to run the world, and to insure a reasonable rate of human progress. The fact is that the safeguarding and development of civilization are and always have been in the exclusive care of a very small minority of human beings of each generation, and that the rest of the human race consists wholly of deadheads. Consider, for example, the telephone, a very characteristic agent of Christian advancement. It has been invented, perfected, organized and brought to every door in our own time by less than 20 men—nay, by less than 10 men. All the others who have made it, financed and installed it have been simply trailers. All the rest of the human race has taken a free ride. The number of such first-rate men in the world is always overestimated, and it is fatuously assumed that they are identical with the wealthier minority of the population. Prof. Dr. McDougall himself falls into this last error. He proves— what everyone knew already—that the children of well-to-do parents are brighter, by pedagogical standards, than the children of poor folk, but this fact is of no significance. If it were, then pedagogues themselves would rank as first-rate men, which is an absurdity; they are, in fact, generally stupid, and seldom produce anything of value to the world. The test of a first-rate man is not to be made by the criteria of schoolmarms. It is to be made by asking the simple question: Has he ever said or done anything that was not said or done before, and is it something of positive and permanent value to the human race? If the answer is yes, then he belongs to the superior minority; if it is no, then he belongs to the mob, no matter how brilliantly he may pass examinations, and no matter how greatly he may prosper under the civilization that his superiors have fostered and developed.

The number of men who can pass this test is always extremely small—vastly smaller than the uncritical worshipers of politicians, university presidents, prima donna theologians, opera singers, lawyers, popular philosophers, successful authors and other such human Fords usually assume. How many exist at the present moment in the United States? I turn to "Who's Who in America" and find 23,443 names. But a brief inspection is sufficient to show that only a small minority are borne by first-rate men. I run over page after page and find nothing but Fords—an army general who has done absolutely nothing save obey orders and draw his pay, three authors of the eighth rate, five or six pedagogues, a theologian or two, a Federal judge—who ever heard of a Federal judge who left the world more intelligent, more virtuous or more efficient than he found it?—a publisher of bad books, two Congressmen, a bishop. I begin to despair. Finally, I find a first-rate man: Bush of the Bush Terminals. One in 35. The proportion, I think, is fair for the whole book. This makes 670 first-rate Americans in our time. Call it 700 to be safe. But race-suicide among the upper classes will make it impossible to produce even the 700 in the next generation? Nonsense! It is not necessary that *every* first-rate man leave children behind him; it is only necessary that a few of them in each generation do so. Nature will do the rest. The first-rate character may be concealed for a generation or two, but soon or late it will reveal itself, and sometimes in many individuals. This explains the common notion that first-rate men are often produced in low life, *i.e.*, the case of Lincoln. They are, but not by low-lifers. Here the devil helps the angels, and the sinfulness of man takes on a high human utility. Often the cross is concealed in forgotten generations. The good blood is apparently lost in the flood of proletarian bilge —but suddenly it begins to run red and clear, and the platitudinarians have another up-from-slavery chapter to wag their ears over. I believe fully that the first-rate men of the world constitute a distinct and separate species—that they have little, if anything, in common with the lower orders of men. But the two races, fortunately for human progress, are mutually fertile. If they ever cease to be, then God help us all! But there is absolutely no sign that they are ceasing to be. So long as they remain as they are there need be no worry about the future of civilization. The danger is that first-rate men may grow too numerous, and so arouse the hatred of the lower orders, as happened in Greece. The United States now accommodates 700. If the number rose to 1000 I fear that the churches, the newspapers, Congress and the American Legion would grow restless, and that the catastrophe dreamed of by Prof. McDougall would begin to cast its shadows before.

Meanwhile, all the current pulling of long faces is absurd. There is not the slightest sign that the basic elements of modern civilization, such as it is, are in any danger, proximately or remotely. Europe, at the moment, is a bit weary, but no actual barbarians are thundering at the gate; all the recognizable barbarians, in fact, are retreating sadly into their native jungles, with troubles of their own. There is no decline in Christian *morale*; if anything, there is far too much Christian *morale* on tap. The one thing that one may say accurately is that there is a struggle for control within the borders of civilization itself, to wit, between the masses of simple and stupid men and various minorities of extremely egoistic and determined men. But neither side is trying to destroy civilization, save in the indignant visions of the other. On the contrary, both are trying their best to preserve it, and whether one side wins or the other it will be duly preserved. Ten years hence it will be just as easy to send a picture postcard or to be beaten by a policeman as it is to-day, and wherever one may buy a picture postcard the arts are safe and wherever one may be beaten by a policeman law and order are safe, and when the arts and law and order are safe, then civilization is also safe. False analogies are at the bottom of most of the current fears—that is, when they are honest. The analogy with Rome, so often cited, is especially nonsensical. A few hundred thousand Romans were surrounded by countless millions of barbarians, and the barbarians had arms quite as good as those of the Romans. Where is any similar horde to be found today? Are the Japs dangerous? Plainly not, save perhaps to the United States. The Japs, with all of the odds on their side, took more than two years to beat the Russians; they would stand up before a European coalition no more than 10 days. The Chinese? They don't want Europe; they want only China. The blacks of Africa? Two German divisions could dispose of all of them, given a fair, stand-up battle, in two hours. Nor is any genuine fear to be deduced from the fate of the late Confederacy in America. The intellectual colapse of the Southern States after the Civil War was purely a local and geographical matter. Most of the surviving Southerners who had been civilized before the war simply moved North, leaving only a few cripples, the darkeys and a mob of poor white trash behind. But civilization in the United States was certainly not affected; in fact, the mixing of Southerners and Northerners in the North probably improved it. Today, a half century afterward, even some of the Southern poor whites are becoming relatively civilized. A book store has been opened in New Orleans, a man in Mobile has bought a violoncello, and only the other day, in Georgia, a white man was actually taken by the constabulary for killing a dozen Negroes.

What the authors of elegies mistake for the collapse of civilization is simply the internal struggle that I have mentioned—the ages-old combat between the haves and the have-nots, now rendered transiently acute by a parlous shortening of the things fought for. The ultimate issue of that struggle seems to me to be plain enough. The have-nots will be given a drubbing, and under the protection of a new and unprecedentedly vigorous and daring capitalism the thing called Christian civilization will be promoted as it has never been promoted before. My arteries harden so fast—a consequence of my constant and quixotic sacrifice of myself to the common weal—that I cannot hope to live into the full flush of that new Golden Age, but I can at least smack my lips over it in anticipation. What I see is a vast horde of inferior men broken, after a hopeless, fruitless fight, to the hard, uninspiring labor of the world—a race of slaves superbly regimented, and kept steadily in order by great brigades of propagandists, official optimists, scare-mongers, Great Thinkers and rev. clergy. And over them a minority of capitalist overlords, well-fed, well-protected, highly respected, politely envied, and lavishly supplied with endless stores of picture postcards, gasoline, silk underwear, mayonnaise, Pontet Canet, toilet soap and phonograph records.

The battle, in fact, is already half won. In France and the United States capitalism can weather any conceivable storm. In England it craftily encourages labor to a combat that will be to a finish, and with capital on top. In Italy it is already in the saddle. In Germany only the Junkers stave off the inevitable victory of money. In Russia the Bolsheviks help capital everywhere by reducing the cause of the have-nots to an absurdity. The other countries are not dogs, but mere tails. . . . The United States, I believe, will see the thing brought to its finest flower. There were no war losses here, but only profits. In all other countries, the conscripts of the war are restless, and inclined to move toward the Left. Here they are already superbly organized to serve capital, and give the final touch of felicity to the situation by serving it for nothing. On the evening of the same day that an American Legionary has his wages reduced 40 per cent. and his hours of labor increased 25 per cent., he goes out at his own risk and expense and helps to tar and feather some visionary who tries to convince him that he has been swindled. Meanwhile, the Supreme Court of New York decides formally that "the courts . . . must stand at all times as the representatives of capital," and the newspapers commend the dictum in lavish terms. . . . I sing Utopia. It is about to burst upon us.

XIII.
On Government

I

"GOVERNMENT," said William Godwin in that "Enquiry Concerning Political Justice" which got Shelley two wives and lost him £6000 a year, "can have no more than two legitimate purposes: the suppression of injustice against individuals within the community, and the common defense against external invasion." The dictum, after a hundred and thirty-one years, remains unimproved and perhaps unimprovable. Today, to be sure, with Darwin behind us, we'd make some change in its terms: what Godwin was trying to say, obviously, was that the central aim of government was to ameliorate the struggle for existence—to cherish and protect the dignity of man in the midst of the brutal strife of *Homo neanderthalensis*. But that change would be simply substituting a *cliché* of the Nineteenth Century for one of the Eighteenth. All the furious discussion of the subject that has gone on in the intervening time has not changed the basic idea in the slightest. To the plain man of to-day, as to the most fanatical Liberal or Socialist, government appears primarily as a device for compensating his weakness, a machine for protecting him in rights that he could not make secure with his own arm. Even the Tory holds the same view of it: its essential function, to him, is to safeguard his property against the lascivious desires of those who, if they were not policed, would be tempted to grab it. "Government," said George Washington, "is not reason, it is not eloquence—it is force." Bad government is that which is weak, irresolute and lacking in constabulary enterprise; when one has defined it, one has also defined a bad bishop, cavalry captain or policeman. Good government is that which delivers the citizen from the risk of being done out of his life and property too arbitrarily and violently—one that relieves him sufficiently from the barbaric business of guarding them to enable him to engage in gentler, more dignified and more agreeable undertakings, to his own content and profit, and the advantage, it may be, of the commonwealth.

Unfortunately, this function is performed only imperfectly by any of the forms of government now visible in Christendom, and Dr. Johnson was perhaps justified in dismissing them all as but various aspects of the same fraud. The citizen of to-day, even in the most civilized states, is not only secured but defectively against other citizens who aspire to exploit and injure him—for example, highwaymen, bankers, quack doctors, clergymen, sellers of oil stock and contaminated liquor, and so-called reformers of all sorts,—and against external foes, military, commercial and philosophical; he is also exploited and injured almost without measure by the government itself—in other words, by the very agency which professes to protect him. That agency becomes, indeed, one of the most dangerous and insatiable of the inimical forces present in his everyday environment. He finds it more difficult and costly to survive in the face of it than it is to survive in the face of any other enemy. He may, if he has prudence, guard himself effectively against all the known varieties of private criminals, from stockbrokers to pickpockets and from lawyers to kidnapers, and he may, if he has been burnt enough, learn to guard himself also against the rogues who seek to rob him by the subtler device of playing upon his sentimentalities and superstitions: charity mongers, idealists, soul-savers, and others after their kind. But he can no more escape the tax-gatherer and the policemen, in all their protean and multitudinous guises, than he can escape the ultimate mortician. They beset him constantly, day in and day out, in ever-increasing numbers and in ever more disarming masks and attitudes. They invade his liberty, affront his dignity and greatly incommode his search for happiness, and every year they demand and wrest from him a larger and larger share of his worldly goods. The average American of today works more than a full day in every week to support his government. It already costs him more than his pleasures and almost as much as his vices, and in another half century, no doubt, it will begin to cost as much as his necessities.

These gross extortions and tyrannies, of course, are all practised on the theory that they are not only unavoidable, but also laudable—that government oppresses its victims in order to confer upon them the great boons mentioned by Godwin. But that theory, I believe, begins to be quite as dishonest as the chiropractor's pretense that he pummels his patient's spine in order to cure his cancer: the actual object, obviously, is simply to cure his solvency. What keeps such notions in full credit, and safeguards them against destructive analysis, is chiefly the survival into our enlightened age of a concept hatched in the black days of absolutism—the concept, to wit, that government is something that is superior to and quite distinct from all other human institutions—that it is, in its essence, not a mere organization of ordinary men, like the Ku Klux Klan, the United States Steel Corporation or Columbia University, but a transcendental organism composed of aloof and impersonal powers, devoid wholly of self-interest and not to be measured by merely human standards. One hears it spoken of, not uncommonly, as one hears the law of gravitation and the grace of God spoken of—as if its acts had no human motive in them and stood clearly above, human fallibility. This concept, I need not argue, is full of error. The government at Washington is no more impersonal than the cloak and suit business is impersonal. It is operated by precisely the same sort of men, and to almost the same ends. When we say that it has decided to do this or that, that it proposes or aspires to do this or that— usually to the great cost and inconvenience of nine-tenths of us—we simply say that a definite man or group of men has decided to do it, or proposes or aspires to do it; and when we examine this group of men realistically we almost invariably find that it is composed of individuals who are not only not superior to the general, but plainly and depressingly inferior, both in common sense and in common decency—that the act of government we are called upon to ratify and submit to is, in its essence, no more than an act of self-interest by men who, if no mythical authority stood behind them, would have a hard time of it surviving in the struggle for existence.

2

These men, in point of fact, are seldom if ever moved by anything rationally describable as public sprit; there is actually no more public spirit among them than among so many burglars or street-walkers. Their purpose, first, last and all the time, is to promote their private advantage, and to that end, and that end alone, they exercise all the vast powers that are in their hands. Sometimes the thing they want is mere security in their jobs; sometimes they want gaudier and more lucrative jobs; sometimes they are content with their jobs and their pay but yearn for more power. Whatever it is they seek, whether security, greater ease, more money or more power, it has to come out of the common stock, and so it diminishes the shares of all other men. Putting a new job-holder to work decreases the wages of every wage-earner in the land—not enough to be noticed, perhaps, but enough to leave its mark. Giving a job-holder more power takes something away from the liberty of all of us: we are less free than we were in proportion as he has more authority. Theoretically, we get something for what we thus give up, but actually we usually get absolutely nothing. Suppose two-thirds of the members of the national House of Representatives were dumped into the Washington garbage incinerator tomorrow, what would we lose to offset our gain of their salaries and the salaries of their parasites? It may be plausibly argued, of course, that the House itself is necessary to our happiness and salvation—that we need it as we need trolley conductors, chiropodists and the men who bite off puppies' tails. But even if that be granted—and I, for one, am by no means disposed to grant it—the plain fact remains that all the useful work the House does might be done just as well by fifty men, and that the rest are of no more utility to the commonwealth, in any rational sense, than so many tight-rope walkers or teachers of mah jong.

The Fathers, when they launched the Republic, were under no illusions as to the nature of government. Washington's view of its inner nature I have already quoted; Jefferson it was who said sagely that "that government is best which governs least." The Constitution in its first form, perhaps, was designed chiefly to check the rising pretensions of the lower orders, drunk with the democratic fustian of the Revolutionary era, but when the Bill of Rights was added to it its guns began to point more especially at the government itself, *i.e.*, at the class of job-holders, ever bent upon oppressing the citizen to the limit of his endurance. It is, perhaps, a fact provocative of sour mirth that the Bill of Rights was designed trustfully to prohibit forever two of the favorite crimes of all known governments: the seizure of private property without adequate compensation and the invasion of the citizen's liberty without justifiable cause and due process of law. It is a fact provocative of mirth yet more sour that the execution of these prohibitions was put into the hands of courts, which is to say, into the hands of lawyers, which is to say, into the hands of men specifically educated to discover legal excuses for dishonest, dishonorable and anti-social acts. The actual history of the Constitution, as everyone knows, has been a history of the gradual abandonment of all such impediments to governmental tyranny. Today we live frankly under a government of men, not of laws. What is the Bill of Rights to a Roosevelt, a Wilson, a Palmer, a Daugherty, a Burns? Under such tin-horn Cæsars the essential enmity between government and citizen becomes only too plain, and one gets all the proof that is needed of the eternal impossibility of protecting the latter against the former. The government can not only evoke fear in its victims; it can also evoke a sort of superstitious reverence. It is thus both an army and a church, and with sharp weapons in both hands it is virtually irresistible. Its personnel, true enough, may be changed, and so may the external forms of the fraud it practises, but its inner nature is immutable.

Politics, as hopeful men practise it in the world, consists mainly of the delusion that a change in form is a change in substance. The American colonists, when they got rid of the Potsdam tyrant, believed fondly that they were getting rid of oppressive taxes forever and setting up complete liberty. They found almost instantly that taxes were higher than ever, and before many years they were writhing under the Alien and Sedition Acts. The French, when they threw off the monarchy at last, looked forward to a Golden Age of peace, plenty and freedom. They are now wrecked by war, bankrupted beyond any chance of recovery, and hag-ridden by an apparently unbreakable combination of the most corrupt and cynical politicians ever seen in the world. The experience of the Russians and Germans is even more eloquent. The former have been ruined by their saviors, and in so far as they have any power of reflection left, long for the restoration of the tyranny they once ascribed to the devil. The latter, delivered from the Hohen-zollerns, now find the Schmidts and Krauses ten times as expensive and oppressive. Six months after the republic was set up a German cabinet minister, for the first time in the history of the nation, was in flight over the border, his loot under his arm. In the first flush of surprise and indignation the people took to assassinating politicians, but before long they gave it up as hopeless: Schmidt fell but Kraus still lived, and so government kept its vitality and its character. Many Germans, reduced to despair, now advocate a complete abolition of political government; if Stinnes had lived they would have tried to make him dictator of the country. But political government, *i.e.*, government by professional job-holders, would have remained in fact, despite its theoretical abolition, and its nature would have been unchanged.

If downright revolution is thus incapable of curing the disease, the ordinary reforms that men believe in sink to the level of bald quackeries. Consider, for example, the history of so-called Civil Service Reform in the United States. It came in on a wave of intense public indignation against the whole governmental imposture; it represented a violent and romantic effort to substitute an ideal of public service for the familiar harsh reality of public exploitation. For fifty years the American people had sweated and suffered under the spoils system, that lovely legacy of the "reforms" of the Jackson era. By the opening of the eighties they were ready to dispose of it by fair means or foul. The job-holder, once theoretically a freeman discharging a lofty and necessary duty, was seen clearly to be no more than a rat devouring the communal corn; his public position was indistinguishable from that of a child-stealer, a well-poisoner or a Sunday-school superintendent; and that of his brother, the government contractor and purveyor, was even lower. Many men of both classes, including some very important ones, were clapped into jail, and many others had to depart for Canada between days, along with the nightly squad of clerical seducers and absconding bank cashiers. Thereupon seers and prophets arose to lead the people out of the wilderness. A few wild ones proposed, in effect, that government be abolished altogether, but the notion outraged democratic sentiment, and so most of them followed the job-holders into jail; some, in fact, were put to death by more or less due process of law. The majority of soothsayers were less revolutionary: they proposed only that the race of job-holders be reformed by force, that government be purged and denaturized.

This was undertaken by what came to be called Civil Service Reform. The essence of Civil Service Reform was the notion that the job-holder, in return for his high prerogatives and immunities, should be compelled to do an honest day's work—that he should fit himself for it by hard effort, as a barber fits himself for cutting hair. Led by such men of Vision as E. L. Godkin, Charles J. Bonaparte and Theodore Roosevelt (that, of course, was before Roosevelt deserted the flag and became himself the archetypical job-holder), the reformers proceeded grimly toward the dreadful purpose of making the job-holder a mere slave, like a bookkeeper in a wholesale house. His pay and emoluments were cut down and his labors were increased. Once the proudest and most envied citizen of the Republic, free to oppress all other citizens to the limit of their endurance, he became at one stroke a serf groaning in a pen, with a pistol pointed at his head. If, despite the bars and artillery surrounding him, his thrift enabled him to make a show of decent prosperity, he was clapped into prison *ipso facto*, and almost without a trial. A few short years saw his fall from the dizziest height of ease to the lowest abyss of misery.

This, of course, could not go on, else politics would have tumbled into chaos and government would have lost its basic character; nay, its very life. What is more, it did *not* go on, for human ingenuity, despite the troubles of the time, was still functioning, and presently it found a remedy for the disease— a remedy so perfect, indeed, that the patient did not know he was taking it. That remedy was achieved by the simple process of making two slight changes in the ideal of Civil Service Reform itself. First the word Reform was lopped off, and then the word Civil. There remained, then, only Service. This Service saved the day for the job-holder; it gave him a new lease upon his job; it diverted public suspicion from him; it converted him from a criminal into a sort of philanthropist. It remains with us today, the heir and assign of the old spoils system, as the bootlegger is the heir and assign of the saloon-keeper.

3

The chief achievement of Service is that it has sucked reform into the governmental orbit, and so made it official and impeccable—more, highly profitable. The old-time reformer was one who got nothing for his psychic corn-cures and shin-plasters—who gave them away freely to all comers, seeking only righteousness himself—who often, indeed, took a beating into the bargain. The new reformer, safe in a government job, with a drastic and complex law behind him, is one who is paid in legal tender, unfailingly proffered, for his passionate but usually unintelligible services to humanity—a prophet of the new enlightenment, a priest at a glittering and immense shrine. He is the fellow who enforces the Volstead Act, the Mann Act, all the endless laws for putting down sin. He is the bright evangelist who tours the country teaching mothers how to have babies, spreading the latest inventions in pedagogy, road-making, the export trade, hog-raising and vegetable-canning, waging an eternal war upon illiteracy, hookworm, the white slave trade, patent medicines, the foot and mouth disease, cholera infantum, adultery, rum. He is, quite as often as not, female; he is a lady Ph.D., cocksure, bellicose, very well paid. Male or female, he represents the new governmental tyranny; he is Vision, vice the spoils system, retired. The old-time job-holder, penned in the cage of the Civil Service, is now only a peon, a brother to the ox. He has to work quite as hard as if he labored for Judge Gary or Henry Ford, and he is very much worse paid. The high prerogatives and usufructs of government have slipped out of his hands. They are exercised and enjoyed today by the apostles of Service, a horde growing daily, vastly and irresistibly, in numbers, impudence, power and pay.

Few of the groaning taxpayers of These States, indeed, realize how far this public merchandizing of buncombe has displaced the old spoils system, or how much it is costing them every year. During the Civil War an army contractor who went to Washington looking for loot announced frankly what he was after; as a result, he was constantly under suspicion, and was lucky if he got away with as much as $100,000; only a few Vanderbilts and Morgans actually stole more. During the late war he called himself a dollar-a-year-man, put on a major's

uniform, took oath to die if need be for the cause of democracy
—and went home with a million, at least. The job-holder has
undergone a similar metamorphosis; maybe apotheosis would
be a better aimed word. In the days of the spoils system he
was, at best, an amateurish and inept performer. The only reason he ever offered for demanding a place at the public trough
was that he deserved it—that he had done his share to elect the
ticket. The easy answer to him was that he was an obvious
loafer and scoundrel, and deserved nothing. But what answer
is to be made to his heir and assign, the evangelist of Service,
the prophet of Vision? He doesn't start off with a bald demand
for a job; he starts off with a Message. He has discovered the
long-sought sure cure for all the sorrows of the world; he has
the infallible scheme for putting down injustice, misery, ignorance, suffering, sin; his appeal is not to the rules of a sinister
and discreditable game, but to the bursting heart of humanity,
the noblest and loftiest sentiments of man. His job is never in
the foreground; it is concealed in his Vision. To get at the former one must first dispose of the latter. Well, who is to do it?
What true-born American will volunteer for the cynical office?
Half are too idiotic and the rest are too cowardly. It takes
courage to flaunt and make a mock of Vision—and where is
courage?

Certainly not in this imperial commonwealth of natural
kneebenders and marchers in parades. Nowhere else in Christendom, save only in France, is government more extravagant,
nonsensical, unintelligent and corrupt than here, and nowhere
else is it so secure. It becomes a sort of crime even to protest
against its villainies; all the late investigations of waste and corruption in Washington were attacked and brought to wreck in
the name of duty, decorum, patriotism. The citizen objecting
to felony by the agents of the sovereign state, acting in its
name, found himself posted as an anarchist! There was, of
course, some logic in this imbecility, as there is in everything
insane. It was felt that too violent an onslaught upon the disease might do gross damage o the patient, that the attempt to
extirpate what was foul and excrescent might imperil what was
useful and necessary. Is government, then, useful and necessary? So is a doctor. But suppose the dear fellow claimed the
right, every time be was called in to prescribe for a bellyache or

a ringing in the ears, to raid the family silver, use the family tooth-brushes, and execute the *droit de seigneur* upon the housemaid? Is it simply a coincidence that the only necessary functionaries who actually perform any comparable brigandage are the lawyers—the very men who, under democracy, chiefly determined the form, policies and acts of the government?

This great pox of civilization, alas, I believe to be incurable, and so I propose no new quackery for its treatment. I am against dosing it, and I am against killing it. All I presume to argue is that something would be accomplished by viewing it more realistically—by ceasing to let its necessary and perhaps useful functions blind us to its ever-increasing crimes against the ordinary rights of the free citizen and the common decencies of the world. The fact that it is generally respected—that it possesses effective machinery for propagating and safeguarding that respect—is the main shield of the rogues and vagabonds who use it to exploit the great masses of diligent and credulous men. Whenever you hear anyone bawling for more respect for the laws, whether it be a Coolidge on his imperial throne or an humble county judge in his hedge court, you have before you one who is trying to use them to his private advantage; whenever you hear of new legislation for putting down dissent and rebellion you may be sure that it is promoted by scoundrels. The extortions and oppressions of government will go on so long as such bare fraudulence deceives and disarms the victims—so long as they are ready to swallow the immemorial official theory that protesting against the stealings of the archbishop's secretary's nephew's mistress' illegitimate son is a sin against the Holy Ghost. They will come to an end when the victims begin to differentiate clearly between government as a necessary device for maintaining order in the world and government as a device for maintaining the authority and prosperity of predatory rascals and swindlers. In other words, they will come to an end on the Tuesday following the first Monday of November preceding the Resurrection Morn.

XIV.
Toward a Realistic Æsthetic

The Nature of Art

THE dominating purpose of man in the world is to conquer Nature, which is to say, to defeat the plain intent of God. God and man are the eternal antagonists. Man makes progress every time he wins a new victory; if he can hold his gains his progress is real. Poetry is one device for defeating God. Its aim is to escape some of the pains of reality by denying boldly that they exist—by saying, in some form or other, that "I am the captain of my soul" and "all's well with the world." This denial gives some comfort to human hearts, particularly to the more romantic sort; it is a poor substitute, perhaps, for the actual conquest of the harsh facts, but it is nevertheless a substitute. Religion operates in precisely the same way; its primary purpose is to read an intelligible and even laudable motive into the inscrutable assaults of God. Poetry, of course, is a cut higher than religion, logically speaking. It denies the facts, but it denies them more or less speciously and sometimes almost convincingly; it seldom, if ever, has to enounce the thumping and obvious absurdities that religion relies upon. But it is nevertheless a denial of reality, and hence very deficient as an agent of progress. Science is far more effective. It does not deny the imbecilities and horrors of Nature; it sets about actually modifying them, and even abolishing them. When science conquers it is usually a conquest that is permanent. We have got rid of wolves, ghosts and yellow fever finally and almost completely; they no longer bother civilized men. In the same way we have got rid of some of the horrors that religion raised—horrors worse than those it sought to lay. Science is not only effective against Nature; it is also effective against the dangerous remedies formerly employed against Nature.

Religion and the arts are thus only second-rate means of achieving man's chief purpose in the world. They give him a lot of comfort, but they expose him to the dangers which always follow the denial of reality. The man who believes that God is personally interested in him and will save him from harm is in a far more perilous situation than the man who knows better; so, also, with the man who believes that what poetry says is true. The other arts, having less ideational content, are a good deal less menacing. The statements that architecture makes, for example, are not against the plain facts but in accord with the plain facts—for example, that St. Thomas' Church is more beautiful than the Jersey marshes or its own rector. So with music, and, to some extent, with painting, though painting is hampered by its function of representing Nature—that is, of reproducing Nature without comment, or with very feeble and ineffective comment. Painting will become a genuinely valuable art when it finally abandons representation. The portrait of an ugly woman, even though the artist tries to ameliorate her ugliness a bit, remains almost as horrible as the ugly woman herself. That is to say, the artist simply multiplies and reinforces the horror already concocted by God.

The arts that avoid representation are like science in this: that they actually improve upon Nature, and so add permanently to man's comfort and happiness in the world. The Parthenon is not a mere idle denial of the facts of life, like poetry; it is a positive improvement upon the facts of life; it makes a Greek hilltop appreciably more beautiful than it was as God made it, and so mitigates the horror of life to man. Music achieves the same thing, and even more effectively. The nine Beethoven symphonies do not deny any palpable fact; they merely create new facts that are more agreeable than those previously existing. There are no sounds in Nature comparable to the lovely sounds that Beethoven evokes. Here man shows himself definitely the superior of God. Poetry, of course, also achieves a measure of genuine and permanent beauty. But it can do so only in its character as a form of music. The blank verse of Shakespeare, as music, is as noble a creation as the symphonies of Beethoven. But all poetry, even the best, is corrupted by its logical content. It almost invariably *says* something, and that something is almost always untrue. When man speaks or believes an untruth he certainly makes no progress with his conquest of Nature. On the contrary, he plainly gives up the battle, at least for the moment. Instead of fighting resolutely and effectively, and so improving his state, he simply buries his head in the sand.

2
The One-Legged Art

To me, at all events, painting seems to be half an alien among the fine arts. Its credentials, of course, are sounder than those of acting, but they are surely not as sound as those of music, poetry, drama, sculpture and architecture. The trouble with painting is that it lacks movement, which is to say, the chief function of life. The best a painter can hope to accomplish is to fix the mood of an instant, the momentary aspect of something. If he suggests actual movement he must do it by palpable tricks, all of which belong to craftsmanship rather than to art. The work that he produces is comparable to a single chord in music, without preparation or resolution. It may be beautiful, but its beauty plainly does not belong to the highest order. The senses soon tire of such beauty. If a man stands before a given painting for more than five or ten minutes, it is usually a sign of affectation: he is trying to convince himself that he has more delicate perceptions than the general. Or he is a painter himself and thus engrossed by the technical aspects of it, as a plumber might be engrossed by the technical aspects of a bathroom. Or he is enchanted by the story that the picture tells, which is to say, by the literature that it illustrates. True enough, he may go back to a painting over and over again, just as a music-lover may strike and re-strike a chord that pleases him, but it can't hold him for long at one session—it can't move his feelings so powerfully that he forgets the real world he lives in.

Sculpture is in measurably better case. The spectator, viewing a fine statue, does not see something dead, embalmed and fixed in a frame; he sees something that moves as he moves. A fine statue, in other words, is not one statue, but hundreds, perhaps even thousands. The transformation from one to another is infinitely pleasing; one gets out of it the same satisfying stimulation that one gets out of the unrolling of a string quartette, or out of such a poem as "Atalanta in Calydon," "Heart of Darkness" or "Faust." So with architecture. It not only revolves; it also moves vertically, as the spectator approaches it. When one walks up a street past a beautiful building one certainly gets an effect beyond that of a mere chord; it is the effect of a whole procession of beautiful chords, like that at the beginning of the slow movement of the "New World" symphony or that in the well-known and much-battered Chopin prélude. If it were a painting it would soon grow tedious. No one, after a few days, would give it a glance.

This intrinsic hollowness of painting has its effects even upon those who most vigorously defend it as the queen of all the fine arts. One hears of such persons "haunting the galleries," but one always discovers, on inquiry, that it is the show-rooms that they actually haunt. In other words, they get their chief pleasure by looking at an endless succession of *new* paintings: the multitude of chords produces, in the end, a sort of confused satisfaction. One never hears of them going to a public gallery regularly, to look at this or that masterpiece. Even the Louvre seldom attracts them more than a dozen or so times in a life-time. The other arts make a far more powerful and permanent appeal. I have read "Huckleberry Finn" at least twenty times and "Typhoon" probably ten times, and yet both pleased me as much (nay, more) the last time as they did the first time. I have heard each of the first eight symphonies of Beethoven more than fifty times, and most of Mozart's, Haydn's, Schubert's and Schumann's quite as often. Yet if Beethoven's C Minor were announced for performance tonight, I'd surely go to hear it. More, I'd enjoy every instant of it. Even second-rate music has this lasting quality. Some time ago I heard Johann Strauss' waltz, "Geschichten aus dem Wiener Wald," for the first time in a long while. I knew it well in my goatish days; every note of it was still familiar. Nevertheless, it gave me exquisite delight. Imagine a man getting exquisite delight out of a painting of corresponding calibre—a painting already so familiar to him that he could reproduce it from memory!

Painters, like barbers and cigarmakers, are able to talk while they are at work, and so they commonly gabble about their art a great deal more than other artists, and the world, in consequence, has come to assume that it is very complex, and full of subtleties. This is not true. Most of its so-called subtleties are manufactured by painters who cannot paint. The genuinely first-rate painters of the world have little to say about the technique of their art, and seem to be unaware that it is difficult. Go back to Leonardo's notes and sketches: you will find him a great deal more interested in anatomy than in painting. In fact, painting was a sort of afterthought with him; he was primarily an engineer, and the engineering that fascinated him most was that of the human body. Come down, then, to Cézanne. He painted in the way that seemed most natural to him, and was greatly astonished when a group of bad painters, seeking to imitate him, began crediting him with a long string of more or less mystical theories, by the Boul' Mich' out of the article on optics in the Encyclopædia Britannica.

The earliest Paleolithic men were already accomplished painters and sculptors. H. G. Wells, in his "Outline of History," says that "they drew astonishingly well." "Paint," he goes on, "was a big fact in their lives. They were inveterate painters." These savages were so low that they had not even invented bows and arrows, usury, the gallows or the notion of baptism by total immersion, and yet they were already accomplished draftsmen. Some of their drawings on the walls of their caves, indeed, remain a great deal more competent than the average magazine illustration of today. They also carved in and modelled in clay, and no doubt they were accomplished poets, as are the lowest Zuñi Indians of our own time. Moreover, they soon began to move out of their caves into artificial houses, and the principles of architectural design that they devised at the very dawn of history have been unchanged ever since, and are poll-parroted docilely every time a sky-scraper thrusts its snout among the cherubim. True enough, they could not draw as accurately as a photographic lens, but they could certainly draw as accurately as, say, Matisse or Gauguin. It remained for modern physicists, *i.e.*, men disdainful of drawing, to improve it. All the progress that has been made in the art during the past fifty or sixty years has been based upon quiet filches from the camera, just as all the progress that has been made in painting has been based upon filches from the spectroscope. When one finds a painter who professes to disdain these scientific aids, one always beholds a painter who is actually unable to draw or paint, and who seeks to conceal his incompetence by clothing it in hocus-pocus. This is the origin of new art that regales us with legs eight feet long, complexions of olive green, and human heads related to the soap-box rather than to the Edam cheese. This is the origin of all the gabble one hears in ratty and unheated studios about cubism, vortism, futurism and other such childish follies.

I regard any human being who, with proper instruction, cannot learn to draw reasonably well as, to all intents and purposes, a moron. He is in a stage of culture actually anterior to that of the Crô-Magnons. As for a human being incapable of writing passable verse, he simply does not exist. It is done, as everyone knows, by children—and sometimes so well that their poems are printed in books and quite solemnly reviewed. But good music is never written by children—and I am not forgetting Mozart, Schubert and Mendelssohn. Music belongs to the very latest stage of culture; to compose it in the grand manner requires long and painful training, and the highest sort of natural skill. It is complex, delicate, difficult. A miraculous youth may show talent for it, but he never reaches any thing properly describable as mastery of it until he is thoroughly mature. The music that all of us think of when we think of the best was written by men a bit bent by experience; it is quite beyond the comprehension of the general. And so with prose. Prose has no stage scenery to hide behind, as poetry has. It cannot use masks and wigs. It is not naïve, but infinitely sophisticated. It is not spontaneous, but must be fabricated by thought and painstaking. Prose is the ultimate flower of the art of words. Next to music, it is the finest of all the fine arts.

To return to music, it must be plain that it is enormously handicapped as an art by the mere fact that its technique is so frightfully difficult. I do not refer, of course, to the technique of the musical executant, but to that of the composer. Any literate man can master the technique of poetry in ten days, and that of the drama—despite all the solemn hocus-pocus of the professors who presume to teach it—in three weeks, but not even the greatest genius could do sound work in the sonata form without years of preparation. To write a good string quartette is not merely an act of creation, like writing a love song; it is also an act of applied science, like cutting out a set of tonsils. I know of no other art that demands so elaborate a professional training. Perhaps the one which comes nearest to it is architecture—that is, modern architecture. As the Greeks practised it, it was relatively simple, for they used simple materials and avoided all delicate problems of stress and strain; and they were thus able to keep their whole attention upon pure design. But the modern architect, with his complex mathematical and mechanical problems, must be an engineer before he is an artist, and the sort of engineering that he must master bristles with technical snares and conundrums. The serious musician is in even worse case. Before he may write at all he must take in and coördinate a body of technical knowledge that is almost as great as the outfit of an astronomer. I say that all this constitutes a handicap on the art of music. What I mean is that it scares off many men who have sound musical ideas and would make good composers, but who have no natural talent or taste for the technical groundwork. For one Schubert who overcomes the handicap by sheer genius there must be dozens who are repelled and discouraged. There is another, and perhaps even worse disadvantage. The potential Schuberts flee in alarm, but the Professor Sawdusts march in bravely. That is to say, music is hard for musicians, but easy for pedants, grinds and examination-passers. Its constant invasion by a hollow formalism is the result. It offers an inviting playground to the bombastic jackass whose delight it is to astonish the bourgeoisie with insane feats of virtuosity.

3
Symbiosis and the Artist

In contemplating the stupendous achievements of such a man as Wagner—achievements so colossal that only a small minority of men, specially trained, can even comprehend and appreciate them—one often finds one's self wondering how much further he would have gone had he not been harassed by his two wives. His first wife, Minna Planer, was frankly and implacably opposed to his life-work, and made deliberate efforts to dissuade him from it. She regarded "Lohengrin" as nonsensical and "Tannhäuser" as downright indecent. It was her constant hope, until Wagner finally kicked her out, that he would give over such stuff, and consecrate himself to the composition of respectable operas in the manner of Rossini, her favorite composer. The only composition of his that genuinely pleased her was a set of variations for the *cornet à piston* that he wrote in Paris. She was a singer, and had the brains of one. It must be plain that the presence of such a woman—and Wagner lived with her for twenty years—must have put a fearful burden upon the man's creative genius. No man can be absolutely indifferent to the prejudices and opinions of his wife. She has too many opportunities to shove them down his throat. If she can't make him listen to them by howling and bawling, she can make him listen by snuffling. To say that he can carry on his work without paying any heed to her is equal to saying that he can carry on his work without paying any heed to his toothache, his conscience, or the boiler-factory next door. In spite of Minna, Wagner composed a number of very fine music dramas. But if he had poisoned her at the beginning of his career it is very likely that he would have composed more of them, and perhaps even better ones.

His second wife, the celebrated Cosima Liszt-von Bülow, had far more intelligence than Minna, and so we may assume that her presence in his music factory was less of a handicap upon the composer. Nevertheless, the chances are that she, too, did him far more harm than good. To begin with, she was extremely plain in face—and nothing is more damaging to the creative faculty than the constant presence of ugliness. Cosima, in fact, looked not unlike a modern woman politician; even Nietzsche, a very romantic young fellow, had to go crazy before he could fall in love with her. In the second place, there is good reason to believe that Cosima, until after Wagner's death, secretly believed that her father, Papa Liszt, was a far better musician. Men's wives almost invariably make some such mistake; to find one who can separate the man of genius from the mere husband, and then estimate the former accurately and fairly, is surely very rare. A woman usually respects her father, but her view of her husband is mingled with contempt, for she is of course privy to the transparent devices by which she snared him. It is difficult for her, being so acutely aware of the shallowness of the man, to give due weight to the dignity of the artist. Moreover, Cosima had shoddy tastes, and they played destructively upon poor Wagner. There are parts of "Parsifal" that suggest her very strongly—more strongly, in fact, than they suggest the author of "Die Götterdämmerung." I do not here decry Wagner; on the contrary, I praise him, and perhaps excessively. It is staggering to think of the work he did, with Minna and Cosima shrilling into his ears. What interests me is the question as to how much further he might have gone had he escaped the passionate affection of the two of them and of their various volunteer assistants. The thought fascinates, and almost alarms. There is a limit beyond which sheer beauty becomes unseemly. In "Tristan und Isolde," in the Ring, and even in parts of "Parsifal," Wagner pushes his music very near that limit. A bit beyond lies the fourth dimension of tone—and madness. Both Beethoven and Brahms, I believe, more than once edged over the line. Two bachelors. Had Beethoven married in 1802, as he seems to have been tempted to do by some scheming wench, it is doubtful that the world would ever have heard the Eroica. In the Eroica there is everything that startles and dismays a loving wife: brilliant novelty, vast complexity, thunderous turmoil, great bursts of undiluted genius. Even Beethoven never wrote anything more astounding than its first movement; the first movement of the C Minor is relatively elemental beside it. Nor is there anything so revolutionary in the Ninth.

The Eroica, indeed, was written precisely at the moment when Beethoven became fully conscious of his extraordinary powers—more accurately, of his singular and unchallengeable *superiority*. It is the work, not only of a man who is absolute master of his materials, but also of a man who disdains his materials, and his customers with them. In the first movement he simply spits into the face of the cosmos. Scarcely ten measures have been played before one suddenly realizes that one is in the presence of something entirely new in music—not merely new in degree, but new in kind. It differs as much from anything written before it, even by Beethoven, as a picture by Cézanne differs from a picture by an English Academician. This first movement has never been sufficiently studied and appraised: it is unutterably stupendous. In the funeral march, I believe, Beethoven descends to some rather cheap tricks, and in the scherzo he is often obvious. But in the first movement, and to a slightly less degree in the last, he takes leave of earth and disports himself among the gods. It is the composition of a colossus. And a bachelor. No normal woman could have watched its genesis without some effort to make it more seemly, more decorous and connubial, more respectable. A faithful wife, present at its first performance, would have blushed, shivered and sworn. Women hate revolutions and revolutionists. They like men who are docile, and well-regarded at the bank, and never late at meals.

XV.

Contributions to the Study
of Vulgar Psychology

I
The Downfall of the Navy

F EW phenomena offer more refined and instructive entertainment to the psychic pathologist than the American
navy's decline in popularity during the past twenty-five years.
At the time of the Spanish-American War, as everyone sentient
in those days will recall, it was easily the premier service in the
popular regard, and in even the least of its exploits the great
masses of the plain people took a violent and vociferous pride.
They were proud, too, of the army, and its heroic efforts
against the Hunnish hordes of Spain, and one of the great captains of that army was made President for his stupendous feats
of blood and blather in the field; but it was the navy that they
cherished most, and the popular heroes that it produced were
more numerous than those of the army, and in the main they
were far more fondly cherished. Even the immortal Roosevelt,
it will be remembered, was half a navy man, and what got
him into the White House, I believe, was less his colossal
butcheries in the land battles of the war, important though
they were to the cause of human liberty, than his long an-
tecedent struggles to free the navy from the politicians, and
make it fit to fight. The navy, indeed, was popular before the
war began, or even threatened. The army could tackle and
massacre a whole tribe of Indians without causing half the
public thrill that followed the bombardment of a Venezuelan
coast village by the White Squadron, with a total loss of but
one blind cripple crippled in the other leg. This White Squadron, I more than suspect, was the actual cause of the war itself.
From the day it first put to sea the plain people watched it with
glowing pride, and longed for a sight of it in action. If it had
not been so handily cruising in Latin-American waters, glittering truculently in the sunshine, there would have been a great
deal less public indignation over the wrongs of the Cubeens.

So superb a fighting arm was surely not designed by God to rust in the scabbard. Thus the fashion arose of drawing it out and poking it into Caribbean and South Atlantic rat-holes. During the half dozen years before the laying of the Spanish dragon was formally undertaken, such heroes as Schley and Fighting Bob Evans carried the White Squadron into half the ports to the southward, and knocked over a few church steeples in most of them. In the end, it was just such an enter-prise that took the *Maine* into Havana harbor, and provided the legal excuse for the war itself.

This was more than a quarter of a century ago. Today, it must be obvious that there is very little public pride in the navy, and almost no public interest. I doubt that one American schoolboy out of ten thousand could name its present ranking officer; between 1890 and 1900 every schoolboy knew all the admirals by face and by name, and most of the captains, and the patriotic epigrams of the more articulate of them were chalked upon every schoolyard fence in the land. I was myself a boy in those days, and remember even today such forgotten heroes of the time as Admiral Gherardi, who commanded the White Squadron in 1893 and 1894, and was retired before the Spanish War; his portrait was on the cigarette cards, along with those of Fighting Bob Evans and Lillian Russell. Later on, having grown more reflective and critical, I specialized in the Sampson-Schley controversy, and was a bitter partisan of Schley, a native of my own Maryland Free State. Dewey, Clark, Evans, Ridley, Hobson (God save us!), Ensign Bagley, Yeoman Ellis, Sigsbee, Wainright—all these eminent tars were as real to the boys of that era as John L. Sullivan or Amos Rusie. Turn now to today. When the newspapers, a year or two ago, an-nounced that a gentleman named Admiral Sims had denied that the German U-boat commanders committed the atroci-ties credited to them during the late war, how many American boys recognized his name? I myself, though I am a historian by profession, boggled him at first glance, mistaking him for a British officer. For the life of me, I could not tell you the name of another American naval officer. . . . Second thought: there was Admiral Benson. But what he did in the war, save involve himself in some controversy that has been forgotten, I can't tell you. No other name occurs to me, though I scratch my head and try various mnemonic dodges. Try me on the names of the commanders who fought the celebrated Creel battle with the U-boats, and I'll have to slide down among the morons. If there was a Hobson in that war, I can't recall him. I remember many English and German commanders—von Tirpitz, von Scheer, Jellicoe, Müller of the Emden, König, and so on—but not a single American.

The fact is, of course, that the part the American navy played in the war, though it was unquestionably important, was quite devoid of the more spectacular varieties of gallantry, and so it failed to make heroes. The battles fought were fought mainly by government press-agents, not by the navy itself; the rest was dangerous but dull policing, with some uninspiring running of ferry-boats. The navy, as everyone knows, became a funk-hole for draft-dodgers. This may account, in some measure, for the present public apathy regarding it; it is not brilliant, and hence it is not charming. But its decay in popularity, I believe, really antedated the war by several years; it was in the shadows long before Admiral Sims transferred his swivel-chair from Washington to London. What caused the change? Is it that the American people have lost their old taste for the sea, and, in particular, their old delight in the sort of heroes that it produces? Or is it that the navy itself has actually lost some of its old romance and color? I incline to think that the latter explanation explains more than the former. My hazard is that the man who made the American navy unpopular was the Hon. Josephus Daniels, and that he did it by trying to convert every battleship into a chautauqua and Sunday-school. In the days when the arrival of a naval vessel in port was the signal for hot times ashore, with the saloons packed to the doors, and all the town's wicked women out *en masse*, and the streets made picturesquely perilous by squads of drunken and roaring gobs—in those days every poor but ambitious boy, when the job of tying up packages and running errands began to palsy him, let his fancy turn toward thoughts of stealing off to foreign parts, the Republic's quarter in his pocket and riotous and attractive company all about him. The sailor of that era was an obscene but highly charming fellow. A great spaciousness was in him. He bore the scars of the constabulary espantoons of distant and romantic lands. He was a wholesale lover, a three-bottle man, a well of astounding profanity. He held the admiration of every adventurous youth. He was romance in baggy breeches, hell-bent down the mysterious by-ways of the world.

Josephus changed all that. A Christian of tender conscience and a firm believer in hell for the sinful, it appalled him to observe that nine-tenths of the young men under his official charge were obviously headed for the fire. When he got his secret reports of their doings in Port Said, Callao, Singapore, Odessa, Smyrna, Vera Cruz, Norfolk, Va., and other such seaboard stews—when these lurid documents began pouring in upon him from missionaries, Y.M.C.A. secretaries and other godly men, he staggered under the horror, and was unfit for business for days afterward. Having recourse to prayer, he was presently given counsel by a voice from the burning bush. To hear was to act. First, he abolished rum from the navy, and forced even the oldest admirals, some of whom had been pickled for years and years, to go upon the dubious water of far-flung and zymotic ports. Secondly, he forbade the enlistment of young men who were fugitives from justice for dog-stealing, moonshining, window-smashing and other such felonies—the mainstays of the navy in the old days. Thirdly, he set up night schools on every battleship, in charge of Christian men like himself, and then day schools, and then schools running both day and night, and to the customary instruction in the three R's he added the whole curriculum of the Y.M.C.A., from double-entry bookkeeping to public speaking, and from show-card writing to venereal prophylaxis. Today a young man goes into the navy from his native farm with nothing in his head save a vast yearning to get away from the smell of cows—and comes out in three years an accomplished paperhanger, with some knowledge of the saxophone, electric wiring and first aid to the injured. The old enlistment posters used to show a gob in a rickshaw with a Japanese cutie; the new ones show him practising as a house and sign painter. The old navy showed the boys the world, and taught them the difference between Swedish punch and Javanese arrak; the new navy converts them into sanitary plumbers and bookkeepers, and teaches them how to lead a prayer-meeting.

Is it any wonder that it declines in popularity—that the

youth of the land is neglectful of its eminent commanders, and has to be lured into enlistments by the arts of the grind-shop auctioneer? The Y.M.C.A. already reigns universally on the dry land of the Republic; only the remotest yokel in the highest hills can hope to escape its tentacles, and even he is fetched by its sinister sister, the chautauqua. When he dreams of the sea, he dreams of a realm that is free from all this—of a realm still barbarous, unchastened and romantic—a realm of free cavorting and exhilarating adventure. But when he gets to the recruiting-office, the first thing he sees is a large lithograph showing a class of gobs being instructed in algebra, grammar and Christian doctrine. The master-at-arms who receives him hasn't got the old naked Venus tattooed on his arm; he has instead a portrait of Dwight L. Moody, and in his button-hole is a button testifying that he has recited 52 successive Golden Texts without an error and brought 20 heathen Danish sailors to the mourners' bench. Instead of the old booby-hatch for souses in this recruiting-office, there is now a gospel hall with a melodeon. The talk is not of the yellow gals in Valparaiso, the powerful red wines of Naples, the all-night shows of Marseilles, the police of Livepool and Kiel, but of the advantages of learning the trades of tin-roofer, cost accountant and hardwood finisher. The rustic candidate, his head buzzing with romance, is floored with statistics and plunged into a bath of bichloride of mercury. No wonder his stomach turns and his heart is broken! And no wonder the navy, thus purged of all its old flavors and juices, has ceased to inflame the imagination of the plain people. Suppose they heard from Hollywood that Charlie Chaplin had become a hard-shell Baptist and opened a pants-pressing parlor?

2

The Mind of the Slave

One of the forgotten divisions between men and men is that separating those who enjoy the work they have to do in the world and those who suffer it only as a necessary evil. The distinction, despite its neglect by sociologists, is probably very important—certainly far more important than the current divisions between producers and exploiters, dolichocephalic

Nordic blonds and brachycephalic Alpines, Darwinians and so-
called Christians, Republicans and Democrats, Protestants and
Catholics, wets and drys. A man's politics, theology and other
vices engage his attention, after all, only in his moments of
leisure, and the shape of his cranium has very little demonstrable influence upon what habitually goes on within it, but the
nature of the work he does in the world conditions every
thought and impulse of his life, and his general attitude toward it
is almost indistinguishable from his general attitude toward
the cosmos.

At the one extreme lies the unmitigated slave—the man who
has to spend his whole life performing tasks that are incurably
uninteresting, and that offer no soothing whatever to his vanity. At the other extreme is what Beethoven called the free
artist—the man who makes a living, with no boss directly over
him, doing things that he enjoys enormously, and that he
would keep on doing gladly, even if all economic pressure
upon him disappeared. To the second category belong all the
happiest men in the world, and hence, perhaps, all the most
useful men. For what is done with joy is always better done,
whether it be fashioning a material object, thinking out a
problem or kissing a pretty girl; and the man who can make
the rest of humanity pay him for being happy is obviously a
better man than the general, or, at all odds, a luckier one. Here
luck and superiority are one and the same. The fact that Joseph
Conrad could write better than I, was in a sense, a matter of
pure chance. He was born with his talent; he did not earn it.
Nevertheless, it was just as real as if he had got it by Christian
endeavor, and his superiority to me was thus perfectly genuine.

The slave is always conscious of his slavery, and makes constant and often desperate efforts to mitigate it or to get rid of
it alogether. Sometimes he seeks that mitigation in outside activities that promise to give him the sense of dignity and importance that his daily labor denies him; sometimes he tries to
give a false appearance of dignity to his work itself. The last
phenomenon must be familiar to every American; it is responsible for various absurd devices to pump up lowly trades by
giving them new and high-sounding names. I point, for example, to those of the real-estate agent and the undertaker.
Neither trade, it must be obvious, offers any stimulation to

men of genuine superiority. One could not imagine a Beethoven, a Lincoln or even a Coolidge getting any joy out of
squeezing apartment-house tenants or pickling Odd Fellows.
Both jobs, indeed, fail to satisfy the more imaginative sort of
men among those compelled to practise them. Hence these
men try to dignify them with hocus-pocus. The real-estate
agent, seeking to conceal his real purpose in life, lets it be
known grandly that he is an important semi-public functionary, that he has consecrated himself to Service and is a man
of Vision—and to prove it he immerses himself in a private
office with a secretary to insult his customers, joins a Rotary
Club, and begins to call himself a realtor, a word as idiotic as
flu, pep or gent. The ambitious washer of the dead—until very
lately a sort of pariah in all civilized societies, like the hangman, the surgeon and the dog-catcher—proceeds magnificently
along the same route. At regular intervals I receive impressive
literature from a trade-union of undertakers calling themselves
the Selected Morticians. By this literature it appears that the
members thereof are professional men of a rank and dignity
comparable to judges or archbishops, and they are hot for the
subtlest and most onerous kind of Service, and even eager to
offer their advice to the national government. In brief, the realtor complex all over again. I do not laugh at these soaring
embalmers; I merely point out that their nonsense proves how
little the mere planting of martyred lodge brothers satisfies
their interior urge to be important and distinguished—an urge
that is in all of us.

But most of the trades pursued by slaves, of course, offer no
such opportunities for self-deceptive flummery. The clerk working in the lime and cement warehouse of some remote town of
the foreign missions belt cannot conceivably convince himself
that his profession is noble; worse, he cannot convince anyone
else. And so with millions of other men in this great Republic,
both urban and rural—millions of poor fellows doomed their
life long to dull, stupid and tedious crafts—the lower sort of
clerks, workmen, wagon-drivers, farmers, farm-laborers, petty
officials, grabbers of odd jobs. They must be downright idiots
to get any satisfaction out of their work. Happiness, the feeling
that they too are somebody, the sense of being genuinely alive,
must be sought in some other direction. In the big cities, that

need is easily met. Here there is a vast and complex machinery for taking the slave's mind off his desolateness of spirit—moving pictures to transport him into a land of romance, where men (whom he always identifies with himself) are brave, rich and handsome, and women (whom he identifies with his wife—or perchance with her younger sister) are clean, well-dressed and beautiful; newspapers to delight and instruct him with their sports pages, their comic strips and their eloquent appeals to his liberality, public spirit and patriotism; public bands and the radio to play the latest jazz for him; circuses and parades; baseball, races, gambling, harlotry and games in arenas; a thousand devices to make him forget his woes. It is this colossal opportunity to escape from life that brings yokels swarming to the cities, not any mere lust for money. The yokel is actually far more comfortable on his native soil; the city crowds and exploits him, and nine times out of ten he remains desperately poor. But the city at least teaches him how to forget his poverty; it amuses him and thrills him while it is devouring him. I once knew an old colored woman, born in Southern Maryland, who lived miserably in one room of a shack in an alley in Baltimore. When asked why she did not go back to her village, where she would have at least had better food and more air, she replied very simply that there were never any parades in the country. It was a profound and intelligent saying.

But millions of the slaves, of course, must remain in the small towns or on the land; the cities can't absorb all of them, nor even half of them. They thus confront the problem of making life bearable out of their own meagre resources. The devices that they adopt—political, religious and social—are familiar to all of us, and account fully, it seems to me, for some of the phenomena of American life that are most puzzling to foreign observers. The hoop-la Methodist revival with its psychopathological basis; the violent bitterness of rural politics; the prosperity of the Ku Klux Klan and all the other clownish fraternal orders; the persistent popularity of lynching, tarring and feathering, barbarities of a dozen other varieties—all these things are no more than manifestations of the poor hind's pathetic effort to raise himself out of his wallow, to justify and dignify his existence, to escape from the sordid realities that daily confront him. To snort and froth at a revival makes him conspicuous, prominent, a man of mark; it is therefore easy to induce him to do it. To hold a petty county office is eminence; hence he struggles for it frantically. To belong to the Ku Klux gives him a mysterious and sinister dignity, and fills him with a sense of power and consequence; he falls for it as quickly as a city intellectual falls for the *Légion d'honneur* or an LL.D. To take a hand in a concrete tarring or lynching—this instantly makes him feel that he has played an heroic rôle in the world, that he has accomplished something large and memorable— above all, that he has had a gaudy good time. In brief, all these things make him forget, transiently or permanently, that he is a miserable worm, and of little more actual importance on earth than his own hogs.

Long ago, I suggested that a good way to diminish lynching in the South would be to establish brass bands in all the country towns. The bad music, I argued, would engage and enchant both the blackamoors and the poor white trash, and so discourage the former from crime and the latter from seeking a savage satisfaction in its punishment. I now improve and embellish that suggestion. That is to say, I propose that the band scheme be shelved, and that bull-fighting be established as a substitute. Why not, indeed? Cattle have to be killed, and the Southern poor white is admittedly a savage. Why not combine the necessary slaughter of horned quadrupeds with a show that will give that savage a thrill and take his mind from his lowly lot, and so turn him from seeking escape in politics, murder and voodoo theology? Bull-fights in the South would not only diminish lynchings; they would also undermine Prohibition. A happy peasantry would have no reason to divert itself with homicide, and neither would it have any reason to belabor the rest of us with the ethical and political manias of its Baptist dervishes. The Ku Klux, it seems to me, is a good influence in the South rather than a bad one, for it tends to regulate and formalize the normal sports of the people, and so restrains excess. The trouble with lynching before the Klan took charge of it was that men of the darker races were often hanged and burned purely arbitrarily, simply because the yokels of some Christian county could not stand boredom any longer. But now rules are laid down and a sort of jurisprudence gets into it. I have heard all kinds of wild charges against the Invisible Empire, but I have never heard anyone allege that its responsible officers have ever countenanced the execution of its laws upon anyone not obviously guilty. This is an improvement. Life is safer and happier in Georgia today that it was before the Rev. Dr. Simmons heard the voice. But it would be even safer and even happier if the pure Anglo-Saxons down there could work off their steam by going weekly to a *plaza de toros*, and there see official *picadores*, *banderilleros*, and *matadors*, all of them good Democrats and baptized men, lynch and burn (or even merely geld) a reluctant and protesting male of *Bos taurus*.

3
The Art Eternal

One of the laudable by-products of the Freudian necromancy is the discovery that lying, in most cases, is involuntary and inevitable—that the liar can no more avoid it than he can avoid blinking his eyes when a light flashes or jumping when a bomb goes off behind him. At its worst, indeed, this necessity tales on a downright pathological character, and is thus as innocent as sciatica or albuminuria. It is part of the morbid baggage of hysterics and neurasthenics: their lying is simply a symptom of their compulsive effort to adjust themselves to an environment which bears upon them too harshly for endurance. The rest of us are not quite so hard pushed, but pushed we all are. In us the thing works through the inferiority complex, which no man can escape. He who lacks it entirely is actually reckoned insane by the fact: his satisfaction with his situation in the world is indistinguishable from a delusion of grandeur. The great majority of us—all, in brief, who are normal —pass through life in constant revolt against our limitations, objective and subjective. Our conscious thought is largely devoted to plans and specifications for cutting a better figure in human society, and in our unconscious the business goes on much more steadily and powerfully. No healthy man, in his secret heart, is content with his destiny. Even the late Woodrow, during his dizzy term as the peer of Lincoln and Washington, was obviously tantalized by the reflection that, in earlier ages, there had been Martin Luther, St. Ignatius Loyola and Paul of Tarsus. We are tortured by such dreams and images as a child is tortured by the thought of a state of existence in which it would live in a candy-store and have two stomachs. The more we try to put the obscene apparition away, the more it haunts and badgers us.

Lying is the product of the unconscious yearning to realize such visions, and if the policeman, conscience, prevents the lie being put into plain words, then it is at least put into more or less plausible acts. We all play parts when we face our fellow-men, as even poets have noticed. No man could bring himself to reveal his true character, and, above all, his true limitations as a citizen and a Christian, his true meannesses, his true imbecilities, to his friends, or even to his wife. Honest autobiography is therefore a contradiction in terms: the moment a man considers himself, even *in petto*, he tries to gild and fresco himself. Thus a man's wife, however realistic her view of him, always flatters him in the end, for the worst she sees in him is appreciably better, by the time she sees it, than what is actually there. What she sees, even at times of the most appalling domestic revelation and confidence, is not the authentic man at all, but a compound made up in part of the authentic man and in part of his projection of a gaudy ideal. The man who is most respected by his wife is the one who makes this projection most vivid—that is, the one who is the most daring and ingratiating liar. He can never, of course, deceive her utterly, but if he is skillful he may at least deceive her enough to make her happy.

Omnis homo mendax: thus the Psalmist. So far the Freudians merely parrot him. What is new in their gospel is the doctrine that lying is instinctive, normal, and unavoidable—that a man is forced into it by his very will-to-live. This doctrine purges the business of certain ancient embarrassments, and restores innocence to the heart. Think of a lie as a compulsion neurose, and you think of it more kindly. I need not add, I hope, that this transfer of it from the department of free will to that of determinism by no means disposes of the penalty that traditionally pursues it, supposing it to be detected and resented. The proponents of free will always make the mistake of assuming that the determinists are simply evil fellows looking

for a way to escape the just consequences of their transgress-
ing. No sense is in that assumption. If I lie on the witness-
stand and am detected by the judge, I am jailed for perjury
forthwith, regardless of my helplessness under compulsion.
Here justice refuses absolutely to distinguish between a misfortune and a tort: the overt act is all it is concerned with. But
as jurisprudence grows more intelligent and more civilized it
may change its tune, to the benefit of liars, which is to say, to
the benefit of humanity. Science is unflinchingly deterministic,
and it has begun to force its determinism into morals. We no
longer flog a child afflicted with nocturnal enuresis; we have
substituted concepts of mental aberration for concepts of crime
in a whole series of cases: kleptomania-shoplifting, pyromania-
arson, etc.; and, in the United States at least, the old savage
punishment of murderers is now ameliorated by considerations of psychiatry and even of honor. On some shining to-
morrow a psychoanalyst may be put into the box to prove that
perjury is simply a compulsion neurose, like beating time with
the foot at a concert or counting the lamp-posts along the
highway.

However, I have but small faith in millenniums, and do not
formally predict this one. Nor do I pronounce any moral judgment, pro or con: moral judgments, as old Friedrich used to
say, are foreign to my nature. But let us not forget that lying,
per se, is not forbidden by the moral code of Christendom.
Holy Writ dismisses it cynically, and statutes of all civilized
states are silent about it. Only the Chinese, indeed, make it a
penal offense. Perjury, of course, is prohibited everywhere,
and also any mendacity which amounts to fraud and deprives a
fellow-man of his property, but that far more common form of
truth-stretching which has only the lesser aim of augmenting
the liar's personal dignity and consequence—this is looked
upon with a very charitable eye. So is that form which has the
aim of helping another person in the same way. In the latter direction lying may even take on the stature of a positive virtue.
The late King Edward VII, when Prince of Wales, attained to
great popularity throughout Christendom by venturing into
downright perjury. Summoned into a court of law to give expert testimony regarding some act of adultery, he lied like a
gentleman, as the phrase goes, to protect a woman. The lie, to

be sure, was intrinsically useless; no one believed that the lady was innocent. Nevertheless, every decent Christian applauded the perjurer for his good intentions, including even the judge on the bench, sworn to combat false witness by every resource of forensics. All of us, worms that we are, occasionally face the alternatives that confronted Edward. On the one hand, we may tell the truth, regardless of conseqences, and on the other hand we may mellow it and sophisticate it to make it humane and tolerable. It is universally held that the man who chooses the first course is despicable. He may be highly moral, but he is nevertheless a cad—as highly moral men have so curious a way of being. But if he lies boldly, then he is held to be a man of honor, and is respected as such by all other men of honor.

For the habitual truth-teller and truth-seeker, indeed, the world has very little liking. He is always unpopular, and not infrequently his unpopularity is so excessive that it endangers his life. Run your eye back over the list of martyrs, lay and clerical: nine-tenths of them, you will find, stood accused of nothing worse than honest efforts to find out and announce the truth. Even today, with the scientific passion become familiar in the world, the general view of such fellows is highly unfavorable. The typical scientist, the typical critic of institutions, the typical truth-seeker in every field is held under suspicion by the great majority of men, and variously beset by posses of relentless foes. If he tries to find out the truth about arterio-sclerosis, or surgical shock, or cancer, he is denounced as a scoundrel by the Christian Scientists, the osteopaths and the antivivisectionists. If he tries to tell the truth about the government, its agents seek to silence him and punish him. If he turns to fiction and endeavors to depict his fellow-men accurately, he has the Comstocks on his hands. In no field can he count upon a friendly audience, and freedom from assault. Especially in the United States is his whole enterprise viewed with bilious eye. The men the American people admire most extravagantly are the most daring liars; the men they detest most violently are those who try to tell them the truth. A Galileo could no more be elected President of the United States than he could be elected Pope of Rome. Both high posts are reserved for men favored by God with an extraordinary genius for swathing the bitter facts of life in bandages of soft illusion.

Behind this almost unanimous distrust of the truth-teller there is a sound and sure instinct, as there is behind every other manifestation of crowd feeling. What it shows is simply this: that the truth is something too harsh and devastating for the majority of men to bear. In their secret hearts they know themselves, and they can suffer the thought of themselves only by idealizing the facts. The more trivial, loathsome and degraded the reality, the more powerful and relentless must be the idealization. An Aristotle, I daresay, may be able occasionally to regard himself searchingly and dispassionately—but certainly not an ordinary man. Here we come back to what we began with: the inferiority complex. The truth-seeker forgets it, and so comes to grief. He forgets that the ordinary man, at bottom, is always afraid of himself, as of some horrible monster. He refuses to sanction the lie whereby the ordinary man maintains his self-respect, just as the bounder, put upon the stand, refuses to support the lie whereby a woman maintains the necessary theory of her chastity. Thus he is unpopular, and deserves to be.

Then why does he go on? Why does he kick up such a bother and suffer such barbarous contumely, all to no end—for the majority of so-called truths, it must be evident, perish as soon as they are born: no one will believe them. The answer probably is that the truth-seeker is moved by the same obscure inner necessity (in Joseph Conrad's phrase) that animates the artist. Something within him, something entirely beyond his volition, forces him to pursue his fanatical and useless quest—some impulse as blind as that which moves a puppy to chase its tail. Again the compulsion neurose! But this one differs materially from that of the liar. The latter is hygienic; it makes for peace, health, happiness. The former makes only for strife and discontent. It invades the immemorial pruderies of the human race. It breeds scandals and heart-burnings. It is essentially anti-social, and hence, by modern theories of criminology, diseased. The truth-seeker thus becomes a pathological case. The average man is happily free from any such malaise. He avoids the truth as diligently as he avoids arson, regicide or piracy on the high seas, and for the same reason: because he believes that it is dangerous, that no good can come of it, that it doesn't pay. The very thought of it is abhorrent to him. This average man, I believe, must be accepted as the normal man, the natural man, the healthy and useful man. He presents a character that is general in the race, and favorable to its security and contentment. The truth never caresses; it stings—and life is surely too short for sane men to be stinging themselves unnecessarily. One would regard it as idiotic even in a flea.

Thus the truth about the truth emerges, and with it the truth about lying. Lying is not only excusable; it is not only innocent, and instinctive; it is, above all, necessary and unavoidable. Without the ameliorations that it offers life would become a mere syllogism, and hence too metallic to be born. The man who lies simply submits himself sensibly to the grand sweep and ripple of the cosmic process. The man who seeks and tells the truth is a rebel against the inner nature of all of us.

XVI.

The American Novel

IT is an ancient platitude of historical criticism that great wars and their sequelæ are inimical to the fine arts, and particularly to the art of letters. The kernel of truth in it lies in the obvious fact that a people engaged in a bitter struggle for existence have no time for such concerns, which demand not only leisure but also a certain assured feeling of security, well-being and self-sufficiency—in brief, the thing often called aristocratic (or sometimes intellectual) detachment. No man ever wrote good poetry with his wife in parturition in the next room, or the police preparing to raid his house, or his shirt-tail afire. He needs to be comfortable to do it, and if not actually comfortable, then at all events safe. Wars tend to make life uncomfortable and unsafe—but not, it must be observed, inevitably and necessarily, not always and invariably. A bitter and demoralizing struggle goes with wars that are lost, and the same struggle goes with wars that are won only by dint of stupendous and ruinous effort, but it certainly does not go with wars that are won easily. These last do not palsy and asphyxiate the artist, as he is palsied and asphyxiated by cholera morbus, suits for damages or marriage. On the contrary, they pump him full of ozone, and he is never more alive and lively than following them.

I point to a few familiar examples. The Civil War, as everyone knows, bankrupted the South and made life a harsh and bitter struggle for its people, and especially for the gentler and more civilized minority of its people. In consequence, the South became as sterile artistically, after Lee's surrender, as Mexico or Portugal, and even today it lags far behind the North in beautiful letters, and even further behind in music, painting and architecture. But the war, though it went on for four years, strained the resources of the North very little, either in men or in money, and so its conclusion found the Northerners very rich and cocky, and full of a yearning to astonish the world, and that yearning, in a few decades, set up a new and extremely vigorous American literature, created an American architecture of a revolutionary character, and even laid the first courses of American schools of music and painting. Mark Twain, Walt Whitman, Henry James and William Dean Howells, all of them draft dodgers in the war itself, were in a very real sense products of the war, for they emerged as phenomena of the great outburst of creative energy that followed it, and all of them, including even James, were as thoroughly American as Jay Gould, P. T. Barnum or Jim Fisk. The stars of the national letters in the years before the war had been Americans only by geographical accident. About Emerson there hung a smell of Königsberg and Weimar; Irving was simply a New York Englishman; Poe was a citizen of No Man's Land; even Hawthorne and Cooper, despite their concern with American themes, showed not the slightest evidence of an American point of view. But Mark Twain, Howells and Whitman belonged to the Republic as palpably as Niagara Falls or Tammany Hall belonged to it, and so did James, though the thought horrified him and we must look at him through his brother William to get the proof. Turn now to Europe. France, harshly used in the war of 1870–71, was sterile for a decade, but the wounds were not deep, and recovery was in full swing by 1880. Germany, injured scarcely at all, produced Nietzsche almost before the troops got home, and was presently offering an asylum and an inspiration to Ibsen, preparing the way for the reform and modernization of the theatre, and making contributions of the utmost value to practically all of the arts and sciences. Spain, after the Armada, gave the world Cervantes and then expired; England produced Shakespeare and founded a literature that is not surpassed in history.

What has thus happened over and over again in the past— and I might pile up examples for pages—may be in process of repetition today, and under our very noses. All Europe, plainly enough, is in a state of exhaustion and depression, and in no department of human activity is the fact more visible than in that of the arts. Not only are the defeated nations, Russia, Germany and Austria, producing nothing save a few extravagant eccentricities; there is also a great lowness of spirit in the so-called victorious nations, for their victory was almost as

ruinous as defeat. France, as after 1870, is running to a pretentious and artificial morbidity in letters, and marking time in
music and painting; Italy is producing little save psychopathological absurdities by such mountebanks as D'Annunzio and
Papini; even England shows all the signs of profound fatigue.
The great English writers of the age before the war are passing.
Meredith is gone; Hardy has put up his shutters; Kipling went
to wreck in the war itself; Conrad is dead; Shaw, once so agile
and diverting, becomes a seer and prophet. Nor is there any
sign of sound progress among the younger men. Arnold Ben-
nett, a star of brilliant promise in 1913, is today a smoking
smudge. Wells has ceased to be an artist and become a prophet
in the Sunday supplements. Masefield has got no further than
he was on August 2, 1914. The rest of the novelists are simply
chasing their own tails. The Georgian poets, having emerged
gloriously during the war, now disappear behind their manners. Only a few women, led by May Sinclair, and a few iconoclastic young men, led by Aldous Huxley, are still indubitably
alive.

It seems to me that, in the face of this dark depression across
the water, the literary spectacle on this side takes on an aspect
that is extremely reassuring, and even a bit exhilarating. For
the first time in history, there begins to show itself the faint
shadow of a hope that, if all goes well, leadership in the arts,
and especially in all the art of letters, may eventually transfer itself from the eastern shore of the Altantic to the western shore.
Our literature, as I have more than once pointed out in the
past, is still oppressed by various heavy handicaps, chiefly resident in the failure of the new aristocracy of money to function
as an aristocracy of taste. The artist among us is still a sort of
pariah, beset by public contempt on the one hand and by academic enmity on the other; he still lacks the public position
that his brothers enjoy in older and more civilized countries.
Nevertheless, it must be obvious to everyone that his condition tends to improve materially—that, in our own time, it *has*
improved materially—that though his rewards remain meagre,
save in mere money, his freedom grows steadily greater. And it
must be obvious, too that he begins to show that that increasing freedom is not wholly wasted upon him—that he knows
how to use it, and is disposed to do so with some gusto. What

all the younger American writers have in common is a sort of new-found elasticity or goatishness, a somewhat exaggerated sense of aliveness, a glowing delight in the spectacle before them, a vigorous and naïve self-consciousness. The school-master critics belabor them for it, and call it a disrespect for tradition, and try to put it down by denouncing it as due to corrupt foreign influences. But it is really a proof of the rise of nationalism—perhaps of the first dawn of a genuine sense of nationality. No longer imitative and timorous, as most of their predecessors were, these youngsters are attempting a first-hand examination of the national scene, and making an effort to represent it in terms that are wholly American. They are the pioneers of a literature that, whatever its defects in the ab-stract, will at least be a faithful reflection of the national life, that will be more faithful, indeed, in its defects than in its mer-its. In England the novel subsides into formulæ, the drama is submerged in artificialities, and even poetry, despite occasional revolts, moves toward scholarliness and emptiness. But in America, since the war, all three show the artless and super-abundant energy of little children. They lack, only too often, manner and urbanity; it is no wonder that they are often shocking to pedants. But there is the breath of life in them, and that life is far nearer its beginning than its end.

The causes of all this are not far to seek. The American Le-gion is right: we won the war. It cost us nothing in men; it brought us a huge profit in money; as Europe has gone down, we have gone up. Moreover, it produced a vast discharge of spiritual electricity, otherwise and more injuriously dissipated in the countries more harshly beset. The war was fought ig-nobly; its first and most obvious effect was to raise up a horde of cads, and set them in authority as spokesmen of the nation. But out of that swinishness there was bound to come reaction, and out of the reaction there was bound to flow a desire to re-examine the whole national pretension—to turn on the light, to reject old formulæ, to think things out anew and in terms of reality. Suddenly the old houses of cards came tumbling down, and the professors inhabiting them ran about in their night-shirts, bawling for the police. The war, first and last, produced a great deal more than John Dos Passos' "Three Soldiers." It also produced Lewis' "Babbitt," and Cabell's "Jurgen," and

Fergusson's "Capitol Hill," and O'Neill's "The Emperor Jones." And, producing them, it ended an epoch of sweetness and light.

2

The young American literatus of today, with publishers ready and eager to give him a hearing, can scarcely imagine the difficulties which beset his predecessor of twenty years ago; he is, indeed, far too little appreciative of the freedom he has, and far too prone to flee from hard work to the solace of the martyr's shroud. When I first began practise as a critic, in 1908, there was yet plenty of excuse for putting it on. It was a time of almost inconceivable complacency and conformity. Hamilton Wright Mabie was still alive and still taken seriously, and all the young pedagogues who aspired to the critical gown imitated him in his watchful stupidity. This camorra had delivered a violent wallop to Theodore Dreiser eight years before, and he was yet suffering from his bruises; it was not until 1911 that he printed "Jennie Gerhardt." Miss Harriet Monroe and her gang of new poets were still dispersed and inarticulate; Miss Amy Lowell, as yet unaware of Imagism, was writing polite doggerel in the manner of a New England schoolmarm; the reigning dramatists of the nation were Augustus Thomas, David Belasco and Clyde Fitch; Miss Cather was imitating Mrs. Wharton; Hergesheimer had six years to go before he'd come to "The Lay Anthony"; Cabell was known only as one who provided the text for illustrated gift-books; the American novelists most admired by most publishers, by most readers and by all practising critics were Richard Harding Davis, Robert W. Chambers and James Lane Allen. It is hard indeed, in retrospect, to picture those remote days just as they were. They seem almost fabulous. The chief critical organ of the Republic was actually the Literary Supplement of the New York *Times.* The *Dial* was down with diabetes in Chicago; the *Nation* was made dreadful by the gloomy humors of Paul Elmer More; the *Bookman* was even more saccharine and sophomoric than it is today. When the mild and pianissimo revolt of the middle 90's—a feeble echo of the English revolt—had spent itself, the Presbyterians marched in and took possession of the works.

Most of the erstwhile revoltés boldly took the veil—notably Hamlin Garland. No novel that told the truth about life as Americans were living it, no poem that departed from the old patterns, no play that had the merest ghost of an idea in it had a chance. When, in 1908, Mrs. Mary Roberts Rinehart printed a conventional mystery story which yet managed to have a trace of sense in it, it caused a sensation. And when, two years later, Dr. William Lyon Phelps printed a book of criticism in which he actually ranked Mark Twain alongside Emerson and Hawthorne, there was as great a stirring beneath the college elms as if a naked fancy woman had run across the campus. If Hergesheimer had come into New York in 1908 with "Cytherea" under his arm, he would have worn out his pantaloons on publishers' benches without getting so much as a polite kick. If Eugene O'Neill had come to Broadway with "The Hairy Ape," he would have been sent to Edward E. Rose to learn the elements of his trade. The devilish and advanced thing, in those days, was for the fat lady star to give a couple of matinées of Ibsen's "A Doll's House."

A great many men and a few women addressed themselves to the dispersal of this fog. Some of them were imaginative writers who found it simply impossible to bring themselves within the prevailing rules; some were critics; others were young publishers. As I look back, I can't find any sign of concerted effort; it was, in the main, a case of each on his own. The more contumacious of the younger critics, true enough, tended to rally 'round Huneker, who, as a matter of fact, was very little interested in American letters, and the young novelists had a leader in Dreiser, who, I suspect, was quite unaware of most of them. However, it was probably Dreiser who chiefly gave form to the movement, despite the fact that for eleven long years he was silent. Not only was there a useful rallying-point in the idiotic suppression of "Sister Carrie"; there was also the encouraging fact of the man's massive immovability. Physically and mentally he loomed up like a sort of headland—a great crag of basalt that no conceivable assault seemed able to touch. His predecessor, Frank Norris, was of much softer stuff. Norris, had he lived longer, would have been wooed and ruined, I fear, by the Mabies, Boyntons and other such Christian critics, as Garland had been wooed and ruined before him.

Dreiser, fortunately for American letters, never had to face any such seduction. The critical schoolmarms, young and old, fell upon him with violence the moment he appeared above the horizon of his native steppe, and soon he was the storm center of a battle-royal that lasted nearly twenty years. The man himself was solid, granitic, without nerves. Very little cunning was in him and not much bellicose enterprise, but he showed a truly appalling tenacity. The pedagogues tried to scare him to death, they tried to stampede his partisans and they tried to put him into Coventry and get him forgotten, but they failed every time. The more he was reviled, sneered at, neglected, the more resolutely he stuck to his formula. That formula is now every serious American novelist's formula. They all try to write better than Dreiser, and not a few of them succeed, but they all follow him in his fundamental purpose—to make the novel true. Dreiser added something, and here following him is harder: he tried to make the novel poignant—to add sympathy, feeling, imagination to understanding. It will be a long while before that enterprise is better managed than he managed it in "Jennie Gerhardt."

Today, it seems to me, the American imaginative writer, whether he be novelist, poet or dramatist, is quite as free as he deserves to be. He is free to depict the life about him precisely as he sees it, and to interpret it in any manner he pleases. The publishers of the land, once so fearful of novelty, are now so hospitable to it that they constantly fail to distinguish the novelty that has hard thought behind it from that which has only some Village mountebank's desire to stagger the wives of Rotarians. Our stage is perhaps the freest in the world—not only to sensations, but also to ideas. Our poets get into print regularly with stuff so bizarre and unearthly that only Christian Scientists can understand it. The extent of this new freedom, indeed, is so great that large numbers of persons appear to be unable to believe in it; they are constantly getting into sweats about the taboos and inhibitions that remain, for example, those nourished by comstockery. But the importance and puissance of comstockery, I believe, is quite as much overestimated as the importance and puissance of the objurgations still hurled at sense and honesty by the provincial professors of American Idealism, the Genius of America, and other such phantasms.

The Comstocks, true enough, still raid an occasional book, particularly when their funds are running low and there is need to inflame Christian men, but that their monkeyshines ever actually *suppress* a book of any consequence I very much doubt. The flood is too vast for them. Chasing a minnow with desperate passion, they let a whole school of whales go by. In any case, they confine their operations to the single field of sex, and it must be plain that it is not in the field of sex that the hottest battles against the old American manner have been fought and won. "Three Soldiers" was far more subversive of that manner than all the stories of sex ever written in America —and yet "Three Soldiers" came out with the imprint of one of the most respectable of American publishers, and was scarcely challenged. "Babbitt" scored a victory that was still easier, and yet more significant, for its target was the double one of American business and American Christianity; it set the whole world to laughing at two things that are far more venerated in the United States than the bodily chastity of women. Nevertheless, "Babbitt" went down so easily that even the alfalfa *Gelehrten* joined in whooping for it, apparently on the theory that praising Lewis would make the young of the national species forget Dreiser. Victimized by their own craft, the *Gelehrten* thus made a foul attack upon their own principles, for if their principles did not stand against just such anarchistic and sacrilegious books, then they were without any sense whatever, as was and is, indeed, the case.

I shall not rehearse the steps in the advance from "Sister Carrie," suppressed and proscribed, to "Babbitt," swallowed and hailed. The important thing is that, despite the caterwauling of the Comstocks and the pedagogues, a reasonable freedom for the serious artist now prevails—that publishers stand ready to print him, that critics exist who are competent to recognize him and willing to do battle for him, and that there is a large public eager to read him. What use is he making of his opportunity? Certainly not the worst use possible, but also certainly not the best. He is free, but he is not yet, perhaps, worthy of freedom. He lets the popular magazine, the movie and the cheap-John publisher pull him too hard in one direction; he lets the vagaries of his politics pull him too hard in another. Back in 1908 I predicted the destruction of Upton Sinclair the

artist by Upton Sinclair the visionary and reformer. Sinclair's
bones now bleach upon the beach. Beside them repose those of
many another man and woman of great promise—for example,
Winston Churchill. Floyd Dell is on his way—one novel and
two doses of Greenwich Village psychology. Hergesheimer
writes novelettes for the *Saturday Evening Post*. Willa Cather
has won the Pulitzer Prize—a transaction comparable to the
election of Charles W. Eliot to the Elks. Masters turns to prose
that somehow fails to come off. Dreiser, forgetting his trilogy,
experiments rather futilely with the drama, the essay, free
verse. Fuller renounces the novel for book reviewing. Tarking-
ton is another Pulitzer prizeman, always on the verge of first-
rate work but always falling short by an inch. Many of the
White Hopes of ten or fifteen years ago perished in the war, as
surely victims of its slaughter as Rupert Brooke or Otto Braun;
it is, indeed, curious to note that practically every American
author who moaned and sobbed for democracy between the
years 1914 and 1919 is now extinct. The rest have gone down
the chute of the movies.

But all this, after all, may signify little. The shock troops
have been piled up in great masses, but the ground is cleared
for those that follow. Well, then, what of the youngsters? Do
they show any sign of seizing their chance? The answer is yes
and no. On the one hand there is a group which, revolving
'round the *Bookman*, talks a great deal and accomplishes
nothing. On the other hand there is a group which, revolving
'round the *Dial* and the *Little Review*, talks even more and
does even less. But on the third hand, as it were, there is a
group which says little and saws wood. There seems to be little
in common between its members, no sign of a formal movement, with its *blague* and its bombast, but all of them have this
in common: that they owe both their opportunity and their
method to the revolution that followed "Sister Carrie." Most
of them are from the Middle West, but they are distinct from
the Chicago crowd, now degenerated to posturing and worse.
They are sophisticated, disillusioned, free from cant, and
yet they have imagination. The raucous protests of the evangelists of American Idealism seem to have no more effect upon
them than the advances of the Expressionists, Dadaists and
other such café-table prophets. Out of this dispersed and ill-

defined group, I believe, something will come. Its members are those who are free from the two great delusions which, from the beginning, have always cursed American letters: the delusion that a work of art is primarily a moral document, that its purpose is to make men better Christians and more docile cannon-fodder, and the delusion that it is an exercise in logic, that its purpose is to prove something. These delusions, lingering beyond their time, are responsible for most of the disasters visible in the national literature today—the disasters of the radicals as well as those of the 100 per cent. dunderheads. The writers of the future, I hope and believe, will carefully avoid both of them.

XVII.

People and Things

The Capital of a Great Republic

THE fourth secretary of the Paraguayan legation. . . .
The chief clerk to the House committee on industrial arts
an expositions. . . . The secretary to the secretary to the Secretary of Labor. . . . The brother to the former Congressman from the third Idaho district. . . . The messenger to the
chief of the Senate folding-room. . . . The doorkeeper outside the committee-room of the House committee on the
disposition of useless executive papers. . . . The chief correspondent of the Toomsboro, Ga., *Banner* in the Senate
press-gallery. . . . The stenographer to the assistant chief en-
tomologist of the Bureau of Animal Industry. . . . The third
assistant chief computor in the office of the Naval Almanac.
. . . The assistant Attorney-General in charge of the investigation of postal frauds in the South Central States. . . . The
former wife of the former secretary to the former member of
the Interstate Commerce Commission. . . . The brother to
the wife of the *chargé d'affaires* of Czecho-Slovakia. . . . The
bootlegger to the ranking Democratic member of the committee on the election of President, Vice-President and representatives in Congress. . . . The acting assistant doorkeeper
of the House visitors' gallery. . . . The junior Senator from
Delaware. . . . The assistant to the secretary to the chief
clerk of the Division of Audits and Disbursements, Bureau of
Stationery and Supplies, Postoffice Department. . . . The
press-agent to the chaplain of the House. . . . The commercial attaché to the American legation at Quito. . . . The
chauffeur to the fourth assistant Postmaster-General. . . .
The acting substitute elevator-man in the Washington monu-
ment. . . . The brother to the wife of the brother-in-law of
the Vice-President. . . . The aunt to the sister of the wife of
the officer in charge of ceremonials, State Department. . . .
The neighbor of the cousin of the step-father of the sister-in-

law of the President's pastor. . . . The superintendent of charwomen in Temporary Storehouse B7, Bureau of Navy Yards and Docks. . . . The assistant confidential clerk to the chief clerk to the acting chief examiner of the Patent Office. . . . The valet to the Chief Justice.

2
Ambassadors of Christ

Fifth avenue rectors with shining morning faces, preaching on Easter to pews packed with stockbrokers, defendants in salacious divorce suits, members of the Sulgrave Foundation and former Zionists. . . . Evangelists of strange, incomprehensible cults whooping and bawling at two or three half-witted old women and half a dozen scared little girls in corrugated iron tabernacles down near the railroad-yards. . . . Mormon missionaries pulling door-bells in Wheeling, W. Va., and Little Rock, Ark., and handing naughty-looking tracts to giggling servant girls. . . . Baptist doctors of divinity calling upon John the Baptist and John D. Rockefeller to bear witness that the unducked will sweat in hell forevermore. . . . Methodist candidates for the sacred frock, sent out to preach trial sermons to backward churches in the mail-order belt, proving magnificently in one hour that Darwin was an ignoramus and Huxley a scoundrel. . . . Irish priests denouncing the Ku Klux Klan. . . . Rabbis denouncing Henry Ford. . . . Presbyterians denouncing Flo Ziegfeld. . . . Fashionable divines officiating at gaudy home weddings, their ears alert for the popping of corks. . . . Street evangelists in Zanesville, O., trying convince a cop and five newsboys that no men will be saved unless he be born again. . . . Missionaries in smelly gospel-shops along the waterfront, expounding the doctrine of the atonement to boozy Norwegian sailors, half of them sound asleep. . . . Cadaverous high-church Episcopalians. . . . Little fat Lutherans with the air of prosperous cheese-mongers. . . . Dunkards with celluloid collars and no neckties. . . . Southern Methodists who still believe in slavery. . . . Former plumbers, threshing-machine engineers and horse-doctors turned into United Brethren bishops. . . . Missionaries collecting money from the mill children in

Raleigh, N.C., to convert the Spaniards and Italians to Calvinism. . . . Episcopal archdeacons cultivating the broad English *a*. . . . Swedenborgians trying to explain the "Arcana
Cœlestia" to flabbergasted newspaper reporters. . . . Polish
clergymen leaping out of the windows at Polish weddings in
Johnstown, Pa., hoping that the next half-dozen beer-bottles
won't hit them. . . . Methodists pulling wires for bishoprics.
. . . Quakers foreclosing mortgages. . . . Baptists busy
among the women.

3
Bilder aus schöner Zeit

The excellent lunch that the illustrious Crispi used to serve
at Delmonico's at five o'clock in the afternoon. . . . The incomparable orange blossom cocktails at Sherry's, and the
plates of salted nuts. . . . The tavern cocktails at the Beaux
Arts, each with its dash of absinthe. . . . The Franziskaner
Mai-Bock at Lüchow's. . . . Dear old Sieg's noble Rhine
wines at the Kaiserhof. . . . The long-tailed clams and Spring
onions at Rogers', with Pilsner to wash them down. . . . The
amazingly good American quasi-Pilsner, made by Herr Abner,
on the Raleigh roof in Washington. . . . The Castel del
Remy at the Brevoort, cheap but perfect. . . . The very dark
Kulmbacher at the Pabst place in 125th street in the last days of
civilization. . . . The burgundy from the Cresta Blanca vine-
yards in California. . . . Michelob on warm Summer evenings,
with the crowd singing "Throw Out the Lifeline!". . . . The
old-time Florestan cocktails—50 per cent. London gin, 25 per
cent. French vermouth and 25 per cent. Martini-Rossi, with a
dash of Angostura bitters—drink half, then drink a glass of
beer, and then drink the other half. . . . That Hoboken red
wine, so strangely smooth and lovely. . . . The bad red wine
(but capital cooking) at the Frenchman's in Lexington avenue. . . . Del Pezzo's superb Chianti. . . . The ale at
Keen's. . . . Obst's herrings, with Löwenbräu to slack
them. . . . The astounding cocktail made by the head waiter
at Henri's. . . . Drinking Faust all night in St. Louis in
1904. . . . The musty ale at Losekam's in Washington. . . .
The draft *Helles* at Krüger's in Philadephia. . . . A Pilsner

luncheon at the old Grand Union, from one to six. . . . A stray bottle of perfect sauterne found in Rahway, New Jersey. . . . A wild night drinking Swedish punch and hot water. . . . Two or three hot Scotch nights. . . . Twenty or thirty Bass' ale nights. Five or six hundred Pilsner nights. . . .

4
The High Seas

The kid who sits in the bucket of tar. . . . The buxom stewardess who comes in and inquires archly if one rang. . . . The humorous piano-tuner who tunes the grand piano in the music-room in the 15-16ths-tone scale. . . . The electric fan which, when a stray zephyr blows in through the porthole, makes a noise like a dentist's drill. . . . The alien ship's printer who, in the daily wireless paper, reports a baseball score of 165 to 3. . . . The free Christian Science literature in the reading-room. . . . The pens in the writing-room. . . . The elderly *Grosshändler* with the young wife. . . . The red-haired girl in the green sweater. . . . The retired boot-legger disguised as a stockbroker. . . . The stockbroker disguised as a United States Senator. . . . The boy who climbs into the lifeboat. . . . The chief steward wearing the No. 18¾ collar. . . . The mysterious pipes that run along the stateroom ceilings. . . . The discovery that one forgot to pack enough undershirts. . . . The night watchman who raps on the door at 3.30 A.M. to deliver a wireless message reading "Sorry missed you. Bon voyage". . . . The bartender who adds a dash of witchhazel to cocktails. . . . The wilting flowers standing in ice-pitchers and spittoons in the hallways. . . . The fight in the steerage. . . . The old lady who gets stewed and sends for the doctor. . . . The news that the ship is in Long. 43°, 41′, 16″ W, Lat. 40°, 23′, 39″ N. . . . The report that the starboard propeller has lost a blade.

5
The Shrine of Mnemosyne

The little town of Kirkwall, in the Orkney Islands, in a mid-Winter mist, flat and charming like a Japanese print. . . . San

Francisco and Golden Gate from the top of Twin Peaks. . . . Gibraltar on a Spring day, all in pastel shades, like the back-drop for a musical comedy. . . . My first view of the tropics, the palm-trees suddenly bulging out of the darkness of dawn, the tremendous stillness, the sweetly acid smell, the immeasurable strangeness. . . . The Trentino on a glorious morning, up from Verona to the Brenner Pass. . . . Central Germany from Bremen to Munich, all in one day, with the apple trees in bloom. . . . Copenhagen on a wild night, with the *Polizei* combing the town for the American who upset the piano. . . . Christiania in January, with the snow-clad statue of Ibsen looming through the gloom like a ghost in a cellar. . . . The beach at Tybee Island, with the faint, blood-curdling rattle of the land-crabs. . . . Jacksonville after the fire in 1902, with the hick militiamen firing their machine-guns all night. . . . The first inauguration of Woodrow, and the pretty suffragette who drank beer with me at the Raleigh. . . . A child playing in the yard of a God-forsaken town in the Wyoming desert. . . . Bryan's farewell speech at the St. Louis Convention in 1904. . . . Hampton Court on Chestnut Sunday. . . . A New Year's Eve party on a Danish ship, 500 miles off the coast of Greenland. . . . The little pile of stones on the beach of Watling's Island, marking the place where Columbus landed. . . . The moon of the Caribbees, seen from a 1000-ton British tramp. . . . A dull night in a Buffalo hotel, reading the American Revised Version of the New Testament. . . . The day I received the proofs of my first book. . . . A good-bye on an Hoboken pier. . . . The Palace Hotel in Madrid.

PREJUDICES
FIFTH SERIES

I.

Four Moral Causes

Birth Control

T HE grotesque failure of the campaign to put down propaganda for birth control in the Republic has a lesson in it for those romantic optimists who believe that in the long run, by some mysterious hook or crook and perhaps with divine help, Prohibition will be enforced. They will not heed that lesson, but it is there nevertheless. Church and state combine to baffle and exterminate the birth controllers. They are threatened with penal servitude and their customers are threatened with hell fire. Yet it must be obvious that they are making progress in the land, for the national birth-rate continues to slide downhill, steadily and rapidly.

Incidentally, it is amusing and instructive to observe that it diminishes with greatest celerity among the educated and highly respectable classes, which is to say, among those who are ordinarily most law-abiding. The same thing is to be noted when one turns to Prohibition. The majority of professional criminals, now as in the old days of sin, are teetotalers, but when one comes to the good citizens who scorn them and demand incessantly that the *Polizei* butcher them and so have done with them, one comes at once upon a high density of scofflaws. I know many Americans of easy means, some of them greatly respected and even eminent. Not two per cent make any pretense of obeying the Volstead Act. And not two per cent of their wives are innocent of birth control. The reason is not far to seek. Both the Volstead Act and the statute aimed at birth control invade the sanctity of the domestic hearth. They take the roof off a man's house, and invite the world to look in. Obviously, that looking in is unpleasant in proportion as the man himself is dignified. If he is a low fellow, he doesn't care much, for he is used to such snooping by his low neighbors. But if he is one who has a high opinion of himself, and is accustomed to seeing it ratified by others, then he is outraged.

And if he has any natural bellicosity in him and resistance seems reasonably safe, he resists with great diligence and vigor.

Here, perhaps, we come upon an explanation of the fact that Prohibition and all other such devices for making men good by force are far less opposed in the country than they are in the cities. The yokel is trained from infancy to suffer espionage. He has scarcely any privacy at all. His neighbors know everything that is to be known about him, including what he eats and what he feeds his quadrupedal colleagues. His religious ideas are matters of public discussion; if he is recusant the village pastor prays for him by name. When his wife begins the sublime biological process of giving him an heir, the news flies around. If he inherits $200 from an uncle in Idaho everyone knows it instantly. If he skins his shin, or buys a new plow, or sees a ghost, or takes a bath it is a public event. Thus living like a goldfish in a glass globe, he acquires a large tolerance of snoutery, for if he resisted it his neighbors would set him down as an enemy of their happiness, and probably burn his barn. When an official spy or two are added to the volunteer pack he scarcely notices it. It seems natural and inevitable to him that everyone outside his house should be interested in what goes on inside, and that this interest should be accompanied by definite notions as to what is nice and what is not nice, supported by pressure. So he submits to governmental tyranny as he submits to the village inquisition, and when he hears that city men resist, it only confirms his general feeling that they are scoundrels. They are scoundrels because they have a better time than he has—the sempiternal human reason. The city man is differently trained. He is used to being let alone. Save when he lives in the slums, his neighbors show no interest in him. He would regard it as outrageous for them to have opinions about what goes on within the four walls of his house. If they offered him advice he would invite them to go to hell; if they tried force he would bawl for the police. So he is doubly affronted when the police themselves stalk in. And he resists them with every means at his command, and believes it is his high duty to do so, that liberty may not perish from the earth.

The birth control fanatics profit by this elemental fact. It is their great good fortune that their enemies have tried to put them down, not by refuting their ideas, but by seeking to shove them into jail. What they argue for, at bottom, remains very dubious, and multitudes of quite honest and intelligent persons are against it. They have by no means proved that a high birth-rate is dangerous, and they have certainly not shown that they know of any sure and safe way to reduce it— that is, any way not already known to every corner druggist. But when an attempt is made to put them down by law, the question whether they are wise falls into the background, and the question whether their rights are invaded comes forward. At once the crowd on their side is immensely reinforced. It now includes not only all the persons who believe in birth control, but also all the persons who believe in free ideas and free speech, and this second group, it quickly appears, is far larger than the first one, and far more formidable. So the birth controllers suddenly find themselves supported by heavy battalions, and that support is sufficient to make them almost invulnerable. Personally, I am inclined to be against them. I believe that the ignorant should be permitted to spawn *ad libitum*, that there may be a steady supply of slaves, and that those of us who are more prudent and sanitary may be relieved of unpleasant work. If the debate were open and fair, I'd oppose the birth controllers with all the subtlest devices of rhetoric, including bogus statistics and billingsgate. But so long as they are denied their plain rights—and, in particular, so long as those rights are denied them by an evil combination of theologians and politicians,—I am for them, and shall remain so until the last galoot's ashore. They have got many more allies on the same terms. And I believe that they are winning.

The law which forbids them to send their brummagem tracts through the mails is obviously disingenuous and oppressive. It is a part of the notorious Postal Act, put on the books by Comstock himself, executed by bureaucratic numskulls, and supported by every variety of witch-burner. I know of no intelligent man or woman who is in favor of the principal of such grotesque legislation; even the worst enemies of the birth controllers would not venture to argue that it should be applied generally. The way to dispose of such laws is to flout them and make a mock of them. The theory that they can be got rid of by enforcing them is nonsense. Enforcing them simply inspires the sadists who advocate them to fresh excesses.

Worse, it accustoms the people to oppression, and so tends to make them bear it uncomplainingly. Wherever, in the United States, there has been any sincere effort to enforce Prohibition, the anti-evolutionists are already on the warpath, and the Lord's Day Alliance is drumming up recruits. No, the way to deal with such laws is to defy them, and thus make them ridiculous. This is being done in the case of the Volstead Act by millions of patriots, clerical and lay. It is being done in the case of the Comstock Act by a small band, but one full of praiseworthy resolution.

Thus I deliver myself of a whoop for the birth controllers, and pass on to pleasanter concerns. Their specific Great Cause, it seems to me, is full of holes. They draw extremely questionable conclusions from a highly dubious body of so-called facts. But they are profoundly right at bottom. They are right when they argue that anyone who tries to silence them by force is the common enemy of all of us. And they are right when they hold that the best way to get rid of such opposition is to thumb the nose at it.

2

Comstockery

In 1873, when the late Anthony Comstock began his great Christian work, the American flapper, or, as she was then called, the young lady, read *Godey's Lady's Book*. To-day she reads—but if you want to find out what she reads simply take a look at the cheap fiction magazines which rise mountain-high from every news-stand. It is an amusing and at the same time highly instructive commentary upon the effectiveness of moral legislation. The net result of fifty years of Comstockery is complete and ignominious failure. All its gaudy raids and alarms have simply gone for naught.

Comstock, of course, was an imbecile; his sayings and doings were of such sort that they inevitably excited the public mirth, and so injured the cause he labored for. But it would be inaccurate, I believe, to put all the blame for its failure upon his imbecility. His successor, in New York, John S. Sumner, is by no means another such unwitting comedian; on the contrary, he shows discretion and even a certain wistful dignity.

Nevertheless, he has failed just as miserably. When he took office "Three Weeks" was still regarded as a very salacious book. The wives of Babbitts read it in the kitchen, with the blinds down; it was hidden under every pillow in every finishing-school in the land. To-day "Three Weeks" is dismissed as intolerably banal by school girls of thirteen. To make a genuine sensation it is not sufficient that a new book be naughty; it must be downright pathological.

I have been reviewing current American fiction pretty steadily since 1908. The change that I note is immense. When I began, a new novel dealing frankly with the physiology and pathology of sex was still something of a novelty. It was, indeed, so rare that I always called attention to it. To-day it is a commonplace. The surprise now comes when a new novel turns out to be chemically pure. Try to imagine an American publisher, in these days, getting alarmed about Dreiser's "Sister Carrie" and suppressing it before publication! The oldest and most dignified houses would print it without question; they print far worse every day. Yet in 1900 it seemed so lewd and lascivious that the publisher who put it into type got into a panic of fright, and hid the whole edition in the cellar. To-day that same publisher is advertising a new edition of Walt Whitman's "Leaves of Grass," with "A Woman Waits for Me" printed in full!

What ruined the cause of the Comstocks, I believe, was the campaign of their brethren of sex hygiene. The whole Comstockian case, as good Anthony himself used to explain frankly, was grounded upon the doctrine that virtue and ignorance were identical—that the slightest knowledge of sin was fatal to virtue. Comstock believed and argued that the only way to keep girls pure was to forbid them to think about sex at all. He expounded that doctrine often and at great length. No woman, he was convinced, could be trusted. The instant she was allowed to peek over the fence she was off to the Bad Lands. This notion he supported with many texts from Holy Writ, chiefly from the Old Testament. He was a Puritan of the old school, and had no belief whatever in virtue *per se*. A good woman, to him, was simply one who was efficiently policed. Unfortunately for him, there rose up, within the bounds of his own sect, a school of uplifters who began to merchant quite contrary ideas. They believed that sin was often caused by ignorance—that many a virtuous girl was undone simply because she didn't know what she was doing. These uplifters held that unchastity was not the product of a congenital tendency to it in the female, but of the sinister enterprise of the male, flowing out of his superior knowledge and sophistication. So they set out to spread the enlightenment. If all girls of sixteen, they argued not unplausibly, knew as much about the dreadful consequences of sin as the average police lieutenant or midwife, there would be no more seductions, and in accordance with that theory, they began printing books describing the discomforts of parturition and the terminal symptoms of lues. These books they broadcasted in numerous and immense editions. Comstock, of course, was bitterly against the scheme. He had no faith in the solemn warnings; he saw only the new and startling frankness, and he believed firmly that its one effect would be to "arouse a libidinous passion . . . in the mind of a modest woman." But he was spiked and hamstrung by the impeccable respectability of the sex hygienists. Most of them were Puritans like himself; some were towering giants of Christian rectitude. One of the most active, the Rev. Dr. Sylvanus Stall, was a clergyman of the first chop—a sorcerer who had notoriously saved thousands of immortal souls. To raid such men, to cast them into jail and denounce them as scoundrels, was palpably impossible. Comstock fretted and fumed, but the thing got beyond him. Of Pastor Stall's books alone, millions were sold. Others were almost as successful; the country was flooded from coast to coast.

Whether Comstock was right or wrong I don't know—that is, whether these sex hygiene books increased or diminished loose living in the Republic I don't know. Some say one thing and some another. But this I *do* know; they had a quick and tremendous influence upon the content of American fiction. In the old-time novel what are now called the Facts of Life were glossed over mellifluously, and no one complained about it, for the great majority of fiction readers, being young and female, had no notion of what they were missing. But after they had read the sex hygiene books they began to observe that what was set out in novels was very evasive, and that much of it was downright untrue. So they began to murmur, to snicker, to boo. One by one the old-time novelists went on the shelf. I could make up a long and melancholy roll of them. Their sales dropped off; they began to be laughed at. In place of them rose a new school, and its aim was to tell it all. With this new school Comstock and his heirs have been wrestling ever since, and with steadily increasing bad fortune. Every year they make raids, perform in the newspapers and predict the end of the world, but every year the average is worse than the worst of the year before. As a practicing reviewer, I have got so used to lewd and lascivious books that I no longer notice them. They pour in from all directions. The most virtuous lady novelists write things that would have made a bartender blush to death two decades ago. If I open a new novel and find nothing about Freudian suppressions in it, I suspect at once that it is simply a reprint of some forgotten novel of 1885, with a new name. When I began reviewing I used to send my review copies, after I had sweated through them, to the Y.M.C.A. Now I send them to a medical college.

The Comstocks labor against this stream gallantly, but, it seems to me, very ineptly. They can't, of course, proceed against every naughty book that comes out, for there are far too many, but they could at least choose their marks far more sagaciously than they do. Instead of tackling the books that are frankly pornographic and have no other excuse for being, they almost always tackle books that have obvious literary merit, and are thus relatively easily defended. In consequence, they lose most of their cases. They lost with "Jurgen," they lost with "The 'Genius,'" they lost with "Mlle. de Maupin," and they have lost countless other times. And every time they lose they grow more impotent and absurd. Why do they pick out such books? Simply because raiding them gets more publicity than raiding more obscure stuff. The Comstock Society, like all other such pious organizations, is chronically short of money, and the way to raise it is to make a noise in the newspapers. A raid on "Night Life in Chicago," or "Confessions of an Escaped Nun" would get but a few lines; an attack on "Jurgen" is first-page stuff for days on end. Christian virtuosi, their libido aroused, send in their money, and so the society is saved. But when the trial is called and the case is lost, contributions fall off again, and another conspicuous victim must be found.

Well, what is the Comstocks' own remedy for this difficulty? It is to be found in what they call the Clean Books Bill. The aim of this bill is to make it impossible for a publisher accused of publishing an immoral book to make any defense at all. If it ever becomes a law the Comstocks will be able to pick out a single sentence from a Dreiser novel of 10,000 pages and base their whole case upon it; the author and publisher will be forbidden to offer the rest of the book as evidence that the whole has no pornographic purpose. Under such a law anyone printing or selling the Bible will run dreadful risks. One typographical error of a stimulating character will suffice to send a publisher to jail. But will the law actually achieve its purpose? I doubt it. Such extravagant and palpably unjust statutes never accomplish anything. Juries revolt against them; even judges punch holes in them. The Volstead Act is an excellent specimen. Has it made the Republic dry?

3
Capital Punishment

Having argued against the death penalty with great heat and eloquence for more than twenty years, I hope I do not go beyond my rights when I now announce that I have begun to wobble, and feel a strong temptation to take the other side. My doubts, in all seriousness, I ascribe to the arguments of the current abolitionists. The more earnestly they set forth those arguments, the more I am harassed by suspicions that they are full of folly. A humane and Christian spirit, to be sure, is in them; but is there any sense? As I hint, I begin to doubt it. Consider the two that are oftenest heard:

1. That hanging a man (or doing him to death in any other such coldblooded way) is a dreadful business, degrading to those who have to do it and revolting to those who have to witness it.

2. That it is useless, for it does not deter others from the same crime.

The first of these arguments, it seems to me, is plainly too weak to need serious refutation. All it says, in brief, is that the work of the hangman is unpleasant. Granted. But suppose it is? It may be quite necessary to society for all that. There are, indeed, many other jobs that are unpleasant, and yet no one thinks of abolishing them. I pass over those connected with surgery, obstetrics, plumbing, military science, journalism and the sacred office, and point to one which, like that of the hangman, has to do with the execution of the laws: to wit, the post of Federal judge under Prohibition. Consider what a judge executing the Volstead Act must do nearly every day. He must assume that men whom he esteems and loves, men of his own profession, even his fellow judges—in brief, the great body of wet and enlightened Christian men—are all criminals. And he must assume that a pack of spies and blackmailers whose mere presence, in private life, would gag him—in brief, the corps of Anti-Saloon League snouters and Prohibition agents—are truth-seekers and altruists. These assumptions are obviously hard to make. Not a few judges, unable to make them, resign from the bench; at least one has committed suicide. But the remaining judges, so long as they sit, must make them as in duty bound, whatever the outrage to their feelings. Many grow callous and suffer no more. So with the hangman, and his even more disagreeable offices. A man of delicate sensibilities, confronting them, would die of horror, but there is no evidence that they are revolting to the men who actually discharge them. I have known hangmen, indeed, who delighted in their art, and practiced it proudly. I have never heard of one who threw up his job.

In the second argument of the abolitionists there is more force, but even here, I believe, the ground under them is very shaky. Their fundamental error consists in assuming that the whole aim of punishing criminals is to deter other (potential) criminals—that we hang or electrocute A simply in order to so alarm B that he will not kill C. This, I believe, is an assumption almost as inaccurate as those which must be made by a Federal judge. It confuses a part with the whole. Deterrence, obviously, is *one* of the aims of punishment, but it is surely not the only one. On the contrary, there are at least half a dozen, and some of them are probably quite as important. At least one of them, practically considered, is *more* important. Commonly, it is described as revenge, but revenge is really not the word for it. I borrow a better term from the late Aristotle: *katharsis*. *Katharsis*, so used, means a salubrious discharge of emotions, a healthy letting off of steam. A schoolboy, disliking his teacher, deposits a tack upon the pedagogical chair; the teacher jumps and the boy laughs. This is *katharsis*. A bootleg-ger, paying off a Prohibition agent, gives him a counterfeit $10 bill; the agent, dropping it in the collection plate on Sunday, is arrested and jailed. This is also *katharsis*. A subscriber to a newspaper, observing his name spelled incorrectly in the re-port of a lodge meeting, spreads a report that the editor of the paper did not buy Liberty Bonds. This again is *katharsis*.

What I contend is that one of the prime objects of judicial punishments is to afford this grateful *katharsis* (a) to the im-mediate victims of the criminal punished, and (b) to the gen-eral body of moral and timorous men. These persons, and particularly the first group, are concerned only indirectly with deterring other criminals. The thing they crave primarily is the satisfaction of seeing the criminal before them suffer as he made them suffer. What they want is the peace of mind that goes with the feeling that accounts are squared. Until they get that satisfaction they are in a state of emotional tension, and hence unhappy. The instant they get it they are comfortable. I do not argue that this yearning is noble; I simply argue that it is almost universal among human beings. In the face of injuries that are unimportant and can be borne without damage it may yield to higher impulses; that is to say, it may yield to what is called Christian charity. But it never so yields when the injury is serious, and gives substantial permanent satisfaction to the person inflicting it. Here Christianity is adjourned, and even saints reach for their sidearms. The better the Christian, in fact, the more violent his demand for *katharsis*—once he has unloaded the Beatitudes. At the time of the Leopold-Loeb trial in Chicago the evangelical pastors of the town bawled for blood unanimously, and even a Catholic priest joined them. On lower levels, it is plainly asking too much of human nature to expect it to conquer so natural an impulse. A keeps a store and has a bookkeeper, B. B steals $700, invests it in Texas oil stocks, and is cleaned out. What is A to do? Let B go? If he does so he will be unable to sleep at night. The sense of injury, of injustice, will keep him awake. So he turns B over to the police, and they send him to prison. Thereafter A can sleep. More, he has pleasant dreams. He pictures B chained to the wall of a dungeon a hundred feet underground, devoured by rats. It is so agreeable that it makes him forget his $700. He has got his *katharsis*.

The same thing precisely takes place on a larger scale when there is a crime which destroys a whole community's feeling of security. Every law-abiding citizen feels menaced and frustrated until the criminals have been struck down—until the communal capacity to get even with them, and more than even, has been dramatically demonstrated. Here the business of deterring others is no more than an afterthought. The main thing is to destroy the scoundrels whose act has alarmed everyone, and thus made everyone unhappy. Until they are brought to book that unhappiness continues; when the law has been executed upon them there is a sigh of relief. In other words, there is *katharsis*.

There is no public demand for the death penalty for ordinary crimes, even for ordinary homicides. Its infliction, say, for necking, for playing poker or for bootlegging would shock all men of normal decency of feeling—that is to say, practically all men save the evangelical clergy and their lay catchpolls. But for crimes involving the deliberate and inexcusable taking of human life, by men openly defiant of all civilized order—for such crimes it seems, to nine men out of ten, a just and proper punishment. Any lesser punishment leaves them feeling that the criminal has got the better of society—that he can add insult to injury by laughing. That feeling is intensely unpleasant, and no wonder! It can be dissipated only by a recourse to *katharsis*, the invention of the aforesaid Aristotle. That *katharsis* is most effectively and economically achieved, as human nature now is, by wafting the criminal to realms of bliss.

4
War

My mail is flooded with the briefs and broadsides of pacifist organizations, damning war as a curse and those who make it as scoundrels. Such literature I always read attentively, for it is full of racy satire against the military, a class of men inevitably more or less ludicrous in time of peace. But does it convert me to the pacifist cause, which, as the pacifists contend, is the cause of God? I can only report simply that it does not. I read it, enjoy it, pass it on to my pastor—and go on believing in war myself. War is the only sport, so far as I know, that is genuinely amusing. And it is the only sport that has any intelligible use.

The arguments that are brought against it are chiefly arguments, not against the thing itself, but only against its political accompaniments and consequences, most of them transient and gratuitous. They reached a high tide of obnoxiousness, revolting to all self-respecting men, during the last great moral combat. That combat was carried on, at least from this side of the fence, in a grossly hysterical, disingenuous, cowardly and sordid manner. The high participating parties were vastly alarmed by the foe, and insanely eager to keep business going as usual, and even better than usual. The result was that the thing began as a sort of Methodist revival and ended as a raid on a gentleman's winecellar, with the Prohibition agents fighting among themselves for the best jugs. The richest of them, once peace came, began sending the others extortionate bills for the brass-knuckles, Bibles and jimmies that all had used in common, and the heroes serving this usurer began demanding tips in cash. But all that swinishness, I submit, had no necessary connection with war itself. It is perfectly possible to conduct war in a gallant and honorable manner, and without using it as a mere cloak to rob noncombatants. More, the thing has been done, and many times in the history of the world. If it has been seldom done by democratic nations, then blame democracy, not war. In democratic nations everything noble and of good account tends to decay and smell badly.

War itself, in its pure form, is something quite different. It is a combat of men who believe that a short and adventurous life, full of changing scenes and high hazards, is better than a safe and dull one—in other words, that it is better to have lived magnificently than to have lived long. In this doctrine I am unable to discern anything properly describable as fallacy. If you argue that, assuming every man to embrace it, the human race would come to an end, I reply at once that you assume something wholly impossible. And if you argue that the life of a warrior is not actually magnificent, then I report that the warrior should be permitted to judge of that himself. Against all such arguments lie the plain facts that the great races of the world have always been more or less warlike, and that war has attracted the talent and satisfied the aspiration of some of their best men. I do not speak of antiquity alone; I speak of our own time. The English, the Germans and the French are all warlike, to-day as always—and if you took away the English, the Germans and the French *Homo sapiens* would be shorn of his stomach, his liver and his ductless glands. If war is immoral, then these great races are all immoral, and so are their greatest men. The pacifists, of course, do not shrink from that absurd argument. But the more they maintain it the more it becomes evident that, as logicians, they are on all fours with the Prohibitionists.

War, so conducted by warriors, is a superb business and full of high uses. It makes for resolution, endurance, enterprise, courage. It puts down the sordid yearnings of ignoble men. Does it, incidentally, shed some blood? Does it cost lives? The pacifists, discussing those lives, always enmesh themselves in the theory that, without war, they would go on forever. It is, I believe, not so. War, at worst, shortens them somewhat. But at the same stroke it speeds up their tempo. The net result is simply a matter of bookkeeping. A man killed at thirty, after six months of war, has lived far longer than a man dead of a belly-ache at sixty, after forty-five years on an office stool.

But I am not on my legs to-day to sing the charms and glories of war; my purpose is to argue that, whether glorious or not, it will remain inevitable on this sad mud-pie so long as the great races of men retain the view of it that I have described, and to deduce therefrom the doctrine that pacifism, as a scheme of practical politics, is thus not only unsound but also very dangerous. All that it could conceivably accomplish, imagining it to succeed anywhere, would be to make the nation embracing it highly vulnerable—in brief, a sort of boozy idealist or unarmored butter-and-egg man, roaming the world unprotected, and so holding out irresistible temptations to less moral and more realistic nations.

War, under the sorry scheme that now passes for civilization, has been degraded—transiently only, I hope and believe—to the uses of robbery. Whoever has gold must have an army to guard it, or resign himself to losing it. Especially must he have a guard for it if his public repute is that of one with a not too fine understanding of the difference between *meum* and *tuum*.

Such a reputation, it must be manifest, is precisely that of the United States to-day. The rest of the world is so passionately convinced that it is a thief that robbing it would take on the high virtue and dignity of a constabulary act. It is not robbed because it is strong. It will not be robbed until it grows weak.

But armed strength, argue the pacifists, does not prevent war: it causes it. Who, reading history, could believe in such transparent nonsense? Let us turn to the late enemy. What kept the peace in Europe for forty-four years if it was not the mighty German army? If it had been weak, France would have struck in 1875, and again in 1882, and again in 1887, and again every two years thereafter. It took nearly half a century to roll up a force sufficient to tackle the colossus, and it took four years to bring it down even then. Our own history is full of examples to the same effect. In 1867 Napoleon III, believing that the United States was war weary and its army disbanded, prepared to move into Mexico and tear the Monroe Doctrine to tatters. He overlooked the large forces engaged in burning barns, robbing hen-roosts and raiding cellars in the late Confederacy. When General Sheridan marched upon the Rio Grande at the head of this army of heroes, Napoleon changed his mind. Three years later he was disposed of by the Germans, and the Continent settled down to forty-four years of peace.

Consider, again, the Venezuela episode. When President Cleveland sent his message to Congress on December 17, 1895, war with England became imminent overnight. What prevented it? Was it the fact that the United States had no army worthy of the name? Or the fact that the United States had a brand-new, highly effective and immensely pugnacious navy, notoriously eager to try its guns? Come, now, to 1898. Of all the nations of Europe, only England sided with us against Spain. The Germans, at Manila, went to great lengths to show their hostility. Did they refrain from attacking Dewey because his fleet was smaller and weaker than theirs, or because it was larger and stronger?

I could multiply instances, but observe the time-keeper reaching for the gong. So far as I know, there is no record in history of a nation that ever gained anything valuable by being unable to defend itself. Such nations, true enough, have sometimes managed to exist for a time—but at what cost! There is the case of Denmark to-day. It is discussing disbanding its army on the ground that any probable or even possible foe could dispose of that army in five days. But what does this mean? It means that the Danes must reconcile themselves to living by the sheer grace of their stronger neighbors—that they must be willing, when the time comes, to see their country made a battle-ground by those neighbors, and without raising a hand. Here I do not indulge in idle talk: I am quoting almost literally a member of the Danish cabinet.

I can't imagine the people of a truly great nation submitting to any such ignominious destiny. The Danes have been forced into acquiescence by their weakness. But why should the United States invite the same fate by putting off its strength?

II.

Four Makers of Tales

Conrad

Some time ago I put in a blue afternoon re-reading Joseph Conrad's "Youth." A *blue* afternoon? What nonsense! The touch of the man is like the touch of Schubert. One approaches him in various and unhappy moods: depressed, dubious, despairing; one leaves him in the clear, yellow sunshine that Nietzsche found in Bizet's music. But here again the phrase is inept. Sunshine suggests the imbecile, barnyard joy of the human kohlrabi—the official optimism of a steadily delighted and increasingly insane Republic. What the enigmatical Pole has to offer is something quite different. If its parallel is to be found in music, it is not in Schubert, but in Beethoven— perhaps even more accurately in Johann Sebastian Bach. It is the joy, not of mere satisfaction, but of understanding—the profound but surely not merry delight which goes with the comprehension of a fundamental fact—above all, of a fact that has been coy and elusive. Certainly the order of the world that Conrad sets forth with such diabolical eloquence and plausibility is no banal moral order, no childish sequence of virtuous causes and edifying effects. Rather it has an atheistic and even demoniacal smack: to the earnest Bible student it must be more than a little disconcerting. The God he visualizes is no loving papa in a house-coat and carpet-slippers, inculcating the great principles of Christian ethics by applying occasional strokes *a posteriori*. What he sees is something quite different: an extremely ingenious and humorous Improvisatore and Comedian, with a dab of red on His nose and maybe somewhat the worse for drink—a furious and far from amiable banjoist upon the human spine, and rattler of human bones. Kurtz, in "Youth," makes a capital banjo for that exalted and cynical talent. And the music that issues forth—what a superb *Hexentanz* it is!

One of the curiosities of critical stupidity is the doctrine that

Conrad is without humor. No doubt it flows out of a more general error; to wit, the assumption that tragedy is always pathetic, that death itself is inevitably a gloomy business. That error, I suppose, will persist in the world until some extraordinary astute mime conceives the plan of playing "King Lear" as a farce—I mean deliberately. That it *is* a farce seems to me quite as obvious as the fact that "Romeo and Juliet" is another, this time lamentably coarse. To adopt the contrary theory—to view it as a great moral and spiritual spectacle, capable of purging and uplifting the psyche like marriage to a red-haired widow or a month in the trenches—to toy with such notions is to borrow the critical standards of a party of old ladies weeping over the damnation of the heathen. In point of fact, death, like love, is intrinsically farcical—a solemn kicking of a brick under a plug-hat—, and most other human agonies, once they transcend the physical—*i.e.*, the unescapably real—have far more of irony in them than of pathos. Looking back upon them after they have eased one seldom shivers: one smiles—perhaps sourly but nevertheless spontaneously. This, at all events, is the notion that seems to me implicit in every line of Conrad. I give you "Heart of Darkness" as the archetype of his whole work and the keystone of his metaphysical system. Here we have all imaginable human hopes and aspirations reduced to one common denominator of folly and failure, and here we have a play of humor that is infinitely mordant and searching. Turn to pages 136 and 137 of the American edition—the story is in the volume called "Youth"—: the burial of the helmsman. Turn then to 178–184: Marlow's last interview with Kurtz's intended. The farce mounts by slow stages to dizzy and breathtaking heights. One hears harsh roars of cosmic laughter, vast splutterings of transcendental mirth, echoing and reëchoing down the black corridors of empty space. The curtain descends at last upon a wild dance in a dissecting-room. The mutilated dead rise up and jig. . . .

It is curious, re-reading a thrice-familiar story, how often one finds surprises in it. I have been amazed, toward the close of "The End of the Tether," to discover that the *Fair Maid* was wrecked, not by the deliberate act of Captain Whalley, but by the machination of the unspeakable Massy. How is one to account for so preposterous an error? Certainly I thought I knew "The End of the Tether" as well as I knew anything in this world—and yet there was that incredible misunderstanding of it, lodged firmly in my mind. Perhaps there is criticism of a sort in my blunder: it may be a fact that the old skipper willed the thing himself—that his willing it is visible in all that goes before—that Conrad, in introducing Massy's puerile infamy at the end, made some sacrifice of inner veracity to the exigencies of what, at bottom, is somewhat too neat and well-made a tale. The story, in fact, belongs to the author's earlier manner; I guess that it was written before "Youth" and surely before "Heart of Darkness." But for all that, its proportions remain truly colossal. It is one of the most magnificent narratives, long or short, old or new, in the English language, and with "Youth" and "Heart of Darkness" it makes up what is probably the best book of imaginative writing that the English literature of the Twientieth Century can yet show. Conrad learned a great deal after he wrote it, true enough. In "Lord Jim," in "Victory," and, above all, in a "A Personal Record," there are momentary illuminations, blinding flashes of brilliance that he was incapable of in those days of experiment; but no other book of his seems to me to hold so steadily to so high a general level—none other, as a whole, is more satisfying and more marvelous. There is in "Heart of Darkness" a perfection of design which one encounters only rarely and miraculously in prose fiction: it belongs rather to music. I can't imagine taking a single sentence out of that stupendous tale without leaving a visible gap; it is as thoroughly *durch componiert* as a fugue. And I can't imagine adding anything to it, even so little as a word, without doing it damage. As it stands it is austerely and beautifully perfect, just as the slow movement of the Unfinished Symphony is perfect.

I observe of late a tendency to examine the English of Conrad rather biliously. This folly is cultivated chiefly in England, where, I suppose, chauvinistic motives enter into the matter. It is the just boast of great empires that they draw in talents from near and far, exhausting the little nations to augment their own puissance; it is their misfortune that these talents often remain defectively assimilated. Conrad remained the Slav to the end. The people of his tales, whatever he calls them, are always as much Slavs as he is; the language in which he describes them

retains a sharp, exotic flavor. But to say that this flavor constitutes a blemish is to say something so preposterous that only
schoolmasters and their dupes may be thought of as giving it
credit. The truly first-rate writer is not one who uses the language as such dolts demand that it be used; he is one who re-
works it in spite of their prohibitions. It is his distinction that
he thinks in a manner different from the thinking of ordinary
men; that he is free from that slavery to embalmed ideas which
makes them so respectable and so dull. Obviously, he cannot
translate his notions into terms of everyday without doing violence to their inner integrity; as well ask a Richard Strauss to
funnel all his music into the chaste jugs of Prof. Dr. Jadassohn.
What Conrad brought into English literature was a new concept of the relations between fact and fact, idea and idea, and
what he contributed to the complex and difficult art of writing
English was a new way of putting words together. His style
now amazes and irritates pedants because it does not roll along
in the old ruts. Well, it is precisely that rolling along in the old
ruts that he tried to avoid—and it was precisely that avoidance
which made him what he is. What lies under most of his alleged sins seems to me to be simple enough: he views English
logically and analytically, and not through a haze of senseless
traditions and arbitrary taboos. No Oxford mincing is in him.
If he cannot find his phrase above the salt, he seeks it below.
His English, in a word, is innocent. And if, at times, there gets
into it a color that is strange and even bizarre, then the fact is
something to rejoice over, for a living language is like a man
suffering incessantly from small internal hemorrhages, and
what it needs above all else is constant transfusions of new
blood from other tongues. The day the gates go up, that day it
begins to die.

A very great man, this Mr. Conrad. As yet, I believe decidedly underestimated, even by many of his post-mortem advocates. Most of his first acclaimers mistook him for a mere
romantic—a talented but somewhat uncouth follower of the
Stevenson tradition, with the orthodox cutlass exchanged for a
Malay *kris*. Later on he began to be heard of as a linguistic and
vocational marvel: it was astonishing that any man bred to Polish should write English at all, and more astonishing that a
country gentleman from the Ukraine should hold a master's

certificate in the British merchant marine. Such banal attitudes are now archaic, but I suspect that they have been largely responsible for the slowness with which his fame has spread in the world. At all events, he is vastly less read and esteemed in foreign parts than he ought to be, and very few Continental Europeans have risen to any genuine comprehension of his stature. When one reflects that the Nobel Prize was given to such third-raters as Benavente, Heidenstam, Gjellerup and Tagore, with Conrad passed over, one begins to grasp the depth and density of the ignorance prevailing in the world, even among the relatively enlightened. One "Lord Jim," as human document and as work of art, is worth all the works produced by all the Benaventes and Gjellerups since the time of Rameses II. It is, indeed, an indecency of criticism to speak of such unlike things in the same breath: as well talk of Brahms in terms of Mendelssohn. Nor is "Lord Jim" a chance masterpiece, an isolated peak. On the contrary, it is but one unit in a long series of extraordinary and almost incomparable works— a series sprung suddenly and overwhelmingly into full dignity with "Almayer's Folly." I challenge the nobility and gentry of Christendom to point to another Opus 1 as magnificently planned and turned out as "Almayer's Folly." The more one studies it, the more it seems miraculous. If it is not a work of absolute genius then no work of absolute genius exists on this earth.

2

Hergesheimer

This gentleman, like Conrad, has been slated very waspishly because his English is sometimes in contempt of Lindley Murray. Once, a few years back, a grammarian writing in the *New Republic* formally excommunicated him for it. A number of his offending locutions were cited, all of them, it must be admitted, instantly recognizable as pathological and against God by any suburban schoolma'm. *Soit!* The plain truth is that Hergesheimer, when it comes to the ultimate delicacies of English grammar, is an ignoramus, as he is when it comes to the niceties of Swedenborgian theology. I doubt that he could tell a noun in the nominative case from a noun in the objective.

But neither could any other man who writes as well as he does. Such esoteric knowledge is the exclusive possession of grammarians, whose pride in it runs in direct ratio to its inaccuracy, unimportance and imbecility. English grammar as a science thus takes its place with phrenology and the New Thought: the more a grammarian knows of it, the less he is worth listening to. Mastering such blowsy nonsense is one thing, and writing sound English is quite another thing, and the two achievements seem to be impossible to the same man. As Anatole France once remarked, nearly all first-rate writers write "bad French"—or "bad English." Joseph Conrad did. France himself did. Dreiser does. Henry James did. Dickens did. Shakespeare did. Thus Hergesheimer need not repine. He is sinful, but in good company. He writes English that is "bad," but also English that is curiously musical, fluent, chromatic, various and caressing. There is in even the worst of his *Saturday Evening Post* novelettes for Main Street a fine feeling for the inner savor of words—a keen ear for their subtler and more fragile harmonies. In "Cytherea," which I like beyond all his works—even beyond "The Three Black Pennys" and "Java Head"—they are handled in so adept and ingenious a way, with so much delicacy and originality, that it is no wonder they offer an intolerable affront to pedagogues.

This novel, as I say, seems to me to be the best that Hergesheimer has yet done. His best writing is in it, and his best observation. What interests him fundamentally is the conflict between the natural impulses of men and women and the conventions of the society that they are parts of. The struggles he depicts are not between heroes and villains, dukes and peasants, patriots and spies, but between the desire to be happy and the desire to be respected. It is, perhaps, a tribute to the sly humor of God that whichever way the battle goes, the result is bound to be disastrous to the man himself. If, seeking happiness in a world that is jealous of it and so frowns upon it, he sacrifices the good will of his fellow men, he always finds in the end that happiness is not happiness at all without it. And if, grabbing the other horn of the dilemma, he sacrifices the free play of his instincts to the respect of those fellow men, he finds that he has also sacrificed his respect for himself. Hergesheimer is no seer. He does not presume to solve the problem; he merely states it with agreeable variations and in the light of a compassionate irony. In "Cytherea" it takes the ancient form of the sexual triangle—old material, but here treated, despite the underlying skepticism, with a new illumination. What we are asked to observe is a marriage in which all the customary causes follow instead of precede their customary effects. To the eye of the world, and even, perhaps, to the eye of the secondary figures in it, the Randon-Grove affair is no more than a standard-model adultery, orthodox in its origin and in its course. Lee Randon, with an amiable and faithful wife, Fanny, at home in Eastlake, Pa., in the Country-Club Belt, with two charming children at her knee, goes to the hell-hole known as New York, falls in love with the sinister Mrs. Savina Grove, and forthwith bolts with her to Cuba, there to encounter a just retribution in the form of her grotesque death. But that is precisely what does *not* happen—that is, interiorly. Savina actually has little more to do with the flight of Randon than the Pullman Company which hauls him southward. It is already inevitable when he leaves Eastlake for New York, almost unaware of her existence. Its springs are to be sought in the very normalcy that it so profoundly outrages. He is the victim, like Fanny, his wife, of a marriage that has turned upon and devoured itself.

Hergesheimer was never more convincing than in his anatomizing of this *débâcle*. He is too impatient, and perhaps too fine an artist, to do it in the conventional realistic manner of piling up small detail. Instead he launches into it with a bold sagittal section, and at once the play of forces becomes comprehensible. What ails Randon, in brief, is that he has a wife who is a shade too good. Beautiful, dutiful, amiable, virtuous, yes. But not provocative enough—not sufficiently the lady of scarlet in the chemise of snowy white. Worse, a touch of stupid blindness is in her: she can see the honest business man, but she can't see the romantic lurking within him. When Randon, at a country-club dance, sits out a hoe-down with some flashy houri on the stairs, all that Fanny can see in it is a vulgar matter, like kissing a chambermaid behind the door. Even when Randon brings home the doll, Cytherea, and gives it a place of honor in their house, and begins mooning over it strangely, she is unable to account for the business in any terms save those of transient silliness. The truth is that Cytherea is to

Randon what La Belle Ettarre is to Cabell's Felix Kennaston—
his altar-flame in a dun world, his visualization of the unattainable, his symbol of what might have been. In her presence he
communes secretly with the outlaw hidden beneath the chairman of executive committees, the gypsy concealed in the
sound Americano. One day, bent upon God's work (specifically, upon breaking up a nefarious affair between a neighboring Rotarian and a moving-picture lady), he encounters the
aforesaid Savina Grove, accidentally brushes her patella with
his own, gets an incandescent glare in return, discovers to his
horror that she is the living image of Cytherea—and ten days
later is aboard the Key West Express with her, bound for San
Cristobal de la Habaña, and the fires eternal.

A matter, fundamentally, of coincidence. Savina, too, has her
Cytherea, though not projected into a doll. She too has toiled
up the long slope of a flabby marriage, and come at last to the
high crags where the air is thin, and a sudden giddiness may be
looked for. To call the thing a love affair, in the ordinary sense,
is rather fantastic; its very endearments are forced and mawk-
ish. What Randon wants is not more love, but an escape from
the bonds and penalties of love—a leap into pure adventure.
And what Savina wants, as she very frankly confesses, is the
same thing. If a concrete lover must go with it, then that lover
must be everything that the decorous William Loyd Grove is
not—violent, exigent, savage, inordinate, even a bit gross. I
doubt that Savina gets her wish any more than Randon gets
his. Good business men make but indifferent Grand Turks,
even when they are in revolt: it is the tragedy of Western civilization. And there is no deliverance from the bonds of habit
and appearance, even with a mistress. Ten days after he reaches
Havana, Randon is almost as securely married as he was at
Eastlake. Worse, Eastlake itself reaches out its long arm and
begins to punish him, and Savina with him. The conventions
of Christendom, alas, are not to be spat upon. Far back in the
Cuban hinterland, in a squalid little sugar town, it is a photo-
graph of Fanny that gives a final touch of gruesomeness to the
drama of Randon and Savina. There, overtaken in her sin by
that banal likeness of the enemy she has never seen, she dies
her preposterous death. An ending profoundly ironical. A curtain that gives a final touch of macabre humor to a tale that,

from first to last, is full of the spirit of high comedy. Hergesheimer never devised one more sardonically amusing, and he
never told one with greater skill.

The reviewers, contemplating it, were shocked by his hedo-
nism in trivialities—his unctuous manner of recording the flavor of a drink, the sheen of a fabric, the set of a skirt, the
furnishings of a room. In all that, I suppose, they saw something Babylonish, and against the Constitution. But this hedo-
nism is really as essential a part of Hergesheimer as moral
purpose is part of a Puritan. He looks upon the world, not as a
trial of virtue, but as a beautiful experience—in part, indeed, as
a downright voluptuous experience. If it is elevating to the
soul to observe the fine colors of a sunset, then why is it not
quite as elevating to observe the fine colors of a woman's hair,
the silk of her frock, a piece of old mahogany, a Jack Rose cocktail? Here it is not actually Hergesheimer's delight in beauty
that gives offense, but his inability to differentiate between the
beauty that is also the good and the true, and the beauty that
is simply beauty. As for me, I incline to go with him in his
heresy. It constitutes a valuable antidote to the moral obsession which still hangs over American letters, despite the collapse of the Puritan *Kultur*. It still seems a bit foreign and
bizarre, but that is because we have yet to achieve a complete
emancipation from the International Sunday-school Lessons.
In "Cytherea," as in "Java Head," it gives a warm and exotic
glow to the narrative. That narrative is always recounted, not
by a moralist, but by an artist. He knows how to give an episode color and reality by the artful use of words and the images
that they bring up—how to manage the tempo, the play of
light, the surrounding harmonies. This investiture is always as
much a part of his story as his tale itself. So is his English style,
so abhorrent to grammarians. When he writes a sentence that
is a bit artificial and complex, it is because he is describing something that is itself a bit artificial and complex. When he varies
his rhythms suddenly and sharply, it is not because he is unable
to write in the monotonous sing-song of a rhetoric professor,
but because he doesn't want to write that way. Whatever such
a man writes is *ipso facto* good English. It is not for pedagogues to criticise it, but to try to comprehend it and teach it.
The delusion to the contrary is the cause of much folly.

3
Lardner

A few years ago a young college professor, eager to make a name for himself, brought out a laborious "critical" edition of "Sam Slick," by Judge Thomas C. Haliburton, eighty-seven years after its first publication. It turned out to be quite unreadable—a dreadful series of archaic jocosities about varieties of *Homo americanus* long perished and forgotten, in a dialect now intelligible only to paleophilologists. Sometimes I have a fear that the same fate awaits Ring Lardner. The professors of his own day, of course, are quite unaware of him, save perhaps as a low zany to be enjoyed behind the door. They would no more venture to whoop him up publicly and officially than their predecessors of 1880 would have ventured to whoop up Mark Twain, or their remoter predecessors of 1837 would have dared to say anything for Haliburton. In such matters the academic mind, being chiefly animated by a fear of sneers, works very slowly. So slowly, indeed, does it work that it usually works too late. By the time Mark Twain got into the text-books for sophomores two-thirds of his compositions, as the Young Intellectuals say, had already begun to date; by the time Haliburton was served up as a sandwich between introduction and notes he was already dead. As I say, I suspect sadly that Lardner is doomed to go the same route. His stories, it seems to me, are superbly adroit and amusing; no other contemporary American, sober or gay, writes better. But I doubt that they last: our grandchildren will wonder what they are about. It is not only, or even mainly, that the dialect that fills them will pass, though that fact is obviously a serious handicap in itself. It is principally that the people they depict will pass, that Lardner's Low Down Americans—his incomparable baseball players, pugs, song-writers, Elks, small-town Rotarians and golf caddies—are flitting figures of a transient civilization, and doomed to be a puzzling and soporific, in the year 2000, as Haliburton's Yankee clock peddler is to-day.

The fact—if I may assume it to be a fact—is certain not to be set against Lardner's account; on the contrary, it is, in its way, highly complimentary to him. For he has deliberately applied himself, not to the anatomizing of the general human soul, but to the meticulous histological study of a few salient individuals of his time and nation, and he has done it with such subtle and penetrating skill that one must belong to his time and nation to follow him. I doubt that anyone who is not familiar with professional ball players, intimately and at first hand, will ever comprehend the full merit of the amazing sketches in "You Know Me, Al"; I doubt that anyone who has not given close and deliberate attention to the American vulgate will ever realize how magnificently Lardner handles it. He has had more imitators, I suppose, than any other living American writer, but has he any actual rivals? If so, I have yet to hear of them. They all try to write the speech of the streets as adeptly and as amusingly as he writes it, and they all fall short of him; the next best is miles and miles behind him. And they are all inferior in observation, in sense of character, in shrewdness and insight. His studies, to be sure, are never very profound; he makes no attempt to get at the primary springs of human motive; all his people share the same amiable stupidity, the same transparent vanity, the same shallow swinishness; they are all human Fords in bad repair, and alike at bottom. But if he thus confines himself to the surface, it yet remains a fact that his investigations on that surface are extraordinarily alert, ingenious and brilliant—that the character he finally sets before us, however roughly articulated as to bones, is so astoundingly realistic as to epidermis that the effect is indistinguishable from that of life itself. The old man in "The Golden Honeymoon" is not merely well done; he is perfect. And so is the girl in "Some Like Them Cold." And so, even, is the idiotic Frank X. Farrell in "Alibi Ike"—an extravagant grotesque and yet quite real from glabella to calcaneus.

Lardner knows more about the management of the short story than all of its professors. His stories are built very carefully, and yet they seem to be wholly spontaneous, and even formless. He has grasped the primary fact that no conceivable ingenuity can save a story that fails to show a recognizable and interesting character; he knows that a good character sketch is always a good story, no matter what its structure. Perhaps he gets less attention than he ought to get, even among the anti-academic critics, because his people are all lowly boors. For your reviewer of books, like every other sort of American, is always vastly impressed by fashionable pretensions. He belongs to the white collar class of labor, and shares its prejudices. He praises F. Scott Fitzgerald's stories of country-club flappers eloquently, and overlooks Fitzgerald's other stories, most of which are much better. He can't rid himself of the feeling that Edith Wharton, whose people have butlers, is a better novelist than Willa Cather, whose people, in the main, dine in their kitchens. He lingers under the spell of Henry James, whose most humble character, at any rate of the later years, was at least an Englishman, and hence superior. Lardner, so to speak, hits such critics under the belt. He not only fills his stories with people who read the tabloids, say "Shake hands with my friend," and buy diamond rings on the instalment plan; he also shows them having a good time in the world, and quite devoid of inferiority complexes. They amuse him sardonically, but he does not pity them. A fatal error! The moron, perhaps, has a place in fiction, as in life, but he is not to be treated too easily and casually. It must be shown that he suffers tragically because he cannot abandon the plow to write poetry, or the sample-case to study for opera. Lardner is more realistic. If his typical hero has a secret sorrow it is that he is too old to take up osteopathy and too much in dread of his wife to venture into bootlegging.

Of late a sharply acrid flavor has got into Lardner's buffoonery. His baseball players and fifth-rate pugilists, beginning in his first stories as harmless jackasses, gradually convert themselves into loathsome scoundrels. The same change shows itself in Sinclair Lewis; it is difficult, even for an American, to contemplate the American without yielding to something hard to distinguish from moral indignation. Turn, for example, to the sketches in the volume called "The Love Nest." The first tells the story of a cinema queen married to a magnate of the films. On the surface she seems to be nothing but a noodle, but underneath there is a sewer; the woman is such a pig that she makes one shudder. Again, he investigates another familiar type: the village practical joker. The fellow in one form or other, has been laughed at since the days of Aristophanes. But here is a mercilessly realistic examination of his dunghill humor, and of its effects upon decent people. A third figure is a successful theatrical manager: he turns out to have the professional competence of a chiropractor and the honor of a Prohibition agent. A fourth is a writer of popular songs: stealing other men's ideas has become so fixed a habit with him that he comes to believe that he has an actual right to them. A fourth is a trained nurse—but I spare you this dreadful nurse. The rest are bores of the homicidal type. One gets the effect, communing with the whole gang, of visiting a museum of anatomy. They are as shocking as what one encounters there—but in every detail they are as unmistakably real.

Lardner conceals his new savagery, of course, beneath his old humor. It does not flag. No man writing among us has greater skill at the more extravagant varieties of jocosity. He sees startling and revelatory likeness between immensely disparate things, and he is full of pawky observations and bizarre comments. Two baseball-players are palavering, and one of them, Young Jake, is boasting of his conquests during Spring practice below the Potomac. "Down South ain't here!" replies the other. "Those dames in some of those swamps, they lose their head when they see a man with shoes on!" The two proceed to the discussion of a third imbecile, guilty of some obscure tort. "Why," inquires Young Jake, "didn't you break his nose or bust him in the chin?" "His nose was already broke," replied the other, "and he didn't have no chin." Such wise cracks seem easy to devise. Broadway diverts itself by manufacturing them. They constitute the substance of half the town shows. But in those made by Lardner there is something far more than mere facile humor: they are all rigidly in character, and they illuminate that character. Few American novelists, great or small, have character more firmly in hand. Lardner does not see situations; he sees people. And what people! They are all as revolting as so many Methodist evangelists, and they are all as thoroughly American.

4
Masters

The case of Masters remains mysterious; more, even, than Sherwood Anderson, his fellow fugitive from a Chicago in decay, he presents an enigma to the prayerful critic. On the one hand there stands "The Spoon River Anthology," unquestionably the most eloquent, the most profound and the most thoroughly national volume of poetry published in America since "Leaves of Grass"; on the other hand stands a great mass of feeble doggerel—imitations of Byron, of Browning, of Lowell, of George H. Boker, of all the bad poets since the dawn of the Nineteenth Century. Of late he turns to prose, and with results almost as confusing. In all of his books there are fine touches, and in one of them, "Mitch Miller," there are many of them. But in all of them there are also banalities so crass and so vast that it is almost impossible to imagine a literate man letting them go by. Consider, for example, the novel, "Mirage." It seems to me to be one of the most idiotic and yet one of the most interesting American novels that I have ever read. Whole pages of it are given over to philosophical discussions that recall nothing so much as the palavers of neighboring barbers between shaves, and yet they are intermingled with observations that are shrewd and sound, and that are set forth with excellent grace and no little eloquence. Some of the characters in the book are mere stuffed dummies, creaking in every joint; others stand out as brilliantly alive as the people of Dreiser or Miss Cather. My suspicion is that there are actually two Masterses, that the man is a sort of literary diplococcus. At his worst, he is intolerably affected, arty and artificial—almost a fit companion for the occult, unintelligible geniuses hymned in the *Dial.* At his best he probably gets nearer to the essential truth about the civilization we suffer under than any other contemporary literatus.

"Mirage," I daresay, is already forgotten, though it was published only in 1924. In substance, it is the story of Skeeters Kirby's quest for the Wonder Woman that all sentimentalists seek, and that none of them finds until drink has brought him to his death-bed, and he sees the fat, affable nurse through a purple haze. Skeeters comes from the town of Mitch Miller, and when we first encounter him he is a lawyer in Chicago. Already the search for the Perfect Doll has begun to leave scars upon his psyche. First there was the sweet one who died before he could get her to the altar; then there was the naughty Alicia, his lawful wife, but, as he would say himself, a lemon. As the story opens, Alicia, divorcing him, had just blackmailed him out of $70,000, almost his whole fortune, as the price of her silence about Mrs. Becky Morris. Becky is the widow of a rich old man, and now enjoys the usufruct of his tenements and hereditaments. She has red hair and a charming manner, and is a great liar. She falsely pretends to have read Schopenhauer's "The World as Will and Idea," and passes in her circle as an intellectual on the strength of it. She tells Skeeters that she is virtuous, or, rather, that she *has* been virtuous, and all the while she is carrying on with one Delaher, a handsome frequenter of the Hotel Ritzdorf in New York. A saucy and poisonous baggage, this Becky, but Skeeters falls violently in love with her, and gladly pays Alicia the $70,000 in order to protect her from scandal. But then she leaves him, writes him a letter of farewell, and refuses flatly to marry him, and when he pursues her to New York, confronts her with her adulteries, and throws up to her the fact that he has gone broke for her, she requites him only with a dreadful slanging. I quote the exact text:

Kirby took a drink of brandy from the flask and came to her, taking her in his arms. "Tell, me, dear, what shall we do? Are we engaged?"

Becky shook her head.

"What do you wish? Shall I treat you as my bride-to-be, or shall we go on as we are now?"

"Go on as we are now!"

"You know I am free now—and it cost me, too, to be free."

"How much?"

"Seventy thousand dollars."

"That's not much."

"It's practically all I have."

"Well, *Alicia won't have such a large income out of it.*"

"And I paid it for you."

Becky opened her eyes. Her face became a bonfire of rage. Her red hair bristled like a wild animal's.

"You're just a liar to say that! And you can't say such things in my room. This is my room; *I pay for it.* And *you can be respectful to me here, or you can go.*"

Kirby did not betray his anger. He concentrated it and went on: "*I beg your pardon.*"

In a voice as soft as oil he asked:

"Did you see Delaher?"

"Yes, I did, and he's a rough-neck."

"Well?"

"None of your business!"

"None of my business, eh?" Kirby said, with a bitter intonation.

"Leave my room," Becky said.

"No, I'll not leave your room."

"*I'll have you put out.*"

"You don't dare, Becky—you don't dare!" . . .

Two pages more of this, and then Becky breaks out grandly:

"What do you want, anyway? You have had everything I have to give: my hospitality, *my bread, my wine, my couch, my affection, gift-tokens of my love*—what do you want?"

Kirby explains that he wants a wife and a soul-mate—"a mind to be the companion of my mind." But Becky refuses to marry him. Instead she goes to her bedroom and then returns with Kirby's letters:

"Here are your letters. You've stayed and had your say out. And now that you've said it, you can see for yourself that *you have no case against me. . . .* Here are your letters."

"I don't want them."

"Very well, I'll tear them up."

She proceeded to do so.

"*Now all the evidence is destroyed,*" he said.

I have thrown in a few italics to point the high spots of this singular colloquy. It goes on for page after page, and the whole book is filled with dialogues like it. What is one to make of such inconceivable banality? Is there worse in "An American Tragedy"? But Masters, you may say, is trying to depict eighth-rate people—frequenters of cabarets and hotel grill-rooms, male and female Elks, dubious hangers-on upon the edges of intelligence and decency—and that is how they actually talk. It may be so, but I note at once two objections to that defense. The first is that Masters does not appear to regard Kirby as eighth-rate; on the contrary, he takes the fellow's moony drabbing quite seriously, and even tries to get a touch of the tragic into it. The second is that precisely the same hollow and meaningless fustian often appears when the author speaks in his own person. The way he tells his story is almost precisely the way it would be told by a somewhat intellectual shoe-drummer in a Pullman smoking-room. Its approach to the eternal sex question, its central theme, is exactly that of such a gentleman; its very phrases, in the main, are his phrases. He actually appears, in fact, as a sort of chorus to the drama, under the name of Bob Haydon. Bob, facing disillusion and death, favors Kirby with many cantos of philosophy. Their general burden is that the prudent man, having marked a sweet one to his taste, uses her person to his wicked ends, and then kicks her out. Kirby's agonies do not move Bob, and neither do they bore him. "Bore me!" he exclaims. "This is better than a circus!"

As I say, I have also enjoyed it myself. It is not, indeed, without its flashes of genuine sagacity; even Bob's stockbroker view of the sexual duel, given such a male as Kirby and such females as Becky, is probably more sound than not. But the chief fascination of the story, I am bound to say, lies in its very deficiencies as a human document and a work of art—in its naïve lack of humor, its elaborate laboring of the obvious, its incredible stiltedness and triteness. There are passages that actually suggest Daisy Ashford. For example: "She was biting her nails while talking to Delaher, and biting them after he left. *Then she put on white cotton gloves to prevent this nervous habit.*" Again (Kirby has abandoned Becky for another girl, Charlotte, formerly his stenographer):

> "*May I say something to you?*" she whispered at last.
> "What is it, Charlotte?"
> "I want a child, and a child with you."

Somehow, this "May I say something to you?" gives me vast delight: the respectful politeness of the perfect stenographer surviving into the most confidential of moments! No such child is achieved—Charlotte, in fact, dies before it can be born—, and so we miss her courteous request for permission to name it after its father. But she and Kirby, alas, sin the sin, and what is worse, they sin it under his mother's roof. What is still worse, they do it with her knowledge and connivance. She is greatly taken, in fact, with Charlotte, and advises Kirby to marry her. I quote her argument:

> "If Byron had mistresses he was also a rider and a fencer and a poet; and if Webster may have been a drinker, he was great as a lawyer and a speaker. If Charlotte has had extra-marital relationships, she is a capable housekeeper, a good secretary, a woman skilled in many things;

and she has all kinds of virtues, like humor and self-control, and the spirit of happiness, and an essential honesty."

I leave the rest to posterity! What will it make of Masters as novelist? When it turns from the heroic and lovely lines of "Ann Rutledge" to the astounding banalities of "Mirage" what will it say?

III.

In Memoriam: W.J.B.

Has it been duly marked by historians that the late William Jennings Bryan's last secular act on this globe of sin was to catch flies? A curious detail, and not without its sardonic overtones. He was the most sedulous fly-catcher in American history, and in many ways the most successful. His quarry, of course, was not *Musca domestica* but *Homo neandertalensis*. For forty years he tracked it with coo and bellow, up and down the rustic backways of the Republic. Wherever the flambeaux of Chautauqua smoked and guttered, and the bilge of Idealism ran in the veins, and Baptist pastors dammed the brooks with the sanctified, and men gathered who were weary and heavy laden, and their wives who were full of Peruna and as fecund as the shad (*Alosa sapidissima*)—there the indefatigable Jennings set up his traps and spread his bait. He knew every country town in the South and West, and he could crowd the most remote of them to suffocation by simply winding his horn. The city proletariat, transiently flustered by him in 1896, quickly penetrated his buncombe and would have no more of him; the cockney gallery jeered him at every Democratic national convention for twenty-five years. But out where the grass grows high, and the horned cattle dream away the lazy afternoons, and men still fear the powers and principalities of the air—out there between the corn-rows he held his old puissance to the end. There was no need of beaters to drive in his game. The news that he was coming was enough. For miles the flivver dust would choke the roads. And when he rose at the end of the day to discharge his Message there would be such breathless attention, such a rapt and enchanted ecstasy, such a sweet rustle of amens as the world had not known since Johann fell to Herod's ax.

There was something peculiarly fitting in the fact that his last days were spent in a one-horse Tennessee village, and that death found him there. The man felt at home in such simple and Christian scenes. He liked people who sweated freely, and were not debauched by the refinements of the toilet. Making his progress up and down the Main street of little Dayton, surrounded by gaping primates from the upland valleys of the Cumberland Range, his coat laid aside, his bare arms and hairy chest shining damply, his bald head sprinkled with dust—so accoutred and on display he was obviously happy. He liked getting up early in the morning, to the tune of cocks crowing on the dunghill. He liked the heavy, greasy victuals of the farmhouse kitchen. He liked country lawyers, country pastors, all country people. He liked the country sounds and country smells. I believe that this liking was sincere—perhaps the only sincere thing in the man. His nose showed no uneasiness when a hillman in faded overalls and hickory shirt accosted him on the street, and besought him for light upon some mystery of Holy Writ. The simian gabble of the cross-roads was not gabble to him, but wisdom of an occult and superior sort. In the presence of city folks he was palpably uneasy. Their clothes, I suspect, annoyed him, and he was suspicious of their too delicate manners. He knew all the while that they were laughing at him—if not at his baroque theology, then at least at his alpaca pantaloons. But the yokels never laughed at him. To them he was not the huntsman but the prophet, and toward the end, as he gradually forsook mundane politics for more ghostly concerns, they began to elevate him in their hierarchy. When he died he was the peer of Abraham. His old enemy, Wilson, aspiring to the same white and shining robe, came down with a thump. But Bryan made the grade. His place in Tennessee hagiography is secure. If the village barber saved any of his hair, then it is curing gall-stones down there to-day.

But what label will he bear in more urbane regions? One, I fear, of a far less flattering kind. Bryan lived too long, and descended too deeply into the mud, to be taken seriously hereafter by fully literate men, even of the kind who write schoolbooks. There was a scattering of sweet words in his funeral notices, but it was no more than a response to conventional sentimentality. The best verdict the most romantic editorial writer could dredge up, save in the humorless South, was to the general effect that his imbecilities were excused by his earnestness—that under his clowning, as under that of the juggler of Notre Dame, there was the zeal of a steadfast soul. But this was apology, not praise; precisely the same thing might be said of Mary Baker G. Eddy, the late Czar Nicholas, or Czolgosz. The truth is that even Bryan's sincerity will probably yield to what is called, in other fields, definitive criticism. Was he sincere when he opposed imperialism in the Philippines, or when he fed it with deserving Democrats in Santo Domingo? Was he sincere when he tried to shove the Prohibitionists under the table, or when he seized their banner and began to lead them with loud whoops? Was he sincere when he bellowed against war, or when he dreamed of himself as a tin-soldier in uniform, with a grave reserved among the generals? Was he sincere when he denounced the late John W. Davis, or when he swallowed Davis? Was he sincere when he fawned over Champ Clark, or when he betrayed Clark? Was he sincere when he pleaded for tolerance in New York, or when he bawled for the faggot and the stake in Tennessee?

This talk of sincerity, I confess, fatigues me. If the fellow was sincere, then so was P. T. Barnum. The word is disgraced and degraded by such uses. He was, in fact, a charlatan, a mountebank, a zany without shame or dignity. His career brought him into contact with the first men of his time; he preferred the company of rustic ignoramuses. It was hard to believe, watching him at Dayton, that he had traveled, that he had been received in civilized societies, that he had been a high officer of state. He seemed only a poor clod like those around him, deluded by a childish theology, full of an almost pathological hatred of all learning, all human dignity, all beauty, all fine and noble things. He was a peasant come home to the barnyard. Imagine a gentleman, and you have imagined everything that he was not. What animated him from end to end of his grotesque career was simply ambition—the ambition of a common man to get his hand upon the collar of his superiors, or, failing that, to get his thumb into their eyes. He was born with a roaring voice, and it had the trick of inflaming half-wits. His whole career was devoted to raising those half-wits against their betters, that he himself might shine. His last battle will be grossly misunderstood if it is thought of as a mere exercise in fanaticism—that is, if Bryan the Fundamentalist Pope is mistaken for one of the bucolic Fundamentalists. There was much more in it than that, as everyone knows who saw him on the

field. What moved him, at bottom, was simply hatred of the
city men who had laughed at him so long, and brought him at
last to so tatterdemalion an estate. He lusted for revenge upon
them. He yearned to lead the anthropoid rabble against them,
to punish them for their execution upon him by attacking the
very vitals of their civilization. He went far beyond the bounds
of any merely religious frenzy, however inordinate. When he
began denouncing the notion that man is a mammal even
some of the hinds at Dayton were agape. And when, brought
upon Darrow's cruel hook, he writhed and tossed in a very
fury of malignancy, bawling against the baldest elements of
sense and decency like a man frantic—when he came to that
tragic climax of his striving there were snickers among the
hinds as well as hosannas.

Upon that hook, in truth, Bryan committed suicide, as a legend as well as in the body. He staggered from the rustic court
ready to die, and he staggered from it ready to be forgotten,
save as a character in a third-rate farce, witless and in poor
taste. It was plain to everyone who knew him, when he came
to Dayton, that his great days were behind him—that, for all
the fury of his hatred, he was now definitely an old man, and
headed at last for silence. There was a vague, unpleasant mangi-
ness about his appearance; he somehow seemed dirty, though
a close glance showed him as carefully shaven as an actor, and
clad in immaculate linen. All the hair was gone from the dome
of his head, and it had begun to fall out, too, behind his ears,
in the obscene manner of the late Samuel Gompers. The reso-
nance had departed from his voice; what was once a bugle
blast had become reedy and quavering. Who knows that, like
Demosthenes, he had a lisp? In the old days, under the magic
of his eloquence, no one noticed it. But when he spoke at Dayton it was always audible.

When I first encountered him, on the sidewalk in front of
the office of the rustic lawyers who were his associates in the
Scopes case, the trial was yet to begin, and so he was still expansive and amiable. I had printed in the *Nation*, a week or so
before, an article arguing that the Tennessee anti-evolution
law, whatever its wisdom, was at least constitutional—that the
rustics of the State had a clear right to have their progeny
taught whatever they chose, and kept secure from whatever

knowledge violated their superstitions. The old boy professed to be delighted with the argument, and gave the gaping bystanders to understand that I was a publicist of parts. Not to be outdone, I admired the preposterous country shirt that he wore—sleeveless and with the neck cut very low. We parted in the manner of two ambassadors. But that was the last touch of amiability that I was destined to see in Bryan. The next day the battle joined and his face became hard. By the end of the week he was simply a walking fever. Hour by hour he grew more bitter. What the Christian Scientists call malicious animal magnetism seemed to radiate from him like heat from a stove. From my place in the courtroom, standing upon a table, I looked directly down upon him, sweating horribly and pumping his palm-leaf fan. His eyes fascinated me; I watched them all day long. They were blazing points of hatred. They glittered like occult and sinister gems. Now and then they wandered to me, and I got my share, for my reports of the trial had come back to Dayton, and he had read them. It was like coming under fire.

Thus he fought his last fight, thirsting savagely for blood. All sense departed from him. He bit right and left, like a dog with rabies. He descended to demagogy so dreadful that his very associates at the trial table blushed. His one yearning was to keep his yokels heated up—to lead his forlorn mob of imbeciles against the foe. That foe, alas, refused to be alarmed. It insisted upon seeing the whole battle as a comedy. Even Darrow, who knew better, occasionally yielded to the prevailing spirit. One day he lured poor Bryan into the folly I have mentioned: his astounding argument against the notion that man is a mammal. I am glad I heard it, for otherwise I'd never believe in it. There stood the man who had been thrice a candidate for the Presidency of the Republic—there he stood in the glare of the world, uttering stuff that a boy of eight would laugh at! The artful Darrow led him on: he repeated it, ranted for it, bellowed it in his cracked voice. So he was prepared for the final slaughter. He came into life a hero, a Galahad, in bright and shining armor. He was passing out a poor mountebank.

The chances are that history will put the peak of democracy in America in his time; it has been on the downward curve among us since the campaign of 1896. He will be remembered perhaps, as its supreme impostor, the *reductio ad absurdum* of its pretension. Bryan came very near being President. In 1896, it is possible, he was actually elected. He lived long enough to make patriots thank the inscrutable gods for Harding, even for Coolidge. Dullness has got into the White House, and the smell of cabbage boiling, but there is at least nothing to compare to the intolerable buffoonery that went on in Tennessee. The President of the United States may be an ass, but he at least doesn't believe that the earth is square, and that witches should be put to death, and that Jonah swallowed the whale. The Golden Text is not painted weekly on the White House wall, and there is no need to keep ambassadors waiting while Pastor Simpson, of Smithville, prays for rain in the Blue Room. We have escaped something—by a narrow margin, but still we have escaped.

That is, so far. The Fundamentalists, once apparently sweeping all before them, now face minorities prepared for battle even in the South—here and there with some assurance of success. But it is too early, it seems to me, to send the firemen home; the fire is still burning on many a far-flung hill, and it may begin to roar again at any moment. The evil that men do lives after them. Bryan, in his malice, started something that it will not be easy to stop. In ten thousand country towns his old heelers, the evangelical pastors, are propagating his gospel, and everywhere the yokels are ready for it. When he disappeared from the big cities, the big cities made the capital error of assuming that he was done for. If they heard of him at all, it was only as a crimp for real-estate speculators—the heroic foe of the unearned increment hauling it in with both hands. He seemed preposterous, and hence harmless. But all the while he was busy among his old lieges, preparing for a *jacquerie* that should floor all his enemies at one blow. He did his job competently. He had vast skill at such enterprises. Heave an egg out of a Pullman window, and you will hit a Fundamentalist almost everywhere in the United States to-day. They swarm in the country towns, inflamed by their *shamans*, and with a saint, now, to venerate. They are thick in the mean streets behind the gas-works. They are everywhere where learning is too heavy a burden for mortal minds to carry, even the vague, pathetic learning on tap in little red schoolhouses. They march with the Klan, with the Christian Endeavor Society, with the Junior Order of United American Mechanics, with the Epworth League, with all the rococo bands that poor and unhappy folk organize to bring some light of purpose into their lives. They have had a thrill, and they are ready for more.

Such is Bryan's legacy to his country. He couldn't be President, but he could at least help magnificently in the solemn business of shutting off the Presidency from every intelligent and self-respecting man. The storm, perhaps, won't last long, as time goes in history. It may help, indeed, to break up the democratic delusion, now already showing weakness, and so hasten its own end. But while it lasts it will blow off some roofs.

IV.
The Hills of Zion

IT was hot weather when they tried the infidel Scopes at Dayton, but I went down there very willingly, for I had good reports of the sub-Potomac bootleggers, and moreover I was eager to see something of evangelical Christianity as a going concern. In the big cities of the Republic, despite the endless efforts of consecrated men, it is laid up with a wasting disease. The very Sunday-school superintendents, taking jazz from the stealthy radio, shake their fire-proof legs; their pupils, moving into adolescence, no longer respond to the proliferating hormones by enlisting for missionary service in Africa, but resort to necking and petting instead. I know of no evangelical church from Oregon to Maine that is not short of money: the graft begins to peter out, like wire-tapping and three-card monte before it. Even in Dayton, though the mob was up to do execution upon Scopes, there was a strong smell of antinomianism. The nine churches of the village were all half empty on Sunday, and weeds choked their yards. Only two or three of the resident pastors managed to sustain themselves by their ghostly science; the rest had to take orders for mail-order pantaloons or work in the adjacent strawberry fields; one, I heard, was a barber. On the courthouse green a score of sweating theologians debated the darker passages of Holy Writ day and night, but I soon found that they were all volunteers, and that the local faithful, while interested in their exegesis as an intellectual exercise, did not permit it to impede the indigenous debaucheries. Exactly twelve minutes after I reached the village I was taken in tow by a Christian man and introduced to the favorite tipple of the Cumberland Range: half corn liquor and half coco-cola. It seemed a dreadful dose to me, spoiled as I was by the bootleg light wines and beers of the Eastern seaboard, but I found that the Dayton illuminati got it down with gusto, rubbing their tummies and rolling their eyes. I include among them the chief local proponents of the Mosaic cosmogony. They were all hot for Genesis, but their faces were far too florid to belong to teetotalers, and when a pretty girl came tripping down the Main street, which was very often, they reached for the places where their neckties should have been with all the amorous enterprise of movie actors. It seemed somehow strange.

An amiable newspaper woman of Chattanooga, familiar with those uplands, presently enlightened me. Dayton, she explained, was simply a great capital like any other great capital. That is to say, it was to Rhea county what Atlanta was to Georgia or Paris to France. That is to say, it was predominantly epicurean and sinful. A country girl from some remote valley of the county, coming into town for her semi-annual bottle of Lydia Pinkham's Vegetable Compound, shivered on approaching Robinson's drug-store quite as a country girl from up-State New York might shiver on approaching the Metropolitan Opera House or the Ritz Hotel. In every village lout she saw a potential white-slaver. The hard sidewalks hurt her feet. Temptations of the flesh bristled to all sides of her, luring her to hell. This newspaper woman told me of a session with just such a visitor, holden a few days before. The latter waited outside one of the town hot-dog and coco-cola shops while her husband negotiated with a hardware merchant across the street. The newspaper woman, idling along and observing that the stranger was badly used by the heat, invited her to step into the shop for a glass of coca-cola. The invitation brought forth only a gurgle of terror. Coca-cola, it quickly appeared, was prohibited by the country lady's pastor, as a levantine and hell-sent narcotic. He also prohibited coffee and tea—and pies! He had his doubts about white bread and boughten meat. The newspaper woman, interested, inquired about ice-cream. It was, she found, not specifically prohibited, but going into a coca-cola shop to get it would be clearly sinful. So she offered to get a saucer of it, and bring it out to the sidewalk. The visitor vacillated—and came near being lost. But God saved her in the nick of time. When the newspaper woman emerged from the place she was in full flight up the street! Later on her husband, mounted on a mule, overtook her four miles out the mountain pike.

This newspaper woman, whose kindness covered city infidels as well as Alpine Christians, offered to take me back in the hills to a place where the old-time religion was genuinely on tap. The Scopes jury, she explained was composed mainly of its customers, with a few Dayton sophisticates added to leaven the mass. It would thus be instructive to climb the heights and observe the former at their ceremonies. The trip, fortunately, might be made by automobile. There was a road running out of Dayton to Morgantown, in the mountains to the westward, and thence beyond. But foreigners, it appeared, would have to approach the sacred grove cautiously, for the upland worshipers were very shy, and at the first sight of a strange face they would adjourn their orgy and slink into the forest. They were not to be feared, for God had long since forbidden them to practice assassination, or even assault, but if they were alarmed a rough trip would go for naught. So, after dreadful bumpings up a long and narrow road, we parked our car in a little woodpath a mile or two beyond the tiny village of Morgantown, and made the rest of the approach on foot, deployed like skirmishers. Far off in a dark, romantic glade a flickering light was visible, and out of the silence came the rumble of exhortation. We could distinguish the figure of the preacher only as a moving mote in the light: it was like looking down the tube of a dark-field microscope. Slowly and cautiously we crossed what seemed to be a pasture, and then we crouched down along the edge of a cornfield, and stealthily edged further and further. The light now grew larger and we could begin to make out what was going on. We went ahead on all fours, like snakes in the grass.

From the great limb of a mighty oak hung a couple of crude torches of the sort that car inspectors thrust under Pullman cars when a train pulls in at night. In the guttering glare was the preacher, and for a while we could see no one else. He was an immensely tall and thin mountaineer in blue jeans, his collarless shirt open at the neck and his hair a tousled mop. As he preached he paced up and down under the smoking flambeaux, and at each turn he thrust his arms into the air and yelled "Glory to God!" We crept nearer in the shadow of the cornfield, and began to hear more of his discourse. He was preaching on the Day of Judgment. The high kings of the earth, he roared, would all fall down and die; only the sanctified would stand up to receive the Lord God of Hosts. One of these kings he mentioned by name, the king of what he called Greece-y. The king of Greece-y, he said, was doomed to hell. We crawled forward a few more yards and began to see the audience. It was seated on benches ranged round the preacher in a circle. Behind him sat a row of elders, men and women. In front were the younger folk. We crept on cautiously, and individuals rose out of the ghostly gloom. A young mother sat suckling her baby, rocking as the preacher paced up and down. Two scared little girls hugged each other, their pigtails down their backs. An immensely huge mountain woman, in a gingham dress, cut in one piece, rolled on her heels at every "Glory to God!" To one side, and but half visible, was what appeared to be a bed. We found afterward that half a dozen babies were asleep upon it.

The preacher stopped at last, and there arose out of the darkness a woman with her hair pulled back into a tight knot. She began so quietly that we couldn't hear what she said, but soon her voice rose resonantly and we could follow her. She was denouncing the reading of books. Some wandering book agent, it appeared, had come to her cabin and tried to sell her a specimen of his wares. She refused to touch it. Why, indeed, read a book? If what was in it was true, then everything in it was already in the Bible. If it was false, then reading it would imperil the soul. This syllogism from Caliph Omar complete, she sat down. There followed a hymn, led by a somewhat fat brother wearing silver-rimmed country spectacles. It droned on for a half a dozen stanzas, and then the first speaker resumed the floor. He argued that the gift of tongues was real and that education was a snare. Once his children could read the Bible, he said, they had enough. Beyond lay only infidelity and damnation. Sin stalked the cities. Dayton itself was a Sodom. Even Morgantown had begun to forget God. He sat down, and a female aurochs in gingham got up. She began quietly, but was soon leaping and roaring, and it was hard to follow her. Under cover of the turmoil we sneaked a bit closer.

A couple of other discourses followed, and there were two or three hymns. Suddenly a change of mood began to make itself felt. The last hymn ran longer than the others, and dropped gradually into a monotonous, unintelligible chant. The leader beat time with his book. The faithful broke out with exulta-

tions. When the singing ended there was a brief palaver that
we could not hear, and two of the men moved a bench into
the circle of light directly under the flambeaux. Then a half-
grown girl emerged from the darkness and threw herself upon
it. We noticed with astonishment that she had bobbed hair.
"This sister," said the leader, "has asked for prayers." We
moved a bit closer. We could now see faces plainly, and hear
every word. What followed quickly reached such heights of
barbaric grotesquerie that it was hard to believe it real. At a
signal all the faithful crowded up to the bench and began to
pray—not in unison, but each for himself! At another they all
fell on their knees, their arms over the penitent. The leader
kneeled facing us, his head alternately thrown back dramatically or buried in his hands. Words spouted from his lips like
bullets from a machine-gun—appeals to God to pull the penitent back out of hell, defiances of the demons of the air, a vast
impassioned jargon of apocalyptic texts. Suddenly he rose to
his feet, threw back his head and began to speak in the tongues
—blub-blub-blub, gurgle-gurgle-gurgle. His voice rose to a
higher register. The climax was a shrill, inarticulate squawk,
like that of a man throttled. He fell headlong across the pyra-
mid of suppliants.

A comic scene? Somehow, no. The poor half-wits were too
horribly in earnest. It was like peeping through a knothole at
the writhings of people in pain. From the squirming and jab-
bering mass a young woman gradually detached herself—a
woman not uncomely, with a pathetic homemade cap on her
head. Her head jerked back, the veins of her neck swelled, and
her fists went to her throat as if she were fighting for breath.
She bent backward until she was like half a hoop. Then she
suddenly snapped forward. We caught a flash of the whites of
her eyes. Presently her whole body began to be convulsed—
great throes that began at the shoulders and ended at the hips.
She would leap to her feet, thrust her arms in air, and then hurl
herself upon the heap. Her praying flattened out into a mere
delirious caterwauling, like that of a Tom cat on a petting
party. I describe the thing discreetly, and as a strict behaviorist.
The lady's subjective sensations I leave to infidel pathologists,
privy to the works of Ellis, Freud and Moll. Whatever they were,
they were obviously not painful, for they were accompanied by

vast heavings and gurglings of a joyful and even ecstatic nature. And they seemed to be contagious, too, for soon a second penitent, also female, joined the first, and then came a
third, and a fourth, and a fifth. The last one had an extraordinary violent attack. She began with mild enough jerks of the
head, but in a moment she was bounding all over the place,
like a chicken with its head cut off. Every time her head came up
a stream of hosannas would issue out of it. Once she collided
with a dark, undersized brother, hitherto silent and stolid. Contact with her set him off as if he had been kicked by a mule. He
leaped into the air, threw back his head, and began to gargle as
if with a mouthful of BB shot. Then he loosed one tremendous, stentorian sentence in the tongues, and collapsed.

By this time the performers were quite oblivious to the profane universe and so it was safe to go still closer. We left our
hiding and came up to the little circle of light. We slipped into
the vacant seats on one of the rickety benches. The heap of
mourners was directly before us. They bounced into us as they
cavorted. The smell that they radiated, sweating there in that
obscene heap, half suffocated us. Not all of them, of course,
did the thing in the grand manner. Some merely moaned and
rolled their eyes. The female ox in gingham flung her great
bulk on the ground and jabbered an unintelligible prayer. One
of the men, in the intervals between fits, put on his spectacles
and read his Bible. Beside me on the bench sat the young
mother and her baby. She suckled it through the whole orgy,
obviously fascinated by what was going on, but never venturing to take any hand in it. On the bed just outside the light
half a dozen other babies slept peacefully. In the shadows, suddenly appearing and as suddenly going away, were vague figures, whether of believers or of scoffers I do not know. They
seemed to come and go in couples. Now and then a couple at
the ringside would step out and vanish into the black night.
After a while some came back, the males looking somewhat
sheepish. There was whispering outside the circle of vision. A
couple of Fords lurched up the road, cutting holes in the darkness with their lights. Once some one out of sight loosed a
bray of laughter.

All this went on for an hour or so. The original penitent, by
this time, was buried three deep beneath the heap. One caught

a glimpse, now and then, of her yellow bobbed hair, but then she would vanish again. How she breathed down there I don't know; it was hard enough six feet away, with a strong five-cent cigar to help. When the praying brothers would rise up for a bout with the tongues their faces were streaming with perspiration. The fat harridan in gingham sweated like a longshoreman. Her hair got loose and fell down over her face. She fanned herself with her skirt. A powerful old gal she was, plainly equal in her day to a bout with obstetrics and a week's washing on the same morning, but this was worse than a week's washing. Finally, she fell into a heap, breathing in great, convulsive gasps.

Finally, we got tired of the show and returned to Dayton. It was nearly eleven o'clock—an immensely late hour for those latitudes —but the whole town was still gathered in the court-house yard, listening to the disputes of theologians. The Scopes trial had brought them in from all directions. There was a friar wearing a sandwich sign announcing that he was the Bible champion of the world. There was a Seventh Day Adventist arguing that Clarence Darrow was the beast with seven heads and ten horns described in Revelation xiii, and that the end of the world was at hand. There was an evangelist made up like Andy Gump, with the news that atheists in Cincinnati were preparing to descend upon Dayton, hang the eminent Judge Raulston, and burn the town. There was an ancient who maintained that no Catholic could be a Christian. There was the eloquent Dr. T. T. Martin, of Blue Mountain, Miss., come to town with a truck-load of torches and hymn-books to put Darwin in his place. There was a singing brother bellowing apocalyptic hymns. There was William Jennings Bryan, followed everywhere by a gaping crowd. Dayton was having a roaring time. It was better than the circus. But the note of devotion was simply not there; the Daytonians, after listening a while, would slip away to Robinson's drug-store to regale themselves with coca-cola, or to the lobby of the Aqua Hotel, where the learned Raulston sat in state, judicially picking his teeth. The real religion was not present. It began at the bridge over the town creek, where the road makes off for the hills.

V.

Beethoven

BEETHOVEN was one of those lucky men whose stature, viewed in retrospect, grows steadily. How many movements have there been to put him on the shelf? At least a dozen in the hundred years since his death. There was one only a few years ago in New York, launched by idiot critics and supported by the war fever: his place, it appeared, was to be taken by such prophets of the new enlightenment as Stravinsky! The net result of that movement was simply that the best orchestra in America went to pot—and Beethoven survived unscathed. It is, indeed, almost impossible to imagine displacing him—at all events, in the concert-hall, where the challenge of Bach cannot reach him. Surely the Nineteenth Century was not deficient in master musicians. It produced Schubert, Schumann, Chopin, Wagner and Brahms, to say nothing of a whole horde of Dvořáks, Tschaikowskys, Debussys, Raffs, Verdis and Puccinis. Yet it gave us nothing better than the first movement of the Eroica. That movement, the first challenge of the new music, remains its last word. It is the noblest piece of absolute music ever written in the sonata form, and it is the noblest piece of program music. In Beethoven, indeed, the distinction between the two became purely imaginary. Everything he wrote was, in a way, program music, including even the first two symphonies, and everything was absolute music, including even the Battle grotesquerie. (Is the latter, indeed, as bad as ancient report makes it? Why doesn't some *Kappellmeister* let us hear it?)

It was a bizarre jest of the gods to pit Beethoven, in his first days in Vienna, against Papa Haydn. Haydn was undeniably a genius of the first water, and, after Mozart's death, had no apparent reason to fear a rival. If he did not actually create the symphony as we know it to-day, then he at least enriched the form with its first genuine masterpieces—and not with a scant few, but literally with dozens. Tunes of the utmost loveliness gushed from him like oil from a well. More, he knew how to manage them; he was a master of musical architectonics. If his music is sniffed at to-day, then it is only by fools; there are at least six of his symphonies that are each worth all the cacophony hatched by a whole herd of Schönbergs and Eric Saties, with a couple of Korngolds thrown in to flavor the pot. But when Beethoven stepped in, then poor old Papa had to step down. It was like pitting a gazelle against an aurochs. One colossal bellow, and the combat was over. Musicians are apt to look at it as a mere contest of technicians. They point to the vastly greater skill and ingenuity of Beethoven—his firmer grip upon his materials, his greater daring and resourcefulness, his far better understanding of dynamics, rhythms and clang-tints —in brief, his tremendously superior musicianship. But that was not what made him so much greater than Haydn—for Haydn, too, had his superiorities; for example, his far readier inventiveness, his capacity for making better tunes. What lifted Beethoven above the old master, and above all other men of music save perhaps Bach and Brahms, was simply his greater dignity as a man. The feelings that Haydn put into tone were the feelings of a country pastor, a rather civilized stockbroker, a viola player gently mellowed by Kulmbacher. When he wept it was with the tears of a woman who has discovered another wrinkle; when he rejoiced it was with the joy of a child on Christmas morning. But the feelings that Beethoven put into his music were the feelings of a god. There was something olympian in his snarls and rages, and there was a touch of hell-fire in his mirth.

It is almost a literal fact that there is not a trace of cheapness in the whole body of his music. He is never sweet and romantic; he never sheds conventional tears; he never strikes orthodox attitudes. In his lightest moods there is the immense and inescapable dignity of the ancient Hebrew prophets. He concerns himself, not with the puerile agonies of love, but with the eternal tragedy of man. He is a great tragic poet, and like all great tragic poets, he is obsessed by a sense of the inscrutable meaninglessness of life. From the Eroica onward he seldom departs from that theme. It roars through the first movement of the C minor, and it comes to a stupendous final statement in the Ninth. All this, in his day, was new in music, and so it caused murmurs of surprise and even indignation.

The step from Mozart's Jupiter to the first movement of the Eroica was uncomfortable; the Viennese began to wriggle in their stalls. But there was one among them who didn't wriggle, and that was Franz Schubert. Turn to the first movement of his Unfinished or to the slow movement of his Tragic, and you will see how quickly the example of Beethoven was followed—and with what genius! But there was a long hiatus after that, with Mendelssohn, Weber, Chopin and company performing upon their pretty pipes. Eventually the day of November 6, 1876, dawned in Karlsruhe, and with it came the first performance of Brahms' C minor. Once more the gods walked in the concert-hall. They will walk again when another Brahms is born, but not before. For nothing can come out of an artist that is not in the man. What ails the music of all the Tschaikowskys, Stravinskys—and Strausses? What ails it is that it is the music of shallow men. It is often, in its way, lovely. It bristles with charming musical ideas. It is infinitely ingenious and workmanlike. But it is as hollow, at bottom, as a bull by Bishop Manning. It is the music of second-rate men.

Beethoven disdained all their artifices: he didn't need them. It would be hard to think of a composer, even of the fourth rate, who worked with thematic material of less intrinsic merit. He borrowed tunes wherever he found them; he made them up out of snatches of country jigs; when he lacked one altogether he contented himself with a simple phrase, a few banal notes. All such things he viewed simply as raw materials; his interest was concentrated upon their use. To that use of them he brought the appalling powers of his unrivaled genius. His ingenuity began where that of other men left off. His most complicated structures retained the overwhelming clarity of the Parthenon. And into them he got a kind of feeling that even the Greeks could seldom match; he was preëminently a modern man, with all trace of the barbarian vanished. In his gorgeous music there went all of the high skepticism that was of the essence of the Eighteenth Century, but into it there also went the new enthusiasm, the new determination to challenge and beat the gods, that dawned with the Nineteenth.

The older I grow, the more I am convinced that the most portentous phenomenon in the whole history of music was the first public performance of the Eroica on April 7, 1805. The

manufacturers of program notes have swathed that gigantic
work in so many layers of childish legend and speculation that
its intrinsic merits have been almost forgotten. Was it dedicated to Napoleon I? If so, was the dedication sincere or ironical? Who cares—that is, who with ears? It might have been
dedicated, just as well, to Louis XIV, Paracelsus or Pontius Pi-
late. What makes it worth discussing, to-day and forever, is the
fact that on its very first page Beethoven threw his hat into the
ring and laid his claim to immortality. Bang!—and he is off!
No compromise! No easy bridge from the past! The Second
Symphony is already miles behind. A new order of music has
been born. The very manner of it is full of challenge. There is
no sneaking into the foul business by way of a mellifluous and
disarming introduction; no preparatory hemming and hawing
to cajole the audience and enable the conductor to find his
place in the score. Nay! Out of silence comes the angry crash
of the tonic triad, and then at once, with no pause, the first
statement of the first subject—grim, domineering, harsh, raucous, and yet curiously lovely—with its astounding collision
with that electrical C sharp. The carnage has begun early; we
are only in the seventh measure! In the thirteenth and fourteenth comes the incomparable roll down the simple scale of E
flat—and what follows is all that has ever been said, perhaps all
that ever *will* be said, about music-making in the grand manner. What was afterward done, even by Beethoven, was done
in the light of that perfect example. Every line of modern music
that is honestly music bears some sort of relation to that
epoch-making first movement.

The rest is Beethovenish, but not quintessence. There is a
legend that the funeral march was put in simply because it was
a time of wholesale butchery, and funeral marches were in
fashion. No doubt the first-night audience in Vienna, shocked
and addled by the piled-up defiances of the first movement,
found the lugubrious strains grateful. But the *scherzo?* Another
felonious assault upon poor Papa Haydn! Two giants boxing
clumsily, to a crazy piping by an orchestra of dwarfs. No
wonder some honest Viennese in the gallery yelled: "I'd give
another kreutzer if the thing would stop!" Well, it stopped
finally, and then came something reassuring—a theme with
variations. Everyone   in   Vienna   knew   and   esteemed

Beethoven's themes with variations. He was, in fact, the rising master of themes with variations in the town. But a joker remained in the pack. The variations grew more and more complex and surprising. Strange novelties got into them. The polite exercises became tempestuous, moody, cacophonous, tragic. At the end a harsh, hammering, exigent row of chords—the C minor Symphony casting its sinister shadow before!

It must have been a great night in Vienna. But perhaps not for the actual Viennese. They went to hear "a new grand symphony in D sharp" (*sic!*). What they found in the Theater-an-der-Wien was a revolution!

VI.

Rondo on an Ancient Theme

IT is the economic emancipation of woman, I suppose, that must be blamed for the present wholesale discussion of the sex question, so offensive to the romantic. Eminent authorities have full often described, and with the utmost heat and eloquence, her state before she was delivered from her fetters and turned loose to root or die. Almost her only feasible trade, in those dark days, was that of wife. True enough, she might also become a servant girl, or go to work in a factory, or offer herself upon the streets, but all of those vocations were so revolting that no rational woman followed them if she could help it: she would leave any one of them at a moment's notice at the call of a man, for the call of a man meant promotion for her, economically and socially. The males of the time, knowing what a boon they had to proffer, drove hard bargains. They demanded a long list of high qualities in the woman they summoned to their seraglios, but most of all they demanded what they called virtue. It was not sufficient that a candidate should be anatomically undefiled; she must also be pure in mind. There was, of course, but one way to keep her so pure, and that was by building a high wall around her mind, and hitting her with a club every time she ventured to peer over it. It was as dangerous, in that Christian era, for a woman to show any interest in or knowledge of the great physiological farce of sex as it would be to-day for a presidential candidate to reveal himself in his cups on the hustings. Everyone knew, to be sure, that as a mammal she had sex, and that as a potential wife and mother she probably had some secret interest in its phenomena, but it was felt, perhaps wisely, that even the most academic theorizing had within it the deadly germs of the experimental method, and so she was forbidden to think about the matter at all, and whatever information she acquired at all she had to acquire by a method of bootlegging.

The generation still on its legs has seen the almost total collapse of that naïve and constabulary system, and of the economic structure supporting it. Beginning with the eighties of the last century, there rose up a harem rebellion which quickly knocked both to pieces. The women of the Western World not only began to plunge heroically into all of the old professions, hitherto sacred to men; they also began to invent a lot of new professions, many of them unimagined by men. Worse, they began to succeed in them. The working woman of the old days worked only until she could snare a man; any man was better than her work. But the working woman of the new days was under no such pressure; her work made her a living and sometimes more than a living; when a man appeared in her net she took two looks at him, one of them usually very searching, before landing him. The result was an enormous augmentation of her feeling of self-sufficiency, her spirit of independence, her natural inclination to get two sides into the bargaining. The result, secondarily, was a revolt against all the old taboos that had surrounded her, all the childish incapacities and ignorances that had been forced upon her. The result, tertiarily, was a vast running amok in the field that, above all others, had been forbidden to her: that of sexual knowledge and experiment.

We now suffer from the effects of that running amok. It is women, not men, who are doing all the current gabbling about sex, and proposing all the new-fangled modifications of the rules and regulations ordained by God, and they are hard at it very largely, I suppose, because being at it at all is a privilege that is still new to them. The whole order of human females, in other words, is passing through a sort of intellectual adolescence, and it is disturbed as greatly as biological adolescents are by the spouting of the hormones. The attitude of men toward the sex question, it seems to me, has not changed greatly in my time. Barring a few earnest men whose mental processes, here as elsewhere, are essentially womanish, they still view it somewhat jocosely. Taking one with another, they believe that they know all about it that is worth knowing, and so it does not challenge their curiosity, and they do not put in much time discussing it, save mockingly. But among the women, if a bachelor may presume to judge, interest in it is intense. They want to know all that is known about it, all that has been guessed and theorized about it; they bristle with ideas of their own about it. It is hard to find a reflective woman, in these days, who is not harboring some new and startling scheme for curing the evils of monogamous marriage; it is impossible to find any woman who has not given ear to such schemes. Women, not men, read the endless books upon the subject that now rise mountain-high in all the book-stores, and women, not men, discuss and rediscuss the notions in them. An acquaintance of mine, a distinguished critic, owns a copy of one of the most revolutionary of these books, by title "The Art of Love," that was suppressed on the day of its publication by the alert Comstocks. He tells me that he has already lent it to twenty-six women and that he has more than fifty applications for it on file. Yet he has never read it himself!

As a professional fanatic for free thought and free speech, I can only view all this uproar in the *Frauenzimmer* with high satisfaction. It gives me delight to see a taboo violated, and that delight is doubled when the taboo is one that is wholly senseless. Sex is more important to women than to men, and so they ought to be free to discuss it as they please, and to hatch and propagate whatever ideas about it occur to them. Moreover, I can see nothing but nonsense in the doctrine that their concern with such matters damages their charm. So far as I am concerned, a woman who knows precisely what a Graafian follicle is is just as charming as one who doesn't—just as charming, and far less dangerous. Charm in women, indeed, is a variable star, and shows different colors at different times. When their chief mark was ignorance, then the most ignorant was the most charming; now that they begin to think deeply and indignantly there is charm in their singular astuteness. But I am inclined to believe that they have not yet attained to a genuine astuteness in the new field of sex. To the contrary, it seems to me that a fundamental error contaminates their whole dealing with the subject, and that is the error of assuming that sexual questions, whether social, physiological, or pathological, are of vast and even paramount importance to mankind in general—in brief, that sex is really a first-rate matter.

I doubt it. I believe that in this department men show better judgment than women, if only because their information is older and their experience wider. Their tendency is to dismiss the whole thing lightly, to reduce sex to the lowly estate of an afterthought and a recreation, and under that tendency there is a sound instinct. I do not believe that the lives of normal men are much colored or conditioned, either directly or indirectly, by purely sexual considerations. I believe that nine-tenths of them would carry on all the activities which engage them now, and with precisely the same humorless diligence, if there were not a woman in the world. The notion that man would not work if he lacked an audience, and that the audience must be a woman, seems to me to be a hollow sentimentality. Men work because they want to eat, because they want to feel secure, because they long to shine among their fellows, and for no other reason. A man may crave his wife's approbation, or some other woman's approbation, of his social graces, of his taste, of his generosity and courage, of his general dignity in the world, but long before he ever gives thought to such things and long after he has forgotten them he craves the approbation of his fellow men. Above all, he craves the approbation of his fellow craftsmen—the men who understand exactly what he is trying to do, and are expertly competent to judge his doing of it. Can you imagine a surgeon putting the good opinion of his wife above the good opinion of other surgeons? If you can, then you can do something that I cannot.

Here, of course, I do not argue absurdly that the good opinion of his wife is nothing to him. Obviously, it is a lot, for if it does not constitute the principal reward of his work, then it at least constitutes the principal joy of his hours of ease, when his work is done. He wants his wife to respect and admire him; to be able to make her do it is also a talent. But if he is intelligent he must discover very early that her respect and admiration do not necessarily run in direct ratio to his intrinsic worth, that the qualities and acts that please her are not always the qualities and acts that are most satisfactory to the censor within him—in brief, that the relation between man and woman, however intimate they may seem, must always remain a bit casual and superficial—that sex, at bottom, belongs to comedy and the cool of the evening and not to the sober business that goes on in the heat of the day. That sober business, as I have said, would still go on if woman were abolished and heirs and assigns were manufactured in rolling-mills. Men would not only work as hard as they do to-day; they would also get almost as much satisfaction out of their work. For of all the men that I know on this earth, ranging from poets to ambassadors and from bishops to statisticians, I know none who labors primarily because he wants to please a woman. They are all hard at it because they want to impress other men and so please themselves.

Woman, plainly enough, are in a far different case. Their emancipation has not yet gone to the length of making them genuinely free. They have rid themselves, very largely, of the absolute need to please men, but they have not yet rid themselves of the impulse to please men. Perhaps they never will: one might easily devise a plausible argument to that effect on biological grounds. But sufficient unto the day is the phenomenon before us: they have got rid of the old taboo which forbade them to think and talk about sex, and they still labor under the old superstition that sex is a matter of paramount importance. The result, in my judgment, is an absurd emission of piffle. In every division there is vast and often ludicrous exaggeration. The campaign for birth control takes on the colossal proportions of the war for democracy. The venereal diseases are represented to be as widespread, at least in men, as colds in the head, and as lethal as apoplexy or cancer. Great hordes of viragoes patrol the country, instructing school-girls in the mechanics of reproduction and their mothers in obstetrics. The light-hearted monogamy which produced all of us is denounced as an infamy comparable to cannibalism. Laws are passed regulating the mating of human beings as if they were horned cattle and converting marriage into a sort of coroner's inquest. Over all sounds the battle-cry of quacks and zealots at all times and everywhere: *Veritas liberabit vos!*

The truth? How much of this new gospel is actually truth? Perhaps two per cent. The rest is idle theorizing, doctrinaire nonsense, mere scandalous rubbish. All that is worth knowing about sex—all, that is, that is solidly established and of sound utility—can be taught to any intelligent boy of sixteen in two hours. Is it taught in the current books, so enormously circulated? I doubt it. Absolutely without exception these books admonish the poor apprentice to renounce sex altogether—to sublimate it, as the favorite phrase is, into a passion for free verse, Rotary or the League of Nations. This admonition is silly, and, I believe, dangerous. It is as much a folly to lock up sex in the hold as it is to put it in command on the bridge. Its proper place is in the social hall. As a substitute for all such nonsense I drop a pearl of wisdom, and pass on. To wit: the strict monogamist never gets into trouble.

VII.

Protestantism in the Republic

HAT Protestantism in this great Christian realm is down with a wasting disease must be obvious to every amateur of ghostly pathology. The denominational papers are full of alarming reports from its bedside, and all sorts of projects for the relief of the patient. One authority holds that only more money is needed to work a cure—that if the Christian exploiters and usurers of the country would provide a sufficient slush fund, all the vacant pews could be filled, and the baptismal tanks with them. Another authority argues that the one way to save the churches is to close all other places of resort and amusement on the Sabbath, from delicatessen shops to road-houses, and from movie parlors to jazz palaces. Yet another proposes a mass attack by prayer, apparently in the hope of provoking a miracle. A fourth advocates a vast augmentation of so-called institutional effort, *i.e.*, the scheme of putting bowling alleys and courting cubicles into church cellars, and of giving over the rest of every sacred edifice to debates on the Single Tax, boxing matches, baby shows, mental hygiene clinics, lectures by converted actors, movie shows, raffles, nonvoluptuous dances, and evening classes in salesmanship, automobile repairing, birth control, interior decoration, and the art and mystery of the realtor. A fifth, borrowing a leaf from Big Business, maintains that consolidation and reorganization are what is needed—that the existence of half a dozen rival churches in every American village profits the devil a great deal more than it profits God. This last scheme seems to have won a great deal of support among the pious. At least a score of committees are now trying to draw up plans for concrete consolidations, and even the Southern and Northern Methodists, who hate each other violently, have been in peaceful though vain negotiation.

On the merits of these conflicting remedies I attempt no pronouncement, but I have been at some pains to look into the symptoms and nature of the disease. My report is that it seems to me to be analogous to that malady which afflicts a star in the heavens when it splits into two halves and they go slambanging into space in opposite directions. That, in brief, is what appears to be the matter with Protestantism in the United States to-day. One half of it is moving, with slowly accelerating speed, in the direction of the Harlot of the Seven Hills: the other is sliding down into voodooism. The former carries the greater part of Protestant money with it; the latter carries the greater part of Protestant enthusiasm, or, as the word now is, pep. What remains in the middle may be likened to a torso without either brains to think with or legs to dance—in other words, something that begins to be professionally attractive to the mortician, though it still makes shift to breathe. There is no lack of life on the higher levels, where the most solvent Methodists and the like are gradually transmogrified into Episcopalians, and the Episcopalians shin up the ancient bastions of Holy Church, and there is no lack of life on the lower levels, where the rural Baptists, by the route of Fundamentalism, the Anti-Saloon League, and the Ku Klux Klan, rapidly descend to the dogmas and practices of the Congo jungle. But in the middle there is desiccation and decay. Here is where Protestantism was once strongest. Here is the region of the plain and godly Americano, fond of devotion but distrustful of every hint of orgy—the honest fellow who suffers dutifully on Sunday, pays his share, and hopes for a few kind words from the pastor when his time comes to die. He stands to-day on a burning deck. It is no wonder that Sunday automobiling begins to get him in its clutches. If he is not staggered one day by his pastor's appearance in surplice and stole, he is staggered the day following by a file of Ku Kluxers marching up the aisle. So he tends to absent himself from pious exercises, and the news goes about that there is something the matter with the churches, and the denominational papers bristle with schemes to set it right, and many up-and-coming pastors, tiring of preaching and parish work, get excellent jobs as the executive secretaries of these schemes, and go about the country expounding them to the faithful.

The extent to which Protestantism, in its upper reaches, has succumbed to the harlotries of Rome seems to be but little apprehended by the majority of connoisseurs. I was myself unaware of the whole truth until last Christmas, when, in the pursuit of a quite unrelated inquiry, I employed agents to attend all the services held in the principal Protestant basilicas of an eminent American city, and to bring in the best reports they could formulate upon what went on in the lesser churches. The substance of these reports, in so far as they related to churches patronized by the well-to-do, was simple: they revealed a head-long movement to the right, an almost precipitate flight over the mountain. Six so-called Episcopal churches held midnight services on Christmas Eve in obvious imitation of Catholic midnight masses, and one of them actually called its service a solemn high mass. Two invited the nobility and gentry to processions, and a third concealed a procession under the name of a pageant. One offered Gounod's St. Cecilia mass on Christmas morning, and another the Messe Solennelle by the same composer; three others, somewhat more timorous, contented themselves with parts of masses. One, throwing off all pretense and euphemism, summoned the faithful to no less than three Christmas masses, naming them by name—two low and one high. All six churches were aglow with candles, and two employed incense.

But that was not the worst. Two Presbyterian churches and one Baptist church, not to mention five Lutheran churches of different synods, had choral services in the dawn of Christmas morning, and the one attended by the only one of my agents who got up early enough—it was in a Presbyterian church— was made gay with candles, and had a palpably Roman smack. Yet worse: a rich and conspicuous Methodist church, patronized by the leading Wesleyan wholesalers and money-lenders of the town, boldly offered a mediæval carol service. Mediæval? What did that mean? The Middle Ages ended on July 16, 1453, at 12 o'clock meridian, and the Reformation was not launched by Luther until October 31, 1517, at 10.15 A.M. If mediæval, in the sense in which it was here used, does not mean Roman Catholic, then I surely went to school in vain. My agent, born a Methodist, reported that the whole ceremony shocked him excessively. It began with trumpet blasts from the church spire and it concluded with an Ave Maria by a vested choir! Candles rose up in glittering ranks behind the chancel rail, and above them glowed a shining electric star.

God help us all, indeed! What next? Will the rev. pastor, on some near to-morrow, defy the lightnings of Jahveh by appearing in alb and dalmatic? Will he turn his back upon the faithful? Will he put in a telephone-booth for auricular confession? I shudder to think of what old John Wesley would have said about that vested choir and that shining star. Or Bishop Francis Asbury. Or the Rev. Jabez Bunting. Or Robert Strawbridge, that consecrated man.

Here, of course, I do not venture into the contumacy of criticising; I merely marvel. A student of the sacred sciences all my life, I am well learned in the dogmas and ceremonials of the sects, and know what they affect and what they abhor. Does anyone argue that the use of candles in public worship would have had the sanction of the *Ur*-Wesleyans, or that they would have consented to *Blasmusik* and a vested choir? If so, let the sciolist come forward. Down to fifty years ago, in fact, the Methodists prohibited Christmas services altogether, as Romish and heathen. But now we have ceremonies almost operatic, and the sweet masses of Gounod are just around the corner! As I have said, the Episcopalians—who, in most American cities, are largely ex-Methodists or ex-Presbyterians, or, in New York, ex-Jews—go still further. In three of the churches attended by my agents Holy Communion was almost indistinguishable from the mass. Two of these churches, according to information placed at my disposal by the police, are very fashionable; to get into one of them is almost as difficult as ordering a suit of clothes from Poole. But the richer the Episcopalian, the more eager he is to forget that he was once baptized by public outcry or total immersion. The Low Church rectors, in the main, struggle with poor congregations, born to the faith but deficient in buying power. As bank accounts increase the fear of the devil diminishes, and there is bred a sense of beauty. This sense of beauty, in its practical effects, is identical with the work of the Paulist Fathers. To-day, indeed, even the Methodists who remain Methodists begin to wobble. Tiring of the dreadful din that goes with the orthodox Wesleyan demonology, they take to ceremonials that grow more and more stately and voluptuous. The sermon ceases to be a cavalry charge, and becomes soft and *pizzicato*. The choir abandons "Throw Out the Life-Line" and "Are You Ready for the Judgment Day?" and toys with Händel. The rev. pastor throws off the uniform of a bank cashier and puts on a gown. It is an evolution that has, viewed from a tree, a certain merit. The stock of nonsense in the world is sensibly diminished and the stock of beauty augmented. But what would the old-time circuit-riders say of it, imagining them miraculously brought back from hell?

So much for the volatilization that is going on above the diaphragm. What is in progress below? All I can detect is a rapid descent to mere barbaric devil-chasing. In all those parts of the Republic where Beelzebub is still as real as Babe Ruth or Dr. Coolidge, and men drink raw fusel oil hot from the still—for example, in the rural sections of the Middle West and everywhere in the South save a few walled towns—the evangelical sects plunge into an abyss of malignant imbecility, and declare a holy war upon every decency that civilized men cherish. First the Anti-Saloon League, and now the Ku Klux Klan and the various Fundamentalist organizations, have converted them into vast machines for pursuing and butchering unbelievers. They have thrown the New Testament overboard, and gone back to the Old, and particularly to the bloodiest parts of it. Their one aim seems to be to break heads, to spread terror, to propagate hatred. Everywhere they have set up enmities that will not die out for generations. Neighbor looks askance at neighbor, the land is filled with spies, every man of the slightest intelligence is suspect. Christianity becomes a sort of psychic cannibalism. Unfortunately, the doings of the rustic gentlemen of God who furnish steam for this movement have been investigated but imperfectly, and in consequence too little is known about them. Even the sources of their power, so far as I know, have not been looked into. My suspicion is that it has increased as the influence of the old-time country-town newspapers has declined. These newspapers, in large areas of the land, once genuinely molded public opinion. They attracted to their service a shrewd and salty class of rustic philosophers, mainly highly alcoholized; they were outspoken in their views and responded only slightly to the prevailing crazes. In the midst of the Bryan uproar, a quarter of a century ago, scores of little weeklies in the South and Middle West kept up a gallant battle for sound money and the Hanna idealism. There were red-hot Democratic papers in Pennsylvania, and others in Ohio; there were Republican sheets in rural Maryland, and even in Virginia. The growth of the big city dailies is what chiefly reduced them to puerility. As communications improved every yokel began following Brisbane, Dr. Frank Crane, and Mutt and Jeff. The rural mail carrier began leaving a 24-page yellow in every second box. The hinds distrusted and detested the politics of these great organs, but enjoyed their imbecilities. The country weekly could not match the latter, and so it began to decline. It is now in a low state everywhere in America. Half of it is boiler-plate and the other half is cross-roads gossip. The editor is no longer the leading thinker of his town; instead, he is commonly a broken and despairing man, cadging for advertisements and hoping for a political job. He used to aspire to the State Senate; now he is content with the post of town bailiff or road supervisor.

His place has been taken by the village pastor. The pastor got into public affairs by the route of Prohibition. The shrewd shysters who developed the Anti-Saloon League made a politician of him, and once he had got a taste of power he was eager for more. It came very quickly. As industry penetrated to the rural regions the new-blown Babbitts began to sense his capacity for safeguarding the established order, and so he was given the job: he became a local Billy Sunday. And, simultaneously the old-line politicians, taught a lesson by the Anti-Saloon League, began to defer to him in general, as they had yielded to him in particular. He was consulted about candidacies; he had his say about policies. The local school-board soon became his private preserve. The wandering cony-catchers of the tin-pot fraternal orders found him a useful man. He was, by now, a specialist in all forms of public rectitude, from teetotalism to patriotism. He was put up on days of ceremony to sob for the flag, vice the county judge, retired. When the Klan burst upon the peasants all of his new duties were synthetized. He was obviously the chief local repository of its sublime principles, theological, social, ethnological and patriotic. In every country town in America to-day, wherever the Klan continues to rowel the hinds, its chief engine is a clerk in holy orders. If the Baptists are strong, their pastor is that engine. Failing Baptists, the heroic work is assumed by the Methodist parson, or the Presbyterian, or the Campbellite. Without these sacerdotal props the Invisible Empire would have faded long ago.

What one mainly notices about these ambassadors of Christ, observing them in the mass, is their vast lack of sound information and sound sense. They constitute, perhaps, the most ignorant class of teachers ever set up to lead a civilized people; they are even more ignorant than the county superintendents of schools. Learning, indeed, is not esteemed in evangelical denominations, and any literate plowhand, if the Holy Spirit inflames him, is thought to be fit to preach. Is he commonly sent, as a preliminary, to a training camp, to college? But what a college! You will find one in every mountain valley of the land, with its single building in its bare pasture lot, and its faculty of half-idiot pedagogues and broken-down preachers. One man, in such a college, teaches oratory, ancient history, arithmetic and Old Testament exegesis. The aspirant comes in from the barnyard, and goes back in a year or two to the village. His body of knowledge is that of a street-car motorman or a vaudeville actor. But he has learned the clichés of his craft, and he has got him a long-tailed coat, and so he has made his escape from the harsh labors of his ancestors, and is set up as a fountain of light and learning.

It is from such ignoramuses that the lower half of American Protestantdom gets its view of the cosmos. Certainly Fundamentalism should not be hard to understand when its sources are inspected. How can the teacher teach when his own head is empty? Of all that constitutes the sum of human knowledge he is as innocent as an Eskimo. Of the arts he knows absolutely nothing; of the sciences he has never so much as heard. No good book ever penetrates to those remote "colleges," nor does any graduate ever take away a desire to read one. He has been warned, indeed, against their blandishments; what is not addressed solely to the paramount business of saving souls is of the devil. So when he hears by chance of the battle of ideas beyond the sky-rim, he quite naturally puts it down to Beelzebub. What comes to him, vaguely and distorted, is unintelligible to him. He is suspicious of it, afraid of it—and he quickly communicates his fears to his dupes. The common man, in many ways, is hard to arouse; it is a terrific job to ram even the most elemental ideas into him. But it is always easy to scare him.

That is the daily business of the evangelical pastors of the Republic. They are specialists in alarms and bugaboos. The rum demon, atheists, Bolsheviki, the Pope, bootleggers, the Jews,—all these have served them in turn, and in the demonology of the Ku Klux Klan all have been conveniently brought together. The old stock company of devils has been retired, and with it the old repertoire of private sins. The American peasant of to-day finds it vastly easier to claw into heaven than he used to. Personal holiness has now been handed over to the Holy Rollers and other such survivors from a harsher day. It is sufficient now to hate the Pope, to hate the Jews, to hate the scientists, to hate all foreigners, to hate whatever the cities yield to. These hatreds have been spread in the land by rev. pastors, chiefly Baptists and Methodists. They constitute, with their attendant fears, the basic religion of the American clodhopper to-day. They are the essence of the new Protestantism, second division, American style.

Their public effects are constantly underestimated until it is too late. I ask no indulgence for calling attention to the case of Prohibition. Fundamentalism, it may be, is sneaking upon the nation in the same disarming way. The cities laugh at the yokels, but meanwhile the politicians take careful notice; such mountebanks as Peay of Tennessee and Blease of South Carolina have already issued their preliminary whoops. As the tide rolls up the pastors will attain to greater and greater consequence. Already, indeed, they swell visibly in power and pretension. The Klan, in its earlier days, kept them discreetly under cover; they labored valiantly in the hold, but only lay go-getters were seen upon the bridge. But now they are everywhere on public display, leading the anthropoid host. The curious thing is that their activity gets little if any attention from the established publicists. Let a lone Red arise to annoy a barroom full of Michigan lumber-jacks, and at once the fire-alarm sounds and the full military and naval power of the nation is summoned to put down the outrage. But how many Americans would the Reds convert to their rubbish, even supposing them free to spout it on every street-corner? Probably not enough, all told, to make a day's hunting for a regiment of militia. The American moron's mind simply does not run in that direction; he wants to keep his Ford, even at the cost of losing the Bill of Rights. But the stuff that the Baptist and Methodist dervishes have on tap is very much to his taste; he gulps it eagerly and rubs his tummy. I suggest that it might be well to make a scientific inquiry into the nature of it. The existing agencies of sociological snooting seem to be busy in other directions. There are elaborate surveys of some of the large cities, showing how much it costs to teach a child the principles of Americanism, how often the average citizen falls into the hands of the cops, how many detective stories are taken out of the city library daily, and how many children a normal Polish woman has every year. Why not a survey of the rustic areas, where men are he and God still reigns? Why not an attempt to find out just what the Baptist dominies have drilled into the heads of the Tennesseeans, Arkansans and Nebraskans? It would be amusing, and it would be instructive. And useful. For it is well, in such matters, to see clearly what is ahead. The United States grows increasingly urban, but its ideas are still hatched in the little towns. What the swineherds credit to-day is whooped to-morrow by their agents and attorneys in Congress, and then comes upon the cities suddenly, with all the force of law. Where do the swineherds get it? Mainly from the only publicists and metaphysicians they know: the gentlemen of the sacred faculty. It was not the bawling of the mountebank Bryan, but the sermon of a mountain Bossuet that laid the train of the Scopes case and made a whole State forever ridiculous. I suggest looking more carefully into the notions that such ignoramuses spout.

Meanwhile, what is the effect of all this upon the Protestant who retains some measure of sanity, the moderate and peaceable fellow—him called by William Graham Sumner the Forgotten Man? He is silent while the bombs burst and the stink bombs go off, but what is he thinking? I believe that he is thinking strange and dreadful thoughts—thoughts that would have frozen his own spine a dozen years ago. He is thinking, *imprimis*, that there must be something in this evolution heresy after all, else Methodist bishops and other such bristling foes to sense would not be so frantically against it. And he is thinking, secondly, that perhaps a civilized man, in the last analysis, would not be worse off if Sherman's march were repeated by the Papal Guard. Between these two thoughts American Protestantism is being squeezed, so to speak, to death.

VIII.

From the Files of a Book Reviewer

I

Counter-Offensive

Is It God's Word? by Joseph Wheless. New York: *Alfred A. Knopf.* [The American Mercury, May, 1926.]

THE author of this book, who is an associate editor of the *American Bar Association Journal*, was trained as a lawyer, but that training, somewhat surprisingly, seems to have left his logical powers unimpaired, and with them his capacity for differentiating between facts and mere appearances. There is no hint of the usual evasions and obfuscations of the advocate in his pages. His business is to examine calmly the authority and plausibility of Holy Writ, both as history and as revelation of the Omnipotent Will, and to that business he brings an immense and meticulous knowledge, an exact and unfailing judicial sense, and a skill at orderly exposition which is quite extraordinary. There is no vaporing of the orthodox exegetes that he is not familiar with, and none that he fails to refute, simply and devastatingly. Nine-tenths of his evidence he takes out of the mouths of his opponents. Patiently, mercilessly, irresistibly, he subjects it to logical analysis, and when he is done at last—his book runs to 494 pages of fine print—there is little left of the two Testaments save a farrago of palpable nonsense, swathed, to be sure, in a very lovely poetry. He exposes all their gross and preposterous contradictions, their violations of common sense and common decency, their grotesque collisions with the known and indubitable facts, their petty tergiversations and fraudulences. He goes behind the mellifluous rhetoric of the King James Version to the harsh balderdash of the originals, and brings it out into the horrible light of day. He exposes the prophecies that have failed to come off. He exhibits the conflicts of romantic and unreliable witnesses, most of them with something to sell. He tracks down ideas to their barbaric sources. He concocts an almost endless series of logical dilemmas. And he does it all with good manners, never pausing to rant and nowhere going beyond the strict letter of the record.

Obviously, there is room and need for such a book, and it deserves to be widely read. For in the America of to-day, after a time of quiescence, the old conflict between religion and science has resumed with great ferocity, and the partisans of the former, not content with denouncing all free inquiry as evil, have now undertaken to make it downright unlawful. Worse, they show signs of succeeding. And why? Chiefly, it seems to me, because the cause of their opponents has been badly handled—above all, because it has lacked vigorous *offensive* leadership. Even the defense is largely an abject running away. We are assured with pious snuffling that there is actually no conflict, that the domains of science and religion do not overlap, that it is quite possible for a man to be a scientist (even a biologist!) and yet believe that Jonah swallowed the whale. No wonder the whoopers for Genesis take courage, and lay on with glad, *sforzando* shouts. At one stroke they are lifted to parity with their opponents, nay, to superority. The bilge they believe in becomes something sacrosanct; its manifest absurdities are not mentioned, and hence tend to pass unnoticed. But meanwhile they are quite free to belabor science with their whole armamentarium of imbecilities. Every cross-roads Baptist preacher becomes an authority upon its errors, and is heard gravely. In brief, science exposes itself to be shot at, but agrees not to shoot back. It would be difficult to imagine any strategy more idiotic.

Or to imagine a Huxley adopting it. Huxley, in his day, followed a far different plan. When the Gladstones, Bishop Wilberforces and other such obscurantists denounced the new biology, he did not waste any time upon conciliatory politeness. Instead, he made a bold and headlong attack upon Christian theology—an attack so vigorous and so skillful that the enemy was soon in ignominious flight. Huxley knew the first principle of war: he knew that a hearty offensive is worth a hundred defensives. How well he succeeded is shown by the fact that even to-day, with theology once more on the prowl and the very elements of science under heavy attack, some of the gaudiest of the ancient theological notions are not heard of. Huxley disposed of them completely; even in Darkest Tennessee the yokels no longer give them credit. But if the Robert Andrews Millikans and other such amiable bunglers continue to boss the scientific camp you may be sure that all these exploded myths and superstitions will be revived, and that the mob will once more embrace them. For it is the natural tendency of the ignorant to believe what is not true. In order to overcome that tendency it is not sufficient to exhibit the true; it is also necessary to expose and denounce the false. To admit the false has any standing in court, that it ought to be handled gently because millions of morons cherish it and thousands of quacks make their livings propagating it—to admit this, as the more fatuous of the reconcilers of science and religion inevitably do, is to abandon a just cause to its enemies, cravenly and without excuse.

It is, of course, quite true that there is a region in which science and religion do not conflict. That is the region of the unknowable. No one knows Who created the visible universe, and it is infinitely improbable that anything properly describable as evidence on the point will ever be discovered. No one knows what motives or intentions, if any, lie behind what we call natural laws. No one knows why man has his present form. No one knows why sin and suffering were sent into this world —that is, why the fashioning of man was so badly botched. Naturally enough, all these problems have engaged the interest of humanity since the remotest days, and in every age, with every sort of evidence completely lacking, men of speculative mind have sought to frame plausible solutions. Some of them, more bold than the rest, have pretended that their solutions were revealed to them by God, and multitudes have believed them. But no man of science believes them. He doesn't say positively that they are wrong; he simply says that there is no proof that they are right. If he admitted, without proof, that they are right, he would not be a man of science. In his view all such theories and speculations stand upon a common level. In the most ambitious soarings of a Christian theologian he can find nothing that differs in any essential way from the obvious hocus-pocus of a medicine man in the jungle. Superficially, of course, the two stand far apart. The Christian theologian, confined like all the rest to the unknowable, has to be more careful than the medicine man, for in Christendom the unknowable covers a far less extensive field than in the jungle. Christian theology is thus, in a sense, more reasonable than voodooism. But it is not more reasonable because its professors know more than the voodoo-man about the unknowable; it is more reasonable simply because they are under a far more rigorous and enlightened scrutiny, and run a risk of being hauled up sharply every time they venture too near the borders of the known.

This business of hauling them up is one of the principal functions of science. Its prompt execution is the gauge of a high and progressive civilization. So long as theologians keep within their proper bounds, science has no quarrel with them, for it is no more able to prove that they are wrong than they themselves are able to prove that they are right. But human experience shows that they never keep within their proper bounds voluntarily; they are always bulging over the line, and making a great uproar over things that they know nothing about. Such an uproar is going on in the United States at the present moment. Hordes of theologians come marching down from the Southern mountains, declaring raucously that God created the universe during a certain single week of the year 4004 B. C., and demanding that all persons who presume to doubt it be handed over to the secular arm. Here, obviously, science cannot suffer them gladly, nor even patiently. Their proposition is a statement of scientific fact; it may be examined and tested like any other statement of scientific fact. So examined and tested, it turns out to be wholly without evidential support. All the known evidence, indeed, is against it, and overwhelmingly. No man who knows the facts—that is, no man with any claim to scientific equipment—is in any doubt about that. He disbelieves it as thoroughly as he believes that the earth moves 'round the sun. Disbelieving it, it is his professional duty, his first obligation of professional honor, to attack and refute those who uphold it. Above all, it is his duty to attack the false evidence upon which they base their case.

Thus an actual conflict is joined, and it is the height of absurdity for the Millikans and other such compromisers to seek to evade it with soft words. That conflict was not begun by science. It did start with an invasion of the proper field of theological speculation by scientific raiders. It started with an invasion of the field of science by theological raiders. Now that it is on, it must be pressed vigorously from the scientific side, and without any flabby tenderness for theological susceptibilities. A defensive war is not enough; there must be a forthright onslaught upon the theological citadel, and every effort must be made to knock it down. For so long as it remains a stronghold, there will be no security for sound sense among us, and little for common decency. So long as it may be used as a recruiting-station and rallying-point for the rabble, science will have to submit to incessant forays, and the same forays will be directed against every sort of rational religion. The latter danger is not unobserved by the more enlightened theologians. They are well aware that, facing the Fundamentalists, they must either destroy or be destroyed. It is to be hoped that the men of science will perceive the same plain fact, and so give over their vain effort to stay the enemy with weasel words.

2

Heretics

ALTGELD OF ILLINOIS, by Waldo R. Browne. New York: *B. W. Huebsch.* THE LAST OF THE HERETICS, by Algernon Sidney Crapsey. New York: *Alfred A. Knopf.* [The American Mercury, October, 1924.]

When I was a boy, in the early nineties of the last century, the reigning hobgoblin of the United States was John P. Altgeld, Governor of Illinois. From this distance the ill-fame that played about him seems almost fabulous. He was a sort of horrendous combination of Trotsky and Raisuli, Darwin and the German Crown Prince, Jesse James and Oscar Wilde, with overtones of Wayne B. Wheeler and the McNamara brothers. We have had, in these later years, no such communal devil. The La Follette of 1917 was a popular favorite compared to him; the Debs of the same time was a spoiled darling. What I gathered from my elders, in the awful years of adolescence, when my voice began to break and vibrissæ sprouted on my lip, was that Altgeld was a shameless advocate of rapine and assassination, an enemy alike to the Constitution and the Ten Commandments—in short, a bloody and insatiable anarchist. I was thus bred to fear him even more than I feared the anonymous scoundrels who had stolen Charlie Ross. When I dreamed, it was of catching him in some public place and cutting off his head, to the applause of the multitude.

The elders that I have mentioned were mainly business men, with a few *Gelehrte* thrown in. I learned later on, by hard experience, that the opinions of such gentlemen, particularly of public matters and public men, were not always sound. Nevertheless, I continued to have a bilious suspicion of the Hon. Mr. Altgeld, and it survived even the discovery, made much later, that men who had actually known him—for example, Theodore Dreiser—regarded him very highly. I remember very well how shocked I was when Dreiser made me privy to this fact. It made a dent, I suppose, in my old view, but it surely did not dispose of it altogether. I continued to believe that Altgeld, though perhaps not an anarchist, as alleged, was at least a blathering Socialist, and hence deserving of a few prophylactic kicks in the pantaloons. I was far gone in my forties before ever I got at the truth. Then I found it in this modest book of Mr. Browne's—a volume that is dreadfully written, but extremely illuminating. That truth may be put very simply. Altgeld was not an anarchist, nor was he a Socialist: he was simply a sentimentalist. His error consisted in taking the college yells of democracy seriously.

I do not go into the evidence, but refer you to the book. It is very completely documented, and it leaves little room for doubt, despite Mr. Browne's obvious prejudice in favor of some of Altgeld's more dubious ideas, especially the idea of government ownership. On the main points his argument is quite beyond cavil. Did Altgeld pardon the Chicago anarchists? Then it was simply because they had been railroaded to jail on evidence that should have made the very judge on the bench guffaw—as men are still railroaded in California to-day. Did he protest against Cleveland's invasion of Chicago with Federal troops at the time of the Pullman strike? Then it was because he knew only too well how little they were needed—and what sinister influences had cajoled poor old Grover into sending them. In brief, Altgeld was one of the first public men in America to protest by word and act against government by usurers and their bashi-bazouks—the first open and avowed advocate of the Bill of Rights since Jackson's time. A romantic fellow, and a firm believer in the virtues of the common people, he couldn't rid himself of the delusion that they would follow him here—that after the yell of rage there would come a resounding cheer. That belief gradually degenerated into a hope, but I doubt that it ever disappeared altogether. The common people met it by turning Altgeld out of office, swiftly and ignominiously. After they had got rid of him as Governor of Illinois, they even rejected him as mayor of Chicago. His experience taught him a lesson, but like that of the Aframerican on the gallows, it came too late.

What lesson is in his career for the rest of us? The lesson, it seems to me, that any man who devotes himself to justice and common decency, under democracy, is a very foolish fellow —that the generality of men have no genuine respect for these things, and are always suspicious of the man who upholds them. Their public relations, like their private relations, are marked by the qualities that mark the inferior man at all times and everywhere: cowardice, stupidity and cruelty. They are in favor of whoever is wielding the whip, even when their own hides must bear the blows. How easy it was to turn the morons of the American Legion upon their fellow-slaves! How heroically they voted for Harding, and then for Coolidge after him—and so helped to put down the Reds! Dog eats dog, world without end. In the Pullman strike at least half the labor unions of the United States were against the strikers, as they were against the more recent steel strikers, and helped to beat them. Altgeld battled for the under dog all his life—and the under dog bit him in the end. A pathetic career, but not without its touches of sardonic comedy. Altgeld, in error at bottom, was often also in error on the surface, and not infrequently somewhat grotesquely. He succumbed to the free silver mania. He supported Bryan—nay more, he may be said to have discovered and made Bryan. It is fortunate for him that he was dead and in hell by 1902, and so not forced to contemplate the later states of his handiwork. He was excessively romantic, but certainly no ignoramus. Imagine him listening to one of good Jennings' harangues against the elements of biology! Such men, indeed, are always happier dead. This world, and especially this Republic, is no place for idealists.

Another proof of it is offered by the career of Dr. Crapsey, whose trial for heresy entertained the damned in 1906. He is still alive as I write, and still full of steam. But I doubt that he is as sure as he used to be that common sense and common honesty pay. Many of the frauds who drove him out of the church, though they know that he was right, are bishops to-day, and licensed to bind and loose. Others have been called by God, and sit upon His right hand. The church itself, as it has grown more sordid and swinish, has only grown more prosperous. In New York City its income approaches that of the bootleggers and it is almost as well regarded. Every new profiteer, even before he tries to horn into the Piping Rock Club, subscribes to its articles. It is robbing the Church of Christ Scientist of all the rich Jews; they are having their sons baptized in its fonts and christened Llewellyn, Seymour and Murray. Certainly it would be difficult to imagine a more gloriously going concern. The rising spires of its steel and concrete cathedrals begin to bulge the floor of heaven; its clergy are sleek, fat and well-oiled; its bishops come next in precedence after movie stars and members of the firm of J. P. Morgan & Company. Lately it threw out another heretic—like Dr. Crapsey, one accused of putting the Sermon on the Mount above the conflicting genealogies of the Preacher. As for Crapsey himself, he has naught to console him in his old age save the thought that hell will at least be warm.

His book is extremely amusing and instructive. Like Altgeld, he confesses to foreign and poisonous blood. The *Stammvater* of the American Crapseii was a fellow named Kropps, apparently a Hessian. But his great-great grandson, the father of the heretic, married the daughter of a United States Senator, and so there is some amelioration of the horror. Like Altgeld again, Crapsey went to the Civil War as a boy scarcely out of knee breeches. Altgeld was so poor that he gladly took the $100 offered by a patriot who had been drafted and wanted a substitute; Crapsey volunteered. Both succumbed to camp fevers and were discharged. Both then took to Service among the downtrodden, Altgeld in politics and the law, and Crapsey in one of the outlying hereditaments of Trinity parish. Both were safe so long as they appeared to be fraudulent; the moment they began to show genuine belief in their doctrines they found themselves in difficulties. So Altgeld became the favorite hobgoblin of the Republic and Crapsey became its blackest heretic.

3
The Grove of Academe

THE GOOSE-STEP, by Upton Sinclair. Pasadena, Calif.: *Published by the Author*. [The Smart Set, May, 1923.]

The doctrine preached in this fat volume—to wit, that the American colleges and universities, with precious few exceptions, are run by stock-jobbers and manned by intellectual prostitutes—this doctrine will certainly give no fillip of surprise to steady readers of my critical compositions. I have, in fact, maintained it steadily since the earliest dawn of the present marvelous century, and to the support of it I have brought forward an immense mass of glittering and irrefragable facts and a powerful stream of eloquence. Nor have I engaged in this moral enterprise *a cappella*. A great many other practitioners have devoted themselves to it with equal assiduity, including not a few reformed and conscience-stricken professors, and the net result of that united effort is that the old assumption of the pedagogue's *bona fides* is now in decay throughout the Republic. In whole departments of human knowledge he has become suspect, as it were, *ex officio*. I nominate, for example, the departments of history and of what is commonly called English language and literature. If a professor in the first field shows ordinary honesty, or, in the second field, ordinary sense, it is now regarded as a sort of marvel, and with sound reason. Barring a scant dozen extraordinary men, no American professor of history has written anything worth reading since the year 1917; nearly all the genuine history published in the United States since then has come from laymen, or from professors who have ceased to profess. And so in the domain of the national letters. The professors, with a few exceptions, mainly belated rice-converts, are unanimously and furiously consecrated to vain attacks upon the literature that is in being. Either, like the paleozoic Beers, of Yale, they refuse to read it and deny that it exists, or, like the patriotic Matthews, of Columbia, they seek to put it down by launching Ku Klux anathemas against it. The net result is that the professorial caste, as a whole, loses all its old dignity and influence. In universities large and small, East, West, North and South, the very sophomores rise in rebellion against the incompetence and imbecility of their preceptors, and in the newspapers the professor slides down gradually to the level of a chiropractor, a press-agent or a Congressman.

Thus there is nothing novel in the thesis of Dr. Sinclair's book, which deals, in brief, with the internal organization of the American universities, and their abject subjection to the Money Power, which is to say, to Chamber of Commerce and Rotary Club concepts of truth, liberty and honor. But there is something new, and very refreshing, in the manner of it, for the learned author, for the first time, manages to tell a long and dramatic story without intruding his private grievances into it. Sinclair's worst weakness, next to his vociferous appetite for Remedies that never cure, is his naïve and almost actorial vanity. As everyone knows, it botched "The Brass Check." So much of that book was given over to a humorless account of his own combats with yellow journals—which, in the main, did nothing worse to him than laugh at him when he was foolish—that he left untold a great deal that might have been said, and with perfect justice and accuracy, about the venality and swinishness of American newspapers. In "The Profits of Religion" he wobbled almost as badly; the subject, no doubt, was much too vast for a single volume; the Methodists and Baptists alone, to say nothing of Holy Church, deserved a whole shelf. But in "The Goose-Step" he tells a straightforward story in a straightforward manner—simply, good-humoredly and convincingly. When he comes into the narrative himself, which is not often, he leaves off his customary martyr's chemise. There is no complaining, no pathos, no mouthing of platitude; it is a plain record of plain facts, with names and dates—a plain record of truly appalling cowardice, disingenuousness, abjectness, and degradation. Out of it two brilliant figures emerge: first the typical American university president, a jenkins to wealth, an ignominious waiter in antechambers and puller of wires, a politician, a fraud and a cad; and secondly, the typical American professor, a puerile and pitiable slave.

Such are the common and customary bearers of the torch in the Republic. Such is the usual machinery and inner nature of the higher learning among us. Its aim, briefly stated, is almost indistinguishable from the aim of the Ku Klux Klan, the American Legion, and Kiwanis. The thing it combats most ardently is not ignorance, but free inquiry; it is devoted to forcing the whole youth of the land into one rigid mold. Its ideal product is a young man who is absolutely correct in all his ideas—a perfect reader for the *Literary Digest*, the *American Magazine*, and the editorial page of the New York *Times*. To achieve this end Big Business has endowed it with unprecedented liberality; there are single American universities with more invested wealth and more income than all the universities of Germany, France or England taken together. But in order to get that ocean of money, and to pay for the piles of pseudo-Gothic that now arise all over the land, scholarship in America has had to sacrifice free inquiry to the prejudices and private interests of its masters—the search for the truth has had to be subordinated to the safeguarding of railway bonds and electric light stocks. As Sinclair shows, there is scarcely a university in the United States, whether maintained out of the public funds or privately endowed, that is not run absolutely, in all departments, by precisely the same men who run the street railways, the banks, the rolling mills, the coal mines and the factories of the country—in brief, by men who have no more respect for scholarship than an ice-wagon driver has for beautiful letters. There is scarcely an American university or college in which the scholars who constitute it have any effective control over its general policies and enterprises, or even over the conduct of their own departments. In almost every one there is some unspeakable stock-broker, or bank director, or railway looter who, if the spirit moved him, would be perfectly free to hound a Huxley, a Karl Ludwig or a Jowett from the faculty, and even to prevent him getting a seemly berth elsewhere. It is not only possible; it has been done, and not once, but scores and hundreds of times.

Sinclair is content to set forth the basic facts; his book, as it is, is very long; he neglects laboring all of the deductions and implications that flow from his thesis, some of them obvious enough. One of them is this: that the control of the universities by Mr. Babbitt is making it increasingly difficult to induce intelligent and self-respecting young men to embrace the birchman's career, and that the personnel of the teaching staffs thus tends to decline in competence, steadily and sharply. This accounts, in large measure, for the collapse of the old public influence of the scholar in America; he begins to be derided simply because he is no longer the dignified man that he once was. In certain departments, of no immediate interest to trustees and contributors, a certain show of freedom, of course, still prevails. What is taught in astronomy, or paleontology, or Greek cannot menace the nail manufacturer on the board, and so he does not issue any orders about it, nor does his agent, the university president. But what is taught in economics, or modern history, or "education," or sociology, or even literature, involves a dealing with ideas that are apt to hit him where he lives, and so he keeps a wary eye upon those departments, and at the slightest show of heresy he takes measures to protect himself. It is in these regions, consequently, that conformity is most comfortable, and that professional character is most lamentably in decay. Even here, to be sure, a few stout-hearted survivors of an earlier day hold out, but they are surely not many, and they will have no successors. The professor of tomorrow, in all departments that have to do with life as men are now living it in the world, will either be a scholastic goose-stepper or he will be out of a job. The screws are tightening every year. In the past the Babbitts have contented themselves with farming out the management of their intellectual brothels to extra-pliant professors, but now they begin to turn to yet more reliable men: army officers, lame-duck politicians, and engineers. The time will come, no doubt, when the president of Columbia will be just as frankly a partner in J. P. Morgan & Company as the head of the Red Cross or the chief vestryman of Trinity Church.

How far will this debauching of education go? Will the universities sink eventually to the level of the public-schools of such barbarous States as Texas, Arkansas and Mississippi? Here education has been reduced to a bald device for multiplying Shriners, Knights of Pythias and Rotarians—in brief, ignoramuses. In the institutions of higher learning one may reasonably look for some resistance to the process, soon or late. I doubt, however, that it will come from the professors; they are already too much cowed and demoralized, as Sinclair shows abundantly. The American Association of University Professors, an organization formed to protect pedagogues against wanton attack by the Babbitts, numbers but 5000 members; the remaining 195,000 American professors are either afraid to join, or already too much battered to want to. How far their degradation has gone was made visible during the late war, when all save an infinitesimal minority of them yielded to the most extravagant manias of the time and thousands gave astounding exhibitions of moronic sadism. The Neandertal qualities thus awakened are still visible in many directions; in the Southern States, I am informed by an exceptional professor, fully five-sixths of his colleagues became charter members of the Ku Klux Klan. It is hopeless to look for a *Freiheitskrieg* among such poor serfs. But the students remain, and in them lies some promise for the future. The American university student, in the past, has been a victim of the same process of leveling that destroyed his teacher. He has been taught conformity, obedience, the social and intellectual goose-step; the ideal held before him has been the ideal of correctness. But that ideal, it must be plain, is not natural to youth. Youth is aspiring, rebellious, inquisitive, iconoclastic, a bit romantic. All over the country the fact is bursting through the chains of repression. In scores of far-flung colleges the students have begun to challenge their professors, often very harshly. After a while, they may begin to challenge the masters of their professors. Not all of them will do it, and not most of them. But it doesn't take a majority to make a rebellion; it takes only a few determined leaders and a sound cause.

4
The Schoolma'm's Goal

THE SOCIAL OBJECTIVES OF SCHOOL ENGLISH, by Charles S. Pendleton. Nashville, Tenn.: *Published by the Author.* [The American Mercury, March, 1925.]

Here, in the form of a large flat book, eight and a half inches wide and eleven inches tall, is a sight-seeing bus touring the slums of pedagogy. The author, Dr. Pendleton, professes the teaching of English (not English, remember, but the teaching of English) at the George Peabody College for Teachers, an eminent seminary at Nashville, in the Baptist Holy Land, and his object in the investigation he describes was, in brief, to find out what the teachers who teach English hope to accomplish by teaching it. In other words, what, precisely, is the improvement that they propose to achieve in the pupils exposed to their art and mystery? Do they believe that the aim of teaching English is to increase the exact and beautiful use of the language? Or that it is to inculcate and augment patriotism? Or that it is to diminish sorrow in the home? Or that it has some other end, cultural, economic or military?

In order to find out, Prof. Pendleton, with true pedagogical diligence, proceeded to list all the reasons for teaching English that he could find. Some he got by cross-examining teachers. Others came from educators of a higher degree and puissance. Yet others he dug out of the text-books of pedagogy in common use, and the dreadful professional journals ordinarily read by teachers. Finally, he threw in some from miscellaneous sources, including his own inner consciousness. In all, he accumulated 1581 such reasons, or, as he calls them, objectives, and then he sat down and laboriously copied them upon 1581 very thin 3x5 cards, one to a card. Some of these cards were buff in color, some were blue, some were yellow, some were pink, and some were green. On the blue cards he copied all the objectives relating to the employment of English in conversation, on the yellow cards all those dealing with its use in literary composition, on the green cards all those having to do with speech-making, and so on. Then he shook up the cards, summoned eighty professional teachers of English, and asked them to sort out the objectives in the order of appositeness and merit. The results of this laborious sorting he now sets before the learned.

Don't be impatient! I won't keep you waiting. Here is the objective that got the most votes—the champion of the whole 1581:

The ability to spell correctly without hesitation all the ordinary words of one's writing vocabulary.

Here is the runner-up:

The ability to speak, in conversation, in complete sentences, not in broken phrases.

And here is No. 7:

The ability to capitalize speedily and accurately in one's writing.

And here is No. 9:

The ability to think quickly in an emergency.

And here are some more, all within the first hundred:

The ability to refrain from marking or marring in any way a borrowed book.

An attitude of democracy rather than snobbishness within a conversation.

Familiarity with the essential stories and persons of the Bible.

And some from the second hundred:

The ability to sing through—words and music—the national anthem.

The ability courteously and effectively to receive orders from a superior.

The avoidance of vulgarity and profanity in one's public speaking.

The ability to read silently without lip movements.

The habit of placing the page one is reading so that there will not be shadows upon it.

The ability to refrain from conversation under conditions where it is annoying or disagreeable to others.

The ability to converse intelligently about municipal and district civic matters.

The ability to comprehend accurately the meaning of all common abbreviations and signs one meets with in reading.

The ability, during one's reading, to distinguish between an author's central theme and his incidental remarks.

I refrain from any more: all these got enough votes to put them among the first 200 objectives—200 out of 1581. Nor do I choose them unfairly; most of those that I have not listed were quite as bad as those I have. But, you may protest, the good professor handed his cards to a jury of little girls of eight or nine years, or to the inmates of a home for the feeble-minded! He did, in fact, nothing of the kind. His jury was very carefully selected. It consisted of eighty teachers of such professional keenness that they were assembled at the University of Chicago for post-graduate study. Every one of them had been through either a college or a normal school; forty-seven of them held learned degrees; all of them had been engaged professionally in teaching English, some for years. They came from Michigan, Nebraska, Iowa, Missouri, Wisconsin, Toronto, Leland Stanford, Chicago and Northwestern Universities; from Oberlin, De Pauw, Goucher, Beloit and Drake Colleges; from a dozen lesser seminaries of the higher learning. They represented, not the lowest level of teachers of English in the Republic, but the highest level. And yet it was their verdict by a solemn referendum that the principal objective in teaching English was to make good spellers, and that after that came breeding of good capitalizers!

I present Dr. Pendleton's laborious work as overwhelming proof of a thesis that I have maintained for years, perhaps sometimes with undue heat: that pedagogy in the United States is fast descending to the estate of a childish necromancy, and that the worst idiots, even among pedagogues, are the teachers of English. It is positively dreadful to think that the young American species are exposed day in and day out to the contamination of such dark minds. What can be expected of education that is carried on in the very sewers of the intellect? How can morons teach anything that is worth knowing? Here and there, true enough, a competent teacher of English is encountered. I could name at least twenty in the whole country. But it does not appear that Dr. Pendleton, among his eighty, found even one. There is not the lightest glimmer of intelligence in all the appalling tables of statistics and black, zig-zag graphs that he has so painfully amassed. Nor any apparent capacity for learning. The sound thing, the sane thing and the humane thing to do with his pathetic herd of A.B.'s would be to take them out in the alley and knock them in the head.

5
The Heroic Age

JEFFERSON AND HAMILTON, by Claude G. Bowers. Boston: *The Houghton Mifflin Company.* JEFFERSON AND MONTI-CELLO, by Paul Wilstach. Garden City, L. I.: *Doubleday, Page &*

Company. CORRESPONDENCE OF JOHN ADAMS AND THOMAS JEFFERSON, 1812–1826, selected by Paul Wilstach. Indianapolis: *The Bobbs-Merrill Company.* [The American Mercury, March, 1926.]

Jefferson, in one of his last letters to Adams, dated March 25, 1826, spoke of the time when both came into fame as the heroic age. The phrase was certainly not mere rhetoric. The two differed enormously, both in their personalities and in their ideas—perhaps quite as much as Jefferson differed from Hamilton or Adams from his cousin Sam—but in one thing at least they were exactly alike: they were men of complete integrity. As Frederick the Great said of the Prussian *Junker*, one could not buy them, and they would not lie. The fact, at times, made them bitter enemies, and the virtues of the one were cancelled by the virtues of the other, to the damage of their common country. But when they stood together, they were irresistible, for complete integrity, when it does not spend itself against itself, is always irresistible—one of the few facts, to me known, that is creditable to the human race. The masses of men, like children, are easily deceived, but in the long run, like children again, they show a tendency to yield to character. Bit by bit it conquers them. They see in it all the high values that they are incapable of reaching themselves. They see the courage that they lack, and the honesty that they lack, and the resolution that they lack. All these things were in both Adams and Jefferson. They fell, in their day, into follies, but I don't think that anyone believes they were ever *pushed* into them. Adams, no doubt, could be bamboozled, but neither he nor Jefferson could be scared.

I fear that the gallant iconoclasts who revise our history-books sometimes forget all this. Engaged upon the destruction of legends, all of them maudlin and many of them downright insane, they also, at times, do damage to facts. One of these facts, it seems to me, ought not to be forgotten, to wit, that it took a great deal of courage, in the Summer of 1776, to sign Jefferson's celebrated exercise in colonial Johnsonese. There were ropes dangling in the air, and they were uncomfortably near. There were wives and children to be considered, and very agreeable estates. However dubious their primary motives, the men who signed took a long chance, quietly, simply, and with their faces to the front. How many of their successors in our own time have ever followed their example? I find it hard to think of one. The politician of to-day lacks their courage altogether; he lacks their incorruptible integrity. He is a complete coward. The whip of the Anti-Saloon League is enough to make him leap and tremble; the shadow of the rope would paralyze him with terror. He is for sale to anyone who has anything valuable to offer him, and the day after he has sold out to A he is ready to sell out to A's enemy, B. His honor is that of a street-walker.

So far we have progressed along the highroad of democracy. The gentleman survives in our politics only as an anachronism; his day is done. Mr. Bowers, in "Hamilton and Jefferson," traces the beggining of the decline; Mr. Wilstach, in the volume of Adams-Jefferson letters, shows it in full tide. Both authors are partial to Jefferson, and present charming portraits of him, especially Mr. Wilstach, in his other book, "Jefferson at Monticello." It seems to me that they often confuse the man and his ideas, especially Mr. Bowers. Jefferson was unquestionably one of our giants. There was more in his head than there has been in the heads of all the Presidents in office since he went out. He was a man of immense intellectual curiosity, profound originality, and great daring. His integrity was of Doric massiveness. But was he always right? I don't think many reflective Americans of to-day would argue that he was. Confronting enemies of great resourcefulness and resolute determination, he was forced, bit by bit, into giving his democratic doctrine a sweep and scope that took it far beyond the solid facts. It became a religious dogma rather than a political theory. Once he was gone, it fell into the hands of vastly inferior men, and soon it had reached its *reductio ad absurdum*. Jefferson died in 1826. By 1829, when Jackson came in, it was a nuisance; by 1837, when he went out, it was a joke.

Jefferson's enthusiasm blinded him to the fact that the liberty to which he had consecrated the high days of his early manhood was a two-headed boon. There was, first, the liberty of the people as a whole to determine the forms of their own government, levy their own taxes, and make their own laws— in brief, freedom from the despotism of the King. There was, second, the liberty of the individual man to live his own life, within the limits of decency and decorum, as he pleased—in brief, freedom from the despotism of the majority. Hamilton was as much in favor of the first kind of liberty as Jefferson: he made, in fact, even greater sacrifices for it. But he saw that it was worth nothing without the second kind—that it might easily become worth less than nothing, for the King, whatever his oppressions *en gros*, at least gave some protection to the isolated subject. Monarchy might be the protector of liberty as well as the foe of liberty. It had been so, in fact, in the Prussia of Frederick. And democracy might be far more the foe than the protector. It was obviously so in the France of the Reign of Terror. Hamilton, a hard-headed man, given to figures rather than to theories, saw all this; Jefferson, a doctrinaire, even in his best moments, saw only half of it. That failure to see together was at the bottom of their difference—and their difference came very near wrecking the United States. Burr's bullet probably prevented a colossal disaster. But it also opened the way for troubles in the years to come. We are in the midst of them yet, and we are by no means near the end of them.

The shadow of Jeffersonism, indeed, is still over us. We are still bound idiotically by the battle-cries of a struggle that was over more than a century ago. We have got the half of liberty, but the other half is yet to be wrested from the implacable fates, and there seems little likelihood that it will be wrested soon. All the fears of Hamilton have come to realization—and some of the fears of Jefferson to fill the measure. Minorities among us have no rights that the majority is bound to respect; they are dragooned and oppressed in a way that would make an oriental despot blush. Yet behind the majority, often defectively concealed, there is always a sinister minority, eager only for its own advantage and willing to adopt any device, however outrageous, to get what it wants. We have a puppet in the White House, pulled by wires, but with dangerous weapons in its hands. Law Enforcement becomes the new state religion. A law is something that A wants and can hornswoggle B, C, D, E and F into giving him—by bribery, by lying, by bluff and bluster, by making faces. G and H are therefore bound to yield it respect—nay, to worship it. It is something sacred. To question it is to sin against the Holy Ghost.

I wonder what Jefferson would think if he could come out of his tomb and examine the Republic that he helped to fashion. He was a man of towering enthusiasms, but he was also sharply intelligent: he knew an accomplished fact when he saw one. My guess is that, at the first Jefferson Day dinner following his emergence, he would make a startling and scandalous speech.

6
The Woes of a 100% American

THE NEW BARBARIANS, by Wilbur C. Abbott. Boston: *Little, Brown & Company.* [The American Mercury, May, 1925.]

It would be easy to poke fun at this disorderly and indignant tract; even, perhaps, to denounce the learned author, in a lofty manner, as a mere jackass. His argument, at more than one place, is so shaky that it tempts ribaldry with a powerful lure, almost a suction. His premises are often gratuitous and absurd; his conclusions are often fantastic. Worse, he argues in circles, and it is frequently hard to make out what he is advocating, and why. Worst of all, the urbanity suitable to a learned gentleman resident in Sparks street, Cambridge, Mass., sometimes yields to a libido far more suitable to an auctioneer, a Federal district attorney or a Methodist bishop, and he rants dreadfully. But against all this there is yet something to be said, and that something, I think, is sufficient to stay the impulse to have at him brutally, either with cackles or with invective. It is, in brief, this: that what he inveighs against, given his natural and laudable prejudices, is plentifully sufficient to excuse all his indignation, and all his incoherence, and even his occasional departures from the strict letter of the record—that it is a merit in any man, facing what he deems to be incubi and succubi, to belabor them in a hearty and vociferous manner, and without too pedantic a respect for the rules of evidence. That merit has nothing to do, at bottom, with his rightness or wrongness; it lies in his mere sincerity. Dr. Abbott is obviously full of sincerity; no fair reader can doubt it for an instant. But he has something more: he has under him a respectable body of facts, sound ones as well as shaky ones. The deductions he draws from them are often extravagant, and now and then he

mingles them with assumptions that seems to me to do violence to the most elemental common sense. Nevertheless, his
basic facts remain, and if I were an Anglo-Saxon as he is I suspect that they would fever me as they fever him.

What he complains of, in a few words, is the assault that has
been made of late upon the old American tradition and the
fundamental canons of American idealism, *i.e.*, upon the body
of ideas that Americans cherish as peculiarly their own, and
believe in with a romantic devotion. What he complains of, especially, is that this assault has been made, in the main, by men
who are not "Anglo-Saxons" (the professor himself quotes the
term: a touching concession to ethnological exactness)—that
it has been largely led by men whose very Americanism, when
they claim to be Americans at all, is open to question. When I
say open to question, I mean, of course, by "Anglo-Saxon"
Americans. Dr. Abbott seems to be firmly convinced that these
are the only ones entitled to the name. They are the pure
stock; their ancestors conquered the continent unaided. They
alone partake of the true national spirit, and may be trusted to
guard the national hearth. All other Americans are in the position of visitors, interlopers, relatives-in-law. They may become
in time, if they are good, creditable assistant Americans, but
they can no more enter into the full national heritage, as free
equals, than they can lift themselves by their boot-straps. The
American tradition, it appears, must forever remain a bit
strange to them; they are the children, not of heroes, but of
serfs. Thus it is no wonder that their political notions, when
they make bold to state them, are exotic and subversive. They
can imagine government only as a power above and beyond
the citizen. If they are not in favor of kaiserism, then they are
in favor of communism, which is simply kaiserism imposed
from below. Their politics is essentially a slave politics. They
stand opposed eternally to that self-reliant and somewhat pugnacious individualism which is the mark of the true "Anglo-
Saxon." If they ever come into power the Constitution will be
destroyed and freedom will perish.

Dr. Abbott's book, as I have said, is somewhat difficult; perhaps I misrepresent him in a few details. But in the main, I
believe, I gather his doctrine correctly; it is, indeed, a doctrine
that has grown very familiar. The Klu Klux has carried it into

every hamlet in the land, and bolstered it with the authority of Holy Writ. I could, if I would, amuse myself by exhibiting the holes in it. Is it a fact, then, that the "Anglo-Saxons" conquered the continent unaided? What of the Spaniards and French? What of the Dutch and Germans? What of the Scotch-Irish? Is it a fact that they invented the American scheme of government? What of Rousseau? Is it a fact all assaults upon that scheme have been made by assistant Americans? What of Jefferson, Jackson, Robert E. Lee, Jeff Davis, Bryan? Is it a fact that all the enemies of the Constitution came from below the salt? What of the Eighteenth Amendment: does it damage the Bill of Rights more or less than the late Dr. La Follette's vaporous schemes? Such questions suggest themselves in great variety. I could roll them off until you stood agape. But I have no desire to press a professor of history unduly; his authority, in the last analysis, cannot be upset by facts. And in the present case, whatever his errors in detail, it seems to me to be quite clear that the fundamental facts are on his side. There *is* unquestionably a difference between the "Anglo-Saxon" American and the non-"Anglo-Saxon"—a difference in their primary instincts, in their reactions to common stimuli, in their ways of looking at the world. And that difference, of late years, *has* come to the estate of a conflict, with the "Anglo-Saxon" striving to keep what he has—his point of view, his cultural leadership, his political hegemony—and the non-"Anglo-Saxon" trying to take it away from him. To deny that conflict is to fall into an absurdity far worse than any Dr. Abbott is guilty of. To admit it is to admit his clear right, nay, his bounden duty, to do battle for his side, passionately, desperately, and with any weapon at hand.

This he does in his book, and up to the limit of his forensic skill, which, I regret to have to add, is not noticeably great. If, at times, he grows a bit muddled, and even maudlin, then let us not hold the fact against him, for a man performing a *pas seul* upon a red-hot stove cannot be expected to achieve an impeccable step. It seems to me that this red-hot stove, at the moment, is under every conscious "Anglo-Saxon" in our great Republic—that he must be an insensate clod, indeed, if he does not feel the heat. The cultural leadership of the country is passing out of his hands, and he is beginning to lose even his political hegemony. I sat in the Democratic National Convention in 1924 as the Hon. Al Smith rolled up his votes, and watched the Ku Kluxers on the floor. They were transfixed with horror: if it was a comedy, then pulling tonsils is also a comedy. Dr. Abbott mentions Dreiser. The influence of Dreiser upon the literature of to-morrow in this land—upon all the youngsters who are now coming to maturity in the universities, and turning away from their ordained professors—will be a hundred times as potent as that of any New Englander now alive. Who is Dreiser? When the grandfathers of the Republic were hanging witches at Salem his forbears were raising grapes on the Rhine. Dr. Abbott professes history at Harvard. During the past ten years but one professor at that great university has materially colored the stream of ideas in America. He has since escaped abroad—and is a Spaniard. Every day a new Catholic church goes up; every day another Methodist or Presbyterian church is turned into a garage. But there is no need to labor the point. The fact is too obvious that the old easy dominance of the "Anglo-Saxon" is passing, that he must be up and doing if he would fasten his notions upon the generations to come. And the fact is equally obvious that his success in that emprise, so far, has been extremely indifferent—that, despite the great advantages that he enjoys, of position, of authority, of ancient right, he is making very heavy weather of it, and not even holding his own. I am frankly against him, and believe, as I have often made known, that he is doomed—that his opponents will turn out, in the long run, to be better men than he is. But I confess that I'd enjoy the combat more if he showed less indignation and more skill.

Dr. Abbott himself reveals many characteristic "Anglo-Saxon" weaknesses. His incoherence I have mentioned. There is also a downright inconsistency, often glaring. On one page he denounces all non-"Anglo-Saxons" as opponents of democracy; on another (for example, page 242) he denounces the fundamental tenets of democracy himself. This inconsistency is visible in nine "Anglo-Saxon" gladiators out of ten. What ails them all is that they have to defend democracy, and yet do not believe in it. Has any good "Anglo-Saxon" ever believed in it? I sometimes doubt it. Did Washington? Did John Adams? Jefferson did, but wasn't there a Celtic strain in him—wasn't he, after all, somewhat dubious, a sort of assistant American? In any case, the surviving Fathers were all apparently against him. In our own time how many "Anglo-Saxons" of the educated class actually believe in democracy? I know of none, and have heard of none. The late war revealed their true faith very brilliantly and even humorously. It was a crusade for democracy, and yet one of the shining partners was the late Czar of Russia! The assault upon the Kaiser was led by Roosevelt! The chief official enemy of absolutism was Wilson! No wonder the whole thing collapsed into absurdity. Dr. Abbott falls into a similar absurdity more than once. His book would be vastly more effective if he took all the idle prattle about democracy out of it, and grounded it upon the forthright doctrine that the "Anglo-Saxons," having got here first, own the country, and have a clear right to impose political disabilities upon later comers—in other words, if he advocated the setting up of an "Anglo-Saxon" aristocracy, with high privileges and prerogatives, eternally beyond the reach of the mongrel commonalty. This, in point of fact, is what he advocates, however much he may cloud his advocacy in democratic terms. I call upon him with all solemnity to throw off his false-face and come out with the bald, harsh doctrine. There is more logic in it than in his present nonsense; he could preach it more powerfully and beautifully. More, he would get help from unexpected quarters. I can speak, of course, only for one spear. I might quibble and protest, but I'd certainly be sorely tempted.

7
Yazoo's Favorite

AN OLD-FASHIONED SENATOR, by Harris Dickson. New York: *The Frederick A. Stokes Company*. [The Nation, October 14, 1925.]

Some time ago, essaying a literary survey of the Republic, I animadverted sadly upon the dreadful barrenness of the great State of Mississippi. Speaking as a magazine editor, I said that I had never heard of a printable manuscript coming out of it. Speaking as a frequenter of the Athenian grove, I said that I had never heard of it hatching an idea. Instantly there was an uproar from Iuka to Pascagoula. The vernacular press had at me with appalling yells; there were demands from the Ku Klux that I come down to Jackson and say it again; Kiwanis joined the Baptist Young People's Society in denouncing me as one debauched by Russian gold. Worse, the Mississippi intelligentsia also had at me. Emerging heroically from the crypts and spring-houses where they were fugitive from Rotary, they bawled me out as ignorant and infamous. Had I never heard, they demanded, of Harris Dickson, the Missisippi Balzac? Had I never heard of John Sharp Williams, the Mississippi Gladstone?

I had, but remained unmoved. I now continue unmoved after reading Balzac's tome on Gladstone. It is, in its small way, a tragic book. Here, obviously, is the best that Mississippi can do, in theme and treatment—and it is such puerile, blowsy stuff that reviewing it realistically would be too cruel. Here the premier literary artist of Mississippi devotes himself *con amore* to the life and times of the premier Mississippi statesman—and the result is a volume so maudlin and nonsensical that it would disgrace a schoolboy. The book is simply mush—and out of the mush there emerges only a third-rate politician, professionally bucolic and as hollow as a jug.

Yet this Williams, during his long years in Congress, passed in Washington as an intellectual. Cloak-room and barroom gossip credited him with a profound education and very subtle parts. Such ideas, when they prevail in Washington, perhaps need and deserve no investigation; the same astute correspondents who propagated this one later coupled the preposterous Coolidge with Pericles. But maybe there was some logic in it, after all; Williams, at some time in the past, had been to Heidelberg and knew more or less German and French. That accomplishment, in a Southern politician, was sufficient to set the capital by the ears. So the Williams legend grew, and toward the end it rose to the dignity of a myth, like that of Dr. Taft's eminence as a constitutional lawyer. Even the learned hero's daily speeches on Teutonic mythology during the war did not drag him out of Valhalla himself. The press-gallery gaped and huzzahed.

But the Heidelberg chapter in Mr. Dickson's book leaves the myth rather sick. It starts off, indeed, with a disconcerting couplet:

> In Germany 'twas very clear
> He'd leave the rapiers for beer.

And what follows is distressingly silent about cultural accretions. Young Williams' main business at Heidelberg, it appears, was putting the abominable Prussian *Junker* in their place. They naturally assumed that their American fellow-student could be thrown about with impunity. Encountering him on the sidewalk, they tried, in the manner made historic by the Creel Press Bureau, to shove him off. Presently one of these fiends in human form came melodramatically to grief. Williams challenged him, and "according to Prussian ethics," named the weapons—pistols. A shock, indeed! The monster expected sabers, at which he was diabolically expert, but Williams didn't intend "to go home with his face all slashed, and have folks jeer at him for getting his jaw cut on a beer glass." Facing cold lead, the Prussian was so scared that he fired prematurely. Worse, he so lost his wits that he addressed his antagonist as Freiherr Williams. That antagonist fired into a snowbank. Some time later, having thus got all that was of worth out of Heidelberg, he came sailing home, "full even then of his ultimate intention: he'd go in for politics, he'd become a professional politican."

A professional politician he remained for thirty years, always in office, first in the House and then in the Senate. His start was slow—he practiced law for a time—, but once he was on the payroll he stayed there until old age was upon him. For a number of years he was Democratic leader in the House; twice he got the party vote for the Speakership. In the Senate he was technically in the ranks, but on great occasions he stepped forward. His specialties, toward the end, were the divine inspiration of Woodrow Wilson, the incomparable valor of the American soldier, the crimes of the Kaiser, the superiority of the "Anglo-Saxon," the godlike bellicosity of the Confederate gentry, and the nature and functions of a gentleman. On these themes he discoursed almost every afternoon. The boys in the press-gallery liked him, and he got plenty of space. Always his rodomontades brought forth dark hints about his esoteric learning, and the news that, next after Henry Cabot Lodge, he was the most cultivated man in the Senate.

Mr. Dickson prints extracts from some of his speeches. Criticism, obviously, is an art not yet in practice in Mississippi, even among the literati. I used to read him in the *Congressional Record*; he was really not so bad as Dickson makes him out. His career, seen in retrospect, seems to have been mainly a vacuum. Once or twice he showed a certain fine dignity, strange in a Southern politician. He opposed the Prohibition frenzy. He voted against the bonus. But usually, despite his constant talk of independence, he ran with the party pack. For years a professional Jeffersonian, he brought his career to a climax by giving lyrical support to the Emperor Woodrow, who heaved the Jeffersonian heritage into the ash-can. During the La Follette uproar he was one of the most vociferous of the witch-burners. He passed out in silence, regretted for his rustic charm, but not much missed.

I commend "An Old-Fashioned Senator" to all persons who are interested in the struggle of the South to throw off its cobwebs. Both as document and as work of art the book makes it very plain why Mississippi's place in that struggle is in the last rank.

8

The Father of Service

THE LIFE STORY OF ORISON SWETT MARDEN, by Margaret Connolly. New York: *The Thomas Y. Crowell Company*. [The American Mercury, February, 1926.]

If Dr. Marden had not written his first book, said Frank A. Munsey one day, he would have been a millionaire. By Munseyan standards, praise could go no higher—and Munsey knew his man, for they were fellow-waiters in a Summer hotel back in the '70's and kept up friendly exchange until Marden's death in 1924. Both sprang from the hard, inhospitable soil of Northern New England, both knew dire poverty in youth, both got somewhere a yearning for literary exercises, and both cherished an immense respect for the dollar. But though fate

brought them together when they were young, they chose
different paths later on. Munsey, with "Afloat in a Great
City," "The Boy Broker," and other inspirational master-
works behind him, abandoned beautiful letters for the stock
market, and eventually gathered in so much money that he
could afford to butcher great newspapers in sheer excess of
animal spirits, as lesser men butcher clay pigeons. Marden,
going the other way, abandoned the hotel business, for which
he seemed to have had genius, for the pen, and devoted the
last thirty years of his life to composition.

His bibliography runs to a hundred or more volumes—a
colossal, relentless, overwhelming deluge of bilge. All his
books have the same subject: getting on in the world. That
was, to him, the only conceivable goal of human aspiration.
Day in and day out, for three decades, he preached his simple
gospel to all mankind, not only in his books, but also in countless pamphlets, in lectures, and in the pages of his magazine,
Success. Its success was instantaneous and durable. His first
book, "Pushing to the Front," rapidly went through a dozen
editions, and was presently translated into a dozen foreign
languages. It remained, to the end, his best-seller, but it had
many formidable rivals. Altogether, his writings in book-form
must have reached a total of 20,000,000 copies, including
3,000,000 in twenty-five tongues other than English. In Germany alone he sold more than 500,000 copies of thirty volumes. He remains to-day the most popular of American
authors in Europe, and by immense odds. I have encountered
translations of his books on the news-stands of remote towns
in Spain, Poland and Czecho-Slovakia. In places where even
Mark Twain is unknown—nay, even Jack London, Upton Sinclair and James Oliver Curwood—he holds aloft the banner of
American literature.

I lack the stomach for the job myself, but I think a lot could
be learned about the psychology of *Homo boobiens* through an
intensive study of Marden's vast shelf of books. The few I have
read seem to be exactly alike; no doubt all the rest resemble
them very closely. What they preach, in brief, is the high value
of hopefulness, hard work, high purpose and unflagging resolution. The appeal is to the natural discontent and vague aspiration of the common man. The remedy offered is partly

practical and partly mystical—practical in its insistence upon
the sound utility of the lowly virtues, mystical in its constant
implication that matter will always yield to mind, that high
thinking has a cash value. An evil philosophy? Surely not. A
valid one? There it is not so easy to answer. Marden is full of
proofs that what he preaches works—but only too often those
proofs show the incredible appositeness and impeccability of
patent-medicine testimonials. How many false hopes he must
have raised in his day! One imagines humble hearts leaping to
the gaudy tales of Judge Elbert Gary, Beethoven and Edison in
the darkest reaches of Montenegro, Norway and Tennessee.
Down went the dose, but was the patient actually cured? Well,
perhaps, he at least *felt* better—and that was something. Marden was not to be pinned down to clinical records; he was, in
his way, a poet, and even more a prophet. A religious exaltation was in him; he knew how to roll his eyes. The first article
of his creed was that it was a sin to despair—that realism was a
black crime against the Holy Ghost. He reduced the Beatitudes to one: Blessed are they that believe in their stars, and
are up and doing.

His infuence was immense, and perhaps mainly for the
good. He soothed his customers with his optimistic taffy, and
made them happier. It is, indeed, small wonder that eminent
figures in finance and industry admired him greatly, and gave
his books to their slaves. He turned the discontents of those
slaves inward; instead of going on strike and breaking windows
they sat up nights trying to generate inspiration and practicing
hope and patience. He was thus a useful citizen in a democratic state, and comparable to the Rev. Dr. Billy Sunday. He
preached a Direct Action of a benign and laudable sort, with
Service running through it. His mark shines brilliantly from the
forehead of every Y.M.C.A. secretary in the land, and from
the foreheads, too, of most of the editorial writers. Many lesser
platitudinarians followed him—for example, Dr. Frank Crane
and the Rev. Dr. Henry van Dyke—, but he kept ahead of all of
them. None other could put the obvious into such mellow and
caressing terms. None other could so completely cast off all
doubts and misgivings. When he spit on his hands and let himself out, the whole world began to sparkle like a Christmas tree.
He was Kiwanis incarnate, with whispers of the Salvation Army.

In early manhood he had cast off the demoniacal theology of his native hills, but one treasure of his Puritan heritage he retained to the end: he knew precisely and certainly what God wanted His children to be and do. God wanted them to be happy, and He wanted them to attain to happiness by working hard, saving money, obeying the boss, and keeping on the lookout for better jobs. Thus, after a hiatus of 137 years, Marden took up the torch of Poor Richard. He was, in his way, the American St. Paul. He was the pa of Kiwanis. He carried the gospel of American optimism to all the four quarters of the world.

9
A Modern Masterpiece

THE POET ASSASSINATED, by Guillaume Apollinaire, translated from the French by Matthew Josephson. New York: *The Broom Publishing Company*. [The American Mercury, March, 1924.]

Whatever may be said against the young literary lions of the Foetal School, whether by such hoary iconoclasts as Ernest Boyd or by such virginal presbyters as John S. Sumner, the saving fact remains that the boys and girls have, beneath their false faces, a sense of humor, and are not shy about playing it upon one another. Such passionate pioneers of the movement as *Broom* and the *Little Review* printed, in their day, capital parodies in every issue, many of them, I believe, deliberate and malicious—parodies of Ezra Pound by the Baroness Elsa von Freytag-Loringhoven, and of the Baroness Elsa Freytag-Loringhoven by E. E. Cummings, and of E. E. Cummings by young Roosevelt J. Yahwitz, Harvard '27. And the thing goes on to this day. Ah, that the rev. seniors of the Hypoendocrinal School were as gay and goatish! Ah, specifically, that Dr. Paul Elmer More would occasionally do a salacious burlesque of Dr. Brander Matthews, and that Dr. Matthews would exercise his forecastle wit upon the Pennsylvania Silurian, Prof. Fred Lewis Pattee!

In the present work, beautifully printed by the *Broom* Press, there is jocosity in the grand manner. For a long while past, as time goes among such neologomaniacs, the youths of the movement have been whooping up one Guillaume Apollinaire. When this Apollinaire died in 1918, so they lamented, there passed out the greatest creative mind that France had seen since the Middle Ages. He was to Jean Cocteau, even, as Cocteau was to Eugène Sue. His books were uncompromising and revolutionary; had he lived he would have done to the banal prose of the Babbitts of letters what Eric Satie has done to the art of the fugue. Such news was not only printed in the *Tendenz* magazines that come and go; it was transmitted by word of mouth from end to end of Greenwich Village. More, it percolated to graver quarters. The estimable *Dial* let it be known that Apollinaire was a profound influence on the literature and perhaps still more on the art and spirit of this modern period. Once, when Dr. Canby was off lecturing in Lancaster, Pa., his name even got into the *Literary Review*.

This electric rumor of him was helped to prosperity by the fact that specific data about him were extremely hard to come by. His books seemed to be rare—some of them, indeed, unprocurable—, and even when one of them was obtained and examined it turned out to be largely unintelligible. He wrote, it appeared, in an occult dialect, partly made up of fantastic slang from the French army. He gave to old words new and mysterious meanings. He kept wholly outside the vocabulary at the back of "College French." Even returning exiles from La Rotonde were baffled by some of his phrases; all that they could venture was that they were unprecedented and probably obscene. But the Village, as everyone knows, does not spurn the cabalistic; on the contrary, it embraces and venerates the cabalistic. Apollinaire grew in fame as he became unscrutable. Displacing Cocteau, Paul Morand, Harry Kemp, T. S. Eliot, André Salmon, Paul Valéry, Maxwell Bodenheim, Jean Giraudoux and all the other gods of that checkered dynasty, he was lifted to the first place in the Valhalla of the Advanced Thinkers. It was Apollinaire's year. . . .

The work before us is the pricking of the bladder—a jest highly effective, but somewhat barbarous. M. Josephson simply translates Apollinaire's masterpiece, adds an *apparatus criticus* in the manner of T. S. Eliot, and then retires discreetly to wait for the yells. They will make a dreadful din, or I am no literary pathologist! For what does "The Poet Assassinated" turn out to be? It turns out to be a dull pasquinade in the manner of a rather atheistic sophomore, with a few dirty words thrown in to shock the *booboisie*. From end to end there is not as much wit in it as you will hear in a genealogical exchange between two taxicab drivers. It is flat, flabby and idiotic. It is as profound as an editorial in the Washington *Star* and as revolutionary as Ayer's Almanac. It is the best joke pulled off on the Young Forward-Lookers since Eliot floored them with the notes to "The Waste Land."

M. Josephson rather spoils its effect, I believe, by rubbing it in—that is, by hinting that Apollinaire was of romantic and mysterious origin—that his mother was a Polish lady of noble name and his father a high prelate of the Catholic Church— that he himself was born at Monte Carlo and baptized in Santa Maria Maggiore at Rome. This is too much. Apollinaire was, like all Frenchmen of humor, a German Jew. His father was a respectable waiter at Appenrodt's, by name Max Spritzwasser: hence the *nom de plume*. His mother was a Mlle. Kunigunda Luise Schmidt, of Holzkirchen, Oberbayern.

10

Sweet Stuff

SIX DAYS OF THE WEEK: A BOOK OF THOUGHTS ABOUT LIFE AND RELIGION, by Henry van Dyke. New York: *Charles Scribner's Sons.* [The American Mercury, March, 1925.]

I offer a specimen:

As living beings we are part of a universe of life.

A second:

Unless we men resolve to be good, the world will never be better.

A third:

Behind Christianity there is Christ.

A fourth:

If Washington had not liberated the American Republic, Lincoln would have had no Union to save.

A fifth:

Some people say that a revolution is coming on in our own age and country. It is possible.

A sixth:

God made us all.

A seventh:

It is a well-known fact that men can lie, and that very frequently they do.

An eighth:

To be foolish is an infirmity. To fool others is a trick.

A ninth:

The Bible was not given to teach science, but religion.

A tenth:

A whole life spent with God is better than half a life.

An eleventh:

Drunkenness ruins more homes and wrecks more lives than war.

A twelfth:

Anything out of the ordinary line will attract notice.

Tupper *est mort*! *Hoch* Tupper! *Hoch, hoch! Dreimal hoch!*

IX.

The Fringes of Lovely Letters

I
Authorship as a Trade

IT is my observation as an editor that most beginning authors are attracted to the trade of letters, not because they have anything apposite and exigent to say, but simply because it seems easy. Let us imagine an ambitious and somewhat gassy young gal, turned out of the public high-school down the street with good marks in English—that is, in the sort of literary composition practiced by schoolma'ms. Having read "Ulysses," "Jurgen" and "Babbitt," she is disinclined to follow her mother too precipitately into the jaws of holy monogamy —or, at all events, she shrinks from marrying such a clod as her father is, and as her brothers and male classmates will be tomorrow. What to do? The professions demand technical equipment. Commerce is sordid. The secretary, even of a rich and handsome man, get up at 7:30 A.M. Most of the fine arts are regarded, by her family, as immoral. So she pays $3 down on a second-hand typewriter, lays in a stock of copy paper, and proceeds to enrich the national literature.

It is such aspirants, I suppose, who keep the pot boiling for the schools of short-story writing and scenario writing that now swarm in the land. Certainly these schools, in so far as I have any acquaintance with them, offer nothing of value to the beginner of genuine talent. They seem to be run, in the main, by persons as completely devoid of critical sense as so many Congressmen, street railway curve-greasers or Methodist revivalists. Their text-books are masses of unmitigated rubbish. But no doubt that rubbish seems impressive enough to the customers I have mentioned, for it is both very vague and very cocksure—an almost irresistible combination. So a hundred thousand second-hand Coronas rattle and jingle in ten thousand remote and lonely towns, and the mail of every magazine editor in America is as heavy as the mail of a get-rich-quick stock-broker.

Unluckily, there is seldom anything in this mail to bulge his eyes and make his heart go pitter-pat. What he finds in it, day in and day out, is simply the same dull, obvious, shoddy stuff —the same banal and threadbare ideas set forth in the same flabby and unbeautiful words. They all seem to write alike, as, indeed, they all seem to think alike. They react to stimuli with the machine-like uniformity and precision of soldiers in a file. The spectacle of life is to all of them exactly the same spectacle. They bring no more to it, of private, singular vision, than so many photographic lenses. In brief, they are unanimously commonplace, unanimously stupid. Free education has cursed them with aspirations beyond their congenital capacities, and they offer the art of letters only the gifts suitable to the lowly crafts of the jazz-baby and the schoolma'm. They come from an intellectual level where conformity seems the highest of goods, and so they lack the primary requisite of the imaginative author: the capacity to see the human comedy afresh, to discover new relations between things, to discover new significances in man's eternal struggle with his fate. What they have to say is simply what any moderately intelligent suburban pastor or country editor would have to say, and so it is not worth hearing.

This disparity between aspiration and equipment runs through the whole of American life; material prosperity and popular education have made it a sort of national disease. Two-thirds of the professors in our colleges are simply cans full of undigested knowledge, mechanically acquired; they cannot utilize it; they cannot think. We are cursed likewise with hordes of lawyers who would be happier and more useful driving trucks, and hordes of doctors who would be strained even as druggists. So in the realm of beautiful letters. Poetry has become a recreation among us for the intellectually unemployed and unemployable: persons who, a few generations ago, would have taken it out on china-painting. The writing of novels is undertaken by thousands who lack the skill to describe a dog-fight. The result is a colossal waste of paper, ink and postage—worse, of binding cloth and gold foil. For a great deal of this drivel, by one dodge or another, gets into print. Many of the correspondence-school students, after hard diligence, learn how to write for the cheap magazines; not a few of them eventually appear between covers, and are solemnly reviewed.

Does such stuff sell? Apparently it does, else the publishers would not print so much of it. Its effect upon those who read it must be even worse than that of the newspapers and popular magazines. They come to it with confident expectations. It is pretentiously bound; *ergo*, there must be something in it. That something is simply platitude. What has been said a thousand times is said all over again. This time it must be true! Thus the standardization of the American mind goes on, and against ideas that are genuinely novel there are higher and higher battlements erected. Meanwhile, on the lower levels, where the latest recruits to letters sweat and hope, this rubbish is laboriously imitated. Turn to any of the cheap fiction magazines, and you will find out how bad it can be at its worst. No, not quite at its worst, for the contributors to the cheap fiction magazines have at least broken into print—they have as they say, made the grade. Below them are thousands of aspirants of even slenderer talents—customers of the correspondence schools, patrons of lectures by itinerant literary pedagogues, patient manufacturers of the dreadful stuff that clogs every magazine editor's mail. Here is the ultimate reservoir of the national literature—and here, unless I err, is only bilge.

The remedy? I know of none. Moreover, I do not believe in remedies. So long as the prevailing pedagogues are not found out, and the absurd effort to cram every moron with booklearning goes on in the Republic, that long there will be too much reading, and too much writing. But let us get out of the fact whatever consolation is in it: too much writing, at worst, is at least a bearable evil. Certainly it is vastly less dangerous than too much religion, and less a nuisance than too much politics. The floggers of Coronas, if they were halted by law, might take to the uplift—as, indeed, many corn-fed pedagogues are already doing, driven out of their jobs by the murrain of Fundamentalism. If I yell against them it is because, on days when the rain keeps me indoors, I am a critic. Perhaps other folks suffer less. Nevertheless, I often wonder what the genuinely competent novelists of the nation think of it—how the invasion of their craft by so many bunglers and numskulls appears to them, and affects them. Surely it must tend to narrow the audience they appeal to, and so do them damage. Who was it who said that, in order that there may be great poets, there must be great audiences too? I believe it was old Walt. He knew. Facing an audience deluged with molasses by Whittier, Felicia Hemans and Fanny Fern, he found the assumptions all against him. He was different, and hence suspicious: it took him two generations to make his way. The competent novelist, setting up shop in America to-day, is confronted by the same flood. If he is pertinacious, he may win in the end, but certainly it takes endurance. Hergesheimer, in his first book, unquestionably had something to say. Its point of view was new; there was a fine plausibility in it; it was worth attending to. But Hergesheimer drove along for eight or ten years, almost in a vacuum. I could add others: Anderson, Cabell, even Dreiser. Cabell became known to the women's clubs with his twelfth book. Meanwhile, a dozen cheesemongers had been adored, and a thousand had made good livings with their sets of rubber-stamps.

2
Authors as Persons

My trade forces me into constant association with persons of literary skill and aspiration, good and bad, male and female, foreign and domestic. I can only report, after a quarter of a century of commerce with them, that I find them, with a few brilliant exceptions, very dull, and that I greatly prefer the society of Babbitts. Is this heresy? If so, I can only offer my sincere regrets. The words are wrung from me, not by any desire to be unpleasant, but simply by a lifelong and incurable affection for what, for want of a better name, is called the truth. Nine-tenths of the literary gents that I know, indeed, are hotter for the dollar than any Babbitt ever heard of. Their talk is not about what they write, but about what they get for it. Not infrequently they get a great deal. I know a number who make more annually than honest bank presidents, even than Christian bank presidents. A few probably top the incomes of railroad purchasing-agents and nose-and-throat specialists, and come close to the incomes of realtors, lawyers and bootleggers. They practice a very profitable trade.

And no wonder, for they pursue it in the most assiduously literate country in Christendom. Our people, perhaps, seldom read anything that is good, but they at least read—day and night, weekdays and Sundays. We have so many magazines of more than 500,000 circulation that a list of them would fill this page. We have at least a dozen above 1,000,000. These magazines have immense advertising revenues, and are thus very prosperous. They can therefore pay high prices for manuscripts. The business of supplying such manuscripts has made a whole herd of authors rich. I do not object to their wealth; I simply report its lamentable effects upon them, and upon the aspirants who strive to imitate them. For those effects go down to the lowest levels. The neophyte, as I have said, seldom shows any yearning to discharge ideas, to express himself, to tackle and master a difficult enterprise; he shows only a desire to get money in what seems to him to be an easy way. Short cuts, quick sales, easy profits—it is all very American. Do we gabble about efficiency? Then the explanation is to be sought in the backwashes of Freudism. Nowhere else on earth is genuine competence so rare. The average American plumber cannot plumb; the average American cook cannot cook; the average American literary gent has nothing to say, and says it with rubber-stamps.

But I was speaking of the literati as persons. They suffer, I believe from two things. The first is what I have just described: their general fraudulence. The second springs out of the fact that their position, in the Republic, is very insecure—that they have no public dignity. It is no longer honorable *per se* to be engaged in travails of the spirit, as it used to be in the New England of the *Aufklärung*; it is honorable only if it pays. I believe that the fact discourages many aspirants who, if they went on, might come to something. They are blasted in their tender years, and so literature loses them. Too sensitive to sit below the salt, they join the hearty, red-blooded men who feast above it, admired by the national gallery. It is, indeed, not surprising that the majority of college graduates, once headed as a matter of course for the grove of Athene, now go into business—that Harvard now turns out ten times as many bond salesmen every year as metaphysicians and martyrs. Business, in America, offers higher rewards than any other human enterprise, not only in money but also in dignity. Thus it tends to attract the best brains of the country. Is Kiwanis idiotic? The answer is that Kiwanis no more represents business than Greenwich Village represents literature. On the higher levels its bilge does not flow—and on those higher levels, as I have hinted, there are shrewder fellows, and more amusing, than ever you will find in the Authors' Club. These fellows, by the strict canons of ethnology, are Babbitts, but it seems to me that they are responsible nevertheless for everything that makes life in the United States tolerable. One finds, in their company, excellent wines and liquors, and one seldom hears any cant.

I don't believe that this is a healthy state of affairs. I believe that business should be left to commonplace and insensitive minds, and that men of originality, and hence of genuine charm, should be sucked automatically into enterprises of a greater complexity and subtlety. It is done in more ancient countries; it has been done from remote antiquity under civilizations that have aged in the wood, and are free from fusel oil. But it is not yet done in These States. Only an overwhelming natural impulse—perhaps complicated by insanity—can urge an American into the writing of fugues or epics. The pull is toward the investment securities business. That pull, yielded to, leads to high rewards. The successful business man among us—and only the sheer imbecile, in such gaudy times as these, is not successful—enjoys the public respect and adulation that elsewhere bathe only bishops and generals of artillery. He is treated with dignity in the newspapers, even when he appears in combat with his wife's lover. His opinion is sought upon all public questions, including the æsthetic. In the stews and wineshops he receives the attention that, in old Vienna, used to be given to Beethoven. He enjoys an aristocratic immunity to most forms of judicial process. He wears the *légion d'honneur*, is an LL.D. of Yale, and is received cordially at the White House.

The literary gent, however worthy, scales no such heights under our *Kultur*. Only one President since the birth of the Republic has ever welcomed men of letters at the White House, and that one, the sainted Roosevelt, judged them by their theological orthodoxy and the hair upon their chests. A few colored poets were added to make the first pages; that was all. The literati thus wander about somewhat disconsolately among us, and tend to become morose and dull. If they enjoy the princely fees of the train-boy magazines, they are simply third-rate business men—successful, perhaps, but without the Larger Vision. If they happen to be genuine artists—and now and then it *does* happen—they are as lonely as life insurance solicitors at a convention of Seventh Day Adventists. Such sorrows do not make for *Gemütlichkeit*. There is much more of it in the pants business.

3
Birth Pangs

I have just said that the typical American author, when he talks intelligibly at all, talks of money. I have said also that his aim in writing is not to rid himself of ideas that bulge and fever his skull, but to get that money in an easy way. Both statements, though true, need a certain qualification. Writing looks easier to the neophyte than any other job open to him, but once he settles down to its practice he finds that it is full of unanticipated pains. So he tends, as he grows older, to talk of those pains almost as much as he talks of their rewards in cash. Here, indeed, all the authors that I know agree, if they agree on nothing else, and in their agreement they show the greatest heat and eloquence. And the beautiful ladies of the trade reënforce and ratify the plaint of the bucks. Writing, they all say, is the most dreadful chore ever inflicted upon human beings. It is not only exhausting mentally; it is also extremely fatiguing physically. The writer leaves his desk, his day's work done, with his mind empty and the muscles of his back and neck full of a crippling stiffness. He has suffered horribly that the babies may be fed and beauty may not die.

The worst of it is that he must always suffer alone. If authors could work in large, well-ventilated factories, like cigarmakers or garment-workers, with plenty of their mates about and a flow of lively professional gossip to entertain them, their labor would be immensely lighter. But it is essential to their craft that they perform its tedious and vexatious operations *a cappella*, and so the horrors of loneliness are added to its other unpleasantnesses. An author at work is continuously and inescapably in the presence of himself. There is nothing to divert and soothe him. So every time a vagrant regret or sorrow assails him, it has him instantly by the ear, and every time a wandering ache runs down his leg it shakes him like the bite of a tiger. I have yet meet an author who was not a hypochondriac. Saving only physicians, who are always ill and in fear of death, the literati are perhaps the most lavish consumers of pills and philtres in this world, and the most willing customers of surgeons. I can scarcely think of one, known to me personally, who is not constantly dosing himself with medicines, or regularly resorting to the knife. At the head of the craft stand men who are even more celebrated as invalids than they are as authors. I know of one who——

But perhaps I had better avoid invading what, after all, may be private confidences, though they are certainly not imparted in confidential tones. The point is that an author, penned in a room during all his working hours with no company save his own, is bound to be more conscious than other men of the petty malaises that assail all of us. They tackle him, so to speak, in a vacuum; he can't seek diversion from them without at the same time suffering diversion from his work. And what they leave of him is tortured and demoralized by wayward and uncomfortable thoughts. It must be obvious that other men, even among the intelligentsia, are not beset so cruelly. A judge on the bench, entertaining a ringing in the ears, can do his work almost as well as if he heard only the voluptuous rhetoric of the lawyers. A clergyman, carrying on his degraded mummery, is not appreciably crippled by a sour stomach: what he says has been said before, and only scoundrels question it. And a surgeon, plying his exhilarating art and mystery, suffers no professional damage from the wild thought that the attending nurse is more sightly than his wife. But I defy anyone to write a competent sonnet with a ringing in his ears, or to compose sound criticism with a sour stomach, or to do a plausible love scene with a head free of private amorous fancies. These things are sheer impossibilities. The poor literatus encounters them and their like every time he enters his work-room and spits on his hands. The moment the door bangs he begins a depressing, losing struggle with his body and his mind.

Why then, do rational men and women engage in so barbarous and exhausting a vocation—for there are relatively intelligent and enlightened authors, remember, just as there are relatively honest politicians, and even bishops. What keeps them from deserting it for trades that are less onerous, and, in the eyes of their fellow creatures, more respectable? The first, and perhaps the foremost reason I have already exposed at length: the thing pays. But there is another, and it ought to be heard too. It lies, I believe, in the fact that an author, like any other so-called artist, is a man in whom the normal vanity of all men is so vastly exaggerated that he finds it a sheer impossibility to hold it in. His overpowering impulse is to gyrate before his fellow men, flapping his wings and emitting defiant yells. This being forbidden by the *Polizei* of all civilized countries, he takes it out by putting his yells on paper. Such is the thing called self-expression.

In the confidences of the literati, of course, it is always depicted as something much more mellow and virtuous. Either they argue that they are moved by a yearning to spread the enlightenment and save the world, or they allege that what steams them and makes them leap is a passion for beauty. Both theories are quickly disposed of by an appeal to the facts. The stuff written by nine authors out of ten, it must be plain at a glance, has as little to do with spreading the enlightenment as the state papers of the late Dr. Warren Gamaliel Harding. And there is no more beauty in it, and no more sign of a feeling of beauty, than you will find in a hotel dining-room or a college yell. The impulse to create beauty, indeed, is rather rare in literary men, and almost completely absent from the younger ones. If it shows itself at all, it comes as a sort of afterthought. Far ahead of it comes the yearning to make money. And after the yearning to make money comes the yearning to make a noise. The impulse to create beauty lingers far behind; not infrequently there is a void where it ought to be. Authors, as a class, are extraordinarily insensitive to beauty, and the fact reveals itself in their customary (and often incredibly extensive) ignorance of the other arts. I'd have a hard job naming six American novelists who could be depended upon to recognize a fugue without prompting, or six poets who could give a rational account of the difference between a Gothic cathedral and a Standard Oil filling-station. The thing goes even further. Most novelists, in my experience, know nothing of poetry, and very few poets have any feeling for the beauties of prose. As for the dramatists, three-fourths of them are unaware that such things as prose and poetry exist at all. It pains me to set down such inconvenient and blushful facts. They will be seized upon, I daresay, by the evangelists of Kiwanis, and employed to support the doctrine that authors are public enemies, and ought to be deported to Russia. I do not go so far. I simply say that many who pursue the literary life are less romantic and high-toned than they might be—that communion with them is anything but the thrilling thing that provincial club ladies fancy. If the fact ought to be concealed, then blame my babbling upon scientific passion. That passion, to-day, has me by the ear.

4
Want Ad

The death of William Dean Howells in 1920 brought to an end a decorous and orderly era in American letters, and issued in a sort of anarchy. One may describe the change, perhaps, by throwing it into dramatic form. Suppose Joseph Conrad and Anatole France were still alive and on their way to the United States on a lecture tour, or to study Prohibition or sex hygiene, or to pay their respects to Henry Ford. Suppose they were to arrive in New York at 2 P.M. to-day. Who would go down the bay on a revenue-cutter to meet them—that is, who in addition to the newspaper reporters and baggage-searchers—who to represent American Literature? I can't think of a single fit candidate. So long as Howells kept to his legs he was chosen almost automatically for all such jobs, for he was the dean of the national letters, and acknowledged to be such by everyone. Moreover, he had experience at the work and a natural gift for it. He looked well in funeral garments. He had a noble and ancient head. He made a neat and caressing speech. He understood etiquette. And before he came to his growth, stretching back into the past, there was a long line precisely like him—Mark Twain, General Lew Wallace, James Russell Lowell, Edmund Clarence Stedman, Richard Watson Gilder, Bryant,

Emerson, Irving, Cooper, and so on back to the dark abysm of time.

Such men performed a useful and highly onerous function. They represented letters in all public and official ways. When there was a grand celebration at one of the older universities they were present in their robes, freely visible to the lowliest sophomore. When there was a great banquet, they sat between generals in the Army and members of the firm of J. P. Morgan & Company. When there was a solemn petition or protest to sign—against fiat money, the massacres in Armenia, municipal corruption, or the lack of international copyright—they signed in fine round hands, not for themselves alone, but for the whole fraternity of American literati. Most important of all, when a literary whale from foreign parts was sighted off Fire Island, they jumped into their frock coats, clapped on their plug-hats and made the damp, windy trip through the Narrows on the revenue-cutter, to give the visitor welcome in the name of the eminent living and the illustrious dead. It was by such men that Dickens was greeted, and Thackeray, and Herbert Spencer, and Max O'Rell, and Blasco Ibáñez, and Matthew Arnold, and James M. Barrie, and Kipling, and (until they found his boot-leg wife under his bed) Maxim Gorky. I name names at random. No worthy visitor was overlooked. Always there was the stately committee on the revenue-cutter, always there was the series of polite speeches, and always there was the general feeling that the right thing had been done in the right way— that American literature had been represented in a tasteful and resounding manner.

Who is to represent it to-day? I search the country without finding a single suitable candidate, to say nothing of a whole posse. Turn, for example, to the mystic nobles of the American Academy of Arts and Letters. I pick out five at random: William C. Brownell, Augustus Thomas, Hamlin Garland, Owen Wister and Henry van Dyke. What is wrong with them? The plain but dreadful fact that no literary foreigner has even heard of them—that their appearance on the deck of his incoming barge would puzzle and alarm him, and probably cause him to call for the police. These men do not lack the homely virtues. They all spell correctly, write neatly, and print nothing that is not constructive. In the five of them there is not enough sin to raise a Congressman's temperature one-hundredth of a degree. But they are completely devoid of what is absolutely essential to the official life: they have, so to speak, no stage presence. There is nothing rotund and gaudy about them. No public and unanimous reverence bathes them. What they write or say never causes any talk. To be welcomed by them, jointly or severally, would appear to Thomas Hardy or Gabriel D'Annunzio as equal to being welcomed by representatives of the St. Joe, Mo., Rotary Club. Nor do I find any better stock among their heirs and apprentices in the National Institute. Put Henry Sydnor Harrison, say, against Howells: it is a wart succeeding Ossa. Match Clayton Hamilton with Edmund Clarence Stedman: Broadway against Wall Street. Shove Robert W. Chambers or Herman Hagedorn into the coat of Lowell: he would rattle in one of its pockets.

Worse, there are no better candidates outside the academic cloister. I daresay that most literate foreigners, asked to name the principal American novelist in practice to-day, would nominate Theodore Dreiser. He would get probably seventy-five per cent of the votes, with the rest scattered among Upton Sinclair, Sinclair Lewis, Cabell, Hergesheimer and Sherwood Anderson. But try to imagine any of these gentlemen togged out in a long-tailed coat, shivering on the deck of a revenue-cutter while Gerhart Hauptman got a grip on himself aboard the *Majestic*! Try to imagine Cabell presiding at a banquet to Knut Hamsun, with Dr. A. Lawrence Lowell to one side of him and Otto Kahn to the other! Try to picture Sinclair handing James Joyce a wreath to put upon the grave of James Whitcomb Riley! The vision, indeed, is more dismal than ludicrous. Howells, the last of his lordly line, is missed tremendously; there is something grievously lacking in the official hospitality of the country. The lack showed itself the instant he was called away. A few weeks later Columbia University gave a soirée in honor of the centenary of Lowell. The president of Columbia, Dr. Nicholas Murray Butler, is a realist. Moreover, he is a member of the American Academy himself, elected as a wet to succeed Edgar Allan Poe. He was thus privy to the deficiencies of his colleagues. To conceal the flabbiness of the evening he shoved them into back seats—and invited John D. Rockefeller, Jr., Tex Rickard, General Pershing and the board of governors of the New York Stock Exchange to the platform!

I believe that, of living masters of letters, H. G. Wells was the first to feel the new chill. When he last visited the Republic he was made welcome by a committee of ship-news reporters. It was as if one of the justices of the King's Bench, landing in America, had been received by a committee of police-court lawyers from Gary, Ind. Later on American literature bestirred itself and gave Wells a banquet in New York. I was present at this feast, and a singular one it was. Not a single author read in Iowa or taught at Harvard was present. The principal literatus at the board was the late Frank A. Munsey, author of "Derringforth" and "The Boy Broker," and the principal address was made by Max Eastman, formerly editor of the *Masses*! . . .

I come to a constructive suggestion. Let the literati of America meet in their respective places of social relaxation, each gang determining the credentials of its own members, and elect delegates to a national convention. Then let the national convention, by open ballot, choose ten spokesmen and ten alternates to represent the national letters on all formal occasions—not only when an eminent foreigner is to be made welcome, but also when Columbia University holds memorial services, when a President is inaugurated, when Harvard meets Yale, when monuments are unveiled—in brief at all times of solemn public ceremonial. Let these representatives practice deportment and elocution. Let them employ good tailors and trustworthy bootleggers. I have, alas, no candidates for the committee. As I have said, there is a dreadful dearth of them. Does Dr. Frank Crane wear whiskers? If so, I nominate him.

5
Literature and the Schoolma'm

With precious few exceptions, all the books on style in English are by writers quite unable to write. The subject, indeed, seems to exercise a special and dreadful fascination over schoolma'ms, bucolic college professors, and other such pseudo-literates. One never hears of treatises on it by George Moore or James Branch Cabell, but the pedagogues, male and female, are at it all the time. In a thousand texts they set forth their depressing ideas about it, and millions of suffering high-school pupils have to study what they say. Their central aim, of course, is to reduce the whole thing to a series of simple rules —the over-mastering passion of their melancholy order, at all times and everywhere. They aspire to teach it as bridge whist, the American Legion flag-drill and double-entry bookkeeping are taught. They fail as ignominiously as that Athenian of legend who essayed to train a regiment of grasshoppers in the goose-step.

For the essence of sound style is that it cannot be reduced to rules—that it is a living and breathing thing, with something of the devilish in it—that it fits its proprietor tightly and yet ever so loosely, as his skin fits him. It is, in fact, quite as securely an integral part of him as that skin is. It hardens as his arteries harden. It has *Katzenjammer* on the days succeeding his indiscretions. It is gaudy when he is young and gathers decorum when he grows old. On the day after he makes a mash on a new girl it glows and glitters. If he has fed well, it is mellow. If he has gastritis it is bitter. In brief, a style is always the outward and visible symbol of a man, and it cannot be anything else. To attempt to teach it is as silly as to set up courses in making love. The man who makes love out of a book is not making love at all; he is simply imitating someone else making love. God help him if, in love or literary composition, his preceptor be a pedagogue!

The schoolma'm theory that the writing of English may be taught is based upon a faulty inference from a sound observation. The sound observation is that the great majority of American high-school pupils, when they attempt to put their thoughts upon paper, produce only a mass of confused and puerile nonsense—that they express themselves so clumsily that it is often quite impossible to understand them at all. The faulty inference is to the effect that what ails them is a defective technical equipment—that they can be trained to write clearly as a dog may be trained to walk on its hind legs. This is all wrong. What ails them is not a defective technical equipment but a defective natural equipment. They write badly simply because they cannot think clearly. They cannot think clearly

because they lack the brains. Trying to teach them is as hopeless as trying to teach a dog with only one hind leg. Any
human being who can speak English understandably has all
the materials necessary to write English clearly, and even beautifully. There is nothing mysterious about the written language;
it is precisely the same, in essence, as the spoken language. If
a man can think in English at all, he can find words enough to
express his ideas. The fact is proved abundantly by the excellent writing that often comes from so-called ignorant men. It
is proved anew by the even better writing that is done on
higher levels by persons of great simplicity, for example, Abraham Lincoln. Such writing commonly arouses little enthusiasm
among pedagogues. Its transparency excites their professional disdain, and they are offended by its use of homely
words and phrases. They prefer something more ornate and
complex—something, as they would probably put it, demanding more thought. But the thought they yearn for is the kind,
alas, that they secrete themselves—the muddled, highfalutin,
vapid thought that one finds in their own text-books.

I do not denounce them because they write so badly; I
merely record the fact in a sad, scientific spirit. Even in such
twilight regions of the intellect the style remains the man. What
is in the head infallibly oozes out of the nub of the pen. If
it is sparkling Burgundy the writing is full of life and charm.
If it is mush the writing is mush too. The late Dr. Harding,
twenty-ninth President of the Federal Union, was a highly self-
conscious stylist. He practiced prose composition assiduously,
and was regarded by the pedagogues of Marion, Ohio, and
vicinity as a very talented fellow. But when he sent a message
to Congress it was so muddled in style that even the late
Henry Cabot Lodge, a professional literary man, could not
understand it. Why? Simply because Dr. Harding's thoughts,
on the high and grave subjects he discussed, were so muddled
that he couldn't understand them himself. But on matters
within his range of customary meditation he was clear and
even charming, as all of us are. I once heard him deliver a brief
address upon the ideals of the Elks. It was a topic close to his
heart, and he had thought about it at length and *con amore*.
The result was an excellent speech—clear, logical, forceful, and
with a touch of wild, romantic beauty. His sentences hung to-

gether. He employed simple words, and put them together with skill. But when, at a public meeting in Washington, he essayed to deliver an oration on the subject of the late Dante Alighieri, he quickly became so obscure and absurd that even the Diplomatic Corps began to snicker. The cause was plain: he knew no more about Dante than a Tennessee county judge knows about the Institutes of Justinian. Trying to formulate ideas upon the topic, he could get together only a few disjected fragments and ghosts of ideas—here an ear, there a section of tibia, beyond a puff of soul substance or other gas. The resultant speech was thus enigmatical, cacophonous and awful stuff. It sounded precisely like a lecture by a college professor on style.

A pedagogue, confronted by Dr. Harding in class, would have set him to the business of what is called improving his vocabulary—that is, to the business of making his writing even worse than it was. Dr. Harding, in point of fact, had all the vocabulary that he needed, and a great deal more. Any idea that he could formulate clearly he could convey clearly. Any idea that genuinely moved him he could invest with charm—which is to say, with what the pedagogues call style. I believe that this capacity is possessed by all literate persons above the age of fourteen. It is not acquired by studying text-books; it is acquired by learning how to think. Children even younger often show it. I have a niece, now eleven years old, who already has an excellent style. When she writes to me about things that interest her—in other words, about the things she is capable of thinking about—she puts her thoughts into clear, dignified and admirable English. Her vocabulary, so far, is unspoiled by schoolma'ms. She doesn't try to knock me out by bombarding me with hard words, and phrases filched from Addison. She is unaffected, and hence her writing is charming. But if she essayed to send me a communication on the subject, say, of Balkan politics or government ownership, her style would descend instantly to the level of that of Dr. Harding's state papers.

To sum up, style cannot go beyond the ideas which lie at the heart of it. If they are clear, it too will be clear. If they are held passionately, it will be eloquent. Trying to teach it to persons who cannot think, especially when the business is attempted by persons who also cannot think, is a great waste of time, and an immoral imposition upon the taxpayers of the nation. It would be far more logical to devote all the energy to teaching, not writing, but logic—and probably just as useless. For I doubt that the art of thinking can be taught at all—at any rate, by school-teachers. It is not acquired, but congenital. Some persons are born with it. Their ideas flow in straight channels; they are capable of lucid reasoning; when they say anything it is instantly understandable; when they write anything it is clear and persuasive. They constitute, I should say, about one-eighth of one per cent. of the human race. The rest of God's children are just as incapable of logical thought as they are incapable of jumping over the moon. Trying to teach them to think is as vain an enterprise as trying to teach a streptococcus the principles of Americanism. The only thing to do with them is to make Ph.D.'s of them, and set them to writing hand-books on style.

6

The Critic and his Job

The assumption that it may be scientific is the worst curse that lies upon criticism. It is responsible for all the dull, blowsy, "definitive" stuff that literary pedagogues write, and it is responsible, too, for the heavy posturing that so often goes on among critics less learned. Both groups proceed upon the theory that there are exact facts to be ascertained, and that it is their business to ascertain and proclaim them. That theory is nonsense. There is, in truth, no such thing as an exact fact in the whole realm of the beautiful arts. What is true therein to-day may be false to-morrow, or vice versa, and only too often the shift is brought about by something that, properly speaking, is not an æsthetic consideration at all.

The case of Whitman comes to mind at once. Orthodox criticism, in his own time, was almost unanimously against him. At his first appearance, true enough, a few critics were a bit dazzled by him, notably Emerson, but they quickly got control of their faculties and took to cover. Down to the time of his death the prevailing doctrine was that he was a third-rate poet and a dirty fellow. Any young professor who, in the sev-

enties or even in the early eighties, had presumed to whoop for
him in class would have been cashiered at once, as both incompetent and immoral. If there was anything definitively established in those days, it was that old Walt was below the salt.
To-day he is taught to sophomores everywhere, perhaps even
in Tennessee, and one of the most unctuously respectable of
American publishing houses brings out "Leaves of Grass" un-
expurgated, and everyone agrees that he is one of the glories
the national letters. Has that change been brought about by a
purely critical process? Does it represent a triumph of criticism
over darkness? It does not. It represents, rather, a triumph of
external forces over criticism. Whitman's first partisans were
not interested in poetry; they were interested in sex. They
were presently reënforced by persons interested in politics.
They were finally converted into a majority by a tatterdemalion horde of persons interested mainly, and perhaps only, in
making a noise.

Literary criticism, properly so-called, had little if anything to
do with this transformation. Scarcely a critic of any recognized
authority had a hand in it. What started it off, after the first
furtive, gingery snuffling over "A Woman Waits for Me" and
the "Calamus" cycle, was the rise of political radicalism in the
early eighties, in reaction against the swinish materialism that
followed the Civil War. I am tempted to say that Terence V.
Powderly had more to do with the rehabilitation of Whitman
than any American critic, or, indeed, than any American poet.
And if you object to Powderly, then I offer you Karl Marx,
with William Jennings Bryan—no less!—peeping out of his
coat-pocket. The radicals made heavy weather of it at the start.
To the average respectable citizen they seemed to be mere criminals. Like the Bolsheviki of a later era, they were represented
by their opponents as the enemies of all mankind. What they
needed, obviously, was some means of stilling the popular fear
of them—some way of tapping the national sentimentality.
There stood Whitman, conveniently to hand. In his sonorous
strophes to an imaginary and preposterous democracy there
was an eloquent statement of their own vague and windy
yearnings, and, what is more, a certificate to their virtue as
sound Americans. So they adopted him with loud hosannas,
and presently he was both their poet and their philosopher.

Long before any professor at Harvard dared to mention him (save, perhaps, with lascivious winks), he was being read to tatters by thousands of lonely Socialists in the mining-towns. As radicalism froze into Liberalism, and so began to influence the intelligentsia, his vogue rose, and by the end of the century even school-teachers had begun to hear of him. There followed the free verse poets, *i.e.*, a vast herd of emerging barbarians with an itch to make an uproar in the world, and no capacity for mastering the orthodox rules of prosody. Thus Whitman came to Valhalla, pushed by political propagandists and pulled by literary mountebanks. The native Taines and Matthew Arnolds made a gallant defense, but in vain. In the remoter denominational colleges some of them still hold out. But Whitman is now just as respectable at Yale as Martin Tupper or Edmund Clarence Stedman.

The point is that his new respectability is just as insecure as his old infamy—that he may be heaved out, on some bright tomorrow, just as he was heaved in, and by a similar combination of purely non-literary forces. Already I hear rumors of a plan to make Dr. Coolidge King. If his conscience stays him, then the throne may go to William Wrigley, Jr., or Judge Elbert H. Gary, LL.D. Democracy, indeed, begins to sicken among us. The doctors at its bedside dose it out of a black bottle, and make sinister signals to the coroner. If it dies, then Whitman will probably die with it. Criticism, of course, will labor desperately to save him, as it once labored to dispose of him, but such struggles are nearly always futile. The most they ever accomplish is to convert the author defended into a sort of fossil, preserved in a showcase to plague and puzzle schoolboys. The orthodox literature books, used in all schools, are simply such showcases. They represent the final effort of pedants to capture zephyrs and chain torrents. They are monuments to the delusion that criticism may be definitive—that appeals to the emotions, which shift and change with every wind, may be appraised and sorted out by appeals to the mind, which is theoretically unchangeable. Certainly every reflective student of any of the fine arts should know that this is not so. There is no such thing as a literary immortality. We remember Homer, but we forget the poets that the Greeks, too, forgot. You may be sure that there were Shakespeares in Carthage, and more of them at the court of Amenophis IV, but their very names are lost. Our own Shakespeare, as year chases year, may go the same way; in fact, his going the same way is quite as certain as anything we can imagine. A thousand years hence, even five hundred years hence, he may be, like Beowulf, only a name in a literature book, to be remembered against examination day and then forgotten.

Criticism is thus anything but scientific, for it cannot reach judgments that are surely and permanently valid. The most it can do, at its best, is to pronounce verdicts that are valid here and now, in the light of living knowledge and prejudice. As the background shifts the verdict changes. The best critic is not that fool who tries to resist the process—by setting up artificial standards, by prattling of laws and principles that do not exist, by going into the dead past for criteria of the present—, but that more prudent fellow who submits himself frankly to the flow of his time, and rejoices in its aliveness. Charles Augustin Sainte-Beuve was a good critic, for he saw everything as a Frenchman of the Second Empire, and if his judgments must be revised to-day it still remains true that they were honest and intelligent when he formulated them. Professor Balderdash is a bad critic, for he judges what is done in the American Empire of 1926 in the light of what was held to be gospel in the pastoral Republic of a century ago. For the rest, the critic survives, when he survives at all, mainly as artist. His judgments, in the long run, become archaic, and may be disregarded. But if, in stating them, he has incidentally produced a work of art on his own account, then he is read long after they are rejected, and it may be plausibly argued that he has contributed something to the glory of letters. No one takes much stock in Macaulay's notions to-day. He is, in fact, fair game for any college tutor who has majored in what is called history. He fell into many gross errors, and sometimes, it is probable, he fell into them more or less deliberately. But his criticism is still read— that is, as much as any criticism is read. It holds all its old charm and address. For Macaulay, when he sat himself down to be critical, did not try fatuously to produce a scientific treatise. What he tried to do was to produce a work of art.

7
Painting and its Critics

Having emerged lately from a diligent course of reading in so-called art criticism, and especially in that variety of it which is concerned with the painters since Cézanne, I can only report that I find it windy stuff, and sadly lacking in clarity and sense. The new critics, indeed, seem to me to be quite as vague and absurd as some of the new painters they celebrate. The more they explain and expound the thing they profess to admire, the more unintelligible it becomes. Criticism, in their hands, turns into a sort of cabbalism. One must prepare for it, as one prepares for the literature of Service or of the New Thought, by acquiring a wholly new vocabulary, and a new system of logic.

I do not argue here that the new painting, in itself, is always absurd. On the contrary, it must be manifest to anyone with eyes that some of its inventions are bold and interesting, and that now and then it achieves a sort of beauty. What I argue is simply that the criticism it has bred does not adequately account for it—that no man of ordinary sense, seeking to find out just what it is about, will get any light from what is currently written about it. All he will get will be a bath of metaphysics, heated with indignation. Polemics take the place of exposition. One comes away with a guilty feeling that one is somehow grossly ignorant and bounderish, but unable to make out why. The same phenomenon is occasionally witnessed in other fields. I have mentioned the cases of Service and the New Thought. There was, a generation ago, the case of Ibsen and the symbolists. These imbeciles read such extravagant meanings into the old man's plays that he was moved, finally, to violent protests. He was not trying to compose cryptograms, he said; he was simply trying to write stage plays. In much the same way Cézanne protested against the balderdash of his earliest disciples and interpreters. He was no messiah, he said; he was only a painter who tried to reduce what he saw in the world to canvas. The Ibsen symbolists eventually subsided into Freudism and other such rubbish, but the Cézannists continue to spoil paper with their highfalutin and occult tosh. I have read nearly all of them, and I denounce all that I have read as quacks.

This tendency to degenerate into a mere mouthing of meaningless words seems to be peculiar to so-called art criticism. There has never been, so far as I know, a critic of painting who wrote about it simply and clearly, as Sainte-Beuve, say, wrote about books, or Schumann and Berlioz about music. Even the most orthodox of the brethren, when he finds himself before a canvas that genuinely moves him, takes refuge in esoteric winks and grimaces and mysterious gurgles and belches. He can never put his feelings into plain English. Always, before he is done, he is sweating metaphysics, which is to say, nonsense. Painters themselves, when they discuss their art, commonly go the same route. Every time a new revolutionist gives a show he issues a manifesto explaining his aims and achievements, and in every such manifesto there is the same blowsy rodomontadizing that one finds in the texts of the critics. The thing, it appears, is very profound. Something new has been discovered. Rembrandt, poor old boy, lived and died in ignorance of it. Turner, had he heard of it, would have yelled for the police. Even Gaugin barely glimpsed it. One can't make out what this new arcanum is, but one takes it on faith and goes to the show. What one finds there is a series of canvases that appear to have been painted with asphalt and mayonnaise, and by a man afflicted with binocular diplopic strabismus. Is this sound drawing? Is this a new vision of color? Then so is your grandmother left-fielder of the Giants. The exceptions are very few. I have read, I suppose, at least two hundred such manifestos during the past twenty years; at one time I even started out to collect them, as odd literary delicatessen. I can't recall a single one that embodied a plain statement of an intelligible idea—that is, intelligible to a man of ordinary information and sanity. It always took a special talent to comprehend them, as it took a special talent to paint the fantastic pictures they discussed.

Two reasons, I believe, combine to make the pronunciamentos of painters so bombastic and flatulent. One lies in the plain fact that painting is a relatively simple and transparent art, and that nothing much of consequence is thus to be said about it. All that is remarkable in even the most profound painting may be grasped by an educated spectator in a few minutes. If he lingers longer he is simply seeing again what he has seen before. His essential experience, in other words, is short-lived. It is not like getting shaved, coming down with the cholera morbus, or going to the wars; it is like jumping out of the way of a taxicab or getting kissed. Consider, now, the position of a critic condemned to stretch this experience into material for a column article or for a whole chapter in a book. Obviously, he soon finds it insufficient for this purpose. What, then, is he to do? Tell the truth, and then shut up? This, alas, is not the way of critics. When their objective facts run out they always turn to subjective facts, of which the supply is unlimited. Thus the art critic begins to roll his eyes inward. He begins to poetize and philosophize his experience. He indulges himself in dark hints and innuendos. Putting words together aimlessly, he presently hits upon a combination that tickles him. He has invented a new cliché. He is a made man. The painter, expounding his work, falls into the same bog. The plain fact, nine times out of ten, is that he painted his picture without any rational plan whatever. Like any other artist, he simply experimented with his materials, trying this combination and then that. Finally he struck something that pleased him. Now he faces the dreadful job of telling why. He simply doesn't know. So he conceals his ignorance behind recondite and enigmatical phrases. He soars, insinuates, sputters, coughs behind his hand. If he is lucky, he, too, invents a cliché. Three clichés in a row, and he is a temporary immortal.

Behind what is written about painting there is always, of course, the immense amount of drivel that is talked about it. No other art is so copiously discussed by its practitioners, or encrusted with so much hollow theorizing. The reason therefor —the second of the two I mentioned above—lies in the obvious fact that painters can talk while they work, and are debarred from working at least half of their waking hours. A poet, when his hormones begin to ferment, not infrequently labors all night; when there is a fog, a thunder-storm or a torch-light parade he is specially inspired. So with a musical composer. But a painter can work only while the light is good, and in the north temperate zone that is not often. So he has much time on his hands, and inasmuch as he seldom has money enough to venture into general society and is usually too ignorant to enjoy reading, he puts in that time talking. Nowhere else on this earth is there so much gabbling as you will find in painters' studios, save it be in the pubs and more or less public bed-rooms that they frequent. It begins as soon as the sun goes down, and it keeps on all night. And it is always about painting, painting, painting. No other class of artists is so self-centered. Once a youth gets a brush into his hand and turpentine in his hair, he appears to join a race apart, and is interested no longer in the general concerns of the world. Even the other arts do not commonly engage any of his attention. If he ventures into music, it is into the banal music of college boys and colored stevedores. If he reads it is only the colicky nonsense that I have been describing. Even his amours are but incidents of his trade. Now put this immense leisure and this great professional keenness against the plain fact that the problems of painting, in the main, are very simple—that very little that is new is to be said about any of them. The result is a vast dilution of ideas, a stormy battle of mere words, an infinite logomachy. And on its higher levels, embellished with all the arts of the auctioneer, it is art criticism.

8
Greenwich Village

The whole saga of Greenwich Village is in Alfred Kreymborg's autobiography, which he calls, very appropriately, "Troubadour." The story begins with an earnest and insolvent young man in a garret, fighting cockroaches and writing free verse. It ends with a respectable gentleman of passing forty, legally married to one very charming wife, and in receipt of a comfortable income in royalties from the 6000 Little Theatres which now freckle and adorn our eminent Republic, distracting the males of the Younger Married Set from the Red Peril and Service, and their wives from millinery and birth control.

Of all the motley revolutionaries who flourished in the Village in its heyday, say fifteen years ago, Kreymborg was surely one of the most engaging, as he was one of the most honest. Most of the others, for all their heroic renunciation of commercialism, were quite as hot for the *mazuma* as other literary artists. With one breath they pledged themselves to poverty—though not, surely, to chastity or obedience!—and denounced

such well-heeled poets as Kipling and Shakespeare as base harlots of the marts. With the next they bargained with such editors
as ventured to buy their wares like Potash tackling One-Eye
Feigenbaum. From this lamentable trafficking Kreymborg
held aloof, a genuine Parnassian. He composed his bad poetry
and his worse novels on a diet of *Schnecken* and synthetic coffee, and paid for that meager fare by teaching Babbitts the elements of chess.

Gradually the tumult died, and Greenwich Village fell into
decay. The poets moved out, and Philistines moved in; it was
all over. But Kreymborg kept the faith—at all events, longer
than most. He continued to write poems like a series of college
yells, plays unearthly and impossible, novels that brought the
Comstocks sliding down their poles like firemen. But gradually
he, too, began to show change. His hair grew thin on top; his
blood grew sluggish. Presently some of his plays were produced; he had at last squeezed through the proscenium arch.
Then he began to accept calls to read his dithyrambs before
provincial Poetry Societies. Then he became an editor and an
anthologist—ten paces behind his ancient enemy, Louis Un-
termeyer. Then he went through two divorces, one of them legal, and married an estimable lady of Brooklyn. Now he is past
forty, has an agent, and pays income-tax. *Schön ist die Jugendzeit; sie kommt nicht mehr!* As I have hinted, there was always
something charming about Kreymborg, even in the days of his
most raucous verse. He threw up a good job with the Aeolian
Company, demonstrating mechanical-piano records, in order
to become a poet, and he stuck to his dream through many a
long year. The waspishness of the other Villagers was not in
him, and he was happily free of their worst imbecilities. Between cantos of free verse, I suspect, he often read Swinburne
and even Tennyson; in his mandolute he concealed Howells
and Mark Twain.

As one who poked many heavy jocosities at it while it lasted,
I hope I may now say with good grace that I believe Greenwich Village did a good service to all the fine arts in this great
land, and left a valuable legacy behind it. True enough, its own
heroes were nearly all duds, and most of them have been forgotten, but it at least broke ground, it at least stirred up the
animals. When it began to issue smoke and flame, the youth of

the country were still under the hoof of the schoolma'm; when it blew up at last they were in full revolt. Was it Greenwich Village or Yale University that cleared the way for Cabell? Was it the Village or the Philharmonic Society that made a place for Stravinsky? Was it the Village on the trustees of the Metropolitan Museum that first whooped for Cézanne? That whooping, of course, did not stop with Cézanne, or Stravinsky, or Cabell. There were whoops almost as loud for Sascha Gilhooly, who painted sunsets with a shaving brush, and for Raoul Goetz, who wrote quartettes for automobile horns and dentist's drills, and for Bruce J. Katzenstein, whose poetry was all figures and exclamation points. But all that excess did no harm. The false prophets changed from day to day. The real ones remained.

X.

Essay in Pedagogy

ON the purely technical side the American novel has obviously made immense progress. As ordinarily encountered, it is very adeptly constructed, and not infrequently it is also well written. The old-time amorphous novel, rambling all over the place and ending with pious platitudes, has pretty well gone out. The American novelists of to-day, and especially the younger ones, have given earnest study to form—perhaps, indeed, too much. For in concentrating their powerful intellects upon it they have lost sight of something that is far more important. I allude, of course, to the observation of character. Thus the average contemporary American novel, though it is workmanlike and well-mannered, fails to achieve its first business. It does not evoke memorable images of human beings. One enjoys reading it, perhaps, but one seldom remembers it. And when it gets beyond the estate of a mere technical exercise, it only too often descends to the even worse estate of a treatise. It attempts to prove something—usually the simple fact that its author is a clever fellow, or a saucy gal. But all a novel of genuine bulk and beam ever proves is that the proper study of mankind is man—the proper study and the most engrossing.

In brief, a first-rate novel is always a character sketch. It may be more than that, but at bottom it is always a character sketch, or, if the author is genuinely of the imperial line, a whole series of them. More, it is a character sketch of an individual not far removed from the norm of the race. He may have his flavor of oddity, but he is never fantastic; he never violates the common rules of human action; he never shows emotions that are impossible to the rest of is. If Thackeray had made Becky Sharp seven feet tall, and given her a bass voice, nine husbands and the rank of lieutenant-general in the British Army, she would have been forgotten long ago, along with all the rest of "Vanity Fair." And if Robinson Crusoe had been an

Edison instead of a normal sailorman, he would have gone the same way.

The moral of all this is not lost upon the more competent minority of novelists in practice among us. It was not necessary to preach it to Miss Cather when she set out to write "My Antonía," nor to Abraham Cahan when he tackled "The Rise of David Levinsky," nor to Sinclair Lewis when he was at work on "Babbitt." All such novelists see the character first and the story afterward. What is the story of "Babbitt"? Who remembers? Who, indeed, remembers the story of "The Three Musketeers"? But D'Artagnan and his friends live brilliantly, and so, too, I believe, will George F. Babbitt live brilliantly—at all events, until Kiwanis ceases to trouble, and his type ceases to be real. Most of the younger American novelists, alas, seem to draw no profit from such examples. It is their aim, apparently, to shock mankind with the vivacity of their virtuosity and the heterodoxy of their ideas, and so they fill their novels with gaudy writing and banal propaganda, and convert their characters into sticks. I read novel after novel without getting any sense of contact with actual human beings. I am, at times, immensely amused and sometimes I am instructed, but I seldom carry away anything to remember. When I do so, it is not an idea, but a person. Like everyone else, I have a long memory for persons. But ideas come and go.

All this becomes the more remarkable when one considers the peculiar richness of the American scene in sharply-outlined and racy characters. Our national ideas, indeed, are mainly third-rate, and some of them are almost idiotic, but taking one year with another we probably produce more lively and diverting people than all the rest of the world taken together. More, these lively and diverting people tend to cluster into types. Mark Twain put half a dozen of them into "Huckleberry Finn" and as many more into "Roughing It," a novel disguised as history. Montague Glass collared a whole flock for his Potash and Perlmutter stories, and Ring Lardner has got another flock into his studies of the American bounder. But the younger novelists, or at least the overwhelming majority of them, stick to their sticks. Thus even the most salient and arresting of American types still lack historians, and seem doomed to perish and be forgotten with the Bill of Rights. Babbitt stood

around for a dozen years, waiting for Lewis; the rest of the
novelists of the land gaped at him without seeing him. How
long will they gape at the American politician? At the American university president? At the American policeman? At the
American lawyer? At the American insurance man? At the Prohibition fanatic? At the revival evangelist? At the bootlegger?
At the Y.M.C.A. secretary? At the butter-and-egg man? At the
journalist?

2

I have put the politician at the top of my list. He probably
embodies more typical American traits than any other; he is,
within his limits, the arch-Americano. Yet how seldom he gets
into a novel! And how seldom, having got there, is he real! I
can recall, indeed, but one American political novel of any
value whatever as a study of character, and that is Harvey Fergusson's story of Washington, "Capitol Hill"—a series of casual sketches, but all of them vivid and true. Fergusson really
understands the American politician. There is, in "Capitol
Hill," no division of the *dramatis personæ* between Democrats
and Republicans, progressives and reactionaries, materialists
and idealists, patriots and traitors; the only division is between
men and women who have something, and men and women
who want it. In that simple fact lies most of the book's curious
reality. For the truth about Washington is that it is not a town
of politics, in the conventional and romantic sense; it is, if anything, a town almost devoid of politics. The people in the industrial cities and out on the farms take political ideas
seriously; what they cherish in that department they refuse passionately to surrender. But so far as I know there are not a
dozen professional politicians in Washington, high or low,
who would not throw overboard, instantly and gladly, every
political idea they are assumed to be devoted to, including especially every political idea that has helped them into public
office, if throwing it overbroad would help them to higher and
gaudier and more lucrative office. I say high or low, and I
mean it literally. There has not been a President of the United
States for half a century who did not, at some time or other in
his career, perform a complete *volte face* in order to further his

career. There is scarcely a United States Senator who does not flop at least three times within the limits of a single session.

The novelists who write about Washington are partly recruited from the ranks of the Washington newspaper correspondents, perhaps the most naïve and unreflective body of literate men in Christendom, and for the rest from the ranks of those who read the dispatches of such correspondents, and take them seriously. The result is a grossly distorted and absurd picture of life in the capital city. One carries off the notion that the essential Washington drama is based on a struggle between a powerful and corrupt Senator and a sterling young uplifter. The Senator is about to sell out the Republic to the Steel Trust, J. P. Morgan or the Japs. The uplifter detects him, exposes him, drives him from public life, and inherits his job. The love interest is supplied by a fair stenographer who steals the damning papers from the Senator's safe, or by an Ambassador's wife who goes to the White House at 3 A.M., and, at the peril of her virtue, arouses the President and tells him what is afoot. All this is poppycock. There are no Senators in Washington powerful enough to carry on any such operations singlehanded, and very few of them are corrupt: it is too easy to bamboozle them to go to the expense of buying them. The most formidable bribe that the average Senator receives from year's end to year's end is a bottle or two of very dubious Scotch, and that is just as likely to come from the agent of the South Central Watermelon Growers' Association as from John D. Rockefeller or the Mikado of Japan. Nor are there any sterling young uplifters in the town. The last was chased out before the Mexican War. There are to-day only gentlemen looking for something for themselves—publicity, eminence, puissance, jobs—especially jobs. Some take one line and some another. Further than that the difference between them is no greater than the difference between a Prohibition agent and a bootlegger, or tweedledum and tweedledee.

Ideas count for nothing in Washington, whether they be political, economic or moral. The question isn't what a man thinks, but what he has to give away that is worth having. Ten years ago a professional Prohibitionist had no more standing in the town than a professional astrologer, Assyriologist or wart-remover; five years ago, having proved that his gang could make or break Congressmen, he got all the deference that belonged to the Chief Justice; now, with the wet wolves chasing him, he is once more in eclipse. If William Z. Foster were elected President to-morrow, the most fanatical Coolidge men of to-day would flock to the White House the day after, and try to catch his eye. Coolidge, while Harding was living, was an obscure and impotent fellow, viewed with contempt by everyone. The instant he mounted the throne he became a Master Mind. Fergusson got all of this into "Capitol Hill," which is not the story of a combat between the True and the False in politics, but the simple tale of a typical Washingtonian's struggle to the front—a tale that should be an inspiration to every Rotarian in the land. He begins as a petty job-holder in the Capitol itself, mailing congressional speeches to constituents on the steppes; he ends at the head of a glittering banquet table, with a Senator to one side of him and a member of the Cabinet to the other—a man who has somehow got power into his hands, and can dispense jobs, and is thus an indubitable somebody. Everybody in Washington who has jobs to dispense is somebody.

This eternal struggle is sordid, but, as Fergusson has shown, it is also extremely amusing. It brings out, as the moralists say, the worst that is in human nature, which is always the most charming. It reduces all men to one common level of ignominy, and so rids them of their customary false-faces. They take on a new humanity. Ceasing to be Guardians of the Constitution, Foes to the Interests, Apostles of Economy, Prophets of World Peace, and such-like banshees, they become ordinary men, like John Doe and Richard Roe. One beholds them sweating, not liquid idealism, but genuine sweat. They hope, fear, aspire, suffer. They are preyed upon, not by J. P. Morgan, but by designing cuties. They go to the White House, not to argue for the World Court, but to hog patronage. From end to end of Fergusson's chronicle there is absolutely no mention of the tariff, or of the farmer and his woes, or of the budget system, or of the Far Eastern question. I marvel that more American novelists have not gone to this lush and delightful material. The supply is endless and lies wide open. Six months in Washington is enough to load an ambitious novelist for all eternity. (Think of what George Moore has made of his one love-affair, back in 1877!) The Washington correspondents, of course, look at it without seeing it, and so do all the Washington novelists save Fergusson. But that is saying nothing. A Washington correspondent is one with a special talent for failing to see what is before his eyes. I have beheld a whole herd of them sit through a national convention without once laughing.

Fergusson, in "Capitol Hill," keeps mainly to that end of Pennsylvania avenue which gives his book its names. I believe that the makings of a far better novel of Washington life are to be found at the other end, to wit, in and about the alabaster cage which houses the heir of Washington, Lincoln and Chester A. Arthur. Why, indeed, has no one ever put *kaiserliche Majestät* into fiction—save, of course, as a disembodied spirit, vaguely radiating idealism? The revelations in the Daugherty inquiry gave a hint of unworked riches—but there is enough dramatic and even melodramatic material without descending to scandal. A President is a man like the rest of us. He can laugh and he can groan. There are days when his breakfast agrees with him, and days when it doesn't. His eyes have the common optical properties: they can see a sweet one as far as they can see a member of the Interstate Commerce Commission. All the funnels of intrigue are aimed at him. He is the common butt of every loud-speaker. No other man in this sad vale has so many jobs to give out, or one-half so many. Try to imagine a day in his life, from dawn to midnight. Do it, and you will have the best American novel ever heard of.

3

But I am forgetting my other candidates—for example, the American university president. I mean, of course, the university president of the new six-cylinder, air-cooled, four-wheel-brake model—half the quack, half the visionary, and wholly the go-getter—the brisk, business-like, confidential, button-holing, regular fellow who harangues Rotary and Kiwanis, extracts millions from usurers by alarming them about Bolshevism, and so builds his colossal pedagogical slaughter-house, with its tens of thousands of students, its professors of cheese-making, investment securities and cheer-leading, its galaxy of football stars, and its general air of Barnum's circus. Why has this

astounding mountebank not got into a book? He fairly yells
for loving embalming *à la* Babbitt. He is not only stupen-
dously picaresque and amusing in himself—the final heir, at
once, of Abelard, Cagliostro, Increase Mather, the Fox sisters,
Pestalozzi, Dr. Munyon, Godey of the *Lady's Book*, and Daniel
Drew—; he is also thoroughly and magnificently characteristic
of the great land we live in. No other country has ever produced anything quite like him. No other country, I suspect,
would tolerate him. But here he lives and flourishes, a superb
and perfect American—and yet our novelists all neglect him.

Worse and more incredible still, they neglect the most American of all Americans, the very *Ur-Amerikaner*—to wit, the
malignant moralist, the Christian turned cannibal, the snout-
ing and preposterous Puritan. Where is there the American
novel in which he is even half limned? There are, to be sure,
glimpses of him in "The Song of the Lark," by Willa Cather,
and in "Babbitt," and there is a more elaborate but still incomplete sketch in E. W. Howe's "The Story of a Country
Town." But Howe, unfortunately, had other fish to fry: he
slapped in his bucolic wowser brilliantly, and then passed on
to melodrama and the agonies of young love. So, too, with
Lewis and Miss Cather. Thus, though the Puritan Father
lies embalmed magnificently in the pages of Hawthorne, his
heir and assign of the present day, the high-powered uplifter,
the prophet of harsh and unenforceable laws, the incurable
reformer and nuisance—this sweet fellow yet awaits his
anatomist.

What a novel is in him! Indeed, what a shelf of novels! For
he has as many forms as there are varieties of human delusion.
Sometimes he is a tin-pot evangelist, sweating to transform
Oklahoma City or Altoona, Pa., into the New Jerusalem.
Sometimes he is a hireling of the Anti-Saloon League, sworn
to Law Enforcement. Sometimes he is a strict Sabbatarian,
bawling for the police whenever he detects his neighbor washing bottles or varnishing the Ford on Sunday morning. Again
he is a vice-crusader, chasing the scarlet lady with fierce Christian shouts. Yet again he is a comstock, wearing out his eyes in
the quest for smut. He may even be female—a lady Ph.D. in a
linoleum hat, patrolling the cow towns and the city slums,
handing out edifying literature, teaching poor Polish women

how to have babies. Whatever his form, he is tremendously grotesque and tremendously amusing—and always he drips with national juices, always he is as thoroughly American as a bootlegger or a college yell. If he exists at all in other lands, it is only in rudimentary and aberrant forms. Try to imagine a French Wayne B. Wheeler, or a Spanish Billy Sunday, or a German William Jennings Bryan. It is as impossible as imagining a Coolidge in the Rome of Julius.

Since the earliest days, as everyone knows, American jurisprudence has been founded upon the axiom that it is the first duty of every citizen to police his neighbors, and especially those he envies, or otherwise dislikes. There is no such thing, in this grand and puissant nation, as privacy. The yokels out in Iowa, neglecting their horned cattle, have a right, it appears—nay, a sacred duty!—to peek into my home in Baltimore, and tell me what I may and may not drink with my meals. An out-at-elbow Methodist preacher in Boston sets himself up to decide what I may read. An obscure and unintelligent job-holder in Washington, inspired by God, determines what I may receive in the mails. I must not buy lottery tickets because it offends the moral sentiment of Kansas. I must keep Sunday as the Sabbath, which is in conflict with Genesis, because it is ordered by persons who believe that Genesis can't be wrong. Such are the laws of the greatest free nation ever seen on earth. We are all governed by them. But a government of laws, of course, is a mere phantasm of political theorists: the thing is always found, on inspection, to be really a government of men. In the United States, it seems to me, the tendency is for such men to come increasingly from the class of professional uplifters. It is not the bankers who run the ostensible heads of the state, as the Liberals believe, nor the so-called bosses, as the bosses themselves believe, but the wowsers. And what is a wowser? What does the word mean? It means precisely what you think of inevitably when you hear it. A wowser is a wowser. He bears a divine commission to regulate and improve the rest of us. He knows exactly what is best for us. He is what Howe calls a Good Man. So long as you and I are sinful, he can't sleep. So long as we are happy, he is after us.

I throw off the guess that there are at least forty novels in the wowser—that is, forty good ones. He has, as I have said, as many forms as the demons who ride him, and every one of them should make a competent novelist, authentically called to the vocation, leap in air with loud hosannas, and spit upon his hands. His psychology remains mysterious. The Freudians, I believe, have misunderstood him, and the psychiatrists have avoided him. What are the springs of his peculiar frenzy to harass and punish his fellow men? By what process of malign eugenics is he hatched? And what is his typical life history? Here is work for the novelist, which is to say, for the professional anatomist of character. I believe that Frank Norris, had he lived, would have tackled it with enthusiasm, and made a great success of its execution. Norris, like Dreiser after him, had a romantic and even a mystical inclination, but at bottom he was a satirist— and the American Puritan was made for satirists as catnip was made for cats. It is easy to laugh at him, but it is hard to hate him. He is eternally in the position of a man trying to empty the ocean with a tin-dipper. He will be mauled, and the chance he offers thrown away, if the novelist who attempts him in the end forgets the tragedy under his comedy. I have known many American wowsers in my time, some of them intimately. They were all intensely unhappy men. They suffered as vastly as Prometheus chained to his rock, with the buzzards exploring his liver. A novelist blind to that capital fact will never comprehend the type. It needs irony—but above all it needs pity.

4

So does another type that also awaits its Thackeray: to wit, the American journalist. Most American novelists, before they challenge Dostoevski, put in an apprenticeship on the public prints, and thus have a chance to study and grasp the peculiarities of the journalistic mind; nevertheless, the fact remains that there is not a single genuine newspaper man, done in the grand manner, in the whole range of American fiction. As in the case of the wowser, there are some excellent brief sketches, but there is no adequate portrait of the journalist as a whole, from his beginnings as a romantic young reporter to his finish as a Babbitt, correct in every idea and as hollow as a jug. Here, I believe, is genuine tragedy. Here is the matter that enters into all fiction of the first class. Here is human character in disintegration

—the primary theme of every sound novelist ever heard of, from Fielding to Zola and from Turgeniev to Joseph Conrad. I know of no American who starts from a higher level of aspiration than the journalist. He is, in his first phase, genuinely romantic. He plans to be both an artist and a moralist—a master of lovely words and a merchant of sound ideas. He ends, commonly, as the most depressing jackass in his community—that is, if his career goes on to what is called success. He becomes the repository of all its worst delusions and superstitions. He becomes the darling of all its frauds and idiots, and the despair of all its honest men. He belongs to a good club, and the initiation fee was his soul.

Here I speak by the book, for I have been in active practice as a journalist for more than a quarter of a century, and have an immense acquaintance in the craft. I could name a man who fits my specifications exactly in every American city east of the Mississippi, and refrain only on the advice of counsel. I do not say that all journalists go that route. Far from it! Many escape by failing; some even escape by succeeding. But the majority succumb. They begin with high hopes. They end with safe jobs. In the career of any such man, it seems to me, there are materials for fiction of the highest order. He is interesting intrinsically, for his early ambition is at least not ignoble—he is not born an earthworm. And he is interesting as a figure in drama, for he falls gradually, resisting all the while, to forces that are beyond his strength. If he can't make the grade, it is not because he is unwilling or weak, but because the grade itself is too steep. Here is tragedy—and here is America. For the curse of this country, as of all democracies, is precisely the fact that it treats its best men as enemies. The aim of our society, if it may be said to have an aim, is to iron them out. The ideal American, in the public sense, is a respectable vacuum.

I heave this typical American journalist to the massed novelists of the Federal Union, and invite them to lay on. There is a capital novel in him—a capital character sketch and a capital picture of the American scene. He is representative and yet he is not commonplace. People will recognize him, and yet they are not familiar with him. Let the fictioneers have at him! But let them bear in mind that, like the wowser, he is not to be done to the tune of superior sneers. He is a wreck, but he has not succumbed to the gales without resistence. Let him be done ironically, as Lewis did Babbitt, but let him be done also with pity. He is not a comedian, but a tragedian. Above all, let him be done without any mouthing of theories. His simple story is poignant enough.

Is he too difficult? Then I offer a substitute: the American policeman. Certainly it is high time for him to get into a book. I dedicate him to the novelists of the nation at once, and provide them simultaneously with all the plot they will need. A moron with an IQ of 53, despairing of ever getting a better job, goes on the force and begins pounding a beat. A chance favor to a saloonkeeper makes a sergeant of him, and thereafter he slowly mounts the ladder. At the end he is an inspector, and in charge of operations against a fabulous crime wave, imagined by the city editor of a tabloid newspaper. Isn't that enough? What a vivid and exhilarating picture of American life could be got out of it! What humors are there, and what genuine drama! Nor are the materials esoteric. Every newspaper reporter's head is stuffed with them. I myself could do such a work in ten volumes folio. Nine young journalists out of ten, I believe, aspire to the novel. Well, here is a chance to write a novel as good as "Babbitt."

XI.

On Living in Baltimore

Some time ago, writing in an eminent Baltimore newspaper upon the Baltimore of my boyhood, I permitted myself an eloquent passage upon its charm, and let fall the doctrine that nearly all of that charm had vanished. Mere rhetoric, I greatly fear. The old charm, in truth, still survives in the town, despite the frantic efforts of the boosters and boomers who, in late years, have replaced all its ancient cobblestones with asphalt, and bedizened it with Great White Ways and suburban boulevards, and surrounded it with stinking steel plants and oil refineries, and increased its population from 400,000 to 800,000. I am never more conscious of the fact than when I return to it from New York. Behind me lies the greatest city of the modern world, with more money in it than all Europe and more clowns and harlots than all Asia, and yet it has no more charm than a circus lot or second-rate hotel. It can't show a single genuinely distinguished street. It hasn't a single park that is more lovely than a cemetery lot. It is without manner as it is without manners. Escaping from it to so ancient and solid a town as Baltimore is like coming out of a football crowd into quiet communion with a fair one who is also amiable, and has the gift of consolation for hard-beset and despairing men.

I have confessed to rhetoric, but I surely do not indulge in it here. For twenty-five years I have resisted a constant temptation to move to New York, and I resist it more easily to-day than I did when it began. I am, perhaps, the most arduous commuter ever heard of, even in that Babylon of commuters. My office is on Manhattan Island and has been there since 1914; yet I live, vote and have my being in Baltimore, and go back there the instant my job allows. If my desk bangs at 3 P.M. I leap for the 3.25 train. Four long hours in the Pullman follow, but the first is the worst. My back, at all events, is toward New York! Behind lies a place fit only for the gross business of getting money; ahead is a place made for enjoying it.

What makes New York so dreadful, I believe, is mainly the

fact that the vast majority of its people have been forced to rid themselves of one of the oldest and most powerful of human instincts—the instinct to make a permanent home. Crowded, shoved about and exploited without mercy, they have lost the feeling that any part of the earth belongs to them, and so they simply camp out like tramps, waiting for the constables to rush in and chase them away. I am not speaking here of the poor (God knows how they exist in New York at all!); I am speaking of the well-to-do, even of the rich. The very richest man, in New York, is never quite sure that the house he lives in now will be his next year—that he will be able to resist the constant pressure of business expansion and rising land values. I have known actual millionaires to be chased out of their homes in this way, and forced into apartments. In Baltimore too, the same pressure exists, to be sure, but it is not oppressive, for the householder can meet it by yielding to it half way. It may force him into the suburbs, even into the adjacent country, but he is still in direct contact with the city, sharing in its life, and wherever he lands he may make a stand. But on Manhattan Island he is quickly brought up by the rivers, and once he has crossed them he may as well move to Syracuse or Trenton.

Nine times out of ten he tries to avoid crossing them. That is, he moves into meaner quarters on the island itself, and pays more for them. His house gives way to a flat—one offering perhaps half the room for his goods and chattels that his house offered. Next year he is in a smaller flat, and three-fourths of his goods and chattels have vanished. A few years more, and he is in two or three rooms. Finally, he lands in an hotel. At this point he ceases to exist as the head of a house. His quarters are precisely like the quarters of 50,000 other men. The front he presents to the world is simply an anonymous door on a gloomy corridor. Inside, he lives like a sardine in a can. Such a habitation, it must be plain, cannot be called a home. A home is not a mere transient shelter: its essence lies in its permanence, in its capacity for accretion and solidification, in its quality of representing, in all its details, the personalities of the people who live in it. In the course of years it becomes a sort of museum of these people; they give it its indefinable air, separating it from all other homes, as one human face is separated from all others. It is at once a refuge from the world, a treasure-house, a castle, and the shrine of a whole hierarchy of peculiarly private and potent gods.

This concept of the home cannot survive the mode of life that prevails in New York. I have seen it go to pieces under my eyes in the houses of my own friends. The intense crowding in the town, and the restlessness and unhappiness that go with it, make it almost impossible for anyone to accumulate the materials of a home—the trivial, fortuitous and often grotesque things that gather around a family, as glories and debts gather around a state. The New Yorker lacks the room to house them; he thus learns to live without them. In the end he is a stranger in the house he lives in. More and more, it tends to be no more than Job No. 16432b from this or that decorator's studio. I know one New Yorker, a man of considerable means, who moves every three years. Every time he moves his wife sells the entire contents of the apartment she is leaving, and employs a decorator to outfit the new one. To me, at all events, such a mode of living would be unendurable. The charm of getting home, as I see it, is the charm of getting back to what is inextricably my own—to things familiar and long loved, to things that belong to me alone and none other. I have lived in one house in Baltimore for nearly forty-five years. It has changed in that time, as I have—but somehow it still remains the same. No conceivable decorator's masterpiece could give me the same ease. It is as much a part of me as my two hands. If I had to leave it I'd be as certainly crippled as if I lost a leg.

I believe that this feeling for the hearth, for the immemorial lares and penates, is infinitely stronger in Baltimore than in New York—that it has better survived there, indeed, than in any other large city of America—and that its persistence accounts for the superior charm of the town. There are, of course, thousands of Baltimoreans in flats—but I know of none to whom a flat seems more than a makeshift, a substitute, a necessary and temporary evil. They are all planning to get out, to find houseroom in one of the new suburbs, to resume living in a home. What they see about them is too painfully not theirs. The New Yorker has simply lost that discontent. He is a vagabond. His notions of the agreeable become those of a vaudeville actor. He takes on the shallowness and unpleasantness of any other homeless man. He is highly sophisticated, and inordinately trashy. The fact no doubt explains the lack of charm that one finds in his town; the fact that the normal man of Baltimore is almost his exact antithesis explains the charm that is there. Human relations, in such a place, tend to assume a solid permanence. A man's circle of friends becomes a sort of extension of his family circle. His contacts are with men and women who are rooted as he is. They are not moving all the time, and so they are not changing their friends all the time. Thus abiding relationships tend to be built up, and when fortune brings unexpected changes, they survive those changes. The men I know and esteem in Baltimore are, on the whole, men I have known and esteemed a long while; even those who have come into my ken relatively lately seem likely to last. But of the men I knew best when I first began going to New York, twenty-five years ago, not one is a friend to-day. Of those I knew best ten years ago, not six are friends. The rest have got lost in the riot, and the friends of to-day, I sometimes fear, will get lost in the same way.

In human relationships that are so casual there is seldom any satisfaction. It is our fellows who make life endurable to us, and give it a purpose and a meaning; if our contacts with them are light and frivolous there is something lacking, and it is something of the very first importance. What I contend is that in Baltimore, under a slow-moving and cautious social organization, touched by the Southern sun, such contacts are more enduring than elsewhere, and that life in consequence is more agreeable. Of the external embellishments of life there is a plenty there—as great a supply, indeed, to any rational taste, as in New York itself. But there is also something much better: a tradition of sound and comfortable living. A Baltimorean is not merely John Doe, an isolated individual of *Homo sapiens*, exactly like every other John Doe. He is John Doe *of* a certain place—of Baltimore, of a definite *house* in Baltimore. It is not by accident that all the peoples of Europe, very early in their history, distinguished their best men by adding *of* this or that place to their names.

XII.

The Last New Englander

THE late Prof. Barrett Wendell, of Harvard, whose letters have been done into a stately volume by M. A. DeWolfe Howe, will probably go down into history as the last flower of the Puritan *Kultur*. Himself by no means a pure New Englander, for his surname was obviously Dutch, he yet had enough New England blood in him to feel himself wholly of that forlorn region, and he was accepted as a fit representative of it by all its tribal headmen. He was steeped in its tradition, and venerated its heroes. What came out of New England seemed to him to be virtuous and lovely, or, as he might have said, gentlemanly; what came out of the rest of the country was simply barbarous.

Nevertheless, Wendell was himself a walking proof that all he admired was passing into the shadows, for, try as he would, he could not, as a contemporary man, squeeze himself into the old Puritan mold. Over and over again he would make an effort to do so, but always, as he struggled with the lid, a diabolical, iconoclastic mood would overcome him, and he would leap up and emit a ribald yell. Harvard, startled and uneasy, never knew what to make of him. His principles were apparently impeccable; he was, in the current phrase, a consistent booster for the lost Golden Age, its glories and high deeds. And yet, whenever the answering cheer came back, he would make a mocking face and say something awful. The Cambridge campus is still warmed by these mockings. What saved him from downright infamy was the fact that, whenever they were actually in contempt of the Puritan mores and gnosiology, they were safely superficial—that is, they never questioned fundamentals. Wendell had a lot to say about the transient excesses and imbecilities of democracy, visible in his time, but he nevertheless believed in all the primary democratic fallacies, and even defended them eloquently. He was a tart critic of the whole educational process, and went to the length, in his own department of English, of denying it any value whatever;

nevertheless, he remained a romantic Harvard man to the end of his days, and venerated *alma mater* with the best of them. He must have seen clearly that there was little that was sound and solid left in the New England culture, that the rest of the country had little need of it and would quickly surpass it; all the same, he clung to the superstition that the preposterous theologians of its early days constituted an intellectual aristocracy, and even wrote a book eulogizing the most absurd of them, Cotton Mather.

Wendell, in fact, was two men, separate and distinct, and they were often at war. One of these men was highly intelligent (though surely not very learned); the other was a romantic under the spell of a disintegrating tradition. The latter was the more charming, but often a prey to mere lyrical fancy. The picture of the American character that Wendell presented to gaping throngs in his Sorbonne lectures was a sort of fantastic chromo of the primeval New England character, seen through nine thicknesses of amber gelatine—in brief, a thing as bizarre as the accounts of the Revolution that used to be in schoolbooks. Fundamentally, he once said somewhere else, we believe in fair play. It would be hard to imagine a more inaccurate saying. If any single quality, indeed, has marked off the Americano from all other civilized men since the start, it is his incapacity to purge combat of passion, his strong disinclination to allow any merit whatever to the other fellow;—in brief, his bad sportsmanship. Our history is a history of minorities put down with clubs. Even the duel, during the few years it flourished in America, took on a ferocity unheard of elsewhere. Gentlemen, going out at daybreak, shot to kill. Aaron Burr was a thorough American; Hamilton was an Englishman. In other fields, Wendell indulged himself in similar sentimentalities. He reacted to the shock of the late war in the correct manner of a State Street banker. He succumbed to the Coolidge buncombe far back in 1920. Yet always the sharply intelligent Wendell hauled up and stayed the orthodox romantic. The tribute to him by Prof. Kuno Francke, quoted by Mr. Howe, is a tribute not only to a gentleman, but also to a man of sense. And even in the midst of his banal speculation whether Coolidge, after all, would not turn out to be a Yankee Lincoln, he saw clearly the "small, hatchet-faced, colorless man, with a tight-shut, thin-lipped mouth"—in other words, the third-rate, small-town attorney, stuffed with copy-book platitudes and quite without imagination. He saw, too, the truth about Wilson, and stated it blisteringly in a letter to his friend R. W. Curtis.

Wendell's actual books, I believe, are now all dead, even his arbitrary and ignorant but highly amusing "Literary History of America." His volume on Shakespeare, published in 1894, is admired by Sir Arthur Quiller-Couch and Mrs. Edith Wharton, but no one else seems to remember it. His novels and dramas are long forgotten. His "English Composition" was and is a school-book; he himself, in his old age, had doubts that it had accomplished even its pedagogic purpose. His political essays, once so salacious, now read like the heresies of the Jefferson era. What remains, then, of Prof. Barrett Wendell. A.B., Litt.D.? A great deal more, I believe, than a mere ghost. When, indeed, the roll of American literati is drawn up at last, and the high deeds of each are set down, it will be found that Wendell, too, did something, and that what he did was of considerable importance. In a few words, he helped to divert criticism from books to life itself—he was one of the first to see that mere literature is, after all, mere literature—that it cannot be understood without knowing something about the society which produced it. Even Poe, masterly critic that he was, overlooked this obvious and all-important fact. His discussion of books went on in a sort of vacuum. He had brilliant (and often sound) opinions about every technical problem imaginable, and about every question of taste, but only too often he overlooked the fact that his author was also a man, and that what the author wrote the man had first to think, feel and endure. Wendell got rid of that narrow bookishness, still lingering in Lowell. He was primarily a critic, not of literary manners and postures, but of human existence under the Republic. There was no scholarly affectation about him, for all his superficial playacting, his delight in impressing sophomores. He did not bury his nose in books; he went out and looked at the world, and what he saw there amused him immensely and filled him with ideas. In Mr. Howe's index the name of Longfellow appears but once, and that of Gilder but once, and that of Aldrich not at all, but that of Blaine is there six times, and after Democracy there are twenty-two entries.

It seems to me that this break with the old American tradition had its high uses, and has left its mark upon American letters. Criticism among us is vastly less cloistered than it once was. Even professors of the loftiest tone, if they would have themselves attended to, must descend from their ivory towers and show themselves at the sea-level. The aloof and austere spirit is now viewed with suspicion. There are, I daresay, ancients who deplore the change. A natural regret, for it has made criticism vastly more difficult. But few deplore it, I believe, who know what literature really is—few, that is, who know the difference between mere intellectual prettiness and a body of living ideas.

As for Wendell's amazing contradictions and inconsistencies, his endless flounderings between orthodoxy and heresy, I believe that an adequate explanation of them is to be found in the compositions of Prof. Dr. Sigmund Freud, the Viennese necromancer. Freud, himself a Jew, discusses in one of his books the curious fact that jokes at the expense of the Jews are chiefly circulated by Jews themselves, and especially by the younger ones. Two Jewish drummers in a Pullman smoking-room fall into an exchange of such jocosities almost automatically. Why? Because, says Freud, they attain thereby to an escape from their Jewishness, which often irks them. It is not that they are ashamed of being Jews; it is that the Jewish practices of their elders are burdensome. They dare not revolt openly, for their sense of filial piety is strong, so they take it out by making jokes. By much the same psychological process, I believe, Wendell arrived at his curious mixture of contrarieties. Sentimentally and emotionally, he was moved powerfully by the New England tradition, and felt a strong impulse to defend it against the world. Intellectually, he saw clearly that it was in collapse around him—worse, that it had been full of defects and weaknesses even when, by his own doctrine, it had been strong. The result was his endless shuttling between worship and ribaldry. The last of the New Englanders, he clung pathetically to a faith which gradually succumbed to doubts. In his later years he thus stood upon a burning deck, whence all but him had fled.

Two things, for all his skepticism, he could never bring himself to admit formally, both obvious: first, that the so-called culture of Puritan New England was largely imaginary, that civilization was actually introduced into the region by anti-Puritans, and second, that when Transcendentalism came in, the leadership of Puritanism passed from New England and went to the South and Middle West. To admit the truth of either proposition was psychically impossible to a man of his romantic feelings. Each, baldly stated, seemed to flout the local Holy Ghost. And yet both were true, and their proofs were visible at a glance. The first, I daresay, will never be granted formally, or even heard patiently, by any genuine New Englander. Only a short while ago Walter Prichard Eaton, a very able Puritan, was arguing eloquently that his blue-nosed ancestors were really lovers of beauty, nay, downright artists— and offering the charming old houses on Nantucket Island as exhibits. Unfortunate examples, alas, alas! The houses on Nantucket were not built until the Puritan theocracy was completely demoralized and impotent—until Boston had a theatre, and was already two-thirds of the way to hell. And if they were actually built by Puritans at all, then it was by Puritans who had gone out into the wide, wide world and savored its dreadful and voluptuous marvels—Puritans who had come back from the Eastern seas with gaudy silks in their sea-chests, and the perfume of strange gals upon their whiskers, and a new glitter to their eyes.

Orthodox history, at least as it appears in school-books, assumes that the witch-burners and infant-damners had it all their own way in New England, even down to Revolutionary times. They actually met with sturdy opposition from the start. All of their sea-ports gradually filled up with sailors who were anything but pious Christian men, and even the back-country had its heretics, as the incessant wars upon them demonstrate. The fact that only Puritans could vote in the towns has deceived the historians; they mistake what was the law for what was really said and done. We have had proofs in our own time that that error is easy. Made by students of early New England, it leads to multiple absurdities. The fact is that the civilization that grew up in the region, such as it was, owed very little to the actual Puritans; it was mainly the product of anti-Puritans, either home-bred or imported. Even the school system, so celebrated in legend, owed whatever value was in it to what were currently regarded as criminals. The Puritans did not found their schools for the purpose of propagating what is now known as learning; they found them simply as nurseries of orthodoxy. Beyond the barest rudiments nothing of any worldly value was taught in them. The principal subject of study, first and last, was theology, and it was theology of the most grotesque and insane sort ever cherished by man. Genuine education began in New England only when the rising minority of anti-Puritans, eventually to become a majority, rose against this theology, and tried to put it down. The revolt was first felt at Harvard; it gradually converted a seminary for the training of Puritan pastors into a genuine educational institution. Harvard delivered New England, and made civilization possible there. All the men who adorned that civilization in the days of its glory—Emerson, Hawthorne and all the rest of them—were essentially anti-Puritans.

To-day, save in its remoter villages, New England is no more Puritan than, say, Maryland or Missouri. There is scarcely a clergyman in the entire region who, if the Mathers could come back to life, would not be condemned by them instantly as a heretic, and even as an atheist. The dominant theology is mild, skeptical and wholly lacking in passion. The evangelical spirit has completely disappeared. Save in a small minority of atavistic fanatics, there is a tolerance that is almost indistinguishable from indifference. Roman Catholicism and Christian Science are alike viewed amiably. The old heat is gone. Where it lingers in America is in far places—on the Methodist prairies of the Middle West, in the Baptist back-waters of the South. There, I believe, it still retains not a little of its old vitality. There Puritanism survives, not merely as a system of theology, but also as a way of life. It colors every human activity. Kiwanis mouths it; it is powerful in politics; learning wears its tinge. To charge a Harvard professor of to-day with agnosticism would sound as banal as to charge him with playing the violoncello. But his colleague of Kansas, facing the same accusation, would go damp upon the forehead, and his colleague of Texas would leave town between days.

Wendell, a sentimentalist, tried to put these facts behind him, though he must have been well aware of them. There got into his work, in consequence, a sense of futility, even when he was discussing very real and important things. He opened paths that he was unable to traverse himself. Sturdier men, following him, were soon marching far ahead of him. He will live in the history of American criticism, but his own criticism is already dead.

XIII.

The Nation

ONE often hears lamentation that the American weeklies of opinion are not as good as their English prototypes—that we have never produced anything in that line to equal, say, the *Athenæum* or the *Saturday Review*. In the notion, it seems to me, there is nothing save that melancholy colonialism which is one of the curses of America. The plain fact is that our weeklies, taking one with another, are quite as well turned out as anything that England has ever seen, and that at least two of them, the *Nation* and the *New Republic*, are a great deal better. They are better because they are more hospitable to ideas, because they are served by a wider and more various range of writers, and because they show an occasional sense of humor. Even the *New Republic* knows how to be waggish, though it also knows, especially when it is discussing religion, how to be cruelly dull. Its Washington correspondence is better than any Parliamentary stuff in any English weekly ever heard of, if only because it is completely devoid of amateur statesmanship, the traditional defect of political correspondence at all times and everywhere. The editors of the English weeklies all ride political hobbies, and many of them are actively engaged in politics. Their American colleagues, I suspect, have been tempted in that direction more than once, but happily they have resisted, or maybe fate has resisted for them.

Of all the weeklies—and I go through at least twenty each week, American and English, including the Catholic *Commonweal* and a Negro journal—I like the *Nation* best. There is something charming about its format, and it never fails to print an interesting piece of news, missed by the daily newspapers. Moreover, there is always a burst of fury in it, and somewhere or other, often hidden in a letter from a subscriber, a flash of wit—two things that make for amusing reading. The *New Republic*, I suspect, is more authoritative in certain fields, —for example, the economic—but it is also more pontifical. The *Nation* gets the air of a lark into many of its most violent

crusades against fraud and folly; one somehow gathers the notion that its editors really do not expect the millennium to
come in to-morrow. Of late they have shown many signs of
forsaking Liberalism for Libertarianism—a far sounder and
more satisfying politics. A liberal is committed to sure cures
that always turn out to be swindles; a Libertarian throws the
bottles out of the window, and asks only that the patient be let
alone.

What the circulation of the *Nation* may be I don't know. In
its sixtieth anniversary number, published in 1925, there was a
hint that the number then sold each week ran far ahead of the
11,000 with which E. L. Godkin began in 1865. I have heard
gabble in the saloons frequented by New York publishers that
the present circulation is above 30,000. But no one, so far as I
know, has ever suggested that it equals the circulation of even
a third-rate daily paper. Such dull, preposterous sheets as the
New York *Telegram*, the Washington *Star*, the Philadelphia
Public Ledger and the Atlanta *Constitution* sell two or three
times as many copies. Such magazines for the herd as *True
Stories* and *Hot Dog* sell fifty times as many. Nevertheless, if I
were a fellow of public spirit and eager to poison the Republic
with my sagacity, I'd rather be editor of the *Nation* than editor
of any of the other journals that I have mentioned—nay, I'd
rather be editor of the *Nation* than editor of all of them together, with every other newspaper and magazine in America,
save perhaps four or five, thrown in. For the *Nation* is unique
in American journalism for one thing: it is read by its enemies.
They may damn it, they may have it barred from libraries, they
may even—as they did during the war—try to have it put
down by the Postoffice, but all the while they read it. That is,
the more intelligent of them—the least hopeless minority of
them. It is to such minorities that the *Nation* addresses itself,
on both sides of the fence. It has penetrated to the capital fact
that they alone count—that the ideas sneaked into them to-
day will begin to sweat out of the herd day after to-morrow.

Is the Creel Press Bureau theory of the late war abandoned?
Is it impossible to find an educated man who is not ashamed
that he succumbed to the Wilson buncombe? Then thank the
Nation for that deliverance, for when it tackled Wilson it tackled him alone. Is the Coolidge Golden Age beginning to be

sicklied o'er with a pale cast of green? Then prepare to thank
the *Nation* again, for it began to tell the harsh, cold truth
about good Cal at a time when all the daily journals of America, with not ten exceptions, were competing for the honor of
shining his shoes. I often wonder, indeed, that the great success of the *Nation* under Villard has made such little impression upon American journalists—that they are so dead to the
lessons that it roars into their ears. They all read it—that is, all
who read anything at all. It prints news every week that they
can't find in their own papers—sometimes news of the very
first importance. It comments upon that news in a tart and
well-informed fashion. It presents all the new ideas that rage in
the world, always promptly and often pungently. To an editorial writer the *Nation* is indispensable. Either he reads it, or he
is an idiot. Yet its example is very seldom followed—that is,
forthrightly and heartily. Editorial writers all over the land steal
ideas from it daily; it supplies, indeed, all the ideas that most of
them ever have. It lifts them an inch, two inches, three inches,
above the sedimentary stratum of Rotarians, bankers and ice-
wagon drivers; they are conscious of its pull even when they
resist. Yet very few of them seem to make the inevitable deduction that the kind of journalism it practices is better and
more effective than the common kind—that they, too, might
amount to something in this world if they would imitate it.

In such matters, alas, change is very slow. The whole press of
the United States, I believe, is moving in the direction of the
Nation—that is, in the direction of independence and honesty.
Even such papers as the New York *Herald-Tribune* are measurably less stupid and intransigeant than they used to be, in their
news if not in their opinions. But the majority of active journalists in the higher ranks were bred on the old-time party organs, and it is very difficult for them to reform their ways.
They still think, not as free men, but as party hacks. On the
one side they put the truth; on the other side they put what
they call policy. Thus there are thousands of them who still sit
down nightly to praise Coolidge—though to the best of my
knowledge and belief there is not a single journalist in the
whole United States who ever speaks of Coolidge in private
without sneering at him. This resistance to change grows all
the more curious when one observes what happens to the oc-

casional paper which abandons it. I offer the Baltimore *Sun-paper* as an example—an especially apposite one, for the influence of the *Nation* upon it must be apparent to everyone familiar with its recent history. It was, a dozen years ago, a respectable but immensely dull journal. It presented the day's news in a formal, unintelligent fashion. It was accurate in small things, and free from sensationalism, but it seldom if ever went beyond the overt event to the causes and motives behind it. Its editorial opinions were flabby, and without influence. To-day it is certainly something far different. It must still go a long, long way, I suspect, before it escapes its old self altogether, but that must be a dull reader, indeed, who cannot see how vastly it has improved. It no longer prints the news formally; it devotes immense energy to discovering and revealing what is behind the news. In opinion it has thrown off all chains of faction and party, and is sharply and often intelligently independent. Its reaction to a new public problem is not that of a party hack, but that of a free man. It is, perhaps, sometimes grossly wrong, but no sane person believes that it is ever deliberately disingenuous.

Well, the point is that this new scheme has been tremendously successful—that it has paid in hard cash as well as in the usufructs of the spirit. There is no sign that the readers of the *Sunpaper*—barring a few quacks with something to sell—dislike its new vigor, enterprise and independence. On the contrary, there is every evidence that they like it. They have increased greatly in numbers. The paper itself rises in dignity and influence. And every other newspaper in America that ventures upon the same innovations, from the *World* in New York to the *Enquirer-Sun* down in Columbus, Ga., rises in the same way. It is my contention that the *Nation* has led the way in this reform of American journalism—that it will be followed by many papers to-morrow, as it is followed by a few to-day. Its politics are sometimes outrageous. It frequently gets into lamentable snarls, battling for liberty with one hand and more laws with the other. It is doctrinaire, inconsistent, bellicose. It whoops for men one day, and damns them as frauds the next. It has no sense of decorum. It is sometimes a bit rowdy. But who will deny that it is honest? And who will deny that, taking one day with another, it is generally right—that its enthusiasms, if they occasionally send it mooning after dreamers, at least never send it cheering for rogues—that its wrongness, when it is wrong, is at all events not the dull, simian wrongness of mere stupidity? It is disliked inordinately, but not, I believe, by honest men, even among its enemies. It is disliked by demagogues and exploiters, by frauds great and small. They have all tasted its snickersnee, and they have all good reason to dislike it.

Personally, I do not subscribe to its politics, save when it advocates liberty openly and unashamed. I have no belief in politicians: the good ones and the bad ones seem to me to be unanimously thieves. Thus I hope I may whoop for it with some grace, despite the fact that my name appears on its flagstaff. How my name got there I don't know; I receive no emolument from its coffers, and write for it very seldom, and then only in contravention of its ideas. I even have to pay cash for my annual subscription—a strange and painful burden for a journalist to bear. But I know of no other expenditure (that is, of a secular character) that I make with more satisfaction, or that brings me a better return. Most of the papers that I am doomed to read are idiotic even when they are right. The *Nation* is intelligent and instructive even when it is wrong.

XIV.

Officers and Gentlemen

H ARD luck pursues the American Navy. It is the common
butt, not only of political mountebanks, but also of all
the brummagem uplifters and soul-snatchers who now sweat
to save us. If a Mr. Secretary Denby is not permitting the Falls
and Dohenys to raid its goods, a Mr. Secretary Wilbur or Josephus Daniels is trying to convert it into a Methodist Sunday-
school. Worse, the Navy gets more than its fair share of the
national dirty work. It is told off to put down free speech in
the Virgin Islands, and it is delegated to flog, hang and butcher
the poor Haitians, and so convert them into black Iowans,
with money in the bank. Elsewhere in the world such disagreeable jobs are given to the Army. The British Army, for example, performs all the massacres that are necessary in India, and
the French Army attends to whatever routine murders and
mayhems are called for in Syria and Morocco. But the American custom puts all such Christian endeavor upon the Navy.

However, unless my agents lie, it is not the gore that revolts
the more high-toned naval officers, but the new rectitude that
has been thrust upon them. They are, as a class, excellent fellows, and full of pride in their uniform. As officers, they are all
theoretically gentlemen, and many of them are so in fact. They
have traveled widely, and are familiar with the usages of the
civilized world. They know what is decent and seemly. Well,
try to imagine how they must feel when they read the daily
papers. One day they read that the Secretary of the Navy has
ordered a group of their colleagues to prosecute a woman
nurse for bringing in a couple of jugs aboard a naval collier.
The next day they observe that a high officer in the Marines
has filled the newspapers with a meticulous and indignant account of what went on at a table where he was a guest, in the
house of one of his subordinates. Explanations of this last
episode have been offered, but they certainly do not explain
it away. The essential and immovable point is that one officer
snitched on another, his host—that the immemorial and

invariable obligations of a guest were sacrificed to Law Enforcement. What would happen to an English naval officer
who made any such assault upon the code? What, indeed
would happen to an honest Elk?

But I am not arguing here that any such things ought to
happen; I am merely calling attention to the fact that, under
democracy, it is becoming increasingly difficult for officers to
be gentlemen, as the term is commonly understood in the
world, and perhaps also increasingly improbable. We are, it
would appear, passing through a time of changing values, and
what was considered decent by our fathers will lose that quality to-morrow. The lower orders of men, having attained to
political power, now proceed to force their ideas upon their
betters, and some of those ideas naturally have to do with
decorum. It is already unlawful in America to take a bottle of
wine to a sick friend; in a few years it may also be indelicate.
And simultaneously, it may become quite proper to go to the
police with anything that is said or done in a friend's house.
Personally, I am inclined to oppose such changes, if only in
sheer hunkerousness, but I am surely under no illusion that
opposing them will stop them. They flow naturally out of the
character of the common man, now in the saddle, and are thus
irresistible. He is extremely and even excessively moral, but the
concept of what is called honor is beyond him. If, for example,
he aspires to public office, he believes that it is entirely proper
to abandon one conviction and take on its opposite in order to
get votes. And, having got into office, he believes that it is entirely proper to hold on at any cost, even at the cost of common decency.

There is a familiar example. I allude to the Cathcart case. In
that case a high officer of State found himself confronting an
uncomfortable dilemma. On the one hand he was bound by
an outrageous law to engage in a public and obscene chase of
a woman taken in adultery. On the other hand he was bound
by the code of all civilized men to refuse and refrain. What was
the way out for him? The way out, obviously, was for him to
resign his office—in other words, to decline flatly to perform
any such ignoble and disgusting duty, and to spurn as insults
the honors and emoluments offered for doing it. But, as far as
I can make out, he never so much as thought of that. Instead

he played the bounder—and kept his dirty job. His conduct, I believe, seemed quite proper to the overwhelming majority of his countrymen. The newspapers, in discussing it, never once suggested that a man of honor, in his boots, would resign forthwith. Instead, they simply denounced him for doing his plain duty under the law—that is, they proposed that he get out of his dilemma by violating his oath of office. The device is characteristically American. Anything is fair and decent that keeps a man his job. That has been the settled American doctrine since Jackson's time.

But it is only of late, I believe, that it has been defended openly, and its antithesis denounced as, in some mysterious fashion, inimical to democracy. We owe that change to the liberation of the lower orders which began with the Civil War. That liberation produced, on one side, an immense increase in political corruption, and, on the other, a rise in moral frenzy. All the characteristic ideas of the mob began to be reflected in public life and legislation. The typical American public officer, who had been a theorist willing to sacrifice anything, including his office, to his notions, became a realist willing to sacrifice anything, including his principles and his honor, to his job. We have him with us to-day, and he smells worse and worse as year chases year. Grover Cleveland was perhaps the last lonely survivor of the old days. He had his faults, God knows, but no one could have imagined him yielding to the mob in order to make votes. Right or wrong, he was his own man—and never more surely than when, by popular standards, he was wrong. In his successor, Dr. Coolidge, we have an almost perfect specimen of the new order. Coolidge is a professional trimmer, who has made his living at the art since his early manhood. It is impossible to imagine him sacrificing his political welfare to his convictions. He has vanity, but nothing properly describable as dignity or self-respect. One automatically pictures him doing, in the Cathcart case, precisely what his subordinate did. He performed many comparable acts during the stinking progress of the Fall case.

This general decay of honor is bound, plainly enough, to drive all the decenter sort of men out of public life among us. The process, indeed, has already gone a long way. I point to Congress. I point to the Federal judiciary. In both directions one observes an increase in trimmers and knee-benders and a decrease in independent and self-respecting men. The bench, in particular, has suffered. The better sort of judges, torn between their lawyer-like respect for all law and their inescapable conviction that many of the new laws they are called upon to enforce are unjust and dishonest, tend to throw off the ermine and go back to practice. And their places are filled by limber nonentities selected—and policed—by the Anti-Saloon League.

Until a few years ago the Army and the Navy escaped this general degradation. Their officers stood apart from the main body of public job-holders. They held office for life, and they were assumed to be innocent of politics. Having no need to curry favor with the mob, they could afford to disdain the common hypocrisies. Inheriting an austere and exact tradition of professional honor, they were what is called gentlemen. They did not blab upon one another. They had the fine tolerance of civilized men. They had dignity. It was as impossible to imagine a naval officer or an army officer playing the spy for the Anti-Saloon League as it was to imagine him using a table-napkin as a handkerchief or getting converted at a Methodist revival. But I fear those days are past. The pressure from outside, exerted through such mountebanks as Mr. Secretary Wilbur, becomes too heavy to be borne. Worse, there is disintegration within, due in part, perhaps, to the packing of the two Services with civilians from the gutter, but in part also to changes in the method of selecting candidates for Annapolis and West Point. Whatever the cause, the effects are already plain. In a few short years, perhaps, we shall see a major-general in the Army preaching Fundamentalism in Tennessee, and an admiral in the Navy going to work for the Anti-Saloon League.

XV.

Golden Age

THE rest of us, struggling onward painfully, must wait in patience for the boons and usufructs of Heaven; Judge Elbert Henry Gary, LL.D., chairman of the United States Steel Corporation, has them here and now. To few men in history, I believe, has it been given to live in a universe so nearly to their hearts' desire. Let the learned ex-jurist look East or West, he will find only scenes to content him. Let him look North or South, and his eye will be caressed and frankincense will spray his gills. The emperor and pope of all the Babbitts, he sits at the center of a Babbitts' paradise. For him and his like there dawns a Golden Age, and its hero is good Cal.

I hope I do not exaggerate. No doubt Judge Gary, in the privacy of his chamber, sweats and fumes against imperfections invisible to the rest of us. He is a man of imagination, and has, I daresay, a bold and soaring fancy. He can imagine a Republic even kinder and more osculatory than this one—that is, to Babbitts. He can even, perhaps, imagine a President more ineffable than Cal. But here we shoot into mere human weaknesses —the voluptuous, Freudian day-dreams of one who, like all of us, has his aberrant, goatish moods. Dr. John Roach Straton, I suppose, can imagine improvements in the Holy Scriptures— here a paragraph excised *pro bonos mores*, there a comma inserted to make sense. I myself have dreamed of a malt liquor better than Pilsner Bürgerbräu. But I do not sign my name to such inordinate speculations, and neither does Dr. Straton. Judge Gary, too, holds his tongue. The rest of us, contemplating him, can only envy him. A vast nation of 110,000,000 human beings, all of them alike, seems to be organized to the one end of making him happy. Whatever he wants it to do, it does. Its laws are framed to his precise taste; its public conscience approves his partisans and execrates his enemies; its high officers of state are his excellent friends, and humble and obedient servants. When he gives a feast, judges and ambassadors leap to grace it. When he would dine out, he is welcome at the White House. The newspapers fawn upon him. Labor licks his hand. His frown is dreaded in the Senate house and on the bench. Altogether, his life is happier than that of a Broadway actor, and if he is not content then it is only because contentment is physiologically impossible to *Homo sapiens.*

The United States, I believe, is the first great empire in the history of the world to ground its whole national philosophy upon business. There have been, of course, eminent trading nations in the past, but none ever went so far. Even in Carthage there was a *Junker* hierarchy that stood above the merchants; in Hannibal it actually had a Crown Prince. And even in England, the nation of shopkeepers of Napoleon's derision, there has always been an aristocracy (made up mainly of military freebooters, enterprising adulterers, the issue of the latter, and, in modern times, shyster lawyers, vaudeville magnates, and the proprietors of yellow newspapers) that has held its own against the men of trade, even at the cost of absorbing the more pugnacious of them. But here in this great Republic of the West the art of trafficking is king—and Judge Gary is its grand vizier, as Cal is its chief eunuch. No other human activity brings such great rewards in money and power, and none is more lavishly honored. The one aim of our jurisprudence is to safeguard business—to make its risks small and its profits sure. If the rights of the citizen get in the way, then the rights of the citizen must be sacrificed. Upon this point our higher courts have delivered themselves more than once, and in eloquent, ringing terms. Judge Gary and his friends prefer dry and dismal slaves to those who are stewed and happy. *Also,* to hell with the Bill of Rights! They prefer, when there is a strike, to win it rather than lose it. Out, then, with the pad of blank junctions! They sweat under criticism, and shiver under attack. To the hoosegow, constable, with the Bolsheviks!

All this, of course, was not achieved without a struggle. For years the Constitution stood in the way—the Constitution and certain national superstitions—the latter sprung from the blather of the Revolutionary stump. But all those impediments are now surmounted. The bench gave Judge Gary to business, and business has reciprocated the favor by providing sound and sane men for the bench. To-day jurisprudence is unfettered. When, a year or so ago, the Supreme Court finally got rid of the Fourth Amendment, that delayed mopping up went almost unnoticed. As I say, Judge Gary ought to be a happy man. The sun shines upon him from all four points of the compass. Congress, well rehearsed, plays soft jazz for him; bishops bring him his toddy; a straw issues from the White House and tickles him behind the ear. But never is his happiness greater, I believe, than when his thoughts turn idly upon the subject of labor, and he contemplates the state of the union movement in the Federal Union.

For this state, it is plain, he has the late Sam Gompers to thank—that great idealist and easy mark. If he sent less than ten hay-wagons of roses to Sam's funeral, then he is a niggard, indeed. For Sam got upon the back of the American labor movement when it was beginning to be dangerous, and rode it so magnificently that at the end of his life it was as tame as a tabby cat. It retains that character to-day, and will continue to do so as long as the Gompersian hierarchy lasts,—that is, so long as Judge Gary and his friends continue to appoint Sam's heirs and assigns to high-sounding committees, and to invite them to gaudy dinners. A plate of puddle duck and a chance to make a speech—that was always enough to fetch Sam. And when Sam was fetched, the 4,000,000 members of the American Federation of Labor were also fetched. Where else in the world is there a great union organization that has so long and honorable a record as a strike-breaker? Or that is so diligently devoted to keeping the lower ranks of labor in due subordination? If it had been conceived and hatched by Judge Gary himself, it could not have been more nearly perfect. Practically considered, it is not a labor organization at all; it is simply a balloon mattress interposed between capital and labor to protect the former from the latter. Gazing upon it, I daresay, Judge Gary feels a glow flickering along the periphery of his gizzard, and if he were not a Christian he would permit himself a guffaw.

I leave the sweetest to the last. The courts might be docile, Congress might be consecrated to right thought, labor might grovel and the bench of bishops might applaud, but if there were an anarchist in the White House it would all go for naught. Imagine, then, Judge Gary's joy in contemplating the incomparable Cal! It is almost as if, in New York, a bootlegger were made king. The man's merits, in the Babbitt view, are almost fabulous. He seems, indeed, scarcely like a man at all, but more like some miraculous visitation or act of God. He is the ideal made visible, if not audible—perfection put into a cutaway coat and trotted up and down like a mannequin in a cloak and suit atelier. Nor was there any long stress of training him—no season of doubt and misgiving. Nature heaved him forth full-blown, like a new star shot into the heavens. In him the philosophy of Babbitt comes to its perfect and transcendental form. Thrift, to him, is the queen of all the virtues. He respects money in each and every one of its beautiful forms— pennies, nickels, dimes, dollars, five-dollar bills, and so on *ad infinitum*. He venerates those who have it. He believes that they have wisdom. He craves the loan and use of that wisdom. He invites them to breakfast, and listens to them. The thing they revere, he reveres. The things they long for, he longs to give them.

Judge Gary is an old man—just how old I do not know, for he withholds the date of his birth from "Who's Who in America," along with the principal suffragettes. He remembers the dreadful days of Roosevelt, with bombs going off every two hours. He remembers the turmoils of the Taft administration. He remembers how *difficile* Woodrow was—how he had to be wooed, flattered, led by the nose, drenched with goose-grease. He remembers the crude carnival under the martyr Harding —Broadway sports, pug managers, small-town Elks at the trough. And then he thinks of Washington to-day, and sees it bathed in pink sunshine. There he is ever welcome. There he is *imperator in imperio*. There is good *Geschäft*. There is the Athens of the new Golden Age.

XVI.
Edgar Saltus

F ORTY years ago Edgar Saltus was a shining star in the national literature, leading the way out of the Egyptian night of Victorian sentimentality. To-day he survives only as the favorite author of the late Warren Gamaliel Harding. I can recall, in the circle of Athene, no more complete collapse. Saltus plunged from the top of the world to the bottom of the sea. His books, of late, have been reissued, and his surviving third wife has printed a biography of him. But all his old following, save for a few romantic die-hards, has vanished.

The causes of the débâcle are certainly not hard to determine. They were set forth twenty-five years ago by that ingenious man, the late Percival Pollard, and you will find them in his book, "Their Day in Court." Saltus was simply a bright young fellow who succumbed to his own cleverness. The gaudy glittering phrase enchanted him. He found early in life that he had a hand for shaping it; he found soon afterward that it had a high capacity for getting him notice. So he devoted himself to its concoction—and presently he was lost. His life after that was simply one long intoxication. He was drunk on words. Ideas gradually departed from him. Day and night, for years and years, he held his nozzle against the jug of nouns, adjectives, verbs, pronouns, prepositions and interjections. Some of his phrases, of course, were good ones. There were enough of that kind in "Imperial Purple," for example, to fascinate the sainted Harding, a voluptuary in all the arts. But the rest quickly wore out—and with them Saltus himself wore out. He passed into the shadows, and was forgotten. When he died, a few years ago, all that remained of him was a vague name.

His wife's biography is encased in an orange slip-cover which announces melodramatically that it is "an extraordinary revealing life." It is, but I doubt that what it reveals will serve to recuscitate poor Saltus. The man who emerges from it is simply a silly and hollow trifler—a mass of puerile pretensions and affectations, vain of his unsound knowledge and full of sentimentalities. He began life by hawking the stale ribaldries of Arthur Schopenhauer, already dead twenty years; he departed to realms of bliss chattering the blowsy nonsense of theosophy. Mrs. Saltus, in the new and appalling fashion of literary wives, is extremely frank. Her Edgar was a handsome dog, but extremely foolish, and even childish. When he was engaged upon his rococo compositions he had to be protected like a queen bee in childbed. The slightest sound dissipated his inspiration, and set him to yelling. If a fish-peddler stopped beneath his window he was done for the day. If a cat came in and brushed his leg he was thrown into hysterics, and had to go to bed. His love affairs were highly complex, and apparently took up a great deal of his time. Early in life, while he was a student at Heidelberg, he had an affair with a lady of noble birth, and even ran away with her. The business was quickly broken up, apparently by the allied sovereigns of Europe. The bride-elect was immured in a convent, and died there "the year following." Saltus then came back to the Republic and married the daughter of a partner in J. P. Morgan & Company. "She was no small catch," but the alliance was doomed. The man was too fascinating to women. His pulchritude charmed them, and his epigrams finished them. In a few years Mrs. Saltus was suing for divorce.

There followed a series of morganatic affairs, culminating in a second marriage. This one also blew up quickly; the bride denounced Saltus as a liar, and even hinted that he had induced her to marry him by fraud. But though she soon left his bed and board, she clung resolutely to her other rights as his wife, and thereafter, for many long years, he devoted all the time he could spare from his writing to efforts to get rid of her. He moved from New York to California, in fact, mainly because the divorce laws on the Coast were easier than in the East. But they were not easy enough to free him. Finally, after endless waiting, he got news one day that the party of the second part was dead. He displayed the correct regrets, but was obviously much relieved. Meanwhile, Wife No. 3 was at call in the anteroom. She had been there, in fact, for years. When Saltus first met her she was a school-girl with her hair down her back, and his attentions to her—he was then rising forty—naturally outraged her family. But her own heart was lost, and so the effort to warn him off failed. He followed her, after that, all over the civilized world. Did she go to London, he was at her heels on the next steamer. Did she move to Los Angeles, he arrived by the next train. In the end they were married in Montreal, on a very hot day and after a pretty lovers' quarrel.

This lady is the author of the biography with the orange slip-cover. Facing page 310 there is a portrait of her showing her "sitting at the table on which her husband wrote his books, burning incense before a Siamese Buddha, and meditating on a stanza from the Bhagavad-Gita." She denies, however, that Saltus took to theosophy under her tutelage. The actual recruiting officer was certain Mr. Colville, of Pasadena, who combined the "enthusiasm of a scholar and the erudition of a sage." This Colville introduced Saltus to the theosophical elements, and later guided his faltering steps. In the end poor old Schopenhauer lost a customer and the art of epigram a gifted and diligent practitioner. Saltus passed into senility with his thoughts concentrated powerfully upon Higher Things.

A grotesque and somewhat pathetic story. The man began life with everything in his favor. His family was well-to-do and of good social position in New York; he was sent to Eton and then to Heidelberg, and apparently made useful friends at both places; he plunged into writing at the precise moment when revolt against the New England Brahmins was rising; he attracted attention quickly, and was given a lavish welcome. No American author of 1885 was more talked about. When his first novel, "The Truth About Tristrem Varick," came out in 1888 it made a genuine sensation. But the stick came down almost as fast as the rocket had gone up. His books set the nation agog for a short while, and were then quickly forgotten. He began as the hope of American letters, and ended as a writer of yellow-backs and a special correspondent for the Hearst papers. What ailed him was simply lack of solid substance. He could be clever, as cleverness was understood during the first Cleveland administration, but he lacked dignity, information, sense. His books of "philosophy" were feeble and superficial, his novels were only facile improvisations, full of satanic melodrama and wooden marionettes.

Of late I have been re-reading them—a sad job, surely, for when I was a schoolboy they were nine-day wonders, barred from all the libraries but devoured eagerly by every aspiring youth. Now their epigrams are dulled, and there is nothing else left. "The Anatomy of Negation" and "The Philosophy of Disenchantment" have been superseded by far better books; "The Truth About Tristrem Varick" reads like one of the shockers of Gertrude Atherton; "Mary Magdalen" is a dead shell; the essays and articles republished as "Uplands of Dream" are simply ninth-rate journalism. Of them all only "Imperial Purple" holds up. A certain fine glow is still in it; it has gusto if not profundity; Saltus's worst faults do not damage it appreciably. I find myself, indeed, agreeing thoroughly with the literary judgment of Dr. Harding. "Imperial Purple" remains Saltus's best book. It remains also, alas, his only good one!

XVII.
Miscellaneous Notes

I
Martyrs

To die for an idea: it is unquestionably noble. But how much nobler it would be if men died for ideas that were true! Searching history, I can find no such case. All the great martyrs of the books died for sheer nonsense—often for trivial matters of doctrine and ceremonial, too absurd to be stated in plain terms. But what of the countless thousands who have perished in the wars, fighting magnificently for their country? Well, show me one who knew precisely what the war he died in was about, and could put it into a simple and plausible proposition.

2
The Ancients

The theory that the ancient Greeks and Romans were men of a vast and ineffable superiority runs aground on the fact that they were great admirers of oratory. No other art was so assiduously practiced among them. To-day we venerate the architecture of Greece far more than we venerate its orators, but the Greeks themselves put the orators first, and so much better records of them are preserved to-day. But oratory, as a matter of fact, is the most primitive and hence the lowest of all the arts. Where is it most respected to-day? Among savages, in and out of civilization. The yokels of the open spaces flock by the thousand to hear imbeciles yawp and heave; the city proletariat glues its ears to the radio every night. But what genuinely civilized man would turn out to hear even the champion orator of the country? Dozens of the most eminent professors of the art show off their tricks every day in the United States Senate. Yet the galleries of the Senate, save when news goes out that some Senator is stewed and about to make an ass of himself, are occupied only by Negroes who have come in to get warm, and hand-holding bridal couples from rural North Carolina and West Virginia.

3
Jack Ketch as Eugenist

Has any historian ever noticed the salubrious effect, on the English character, of the frenzy for hanging that went on in England during the Eighteenth Century? When I say salubrious, of course, I mean in the purely social sense. At the end of the Seventeenth Century the Englishman was still one of the most turbulent and lawless of civilized men; at the beginning of the Nineteenth he was the most law-abiding; *i.e.*, the most docile. What worked the change in him? I believe that it was worked by the rope of Jack Ketch. During the Eighteenth Century the lawless strain was simply choked out of the race. Perhaps a third of those in whose veins it ran were actually hanged; the rest were chased out of the British Isles, never to return. Some fled to Ireland, and revivified the decaying Irish race: in practically all the Irish rebels of the past century there have been plain traces of English blood. Others went to the Dominions. Yet others came to the United States, and after helping to conquer the Western wilderness, begat the yeggman, Prohibition agents, footpads and hijackers of to-day.

The murder rate is very low in England, perhaps the lowest in the world. It is low because nearly all the potential ancestors of murderers were hanged or exiled in the Eighteenth Century. Why is it so high in the United States? Because most of the potential ancestors of murderers, in the late Eighteenth and early Nineteenth Centuries, were *not* hanged. And why did they escape? For two plain reasons. First, the existing government was too weak to track them down and execute them, especially in the West. Second, the qualities of daring and enterprise that went with their murderousness were so valuable that it was socially profitable to overlook their homicides. In other words, the job of occupying and organizing the vast domain of the new Republic was one that demanded the aid of men who, among other things, occasionally butchered their fellow men. The butchering had to be winked at in order to get their help. Thus the murder rate, on the frontier, rose to

unprecedented heights, while the execution rate remained
very low. Probably 100,000 men altogether were murdered in
the territory west of the Ohio between 1776 and 1865; probably
not 100 murderers were formally executed. When they were
punished at all, it was by other murderers—and this left the
strain unimpaired.

4
Heroes

Of human eminence there are obviously two varieties: that
which issues out of the inner substance of the eminent individual and that which comes to him, either partially or wholly,
from without. It is not difficult to recognize men at the two
extremes. No sane person would argue seriously that the eminence of such a man, say, as Richard Wagner was, in any plausible sense, accidental or unearned. Wagner created "Tristan
und Isolde" out of his own inherent substance. Allowing
everything for the chances of his education and environment,
the massive fact remains that no other man of the same general
education and environment has ever created anything even remotely comparable to it. Wagner deserved the eminence that
came to him quite as certainly as the Lord God Jehovah deserves that which attaches to Him. He got it by differing
sharply from other men, and enormously for the better, and by
laboring colossally and incessantly to make that difference visible. At the other extreme lies such a fellow, say, as young John
D. Rockefeller. He is, by all ordinary standards, an eminent
man. When he says anything the newspapers report it in full. If
he fell ill of gallstones to-morrow, or eloped with a lady Ph.D.,
or fell off the roof of his house, or was taken in a rum raid the
news would be telegraphed to all parts of the earth and at least
a billion human beings would show some interest in it. And if
he went to Washington and pulled the White House bell he
would be let in infallibly, even if the Heir of Lincoln had to
quit a saxophone lesson to see him. But it must be obvious
that young John's eminence, such as it is, is almost purely fortuitous and unearned. He is attended to simply because he
happens to be the son of old John, and hence heir to a large
fortune. So far as the records show, he has never said anything

in his life that was beyond the talents of a Rotary Club orator
or a newspaper editorial writer, or done anything that would
have strained an intelligent bookkeeper. He is, to all intents
and purposes, a vacuum, and yet he is known to more people,
and especially to more people of means, than Wagner, and admired and envied vastly more by all classes.

Between Wagner and young John there are infinite grada-
tions, and sometimes it is a hard matter to distinguish between
them. To most Americans, I daresay, a Harding or a Coolidge
appears to enjoy an eminence that is not only more gaudy but
also more solid than that of, say, an Einstein. When Einstein
visited the United States, a few years ago, he was taken to
see Harding as a sort of treat, and many worthy patriots, no
doubt, regarded it as somewhat too rich for him, an enemy
alien and a Jew. If Thomas Hardy came here to-morrow, his
publisher would undoubtedly try to get an invitation to the
White House for him, not merely to advertise his books but
also to honor the man. Yet it must be plain that the eminence
of Coolidge, however vastly it may be whooped up by gentlemen of enlightened self-interest, is actually greatly inferior to
that of either Einstein or Hardy. These men owe whatever
fame they have to actual accomplishments. There is no doubt
whatever that what they have is wholly theirs. They owe nothing to anyone, and no conceivable series of accidents could
have made them what they are. If superiority exists among
men, then they are indubitably superior. But is there any sign
of superiority in Coolidge? I can find none. His eminence is
due entirely to two things: first, a series of accidents, and secondly, the possession of qualities that, in themselves, do not
mark a superior man, but an inferior. He is a cheap, sordid and
grasping politician, a seeker of jobs all his life, willing to do
almost anything imaginable to get them. He has never said a
word worth hearing, or done a thing requiring genius, or even
ordinary skill. Put into his place and given the opportunities
that have arisen before him in a long succession, any other ninth-
rate lawyer in the land could have got as far as he has got.

Now for my point. It is, in brief, that the public estimation
of eminence runs almost directly in inverse ratio to its gen-
uineness. That is to say, the sort of eminence that the mob es-

teems most highly is precisely the sort that has least grounding in solid worth and honest accomplishment. And the reason therefor is not far to seek. The kind of eminence that it admires is simply the kind that it can understand—the kind that it can aspire to. The very puerility of a Coolidge, in fact, is one of the principal causes of the admiration he excites. What he has done in the world is within the capacities, given luck enough, of any John Smith. His merits, such as they are, are almost universal, and hence perfectly comprehensible. But what a Wagner or an Einstein does is wholly beyond the understanding of an ordinary ignoramus, and so it is impossible for the ignoramus to admire it. Worse, it tends to arouse his suspicion, and hence his animosity. He is not merely indifferent to the merits of a Wagner; he will, if any attempt is made to force them upon his attention, challenge them sharply. What he admires fundamentally, in other words, is himself, and in a Coolidge, a Harding, a baseball pitcher, a movie actor, an archbishop, or a bank president he can see himself. He can see himself, too, though perhaps more dimly, in a Dewey, a Pershing, a Rockefeller or a Jack Dempsey. But he can no more see himself in a Wagner or an Einstein than he can see himself on the throne of the Romanoffs, and so he suspects and dislikes such men, as he suspects and dislikes Romanoffs.

Unluckily, it is one thing to denounce his stupidity, and quite another thing to escape its consequences. The history of mankind is peopled chiefly, not with the genuinely great men of the race, but with the flashy and hollow fellows who appealed to the mob. Every American remembers vividly the contribution that Theodore Roosevelt made to the building of the Panama Canal—a contribution that might have been made by any other American thrown fortuitously into his place, assuming only that the substitute shared his normal American lack of a sense of honor. But who remembers the name of the man who actually designed the canal? I turn to the New International Encyclopedia and find nine whole pages about the canal, with many drawings. There is eloquent mention of Col. Goethals—who simply carried out the designer's plans. There is mention, too, of Col. Gorgas—whose sanitary work was a simple application of other men's ideas. There is ample space for Roosevelt, and his blackjacking of Colombia. But so far as I can find, the name of the designer is not there. The mob did not admire him, and so history has overlooked him.

5
An Historic Blunder

The Southern gentry made a thumping mistake when, after the Civil War, they disfranchised the blacks. Had they permitted the latter to vote, they would have retained political control of all the Southern States, for the blacks, like the peasants everywhere else, would have followed their natural masters. As it was, control quickly passed to the poor white trash, who still maintain it, though many of them have ceased to be poor. The gentry struggle in vain to get back in the saddle; they lack the votes to achieve the business unaided, and the blacks, who were ready to follow them in 1870, are now incurably suspicious of them. The result is that politics in the South remain fathomlessly swinish. Every civilized Southerner knows it and is ashamed of it, but the time has apparently passed to do anything about it. To get rid of its Bleases, Mayfields, Slemps, Peays and Vardamans, the South must wait until the white trash are themselves civilized. This is a matter demanding almost as much patience as the long vigil of the Seventh Day Adventists.

6
On Cynicism

One of the most curious of human delusions lies in the theory that cynics are unhappy men—that cynicism makes for a general biliousness and malaise. It is a false deduction, I believe, from the obvious fact that cynics make *other* men unhappy. But they are themselves among the most comfortable and serene of mammals; perhaps only bishops, pet dogs and actors are happier. For what a cynic believes, though it may be too dreadful to be put into formal words, at least usually has the merit of being true—and truth is ever a rock, hard and harsh, but solid under the feet. A cynic is chronically in the position of a wedding guest who has known the bride for nine years, and has had her confidence. He is a great deal less happy, theoretically, than the bridegroom. The bridegroom, beautifully barbered and arrayed, is about to launch into the honeymoon. But the cynic looks ahead two weeks, two months, two years. Such, to borrow a phrase from the late Dr. Eliot, are the durable satisfactions of life.

7

Music and Sin

Among Christian workers and other intellectual cripples the delusion seems to persist that jazz is highly aphrodisiacal. I never encounter a sermon on the subject without finding it full of dark warnings to parents, urging them to keep their nubile daughters out of the jazz palaces on the ground that the voluptuous music will inflame their passions and so make them easy prey to bond salesmen, musicians and other such carnal fellows. All this seems to me to be nonsense. Jazz, in point of fact, is not voluptuous at all. Its monotonous rhythm and puerile tunes make it a sedative rather than a stimulant. If it is an aphrodisiac, then the sound of riveting is also an aphrodisiac. What fetches the flappers who come to grief in the jazz parlors is not the music at all, but the alcohol. Drinking it out of flasks in the washrooms, they fail to keep the dose in harmony with their natural resistance, and so they lose control of their faculties, and what follows is lamentable. Jazz, which came in with Prohibition, gets the blame that belongs to its partner. In the old days, when it was uncommon for refined women to get drunk at dances, it would have been quite harmless. To-day even Chopin's funeral march would be dangerous.

The truth is that jazz is probably the least voluptuous variety of music commonly heard in Christendom. There are plenty of Methodist hymns that are ten times as aphrodisiacal, and the fact is proved by the scandals that follow every camp-meeting. In most parts of the United States, indeed, the Methodists have begun to abandon camp-meetings as subversive of morality. Where they still flourish it is not unusual for even the rev. clergy to be taken in byzantine practices. But so-called good music is yet worse than the Methodist hymns. Has the world so soon forgotten James Huneker's story of the prudent opera mamma who refused to let her daughter sing Isolde, on the ground that no woman could ever get through the second act without forgetting God? That second act, even so, is much overestimated. There are piano pieces of Chopin that are a hundred times worse; if the Comstocks really had any sense, they would forbid their performance. And what of the late Puccini? If "La Bohème" is not an aphrodisiac, then what is it? Yet it is sung publicly all over the world. Only in Atlanta, Ga., is there a law against it, and even that law was probably inspired by the fact that it was written by a Catholic and not by the fact that it has brought hundreds of thousand of Christian women to the edge of the abyss.

Old Ludwig himself was not without guilt. His "Egmont" overture is a gross and undisguised appeal to the medulla oblongata. And what of his symphonies and quartettes? The last movement of his Eroica is not only voluptuous to the last degree; it is also Bolshevistic. Try to play it with your eyes on a portrait of Dr. Coolidge. You will find the thing as impossible as eating ice-cream on roast beef. At the time of its first performance in Vienna the moral sense of the community was so greatly outraged that Beethoven had to get out of town for a while. I pass over Wagner, whose "Tristan und Isolde" was probably his most decorous work, despite Huneker—think of "Parsifal"!—and come to Richard Strauss. Here I need offer no argument: his "Salomé" and "Elektra" have been prohibited by the police, at one time or another, in nearly every country in the world. I believe that "Der Rosenkavalier" is still worse, though the police leave it unmolested. Compare its first act to the most libidinous jazz ever heard of on Broadway. It is like comparing vodka to ginger-pop. No woman who hears it is ever the same again. She may remain within the law, but her thoughts are wayward henceforth. Into her ear the sirens have poured their abminable song. She has been beset by witches. There is a sinister glitter in her eye.

8
The Champion

Of the forty-eight sovereign States of this imperial Federation, which is the worst? In what one of them is a civilized man most uncomfortable? Over half the votes, if the question were put to a vote, would probably be divided between California and Tennessee. Each in its way, is almost unspeakable. Tennessee, of course, has never been civilized, save in a small area; even in the earliest days of the Republic it was regarded as barbaric by its neighbors. But California, at one time, promised to develop a charming and enlightened civilization. There was a touch of tropical balm in its air, and a touch of Latin and oriental color in its ideas. Like Louisiana, it seemed likely to resist Americanization for many years; perhaps forever. But new California, the old California, is simply extinct. What remains is an Alsatia of retired Ford agents and crazy fat women—a paradise of 100% Americanism and the New Thought. Its laws are the most extravagant and idiotic ever heard of Christendom. Its public officers, and particularly its judges, are famous all over the world for their imbecilities. When one hears of it at all, one hears that some citizen has been jailed for reading the Constitution of the United States, or that some new swami in a yellow bed-tick has got all the realtors' wives of Los Angeles by the ears. When one hears of it further, it is only to learn that some obscure movie lady in Hollywood has murdered another lover. The State is run by its Chambers of Commerce, which is to say, by the worst variety of resident shysters. No civilized man ever seems to take any part in its public life. Not an idea comes out of it—that is, not an idea beyond the grasp of a Kiwanis Club secretary, Christian Science sorcerer, or a grand goblin of the American Legion. Twice, of late, it has offered the country candidates for the presidency. One was the Hon. Hiram Johnson and the other was the Hon. William Gibbs McAdoo! Only Vermont can beat that record.

The minority of civilized Californians—who lately, by the way, sent out a call from Los Angeles for succor, as if they were beset by wolves!—commonly lay the blame for this degeneration of a once-proud commonwealth upon the horde of morons that has flowed in from Iowa, Nebraska and the other cow-States, seeking relief from the bitter climate of the steppes. The California realtors have been luring in these hinds for a generation past, and they now swarm in all the southern towns, especially Los Angeles. They come in with their savings, are swindled and sent home, and so make room for more. While they remain and have any part of their money left, they patronize the swamis, buy oil stock, gape at the movie folk, and pack the Methodist churches. Unquestionably, the influence of such vacuums has tended to degrade the general tone of California life; what was once a Spanish *fiesta* is now merely an upper Mississippi valley street-carnival. But it is not to be forgotten that the Native Sons have gone down the chute with the newcomers—that there is no more sign of intellectual vigor in the old stock than there is in the new stock. A few intransigeants hold out against the tide of 100% Americanism, but only a few. The rest bawl against the Reds as loudly as any Iowa steer-stuffer.

The truth is that it is unjust to blame Iowa for the decay of California, for Iowa itself is now moving up, not down. And so is Nebraska. A few years ago both States were as sterile, intellectually, as Spain, but both are showing signs of progress to-day, and in another generation or two, as the Prohibition lunacy passes and the pall of Methodism begins to lift, they will probably burst into very vigorous activity. Some excellent stock is in them; it is very little contaminated by what is called Anglo-Saxon blood. Iowa, even to-day, is decidedly more civilized than California. It is producing more ideas, and, more important still, it is carrying on a much less violent war *against* ideas. I doubt that any man who read the Constitution in Davenport or Des Moines would be jailed for it, as Upton Sinclair (or one of his friends) was in Pasadena. The American Legion would undoubtedly protest, but the police would probably do nothing, for the learned judges of the State would not entertain the charge.

Thus California remains something of a mystery. The whole United States, of course, has been going down hill since the beginning of the century, but why should one State go so much faster than the others? Is the climate to blame? Hardly. The climate of San Francisco is thoroughly un-Californian, and yet San Francisco is almost as dead as Los Angeles. It was there, indeed, that that California masterpiece, the Mooney case, was staged; it was here that the cops made three efforts to convict poor Fatty Arbuckle of murder in the first-degree; it

was there that the late Dr. Abrams launched a quackery that
went Mother Eddy one better. San Francisco, once the home
of Mark Twain and Bret Harte, is now ravaged by Prohibition
enforcement officers. But if the climate is not to blame, then
what is? Why should a great State, lovely physically and of romantic history, so violently renounce all sense and decency?
What has got into it? God alone knows!

9
Honor in America

Some time ago I enjoyed the distinguished honor of entertaining an American university professor in my house. The fellow had a resilient gullet, and in the course of the evening we
got down a quart of Scotch. Made expansive by the liquor, he
told me this story:

A short while before, at his university, one of the professors
gave a booze party for a group of colleagues, including the
president of the institution. It was warm weather, and they
sat on the veranda, guzzling moonshine and ginger-ale. There
was so much chatter that they didn't hear a student coming
up the path. Suddenly he was on them, and they almost
fainted. . . .

At this point I asked why they were alarmed.

"Well," said my visitor, "suppose the student had turned out
to be a Christian? He would have babbled, and then our host
would have lost his chair. The president would have been
forced to cashier him."

"But the president," I argued, "was a guest in the man's
house. How could he have dismissed him?"

"What else would there have been for him to do?" asked the
professor.

"Resign at once," I replied. "Wasn't he under the obligations of a guest? Wasn't he *particeps criminis*? How could he
separate himself from his host? How could he sit as judge upon
his host, even if only formally?"

But the professor couldn't see the point. I began to fear that
he was in his cups, but it soon appeared that he was quite clear.
We argued for half an hour: he was still unable to see the point.

The duty of a president to enforce an unwilling and dishonest obedience to an absurd law—this duty was superior to his duty as a guest, *i.e.*, it was superior to his obligation as a man of honor! We passed on to another point.

"What of the student?" I asked. "I take it that he turned out to be a gentleman. Suppose he had been a Christian? Suppose he had blabbed? What would the other boys have done to him?"

The professor stared at me blankly.

"Nothing," he said at length. "After all, we *were* boozing."

This professor, I should add, was a man of the old American stock—in fact, a fellow very proud of his colonial ancestry. When he got back to his university he joined in signing a public statement that Prohibition was a great success there.

I proceed to another case. One day in the Summer of 1924, during the Republican National Convention at Cleveland, I met an eminent American publicist in a hotel lobby there. He told me at once that he was suffering from a dreadful bellyache. I had a jug in my room, but my own hotel was far away, so I suggested that help might be got from a journalist on the premises. We went to his room, and I introduced the publicist. The journalist promptly got out a bottle and gave him a policeman's drink. The publicist had recovered in three minutes. . . . When he got home, he joined, like the professor, in signing a public statement praising Prohibition.

10
Note in the Margin of a Treatise on Psychology

As I stoop to lace my shoe you hit me over the coccyx with a length of hickory (*Carya laciniosa*). I conclude instantly that you are a jackass. This is the whole process of human thought in little. This also is free will.

11
Definition

Democracy is that system of government under which the people, having 35,717,342 native-born adult whites to choose from, including thousands who are handsome and many who are wise, pick out a Coolidge to be head of the State. It is as if a hungry man, set before a banquet prepared by master cooks and covering a table an acre in area, should turn his back upon the feast and stay his stomach by catching and eating flies.

XVIII.
Catechism

Q. If you find so much that is unworthy of reverence in the United States, then why do you live here?

A. Why do men go to zoos?

PREJUDICES
SIXTH SERIES

I.
Journalism in America

I

ONE of the agreeable spiritual phenomena of the great age
in which we live is the soul-searching now going on
among American journalists. Fifteen years ago, or even ten
years ago, there was scarcely a sign of it. The working newspaper men of the Republic, of whom I have had the honor to
be one since the last century, were then almost as complacent
as so many Federal judges, movie magnates, or major-generals
in the army. When they discussed their puissant craft at all, it
was only to smack their chests proudly, boasting of their vast
power in public matters, of their adamantine resistance to all
the less tempting varieties of bribes, and of the fact that a
politician of enlightened self-interest, giving them important
but inaccurate news confidently, could rely upon them to man-
gle it beyond recognition before publishing it. I describe a sort
of Golden Age, and confess frankly that I can't do so without
a certain yielding to emotion. Salaries had been going up since
the dawn of the new century, and the journalist, however
humble, was beginning to feel his oats. For the first time in
history he was paid as well as the human cranes and steam-
shovels slinging rolls of paper in the cellar. He began to own
two hats, two suits of clothes, two pairs of shoes, two walking-
sticks, even two belts. He ceased to feed horribly in one-arm
lunch-rooms and began to dine in places with fumigated wait-
resses, some of a considerable pulchritude and amiability, and
red-shaded table lamps. He was, as such things are reckoned,
happy. But at the heart of his happiness, alas, there yet gnawed
a canker-worm. One enemy remained in his world, unscotched
and apparently unscotchable, to wit, the business manager.
The business manager, at will, could send up a blue slip and
order him fired. In the face of that menace from below-stairs
his literary superiors were helpless, up to and including the
editor-in-chief. All of them were under the hoof of the business
manager, and all the business manager ever thought of was

advertising. Let an advertiser complain that his honor had been impugned or his *clavi* abraded, and off went a head.

It was the great war for human freedom, I suspect and allege, that brought the journals deliverance from that last and most abominable hazard: he was, perhaps, one of the few real beneficiaries of all the carnage. As the struggle grew more savage on Flanders fields and business grew better and better at home, reporters of any capacity whatever got to be far too scarce to fire loosely. Moreover, the business manager, with copy pouring over his desk almost unsolicited, began to lose his old dread of advertisers, and then even some of his natural respect for them. It was a sellers' market, in journalism as in the pants business. Customers were no longer kissed; the lesser among them actually began to stand in line. The new spirit, so strange and so exhilarating, spread like a benign pestilence, and presently it began to invade even the editorial rooms. In almost every American city, large or small, some flabbergasted advertiser, his money in his hand, sweat pouring from him as if he had seen a ghost, was kicked out with spectacular ceremonies. All the principal papers, suddenly grown rich, began also to grow independent, virtuous, touchy, sniffish. No — — — — could dictate to them, God damn! So the old free reading notices of the Bon Marché and the Palais Royal disappeared, salaries continued to climb, and the liberated journalist, taking huge breaths of thrilling air, began to think of himself as a professional man.

Upon that cogitation he is still engaged, and all the weeklies that print the news of the craft are full of its fruits. He elects representatives and they meet in lugubrious conclave to draw up codes of ethics. He begins to read books dealing with professional questions of other sorts—even books not dealing with professional questions. He changes his old cynical view of schools of journalism, and is lured, now and then, into lecturing in them himself. He no longer thinks of his calling as a business, like the haberdasher's or tallow chandler's, or as a game, like the stockbroker's or faro-dealer's, but as a profession, like the jurisconsult's or gynecologist's. His purpose is to set it on its legs as such—to inject plausible theories into its practise, and rid it of its old casualness and opportunism. He no longer sees it as a craft to be mastered in four days, and abandoned at the first sign of a better job. He begins to talk darkly of the long apprenticeship necessary to master its technic, of the wide information and sagacity needed to adorn it, of the high rewards that it offers—or may offer later on—to the man of true talent and devotion. Once he thought of himself, whenever he thought at all, as what Beethoven called a free artist—a gay adventurer careening down charming highways of the world, the gutter ahead of him but ecstasy in his heart. Now he thinks of himself as a fellow of weight and responsibility, a beginning publicist and public man, sworn to the service of the born and unborn, heavy with duties to the Republic and to his profession.

In all this, I fear, there is some illusion, as there always is in human thinking. The journalist can no more see himself realistically than a bishop can see himself realistically. He gilds and engauds the picture, unconsciously and irresistibly. For one thing, and a most important one, he is probably somewhat in error about his professional status. He remains for all his dreams, a hired man—the owner downstairs, or even the business manager, though he doesn't do it very often now, is still free to demand his head—, and a hired man is not a professional man. The essence of a professional man is that he is answerable for his professional conduct only to his professional peers. A physician cannot be fired by any one, save when he has voluntarily converted himself into a job-holder; he is secure in his livelihood so long as he keeps his health, and can render service, or what they regard as service, to his patients. A lawyer is in the same boat. So is a dentist. So, even, is a horse-doctor. But a journalist still lingers in the twilight zone, along with the trained nurse, the embalmer, the rev. clergy and the great majority of engineers. He cannot sell his services directly to the consumer, but only to entrepreneurs, and so those entrepreneurs have the power of veto over all his soaring fancies. His codes of ethics are all right so long as they do not menace newspaper profits; the moment they do so the business manager, now quiescent, will begin to growl again. Nor has he the same freedom that the lawyers and the physicians have when it comes to fixing his own compensation; what he faces is not a client but a boss. Above all, he is unable, as yet, to control admission to his craft. It is constantly recruited, on its lowest levels, from men who have little professional training or none at all, and some of these men master its chief mysteries very quickly. Thus even the most competent journalist faces at all times a severe competition, easily expanded at need, and cannot afford to be too saucy. When a managing editor is fired there is always another one waiting to take his place, but there is seldom another place waiting for the managing editor.

All these things plainly diminish the autonomy of the journalist, and hamper his effort to lift his trade to professional rank and dignity. When he talks of codes of ethics, indeed, he only too often falls into mere tall talk, for he cannot enforce the rules he so solemnly draws up—that is, in the face of dissent from above. Nevertheless, his discussion of the subject is still not wholly absurd, for there remain plenty of rules that he *can* enforce, and I incline to think that there are more of them than of the other kind. Most of the evils that continue to beset American journalism to-day, in truth, are not due to the rascality of owners nor even to the Kiwanian bombast of business managers, but simply and solely to the stupidity, cowardice and Philistinism of working newspaper men. The majority of them, in almost every American city, are still ignoramuses, and proud of it. All the knowledge that they pack into their brains is, in every reasonable cultural sense, useless; it is the sort of knowledge that belongs, not to a professional man, but to a police captain, a railway mail-clerk, or a board-boy in a brokerage house. It is a mass of trivialities and puerilities; to recite it would be to make even a barber beg for mercy. What is missing from it, in brief, is everything worth knowing—everything that enters into the common knowledge of educated men. There are managing editors in the United States, and scores of them, who have never heard of Kant or Johannes Müller and never read the Constitution of the United States; there are city editors who do not know what a symphony is, or a streptococcus, or the Statute of Frauds; there are reporters by the thousand who could not pass the entrance examination for Harvard or Tuskegee, or even Yale. It is this vast and militant ignorance, this wide-spread and fathomless prejudice against intelligence, that makes American journalism so pathetically feeble and vulgar, and so generally disreputable. A man with so little intellectual enterprise that, dealing with news daily, he can go through life without taking in any news that is worth knowing—such a man, you may be sure, is lacking in professional dignity quite as much as he is lacking in curiosity. The delicate thing called honor can never be a function of stupidity. If it belongs to those men who are genuinely professional men, it belongs to them because they have lifted themselves to the plane of a true aristocracy, in learning as well as in liberty— because they have deliberately and successfully separated themselves from the great masses of men, to whom learning is an insult and liberty an agony. The journalists, in seeking to acquire that status, put the cart before the horse.

2

The facts that I here set forth are well known to every American newspaper man who rises above the ice-wagon driver level, and in those sad conferences which mark every gathering of the craft they do not go undiscussed. Even the American Society of Newspaper Editors, *i.e.*, of those journalists who have got into golf clubs and become minor Babbitts, has dealt with them at some of its annual pow-wows, albeit very gingerly and with many uneasy glances behind the door. But in general journalism suffers from a lack of alert and competent professional criticism; its slaves, afflicted by a natural inferiority complex, discountenance free speaking as a sort of treason; I have myself been damned as a public enemy for calling attention, ever and anon, to the intolerable incompetence and quackery of all save a small minority of the Washington correspondents. This struthion fear of the light is surely not to be noted in any of the actual professions. The medical men, in their trade journals, criticise one another frankly and sharply, and so do the lawyers in theirs: the latter, indeed, are not above taking occasional hacks at the very judges, their lawful fathers and patterns of grace. As for the clergy, every one knows that they devote a large part of their professional energy to refuting and damning their brethren, and that not a few of them do it on public stumps, with the laity invited. So, also, in the fine arts. It is impossible for an architect to affront humanity with a blotch without hearing from other architects, and it is impossible for a poet to print anything at all without tasting the clubs of other poets. Even dramatists, movie actors, chiropractors and politicians criticise one another, and so keep themselves on tiptoe. But not journalists. If a Heywood Broun is exasperated into telling the truth about the manhandling of a Snyder trial, or a Walter Lippmann exposes the imbecility of the Russian "news" in a New York *Times*, or an Oswald Garrison Villard turns his searchlight on a Boston *Herald* or a Washington *Star*, it is a rarity and an indecorum. The organs of the craft—and there are journals for journalists, just as there are doctors for doctors—are all filled with bilge borrowed from Rotary and Kiwanis. Reading them, one gathers the impression that every newspaper proprietor in the United States is a distinguished public figure, and every circulation manager a wizard. The editorial boys, it appears, never fall down on their jobs; they are not only geniuses, but also heroes. Some time ago, having read all such journals assiduously for years, I stopped my subscriptions to them. I found that I preferred the clip-sheet of the Methodist Board of Temperance, Prohibition and Public Morals.

But if there is thus little or no frank and open discussion of the evils that beset journalism in the Republic, there is a great deal of private discontent and soul-searching, and it shows itself in all the fantastic codes of ethics that issue from embattled professors of journalism in the great rolling-mills of learning, and from editorial associations in the cow States. In such codes, I am sorry to have to repeat, I take no stock. Most of them are the handiwork of journalists of no professional importance whatever, and, what is worse, of no apparent sense. They run the scale from metaphysical principia worthy of Rotary to sets of rules fit only for the government of a Y.M.C.A. lamasery or a State's prison. They concern themselves furiously with abuses which are not peculiar to journalism but run through the whole of American life, and they are delicately silent about abuses that are wholly journalistic, and could be remedied quickly and without the slightest difficulty. Their purpose, I believe, is largely rhetorical. They give a certain ease and comfort to the laboring patient without letting any of his blood. Nevertheless, I am glad to see them multiply, for though most of them may be hollow to-day, there is always a chance that some solid substance may get into them to-morrow. If they accomplish nothing else at the moment, they at least accustom the journalist to the notion that his craft needs an overhauling. His old romantic optimism oozes out of him. He is no longer quite happy. Out of his rising discomforts, I believe, there will issue eventually a more realistic attitude toward the problems that confront him, and on some bright day in the future he may address himself rationally to the hard business of solving them. Most of them, I believe, are clearly soluble. More, most of them can be solved by working newspaper men, without any help from experts in ethics. What they call for is not any transcendental gift for righteousness, but simply ordinary professional competence and common sense.

For example, the problem of false news. How does so much of it get into the American newspapers, even the good ones? Is it because journalists, as a class, are habitual liars, and prefer what is not true to what is true? I don't think it is. Rather, it is because journalists are, in the main, extremely stupid, sentimental and credulous fellows—because nothing is easier than to fool them—because the majority of them lack the sharp intelligence that the proper discharge of their duties demands. The New York *Times* did not print all its famous blather and balderdash about Russia because the Hon. Mr. Ochs desired to deceive his customers, or because his slaves were in the pay of Russian reactionaries, but simply and solely because his slaves, facing the elemental professional problem of distinguishing between true news and false, turned out to be incompetent. All around the borders of Russia sat propagandists hired to fool them. In many cases, I have no doubt, they detected that purpose, and foiled it; we only know what they printed, not what they threw into their wastebaskets. But in many other cases they succumbed easily, and even ridiculously, and the result was the vast mass of puerile rubbish that Mr. Lippmann later made a show of. In other words, the editors of the American newspaper most brilliantly distinguished above its fellows for its news-gathering enterprise turned out to be unequal to a job of news-gathering presenting special but surely not insuperable difficulties. It was not an ethical failure, but a purely technical failure. And so was the same eminent newspaper's idiotic misreporting of the news from China in the early part of 1927, and the grotesque paralysis of the whole American press in the face of the Miami hurricane in 1926.

Obviously, the way to diminish such failures in future is not to adopt sonorous platitudes borrowed from the realtors, the morticians, the sanitary plumbers and Kiwanis, but to undertake an overhauling of the faulty technic, and of the incompetent personnel responsible for it. This overhauling, of course, will take some intelligence, but I don't think it will make demands that are impossible. The bootlegging, legal or delicatessen professions, confronted by like demands, would quickly furnish the talent necessary to meet them; I see no reason why the profession of journalism should not measure up as well. What lies in the way of it is simply the profound, maudlin sentimentality of the average American journalist—his ingenuous and almost automatic belief in everything that comes to him in writing. One would think that his daily experience with the written word would make him suspicious of it; he himself, in fact, believes fondly that he is proof against it. But the truth is that he swallows it far more often than he rejects it, and that his most eager swallowing is done in the face of the plainest evidence of its falsity. Let it come in by telegraph, and his mouth flies open. Let it come in by telegraph *from a press association* and down it goes at once. I do not say, of course, that *all* press association news is thus swallowed by news editors. When the means are readily at hand, he often attempts to check it, and sometimes even rejects it. But when such checking presents difficulties—in other words, when deceit is especially easy, and hence should be guarded most vigilantly—he succumbs nine times out of ten, and without a struggle. It was precisely by this process that the editors of the *Times*, otherwise men of extraordinary professional alertness, were victimized by the Russian "news" that made that paper ridiculous. In the face of great improbabilities, they interpreted their inability to dispose of them as a license to accept them as truth. Journalism will be a sounder and more dignified profession when a directly contrary interpretation of the journalist's duty prevails. There will then be less news in the papers, but it will at least have the merit of being true.

Nor is the typical American journalist's credulity confined to such canards and roorbacks from far places. He is often victimized just as easily at home, despite his lofty belief that he is superior to the wiles of press agents. The plain fact is that most of the stuff he prints now emanates from press agents, and that his machinery for scrutinizing it is lamentably defective. True enough, the bold, gay liars employed by theatrical managers and opera singers no longer fool him as they used to; he has grown so suspicious of them that he often turns them out when they have real news. But what of the press agents of such organizations as the Red Cross, the Prohibition Unit, the Near-East Relief, the Chamber of Commerce of the United States, the Department of Justice, the Y.M.C.A., and the various bands of professional patriots? I do not say that the press agents of such bodies are always or necessarily liars; all I say is that, nine times out of ten, their statements are accepted as true by the newspapers without any attempt to determine accurately whether they are true or not. They may be simple statements of plain fact; they may, on the contrary, conceal highly dubious purposes, of organizations and individuals. In both cases they are set forth in the same way—solemnly and without comment. Who, ordinarily, would believe a Prohibition agent? Perhaps a Federal judge in his robes of office and full of seized evidence; I can think of no one else. Yet the American newspapers are filled every day with the dreadful boasts and threats of such frauds: it is set before the people, not as lies, but as news. What is the purpose of such rubbish? Its purpose, obviously, is to make it appear that the authors are actually enforcing Prohibition—in other words, to made them secure in their jobs. Every newspaper man in America knows that Prohibition is not being enforced—and yet it is rarely that an American newspaper comes out in these days without a gaudy story on its first page, rehearsing all the old lies under new and blacker headlines.

I do not argue here, of course, that only demonstrable facts are news. There are times and occasions when rumor is almost as important as the truth—when a newspaper's duty to its readers requires it to tell them not only what has happened, but also what is reported, what is threatened, what is merely said. What I contend is simply that such quasi-news, such half-baked and still dubious news, should be printed for exactly what it is—that it ought to be clearly differentiated from news that, by an overwhelming probability, is true. That differentiation is made easily and as a matter of course by most European newspapers of any dignity. When they print a dispatch from the Russian border they indicate its source, and not infrequently follow it with a cynical comment. If they had Prohibition agents on their hands, they would print the fulminations of those gentlemen in the same way—with plain warnings to stop, look and listen. In brief, they make every reasonable effort to make up for their own technical limitations as newsgatherers—they do the best they can, and say so frankly when it is not very good. I believe that American newspapers might imitate them profitably. If it were done, then the public's justifiable distrust of all newspapers, now rising, would tend to ebb. They would have to throw off their present affectation of omniscience, but they would gain a new repute for honesty and candor; they would begin to seem more reliable when they failed than they now seem when they succeed. The scheme I propose would cost nothing; on the contrary, it would probably save expense. It would throw no unbearable burden upon the journalistic mind; it would simply make it more cautious and alert. Best of it, it would increase the dignity of journalism without resort to flapdoodlish and unenforceable codes of ethics, by Mush out of Tosh.

3

In private communions, though seldom in public, the more conscientious and unhappy variety of journalists commonly blame the woes of the craft upon the entrance into newspaper ownership of such opulent vacuums as Cyrus H. K. Curtis and the late Frank A. Munsey. As a result of the application of chain-store methods to journalism by these amiable Vandals there are fewer papers than there used to be, and the individual journalist is less important. All the multitudinous Hearst papers are substantially identical, and so are all the Scripps-Howard papers, and all the Curtis papers, and so were the Munsey papers in the great days of that pathetic man. There is little room, on the papers of such chains, for the young man who aspires to shine. Two-thirds of their contents are produced in great factories, and what remains is chiefly a highly standard-ized bilge. In the early days of Hearst, when he had only a few widely-scattered papers, his staffs were manned by men of great professional enterprise and cunning, and some of them became celebrated in the craft, and even generally. But now a Hearst paper, however inflammatory, is no more than a single unit in a long row of filling-stations, and so it tends to attract only the duller and less picturesque sort of men. There is scarcely a Hearst managing editor to-day who amounts to any-thing professionally, or is heard of outside his own dung-hill. The platitudes of Brisbane and Dr. Frank Crane serve as pabu-lum for all of them. What they think is what the machines at the central factory think; what they do is determined by men they have never seen. So with the Scripps-Howard slaves, and the slaves of Cox, and those of Curtis, and all the rest. Their predecessors of a generation ago were gaudy adventur-ers, experimenters, artists; they themselves are golf-players, which is to say, blanks. They are well paid, but effectively knee-haltered. The rewards of trade used to come in freedom, op-portunity, the incomparable delights of self-expression; now they come in money.

But the sweet goes with the bitter. The newspapers of to-day, though they may be as rigidly standardized as Uneeda biscuits, are at least solvent: they are no longer the paltry free-booters that they used to be. A Munsey, perhaps, is a jackass, but he is at least honest; no one seriously alleges that his papers are for sale; even the sinister Wall Street powers that Liberals see in the background must get what they want out of him by being polite to him, not by simply sending him orders. The old-timers, contemplating the ghastly spectacle of a New York *Sun* submerged in the Munsey swamp and an *Evening Post* descending from a Villard to a Curtis, forget conveniently how bad most of the papers they once worked for really were. In the town where I began there were five papers, and four of them were cheap, trashy, stupid and corrupt. They all played politics for what there was in it, and leaped obscenely every time an advertiser blew his nose. Every other American city of that era was full of such papers—dreadful little rags, venal, vulnerable and vile. Not a few of them made great preten-sions, and were accepted by a naïve public as organs of the enlightenment. To-day, I believe, such journalistic street-walkers are very rare. The consolidations that every old-timer deplores have accomplished at least one good thing: they have got the newspapers, in the main, out of the hands of needy men. When orders come from a Curtis or a Munsey to-day the man who gets them, though he may regard them as ill-advised and even as idiotic, is seldom in any doubt as to their good faith. He may execute them without feeling that he has been made an unwilling party to an ignominious barter. He is not condemned daily to acts whose true purpose he would not dare to put into words, even to himself. His predecessor, I believe, often suffered that dismaying necessity: he seldom had any illusions about the *bona fides* of his boss. It took the whole force of his characteristic sentimentality to make him believe in his paper, and not infrequently even that sentimentality was impotent without the aid of ethyl alcohol.

Thus there is something to be said for the new newspaper Babbitts, as reluctant as every self-respecting journalist must be to say it. And in what is commonly said against them there is not infrequently a certain palpable exaggeration and injustice. Are they responsible for the imbecile editorial policies of their papers, for the grotesque lathering of such mountebanks as Coolidge and Mellon, for the general smugness and lack of intellectual enterprise that pervades American journalism? Perhaps they are. But do they issue orders that their papers shall be printed in blowsy, clumsy English? That they shall stand against every decent thing, and in favor of everything that is meretricious and ignoble? That they shall wallow in trivialities, and manhandle important news? That their view of learning shall be that of a bartender? Has any newspaper proprietor ever issued orders that the funeral orgies of a Harding should be described in the language of a Tennessee revival? Or that helpless men, with the mob against them, should be pursued without fairness, decency or sense? I doubt it. I doubt, even, that the Babbitts turned Greeleys are responsible, in the last analysis, for the political rubbish that fills their papers—the preposterous anointing of Coolidge, the craven yielding to such sinister forces as the Ku Klux Klan and the Anti-Saloon League, the incessant, humorless, degrading hymning of all sorts of rogues and charlatans. The average newspaper proprietor, I suspect, gets nine-tenths of his political ideas from his own men. In other words, he is such an ass that he believes political reporters, and especially his own political reporters. They have, he fancies, wide and confidential sources of information: their wisdom is a function of their prestige as his agents. What they tell him is, in the long run, what he believes, with certain inconsiderable corrections by professionals trying to work him. If only because they have confidential access to him day in and day out, they are able to introduce their own notions into his head. He may have their jobs in his hands, but they have his ears and eyes, so to speak, in theirs.

Even the political garbage that emanates from Washington, and especially from the typewriters of the more eminent and puissant correspondents there resident, is seldom inspired, I am convinced, by orders from the Curtis or Munsey at home: its sources are rather to be sought in the professional deficiencies of the correspondents themselves—a class of men of almost incredible credulity. In other words, they are to be sought, not in the corruption and enslavement of the press, but in the incompetence of the press. The average Washington correspondent, I believe, is honest enough, as honesty goes in the United States, though his willingness to do press work for the National Committees in campaign time and for other highly dubious agencies at other times is not to be forgotten. What ails him mainly is that he is a man without sufficient force of character to resist the blandishments that surround him from the moment he sets foot in Washington. A few men, true enough, resist, and their papers, getting the benefit of it, become notable for their independence and intelligence, but the great majority succumb almost at once. A few months of associating with the gaudy magnificoes of the town, and they pick up its meretricious values, and are unable to distinguish men of sense and dignity from mountebanks. A few clumsy overtures from the White House, and they are rattled and undone. They come in as newspaper men, trained to get the news and eager to get it; they end as tin-horn statesmen, full of dark secrets and unable to write the truth if they tried. Here I spread no scandal and violate no confidence. The facts are familiar to every newspaper man in the United States. A few of the more intelligent managing editors, cynical of ever counteracting the effects of the Washington miasma, seek to evade them by frequently changing their men. But the average managing editor is too stupid to deal with such difficulties. He prints balderdash because he doesn't know how to get anything better—perhaps, in many cases, because he doesn't know that anything better exists. Drenched with propaganda at home, he is quite content to take more propaganda from Washington. It is not that he is dishonest, but that he is stupid—and, being stupid, a coward. The resourcefulness, enterprise and bellicosity that his job demands are simply not in him. He doesn't wear himself out trying to get the news, as romance has it; he slides supinely into the estate and dignity of a golf-player. American journalism suffers from too many golf-players. They swarm in the Washington Press Gallery. They, and not their bosses, are responsible for most of the imbecilities that now afflict their trade.

4

The journalists of the United States will never get rid of those afflictions by putting the blame on Dives, and never by making speeches at one another in annual conventions, and never by drawing up codes of ethics that most of their brethren will infallibly laugh at, as a Congressman laughs at a gentleman. The job before them—that is, before the civilized minority of them—is to purge trade before they seek to dignify it—to clean house before they paint the roof and raise a flag. Can the thing be done? It not only can be done; it *has* been done. There are at least a dozen newspapers in the United States that already show a determined effort to get out of the old slough. Any managing editor in the land, if he has the will, can carry his own paper with them. He is under no compulsion, save rarely, to employ this or that hand; it is not often that owners, or even business managers, take any interest in that business, save to watch the payroll. Is his paper trifling, ill-informed, petty and unfair? Is its news full of transparent absurdities? Are its editorials ignorant and without sense? Is it written in English full of *clichés* and vulgarities—English that would disgrace a manager of prize-fighters or a county superintendent of schools? Then the fault belongs plainly, not to some remote man, but to the proximate man—to the man who lets such drivel go by. He could get better if he wanted it, you may be sure. There is in all history no record of a newspaper owner who complained because his paper was well-edited. And I know of no business manager who objected when the complaints pouring in upon him, of misrepresentations, invasions of privacy, gross inaccuracies and other such nuisances, began to lighten.

Not a few managing editors, as I say, are moving in the right directions. There has been an appreciable improvement, during the past dozen years, in the general tone of American newspapers. They are still full of preposterous blather, but they are measurably more accurate, I believe, than they used to be, and some of them are better written. A number of them are less absurdly partisan, particularly in the smaller cities. Save in the South and in the remoter fastnesses of New England the old-time party organ has gone out of fashion. In the big cities the faithful hacks of the New York *Tribune* type have begun to vanish. With them has gone the old-time drunken reporter, and in his place is appearing a young fellow of better education, and generally finer metal. The uplifters of the craft try to make him increase, and to that end encourage schools of journalism. But these seminaries, so far, show two palpable defects. On the one hand, they are seldom manned by men of any genuine professional standing, or of any firm notion of what journalism is about. On the other hand, they are nearly all too easy in their requirements for admission. Probably half of them, indeed, are simply refuges for students too stupid to tackle the other professions. They offer snap courses, and they promise quick jobs. The result is that the graduates coming out of them are mainly second-raters—that young men and women issuing from the general arts courses make better journalistic material.

What ails these schools of journalism is that they are not yet professional schools, but simply trade schools. Their like is to be found, not in the schools of medicine and law, but in the institutions that teach barbering, bookkeeping and scenario-writing. Obviously, the remedy for their general failure is to borrow a leaf from the book of the medical men, and weed out the incompetents, not after they have finished, but before they have begun. Twenty-five years ago any yokel who had got through the three R's was free to study medicine in the United

States. In three years, and sometimes in two years, he was turned out to practice upon his fellow hinds, and once he had his license it was a practical impossibility to challenge him. But now there is scarcely a medical school in the United States that does not demand a bachelor's degree or its equivalent as a prerequisite to entrance, and the term of study in all of them is four years, and it must be followed by at least one year of hospital service. This reform was not achieved by passing laws against the old hedge schools: it was achieved simply by setting up the competition of good schools. The latter gradually elbowed the former out. Their graduates had immense advantages. They had professional prestige from the moment of their entrance into practice. The public quickly detected the difference between them and their competitors from the surviving hedge schools. Soon the latter began to disintegrate, and now all save a few of them have disappeared. The medical men improved their profession by making it more difficult to become a medical man. To-day the thing is a practical impossibility to any young man who is not of genuine intelligence.

But at least two-thirds of the so-called schools of journalism still admit any aspirant who can make shift to read and write. The pedagogues who run them cannot be expected to devote much thought or money to improving them; they are in the position of the quacks who used to run the hedge medical schools. The impulse toward improvement, if it ever comes at all, must come from the profession they presume to serve. Here is a chance for the editorial committees and societies of journalists that now spring up on all sides. Let them abandon their vain effort to frame codes of ethics and devote themselves to the nursery. If they can get together a committee on schools of journalism as wise and as bold as the Council on Medical Education of the American Medical Association they will accomplish more in a few years than they can hope to accomplish with academic codes of ethics in a half century.

All the rest will follow. The old fond theory, still surviving in many a newspaper office, that it is somehow discreditable for a reporter to show any sign of education and culture, that he is most competent and laudable when his intellectual baggage most closely approaches that of a bootlegger—this theory will fall before the competition of novices who have been adequately trained, and have more in their heads than their mere training. Journalism, compared to the other trades of literate men, is surely not unattractive, even to-day. It is more amusing than the army or the cloth, and it offers a better living at the start than either medicine or the law. There is a career in it for the young man of original mind and forceful personality—a career leading to power and even to a sort of wealth. In point of fact, it has always attracted such young men, else it would be in an even lower state than it is now. It would attract a great many more of them if its public opinion were more favorable to them—if they were less harassed by the commands of professional superiors of no dignity, and the dislike of fellows of no sense. Every time two of them are drawn in they draw another. The problem is to keep them. That is the central problem of journalism in the United States to-day.

I seem to be in a mood for constructive criticism. Let me add one more pearl of wisdom before I withdraw. I put it in the form of a question. Suppose the shyster lawyers of every town organized a third-rate club, called it the Bar Association, took in any Prohibition agent or precinct politician who could raise the dues, and then announced publicly, from the Courthouse steps, that it represented the whole bar, and that membership in it was an excellent form of insurance—that any member who paid his dues would get very friendly consideration, if he ever got into trouble, from the town's judges and district attorney. And suppose the decent lawyers of the town permitted this preposterous pretension to go unchallenged—and some of them even gave countenance to it by joining the club. How long would the legal profession in that town retain its professional honor and dignity? How many laymen, after two or three years, would have any respect left for *any* lawyer, even a judge?

Yet the journalists of the United States permit that precise thing to go on under their noses. In almost every city of the country there is a so-called Press Club, and at last three-fourths of them are exactly like the hypothetical Bar Association that I have described. They are run by newspaper men of the worst type—many of them so incompetent and disreputable that they cannot even get jobs on newspapers. They take the money of all the town grafters and rascals on the pretense that newspaper favors go with its receipt. They are the resorts of idlers and blackmailers. They are nuisances and disgraces. Yet in how many towns have they been put down? In how many towns do the decent newspaper men take any overt action against them? My proposal is very simple. I propose that they be shut up, East, West, North and South, before anything more is said about codes of newspaper ethics.

II.

From the Memoirs of a Subject
of the United States

I
Government by Bounder

Of government, at least in democratic states, it may be said briefly that it is an agency engaged wholesale, and as a matter of solemn duty, in the performance of acts which all self-respecting individuals refrain from as a matter of common decency. The American newspapers supply examples every day, chiefly issuing out of Federal tribunals, judicial and administrative. The whole process of the Federal law, indeed, becomes a process of bounderism. Its catchpolls are not policemen, in any rational and ordinary sense, but simply sneaks and scoundrels with their eyes glued eternally to knot-holes. Imagine a man of ordinary decency discovering his son reading an account of the proceedings against the once celebrated Lady Cathcart, now happily forgotten? Would his exposition of the case take the form of patriotic hallelujahs, or would he caution the boy that such things are not done by gentlemen? No wonder the teaching of patriotism in the Republic is being handed over to virgin schoolma'ms, who know of honor only as an anatomical matter! The business becomes too difficult for men who must face their fellow-men daily, and therewith the ancient prejudices of the race. Those prejudices, for unnumbered centuries, have run against the man who mouths the frailties of a fair one in the market-place. But the commission of Uncle Sam, it appears, repeals that obligation of elemental honor, as it repeals every other. One sworn to uphold the Constitution becomes straightway a licentiate in swinishness, with a mandate to examine the female guests of the nation publicly, and to denounce all who are not *virgo intacta*. This mandate covers not only the lowly ruffians told off to guard the ports, but also magnificoes of ministerial rank. The Cabinet of a great Christian nation meets behind locked doors to perform a business which, if done by an honest Elk, would bring his board of governors together to kick him out.

If such obscenities were rare one might set them down to moral profit and loss, and so try to forget them. But they happen every day. If a Cathcart case is not on the front pages, then a Whitney case or a Kollontai case is there. And day in and day out the newspapers are filled with the revolting muckeries of Prohibition agents, and their attendant district attorneys and judges. The whole trend of American legislation, and with it of jurisprudence, seems to be toward such ideas of dignity and decency as prevail in remote and forlorn country villages, among the human débris of Puritanism. A court of justice, once a place where the state intervened to curb the savagery of the strong, is now an arena of savagery both cruel and cynical. The notion seems to be that any device of deceit or brutality is fair, so long as it helps to fill the jails. The government, through its authorized agents, sets itself deliberately to lure men into so-called crime, and then punishes them mercilessly for succumbing. Is there such a thing as a *contrat social*? Then certainly it is getting heavy blows in the Federal Union. For if it is not based upon the expectation that one citizen will treat another with common decency, it is based upon nothing more than a shadow—and that expectation is fast becoming vain among us. The natural confidence that every man should have in his fellows—that they will not hit below the belt, that they will not abuse his natural trust, that he may rely upon them, in a given situation, to act according to the principles of fair-play prevailing immemorially among civilized men—this confidence, when it touches American officialdom, has no longer any basis in fact. The government, under the Volstead Act, is a spy and a snitcher, just as, under the Immigration Act, it is a brute and blackguard, and under the Alien Property Act, a common thief.

Obviously, such things cannot go on without having profound effects upon the general American character. A government, though it may be worse than the average man it governs, is still made up of just such average men. If, by some process of legal decay, it is set to disgusting acts, then the consequence must be that, in the long run, they will become less disgusting. How the business has worked in other lands has been displayed with much snuffling by specialists in American-ism; unfortunately, they seem to show no interest in the phe-nomena when it is repeated at home. I have spoken then of the father with a son ripe for instruction in the traditional decen-cies. Unfecund myself, I can only imagine his difficulties, but it must be obvious that they are serious. How, indeed, is he to interpret such an inescapable transaction as the Cathcart up-roar? Is it his duty to tell his son that gentlemen set their dogs upon loose women? Or is it his duty to say that the United States is not a gentleman—nay, not even a decent thug?

Such doings, it seems to me, flow quite naturally out of the democratic theory. It holds, *imprimis*, that cads make just as good governors as civilized and self-respecting men, and it holds, *secundo*, that the notions of propriety and decency held by the mob are good enough for the state, and ought, in fact, to have the force of law. Thus it becomes increasingly difficult to be a good American, as the thing is officially defined, and remain what all the other peoples of the world regard as a good citizen—that is, one who views the acts and ideas of his fellows with a tolerant and charitable eye, and wishes them to be free and happy. The whole tendency of American law, in this day, is to put down happiness wherever it is encountered, and the *mores* of the land march with the law. The doctrine seems to be that it is the highest duty of the citizen to police his fellows. What they naturally want to do is precisely what they must be kept from doing. To this business a large and in-creasing class of professional snouters and smellers addresses itself. How many noses it can muster, God only knows, but the number must be immensely large. In the single State of Ohio, with the Anti-Saloon League in the saddle, there are certainly at least five thousand, and every prowling village deacon and petty urban blackmailer is free to join the force as a volunteer. And in more civilized regions, where public opinion, even in the mob, runs against such putridities, the Federal govern-ment supplies the scoundrels.

This antagonism between democratic Puritanism and com-mon decency is inherent in the nature of the two things, and leads to conflicts in all so-called "free" countries, but it is only in the United States that it has reached the stage of open and continuous war, with Puritanism sweeping the field and common decency in flight. Thus life in the Republic grows increasingly uncomfortable to men of the more urbane and seemly sort, and, despite the great material prosperity of the country, the general stock of happiness probably diminishes steadily. For the thing that makes us enjoy the society of our fellows is not admiration of their inner virtues but delight in their outward manners. It is not enough that they are headed for heaven, and will sit upon the right hand of God through all eternity; it is also necessary that they be polite, generous, and, above all, trustworthy. We must have confidence in them in order to get any pleasure out of associating with them. We must be sure that they will not do unto us as we should refuse, even for cash in hand, to do unto them. It is the tragedy of the Puritan that he can never inspire this confidence in his fellowmen. He is by nature a pedant in ethics, and hence he is by nature a mucker. With the best of intentions he cannot rid himself of the belief that it is his duty to save us from our follies—*i.e.*, from all the non-puritanical acts and whimsies that make life charming. His duty to let us be happy takes second, third or fourth. A Puritan cannot be tolerant—and with tolerance goes magnanimity. The late Dr. Woodrow Wilson was a typical Puritan—of the better sort, perhaps, for he at least toyed with the ambition to appear as a gentleman, but nevertheless a true Puritan. Magnanimity was simply beyond him. Confronted, on his death-bed, with the case of poor old Debs, all his instincts compelled him to keep Debs in jail. I daresay that, as a purely logical matter, he saw clearly that the old fellow ought to be turned loose; certainly he must have known that Washington would not have hesitated, or Lincoln. But Calvinism triumphed as his intellectual faculties decayed. In the full bloom of health, with a plug hat on his head, he aped the gentry of his wistful adoration very cleverly, but lying in bed, stripped like Thackeray's Louis XIV, he reverted to his congenital Puritanism, which is to say, bounderism.

Of such sort are the grand seigneurs of the nation—the custodians of its dignity and honor. They speak for it to the world. They set the tone of the national life at home. Is there any widespread murmuring against them? I wish I could report that there was, but I see no sign of it. Instead, there seems to be only a resigned sort of feeling that nothing can be done about

it—that the swinishness of government lies in the very nature
of things, and so cannot be changed. Even the popular discontent with Prohibition is not a discontent with its sneaking and
knavishness—its wholesale turning loose of licensed blacklegs
and blackmailers, its appalling degradation of the judiciary, its
corruption of Congress, its disingenuous invasion of the Bill of
Rights. What is complained of is simply the fact that Scotch is
dubious and costs too much. As bootlegging grows more efficient, I suppose, even that complaint will sink to a whisper,
perhaps in the form of a snigger. Of any forthright grappling
with the underlying indecency there is little show. It would be
difficult, in most American communities, to get signers for
even the most academic protest against it. The American, played
upon for years by a stream of jackass legislation, takes refuge in
frank skulking. He first dodges the laws, and then he dodges
the duty of protesting against them. His life becomes a process
of sneaking through back-alleys, watching over one shoulder
for the cop and over the other for his neighbor. Thus a-tremble
(and with a weather eye open for Bolsheviks, atheists and loose
women), he serves the high oath that government of the
people, by the people, and for the people shall not perish from
the earth.

2

Constructive Proposal

A mood of constructive criticism being upon me, I propose
forthwith that the method of choosing legislators now prevailing in the United States be abandoned and that the method
used in choosing juries be substituted. That is to say, I propose
that the men who make our laws be chosen by chance and
against their will, instead of by fraud and against the will of all
the rest of us, as now. But isn't the jury system itself imperfect?
Isn't it occasionally disgraced by gross abuse and scandal?
Then so is the system of justice devised and ordained by the
Lord God Himself. Didn't He assume that the Noachian
Deluge would be a lasting lesson to sinful humanity—that it
would put an end to all manner of crime and wickedness, and
convert mankind into a race of Methodists? And wasn't Noah
himself, its chief beneficiary, lying drunk, naked and uproarious

within a year after the ark landed on Ararat? All I argue for the
jury system, invented by man, is that it is measurably better
than the scheme invented by God. It has its failures and its absurdities, its abuses and its corruptions, but taking one day
with another it manifestly works. It is not the fault of juries
that so many murderers go unwhipped of justice, and it is not
the fault of juries that so many honest men are harassed by preposterous laws. The juries find the gunmen guilty: it is the
judges higher up who deliver them from the noose, and turn
them out to resume their butcheries. It is from judges again,
and not from juries, that Volsteadian padlocks issue, and all the
other devices for making a mock of the Bill of Rights. Are juries occasionally sentimental? Then let us not forget that it was
their sentimentality, in the Eighteenth Century, that gradually
forced a measure of decency and justice into the English Criminal Law. It was a jury that blocked the effort of the Department of Justice to railroad Senator Wheeler to prison on false
charges. It was another jury that detected and baffled the same
Department's perjurers in the O'Leary case, during the late
war. And it was yet another jury that delivered the eminent
Fatty Arbuckle from what was, perhaps, the most disingenuous and outrageous persecution ever witnessed in a civilized
land.

Would any American Legislature, or Congress itself, have
resisted the vast pressure of the bureaucracy in these cases? To
ask the question is to answer it. The dominant character of
every legislative body ever heard of, at least in this great free
Republic, is precisely its susceptibility to such pressure. It not
only leaps when the bureaucracy cracks the whip; it also leaps
to the whip-cracking of scores of extra-legal (and often, indeed, *il*legal) agencies. The Anti-Saloon League, despite its
frequent disasters, is still so powerful everywhere that four legislators out of five obey it almost instinctively. When it is
flouted, as has happened in a few States under an adverse pressure yet more powerful, the thing is marvelled at as a sort of
miracle. The bureaucracy itself is seldom flouted at all. When it
is in a moral mood, and heaving with altruistic sobs, the thing
simply never happens. Is it argued that Congress has nevertheless defied it, and Dr. Coolidge with it? Then the argument
comes from persons whose studies of Washington pathology

have been very superficial. At least nine-tenths of the idiocies advocated by Dr. Coolidge and his highly dubious friends have been swallowed by both Houses with no more than a few reflex gags. Even the celebrated Warren appointment was defeated in the Senate by only a few votes—and the few votes were delivered, as connoisseurs will recall, by a process indistinguishable from an act of God. It is my contention that a jury of plain men, issuing unwilling from their plumbing-shops and grocery-stores and eager to get back to work, would have rejected Warren without leaving their box, and that the same jury, confronted by such things as the World Court imbecility, would dispose of them just as quickly.

Why were the learned Senators so much less intelligent and so much less resolute? For a plain reason. Fully two-thirds of them were not thinking of Warren as they voted; they were thinking of their jobs. The problem before them was not whether elevating the preposterous Warren was a reasonable and laudable measure, likely to benefit and glorify the United States, but whether voting for Warren would augment or diminish their chance of reëlection. In other words, they were not free agents, and in consequence not honest men. They had sought their jobs on their bellies, and they were eager to keep them, even at the cost of groveling on their bellies again. Say the worst you can say against a box of twelve jurymen, and you can never say that. Not one among them sought his job. Not one among them wants to keep it. The business before them presents itself as a public duty to be done, not as an opportunity for private advantage. They are eager only to get it done decently, and go home.

So my proposal is that our Legislatures be chosen as our juries are now chosen—that the names of all the men eligible in each assembly district be put into a hat (or, if no hat can be found that is large enough, into a bathtub), and that a blind moron, preferably of tender years, be delegated to draw out one. Let the constituted catchpolls then proceed swiftly to this man's house, and take him before he can get away. Let him be brought into court forthwith, and put under a stupendous bond to serve as elected, and if he cannot furnish the bond, let him be kept until the appointed day in the nearest jail.

The advantages that this system would offer are so vast and

so obvious that I hesitate to venture into the banality of re-hearsing them. It would, in the first place, save the common-wealth the present excessive cost of elections, and make political campaigns unnecessary. It would, in the second place, get rid of all the heart-burnings that now flow out of every contest at the polls, and block the reprisals and charges of fraud that now issue from the heart-burnings. It would, in the third place, fill all the State Legislatures with men of a peculiar and unprecedented cast of mind—men actually convinced that public service is a public burden, and not merely a private snap. And it would, in the fourth and most important place, completely dispose of the present degrading knee-bending and trading in votes, for nine-tenths of the legislators, having got into office unwillingly, would be eager only to finish their du-ties and go home, and even those who acquired a taste for the life would be unable to do anything to increase the probability, even by one chance in a million, of their reëlection.

The disadvantages of the plan are very few, and most of them, I believe, yield readily to analysis. Do I hear argument that a miscellaneous gang of tin-roofers, delicatessen dealers and retired bookkeepers, chosen by hazard, would lack the vast knowledge of public affairs needed by makers of laws? Then I can only answer (*a*) that no such knowledge is actually neces-sary, and (*b*) that few, if any, of the existing legislators possess it. The great majority of public problems, indeed, are quite simple, and any man may be trusted to grasp their elements in ten days who may be—and is—trusted to unravel the obfusca-tions of two gangs of lawyers in the same time. In this depart-ment the so-called expertness of so-called experts is largely imaginary. The masters of the tariff who sit at Washington know little about the fundamental philosophy of protection, and care less; the subject, if discussed on the floor, would send the whole House flying to the Capitol bootleggers. The knowledge that these frauds are full of is simply knowledge of how many votes an extra ten cents on aluminum dishpans may be counted on producing, and how much the National Associ-ation of Brass Cuspidor Manufacturers deserves to be given for its campaign contribution of $10,000. Such is the science of the tariff as it is practiced by the professors who now flourish. It is my contention that a House of malt-and-hop dealers, garage mechanics and trolley conductors, brought in by the common hangman, would deal with the question with quite as much knowledge, and with a great deal more honesty. It might make mistakes, but it would not, at least, be pledged to them in advance. Some of its members might sell out, but there would remain, at worst, a workable minority of honest men.

The tariff, in any case, is no longer an issue. Neither are most of the other great politico-economical puzzles that harassed the statesmen of an elder day. They have all been solved; the two great parties agree upon them, with a few wild fellows dissenting. But as economics and finance go out, morals come in. The legislation of to-day is chiefly made up of quack cure-alls, invented by fanatics and supported by the bureaucracy. Well, I ask you what sort of Legislature is the more likely to swallow these cure-alls: one made up of professionals eager to hold their jobs, or one made up of amateurs eager only to get rid of their jobs?

My scheme would have the capital merit, if it had no other, of barring the professionals from the game. They would lose their present enormous advantages as a class, and so their class would tend to disappear. Would that be a disservice to the state? Certainly not. On the contrary, it would be a service of the first magnitude, for the worst curse of democracy, as we suffer under it to-day, is that it makes public office a monopoly of a palpably inferior and ignoble group of men. They have to abase themselves in order to get it, and they have to keep on abasing themselves in order to hold it. The fact reflects itself in their general character, which is obviously low. They are men congenitally capable of ignoble acts, else they would not have got into public life at all. There are, of course, exceptions to that rule among them, but how many? What I contend is simply that the number of such exceptions is bound to be smaller in the class of professional job-seekers than it is in any other class, or in the population in general. What I contend, second, is that choosing legislators from that population, by chance, would reduce immensely the proportion of such crawling, slimy men in the halls of legislation, and that the effects would be instantly visible in a great improvement in the justice and reasonableness of the laws.

Are juries ignorant? Then they are still intelligent enough to be entrusted with your life and mine. Are they venal? Then they are still honest enough to take our fortunes into their hands. Such is the fundamental law of the Germanic peoples, and it has worked for nearly a thousand years. I have launched my proposal that it be extended upward and onward, and the mood of constructive criticism passes from me. My plan belongs to any reformer who cares to lift it.

3
The Nature of Government

What ails the world mainly, at least in the political sense, is that its governments are too strong. It has been a recurrent pest since the dawn of civilization. Government is always depicted, in the orthodox texts, as the creation of the people governed; the theory is that they created it in order to secure their own safety and promote their daily business. But no Professor Oppenheimer was needed to demonstrate that it is really something imposed from without, or, at all events, the heir and assign of something imposed from without. Its interests and those of the people it governs are the same only occasionally, and then usually accidentally. True enough, it must sometimes throw them bones, and even beefsteaks, lest they grow desperate and attempt to destroy it, but such concessions are always made grudgingly, and withdrawn very promptly the moment it looks safe.

The history of the United States would make all this plain enough, if that history were studied realistically. Consider, for example, the matter of liberty. The American people profess to esteem liberty very highly—so highly, in fact, that their common talk about it seems somewhat lyrical and excessive to the people of most other nations. They seem to believe that there is more of it on tap in the Republic than anywhere else on earth—that the Republic was actually founded for the sole purpose of giving it to them. Yet it must be obvious that their hold upon it is always precarious, and that their government tries to take it away from them whenever possible—not completely, perhaps, but always substantially. That government resisted their demand for it at the very start, and yielded only after a very severe struggle. The Bill of Rights was not in the original Constitution; it got in only as amendments. Ever since then, at every opportunity, the government has tried to weaken it. Here parties and personalities count for very little. The most successful raids upon the Bill of Rights so far recorded were made by Abraham Lincoln, a Republican and the spokesman (in theory) of the inferior man, and by Woodrow Wilson, a Democrat and the agent of what passes, in the United States, for an aristocracy.

The men who constitute the government always try to make it appear, of course, that they carry on their activities in a patriotic and altruistic way—in brief, they are full of public spirit. But that pretension deceives no one, not even *Homo boobiens.* The average man, whatever his errors otherwise, at least sees clearly that the government is something lying outside him and outside the generality of his fellow men—that it is a separate, independent and often hostile power, only partly under his control, and capable, on occasion, of doing him great harm. In his romantic moments, he may think of it as a benevolent father or even a sort of *jinn* or god, but he never thinks of it as part of himself. In times of trouble he looks to it to perform miracles for his benefit; at other times he sees it as an enemy with which he must do constant battle. Is it a fact of no significance that robbing the government is everywhere regarded as a crime of less magnitude than robbing an individual, or even a corporation? In the United States to-day it is punished only when it is complicated by some secondary, and, in the public judgment, worse offense—for example, depriving crippled war veterans of their lawful relief. Otherwise, it carries a smaller penalty and infinitely less odium than acts that are intrinsically trivial—for example, spitting on the sidewalk or marrying two wives. None of the thieves who robbed the government at Hog Island during the war has ever gone to jail. The airship contractors, though they made off with nearly a billion dollars, are still all at large. So are all the camp contractors. More, the man who broke up the feeble and abortive effort to punish these scoundrels—who denounced that effort as, in some mysterious way, an *attentat* against public morality—that man is now first in succession to the presidency of the

Republic. His indignation plainly had public sentiment behind it. He was and is an accomplished professor of the mind of man under democracy.

Other politicians, less gifted in that science, often take the other side, and so come to grief. They assume absurdly that the public conscience is opposed to robbing the government, and try to climb into popularity and high office by pursuing the gay fellows who do it. The attempt almost always fails. The great masses of the plain people, true enough, enjoy the chase, as they enjoy, indeed, *any* chase. The damning evidence, as it unrolls, delights them; they devour every accusation, however ill supported. But it usually turns out in the end that they do not care to eat the game. The minute the evidence is all in they lose interest; there is no demand from them for the jailing of the accused. On the contrary, they sympathize with the accused, and show it actively when the time comes to supply conscripts for the trial jury. Perhaps the safest men in the whole United States to-day are the gentlemen who have been indicted for robbing the government. Every such indictment is a sort of policy of insurance against going to jail.

What lies behind all this, I believe, is a deep sense of the fundamental antagonism between the government and the people it governs. It is apprehended, not as a committee of citizens chosen to carry on the communal business of the whole population, but as a separate and autonomous corporation, mainly devoted to exploiting the population for the benefit of its own members. Robbing it is thus an act almost devoid of infamy—an exploit rather resembling those of Robin Hood and the eminent pirates of tradition. When a private citizen is robbed a worthy man is deprived of the fruits of his industry and thrift; when the government is robbed the worst that happens is that certain rogues and loafers have less money to play with than they had before. The notion that they have earned that money is never entertained; to most men it would seem extremely ludicrous. They are simply rascals who, by accidents of law, have a somewhat dubious right to a share in the earnings of their fellowmen. When that share is diminished by private enterprise the business is, on the whole, far more laudable than not.

The average man, when he pays taxes, certainly does not believe that he is making a prudent and productive investment of his money; on the contrary, he feels that he is being mulcted in an excessive amount for services that, in the main, are useless to him, and that, in substantial part, are downright inimical to him. He may be convinced that a police force, say, is necessary for the protection of his life and property, and that an army and navy safeguard him from being reduced to slavery by some vague foreign kaiser, but even so he views these things as extravagantly expensive—he sees in even the most essential of them an agency for making it easier for the exploiters constituting the government to rob him. The policeman, in fact, is his symbol for a thief. The army and navy, as he sees them, are blankets for mere display, ostentation and waste—of his hard-earned money. The rest of the government is purely predatory and useless; he believes that he gets no more benefit from its vast and costly operations than he gets from the money he lends to his wife's brother. It is a power that stands over him constantly, ever alert for new chances to squeeze him. If it could do so safely it would strip him to his hide. If it leaves him anything at all, it is simply prudentially, as a farmer leaves a hen some of her eggs.

Thus he sees nothing wrong, in the sense that robbing a neighbor is wrong to him, in turning the tables upon it whenever the opportunity offers. When he steals anything from it he is only recovering his own, with fair interest and a decent profit. Two gangs thus stand confronted: on the one hand the gang of drones and exploiters constituting the government, and on the other hand the body of prehensile and enterprising citizens. The latter is certainly not made up exclusively, as the Liberals and other such romantics seem to think, of bankers, railroad stockholders, great industrialists and other such magnificoes. There is plenty of room in it for more lowly men, if only they have the courage to horn in. During the late war all the union men of the nation, by pooling their strength and so dispersing the risk, made a magnificent and successful effort to get their share: they stole almost as much, in all probability, as the dollar-a-year men. And when the war was over the soldiers, deprived of their chance while the going was good, demanded it belatedly. The chief argument for the bonus was not that the veterans of the war had leaped gallantly to the defense of democracy, for at least two-thirds of them, as everyone knows, tried their best to evade service. The chief argument was that they were forced into the army against their will and in violation of their private interests—that they didn't get their fair chance at the loot. They did not demand the punishment of those who looted while they served; they only demanded a rectification of the injustice which kept them honest themselves.

The difference between the two gangs—of professionals and of amateurs—is that the former has law on its side, and so enjoys an unfair advantage. Worse, it makes the very laws it profits by. Yet worse, it controls all the agencies which execute them, including the courts. The other gang is almost unarmored. The government is always able, when it happens to be so disposed, to single out a few of its ring-leaders and clap them into jail. Such proceedings, of course, are unpopular, but they are nevertheless possible. But the government gang is well-nigh immune to punishment. Its worst extortions, even when they are baldly for private profit, carry no certain penalties under our laws. Since the first days of the Republic less than a dozen of its members have been impeached, and only a few obscure understrappers have ever been put into prison. The number of men sitting at Atlanta and Leavenworth for revolting against the extortions of the government is always ten times as great as the number of government officials condemned for oppressing the tax-payers to their own gain. Thus the combat which goes on is not unlike that between the Anti-Saloon League and the bootleggers. The Anti-Saloon League, it must be manifest, is quite as criminal as the bootleggers; it devotes itself professionally to violating the Bill of Rights; its kept judges have pretty well disposed of all the constitutional guarantees of the citizen. But its control of the government puts it above the law. Its agents, on and off the bench, commit their crimes almost unmolested; only one of them, in fact, has ever got into jail—and that was by a sort of accident.

But public opinion is mainly on the side of the bootleggers. They represent, in the combat, the plain man, eternally oppressed and robbed by his overlords. In their popularity is to be seen the first glimmers of a revolt that must one day shake the world—a revolt, not against this or that form of government, but against the tyranny at the bottom of *all* government. Government, to-day, is growing too strong to be safe.

There are no longer any citizens in the world; there are only subjects. They work day in and day out for their masters; they are bound to die for their masters at call. Out of this working and dying they tend to get less and less. On some bright to-morrow, a geological epoch or two hence, they will come to the end of their endurance, and then such newspapers as survive will have a first-page story well worth its black head-lines.

4
Freudian Footnote

That the life of man is a struggle and an agony was remarked by the Brisbanes and Dr. Frank Cranes of the remotest antiq-uity. The earliest philosophers busied themselves with the fact, and so did the earliest poets. It runs like a *Leitmotif* through the literature of the Greeks and the Jews alike. "Vanity of van-ities," saith the Preacher, "vanity of vanities; all is vanity!" "O ye deathward-going tribes of men," chants Sophocles, "what do your lives mean except that they go to nothingness?" But not placidly, not unresistingly, not without horrible groans and gurgles. Man is never honestly the fatalist, nor even the stoic. He fights his fate, often desperately. He is forever entering bold exceptions to the rulings of the bench of gods. This fight-ing, no doubt, makes for human progress, for it favors the strong and the brave. It also makes for beauty, for lesser men try to escape from a hopeless and intolerable world by creating a more lovely one of their own. Poetry, as every one knows, is a means to that end—facile, and hence popular. The aim of poetry is to give a high and voluptuous plausibility to what is palpably not true. I offer the Twenty-third Psalm as an exam-ple: "The Lord is my shepherd; I shall not want." It is im-mensely esteemed by the inmates of almshouses, and by gentlemen waiting to be hanged. I have to limit my own read-ing of it, avoiding soft and yielding moods, for I too, in my way, am a gentleman waiting to be hanged, as you are. If the air were impregnated with poetry, as it is with carbon in Pitts-burgh, and alcohol in Hoboken, N.J., and stale incense in Boston, the world would be a more comfortable and caressing place, but the service of the truth would be neglected. The truth is served by prose. The aim of prose is not to conceal the facts, but to display them. It is thus apt to be harsh and painful. All that the philosophers and metaphysicians of the world have accomplished, grinding away in their damp cells since man became cryptococcygeal, is to prove that *Homo sapiens* and *Equus asinus* are brothers under their skins. As for the more imaginative *prosateurs*, they have pretty well confined themselves, since the earliest beginnings of their craft, to the lugubrious chronicle of man's struggle and defeat. I know of no first-rate novel that hasn't this theme. In all of them, from "Don Quixote" to "The Brothers Karamazov" and from "Vanity Fair" to "McTeague," we are made privy to the agonies of a man resisting his destiny, and getting badly beaten.

The struggle is always the same, but in its details it differs in different ages. There was a time, I believe, when it was mainly a combat between the natural instincts of the individual and his yearning to get into Heaven. That was an unhealthy time, for throttling the instincts is almost as deleterious as breathing bad air; it makes for an unpleasant clamminess. The Age of Faith, seen in retrospect, looks somehow pale and puffy: one admires its saints and anchorites without being conscious of any very active desire to shake hands with them and smell them. To-day the yearning to get into Heaven is in abeyance, at least among the vast majority of humankind, and so the ancient struggle takes a new form. In the main, it is a struggle of man with society—a conflict between his desire to be respected and his impulse to follow his own bent. It seems to me that society usually wins. There are, to be sure, free spirits in the world, but their freedom, in the last analysis, is not much greater than that of a canary in a cage. They may leap from perch to perch; they may bathe and guzzle at their will; they may flap their wings and sing. But they are still in the cage, and soon or late it conquers them. What was once a great itch for long flights and the open spaces is gradually converted into a fading memory and nostalgia, sometimes stimulating but more often merely blushful. The free man, made in God's image, is converted into a Freudian case.

Such Freudian cases swarm in modern society; they are hidden in all sorts of unexpected places. Observing a Congressman, one sees only a gross and revolting shape, with dull eyes and prehensile hands. But under that preposterous mask there may be yearnings, and some of them may be of high voltage and laudable delicacy. There are Congressmen, I have no doubt, who regret their lost honor, as women often do in the films. Tossing in their beds on hot, sticky Washington nights, their gizzards devoured by bad liquor, they may lament the ruin that the service of Demos has brought to their souls. For Congressmen, despite their dishonorable trade, are exactly like the rest of us at bottom, and respond to the same biogenetic laws. In infancy they go to Sunday-school. Passing through adolescence, they are idealists, and dream of saving the world. Come to young manhood, they suffer the purifying pangs of love. The impulse to seek political preferment, when it arises in them, is not always, nor primarily, an impulse to grab something, to victimize and exploit the rest of us. That comes later: even Penrose and Roosevelt started out as altruists and reformers. But the rules of the game run one way, and common honesty and common decency run another. There comes a time when the candidate must surrender either his ideals or his aspirations. If he is in Congress it is a sign that he has preserved the latter.

Democracy produces swarms of such men, in politics and on other planes, and their secret shames and sorrows, I believe, are largely responsible for the generally depressing tone of democratic society. Old Freud, living in a more urbane and civilized world, paid too little heed to that sort of repression. He assumed fatuously that what was repressed was always, or nearly always, something intrinsically discreditable, or, at all events, anti-social—for example, the natural impulse to neck a pretty woman, regardless of her husband's protests. But under democracy that is only half the story. The democrat with a yearning to shine before his fellows must not only repress all the common varieties of natural wickedness; he must also repress many of the varieties of natural decency. His impulse to speak his mind freely, to tell the truth as he sees it, to be his own man, comes into early and painful collision with the democratic dogma that such things are not nice—that the most worthy and laudable citizen is that one who is most like all the rest. In youth, as every one knows, this dogma is frequently challenged, and sometimes with great asperity, but the rebellion, taking one case with another, is not of long duration. The campus Nietzsche, at thirty, begins to feel the suction of Rotary; at forty he is a sound Mellon man; at fifty he is fit for Congress.

But his early yearning for freedom and its natural concomitants is still not dead; it is merely imprisoned in the depths of his subconscious. Down there it drags out its weary and intolerable years, protesting silently but relentlessly against its durance. We know, by Freud's appalling evidence, what the suppression of the common wickednesses can do to the individual —how it can shake his reason on its throne, and even give him such things as gastritis, migraine and angina pectoris. Every Sunday-school in the land is full of such wrecks; they recruit the endless brigades of lady policemen and male wowsers. A vice-crusader is simply an unfortunate who goes about with a brothel in his own cellar; a Prohibitionist is one who has buried rum, but would have been safer drinking it. All this is now a commonplace of knowledge to every American school-girl. The wowsers themselves give the facts a universal dispersion by trying to suppress them. But so far no psychoanalyst has done a tome on the complexes that issue out of moral struggles against common decency, though they are commoner under democracy than the other kind, and infinitely more ferocious. A man who has throttled a bad impulse has at least some consolation in his agonies, but a man who has throttled a good one is in a bad way indeed. Yet this great Republic swarms with such men, and their sufferings are under every eye. We have more of them, perhaps, than all the rest of Christendom, with heathendom thrown in to make it unanimous.

I marvel that no corn-fed Freud or Adler has ever investigated the case of the learned judges among us, and especially those of the Federal rite. Prohibition, I suspect, has filled them with such repressions that even a psychoanalyst, plowing into the matter, would be shocked. Enforcing its savage and antisocial mandates, with fanatics pulling them and blacklegs pushing them, has obviously compelled them to make away with all the pruderies that are natural to men of their class and condition. There may be individuals among them, to be sure, who were born without any pruderies and hence do not suffer, just as there are individuals who were born without any capacity for affection and hence show no trace of the Œdipus complex, but such men must be very rare, even among politicians, even among lawyers. The average judge, I take it, is much like the rest of us. When he is free to do it, he does the decent thing. His natural impulse is to speak the truth as he sees it, to challenge error and imposture, to frown upon fraud. What, now, if his high and solemn duties compel him to treat fraud as if it were divine revelation? What if he must spend his days prospering rogues and oppressing honest men? What if his oath wars horribly with his conscience? No Freud was needed to argue that the effect upon him must be very evil. He cannot perform his work without assassinating his inner integrity. Putting on his black gown, he must simultaneously cram his unconscious with all the sound impulses and natural decencies that make him the noble fellow that he is.

The clinical effects are certainly not occult. One hears constantly of judges coming down with symptoms which, in ordinary men, would be accepted as proofs of inner turmoils, insusceptible to correction by the pharmacopœia. They break into hysterical tirades from the bench; they speak in unintelligible language; they deliver judgments that upset the laws of logic; they complain of buzzings in the ears, flashes before the eyes, and vague bellyaches. Two Federal judges, of late, have committed suicide. One climbed a high mountain in his motorcar, and then leaped into space: a monstrous act, and no doubt of plain significance to a Freudian adept. The other left a note saying frankly that Prohibition had wrecked him. The faculty has at such disturbances of the psyche by hunting for focal infections and pulling teeth: the whole judiciary tends to become toothless. But it would be easier and cheaper and more effective, I am convinced, to send for a psychoanalyst. The stricken judge would come out of the room cured, and the psychoanalyst would come out with a new outfit of complexes.

I speak of the judges because their sufferings are palpable. But there must be swarms of other victims in this eminent free nation. Every one of us has been under the steam-roller; every one of us, in this way or that, confirms unwillingly, and has the corpse of a good impulse belowstairs. There are probably no exceptions. Psychoanalyze a Methodist bishop, and you'll probably find him stuffed with good impulses, all of them repressed. On blue afternoons, perhaps, there sneaks out of his unconscious a civilized yearning for a decent drink; in the dark watches of the night he remembers a Catholic girl of his youth, and weeps that she was so fair; he may even, passing a public library, feel a sudden, goatish inclination to go in and read a good book. Suppressed, such appetites make him uncomfortable, unhappy, desperate, an enemy to society. Dredged up by some super-Freud, and dissipated in the sunlight, they would leave him an honest and happy man.

5

Bach to Bach!

Ah, at evening, to be drinking from the glassy pond, to have—oh, better than all marrow-bones!—the fresh illusion of lapping up the stars!

I take the thought from Patou, the forward-looking hound-dog in Rostand's "Chantecler." Let him stand as a symbol of the whole melancholy company of crib-haltered but aspiring Americans, their hands doomed to go-getting but their hearts leaping into interstellar space. Patou, lifted to his hind legs and outfitted with pantaloons, would have made a capital Rotarian. Condemned by destiny to a kennel in a barnyard, he yet had that soaring, humorless Vision which is the essence of Rotary, and the secret, no doubt, of its firm hold upon otherwise un-poetical men. For even in the paradise of Babbitt, Babbitt is vaguely uneasy and unhappy. He needs something more, he finds, than is to be found in bulging order-books; in innumerable caravans of prospects, and in belching chimneys and laden trains. He needs something more than is to be got out of blowing spitballs and playing golf. So he searches for that something in the realm of the fancy, where the husks of things fall and their inner sap is revealed. He reads the dithyrambs of Edgar Albert Guest, Arthur Brisbane, and Dr. Frank Crane. He listens to the exhortations of itinerant rhetoricians, gifted and eloquent men, specialists in what it is all about. He intones "Sweet Adeline," and is not ashamed of the tear that babbles down his nose. Thus Babbitt, too, is tantalized by a Grail; he seeks it up and down the gorgeous corridors of his Statler

Hotel, past the cigar-stand and the lair of the hat-check gal, and on to the perfumed catacombs of the lovely manicurist and the white-robed chirotonsor. *Non in solo pane vivit homo.* Man cannot live by bread alone. He must hope also. He must dream. He must yearn.

The fact explains the Rotarian and his humble brother, the Kiwanian; more, it strips them of not a little of their superficial obnoxiousness. They are fools, but they are not quite damned. If their quest is carried on in motley, they at least trail after better men. And so do all their brethren of Service, great and small—the Americanizers, the Law Enforcers, the boosters and boomers, and the endless others after their kind. At first glance, one sees in these visionaries only noisy and preposterous fellows, disturbing the peace of their betters. But a closer examination is more favorable to them. They are tortured, in their odd, clumsy fashion, by the same ringing in the ears that maddened Ludwig van Beethoven. They suffer from the same optical delusions, painful and not due to sin, that set the prophets of antiquity to howling: they look at a Harding or a Coolidge and see a Man. What lures them to their bizarre cavortings—and it is surely not to be sniffed at *per se*—is a dim and disturbing mirage of a world more lovely and serene than the one the Lord God has doomed them to live in. What they lack in common, thus diverging from the prophets, is a rational conception of what it ought to be, and might be.

It is somewhat astonishing that 100% Americans should wander so helplessly in this wilderness. For there is a well-paved road across the whole waste, and it issues, at its place of beginning, from the tombs of the Fathers, and their sacred and immemorial dust. Straight as a pistol so it runs, until at the other end it sweeps up a glittering slope to a shrine upon a high hill. This shrine may be seen on fair days for many leagues, and presents a magnificent spectacle. Its base is confected of the bones of Revolutionary heroes, and out of them rises an heroic effigy of George Washington, in alabaster. Surrounding this effigy, and on a slightly smaller scale, are graven images of Jefferson, Franklin, Nathan Hale, old Sam Adams, John Hancock and Paul Revere, each with a Bible under his arm and the Stars and Stripes fluttering over his shoulder. A bit to the rear, and without the Bible, is a statue of Thomas Paine.

Over the whole structure stretch great bands of the tricolor, in silk, satin and other precious fabrics. Red and white stripes run up and down the legs of Washington, and his waistcoat is spattered with stars. The effect is the grandiose one of a Democratic national convention. At night, in the American manner, spotlights play upon the shrine. Hot dogs are on sale nearby, that pilgrims may not hunger, and there is a free park for Fords, with running water and booths for the sale of spare parts. It is the shrine of Liberty!

But where are the pilgrims? One observes the immense parking space and the huge pyramids of hot dogs, and one looks for great hordes of worshipers, fighting their way to the altar-steps. But they are *non est*. Now and then a honeymoon couple wanders in from the rural South or Middle West, to gape at the splendors hand in hand, and now and then a schoolma'm arrives with a flock of her pupils, and lectures them solemnly out of a book. More often, perhaps, a foreign visitor is to be seen, with a *couronne* of tin bay-leaves under his arm. He deposits the *couronne* at the foot of Washington, crosses himself lugubriously, and retires to the nearest hot dog stand. But where are the Americanos? Where are the he-men, heirs to the heroes whose gilded skulls here wait the Judgment Day? Where are the Americanizers? Where are the boosters and boomers? Where are the sturdy Coolidge men? Where are the Rotarians, Kiwanians, Lions? Where are the authors of newspaper editorials? The visionaries of Chautauqua? The keepers of the national idealism? Go search for them, if you don't trust the first report of your eyes! Go search for honest men in Congress! They are simply not present. For among all the visions that now inflame forward-looking and up-and-coming men in this great Republic, there is no sign any more of the one that is older than all the rest, and that is the vision of Liberty. The Fathers saw it, and the devotion they gave to it went far beyond three cheers a week. It survived into Jackson's time, and its glow was renewed in Lincoln's. But now it is no more.

The phenomenon is curious, and deserves far more study by eminent psychologists than it has got. I may undertake that study as an amateur in a work reserved for my senility; at the moment I can only point to the fact. Liberty, to-day, not only lacks its old hot partisans and romantic fanatics in America; it has grown so disreputable that even to mention it, save in terms of a fossilized and hollow rhetoric, becomes a sort of indecorum. I know of but one national organization that advocates it with any genuine heartiness, and that organization, not long ago, was rewarded with a violent denunciation on the floor of the House of Representatives: only the lone Socialist, once in jail himself for the same offense, made bold to defend it. From the chosen elders of the nation, legislative, executive and judicial, one hears only that demanding it is treason. It is the first duty of the free citizen, it appears, to make a willing sacrifice of the Bill of Rights. He must leap to the business gladly, and with no mental reservations. If he pauses, then he is a Bolshevik.

I venture to argue that this doctrine is evil, and that renouncing it would yield a sweeter usufruct to the American people than all the varieties of Service that now prevail. Of what use is it for Kiwanis to buy wooden legs for one-legged boys if they must grow up as slaves to the Anti-Saloon League? What is the net gain to a boomed and boosted town if its people, coincidentally, lose their right to trial by jury and their inviolability of domicile? Who gives a damn for the Coolidge idealism if its chief agent and executor, even the Cabinet, is the Board of Temperance, Prohibition and Public Morals of the Methodist Episcopal Church, *i.e.*, a gang of snooty ecclesiastics, committed unanimously to the doctrines that Christ should have been jailed for the business at Cana, that God sent she-bears to "tare" forty-two little children because they had made fun of Elisha's bald head, and that Jonah swallowed the whale? Imagine an immigrant studying the new science of Americanism, and coming to the eighteen amendments to the Constitution. What will he make of the discovery that only the Eighteenth embodies a categorical imperative—that all the others must yield to it when they conflict with it—that the Fourteenth and Fifteenth are not binding upon the Prohibitionists of the South and that the First, Fourth, Fifth and Sixth are not binding upon Prohibitionists anywhere?

I preach reaction. Bach to Bach! I can't find the word Service in the Constitution, but what is there is sounder and nobler than anything ever heard of where Regular Fellows meet to slap backs and blow spitballs—or, at all events, it *was* there before January 16, 1920. The Fathers, too, had a Vision. They were, in their way, forward-lookers; they were even go-getters. What they dreamed of and fought for was a civilization based upon a body of simple, equitable and reasonable laws— a code designed to break the chains of lingering medivælism and set the individual free. The thing they imagined was a commonwealth of free men, all equal before the law. Some of them had grave doubts about it, and put off making it a reality as long as possible, but in the end the optimists won over the doubters, and they all made the venture together. I am myself no partisan of their scheme. It seems to me that there were fundamental defects in it—that some of their primary assumptions were false. But in their intention, at least, there was something exhilarating, and in it there was also something sound. That something was the premiss that the first aim of civilization is to augment and safeguard the dignity of man— that it is worth nothing to be a citizen of a commonwealth which holds the humblest citizen cheaply and uses him ill.

This is what we have lost, and not all the whooping and yelling of new messiahs can cover the fact. The government, as I have shown, becomes the common enemy of all well-disposed and decent men. It commandeers and wastes their money, it assaults and insults them with outrageous and extravagant laws, and it turns loose upon them a horde of professional blackguards, bent only upon destroying their liberties. The individual, facing this pestilence of tyranny and corruption, finds himself quite helpless. If he goes to the agents of the government itself with his protest, he gets only stupid reviling. If he turns to his fellow victims for support, he is lucky to escape jail. Worse, he is lucky to escape lynching. For the thing has gone so far that the great majority of dull and unimaginative men have begun to take it as a matter of course—almost as the order of nature. The Bill of Rights becomes a mere series of romantic dithyrambs, without solid substance or meaning— say, like the Sermon on the Mount. The school-books of the next generation will omit it. The few fanatics who remember it will keep it on the top shelf, along with the Family Doctor

Book, the scientific works of Dr. Marie Stopes, and "Only a Boy."

Against all this I protest, feebly and too late. The land swarms with Men of Vision, all pining for Service. What I propose is that they forget their brummagem Grails for one week, and concentrate their pep upon a chase that really leads uphill. Let us have a Bill of Rights Week. Let us have a Common Decency Week.

III.

The Human Mind

I

On Metaphysicians

IN the Summer of the year, when the weather on my estates in the Maryland jungles is too hot for serious mental activity, I always give over a couple of weeks to a re-reading of the so-called philosophical classics, with a glance or two at the latest compositions of the extant philosophers. It is a far from agreeable job, and I undertake it sadly, as a surgeon, after an untoward and fatal hemorrhage, brushes up on anatomy; there is, somewhere down in my recesses, an obscure conviction that I owe a duty to my customers, who look to me to flatter them with occasional dark references to Aristotle, Spinoza and the categorical imperative. Out of the business, despite its high austerity, I always carry away the feeling that I have had a hell of a time. That is, I carry away the feeling that the art and mystery of philosophy, as it is practiced in the world by professional philosophers, is largely moonshine and wind-music—or, to borrow Henry Ford's searching term, bunk.

Is this anarchy and atheism? Has Russian gold got to me at last? Am I in training for the abattoir of the Department of Justice? In stay of execution I can only point to the philosophy books themselves. For three millenniums their authors have been searching the world and its suburbs for the truth—and they have yet to agree upon so much as the rules of the search. Since the dawn of time they have been trying to get order and method into the thinking of *Homo sapiens*—and *Homo sapiens*, when he thinks at all, is still a brother to the lowly ass (*Equus africanus*), even to the ears and the bray. I include the philosophers themselves, unanimously and especially. True enough, one arises now and then who somehow manages to be charming and even plausible. I point to Plato, to Nietzsche, to Schopenhauer. But it is always as poet or politician, not as philosopher. The genuine professional, sticking to his gloomy speculations, is as dull as a table of logarithms. What man in human history ever wrote worse than Kant? Was it, perhaps, Hegel? My own candidate, if I were pushed, would be found among the so-called Critical Realists of to-day. They achieve the truly astounding feats of writing worse than the New Thoughters, whom they also resemble otherwise—nay, even worse than the late Warren Gamaliel Harding.

What reduces all philosophers to incoherence and folly, soon or late, is the lure of the absolute. It tortures them as the dream of Law Enforcement tortures Prohibitionists. Now and then, when they forget it transiently, they grow relatively rational and even ingratiating, but in the long run they always resume their chase of it, and that chase carries them inevitably into the intellectual Bad Lands. For the absolute, of course, is a mere banshee, a concept without substance or reality. No such thing exists. When, by logical devices, it is triumphantly established, the feat is exactly on all fours with that of the mathematician who proved that twice two was double once two. Who believes in Kant's categorical imperatives to-day? Certainly not any student of psychology who has got beyond the first page of his horn-book. There is, in fact, no idea in any man that may be found certainly in all men. Only the philosophers seem to cling to the doctrine that there is. Functioning as theologians, for example, they still argue for the immortality of the soul on the ground that a yearning for immortal life is in all of us. But that is simply nonsense. I know scores of men in whom no such yearning is apparent, either outwardly or in their consciousness. I have seen such men die, and they passed into what they held to be oblivion without showing the slightest sign of wishing that it was something else. All the other absolutes, whether theological, ethical or philosophical in the strict sense, are likewise chimeras. On inspection it always turns out that they are no more the same to all men than a woman A or a cocktail B is the same to all men. They are even different to the same man at different times. I cherished ethical postulates at the age of twenty-one that seem puerile to me to-day, and to-day I am cherishing postulates that would have shocked me then. *Quod est veritas?* Simply something that seems to me to be so—now, and to me. It has no more objective character than the sweet and dreadful passion of love. It is as tenderly personal and private as a gallstone.

The common sense of mankind, which is immensely superior to the anæmic, camphor-smelling wisdom of philosophers, long ago revolted against the quest of the absolute. Men found back in Mousterian days that it got them nowhere, but left them, intellectually speaking, with one leg up and one leg down. So they began to set up arbitrary values, if only to get some peace. Religion is a series of such arbitrary values. Most of them are dubious, and many of them are palpably false, but the experience of the race has shown that, for certain types of mind and in certain situations, they work. So they are accepted as, if not quite true, then as true enough, and the gloomy business of rectifying them, when they need it, is turned over to theologians, who are enemies of mankind anyhow, and thus deserve and get no sympathy when they suffer. Arbitrary values of the same sort are made use of every day in all the fields of human speculation and activity. They are brilliantly visible in the field of politics and government. Here they are rammed into children in the little red schoolhouse, and questioning them later in life becomes a crime against the Holy Ghost. Is it therefore to be assumed that they are true? Not at all. Many of them are so transparently dubious that even patriots, preparing to mumble them, have to make ready for it by closing their eyes and taking long breaths. But they at least work. They at least get some semblance of order into the complicated and dangerous business of living together in society. They at least relieve the mind. And so they are cherished.

Unfortunately, human existence is not static but dynamic, and in consequence the axioms that work well to-day tend to work less well to-morrow. Now and then, as the social organization changes, certain ancient and honorable ones have to be abandoned. This is always a perilous business, and usually it is accomplished only by a letting of blood. The fact is not without its significance. In the long run, I believe, it will be found that (as the Behaviorists argue even now) human ideas come out of the liver far more often than they come out of the soul, and that changing them is a job for surgeons rather than for metaphysicians. The thought leads at once to a constructive suggestion, and in the exalted field of pedagogy. What is the present aim of education, as the professors thereof expound it? To make good citizens. And what is a good citizen? Simply one who never says, does or thinks anything that is unusual. Schools are maintained in order to bring this uniformity up to the highest possible point. A school is a hopper into which children are heaved while they are still young and tender; therein they are pressed into certain standard shapes and covered from head to heels with official rubber-stamps. Unluckily, it is a very inefficient machine. Many children, though squeezed diligently, do not take the standard shapes. Others have hides so oily that the most indelible of rubber-stamps is washed from them by the first rain, or even blown from them by the first wind.

It is my notion that surgery will one day find a remedy for this unpleasant and dangerous state of affairs. It will first perfect means of detecting such aberrant children in their early youth, and then it will devise means of curing them. The child who laughs when the Bill of Rights is read will not be stood in a corner and deprived of chewing-gum, as now; it will be sent to the operating-table, and the offending convolution, or gland, or tumor, or whatever it is will be cut out. While it is lying open all other suspicious excrescences will be removed, and so it will be returned to the class-room a normal 100% American. This scheme, if it turns out to be practicable, will add a great deal to the happiness of the American people. It will not only protect those of us who are naturally respectable from the menace of strange and disturbing ideas; it will also relieve the present agonies of those who cherish them. For the search for imaginary absolutes—*i.e.*, for the truth, that ghost —is not pleasant, as poets allege, but intensely painful. There is no record in human history of a happy philosopher: they exist only in romantic legend. Many of them have committed suicide; practically all of them have turned their children out of doors and beaten their wives. And no wonder! If you want to find out how a philosopher feels when he is engaged in the practice of his profession, go to the nearest zoo and watch a chimpanzee at the wearying and hopeless job of chasing fleas. Both suffer damnably, and neither can win.

2
On Suicide

The suicide rate, so I am told by an intelligent mortician, is going up everywhere on earth. It is good news to his profession, which has been badly used of late by the progress of medical science, and scarcely less so by the rise of cut-throat, go-getting competition within its own ranks. It is also good news to those romantic optimists who like to believe that the human race is capable of rational acts. What could be more logical than suicide? What could be more preposterous than keeping alive? Yet nearly all of us cling to life with desperate devotion, even when the length of it remaining is palpably slight, and filled with agony. Half the time of all medical men is wasted keeping life in human wrecks who have no more intelligible reason for hanging on than a cow has for mooing.

In part, no doubt, this absurd frenzy has its springs in the human imagination, or, as it is more poetically called, the human reason. Man, having acquired the high faculty of visualizing death, visualizes it as something painful and dreadful. It is, of course, seldom anything of the sort. The proceedings anterior to it are sometimes (though surely not always) painful, but death itself appears to be almost devoid of sensation, either psychic or physical. The candidate, facing it at last, simply loses his faculties. Death is no more to him than it is to a coccus. The dreadful, like the painful, is not in it. It is far more likely to show elements of the grotesque. I speak here, of course, of natural death. Suicide is plainly more unpleasant, if only because there is some uncertainty about it. The candidate hesitates to shoot himself because he fears, with some show of reason, that he may fail to kill himself, and only hurt himself. Moreover, this shooting, along with most of the other more common aids to an artificial exitus, involves a kind of affront to his dignity: it is apt to make a mess. But that objection, it seems to me, is one that is bound to disappear with the progress of science. Safe, sure, easy and sanitary methods of departing this life will be invented. Some, in truth, are already known, and perhaps the fact explains the steady increase in suicides, so satisfactory to my mortician friend.

I pass over the theological objections to self-destruction as too transparently sophistical to be worth a serious answer. From the earliest days Christianity has depicted life on this earth as so sad and vain that its value is indistinguishable from that of a damn. Then why cling to it? Simply because its vanity and unpleasantness are parts of the will of a Creator whose love for His creatures takes the form of torturing them. If they revolt in this world they will be tortured a million times worse in the next. I present the argument as a typical specimen of theological reasoning, and proceed to more engaging themes. Specifically, to my original thesis: that it is difficult, if not impossible, to discover any evidential or logical reason, not instantly observed to be full of fallacy, for keeping alive. The fact that we nevertheless do it is no more than proof that reason is mainly only a sort of afterthought. I enjoy the effects of alcohol when I am sad. *Ergo*, all Prohibitionists are fools and most of them are scoundrels. Alcohol makes me ill and killed my Uncle Emil. *Ergo*, it ought to be prohibited by law, as it is by the Holy Scriptures, though in a passage that, at the moment, I can't recall. I admire and enjoy Americans, particularly when they make asses of themselves. *Ergo*, any foreigner who essays to butcher them is a fiend from Hell. Americans fatigue me. *Ergo*, the same foreigner is a charming fellow.

But sometimes these second thoughts—and *all* thoughts are second thoughts—are unanimous, and then they become what is called universal wisdom. The universal wisdom of the world long ago concluded that life is mainly a curse. Turn to the proverbial philosophy of any race, and you will find it full of a sense of the futility of the mundane struggle. Anticipation is better than realization. Disappointment is the lot of man. We are born in pain and die in sorrow. The lucky man died a' Wednesday. He giveth His beloved sleep. I could run the list to pages. If you disdain folk-wisdom, secular or sacred, then turn to the immortal works of William Shakespeare. They drip with such pessimism from end to end. If there is any general idea in them, it is the idea that human existence is a painful futility. Out, out, brief candle!

Yet we cling to it in a muddled physiological sort of way—or, perhaps more accurately, in a pathological way—and even try to fill it with gaudy hocus-pocus. All men who, in any true sense, are sentient strive mightily for distinction and power, *i.e.*, for the respect and envy of their fellowmen, *i.e.*, for the ill-natured admiration of an endless series of miserable and ridiculous bags of rapidly disintegrating amino acids. Why? If I knew, I'd certainly not be writing books in this infernal American climate; I'd be sitting in state in a hall of crystal and gold, and people would be paying $10 a head to gape at me through peep-holes. But though the central mystery remains, it is possible, perhaps, to investigate the superficial symptoms to some profit. I offer myself as a laboratory animal. Why have I worked so hard for thirty years, desperately striving to accomplish something that remains impenetrable to me to this day? Is it because I desire money? Bosh! I can't recall ever desiring it for an instant: I have always found it easy to get all I wanted. Is it, then, notoriety that I am after? Again the answer must be no. The attention of strangers is unpleasant to me, and I avoid it as much as possible. Then is it a yearning to Do Good that moves me? Bosh and blah! If I am convinced of anything, it is that Doing Good is in bad taste.

Once I ventured the guess that men worked in response to a vague inner urge for self-expression. But that was probably a feeble theory, for some men who work the hardest have nothing to express. An hypothesis with rather more plausibility in it now suggests itself. It is that men work simply in order to escape the depressing agony of contemplating life—that their work, like their play, is a mumbo-jumbo that serves them by permitting them to escape from reality. Both work and play, ordinarily, are illusions. Neither serves any solid and permanent purpose. If work has what is called value, then it only condemns more human beings to work. But life, stripped of such illusions, instantly becomes unbearable. Man cannot sit still, contemplating his destiny in this world, without going frantic. So he invents ways to take his mind off the horror. He works. He plays. He accumulates the preposterous nothing called property. He strives for the coy eye-wink called fame. He founds a family, and spreads his curse over others. All the while the thing that moves him is simply the yearning to lose himself, to forget himself, to escape the tragi-comedy that is himself. Life, fundamentally, is not worth living. So he confects artificialities to make it so. So he erects a gaudy structure to conceal the fact that it is *not* so.

Perhaps my talk of agonies and tragi-comedies may be a bit misleading. The basic fact about human existence is not that it is a tragedy, but that it is a bore. It is not so much a war as an endless standing in line. The objection to it is not that it is predominantly painful, but that it is lacking in sense. What is ahead for the race? Even theologians, to whom devils are easily visible, can see nothing but a gray emptiness, with a burst of irrational fireworks at the end. But there is such a thing as human progress. True. It is the progress that a felon makes from the watch-house to the jail, and from the jail to the death-house. Every generation faces the same intolerable boredom.

I speak as one who has had what must be regarded, speaking statistically, as a happy life. I work a great deal, but working is more agreeable to me than anything else I can imagine. I am conscious of no vast, overwhelming and unattainable desires. I want nothing that I can't get. But it remains my conclusion, at the gate of senility, that the whole thing is a grandiose futility, and not even amusing. The end is always a vanity, and usually a sordid one, without any noble touch of the pathetic. The means remain. In them lies a secret of what is called contentment, *i.e.*, the capacity to postpone suicide for at least another day. They are themselves without meaning, but at all events they offer a way of escape from the paralyzing reality. The central aim of life is to simulate extinction. We have been yelling up the wrong rain-spout.

3
On Controversy

Any man engaged habitually in controversy, as I have been for twenty years past, must enter upon his declining days with a melancholy sense of its hollowness and futility. Especially in this great Republic, where all ideas are suspect, it tends almost inevitably to degenerate into a mere exchange of nonsense. Have you ever examined carefully the speeches made by the candidates in a Presidential campaign? If so, you know that they are of bilge and blather all compact. Now and then, true enough, one of the august aspirants to the Washingtonian breeches is goaded or misled into saying something pungent and even apposite, but not often, not deliberately. His daily stint is simply balderdash.

It is rare, indeed, to encounter a controversialist who states his own case clearly, or who shows any sign of understanding his opponent's. Turn, for example, to the current combat between the Fundamentalists and the Modernists—an academic and puerile duel in our great Sodoms and Ninevehs, but raging like an oil fire in the Bible and Hookworm Belt, where men are he and Hell yawns. Both sides wallow in pishposh. The Fundamentalists, claiming a monopoly of faith, allege that they believe the whole Bible *verbatim et literatim*, which is not true, for at least 99% of them reject Exodus XXII, 18, to say nothing of I Timothy V, 23. And the Modernists argue that there is no conflict between science and Holy Writ, which is even less true. This controversy, in fact, is almost classical in character. Neither side is able to stick to the question at issue. Each tries to dispose of the other by delivering mighty wallops below the belt—the Fundamentalists by passing laws converting the Modernists into criminals (that is, as criminality is now defined by American jurisprudence), and the Modernists by depicting the Fundamentalists as a horde of gibbering baboons, sworn to uproot civilization and not above suspicion of cannibalism.

I have had a hand in this great battle of scattered wits myself, striving in an austere and lofty manner to introduce the sublime principles of Aristotle's "Organon" into it. I have got the traditional reward of one stopping to preach in front of a house afire. The more extreme Modernists—which is to say, the professional atheists,—discontented because I haven't advocated hanging the Fundamentalists, denounce me as a Crypto-Calvinist, and hold me up to obloquy in their papers. The Fundamentalists, suspecting me of a partiality for Darwin, accuse me of trying to upset the Ten Commandments, and one of the most eminent of them lately hinted that I have personally had a bout with No. 7, and come to grief in the manner described by the late Dr. Sylvanus Stall, in his well-known work on pathology, "What Every Boy of Fourteen Should Know." This last accusation was novel, but, as they run in such affairs, very mild. The usual charge against an opponent, in the

America of to-day, is that he is a Bolshevist, and in receipt of traitor's gold. It has been leveled at me so often that probably a majority of the persons who have heard of me at all believe it, and there are even dismal days when I half believe it myself, though I have been denouncing Socialism publicly for twenty years, and am, in fact, an incurable Tory in politics. A short while ago a Boston critic, becoming aware of the latter fact by some miracle, at once proceeded to denounce me because my radicalism, as he thought he had discovered, was bogus.

During the decade 1910–1920 I was chiefly engaged in literary controversies, and so my politics were aside from the issue. But when the great wave of idealism engulfed the United States in 1917, I was at once bawled out as a German spy, and open demands were made that my purely æsthetic heresies be put down by the *Polizei*. One of my opponents, in those days, was an eminent college professor, now unhappily deceased. He not only attempted to dispose of my literary judgments by arguing that they were inspired by the Kaiser; he even made the same charge against the works of the writers I was currently whooping up. And so did many of his learned colleagues. It was not easy to meet this onslaught by logical devices; logic, in those days, was completely adjourned, along with the Bill of Rights. Moreover, there was a considerable plausibility in the general charge. So I attempted no defense; it is, indeed, against my nature to take the defensive. Instead, I launched into an elaborate effort to prove that all college professors, regardless of their politics, were hollow and preposterous asses, and to this business I brought up all the ancient and horrifying devices of the art of rhetoric.

The issue of the controversy was characteristic: thus all combats in the realm of so-called ideas end. The moment the War to End War was over there came a revulsion against its blather, and so it was no longer damaging to me to be accused of taking the money of the Hohenzollern. Thus the professor I have mentioned suddenly found his principal ammunition gone, and in an effort to unearth more he began reading the books I had been advocating. To his surprise he found that many of them were works of high merit, whereupon he began whooping for them himself, and even going beyond my loudest hurrahs. In the end he was actually searching them for evidences of Teutonic influence, and hailing it with enthusiasm when found! His poor fellow-professors, meanwhile, were the goats. I ceased to revile them, once the war was over, and devoted myself mainly to political and moral concerns, but various other controversialists took up the jehad where I left off, and in a short time it was raging from coast to coast. It got far beyond anything I had myself dreamed of. Indignant publicists, quite unknown to me, began grouping all professors with chiropractors, Congressmen and spiritualists. In dozens of colleges large and small, North, East, South and West, the students began holding meetings and flinging insults at their tutors. Scores of college papers, for flouting them in contumacious terms, had to be suppressed. In several great institutions of learning the thing actually reached the form of physical assault. When the smoke cleared away the professor, once so highly respected by every one, found himself a sort of questionable character, and he remains so to this day. In many cases, I believe, he actually is, but surely not in all. The point is that the virtuous have suffered with the guilty. Many an honest and God-fearing professor, laboriously striving to ram his dismal nonsense into the progeny of Babbitts, is bombarded with ribald spit-balls as a result of a controversy which begun quite outside his ken and speedily got far beyond the issue between the original combatants.

Such are the ways of war in the psychic field. Why they should be so I don't know, but so they are. No controversy to my knowledge has ever ended on the ground where it began. Even the historic one between Huxley and Wilberforce, two of the most eminent men of their time in England, ranged all over the landscape before the contestants had enough. It began with Huxley trying to prove that Darwin's "Origin of Species" was a sound book; it ended with Bishop Wilberforce trying to prove that Huxley's grandfather was a gorilla. What was its issue? Did Huxley convert Wilberforce? Did Wilberforce make any dent in the armor of Huxley? I apologize for wasting your time with silly rhetorical questions. Did Luther convert Leo X? Did Grant convert Lee?

4
On Faith

Some time ago I received a letter from a learned Socialist, one very active in the movement, but long since retired. It was stuffed with circulars advertising a new sure cure for all human ills, from bellyache to cancer. This invention, the Socialist assured me, was no fake. He had personally seen it snatch back men and women from the brink of the grave. It would be in use everywhere, he said, and saving hundreds of thousands of lives a year, if it were not for the hellish conspiracies of the American Medical Association.

It all seemed familiar. More, it all seemed quite natural. For who has ever heard of a Socialist who did not also believe in some other quackery? I have known all of the principal gladiators of the movement in my time, at least in America; I have yet to meet one who was not as gullible as a Mississippi darkey, nay, even a Mississippi white man. Didn't Karl Marx himself carry a madstone and believe in astrology? If not, then it was strange indeed. Didn't Debs believe that quinine would cure a cold? If not, then he was not a genuine Socialist.

The leading living Socialist of this great Republic is Upton Sinclair. Perhaps, indeed, he is the only leader the movement has left, for Debs is dead, and most of the rest leaped down the sewers during the late war. Well, Sinclair believes in so many different kinds of nonsense that he needs two thick volumes to record them. He was one of the earliest believers in the fasting cure for catarrh, and he was one of the first dupes to be roped in by the late Dr. Albert Abrams, the San Francisco swindler. I do not hold all this against Sinclair: he is a charming fellow otherwise. I merely say that such credulity is natural to Socialists. Turn to England, where one of the late heroes of the movement is young Oliver Baldwin, son of the Prime Minister. Some time ago the Associated Press was reporting from London that Oliver had taken to spiritualism and was hearing "spirit voices coming from all parts of the room in no fewer than five languages."

As I have said, practically all of the more eminent Socialists of the United States took to the sewers in 1917. When the gunmen of the Hon. A. Mitchell Palmer began rounding up the

lesser comrades, and pliant Federal judges began sending them
to Atlanta for five, ten and twenty years, the high-toned members of the movement saw a great light, and began to bawl and
sob for the flag. Now, with the danger over, they can't get
back: the surviving comrades won't have anything to do with
them, and even denounce them bitterly as scabs. But if the
Marxian grove is thus closed to them, there is plenty of room
for them around other flambeaux, and all of them seem to be
crowding up. A considerable number, in 1920, became violent
Prohibitionists, and began predicting that the country would
be bone-dry in two years. Others became chiropractors. Yet
others announced that they were converted to the League of
Nations. Many became spiritualists, and a few, I believe, followed Sinclair in succumbing to Dr. Abrams. The rest went in
for free love, Fundamentalism, mental telepathy, the Harding
idealism, Texas oil stocks, numerology, the poetry of T. S.
Eliot, the music of Erik Satie, or the ouija board. One or two
became professional sorcerers. The point is that every last one
of them found some sort of satisfaction and solace for the imperative need of his nature—every one found something outlandish and preposterous to believe in. For all of them, as
ex-Socialist, had believing minds. They could get rid of their
Socialism, especially when helped by the *Polizei*, but they
could no more get rid of their believing minds than they could
get rid of the shapes of their heads. A Socialist, in brief, is simply a man suffering from an overwhelming compulsion to
believe what is not true. He yearns for it as a cow yearns for
the milkmaid, lowing in the cool of the evening. He pines for
it as a dry Congressman pines for a drink.

Of all the things that are palpably not true Socialism is one
of the most satisfying to men of that romantic kidney, and so
nine-tenths of them, at one time or another in their lives, are
Socialists, or, if not Socialists, then at least Progressives, or
Single Taxers, or evangelists of Farm Relief. But Socialism,
though it is sweet, is never enough for them, and neither is
the Single Tax. They always reach out for something else.
They always succumb to some other and worse Marx, with
longer whiskers and dirtier finger-nails. Years ago, when the
Single Taxers were still making a noise in the land, I made a
roster of the princes of the movement, setting down beside

each name the varieties of balderdash that its owner believed in. There was not a single name without two entries and some of them had a dozen. One of the leading Single Taxers was also president of the League for Medical Freedom, a verein of quacks organized to oppose vaccination. Another was militant anti-vivisectionist, and proposed that the Johns Hopkins Medical School be closed by the police. A third was an anthropophagous atheist of the kind that proselytes, especially among peaceable old ladies. A third was a table-tapper, and a fourth got messages from the ghosts of Martin Luther, Lucy Stone and Sitting Bull. A fifth deserted his wife for a cutie with pansy eyes, and lost, in consequence, his job as a college professor. A sixth, believing that he was Millard Fillmore, was put away by his family.

What lies beneath all this is simply an ancient fact, noted long ago by William James, and before him by Friedrich Wilhelm Nietzsche, and before him by the Greeks, and before the Greeks by the first human politicians. It is the fact that the race of men is divided sharply into two classes: those who are what James called tough-minded, and demand proofs before they will believe, and those who are what he called tender-minded, and are willing to believe anything that seems to be pleasant. It is the tender-minded who keep quacks of all sorts well-fed and active, and hence vastly augment the charm of this world. They find it wholly impossible to distinguish between what is subjectively agreeable and what is objectively true. Would it be nice if the whole world turned sober overnight, and even flappers put away the jug? If so, then there must be a quick and sure way to accomplish it. Does Prohibition promise to do so? If so, then Prohibition must be true. This is precisely the route by which Sinclair became a Prohibitionist—one of his follies that I forgot to mention above. And this is the route by which multitudes of his tender-hearted brethren and sistren followed him into the jaws of the Anti-Saloon League.

Socialism, while it was still vague and untested, appealed powerfully to all such persons. Fifteen or twenty years ago it was making immense progress in the United States, vice Free Silver, deceased. All the young college professors, in those days, were Socialists, as they are now eugenists and birth controllers. It swept and enchanted the tender-minded. Fat women wept over it, as they now weep over the Armenians. But one day it collided slambang with the harsh and horrible facts. One day it was put to the test in Russia,—and promptly blew up. Even the tender-minded could not dodge the appalling proofs. So they fled in this direction and that. Some took to spiritualism, some to chiropractic, some to Genesis. Some, like Sinclair, took to Prohibition, the Single Tax, fasting, and the electronic vibrations of Dr. Abrams. But not one, so far as I can make out, took to sense.

IV.
Clarion Call to Poets

ONE of the crying needs of the time in this incomparable Republic—the goal and despair of all other and hence lesser states—is for a suitable Burial Service for the admittedly damned. I speak as one who has of late attended the funeral orgies of several such gentlemen, each time to my æsthetic distress. The first of these gentlemen, having a great abhorrence of rhetoric in all its branches, left strict orders that not a word was to be said at his obsequies. The result was two extremely chilly and uncomfortable moments: when six of us walked into his house in utter silence and carried out his clay, and when we shoved it, in the same crawling silence, into the yawning firebox of the crematory. The whole business was somehow unnatural and even a shade indecent: it violated one of the most ancient sentiments of *Homo sapiens* to dispatch so charming a fellow in so cavalier a fashion. One felt almost irresistibly impelled to say good-by to him in some manner or other, if only, soldier fashion, by blowing a bugle and rolling a drum. Even the mortician, an eminent star of one of the most self-possessed of professions, looked a bit uneasy and ashamed.

The second funeral was even worse. The deceased had been a Socialist of the militantly anti-clerical variety, and threatened, on his death-bed, to leap from his coffin with roars if a clergyman were hired to snuffle over him. His widow accordingly asked two of his Socialist colleagues to address the mourners. They prepared for the business by resorting to a bootlegger, and in consequence both of them were garrulous and injudicious. One of them traced the career of Karl Marx in immense detail, and deduced from it a long series of lessons for ambitious American boys. The other, after first denouncing the New York *Times*, read twenty or thirty cantos of execrable poetry from the *Freethinker*. If the widow had not performed a series of very realistic sobs—leaning for support, I may add, upon a comrade who soon afterward succeeded to the rights of the deceased in her person and real estate—the ceremony would have been indistinguishable from a session of the House of Representatives.

The third funeral was conducted by Freemasons, who came in plug hats and with white aprons over their cow-catchers. They entered the house of mourning in a long file, with their hats held over their left breasts in the manner of a President reviewing an inaugural parade, and filed past the open coffin at a brisk parade march. As each passed he gave a swift, mechanical glance at the fallen brother: there was in it the somewhat metallic efficiency of an old hand. These Freemasons brought their own limousines and took a place in the funeral procession ahead of the hearse. At the cemetery they deployed around the grave, and as soon as the clergyman had finished his mumbo-jumbo, began a ceremonial of their own. Their leader, standing at the head of the grave with his plug hat on, first read a long series of quasi-theological generalities—to the general effect, so far as I could make out, that Freemasons are immune to Hell, as they are notoriously immune to hanging—, and then a brother at the foot of the grave replied. After that there was a slight pause, and in rather ragged chorus the rest of the brethren said "So mote it be!" This went on almost endlessly; I was heartily glad when it as over. The whole ceremony, in fact, was tedious and trashy. As for me, I'd rather have been planted by a Swedenborgian, whiskers and all. Or even by a grand goblin of the Ethical Culture Society.

What is needed, and what I bawl for politely, is a service that is free from the pious but unsupported asseverations that revolt so many of our best minds, and yet remains happily graceful and consoling. It will be very hard, I grant you, to concoct anything as lasciviously beautiful as the dithyrambs in the Book of Common prayer. Who wrote them originally I don't know, but whoever did it was a poet. They put the highly improbable into amazingly luscious words, and the palpably not-true into words even more caressing and disarming. It is impossible to listen to them, when they are intoned by a High Church rector of sepulchral gifts, without harboring a sneaking wish that, by some transcendental magic, they could throw off their lowly poetical character and take on the dignity and reliability of prose—in other words, that the departed could be actually imagined as leaping out of the grave on the Last

Morn, his split colloids all restored to their pristine complexity, his clothes neatly scoured and pressed, and every molecule of him thrilling with a wild surmise. I have felt this wish at the funerals of many virtuous and earnest brethren, whose sole sin was their refusal to swallow such anecdotes as the one in II Kings II, 23–24. It seems a pity that men of that sort should be doomed to Hell, and it seems an even greater pity that they should be laid away to the banal chin-music of humorless Freemasons and stewed Socialists.

But, so far as I know, no suitable last rites for them have ever been drawn up. Between the service in the Book of Common Prayer (and its various analogues, nearly all of them greatly inferior) and the maudlin mortuary dialogues of the Freemasons, Ku Kluxers, Knights of Pythias and other such assassins of beauty there is absolutely nothing. Even the professional agnostics, who are violently literary, have never produced anything worthy to be considered; their best is indistinguishable from the text of a flag-drill or high-school pageant. Thus the average American skeptic, when his time comes to return to earth, is commonly turned off with what, considering his prejudices, may be best described as a razzing. His widow, disinclined to risk scandal by burying him without any ceremonies at all, calls in the nearest clergyman, and the result is a lamentable comedy, creditable neither to honest faith nor to honest doubt. More than once, in attendance upon such an affair, I have observed a sardonic glitter in the eye of the pastor, especially when he came to the unequivocal statement that the deceased would infallibly rise again. Did he secretly doubt it? Or was he poking fun at a dead opponent, now persuaded of the truth of revelation at last? In either case there was something unpleasant in the spectacle. A suitable funeral for doubters, full of lovely poetry but devoid of any specific pronouncement on the subject of a future life, would make such unpleasantness unnecessary.

We have the poets for the job, and I incline to suspect that their private theological ideas fit them for it. Skepticism, in fact, runs with their cynical trade. Most Americans, as every one knows, give their ecclesiastical affiliations in "Who's Who in America"—especially Congressmen, pedagogues, bank presidents and uplifters. But not the poets. The sole exception, so far as I can make out, is Vachel Lindsay, who reports that he is a member of the "Christian (Disciples) Church," a powerful sect in the No-More-Scrub-Bulls Belt, with a private Hell of its own, deep and hot. Even Edgar Albert Guest is silent on the subject, though he mentions the fact that he is a 33° Mason. Frost, Robinson, Sandburg and Masters keep suspiciously mum. I suggest that they meet in some quiet saloon and draw up the ritual I advocate. Let Masters be chairman of the committee: he is a lawyer as well as a poet, and may be trusted to keep within the statutes. And let Edna St. Vincent Millay be added to give the thing a refined voluptuousness, and James Weldon Johnson to put music into it, that it may be intoned without getting the celebrant out of breath. Here Holy Church shows the way. Its funeral service is a great deal less forensic than operatic.

There is some need, too, for a Marriage Service for the damned, and at different times attempts have been made to supply it. But all such works seem to emanate from radicals showing a characteristic lack of humor—and humor is as necessary to a Marriage Service as poetry is to a Funeral Service: a fact that the astute authors of the Book of Common Prayer did not overlook. However, the need here is not pressing, for in most American States civil marriage is sufficient, and heretics may be safely united without going before a sorcerer at all. Court clerks and police magistrates perform the job, mumbling unintelligibly out of a mysterious book, perhaps only a stolen Gideon Bible, excavated to hold cigarettes. The main thing is to pay the fee. Marriages after midnight cost double, and if the bridegroom has the fumes of wine in his head, he is apt to lose his watch as well as his liberty.

As I say, the Marriage Services drawn up by antinomians for the use of unbelievers lack humor. Worse, they are full of indignation—against the common theory that a wife is bound to give some care to her husband's goods, against the convention that she shall adopt his surname, and so on. It is hard to give serious attention to such grim notions at a time immemorially viewed as festive and jocose. One hears frequently of wedding guests getting drunk and fighting—not long ago a Methodist pastor in Missouri was protesting against it publicly—, but when they are drawn into sociological controversy it is too much. Such revolutionary Marriage Services, in point of fact, have never gained much popularity. Now and then a pair of Socialists resorts to one, but even Socialists appear to prefer the harsh, mechanical offices of a court clerk.

Nor is there any active demand for a non-theological Baptismal Service. I am constantly amazed, as a bachelor, by the number of children growing up, in these iconoclastic modern days, without any formal naming at all. Not only do heretics spurn the ceremony; even professing Christians often neglect it. In my own nonage practically all babies, at least of the more respectable tribes of the race, were christened. There was a general feeling that failing to put them through the sacrament was, in some obscure way, a tort against them—that it would bring them bad luck, and perhaps lead to difficulties in after life. It is so believed to this day nearly everywhere in Europe, and for sound reasons. Whenever a citizen in those decaying lands comes into contact with the state, which is very often, its agents demand his baptismal certificate as well as his birth certificate. So far, the imbeciles at Washington have not come to that, but it must be plain that they will come to it soon or late, and when the time is finally upon us there will be trouble for all those Americanos whose naming is now trusted to acclamation. They will have to dig up senile aunts and uncles, and produce affidavits that they were known to every one as so-and-so at some date far in the past, just as they now have to get such affidavits, more often than not, when they want passports. The bureaucracy grinds slowly, but it grinds exceeding fine. Recruited from the mentally deficient, it runs to circular insanities. Let it be proved to-morrow that some John Doe, suspected of favoring the recognition of Russia, was actually baptized Johannes, and it will be sufficient excuse for a regulation requiring all of us to prove that we are legally entitled to the names we sign to checks.

But all these are side issues. The main thing is that the poets, though most of them seem to have departed from the precincts and protection of Holy Church and her schismatic colonies—since when has a first-rate American poet written a hymn?—have failed, so far, to rise to the occasion when, even among heretics, poets are most pressingly needed. I have suggested that they meet in some convenient speak-easy and remedy the lack gloriously, but I don't insist, of course, that their service for the doubting dead be wholly original. The authors of the Book of Common Prayer, though they were poets of great talent, certainly did not trust only to their private inspiration. They borrowed copiously from the old missals, and they borrowed, too, directly from Holy Writ. What they concocted finally was a composite, but it was very discreetly and delicately put together, and remains impregnable to this day, despite many furious efforts to undo it.

All I propose is that the committee of poets imitate them, but with an avoidance of strophes objectionable in doctrine. Isn't there material enough in the books? There is enough, and to spare. I point to the works of Walt Whitman, now at last passing freely through the mails—to those parts, of course, of a non-erotic and non-political nature. I point to certain memorable stanzas of William Cullen Bryant. I point to Blake, Tennyson, Milton, Shelley, Keats, even Swinburne; what gaudy stuff for the purpose is in "Ave Atque Vale," "Tristram of Lyonesse" and "Atalanta in Calydon"! There is here a sweet soothing, a healing reassurance, a divine booziness—in brief, all the stuff of A No. 1 poetry. It would bring comfort, I believe, to many a poor widow who now groans as the Freemasons intone their balderdash, or flounces her veil, fidgets and blushes as a Socialist orator denounces Omnipotence for permitting stock dividends—it would bring her a great deal more comfort, certainly, than the positive statement, made defiantly by the unwilling rector of the parish, that her departed John, having been colloidal and as the beasts, has now become gaseous and immortal. Such a libretto for the inescapable last act would be humane and valuable. I renew my suggestion that the poets spit upon their hands and confect it at once.

V.
Souvenirs of a Book Reviewer

I
The Emperor of Wowsers

ANTHONY COMSTOCK: ROUNDSMAN OF THE LORD, by Heywood Broun and Margaret Leech. New York: *Albert & Charles Boni.* [Books, March 6, 1927.]

IN an appendix to this amusing and instructive work, Mr. Broun states the case against comstockery in a neat, realistic and unanswerable manner, but the book itself is by no means a philippic against old Anthony. On the contrary, it deals with him in a very humane and even ingratiating way. And why not? He was, in point of fact, a man of manifold virtues, and even his faults showed a rugged, Berserker quality that was sneakingly charming. It is quite impossible, at this distance, to doubt his *bona fides*, and almost as difficult, despite his notorious extravagances, to question his essential sanity. Like all the rest of us in our several ways, he was simply a damned fool. Starting out in life with an idea lying well within the bounds of what most men would call the rational, he gradually pumped it up until it bulged over all four borders. But he never departed from it altogether; he never let go his hold upon logic; he never abandoned reason for mere intuition. Once his premises were granted, the only way to escape his conclusions was to forsake Aristotle for Epicurus. Such logical impeccability, as all connoisseurs must know, is very common among theologians; they hold, indeed, almost a monopoly of it. The rest of us, finding that our ratiocination is leading us into uncomfortable waters, give it the slip and return to dry land. But not the theologians. They have horribly literal minds; they are less men than intellectual machines. I defy any one to find a logical flaw in their proofs of the existence of Hell. They demonstrate it magnificently and irrefutably. Do multitudes of wise men nevertheless deny it? Then that is only because very few wise men have any honest belief in the reality of the thing that the theologians and other logicians call truth.

Mr. Broun, in his appendix, tries to find holes in Anthony's logic, but it turns out to be far from easy: what he arrives at, in the end, is mainly only proof that a logician is an immensely unpleasant fellow. Turn, for example, to a typical and very familiar comstockian syllogism. First premiss: The effect of sexual images, upon the young, is to induce auto-erotism. Second premiss: the effects of auto-erotism are idiocy, epilepsy and locomotor ataxia. *Ergo*, now is the time for all good men to put down every book or picture likely to evoke sexual images. What is wrong with all this? Simply that Mr. Broun and you and I belong to a later generation than Anthony's, and are thus skeptical of his premisses. But let us not forget that they were true for him. His first came out of the hard, incontrovertible experience of a Puritan farm-boy, in executive session behind the barn. His second was supported, when he was getting his education, by the almost unanimous medical opinion of Christendom. And so his conclusion was perfect. We have made no progress in logic since his time; we have simply made progress in skepticism. All his grand truths are now dubious, and most of them are laughed at even by sucklings.

I think that he himself had a great deal to do with upsetting them. The service that he performed, in his grandiose way, was no more than a magnification of the service that is performed every day by multitudes of humble Y.M.C.A. secretaries, evangelical clergymen, and other such lowly fauna. It is their function in the world to ruin their ideas by believing in them and living them. Striving sincerely to be patterns to the young, they suffer the ironical fate of becoming horrible examples. I remember very well, how, as a boy of ten, I was articled to the Y.M.C.A.: the aim was to improve my taste for respectability, and so curb my apparently natural flair for the art and mystery of the highwayman. But a few months of contact with the official representatives of that great organization filled me with a vast loathing, not only for the men themselves, but also for all the ideas they stood for. Thus, at the age of eleven, I abandoned Christian Endeavor forevermore, and have been an antinomian ever since, contumacious to holy men and resigned to Hell. Old Anthony, I believe, accomplished much the same thing that the Y.M.C.A. achieved with me, but on an immeasurably larger scale. He did more than any other man to ruin Puritanism in the United States. When he began his long and brilliant career of unwitting sabotage, the essential principles of comstockery were believed in by practically every reputable American. Half a century later, when he went upon the shelf, comstockery enjoyed a degree of public esteem, at least in the big cities, halfway between that enjoyed by phrenology and that enjoyed by homosexuality. It was, at best, laughable. It was, at worst, revolting.

So much did one consecrated man achieve in the short span of his life. I believe that it was no mean accomplishment. Anthony managed it, not because there was any unusual ability in him, but simply because he had a congenital talent for giving shows. The fellow, in his way, was a sort of Barnum. A band naturally followed him, playing in time to his yells. He could not undertake even so banal a business as raiding a dealer in abortifacient pills without giving it the melodramatic air of a battle with a brontosaurus. So a crowd always followed him, and when he made a colossal ass of himself, which was very frequently, the fact was bruited about. Years of such gargantuan endeavor made him one of the national clowns—and his cause one of the national jokes. In precisely the same way, I believe, such gaudy zanies as the Rev. Dr. Billy Sunday and the Rev. John Roach Straton are ruining the evangelical demonology in the Bible Belt. They make so much uproar that no one can fail to notice them. The young peasants, observing them, are gradually enlightened by them—unintentionally, but none the less surely. The men themselves are obviously charlatans; *ergo*, their ideas must be fraudulent too. What has been the net effect of the Scopes trial, with its solemn martyrdom of William Jennings Bryan? Its chief effect seems to be that societies of young atheists are now flourishing in all the Southern colleges. Has the study of Darwin been put down? Far from it. Darwin is now being read below the Potomac, and by the flower of Christian youth, as assiduously as "Only a Boy" used to be read in New York in the great days of Anthony's historic offensive against it.

Comstockery, of course, still lives, but it must be manifest that its glories have greatly faded. There is, anon, a series of raids and uproars, but they soon pass, and the work of the Devil goes on. It would be hard to imagine Anthony taking

orders from district attorneys, or going into amicable conference with his enemies (and God's), or consenting to the appointment of joint committees (mainly made up of obvious
anti-Puritans) to discover and protect the least dirty among
the dirty plays of Broadway; he would have raided them all,
single-handed and alone. His heirs and assigns are far milder
men, and hence, I sometimes fear, more dangerous. Their
sweet reasonableness is disarming; it tends to conceal the fact
that they are nevertheless blue-noses at heart, and quite as eager to harry and harass the rest of us as Anthony was. Those
opponents who now parley with them had better remember
the warning against making truces with Adam-Zad. They may
end by restoring to comstockery some of its old respectability,
and so throw us back to where we were during the Grant
administration. I sound the warning and pass on. It will take,
at best, a long time, and I'll be beyond all hope or caring
before it is accomplished. For Anthony's ghost still stalks the
scenes of his old endeavors, to plague and palsy his successors.
His name has given a term of opprobrium to the common
tongue. Dead, and—as Mr. Broun and Miss Leech so beautifully suggest, an angel with harp, wings and muttonchops—he
is yet as alive as Pecksniff, Chadband or Elmer Gantry.

Well, here is his story, done fully, competently, and with
excellent manners. There is much in it that you will not find
in the earlier biography by Charles Gallaudet Trumbull, for
Trumbull wrote for the Sunday-schools, and so had to do a lot
of pious dodging and snuffling. The additional facts that Mr.
Broun and Miss Leech set forth are often very amusing, but I
must add at once that they are seldom discreditable. Old Anthony was preposterous, but not dishonest. He believed in his
idiotic postulates as devotedly as a Tennessee Baptist believes
that a horse-hair put into a bottle of water will turn into a
snake. His life, as he saw it, was one of sacrifice for righteousness. Born with a natural gift for the wholesale drygoods
trade, he might have wrung a fortune from its practice, and so
won an heroic equestrian statue in the Cathedral of St. John
the Divine. Perhaps there were blue days when regret crept
over him, shaking his Christian resolution. His muttonchop
whiskers, the stigma and trademark of the merchant princes of
his era, had a pathetic, Freudian smack. But I don't think he

wobbled often. The Lord was always back of him, guiding and stimulating his fighting arm. So he was content to live in a drab suburb on the revenues of a second-rate lawyer, with his elderly, terrified wife and his half-witted foster-daughter. There was never any hint, in that humble home, of the gaudy connubial debaucheries that the modern sex hygienists describe so eloquently. Anthony had to go outside for his fun. Comstockery was his corner saloon.

I confess to a great liking for the old imbecile. He is one of my favorite characters in American history, along with Frances E. Willard, Daniel Drew and Brigham Young. He added a great deal to the joys of life in the Federal Republic. More than any other man, he liberated American letters from the blight of Puritanism.

2
Thwacks From the Motherland

THE BABBITT WARREN, by C.E.M. Joad. New York: *Harper & Brothers*. [The Nation, April 20, 1927.]

Mr. Joad, who is a philosopher by trade, prefaces his thunderous philippic against all things Yankee and accursed with a disarming quotation from the late Filippo G. Bruno, of Nola, Italy: "*Se non è vero, è ben trovato.*" He needs this plea in confession and avoidance, and very badly, for he admits frankly that he "has not had the privilege of visiting the United States," and the fact is visible on almost every page of his book. Much of the evidence he relies on, indeed, seems to have been derived from the travelers' tales of returning English actors and the confidences of the more humorous and ingenious members of the corps of cabin-stewards of the Cunard line. Thus, on page 83, he begins a long diatribe with the postulate that "the films are the literature of America"—which is to say, the *only* literature—and on page 89 he permits himself the grave announcement that the lamented J. Gordon Coogler was "the one famous Southern American poet." The one criterion of eminence in the Republic, according to the agents he appears to trust, is money. "The artist, the scientist, the musician, the statesman, and the author are held of no account unless their claims to consideration are backed by money." A rich man, regardless of his private virtue, "is king of any company he chooses to enter." This preëminence, it seems, takes on a transcendental character, and so works miracles. "Thus a rich man who had lost his eye recently purchased another from a poor man, the transfer of optics being hailed as a marvel of medical science." And no wonder!

But it is not necessary to swallow all of Mr. Joad's evidence in order to discuss his conclusions. They are, in brief, that the machine civilization which now threatens the whole world has reached its highest development in the United States, that the influence of American gold is rapidly extending it, and that if its proliferation is not checked it will destroy most the values that men have cherished for ten thousand years. I see nothing against reason here. The facts, in truth, are apparent to every one, and even some of the most startling testimony that Mr. Joad introduces, though it is not true, is at least consonant with what is. We have surely not yet come to the pass that "a rich man is king of any company he chooses to enter," but we have certainly developed a respect for bare money which goes far beyond the bounds of the seemly and ordinate. I know of no other country in which the hollow imbecilities of a Judge Gary would get the respect they got here, nor in which so preposterous a vacuum as Andy Mellon would be venerated as a great statesman. The English also bend the knee to men of money, and so do the Germans and the French, but they have not yet come to the point of mistaking them for philosophers. The English had a fair chance to venerate Otto H. Kahn, but seem to have muffed him. The Germans, I fear, if Charlie Schwab went to live and make speeches among them, would regard him as a comic character. Even the Portuguese, Serbs, Rumanians, and Greeks would probably laugh at Cal.

Thus Mr. Joad is often right in essence, even when he is wrong in his specification. It is not true, literally, that J. Gordon Cooglar was "the one famous Southern American poet," but nevertheless there is an inner plausibility in the dictum that makes it somehow disconcerting: if the majority of Southern fanciers had their way it *would* be true. Similarly, it is not true, literally, that the dreadful bilge of the movie-parlors is the only American literature now in being, but there remains an uncomfortable possibility that it may be true on some not distant to-morrow. Try to put together a list of American imaginative authors, all of the first chop, who have never taken the film shilling. I can think of Cabell and Sherwood Anderson, but there I begin to wabble; the complete roster is surely not long. The rest of the scrivening boys and girls have all submitted to the loathsome embraces of the Hollywood art-fosterers. The effects of this psychic fornication are not concealed from Mr. Joad's eyes. The movie rubber-stamp, he observes, begins to show itself upon even the swellest varieties of our national swell letters. The self-same novelists who, but a decade and a half ago, swore upon Alps of Bibles (and meant it) that they'd never yield to the foul caresses of Hamilton Wright Mabie and Anthony Comstock—these same novelists, planning their masterpieces to-day, find it a sheer impossibility to rid themselves of sneaking, Freudian thoughts of Gloria Swanson and Jack Gilbert. It is sad, but it is *vero*.

Such sadnesses fill Mr. Joad's tome—an instructive work, but extremely depressing. Purge it of all its errors of fact— some of them really shocking—and its general thesis remains defensible. More, its general thesis remains a fair statement of the view of the Republic held by civilized Europeans. That view is not only critical; it is downright indignant. We are, it appears, not only a nation of barbarians; we are actually hard to distinguish from criminals. Unless we are dissuaded from our course by remonstrance, and, if remonstrance fails, by a resort to *force majeure*, the civilization that men have been struggling for since the dawn of history will go to pot. The wisdom of the late Gary will supplant that of Plato and Aristotle; Henry Ford will displace Thucydides; Luther and St. Francis will be shelved for the Rev. Dr. Billy Sunday and the beauteous Aimée Semple McPherson; the epic and the sonnet will be alike engulfed by the scenario; and the whole world will read the *Saturday Evening Post.* I do not argue that these transformations would ruin humanity, or that they are sure to come to pass; I merely report that a fear of them is widespread in the world. Mr. Joad simply puts into a convenient book, weighing exactly one pound (it is printed on feather-weight paper), what gnaws at the hearts of hundreds of thousands of the European *intelligentsia*. One cannot pick up an English

newspaper without getting some flavor of that dread and indignation. It is an ironical situation, and no doubt full of lessons for specialists in the historical and ethical sciences. The
Yankee saved civilization, and now civilization damns him to
Hell. He put down the accursed Hun, and now the Hun,
compared to him, becomes an archangel. As a professional patriot I resent all this. But on days when my patriotism passes a
dividend I confess that I am consoled by certain *pizzicato*
snickers, or, as they say in the Motherland, sniggers.

3
The Powers of the Air

THE HISTORY OF WITCHCRAFT AND DEMONOLOGY, by Montague
Summers. New York: *Alfred A. Knopf.* [The American Mercury,
May, 1927.]

This tome is learned, honest and amusing. Its author, an English clergyman—his full name is the Rev. Alphonsus Joseph-
Mary Augustus Montague, M.A.—wastes no time trying to
reconcile religion and science, a folly that has brought so many
American scientists, including the eminent but mushy Dr.
Robert Andrews Millikan, to grief. He is in favor of religion,
not of science, and with it, in the manner of a true believer, he
goes the whole hog. Does Exodus XXII, 18, say flatly that
witches exist, and that it is the duty of every righteous man to
butcher them when found? Then Dr. Summers accepts the
fact and the duty without evasion, and proceeds to elaborate
on both. He can't imagine a Christian who refuses to believe
in demoniacal possession, and no more can I. Marshaling an
array of proofs that must shake even an atheistic archbishop,
he demonstrates with fine eloquence and impeccable logic that
the air is full of sinister spirits, and that it is their constant
effort to enter into the bodies of men and women, and so convert good Christians, made in God's image, into witches, sorcerers, spiritualists, biologists, and other such revolting shapes.
The Bible is the rock of his argument, but he also makes frequent and very effective use of the revelations vouchsafed to
Holy Church. There has never been a time in Christian history, he shows, when its chief experts and wiseacres did not
believe in demons. The Roman rite, accepting their existence

as indubitable, provides elaborate machinery for their scotch-ing to this day. That machinery, to be sure, is not put into effect lightly. So long as the medical faculty is convinced that the patient is suffering from nothing worse than a leaping tapeworm or delirium tremens, and hope of his cure by chem-ical and mechanical means is thus held out, he is resigned to the secular arm. But once it becomes manifest that a fiend or goblin has got into him, the business becomes a matter for su-pernatural intervention, and the subsequent proceedings must be carried on by an ordained pastor, and according to a for-mula set forth in the "Rituale Romanum," and in use since the pontificate of Peter I.

This formula is extremely complicated, and I suspect that using it must be somewhat fatiguing to the officiating clergy-man. He must be himself a man of mature years, guiltless of anything even approaching loose living, and, according to Mr. Summers, "a systematic student, and well versed in the latest trends and developments of psychological science." He is re-quired to make himself quite sure, before he begins his exor-cism, that the patient before him is actually possessed by a demon—that he is not confronting a mere case of insanity, or, worse still, imposture. Once convinced, he proceeds with the utmost heat and diligence, never relenting until the unclean spirit takes wing, and so returns to Hell. Mr. Summers gives the words of the exorcism, translated into English; they are so terrifying that I hesitate to reprint them in a volume designed for reading aloud at the domestic hearth. The demon is de-nounced in words that sting like scorpions: no Baptist pastor, damning Clarence Darrow, ever scorched the air with worse. And if, at the first attack, they fail to dislodge him they are to be used again, and then again, and so on until the exorcism is completed. The patient, it appears, is apt to fall asleep while they are being intoned: making him do so is one of the Devil's favorite tricks. If it happens, then the exorcist must awaken him, and by any device that seems workable, including smart blows *a posteriori*. Ordinarily, all this must be done in a church, but if the patient is too ill to leave his bed the exorcist may visit him in his own boarding-house. Idle spectators are forbidden, but the canon requires that, as at a baptism or electrocution, a number of official witnesses, of known piety and sober mien, shall be present. No unnecessary conversation with the demon is permitted. If he speaks through the mouth of the patient, he is to be heard politely, but when he has had a sufficient say he is to be shut off. In particular, he is not to be permitted to indulge in ribaldries.

It is commonly believed that Protestantism questions the actuality of demoniacal possession, but this is not so. True enough, the Unitarians and Universalists have doubts about it, but so far as I am aware no other Protestant sect has ever formally repudiated it. There is a canon of the Church of England which forbids a priest to exorcise demons without the "license or direction (*mandatum*)" of his Bishop, but there is nothing to prevent a Bishop issuing such a *mandatum*. If Bishop Manning became convinced tomorrow that Sinclair Lewis or any other such antinomian was possessed, he could, I believe, give Dr. William N. Guthrie a *mandatum* to exorcise the invading gaseous organism. I do not allege that Dr. Manning would do it or that Dr. Guthrie would take advantage of the license; all I argue is that the transaction would lie within the confines of canon law. The Lutherans, who are very orthodox, all believe in demoniacal possession, and hence, by a necessary inference, in witches; if they did not they would have to put Martin Luther down as a liar. As for the Methodists, the Baptists and other such proletarians of the Lord, it must be obvious that doubts among them are confined to a few advanced intellectuals, debauched by reading the epicurean poetry of Edgar A. Guest. The Baptists, at least in the South, even believe in ghosts, especially the colored brethren. The colored pastors have an elaborate ceremonial for exorcising all varieties of spirits, good or evil; an important part of it is the free-will offering just before the curative anathema is launched. In my own native republic, the Saorstát Maryland, I once made an attempt to ascertain the number of people, regardless of creed, who believed in ghosts and witches. After elaborate inquiries through prudent agents, I came to the conclusion that 92% of the population believed in ghosts, and that 74% also believed in witches. In the latter group was the then Governor of the State. He believed that rheumatism was caused by witchcraft, and wore a string around his middle to ward it off. The Marylanders are a gay and liberty-loving people, and drink and drab, perhaps, somewhat more than is good for them, but atheism has never made much progress among them. At least one of the eminent professors in the Johns Hopkins Medical School, at Baltimore, has been publicly accused of believing in witches, and has never, so far as I know, made a categorical denial of it.

Dr. Summers is equally honest, and I think he deserves all praise for being so. Most ecclesiastics, when they write upon such subjects, try to evade the clear issue. They seem to be convinced—on what ground I don't know—that the old belief in demons is now dying out in the world, and to be afraid that they will be laughed at if they confess to it. All I can say is that that is a poor way to get into Heaven *post mortem*. Such duckers and skulkers, you may be sure, will have extremely unpleasant sessions with St. Peter when they reach the Gates, and Peter will be well justified in razzing them. Either the Christian religion involves a belief in disembodied powers, good and evil, or it doesn't. If it doesn't, then its Sacred Scriptures are a mass of nonsense, and even its Founder was grossly misinformed. If it does, then every one adhering to it ought to confess the fact frankly, and without ignominious equivocation. This is what Dr. Summers does. In detail, his colleagues in theology may sometimes reasonably challenge him, as when, for example, he lays down the doctrine that the heaving of tables at spiritualist séances is performed by demons from Hell. But his fundamental postulates stand beyond refutation. If he is wrong, then the whole science of Christian theology is a degraded imposture—something which no right-thinking, law-abiding, home-loving American, I am sure, will want to allege. I rejoice to find a holy man so forthright and courageous, and so irresistibly convincing. He has rescued demonology from its long neglect, and restored it to its old high place among the sacred sciences. What a knock-out he would be on an American lecture tour! I offer him $1,000 in advance for his Jackson, Miss., house, with an offer of the fattest pastorate in the town thrown in.

4
To the Glory of an Artist

LIFE AND LETTERS OF HENRY WILLIAM THOMAS, MIXOLOGIST,
by Various Hands. Washington: *Privately Printed.* [The American
Mercury, February, 1927.]

This entertaining and instructive work is, in form, a *Fest-schrift* in honor of Mr. Thomas, for many years one of the most eminent of Washington bartenders. He pontificated, in the closing days of the Bill of Rights (*selig!*), in various celebrated Washington bars, including Loehl's, Shoomaker's, Arman's, and George Driver's, and those of the Shoreham, Willard, Raleigh and Metropolitan Hotels. His longest term of service was at Driver's, which was the first really high-toned saloon encountered in Pennsylvania avenue as one left the halls of Congress. Here his clients included all the most distinguished statesmen of the Republic, and many of its heroic warriors, gifted publicists and opulent men of affairs. His acquaintance among such men was wide and intimate: he lived in an atmosphere of greatness that was denser and more exhilarating, even, than that surrounding Col. George B. M. Harvey or Dr. Otto H. Kahn. His professional or bedside manner, like that of every other salient man of his craft, was delicate, discreet and judicious. If a Congressman, coming in from a committee meeting, raced his metabolism by drinking too fast and so began to blab high matters of state, Mr. Thomas would knock him off with a reliable silencer, and save him from ruin. If a Senator came in with a constituent who seemed suspiciously Christian, Mr. Thomas would express regret at not having seen him (the Senator) for a long, long time. If even higher dignitaries began to sway dizzily and clutch the bar-rail, Mr. Thomas would summon a pair of trustworthy Negroes and have them carted home. Such thoughtfulness and humanity, when combined with a high professional competence, naturally made him popular in the town, and when the Methodist Board of Temperance, Prohibition and Public Morals supplanted Congress in the government of the District, and all the saloons were closed, and Mr. Thomas moved out to Chevy Chase, and began serving limeade and coca-cola at what was once the bar of the club there—when these events fell like thunderclaps there was widespread woe in the highest circles, and congressional funerals began to multiply. Now his surviving friends, to honor him in his declining years, print the present *Festschrift*.

It is a mellow and charming volume, and the pity is that it is printed for private circulation only, and will thus not get into the public libraries, for the instruction of future generations. Prohibition, as every one knows, has not actually cut off the supply of strong drink, nor has it diminished the consumption. On the contrary, it has made drinking more common than ever before, especially among the young. But the young miss something that their fathers enjoyed: the privilege of contact with amiable and accomplished bartenders. They drink in washrooms, surrounded by bootblacks, busboys and subway tiles; their fathers drank in front of mahogany bars, with men of the world serving them. In the more high-toned of the old-time saloons American civilization, such as it is, probably reached its highest point. The society was of the best. The most obscure man, if he were decently clad, could meet United States Senators, the Governors of great States, men distinguished in all the arts and sciences, and the principal industrial and financial heads of the nation. It was a charming and admirable school for youngsters just coming to maturity, not only in manners but also in all the ideas and fancies that engrossed the superior minority. They heard the great problems of statecraft discussed in an offhand and confidential way. They saw notable men in mufti, so to speak, with their cares laid off, and their minds functioning brilliantly. They came into contact with every class making up the world of affairs, from members of the Cabinet to champion pugilists, and from scientific men of the first caliber to the greatest artists and manufacturers of the nation. All this was especially true in Washington. The saloons of that town, during the half century before Prohibition, were the true centers of its intellectual activity. Its great men frequented them incessantly. They entertained all its eminent guests. Naturally enough, such customers would shrink from being served by roughnecks: they demanded bartenders of the highest skill and most delicate prudence. Such a bartender was Henry

William Thomas. The statesmen and others who have collabo-
rated in the *Festschrift* in his honor do honor to themselves.

The volume is small, as befits the modesty of the man whose
virtues it celebrates, but it is packed with good things. It opens
with a series of quotations from the greatest authors of all time
—Homer, Shakespeare, Cervantes and so on—, every one of
them a conscientious wet. Lesser men are also included—
Longfellow, Sheridan, Villon, Irving, Pepys, Omar, Horace,
Ben Johnson and company—all of them equally wet. There
follows a series of original toasts by some of the collaborators
in the *Festschrift*, and after that comes a page of music and a
sketch of the life and times of Mr. Thomas. Some curious details are in it, and not a few of them are pathetic. In the days of
his service at Driver's, it appears, the common price of French
and Italian vermouth, in case lots, was $6 a case. Absinthe cost
$15 a case, and the best gins were obtainable at from $10 to
$18. Scotch ran from $14 to $30, and rye from $6 to $16.
Fourteen-year-old brandy cost $20, and sixty-year-old brandy
$50. The booticians of to-day, though they gradually perfect
their art, will never be able to offer sound goods at such prices.
If, by the end of the fifth or sixth Coolidge administration,
Scotch drops to $50 a case, as the public relations counsel of
the New York booters lately predicted, it will still cost four
times as much as the average Scotch of Mr. Thomas' prime.
Moreover, it will be inferior in quality. Such bars as Driver's
served only the choicest goods. They didn't buy labels, but
Scotch. To-day it runs the other way. The last part of the
Festschrift is given over to a long and voluptuous discussion of
the drinks that Mr. Thomas used to compound. Many of the
materials mentioned are almost unobtainable to-day. The
booters bring in plenty of so-called Scotch whiskey and English gin, and immense supplies of highly dubious champagne,
but it would be hard, I believe, to find one able to furnish a
plausible Sloe gin, or a sound Hollands, or a genuine St. Croix
rum. Such delicatessen have simply gone out of the répertoire.
They have gone out with the old-time bartenders—men of
fine feelings and high gifts, their lives consecrated to an art
that made men happy. Of these great craftsmen Mr. Thomas
was one of the best. The frontispiece of the *Festschrift* shows
him as he is to-day, still vigorous and handsome, but with the

light of tragedy in his eyes. He looks as Shakespeare would have looked had he (Shakespeare) lived into the bleak, sour days of the Commonwealth. He looks as Washington would have looked if he had lived to see Coolidge.

5
God Help the South!

THE ADVANCING SOUTH, by Edwin Mims. Garden City, L. I.: *Doubleday, Page & Company* [The American Mercury, August, 1926.]

Dr. Mims, who hails from Arkansas, is professor of English at Vanderbilt University, in the great Christian *Polizeistaat* of Tennessee, and a member of the Joint Hymn-Book Committee of the Methodist Episcopal Church. He has lectured at Chautauqua, N.Y., and is secretary of the Tennessee Law and Order League. He thus makes the grade, by Southern standards, as a critic of literature and life. But in the less Christian North, I suspect, there will be scoffers to cavil at him, especially when it is noted that he is very suspicious of James Branch Cabell, and in fact puts Ellen Glasgow above him. And even in the South there will be heretics to repine that a more competent and sympathetic historian was not found to tell the story of their heroic (and perhaps vain) struggle to haul the Confederacy out of its wallow. For the good Dr. Mims, despite a laudable diligence and a high degree of uplifting enthusiasm, constantly gives one the impression of a scrivener laboring valiantly with a theme that he doesn't quite understand. Perhaps I may throw some light upon his equipment by observing that, when he comes to discuss Southern journalists, he has high and sweet praises for the late Mooney of Memphis, the most passionate defender of the Bryan theological imbecilities ever heard of even in Tennessee, and not a word for Hall of Montgomery, Wright of Columbia, S.C., Jaffe of Norfolk, Dabney of Richmond, or Sanders of Mooney's own town. In brief, Dr. Mims seems to know little more about the current journalistic situation in the South, and hence about the political and cultural situation, than a somewhat advanced village schoolma'm. He has heard of Johnson of Greensboro, now that Johnson has left the South, and of Harris of Columbus, Ga., now that Harris has the Pulitzer prize, and of such women as Miss Frances Newman, Miss Nell Battle Lewis and Miss Sara Haardt, now that the North has discovered them, but one cannot escape the suspicion that they were outside his ken in the days of their first and hardest labors, as their heirs and assigns are outside his ken to-day. Call me a Union spy if you will, but I give you my solemn word that in his book of 319 pages, devoted largely, if not principally, to the renaissance of literary endeavor below the Potomac, there is absolutely no mention of Emily Clark, of Richmond, founder of the *Reviewer*! Or of Mrs. Julia Peterkin! Or of T. S. Stribling! Or of Clement Wood! Or of J. W. Krutch!

It is, perhaps, the worst of all the curses of the South that it is interpreted for the nation by just such depressing obfuscators. They love it as no Scotsman ever loved his smoky crags, and their yearning to see it go forward has all the violent passion of an evangelical religion, but they are seldom clear as to what is the matter with it, and they seldom differentiate accurately between its genuinely enlightened leaders—mainly young and extremely unpopular—and its mere windjammers. Dr. Mims, I should say in all fairness, is better than most, but he is still far too much the orthodox Southerner to see what is the matter with the South. A resident of Tennessee for a generation, he shows all the peculiar Tennessee prejudices and puerilities. For the pious Mooney, bawling for Genesis, he has high praises; for the intelligent and courageous John R. Neal he has only sneers. Where was he himself when Bryan marched in, and the hill-billies came down to drive all sense and decency out of the State? Was he in the forefront of the fray? Was he heard at Dayton, on the side of educated and self-respecting men? If so, his voice was small indeed, for I got no echo of it in the courtroom. Like all the other so-called intellectuals of the State, journalistic, legal and pedagogical, he left the heavy burden of the fight to Dr. Neal, and now all he can say of Neal is that he is "a local attorney" and "an often defeated politician." It is the tragedy of Tennessee that such men as Neal are defeated and such men as the mountebank Peay are kept in high office. It is the greater tragedy of the South that when, by some act of God, a Neal springs out of the land all the Mimses combine to cry him down.

That they succeed only too well is proved by Mims' own evidence. His book is strewn with the names of Southerners who have been forced to come North for air—Walter Hines Page, William E. Dodd, John Spencer Bassett, W. P. Trent, Woodrow Wilson, Ashby Jones. Of some of these men, especially on the political side, I am surely no romantic admirer, but they were the best that the South could produce, and the South obviously needed them. All came North—and the younger men and women of to-day are following them. Perhaps the best newspaper editorial writer that the South has produced in my time is Gerald W. Johnson: he is now in Baltimore. The best newspaper reporter is Paul Y. Anderson: he is now in St. Louis. The most promising critic of letters and life is Joseph W. Krutch: he is now in New York. The list might be lengthened almost endlessly. In particular, the names of many women are on it, for the South, despite its gabble of chivalry, still knows how to be unpleasant to a woman who is intelligent. True enough, a few hard-boiled and heroic men, their veins filled with manganese, manage to hold out: for example, W. L. Poteat, John D. Wade, Paul Green, and Howard W. Odum. But Poteat is of such years that his mere antiquity now begins to protect him, and Wade, Green and Odum, though they remain in the South to-day, will probably be on their way to-morrow. The kind of "leader" who survives down there is mainly the yellow dog kind. The Underwoods pass out and the Peays and Bleases come in. The South loses Johnson and keeps Clark Howell, Douglas Freeman, and the incredible Sullens, of Mississippi; it lets the *Reviewer* die and reads and admires the *Manufacturers' Record*. The enlightened Pastor Jones departs for Kansas City and the preposterous Bishop Candler, with his coca-cola theology, holds the fort. Who *goes* South? I recall two salient emigrants: William Jennings Bryan and the Rev. Dr. John Roach Straton.

What is to be noted in all this is that the South is by no means sterile. It still produces a very respectable annual crop of bright young men and women. Considering its backwardness in education, indeed, it probably produces more of them, relatively, than some of the States of the North—for example, New Jersey, Ohio and Vermont. The best blood of the South, I am inclined to think, is the best in the whole Republic—that is, taking account only of so-called Anglo-Saxons. But that best blood, save in a few areas, mainly along tide-water, is no longer dominant. The lower orders of Southerners, having been lifted out of poverty by the general economic rise of the region, have got the reins of political power into their hands, and through the medium of politics they are trying to force their ignorance upon their betters. Every emerging leader must pass their tests—and their tests are scarcely to be distinguished from those of the savages in the Borneo jungle. Culturally, indeed, they are precisely on the level of the anthropoid blacks surrounding them. They share the same suspicion of knowledge, they show the same primitive emotionality, and they practice the same barbaric and revolting religion. This religion, as is always the case with people only superficially civilized, colors their whole lives. The *shaman* is the principal functionary among them, and his fiats have the force of divine revelation. Nothing can be undertaken that does not meet his approval; nothing is regarded as sound, or even as decent, that violates the tenets of his hog-wallow theology. The troubles of the South, it seems to me, all revolve around that simple fact. The *shaman*, who has been reduced to innocuousness in more civilized regions, is still too powerful down there. All the Southern politicians flatter and cajole him, and he is treated with elaborate respect by practically all the Southern newspapers. No wonder he believes in his own magic! And no wonder it is difficult, in the face of his ignorance and his power, to launch a sound idea!

It seems to me that the more intelligent Southerners, rising one by one out of the general darkness, are all doomed to failure until they concentrate upon this chartered enemy of every intellectual dignity and decency, and clear him off the scene. Their error, at the moment, consists in trying to compromise with him. They are all too eager to avoid violating the pious pruderies of his victims. It is an error that is not new in the world, and wherever it has been followed it has greatly prospered *shamans*. In its final form it converts itself into the doctrine that any and every theological notion, however insane and outageous, deserves respect. I can imagine nothing more unsound. If the men of past ages had cherished that delusion we'd still be sweating under the Inquisition—nay, we'd be consulting oracles and trembling before sorcerers. In other words, the whole human race would still be on the level of the Haitian voodoo-worshipers and the Georgia Baptists. The way to get rid of such ideas is not to walk softly before them, but to attack them vigorously and with clubs. If Mims and his fellow pussy-footers had done that in Tennessee, there would have been no Scopes trial, and no ensuing disgrace of the State. I don't think the yokels themselves were to blame for that obscenity. Such of them as I met during the trial seemed to me to be decidedly above the general level of American peasants, They were not noticeably stupid; they were simply grossly misinformed. The rubbish that was preached to them four times a week by their pastors went unchallenged. The Mimses hesitated to attack it, I daresay, for fear of being accused of attacking religion. Well, why should religion *not* be attacked when it is idiotic? What gives a theological imbecility superiority over any other imbecility? Why should a moron dressed up as a Methodist preacher get any more respect than a moron behind a plow? The doctrine that there are differences here greatly burdens the South. If it is ever to have a general intellectual awakening, and not merely a series of gallant but unimportant one-man revolts, it must first get rid of its superstitious reverence for sacerdotal mountebanks. They are the common enemies of every enlightened Southerner, including such liberal but faithful churchmen as Dr. Jones and Dr. Poteat quite as much as such skeptics as Miss Newman and Cabell. No tolerant and progressive civilization will ever rise in the South with their consent.

Thus the fundamental struggle there is a *Kulturkampf* in the strictest Bismarckian sense, and soon or late its challenge must be squarely met. The question is whether the South is to be run by its educated and intelligent men, or by a rabble of hedge theologians, led by blood-sweating fanatics and followed by a docile tail of crooked politicians and boot-licking editors. As I have said, it produces plenty of admirable candidates for leadership—perhaps more, relatively, than any other American section save the Northeastern seaboard. But they are driven out almost as fast as they arise. The village pastors flush them instantly, and they are soon in full flight, with a baying pack of Ku Kluxers, Methodist bishops, Fundamentalist legislators, Daughters of the Confederacy, and professional wowsers after them. Suppose that, by some miracle, a competent biologist were produced at Vanderbilt University, at Nashville, which Dr. Mims serves as a professor. Where could he pass on his learning in Tennessee, save at Vanderbilt University? Suppose a competent journalist arose in Mississippi. What paper in that State would employ him? Certainly the same questions could not be asked in Illinois, say, or in Wisconsin, or in Maryland, or even in Pennsylvania, as dull and degraded as it is. Such States utilize their own good men. They welcome the free play of ideas. They have got beyond that elemental stage of civilization in which all questions are questions of faith. They have thrown off the tyranny of the *shaman*. The South, I believe, will some day follow them. But the road is long and full of perils, and many a head will be cracked before the end of it is reached.

6
The Immortal Democrat

JEFFERSON, by Albert Jay Nock. New York: *Harcourt, Brace & Company.* [The American Mercury, September, 1926.]

This book has a fine surface: it is the work of a subtle and highly dexterous craftsman. What publicist among us, indeed, writes better than Nock? His editorials during the three brief years of the *Freeman* set a mark that no other man of his trade has ever quite managed to reach. They were well-informed and sometimes even learned, but there was never the slightest trace of pedantry in them. In even the least of them there were sound writing and solid structure. Nock has an excellent ear. Thinking in English, he thinks in charming rhythms. There is never any cacophony in his sentences, as there is never any muddling in his ideas. One may reject his doctrines as evil and against God, but one never finds any flaws in his actual syllogisms. In the present volume he is completely at home. Jefferson has been his Baal since his nonage, and he is soaked in Jeffersoniana as the late Dr. Harding was soaked in the idealism of the Elks.

What emerges here is in no sense a formal biography, nor

even a political history. It is, rather, an elaborate psychological study of the man—an attempt to search out the origins of his chief ideas, to discern and delimit the forms that they finally took in his mind, and to estimate them in the light of the problems to which they were applied, and of the experience that has accumulated in the century since Jefferson's death. In brief, the book is a sort of critical analysis of Jeffersonism, done with constant sympathy and yet with a sharp outlook for fallacy and folly. It is accurate, it is shrewd, it is well ordered, and above all it is charming. I know of no other book on Jefferson that penetrates so persuasively to the essential substance of the man. There are no weak spots in it, and no false notes. It is overwhelmingly convincing as polemic and it is unfailingly caressing as work of art.

It goes without saying that much of Nock's attention is directed toward clearing off the vast mountain of doctrinaire rubbish that has risen above Jefferson's bones. In that Hell where politicians go the Sage of Monticello, I daresay, has suffered far more than most. Imagine his ghost contemplating Bryan, Alton B. Parker, Jimmie Cox, Al Smith, Jimmie Walker, W. G. McAdoo, Cole Blease, Ma and Pa Ferguson, John W. Davis, Tom Taggart, even Woodrow Wilson and Grover Cleveland! It is, indeed, one of the fine ironies of history that the party which professes to follow him has been led almost exclusively, for a hundred years, by leaders wholly unable to grasp the elements of his political philosophy. It stands as far from him to-day as the Methodist Board of Temperance, Prohibition and Public Morals stands from Christ. That is to say, it stands as far off as it is humanly possible to get. Its titular leader, in 1924, was the preposterous Davis: he led it to disaster, but nevertheless he led it. Well, this Davis was, and is, the perfect embodiment of everything that Jefferson distrusted and disliked. He is precisely the sort of man whose oblique doings, in the years between 1810 and 1825, tortured old Tom with his dreams of monocrats. The rest are even worse: McAdoo and his Ku Kluxers, Al Smith and his Tammany gorillas, the Southern State bosses and their tatterdemalion hordes of boozy Prohibitionists. In the whole outfit there is but one man, I suspect, who would get any politeness from Jefferson, imagining him come back to earth. That man, by a coincidence that is surely not strange, was long in formal exile from the Democratic party. He was excommunicated by the late Woodrow; in the Cox convention he was denied a seat; in the Davis convention he took no part. But he remains nearer to Jefferson than all the rest.

Of the Jeffersonian system Mr. Nock offers a clear and comprehensive account, disentangling it from the trivialities that party history has thrown about it. The essence of it, he says, is to be found in what would be called, to-day, Jefferson's class consciousness. He divided all mankind into two classes, the producers and the exploiters, and he was for the former first, last and all the time. But there is no consolation in the fact for the Marxians who now rage in the world, for to Jefferson producers meant far more than mere handworkers. A manufacturer, if he made some useful thing, was also a producer; so was a large landowner, if only he worked his land; Jefferson regarded himself as a producer, and his friend Jimmie Madison as another. Living in our own time, no doubt, he would put Henry Ford in that category; Henry, in fact, puts himself there, and with no little show of reason. The only genuine non-producer, in the Jefferson lexicon, was the speculator— that is to say, the banker, the promoter, the usurer, the jobber. It was against this class that he launched all his most awful thunderbolts of invective; it was this class that he sought to upset and destroy in the ferocious and memorable campaign of 1800. His failure was colossal. Driving that class out of the executive offices and making life very warm for it in the halls of legislation, he only shoved it into the courts, and there it has survived gloriously ever since, gradually extending and consolidating its power. Since Marshall's day the American courts have suffered many vicissitudes and entertained many heresies, but in one department, at least they have kept the faith heroically: they have always protected the virtuous and patriotic bond-holder.

Jefferson has come down in legend as the most adroit of all the early American politicians—that is, after Sam Adams. He is credited with having conjured up, almost out of the air, the party which still disgraces him. He is accused of almost fabulous feats of demagogy. I see little evidence for all this in his actual history. He was, in fact, far less the practical politician than the political philosopher. Office seems to have had few attractions for him, and he was quite devoid of the sense of party regularity. His so-called demagogy turns out, on inspection, to have been simply a realistic statement of fundamental democratic theory. There is little in even his most startling pronouncements that is not implicit in the Bill of Rights. He was far less the foe of the Federalists than of government in general. He believed that it tended inevitably to become corrupt—that it was the common enemy of all well-disposed, industrious and decent men. The less there was of it, the better he liked it, and the more he trusted it. Well, that was a century ago, and wild doctrines from the barricades were still in the air. Government has now gone far beyond anything dreamed of in Jefferson's day. It has taken on a vast mass of new duties and responsibilities; it has spread out its powers until they penetrate to every act of the citizen, however secret; it has begun to throw around its operations the high dignity and impeccability of a state religion; its agents become a separate and superior caste, with authority to bind and loose, and their thumbs in every pot. But it still remains, as it was in the beginning, the common enemy of all well-disposed, industrious and decent men.

7
Fides Ante Intellectum

A SCIENTIFIC MAN AND THE BIBLE, by Howard A. Kelly. Philadelphia: *The Sunday-School Times Company*. [The American Mercury, February, 1926.]

The author of this astounding and depressing book is professor emeritus of gynecological surgery at the Johns Hopkins, and one of the most celebrated surgeons in the United States. This is what his own university says of him in an official document:

His contribution to the development of genito-urinary surgery for women has been unparalleled. Step by step he unraveled the diseases of the bladder, ureter and kidney. . . . His methods of examination revolutionized gynecological diagnosis.

And much more to the same effect. In brief, a medical man of the first caliber: when he speaks of himself as a scientist, as he does very often in his book, he has every right to use the word. His life has been devoted to exact observation, and that observation has been made so competently and interpreted so logically that the result has been a series of immensely valuable improvements in the healing art and craft. And yet—and yet— How am I to make you believe that such a man has actually written such a volume as this one? How am I to convince you that one of four men who laid the foundations of the Johns Hopkins Medical School—the daily associate and peer of Osler, Welch and Halsted—is here on exhibition as a Fundamentalist of the most extreme wing, compared to whom Judge Raulston, of Dayton, Tenn., seems almost an atheist?

Yet it is so—and I go, for the appalling proof, behind the book and to the man himself. I have known Dr. Kelly for twenty years, and at different times have seen a great deal of him. Hours on end I have discussed his theological ideas with him, and heard his reasons for cherishing them. They seem to me now, as they seemed when I first heard them, to be completely insane—yet Kelly himself is surely not insane. Nor is there the remotest suspicion of insincerity about him. It would be of vast benefit to him professionally to throw over his great cargo of supernatural rubbish, and trim his course as his colleagues trim theirs. If he did so, the Johns Hopkins would be illuminated with Roman candles, star shells and incandescent bock beer signs, and the very cadavers in the deadhouse would have their backs slapped. But he will not budge. He believes that God created the world in six calendar days, and rested on the seventh. He believes that God caused forty-two little children to be devoured by she-bears because they made fun of Elijah's bald head. He believes that Jonah was three days and three nights in the belly of a whale (*Physeter macrocephalus*), and then came out alive. *Medicinæ doctor* though he be, he believes that the hallucinations of John on the island of Patmos were real. An LL.D. of Aberdeen, he believes (Exodus XXII, 18) that witches exist and should be put to death. An honorary member of learned societies in Paris, Vienna, Rome, Berlin, Leipzig, Bucharest and Moscow, he believes in both the Virgin Birth (Matthew I, 18–25), and in the descent of Jesus from

David through Joseph (Matthew I, 1–17). All this, and much more, he believes absolutely without reservation, as a Tennessee hind believes it. "I accept the *whole* Bible," he says, "as God's Word." And he adds something that even the hind balks at: he believes in the Second Coming—"at any moment"!

In his book Dr. Kelly offers powerful argument for his amazing credo, but I can only report that, in cold type as *viva voce*, it leaves me full of what the lawyers call reasonable doubt. His logic has a curious habit of going halfway to a plausible conclusion, and then blowing up completely. For example, he starts off, in one place, by showing how the early criticism of the Gospel of John has broken down—and then proceeds gaily to the assumption that proving an error in criticism is identical with proving the complete authenticity of the thing criticized. Again, he denounces the effort to raise up doubts of the Mosaic authorship and divine inspiration of the Pentateuch—and then clinches his case by showing that the Bible itself "claims in all its parts" that it is "the very literal Word of God." But the record of a personal experience exhibits the workings of his mind even more beautifully. Early in manhood he had to give up his medical studies on account of ill-health, and went West to recuperate. In Colorado, during a blizzard, he was beset by snow blindness, and had to take to his bed. Suddenly there came upon him "an overwhelming sense of a great light in the room." How would any ordinary medical student interpret that great light? How would any ordinary ice-wagon driver, or chiropractor, or Methodist bishop, or even catfish interpret it? Obviously, he would refer it to the violent conjunctivitis from which he was suffering—in other words, to a purely physical cause. But not Kelly. After nearly fifty years of active medical practice he still believes that the glare was due to the presence of God! This divine visitation he speaks of very simply as "the chief event" of his life! It surely was—if it was real!

What I'd like to read is a scientific review, by a scientific psychologist—if any exists—of "A Scientific Man and the Bible." By what route do otherwise sane men come to believe such inconceivable nonsense? How is it possible for a human brain to be divided into two insulated halves, one functioning normally, naturally and even brilliantly, and the other capable only of the ghastly balderdash which issues from the minds of

Baptist evangelists? Such balderdash takes various forms, but it is at its worst when it is religious. Why should this be so? What is there in religion that completely flabbergasts the wits of those who believe in it? I see no logical necessity for that flabbergasting. Religion, after all, is nothing but an hypothesis framed to account for what is evidentially unaccounted for. In other fields such hypotheses are common, and yet they do no apparent damage to those who incline to them. But in the religious field they quickly rush the believer to the intellectual Bad Lands. He not only becomes anæsthetic to objective fact; he becomes a violent enemy of objective fact. It annoys and irritates him. He sweeps it away as something somehow evil.

This little book I commend to all persons interested in the mysteries of the so-called mind of man. It is a document full of fascination, especially to the infidel and damned. There is a frankness about it that is refreshing and commendable. The author does not apologize for his notions, nor does he try to bring them into grotesque and incredible harmony with scientific facts. He believes the Bible from cover to cover, fly-specks and all, and he says so (considering his station in life) with great courage.

8
Speech Day in the Greisenheim

ACADEMY PAPERS: ADDRESSES ON LANGUAGE, by Members of the American Academy of Arts and Letters. New York: *Charles Scribners' Sons.* [The American Mercury, January, 1926.]

The contributors to this volume, with their academic dignities, and their ages at the time it was published, are as follows:

Paul Elmer More, A.B., A.M., LL.D., 3(Litt.D.)	61 years
Bliss Perry, A.B., 2(A.M.), 3(L.H.D.), Litt.D., 2(LL.D.)	64 ”
Paul Shorey, A.B., Ph.D., 7(LL.D.), 2(Litt.D.)	69 ”
Brander Matthews, A.B., A.M., LL.B., D.C.L., Litt.D., LL.D.	73 ”
Henry van Dyke, A.M., 3(D.D.), 3(LL.D.), D.C.L.	73 ”

Robert Underwood Johnson, B.S., A.M., Ph.D.,
    L.H.D.   73   "
William M. Sloane, A.B., A.M., Ph.D., L.H.D.,
    2(LL.D.)   75   "
William Crary Brownell, A.B., L.H.D., Litt.D.,
    LL.D.   75   "

This works out to an average of a little more than seventy—
the age, according to Psalms XC, 10, of extreme unction. Is it
surprising that the dullness of the different papers runs in
almost direct ratio to the years of their authors? Surprising or
not, it is a fact. Dr. More, though he has nothing to say, and
seems to have noticed little about the language he writes save
that the English also use it, nevertheless offers a paper that has
a certain stealthy liveliness, and even a touch of sauciness. He
opens it, indeed, with a quotation from "The Merchant of
Venice" which, flung at them by a barbarian, would have
caused the most potent, grave and reverend signiors of the
Academy to wince. But youth must kick up its legs, and Dr.
More of the time of his cavorting, was only sixty-one. Ten
years will mellow him, and give him a softer patina.

Dr. Perry, who is three years older and has been in cold stor-
age at Harvard for years, is also somewhat goatish. He even
goes to the length of presenting three ideas, one of which is
actually new. The first, apparently borrowed from the philolo-
gians of the Invisible Empire, is that the secular arm should be
summoned to safeguard the mother-tongue in the Republic—
that is, that the process of Americanization should be pushed
by law. The second is that the Academy should establish a
grand prize for diction—to be given annually, it would seem,
to some English *cabotin*, for the only virtuosi of "distinguished diction" that Dr. Perry mentions are George Arliss
and Edith Wynne Matthison. The third suggestion, and the
only one that is original, is that the Academy should also set
up rewards for those authors, apparently American in this
case, whose books "are characterized by distinction of style."
A good idea, but full of dynamite. How would the old
boys dodge giving an occasional gold medal, or India-paper
Bible, or basket of Moët et Chandon, or silk American flag, or

whatever the prize was, to James Branch Cabell? And what would they do with Cabell's blistering reply, having received and read it?

Dr. Shorey comes next—and with an unfair advantage. He is not a bad author and no more, like the rest, but a professor of Greek, and denoted all his life to Plato *geb.* Aristocles. (The rest, I venture, know so little Greek that they can scarcely shine their own shoes.) His paper is that of an innocent but amiable bystander. He denies that there is an American dialect of English, and then proves very charmingly that there is. He is full of amusing anecdotes and shrewd observations. He closes with an engaging, but, I regret to have to add, far from convincing plea for the study of Latin. The day he read his paper before the Academy must have been a pleasant one for the janitor, staff surgeon, newspaper reporters, wheel-chair motormen, trained nurses and embalmers in attendance. But I guess that more than one immortal blew his nose sadly as wheeze followed wheeze, and cackles rippled through the audience. Shorey was then only sixty-nine and had lived at Bonn, Leipzig, Munich and Athens.

Over seventy Academicians jell. Dr. Matthews' paper is heavy and hollow stuff—the sort of thing he used to write for *Munsey's Magazine* in the days when he and it were ornaments to the national letters, and the Kaiser had not yet sent in such men as Cabell, Lewis and Dreiser to annoy him. Dr. Brownell contributes two dull papers in his baroque and tedious style, with occasional descents to dubious English. (See, for example, the first two lines of page 42.) Pastor van Dyke, turning aside from his combat of Golden Texts with Dr. Frank Crane, offers an essay in which he denounces Carl Sandburg and says of "The Spoon River Anthology" that "to call it poetry is to manhandle a sacred word." (Has the rev. gentleman ever come to the page containing "Ann Rutledge"?) Finally, Dr. Johnson, after joining in the butchery of Sandburg, delivers a whoop for the old-style poetry—by which, on his own showing, he means poetry full of moral purpose—and then ends with a tart reference, in execrable taste, to the poetry printed by the *Century Magazine* since his retirement as its editor.

Thus the ancients of the American Academy of Arts and Letters. Eight of them join forces to write a book of 282 pages

—and the result is sheer emptiness, signifying nothing. Their subject is the language all of them are supposed to write, not merely well but better than any other eight men in the country—and what seven of them have to say of it is simply what one would expect from a baker's half-dozen of school-ma'ms, chosen at random.

9
Professors of English

THE STANDARDS OF AMERICAN SPEECH, AND OTHER PAPERS, by Fred Newton Scott. Boston: *Allyn & Bacon.* HOW TO DESCRIBE AND NARRATE VISUALLY, by L. A. Sherman. New York: *The George H. Doran Company.* [The American Mercury, October, 1926.]

Scott is an A.B., an A.M. and a Ph.D.; he has professed at the University of Michigan since 1887 and is now professor of rhetoric and journalism there and university editor; he has been president of the Modern Language Association, of the National Council of Teachers of English, of the North Central Association of Colleges and Secondary Schools, and of the American Association of Teachers of Journalism; he is a member of the Modern Language Research Association, the American Association for the Advancement of Science, and the British Association, and represented the literati of the Republic at the Conference of American and British Professors of English at London in 1920; he is the author of many works, including an English grammar, a treatise on literary criticism and another on æsthetics, and the editor of many more, including two volumes of gems from Holy Writ. Sherman is an A.B., a Ph.D. and an LL.D.; he has professed English at the University of Nebraska since 1882, and is now dean of the graduate college there; he is a member of Phi Beta Kappa, Alpha Delta Phi and other learned lodges; he has composed a book called "What is Shakespeare?" and another called "Analytics of Literature"; his textbooks are in wide use.

Well, what have these powerfully learned and eminent men to say in their present volumes? Scott devotes a chapter to proving that "of the 10,565 lines of 'Paradise Lost,' 670, or 6.3%, contain each two or more accented alliterating vowels," another proving that in such word-groups as "rough and ready,"

68% put the monosyllable first and the dissyllable second, and 42% put the dissyllable first and the monosyllable second, and a third (very long) to developing John Stuart Mill's well-known saying that "eloquence is heard; poetry is overheard," *i.e.*, that the primary aim of prose is persuasion, whereas that of poetry is simply self-expression. So much for Scott. Sherman fills 364 pages with windy platitudes on the writing of English, and lays chief stress on the revolutionary discovery that visual images are very effective. At the end of each chapter he sets a dozen or more tests for students. I offer a few specimens:

Detail the points of exposition as gathered from some recent sermon.

Draw a character by the use of imaginative appeals of degree.

From some outgrown or discarded theme, find what sentences are not of the first or second grade of value.

Describe, by form-types, the safety chain.

Devise a new system of ten points, five of matter, five of manner, and by it evaluate three debates prepared on the same side of some live question of the hour.

Find or recall an example of summarizing narration that seems to you worthy of being told in the consecutive manner, and give reasons for your criticism.

Such are two of the great whales of literary science among us. God help the poor yokels who have to sweat through their books! God help the national letters!

VI.
Five Little Excursions

I
Brahms

MY excuse for writing of the above gentleman is simply that, at the moment, I can think of nothing else. A week or so ago, on a Baltimore Summer evening of furious heat, I heard his sextette for strings, opus 18, and ever since then it has been sliding and pirouetting through my head. I have gone to bed with it and I have got up with it. Not, of course, with the whole sextette, nor even with any principal tune of it, but with the modest and fragile little episode at the end of the first section of the first movement—a lowly thing of nine measures, thrown off like a perfume, so to speak, from the second subject:

What is the magic in such sublime trivialities? Here is a tune so slight and unassuming that it runs to but eight measures and uses but six of the twelve tones in the octave, and yet it rides an elderly and unromantic man, weighing 180 pounds and with a liver far beyond pills or prayer, as if it were the very queen of the succubi. Is it because I have a delicately sensitive ear? Bosh! I am almost tone-deaf. Or a tender and impressionable heart? Bosh again! Or a beautiful soul? *Dreimal* bosh! No theologian not in his cups would insure me against Hell for cent per cent. No, the answer is to be found in the tune, not in the man. Trivial in seeming, there is yet in it the power of a thousand horses. Modest, it speaks with a clarion voice, and having spoken, it is remembered. Brahms made many another like it. There is one at the beginning of the trio for violin, 'cello and piano, opus 8—the loveliest tune, perhaps, in the whole range of music. There is another in the slow movement of the quintette for piano and strings, opus 34. There is yet another in the double concerto for violin and 'cello, opus 102— the first subject of the slow movement. There is one in the coda of the Third Symphony. There is an exquisite one in the Fourth Symphony. But if you know Brahms, you know all of them quite as well as I do. Hearing him is as dangerous as hearing Schubert. One does not go away filled and satisfied, to resume business as usual in the morning. One goes away charged with a something that remains in the blood a long while, like the toxins of love or the pneumococcus. If I had a heavy job of work to do on the morrow, with all hands on deck and the cerebrum thrown into high, I'd certainly not risk hearing any of the Schubert string quartettes, or the incomparable quintette with the extra 'cello, or the Tragic Symphony. And I'd hesitate a long time before risking Brahms.

It seems an astounding thing that there was once a war over him, and that certain competent musicians, otherwise sane, argued that he was dull. As well imagine a war over Beauvais Cathedral or the Hundred-and-third Psalm! The contention of these foolish fellows, if I recall it aright, was that Brahms was dull in his development sections—that he flogged his tunes to death. I can think of nothing more magnificently idiotic. Turn to the sextette that I have mentioned, written in the early '60's of the last century, when the composer was barely thirty. The development section of the first movement is not only fluent and workmanlike: it is a downright masterpiece. There is a magnificent battle of moods in it, from the fieriest to the tenderest, and it ends with a coda that is sheer perfection. True enough, Brahms had to learn—and it is in the handling of thematic material, not in its invention, that learning counts. When he wrote his first piano trio, at twenty-five or thereabout, he started off, as I have said, with one of the most lovely tunes ever put on paper, but when he came to develop it his inexperience showed itself, and the result was such that years later he rewrote the whole work. But by the time he came to his piano concerto in D he was the complete master of his materials, and ever thereafter he showed a quality of work-

manship that no other composer has ever surpassed, not even
Beethoven. The first movement of the Eroica, I grant you, is
sui generis: it will never be matched until the time two great
geniuses collide again. But what is in the rest of the first eight
symphonies, even including the Fifth and Ninth, that is clearly
better than what is in the four of Brahms? The first performance of his First, indeed, was as memorable an event in the
history of music as the first performance of the Eroica. Both
were furiously denounced, and yet both were instantaneous
successes. I'd rather have been present at Karlsruhe on November 6, 1876, I think, than at the initiation of General Pershing
into the Elks, or even than at the baptism of Coolidge. And I'd
rather have been present at Vienna on April 7, 1805, than at the
landing of Columbus.

In music, as in all the other arts, the dignity of the work is
simply a reflection of the dignity of the man. The notion that
shallow and trivial men can write masterpieces is one of the follies that flow out of the common human taste for scandalous
anecdote. Wagner wore a velvet cap and stole another man's
wife; *ergo*, nothing is needed to write great music save the talents of a movie actor. What could be more preposterous? More
than any other art, perhaps, music demands brains. It is full of
technical complexities. It calls for a capacity to do a dozen
things at once. But most of all it is revelatory of what is called
character. When a trashy man writes it, it is trashy music.

Here is where the immense superiority of such a man as
Brahms becomes manifest. There is less trashiness in his music
than there is in the music of any other man ever heard of, with
the sole exception, perhaps, of Johann Sebastian Bach. It was
simply impossible for him, at least after he had learned his
trade, to be obvious or banal. He could not write even the
baldest tune without getting into it something of his own high
dignity and profound seriousness; he could not play with that
tune, however light his mood, without putting an austere and
noble stateliness into it. Hearing Brahms, one never gets any
sense of being entertained by a clever mountebank. One is facing a superior man, and the fact is evident from the first note.
I give you his "Deutsches Requiem" as an example. There is
no hint of what is commonly regarded as religious feeling in it.
Brahms, so far as I know, was not a religious man. Nor is there

the slightest sign of the cheap fustian of conventional patriotism. Nevertheless, a superb emotion is there—nay, an overwhelming emotion. The thing is irresistibly moving. It is moving because a man of the highest intellectual dignity, a man of exalted feelings, a man of brains, put into it his love for and pride in his country. Lucky the country which produces such men!

But in music emotion is only half the story. Mendelssohn had it, and yet he belongs to the second table. Nor is it a matter of mere beauty—that is, of mere sensuous loveliness. If it were, then Dvořák would be greater than Beethoven, whose tunes are seldom inspired, and who not infrequently does without them altogether. What makes great music is the thing I have mentioned: brains. The greatest musician is a man whose thoughts and feelings are above the common level, and whose language matches them. What he has to say comes out of a wisdom that is not ordinary. Platitude is impossible to him. He is the precise antithesis of Mr. Babbitt. Above all, he is a master of his craft, as opposed to his art. He gets his effects in new, difficult and ingenious ways—and they convince one instantly that they are inevitable. One can easily imagine improvements in the human eye, and in the Alps, and in the art of love, and even in the Constitution, but one cannot imagine improvements in the first movement of the Eroica. The thing is completely perfect, even at the places where the composer halts to draw breath. Any change in it would damage it. But what is inevitable is never obvious. John Doe would not and could not write thus. The immovable truths that are there —and there are truths in the arts as well as in theology —became truths when Beethoven formulated them. They did not exist before. They cannot perish hereafter.

So with Brahms. There are plenty of composers of more romantic appeal. I need mention only Schubert. Schubert, had he lived, might have been the greatest of them all, but he died before any patina had formed on him; he was still going to school in his last days. But Brahms seems to have come into the world full-blown. A few experiments, brilliant even when they failed, and he was a master beside Beethoven and Bach. In all his music done after his beard had sprouted, there is not the slightest sign of bewilderment and confusion, of trial and error, of uncertainty and irresolution. He knew precisely what he wanted to say, and he said it colossally.

2
Johann Strauss

The centenary of John Strauss the Younger passed almost unnoticed in the United States. In Berlin and in Vienna it was celebrated with imposing ceremonies, and all the German radio stations put "Wein, Weib und Gesang" and "Rosen aus dem Süden" on the air. Why wasn't it done in this great country? Was the pestilence of jazz to blame—or was it due to the scarcity of sound beer? I incline to Answer No. 2. Any music is difficult on well-water, but the waltz is a sheer impossibility. "Man Lebt Nur Einmal" would be as dreadful in a dry town as a Sousa march at a hanging.

For the essence of a Viennese waltz, and especially of a Strauss waltz, is merriment, good humor, happiness, *Gemüt-lichkeit*. It reflects brilliantly the spirits of a people who are eternally gay, war or no war. Sad music, to be sure, has been written in Vienna—but chiefly by foreigners: Haydn, who was a Croat; Beethoven, whose pap had been a sour Rhine wine; Brahms, who came from the bleak Baltic coast. I come upon Schubert—but all rules go to pot when he appears. As for Strauss, he was a 100% Viennese, and could no more be sad than he could be indignant. The waltz wandered into the minor keys in Paris, in the hands of the sardonic Alsatian Jew, Waldteufel. At home old Johann kept it in golden major, and so did young Johann after him. The two, taking it from Schubert and the folk, lifted it to imperial splendor. No other dance-form, not even the minuet, has ever brought forth more lovely music. And none other has preserved so perfectly the divine beeriness of the peasant dance. The best of the Strauss waltzes were written for the most stilted and ceremonious court in Europe, but in every one of them, great and little, there remains the boggy, expansive flavor of the village green. Even the stately "Kaiser" waltz, with its preliminary heel-clicks and saber-rattling, is soon swinging jocosely to the measures of the rustic *Springtanz*.

It is a curious, melancholy and gruesome fact that Johann

Strauss II was brought up to the variety of thieving known as the banking business. His father planned that he should be what in our time is called a bond salesman. What asses fathers are! This one was himself a great master of the waltz, and yet he believed that he could save all three of his sons from its lascivious allurements! Young Johann was dedicated to investment banking, Josef to architecture, and Eduard, the baby, to the law. The old man died on September 25, 1849. On September 26 all three were writing waltzes. Johann, it quickly appeared, was the best of the trio. In fact, he was the best musician who ever wrote waltzes for dancing, and one of the really first-rate musicians of his time. He took the waltz as his father left it, and gradually built it up into a form almost symphonic. He developed the introduction, which had been little more than an opening fanfare, into a complex and beautiful thing, almost an overture, and he elaborated the coda until it began to demand every resource of the composer's art, including even counterpoint. And into the waltz itself he threw such lush melodic riches, so vastly a rhythmic inventiveness and so adept a mastery of instrumentation that the effect was overwhelming. The Strauss waltzes, it seems to me, have never been sufficiently studied. That other Strauss, Richard, knows what is in them, you may be sure, for the first act of "Der Rosenkavalier" proves it, but the musical pedants and pedagogues have kept aloof. What they miss! Consider, for example, the astonishing skill with which Johann manages his procession of keys—the inevitable air which he always gets into his choice! And the immense ingenuity with which he puts variety into his bass—so monotonous in Waldteufel, and even in Lanner and Gung'l! And the endless resourcefulness which marks his orchestration—never formal and obvious for an instant, but always with some new quirk in it, some fresh and charming beauty! And his codas—how simple they are, and yet how ravishing!

Johann certainly did not blush unseen. He was an important figure at the Austrian court, and when he passed necks were craned as if at an ambassador. He traveled widely and was received with honor everywhere. His waltzes swept the world. His operettas, following them, offered formidable rivalry to the pieces of Gilbert and Sullivan. He was plastered with orders like a Doug Fairbanks or an Otto Kahn. He took in, in his time, a great deal of money, and left all his wives well provided for. More, he had the respect and a little of the envy of all his musical contemporaries. Wagner delighted in his waltzes and so did Brahms. Brahms once gave the score of one of them to a fair admirer with the inscription, "Leider *nicht* von Johannes Brahms"—Unfortunately, *not* by Johannes Brahms. Coming from so reserved a man, it was a tremendous compliment indeed,—perhaps the most tremendous recorded in history— nor was there any mere politeness in it, for Brahms had written plenty of waltzes himself, and knew that it was not as easy as it looked. The lesser fish followed the whales. There was never any clash of debate over Strauss. It was unanimously agreed that he was first-rate. His field was not wide, but within that field he was the unchallenged master. He became, in the end, the dean of a sort of college of waltz writers, centering at Vienna. The waltz, as he had brought it up to perfection, became the standard ball-room dance of the civilized world, and though it had to meet rivals constantly, it held its own for two generations, and even now, despite the murrain of jazz, it threatens to come back once more. Disciples of great skill began to appear in the Straussian wake—Ziehrer, with the beautiful "Weaner Mad'l," Lincke with "Ach, Frühling, Wie Bist Du So Schön," and many another. But old Johann never lost his primacy. Down to the very day of his death in 1899 he was *primus inter omnes.* Vienna wept oceans of beery tears into his grave. A great Viennese—perhaps the ultimate flower of old Vienna—was gone.

Now he is dead a hundred years. But surely not forgotten, despite shadows over the moon here and there. The man who makes lovely tunes has the laugh on Father Time. Oblivion never quite fetches him. He goes out of fashion now and then, but he always returns. There was a time when even Bach seemed to be forgotten. What a joke! Bach will last as long as human beings are born with ears; in the end, perhaps, he will be all that the world remembers of the Eighteenth Century. And Strauss, I suspect, will keep on bobbing up in the memory of the race so long as men have legs and can leap in 3–4 time, —at all events, so long as there is good malt liquor anywhere in the world. World-wide Prohibition, it is conceivable, may eventually kill him; in a dry universe he would be *contra bonus mores*. But jazz can do him no more permanent damage than a dog visiting his grave.

3
Poetry in America

The New Poetry Movement in America, so full of life and even of malicious animal magnetism a dozen years ago, is now obviously down with cholelithiasis, and no literary pathologist of genuine gifts would be surprised to hear, at any moment, of its death. Most of its former ornaments, indeed, begin to flee its bedside. Miss Lowell, in her last years, devoted herself to prose, and Masters goes the same way. Vachel Lindsay and Robert Frost take to college professing. Carl Sandburg has joined the minstrels. All the principal Greenwich Village poets, harassed by the morals squad, fled long ago to Paris, where landlords are less prying, and even artists may lead their own lives.

This slackening of effort is visible in all the little poetry magazines. Most of them continue to come out, and in the backwaters of the Republic, where all varieties of human progress are behind schedule, there are even occasional appearances of new ones, but there is little in any of them that is worth reading, and almost no actual poetry. What they print, in the main, is simply a series of exercises in the new prosody. It turns out, on examination, to be quite as tight and arbitrary as the old kind. For one thing that a poet of 1885 could not do there are ten things that a poet of 1927 cannot do. Thus the revolt against form expires in a new and worse formalism. The fact is most visible, of course, on the edges of the movement—that is, among the poets of Greenwich Village. What one observes in the advanced and atrabilious magazines which they publish is simply a sort of organized imbecility. The poet is strictly forbidden to make use of any of the traditional materials of his craft, or to concede anything to its traditional idioms. He must eschew all rhyme that really rhymes, he must eschew all the orthodox rhythms, and he must eschew all direct attack upon the emotions. In other words, he must eschew poetry. What he writes, it must be confessed, is sometimes very interesting, in its bizarre, unearthly way—just as a college yell, say, is interesting, or an act of Congress. But it is no more poetry than the college yell is music or the act of Congress wisdom.

The trouble with most of the new poets, whether in or out of Greenwich Village, is that they are too cerebral—that they attack the problems of a fine art with the methods of science. That error runs through all their public discussions of the business. Those discussions are full of theories, by the new psychology out of the cant of the studios, that do not work and are not true. The old-time poet did not bother with theories. When the urge to write was upon him, he simply got himself into a lather, tied a towel around his head, and then tried to reduce his feelings to paper. If he had any skill the result was poetry; if he lacked skill it was nonsense. But even his worst failure still had something natural and excusable about it—it was the failure of a man admittedly somewhat feverish, with purple paint on his nose and vine-leaves in his hair. The failure of the new poet is the far more grotesque failure of a scientist who turns out to be a quack—of a mathematician who divides 20 by 4 and gets 6, of a chiropractor who looks in the vertebrae for the cause of cross-eyes, of a cook who tries to make an omelette of china doorknobs. Poetry can never be concocted by any purely intellectual process. It has nothing to do with the intellect; it is, in fact, a violent and irreconcilable enemy to the intellect. Its purpose is not to establish facts, but to evade and deny them. What it essays to do is to make life more bearable in an intolerable world by concealing and obliterating all the harsher realities. Its message is that all will be well to-morrow, or, at the latest, next Tuesday, that the grave is not cold and damp but steam-heated and lined with roses, that serving in the trenches is far more amusing and comfortable than serving in the United States Senate, that a girl is not a viviparous mammal, full of pathogenic organisms and enlightened self-interest, but an angel with bobbed wings and a heart of gold. Take this denial of the bald and dreadful facts out of poetry—make it scientific and sensible—and it simply ceases to be what it pretends to be. It may remain good prose; it may even remain beautiful prose. But it cannot stir the blood as true poetry does; it cannot offer that soothing consolation, that escape from reality, that sovereign balm for every spiritual itch and twinge which is the great gift of poetry to man. The best poetry is always palpably untrue; it is its eloquent untruth that makes it so lovely. The other day I read of a gentleman, condemned to death in one of the Southern States, who went to the electric chair reciting the Twenty-third Psalm. It is a pity he had to die; he would have made an excellent critic, for he understood perfectly the nature and purpose of poetry.

The new poets, now passing into the shadows, not only made the mistake of trying to rationalize poetry, an enterprise comparable to trying to rationalize necking, drunkenness or the use of hasheesh; they also tried to detach themselves from the ordinary flow of American ideas, and to convert themselves into an intellectual aristocracy. Some of them, true enough, quickly found the thing impossible, and so turned back, notably Sandburg and Lindsay, but nearly all at least made the attempt. Miss Lowell, perhaps, went furthest; there was a time when even Boston felt bucolic and loutish, and hence very uneasy, in her presence. The result was that nine-tenths of the compositions the fraternity produced simply shot into space. The great heart of the folk reacted to them as feebly as it might have reacted to polemics between astronomers. When poetry fails in this way it fails all over. I do not argue that it ought to reach and soothe the nether herd, though some of the very best poetry ever written actually does—for example, the poetry in the Bible. All I contend is that it ought to reach the generality of the literate. If literary pastors are not moved by it, if it fails to supply phrases for editorial writers, if it is not quoted by stewed Congressmen at the endless memorial services on Capitol Hill, then it has obviously missed fire. Of all the stuff produced by the new poets precious little has ever gone that far. I can recall a few poems by Sandburg and Lindsay, perhaps one or two by Frost, and none other. The whole body of verse of Miss Lowell is as dead as if it had been written in Choctaw. Meanwhile, certain old-fashioned poets, notably Miss Reese and Miss Teasdale, have written things that will probably live. They will live because they are alive.

I sometimes think, indeed, that the real poetry of our era has been written, not by poets at all, but by men who would be as indignant, if you called them poets, as if you called them kidnapers, violoncellists or Socialists. I allude to the earnest rhetoricians who roam the chautauquas and the Kiwanis Clubs, waving the banner of idealism. What these fellows say is almost always nonsense, but it is at least the sort of nonsense that the American people yearn to cherish and believe in—it somehow fills their need. I point, for example, to their gabble about Service—already the source of phrases that Congressmen, clergymen, editorial writers and so on mouth every day. Here is the essential poetry of the Americano: his life is sordid, but he tries to escape from the fact by leering at the stars. It is a comprehensible impulse, and even worthy. The poets of his country have not helped him to attain his heart's desire. He has had to turn to traveling go-getters and forward-lookers.

Alas, whenever one thus discusses the nature and function of poetry—that is, whenever one tries to be realistic about it—one is sure to be accused of being an enemy to the art itself. But does this necessarily follow? I am sure it does not. The social value of poetry is not diminished in the slightest by looking at it without illusion. It still offers its old escape from reality; it still offers consolation to *Homo sapiens* in his woeful journey through this inclement vale. To denounce it out of hand would be as absurd as to denounce religion or anesthetics. The purpose of anesthetics is to get rid of the harsh torture of pain and substitute the sweet peace of sleep. The purpose of even the highest poetry is almost precisely the same. Chloroform tells a man that he is not having his leg cut off, but lying drunk on a feather-bed, with fireworks to entertain him. Poetry tells him that his girl is as beautiful as Venus and is marrying him without a single thought of his tenements and hereditaments, that his country is a Galahad among the nations and wholly devoid of the rascality prevailing everywhere else, that he himself is a noble fellow and will go to Heaven when he dies. All these things, I suspect, are false. But all of them make life more bearable. Poets are simply men who devote themselves to spreading them, often at great sacrifice of income. They are liars, but their lies, I believe, will be viewed very generously on the Resurrection Morn.

4
Victualry As A Fine Art

Some time ago, functioning as a magazine editor, I essayed to get hold of some articles on the American cuisine. At once I discovered that the number of American authors capable of writing upon the subject, charmingly and at first hand, was so small as to be substantially equal to the number of honest Prohibition agents. After six months' search, in fact, I found but three, and one of them had been living abroad for years and the other had lived there since childhood. Even the third was scarcely a 100% American, for he had traveled extensively in heathen lands, and though he was holding a public office in Washington when I found him, he confessed in the first sentence of his article that he wished the Volstead Act were repealed and the Hon. Mr. Volstead himself in Hell.

I speak here, of course, of authors competent to write of victualing as a fine art. Of cooking-school ma'ms, of course, we have a plenty, and we also have a vast and cocksure rabble of dietitians, some of them more or less scientific. But it must be obvious that the cooking-school ma'm knows very little about voluptuous eating, and that the dietitian is its enemy. The ma'm, indeed, seldom shows any sign that the flavor of victuals interests her. The thing she is primarily interested in, to borrow a term from surgery, is the cosmetic effect. In the women's magazines she prints pretty pictures of her masterpieces, often in full color. They look precisely like the dreadful tit-bits one encounters in the more high-toned sort of tea-rooms, and at wedding breakfasts. One admires them as spectacles, but eating them is something else again. Moreover, the ma'm is primarily a cook, not an epicure. She is interested in materials and processes, not in gustatory effects. When she invents a new way to utilize the hard heel of a ham, she believes that she has achieved something, though even the house-cat may gag at it. Her efforts are to the art of the *cordon bleu* what those of a house-painter are to those of a Cézanne. She is a pedagogue, not an artist. The fact that she is heeded in the land, and her depressing concoctions solemnly devoured, is sufficient proof, if any were needed, that Americans do not respect the dignity of their palates.

Why this should be so I don't know, for here in this great
Republic we have the materials for the most superb victuary
the world has ever seen, and our people have the money to pay
for it. Even the poorest Americano, indeed, eats relatively expensive food: his wife knows nothing of the hard pinching that
entertains her French sister. He has meat in abundance and in
considerable variety, and a great wealth of fruits and vegetables. Yet he eats badly, gets very little enjoyment out of his
meals, and is constantly taking pills. The hot dog is the *reductio ad absurdum* of American eating. The Sicilian in the ditch,
though he can never be President, knows better: he puts a slice
of onion between his slabs of bread, not a cartridge filled with
the sweepings of the abattoir. This national taste for bad food
seems all the more remarkable when one recalls that the
United States, more than any other country of the modern
world, has been enriched by immigrant cuisines. Every fresh
wave of newcomers has brought in new dishes, and many of
them have been of the highest merit. But very few of them
have been adopted by the natives, and the few have been
mainly inferior. From the Italians, for example, we have got
only spaghetti; it is now so American that it is to be had in
cans. But spaghetti is to the Italian cuisine simply what eggs
are to the Spanish: a raw material. We eat it as only those Italians eat it who are on the verge of ceasing to eat at all. Of the
multitudinous ways in which it may be cooked and garnished
we have learned but one, and that one is undoubtedly the
worst. So with the German sauerkraut—a superb victual when
properly prepared for the table. But how often, in America, is
it properly prepared? Perhaps once in 100,000 times. Even the
Germans, coming here, lose the art of handling it as its inner
nature deserves. It becomes in their hands, as in the hands of
American cooks, simply a sort of stewed hay, with overtones of
the dishpan. To encounter a decent dish of it in an American
eating-house would be as startling as to encounter a decent
soup.

What ails our victualry, principally, is the depressing standardization that ails everything else American. There was a
time when every American eating-house had its specialties, and
many of them were excellent. One did not expect to find the
same things everywhere. One went to one place for roast

goose, and to another for broiled soft crabs, and to another for oysters, and to yet another for mutton chops. Rolls made the old Parker House in Boston famous, and terrapin *à la* Maryland did the same for Barnum's and Guy's Hotels in Baltimore. This specialization still prevails in Europe. The best restaurants in Paris—that is, the best in the epicurean, not in the fashionable sense—do not profess to offer the whole range of the French cuisine. Each has its specialty, and upon that specialty the art of the chef is lavished, aided by prayer and fasting. His rivals in other places do not try to meet and best him on his own ground. They let him have his masterpiece, and devote themselves to perfecting masterpieces of their own. Thus victualing in France continues to show a great variety, and a never-failing charm. One may eat superbly every day, and never encounter a dish that is merely eatable. The Parisians look forward to dinner as a Mississippian looks forward to his evening necking of the Scriptures. But in America the public cooks have all abandoned specialization, and every one of them seems bent upon cooking as nearly as possible like all the rest. The American hotel meal is as rigidly standardized as the parts of a Ford, and so is the American restaurant meal. The local dishes, in all eating-houses pretending to any tone, are banned as low. So one hunts in vain in Boston for a decent plate of beans, and in Baltimore for a decent mess of steamed hard crabs, and in St. Louis for a decent rasher of catfish. They are obtainable, perhaps, but only along the wharves. One must take a squad of police along to enjoy them in safety.

What remains? A series of dishes fit only for diners who are hurrying to catch trains—tasteless roasts, banal beefsteaks, cremated chops, fish drenched in unintelligible sauces, greasy potatoes, and a long répertoire of vegetables with no more taste than baled shavings. The bill-of-fare is the same everywhere, and nowhere is it interesting. Within the past year I have been in the heart of New England and in the heart of the South. In both places the hotels offered the same standardized cuisine. In neither was there any culinary sign that I was not in Chicago or New York. In New England the brown bread was indistinguishable from the stuff served on railway dining-cars, and in the South there was no corn-bread at all.

I daresay that the railway diner has done much to bring in

this standardization. Distances are so great in the Federal Union that the man who does much traveling eats most of his meals on trains. So he gets used to dishes that all taste alike, whatever their ostensible contents, and ends by being unable to distinguish one from another. Thus he is indifferent to novelty, and perhaps hostile to it. The hotels give him what he wants. If he protested often enough and loudly enough, they would turn out their present crews of street-railway curve-greasers and locomotive firemen and put in cooks.

I leave the meals served on railway diners for a separate treatise, to be undertaken later in life. They are botched by the effect to give them the delusive variety of the appalling meals served in American hotels. In a kitchen two feet wide and eleven feet long, four or five honest but uninspired Aframericans try to concoct fifteen or twenty different dishes. They naturally spoil all of them. On the Continent of Europe all meals served on trains are *table d'hôte*. Their principal dishes are cooked, not on the train, but at the terminals. They are always appetizing and often excellent. Light wines and beers wash them down. The dining-cars are hideous with gaudy advertisements—one sees inside what one sees outside in America—but the chow does not insult the palate. At home I have to eat many meals in railway diners. I always order the same thing. It is impossible for even a cook traveling seventy miles an hour to spoil ham and eggs.

5

The Libido For the Ugly

On a Winter day, not long ago, coming out of Pittsburgh on one of the swift, luxurious expresses of the eminent Pennsylvania Railroad, I rolled eastward for an hour through the coal and steel towns of Westmoreland county. It was familiar ground; boy and man, I had been through it often before. But somehow I had never quite sensed its appalling desolation. Here was the very heart of industrial America, the center of its most lucrative and characteristic activity, the boast and pride of the richest and grandest nation ever seen on earth—and here was a scene so dreadfully hideous, so intolerably bleak and forlorn that it reduced the whole aspiration of man to a macabre and depressing joke. Here was wealth beyond computation, almost beyond imagination—and here were human habitations so abominable that they would have disgraced a race of alley cats.

I am not speaking of mere filth. One expects steel towns to be dirty. What I allude to is the unbroken and agonizing ugliness, the sheer revolting monstrousness, of every house in sight. From East Liberty to Greensburg, a distance of twenty-five miles, there was not one in sight from the train that did not insult and lacerate the eye. Some were so bad, and they were among the most pretentious—churches, stores, warehouses, and the like—that they were downright startling: one blinked before them as one blinks before a man with his face shot away. It was as if all the more advanced Expressionist architects of Berlin had been got drunk on *Schnapps*, and put to matching aberrations. A few masterpieces linger in memory, horrible even there: a crazy little church just west of Jeannette, set like a dormer-window on the side of a bare, leprous hill; the headquarters of the Veterans of Foreign Wars at Irwin; a steel stadium like a huge rat-trap somewhere further down the line. But most of all I recall the general effect—of hideousness without a break. There was not a single decent house within eye-range from the Pittsburgh suburbs to the Greensburg yards. There was not one that was not misshapen, and there was not one that was not shabby.

The county itself is not uncomely, despite the grime of the endless mills. It is, in form, a narrow river valley, with deep gullies running up into the hills. It is thickly settled, but not noticeably overcrowded. There is still plenty of room for building, even in the larger towns, and there are very few solid blocks. Nearly every house, big and little, has space on all four sides. Obviously, if there were architects of any professional sense or dignity in the region, they would have perfected a châlet to hug the hillsides—a châlet with a high-pitched roof, to throw off the heavy Winter snows, but still essentially a low and clinging building, wider than it was tall. But what have they done? They have taken as their model a brick set on end. This they have converted into a thing of dingy clapboards, with a narrow, low-pitched roof. And the whole they have set upon thin, preposterous brick piers. What could be more appalling? By the hundreds and thousands these abominable houses cover the bare hillsides, like gravestones in some gigantic and decaying cemetery. On their deep sides they are three, four and even five stories high; on their low sides they bury themselves swinishly in the mud. Not a fifth of them are perpendicular. They lean this way and that, hanging on to their bases precariously. And one and all they are streaked in grime, with dead and eczematous patches of paint peeping through the streaks.

Now and then there is a house of brick. But what brick! When it is new it is the color of a fried egg. When it has taken on the patina of the mills it is the color of an egg long past all hope or caring. Was it necessary to adopt that shocking color? No more than it was necessary to set all of the houses on end. Red brick, even in a steel town, ages with some dignity. Let it become downright black, and it is still sightly, especially if its trimmings are of white stone, with soot in the depths and the high spots washed by the rain. But in Westmoreland they prefer that uremic yellow, and so they have the most loathsome towns and villages ever seen by mortal eye.

I award this championship only after laborious research and incessant prayer. I have seen, I believe, all of the most unlovely towns of the world; they are all to be found in the United States. I have seen the mill towns of decomposing New England and the desert towns of Utah, Arizona and Texas. I am familiar with the back streets of Newark, Brooklyn, Chicago and Pittsburgh, and have made bold scientific explorations to Camden, N.J. and Newport News, Va. Safe in a Pullman, I have whirled through the gloomy, Godforsaken villages of Iowa and Kansas, and the malarious tide-water hamlets of Georgia. I have been to Bridgeport, Conn., and to Los Angeles. But nowhere on this earth, at home or abroad, have I seen anything to compare to the villages that huddle along the line of the Pennsylvania from the Pittsburgh yards to Greensburg. They are incomparable in color, and they are incomparable in design. It is as if some titanic and aberrant genius, uncompromisingly inimical to man, had devoted all the ingenuity of Hell to the making of them. They show grotesqueries of ugliness that, in retrospect, become almost diabolical. One cannot imagine mere human beings concocting such dreadful things, and one can scarcely imagine human beings bearing life in them.

Are they so frightful because the valley is full of foreigners— —dull, insensate brutes, with no love of beauty in them? Then why didn't these foreigners set up similar abominations in the countries that they came from? You will, in fact, find nothing of the sort in Europe—save perhaps in a few putrefying parts of England. There is scarcely an ugly village on the whole Continent. The peasants, however poor, somehow manage to make themselves graceful and charming habitations, even in Italy and Spain. But in the American village and small town the pull is always toward ugliness, and in that Westmoreland valley it has been yielded to with an eagerness bordering upon passion. It is incredible that mere ignorance should have achieved such masterpieces of horror. There is a voluptuous quality in them—the same quality that one finds in a Methodist sermon or an editorial in the New York *Herald-Tribune*. They look deliberate.

On certain levels of the human race, indeed, there seems to be a positive libido for the ugly, as on other and less Christian levels there is a libido for the beautiful. It is impossible to put down the wallpaper that defaces the average American home of the lower middle class to mere inadvertence, or to the obscene humor of the manufacturers. Such ghastly designs, it must be obvious, give a genuine delight to a certain type of mind. They meet, in some unfathomable way, its obscure and unintelligible demands. They caress it as "The Palms" caresses it, or the art of Landseer, or the ecclesiastical architecture of the United Brethren. The taste for them is as enigmatical and yet as common as the taste for vaudeville, dogmatic theology, sentimental movies, and the poetry of Edgar A. Guest. Or for the metaphysical speculations of Arthur Brisbane. Thus I suspect (though confessedly without knowing) that the vast majority of the honest folk of Westmoreland county, and especially the 100% Americans among them, actually admire the houses they live in, and are proud of them. For the same money they could get vastly better ones, but they prefer what they have got. Certainly there was no pressure upon the Veterans of Foreign Wars at Irwin to choose the dreadful edifice that bears their banner, for there are plenty of vacant buildings along the trackside, and some of them are appreciably better. They might, indeed, have built a better one of their own. But they chose that clapboarded horror with their eyes open, and having chosen it, they let it mellow into its present shocking depravity. They like it as it is: beside it, the Parthenon would no doubt offend them. In precisely the same way the authors of the rat-trap stadium that I have mentioned made a deliberate choice. After painfully designing and erecting it, they made it perfect in their own sight by putting a completely impossible pent-house, painted a staring yellow, on top of it. The effect is truly appalling. It is that of a fat woman with a black eye. It is that of a Presbyterian grinning. But they like it.

Here is something that the psychologists have so far neglected: the love of ugliness for its own sake, the lust to make the world intolerable. Its habitat is the United States. Out of the melting pot emerges a race which hates beauty as it hates truth. The etiology of this madness deserves a great deal more study than it has got. There must be causes behind it; it arises and flourishes in obedience to biological laws, and not as a mere act of God. What, precisely, are the terms of those laws? And why do they run stronger in America than elsewhere? Let some honest *Privat Dozent* apply himself to the problem.

VII.

Hymn to the Truth

ON December 28, 1917, in the midst of war's alarums, I printed in the New York *Evening Mail*, a journal now happily extinct, an article purporting to give the history of the bathtub. This article, I may say at once, was a tissue of somewhat heavy absurdities, all of them deliberate and most of them obvious. I alleged that the bathtub was unknown in the world until the '40's of the last century, and that it was then invented in Cincinnati by a contemporary of *Stammvater* Longworth. I described how the inventor, in the absence of running water in the town, employed Aframericans to haul it in buckets from the adjacent Ohio river. I told how a bathtub was put into the White House in the '50's, and how the intrepid Millard Fillmore, of Cayuga, N.Y., took the first presidential bath. I ended by saying that the medical faculty of the Republic opposed the new invention as dangerous to health, and that laws against it were passed by the legislators of Virginia, Pennsylvania and Massachusetts.

This article, plainly enough, was of spoofing all compact. I composed it, in fact, to sublimate and so make bearable the intolerable libido of the war for democracy, and I confess that I regarded it, when it came out in the *Mail*, with a certain professional satisfaction. It was promptly reprinted by various other great organs of the enlightenment, sometimes with credit, and after a while a stream of letters began to reach me from persons who had read it. Then, of a sudden, all my satisfaction turned to consternation. For it quickly appeared that at least nine-tenths of these readers took my idle jocosities with complete seriousness! Some of them, of antiquarian tastes, asked for further light upon this or that phase of the subject. Others offered corrections in detail. Yet others offered me corroboration! But the worst was to come. Soon I began to discover my preposterous "facts" in the writings of other men, some of them immensely earnest. The chiropractors and other such quacks collared them for use as evidence of the stupidity of

476

medical men. They were cited by medical men as proof of the progress of public hygiene. They got into learned journals and the transactions of learned societies. They were alluded to on the floor of Congress. The editorial writers of the land, borrowing them in toto and without mentioning my begetting of them, began to labor them in their dull, indignant way. They crossed the dreadful wastes of the North Atlantic, and were discussed horribly by English uplifters and German professors. Finally, they got into the standard works of reference, and began to be taught to the young.

For a while I was alarmed; then I was amused; then I began to be alarmed again. In the early part of 1926, having undergone a spiritual rebirth and put off sin, I resolved to confess, and so put an end to the imposture. This I did formally on May 23. I admitted categorically that I had invented the whole tale, and that there was not a word of truth in it. I pointed out its obvious and multitudinous absurdities. I called upon the pedagogues of the land to cease teaching such appalling nonsense to the young, and upon the historians to take it out of their books. This confession and appeal were printed simultaneously in thirty great American newspapers, with a combined circulation, according to their sworn claims, of more than 250,000,000. One of them, and perhaps the greatest of them all, was the eminent Boston *Herald*, organ of the New England illuminati. The *Herald*, on that bright May Sunday, printed my article on a leading page of its so-called Editorial Section, under a black and beetling four-column head, and with a two-column cartoon labeled satirically "The American Public Will Swallow Anything." And then, three weeks later, on June 13, in the same Editorial Section, but promoted to page one, the same *Herald* reprinted my ten-year-old fake—soberly and as a piece of news!

Do not misunderstand me: I am not seeking to cast a stone at the *Herald*, or at its talented and patriotic editors. It is, as every one knows, one of the glories of American journalism, and is awarded Pulitzer prizes almost as often as the Pulitzer papers themselves. It labors unceasingly for public morality, the Andy Mellon idealism, and the flag. If it were suppressed by the Watch and Ward Society to-morrow New England would revert instantly to savagery, wolves and catamounts

would roam in Boylston Street, and the Harvard Law School
would be engulfed by Bolshevism. Little does the public reck
what great sums such journals expend to establish and dissem-
inate the truth. It may cost $10,000 and a reporter's leg to get
a full and accurate list of the guests at a Roxbury wake, with
their injuries. My point is that, despite all this extravagant
frenzy for the truth, there is something in the human mind
that turns instinctively to fiction, and that even the most gifted
journalists succumb to it. A German philosopher, Dr. Hans
Vaihinger, has put the thing into a formal theory, and you will
find it expounded at length in his book, "The Philosophy of
As If." It is a sheer impossibility, says Dr. Vaihinger, for human
beings to think exclusively in terms of the truth. For one
thing, the stock of indubitable truths is too scanty. For another
thing, there is the instinctive aversion to them that I have mentioned. All of our thinking, according to Vaihinger, is in terms
of assumptions, many of them plainly not true. Into our most
solemn and serious reflections fictions enter—and three times
out of four they quickly crowd out all the facts.

That this truth about the so-called truth is true needs no argument. Every man, thinking of his wife, has to assume that
she is beautiful and amiable, else despair will seize him and he
will be unable to think at all. Every 100% American, contemplating Dr. Coolidge, is psychically bound to admire him: the
alternative is anarchy. Every Christian, viewing the clergy, is
forced into a bold theorizing to save himself from Darwinism
and Hell. And all of us, taking stock of ourselves, must resort
to hypothesis to escape the river. What ails the bald truth is
that it is mainly uncomfortable, and never caressing. What the
actual history of the bathtub may be I don't know: digging it
out would be an endless job, and the result, after all the labor,
would probably be only a string of banalities. The fiction I
concocted back in 1917 was at least better than that. It lacked
sense, but it was certainly not without a certain charm. There
were heroes in it, and villains. It revealed a conflict, with virtue
winning. So it was embraced by mankind, precisely as the story
of George Washington and the cherry-tree was embraced, and
it will live, I daresay, until it is displaced by something worse—
and hence better.

In other words, it was poetry, which is to say, a mellifluous and caressing statement of the certainly not true. The two elements, of untruth and of beauty, are both important, and perhaps equally. It is not sufficient that the thing said in poetry be untrue: it must also be said with a certain grace—it must soothe the ear while it debauches the mind. And it is not sufficient that it be voluptuous: it must also offer a rock and a refuge from the harsh facts of everyday. Poets, of course, protest against this doctrine. They argue that they actually deal in the truth, and that their brand of truth is of a peculiarly profound and esoteric quality—in other words, that their compositions add to the sum of human wisdom. It is sufficient answer to them to say that the chiropractors make precisely the same claim, and with exactly the same plausibility. Both actually deal in fictions. Those fictions are not truths; they are not even truths in decay. They are simply better-than-truths. They make life more comfortable and happy. They turn and dull the sharp edge of reality.

It is commonly held that the vast majority of men are anæsthetic to the poetry, as they are alleged to be anæsthetic to other forms of beauty, but this is itself a fiction, devised by poets to dignify their trade, and make it seem high-toned and mysterious. The fact is that the love of poetry is one of the most primitive of human traits, and that it appears in children almost as soon as they learn to speak and steal. I do not refer here to the love of verbal jingles, but to the love of poetry properly-so-called—that is, to the love of the agreeably not-so. A little girl who nurses a rag-doll is a poet, and so is a boy who plays at soldiers with a box of clothes-pins. Their ma is another poet when she brags about them to the neighbors, and their pa when he praises the cooking of their ma. The more simple-minded the individual, indeed, the greater his need of poetry, and hence the more steady his demand for it. No poet approved by the *intelligentsia* ever had so many customers as Edgar A. Guest. Are Guest's dithyrambs laughed at by the *intelligentsia*? Then it is not because the things they say are not so, but because the fiction in them is of a kind not satisfying to sniffish and snooty men. It is fiction suitable to persons of a less critical habit. It preaches the joys open to the humble. It glorifies their dire necessities. It cries down their lacks. It promises them happiness, and if not happiness, then at least contentment. No wonder it is popular! No wonder it is intoned every time Kiwanians get together, and the reassuring slapping of backs begins. It is itself a sort of back-slapping. And so is all other poetry. The strophes of Robert Browning elude the Kiwanian, but they are full of soothing for the young college professor, for they tell him that it is a marvelous and exhilarating thing to be as intellectual as he is. This, of course, is not true—which is the chief reason why it is pleasant. No normal human being wants to hear the truth. It is the passion of a small and aberrant minority of men, most of them pathological. They are hated for telling it while they live, and when they die they are swiftly forgotten. What remains to the world, in the field of wisdom, is a series of long-tested and solidly agreeable lies. It is out of such lies that most of the so-called knowledge of humanity flows. What begins as poetry ends as fact, and is embalmed in the history books. One recalls the gaudy days of 1914–1918.

But I am forgetting the coda to my story. On July 25, six weeks after the *Herald's* astounding *faux pas* and nine weeks after my exposure of the original fraud, I printed another article on the subject, disclosing the complete facts once more, and cackling over the joke at the *Herald's* expense. This second article got a great deal of attention: it was reprinted from end to end of the Republic, and discussed in such remote and barbarous places as Liverpool, Melbourne and Cape Town. And then, early in 1927, the distinguished *Scribner's Magazine* printed a learned article on the history of bathing, and in it all my stale nonsense was once more set forth as fact!

VIII.

The Pedagogy of Sex

IT is a curious and instructive fact that in all the vast literature of so-called sex hygiene emitted from the American presses for twenty years past there is scarcely a book of any sound and practical value. I have been through, I should say, at least a hundred such volumes, and I can recall but one that was even completely honest. That one was a little pamphlet called "The Sex Side of Life," by Mrs. Mary Ware Dennett, a birth controller but an intelligent woman. Naturally enough, it was suppressed by the wowsers of the Postoffice, and is now contraband. All the rest of the expository and hortatory manuals, large and small, are full of evasions, with many descents to downright false pretenses. It is difficult to imagine such prissy rubbish deceiving the adolescents to whom it is ostensibly addressed. For youth, though it may lack knowledge, is certainly not devoid of intelligence: it sees through shams with sharp and terrible eyes. When a schoolmaster is an ass, which happens in Christendom more often than not, you may be sure that even the dullest of his pupils is well aware of it.

The teachers of sex hygiene fall almost unanimously into that melancholy category. Very few such books appear to be written by adults of worldly experience and sound sense. They are, like the school physiology books, mainly the product of authors cursed with the *furor pedagogicus*—which is to say, of authors whose yearning to teach is unaccompanied by anything properly describable as useful knowledge or civilized discretion. I have read such books that were downright idiotic, and I have read others that were palpably dangerous. What ails most of them is simply the fact that their composers, as pedagogues, are moralists first, and scientists only afterward. Dealing with a subject in which only the plain and unequivocal facts can be of any imaginable value, they swathe those facts in such endless yards of pious platitude that not even a modern puella, appalling keen though her wits may be, can be expected to penetrate to the core of wisdom that is theoretically concealed within them.

Several common defects run through these lamentable tomes. One is the thumping *non sequitur* that is in them—the gross disparity between their premisses and their conclusions. They start off with attempts to show that the phenomena of sex in the lower organisms—usually dahlias, herring or frogs— are beautiful and instructive, and they close with horrible warnings that the phenomena of sex in man are ugly and not to be mentioned. I do not forget, of course, their frequent high praise of maternity, their florid descriptions of the ineffable joys of philoprogenitiveness. But maternity, as they picture it, is scarcely more sexual than playing the piano. It is, in fact, set up as something definitely anti-sexual, and virtuous thereby, —as a sweet boon that must be forfeited if sex is yielded to. I do not know how this logical swamp is to be got around. It may present, indeed, a difficulty that no one will ever resolve. All I presume to do is to point out that the authors of the sex hygiene books have certainly not disposed of it, and that most of them seem to be happily unaware that it exists. First they describe romantically the mating of the calla-lilies and the June bugs, and then they plunge furiously into their revolting treatises upon *ophthalmia neonatorum*, lues, prostatitis, female weakness, and the fires of Hell. First they paint a picture fit for a Christmas card, and then they turn it around and show a panorama of jails, gutters and dissecting-rooms. It is the old juristic error of trying to put down crime by converting trivial misdemeanors into thumping felonies, with capital punishment. I don't believe that it works. Personally, I do not frequent adolescent society, but if those who do so are to be believed it is looser to-day than it ever was before. That is to say, the era of sex hygiene books—pouring from the presses by the million—is an era of rapidly increasing sexual recklessness. Is there any relation of cause and effect here? I incline to think that there may be. Youth, with its highly efficient eyes, sees plainly that many, at least, of the dangers described are enormously exaggerated. What more natural than for it to conclude that the rest are exaggerated, too?

There is another defect common to most of these books, and it is quite as serious as the first. It lies in their evasion of the plain fact that sex would be unimportant if it were not for its capacity to produce an overwhelming ecstasy—that the average human being seldom thinks of it in any other aspect, and almost never hears of it. This ecstasy, of course, does not have to be taught; it is known by every flapper who has been kissed by her first beau. But when, in a treatise upon the subject, it is not mentioned at all—or, if mentioned, passed over gingerly—, then it is certainly not surprising if the young reader drops the book as ignorant and fraudulent, and is lost to the moral lessons it inculcates. Only Mrs. Dennett, of all the sexual pedagogues I have read, so much as hints that the exercise of the reproductive faculty is immensely agreeable—and Mrs. Dennett, as I have said, is under the ban of the Postoffice. The rest of the sex hygienists depict it either as something inert and banal, like having one's hair cut, or as something painful and dangerous, like having one's appendix out. There is, on the one hand, the chaste and arctic philandering of the rose, and there is on the other hand a complex of pathological horrors. The average youngster, male or female, is deceived by neither picture. It is well known, even in the primary grades, that kissing is far more pleasant than gargling or sneezing, and it is unanimously suspected that what instinct suggests ought to follow is more pleasant still. Those ensuing proceedings constitute the fundamental mystery of sex, as the young confront it—and yet it is precisely there that the sex hygiene books are least illuminating. They are full of alarming news about the remotest and most improbable consequences of a phenomenon, and leave the phenomenon itself undescribed. Thus they fail to satisfy the very curiosity that ostensibly brought them into being—the very curiosity they so ineptly inflame. Is it any wonder that intelligent young readers—and even a moron, at twelve, is still intelligent—cast them aside as buncombe, and carry away nothing from them save the notion that what is so dangerous must be immensely fascinating, else the human race would have committed suicide long ago by avoiding the risk?

As I have hinted, it may be that these defects in the sex hygiene books—and I could list many more—are inescapable. It may be that the subject is inherently and incurably resistant to pedagogical science. But I prefer to take a more optimistic view. The human mind is a pliant and puissant organ. It has solved many occult and vexatious problems. Perhaps, in the long run, it will solve this one too. Perhaps, indeed, the solution would be possible to-morrow—if the higher powers of the mind were applied to it. In the sex hygiene books, so far as I can make out, only the lower powers are in action. Such books, it appears, are not ordinarily written by persons of sound information and ordinary sense. On the contrary, they seem to be mainly the product of Freudian cripples who know very little about the subject they discuss, and have nothing to say about it that is apposite and worth hearing. They are moral exhorters, not seekers of the truth. Their aim is hortatory, not scientific. They apply themselves to what ought to be, not to what is.

I believe that the remedy lies in trying to enlist performers of a better grade—that is, performers who have taken the trouble to investigate the matters they deal with, calmly and thoroughly, and who have the degree of common sense that one ordinarily looks for in a railroad conductor or an ice-man. There must be plenty of such men, not to mention women. Their writings, indeed, are already available—pursued by the wowsers, but not yet quite scotched. I have mentioned Mrs. Dennett and offer Havelock Ellis as another example. But most such authors, of course, address adults—what is more, highly sophisticated adults. What remains is for them to bring their knowledge down to the comprehension of the young. I believe that it can be done, and that on some near to-morrow it will be done. When the day comes at least nine-tenths of the sex hygiene books that now stand in the book-shops will be thrown out as rubbish.

IX.

Metropolis

I^T is astonishing how little New York figures in current
American literature. Think of the best dozen American
novels of the last ten years. No matter which way your taste
and prejudice carry you, you will find, I believe, that Manhattan Island is completely missing from at least ten of them, and
that in the other two it is little more than a passing scene,
unimportant to the main action. Perhaps the explanation is to
be sought in the fact that very few authors of any capacity live
in the town. It attracts all the young aspirants powerfully, and
hundreds of them, lingering on, develop into very proficient
hacks and quacks, and so eventually adorn the Authors'
League, the Poetry Society, and the National Institute of Arts
and Letters. But not many remain who have anything worth
hearing to say. They may keep quarters on the island, but they
do their writing somewhere else.

Primarily, I suppose, it is too expensive for them: in order to
live decently they must grind through so much hack work for
the cheap magazines, the movies and the Broadway theaters
that there is no time left for their serious concerns. But there is
also something else. The town is too full of distractions to be
comfortable to artists; it is comfortable only to performers. Its
machinery of dissipation is so vastly developed that no man
can escape it—not even an author laboring in his lonely room,
the blinds down and chewing-gum plugging his ears. He hears
the swish of skirts through the key-hole; down the area-way
comes the clink of ice in tall glasses; some one sends him a pair
of tickets to a show which whisper promises will be the dirtiest
seen since the time of the Twelve Apostles. It is a sheer impossibility in New York to escape such appeals to the ductless
glands. They are in the very air. The town is no longer a place
of work; it is a place of pleasure. Even the up-State Baptist,
coming down to hear the Rev. Dr. John Roach Straton tear
into sin, must feel the pull of temptation. He wanders along
Broadway to shiver dutifully before the Metropolitan Opera

House, with its black record of lascivious music dramas and adulterous tenors, but before he knows what has struck him he is lured into a movie house even gaudier and wickeder, to sweat before a film of carnal love with the lewd music of Tschaikowsky dinning in his ears, or into a grindshop auction house to buy an ormolu clock disgraceful to a Christian, or into Childs' to debauch himself with such victuals as are seen in Herkimer county only on days of great ceremonial.

Such is the effect of organized badness, operating upon imperfect man. But what is bad is also commonly amusing, and so I continue to marvel that the authors of the Republic, and especially the novelists, do not more often reduce it to words. Is there anything more charming and instructive in the scenes that actually engage them? I presume to doubt it. There are more frauds and scoundrels, more quacks and cony-catchers, more suckers and visionaries in New York than in all the country west of the Union Hill, N.J., breweries. In other words, there are more interesting people. They pour in from all four points of the compass, and on the hard rocks of Manhattan they do their incomparable stuff, day and night, year in and year out, ever hopeful and ever hot for more. Is it drama if Jens Jensen, out in Nebraska, pauses in his furrow to yearn heavily that he were a chiropractor? Then why isn't it drama if John Doe, prancing in a New York night club, pauses to wonder who the fellow was who just left in a taxi with Mrs. Doe? Is it tragedy that Nils Nilsen, in South Dakota, wastes his substance trying to horn into a mythical Heaven? Then why isn't it tragedy when J. Eustace Garfunkel, after years of effort, fails to make the steep grade of St. Bartholomew's Church?

New York is not all bricks and steel. There are hearts there, too, and if they do not break, then they at least know how to leap. It is the place where all the aspirations of the Western World meet to form one vast master aspiration, as powerful as the suction of a steam dredge. It is the icing on the pie called Christian civilization. That it may have buildings higher than any ever heard of, and gin enough to keep it gay, and bawdy shows enough, and door-openers enough, and noise and confusion enough—that these imperial ends may be achieved, uncounted millions sweat and slave on all the forlorn farms of the earth, and in all the miserable slums, including its own. It pays more for a meal than an Italian or a Pole pays for a wife, and the meal is better than the wife. It gets the best of everything, and especially of what, by all reputable ethical systems, is the worst. It has passed beyond all fear of Hell or hope of Heaven. The primary postulates of all the rest of the world are its familiar jokes. A city apart, it is breeding a race apart. Is that race American? Then so is a bashi-bazouk American. Is it decent? Then so is a street-walker decent. But I don't think that it may be reasonably denounced as dull.

What I marvel at is that the gorgeous, voluptuous color of this greatest of world capitals makes so little showing in the lovely letters of the United States. I am not forgetting such things as John Dos Passos' "Manhattan Transfer" and Felix Riesenberg's "East Side, West Side"—but neither am I admitting that they fill my bill. If only as spectacle, the city is superb. It has a glitter like that of the Constantinople of the Comneni. It roars with life like the Bagdad of the Sassanians. These great capitals of antiquity, in fact, were squalid villages compared to it, as Rome was after their kind, and Paris, Berlin and London are to-day. There is little in New York that does not issue out of money. It is not a town of ideas; it is not even a town of causes. But what issues out of money is often extremely brilliant, and I believe that it is more brilliant in New York than it has ever been anywhere else. A truly overwhelming opulence envelops the whole place, even the slums. The slaves who keep it going may dwell in vile cubicles, but they are hauled to and from their work by machinery that costs hundreds of millions, and when they fare forth to recreate themselves for tomorrow's tasks they are felled and made dumb by a gaudiness that would have floored John Paleologus himself. Has any one ever figured out, in hard cash, the value of the objects of art stored upon Manhattan Island? I narrow it to paintings, and bar out all the good ones. What would it cost to replace even the bad ones? Or all the statuary, bronzes, hangings, pottery, and bogus antiques? Or the tons of bangles, chains of pearls stomachers, necklaces, and other baubles? Assemble all the diamonds into one colossal stone, and you will have a weapon to slay Behemoth. The crowds pour in daily, bringing the gold wrung from iron and coal, hog and cow. It is invisible, for they carry it in checks, but it is real for all that. Every dollar earned in

Kansas or Montana finds its way, soon or late, to New York, and if there is a part of it that goes back, there is also a part of it that sticks.

What I contend is that this spectacle, lush and barbaric in its every detail, offers the material for a great imaginative literature. There is not only gaudiness in it; there is also a hint of strangeness; it has overtones of the fabulous and even of the diabolical. The thing simply cannot last. If it does not end by catastrophe, then it will end by becoming stale, which is to say, dull. But while it is in full blast it certainly holds out every sort of stimulation that the gifted literatus may plausibly demand. The shocking imbecility of Main Street is there and the macabre touch of Spoon River. But though Main Street and Spoon River have both found their poets, Manhattan is still to be adequately sung. How will the historian of the future get at it, imagining a future and assuming that it will have historians? The story is not written anywhere in official records. It is not in the files of the newspapers, which reflect only the surface, and not even all of that. It will not go into memoirs, for the actors in the melodramatic comedy have no taste for prose, and moreover they are all afraid to tell what they know. What it needs, obviously, is an imaginative artist. We have them in this bursting, stall-fed land—not many of them, perhaps—not as many as our supply of quacks—but nevertheless we have them. The trouble is that they either hate Manhattan too much to do its portrait, or are so bedazzled by it that their hands are palsied and their parts of speech demoralized. Thus we have dithyrambs of Manhattan—but no prose.

I hymn the town without loving it. It is immensely amusing, but I see nothing in it to inspire the fragile and shy thing called affection. I can imagine an Iowan loving the black, fecund stretches of his native State, or a New Englander loving the wreck of Boston, or even a Chicagoan loving Chicago, poets, Loop, stockyards and all, but it is hard for me to fancy any rational human being loving New York. Does one love bartenders? Or interior decorators? Or elevator starters? Or the head-waiters of night clubs? No, one delights in such functionaries, and perhaps one respects them and even reveres them, but one does not love them. They are as palpably cold and artificial as the Cathedral of St. John the Divine. Like it, they are mere functions of solvency. When the sheriff comes in they flutter away. One invests affection in places where it will be safe when the winds blow.

But I am speaking now of spectacles, not of love affairs. The spectacle of New York remains—infinitely grand and gorgeous, stimulating like the best that comes out of goblets, and none the worse for its sinister smack. The town seizes upon all the more facile and agreeable emotions like band music. It is immensely trashy—but it remains immense. Is it a mere Utopia of rogues, a vast and complicated machine for rooking honest men? I don't think so. The honest man, going to its market, gets sound value for his money. It offers him luxury of a kind never dreamed of in the world before—the luxury of being served by perfect and unobtrusive slaves, human and mechanical. It permits him to wallow regally—nay, almost celestially. The Heaven of the Moslems is open to any one who can pay the *couvert* charge and honorarium of the hat-check girl—and there is a door, too, leading into the Heaven of the Christians, or, at all events, into every part of it save that devoted to praise and prayer. Nor is all this luxury purely physiological. There is entertainment also for the spirit, or for what passes for the spirit when men are happy. There were more orchestral concerts in New York last Winter than there were in Berlin. The town has more theaters, and far better ones, than a dozen Londons. It is, as I have said, loaded with art to the gunwales, and steadily piling more on deck. Is it unfecund of ideas? Perhaps. But surely it is not hostile to them. There is far more to the show it offers than watching a pretty gal oscillate her hips; one may also hear some other gal, only a shade less sightly, babble the latest discoveries in antinomianism. All kinds, in brief, come in. There are parts for all in the *Totentanz*, even for moralists to call the figures. But there is, as yet, no recorder to put it on paper.

X.

Dives into Quackery

Chiropractic

THIS preposterous quackery is now all the rage in the back reaches of the Republic, and even begins to conquer the less civilized of the big cities. As the old-time family doctor dies out in the country towns, with no trained successor willing to take over his dismal business, he is followed by some hearty blacksmith or ice-wagon driver, turned into a chiropractor in six months, often by correspondence. In Los Angeles the damned there are more chiropractors than actual physicians, and they are far more generally esteemed. Proceeding from the Ambassador Hotel to the heart of the town, along Wilshire boulevard, one passes scores of their gaudy signs; there are even many chiropractic "hospitals." The morons who pour in from the prairies and deserts, most of them ailing, patronize these "hospitals" copiously, and give to the chiropractic pathology the same high respect that they accord to the theology of Aimée McPherson and the art of Cecil De Mille. That pathology is grounded upon the doctrine that all human ills are caused by the pressure of misplaced vertebra upon the nerves which come out of the spinal cord—in other words, that every disease is the result of a pinch. This, plainly enough, is buncombe. The chiropractic therapeutics rest upon the doctrine that the way to get rid of such pinches is to climb upon a table and submit to an heroic pummeling by a retired piano mover. This, obviously, is buncombe doubly damned.

Both doctrines were launched upon the world by an old quack named Andrew T. Still, the father of osteopathy. For years his followers merchanted them, and made a lot of money at the trade. But as they grew opulent they grew ambitious, *i.e.*, they began to study anatomy and physiology. The result was a gradual abandonment of Papa Still's ideas. The high-toned osteopath of to-day is a sort of eclectic. He tries anything that promises to work, from tonsillectomy to the vibrations of the late Dr. Abrams. With four years' training behind him, he probably knows more anatomy than the average graduate of the Johns Hopkins Medical School, or, at all events, more osteology. Thus enlightened, he seldom has much to say about pinched nerves in the back. But as he abandoned the Still revelation it was seized by the chiropractors, led by another quack, one Palmer. This Palmer grabbed the pinched nerve nonsense and began teaching it to ambitious farm-hands and out-at-elbow Baptist preachers in a few easy lessons. To-day the backwoods swarm with chiropractors, and in most States they have been able to exert enough pressure on the rural politicians to get themselves licensed. Any lout with strong hands and arms is perfectly equipped to become a chiropractor. No education beyond the elements is necessary. The whole art and mystery may be imparted in a few months, and the graduate is then free to practice upon God's images. The takings are often high, and so the profession has attracted thousands of recruits—retired baseball players, plumbers, truck-drivers, longshoremen, bogus dentists, dubious preachers, village school superintendents. Now and then a quack doctor of some other school—say homeopathy—plunges into it. Hundreds of promising students come from the intellectual rank of hospital orderlies.

In certain States efforts have been made, sometimes by the medical fraternity, to make the practice of chiropractic unlawful. I am glad to be able to report that practically all of them have failed. Why should it be prohibited? I believe that every free-born man has a clear right, when he is ill, to seek any sort of treatment that he yearns for. If his mental processes are of such a character that the theory of chiropractic seems plausible to him, then he should be permitted to try chiropractic. And if it be granted that he has a right to do so, then it follows clearly that any stevedore privy to the technique of chiropractic has a right to treat him. To preach any contrary doctrine is to advocate despotism and slavery. The arguments for such despotism are all full of holes, and especially those that come from medical men who have been bitten by the public hygiene madness, *i.e.*, by the messianic delusion. Such fanatics infest every health department in the land. They assume glibly that the whole aim of civilization is to cut down the death-rate, and to attain that

end they are willing to make a sacrifice of everything else imaginable, including their own sense of humor. There is, as a
matter of fact, not the slightest reason to believe that cutting
down the death-rate, in itself, is of much benefit to the human
race. A people with an annual rate of 40 a thousand might still
produce many Huxleys and Darwins, and one with a rate of
but 8 or 9 might produce nothing but Coolidges and Billy
Sundays. The former probability, in truth, is greater than the
latter, for a low rate does not necessarily mean that more superior individuals are surviving; it may mean only that more of
the inferior are surviving, and that the next generation will be
burdened by their get.

Such quackeries as Christian Science, osteopathy and chiropractic work against the false humanitarianism of the hygienists and to excellent effect. They suck in the botched, and help
them on to bliss eternal. When these botched fall into the
hands of competent medical men they are very likely to be
patched up and turned loose upon the world, to beget their
kind. But massaged along the backbone to cure their lues, they
quickly pass into the last stages, and so their pathogenic heritage perishes with them. What is too often forgotten is that
nature obviously intends the botched to die, and that every
interference with that benign process is full of dangers. Moreover, it is, like birth control, profoundly immoral. The chiropractors are innocent in both departments. That their labors
tend to propagate epidemics and so menace the lives of all of
us, as is alleged by their medical opponents—this I doubt. The
fact is that most infectious diseases of any seriousness throw
out such alarming symptoms and so quickly that no sane chiropractor is likely to monkey with them. Seeing his patient
breaking out in pustules, or choking, or falling into a stupor,
he takes to the woods at once, and leaves the business to the
nearest medical man. His trade is mainly with ambulant patients; they must come to his studio for treatment. Most of
them have lingering diseases; they tour all the neighborhood
doctors before they reach him. His treatment, being entirely
nonsensical, is in accord with the divine plan. It is seldom, perhaps, that he actually kills a patient, but at all events he keeps
many a worthy soul from getting well.

Thus the multiplication of chiropractors in the Republic

gives me a great deal of pleasure. It is agreeable to see so many morons getting slaughtered, and it is equally agreeable to see so many other morons getting rich. The art and mystery of scientific medicine, for a decade or more past, has been closed to all save the sons of wealthy men. It takes a small fortune to go through a Class A medical college, and by the time the graduate is able to make a living for himself he is entering upon middle age, and is commonly so disillusioned that he is unfit for practice. Worse, his fees for looking at tongues and feeling pulses tend to be cruelly high. His predecessors charged fifty cents and threw in the pills; his own charges approach those of divorce lawyers, consulting engineers and the higher hetæræ. Even general practice, in our great Babylons, has become a sort of specialty, with corresponding emoluments. But the chiropractor, having no such investment in his training, can afford to work for more humane wages, and so he is getting more and more of the trade. Six weeks after he leaves his job at the filling-station or abandons the steering-wheel of his motor-truck he knows all the anatomy and physiology that he will ever learn in this world. Six weeks more, and he is an adept at all the half-Nelsons and left hooks that constitute the essence of chiropractic therapy. Soon afterward, having taken postgraduate courses in advertising, salesmanship and mental mastery, he is ready for practice. A sufficiency of patients, it appears, is always ready, too. I hear of no complaint from chiropractors of bad business. New ones are being turned out at a dizzy rate, but they all seem to find the pickings easy. Some time ago I heard of a chiropractor who, having once been a cornet-player, had abandoned chiropractic in despair, and gone back to cornet-playing. But investigation showed that he was really not a chiropractor at all, but an osteopath.

The osteopaths, I fear, are finding this new competition serious and unpleasant. As I have said, it was their Hippocrates, the late Dr. Still, who invented all of the thrusts, lunges, yanks, hooks and bounces that the lowly chiropractors now employ with such vast effect, and for years the osteopaths had a monopoly of them. But when they began to grow scientific and ambitious their course of training was lengthened until it took in all sorts of tricks and dodges borrowed from the regular doctors, or resurrection men, including plucking of tonsils, adenoids and appendices, the use of the stomach-pump, and even some of the legerdemain of psychiatry. They now harry their students furiously, and turn them out ready for anything from growing hair on a bald head to frying a patient with the *x*-rays. All this new striving, of course, quickly brought its inevitable penalties. The osteopathic graduate, having sweated so long, was no longer willing to take a case of sarcoma for $2, and in consequence he lost patients. Worse, very few aspirants could make the long grade. The essence of osteopathy itself could be grasped by any lively farm-hand or night watchman in a few weeks, but the borrowed magic baffled him. Confronted by the phenomenon of gastrulation, or by the curious behavior of heart muscle, or by any of the current theories of immunity, he commonly took refuge, like his brother of the orthodox faculty, in a gulp of laboratory alcohol, or fled the premises altogether. Thus he was lost to osteopathic science, and the chiropractors took him in; nay, they welcomed him. He was their meat. Borrowing that primitive part of osteopathy which was comprehensible to the meanest understanding, they threw the rest overboard, at the same time denouncing it as a sorcery invented by the Medical Trust. Thus they gathered in the garage mechanics, ash-men and decayed welter-weights, and the land began to fill with their graduates. Now there is a chiropractor at every cross-roads, and in such sinks of imbecility as Los Angeles they are as thick as bootleggers.

I repeat that it eases and soothes me to see them so prosperous, for they counteract the evil work of the so-called science of public hygiene, which now seeks to make morons immortal. If a man, being ill of a pus appendix, resorts to a shaved and fumigated longshoreman to have it disposed of, and submits willingly to a treatment that involved balancing him on McBurney's spot and playing on his vertebræ as on a concertina, then I am willing, for one, to believe that he is badly wanted in Heaven. And if that same man, having achieved lawfully a lovely babe, hires a blacksmith to cure its diphtheria by pulling its neck, then I do not resist the divine will that there shall be one less radio fan in 1967. In such matters, I am convinced, the laws of nature are far better guides than the fiats and machinations of the medical busybodies who now try to run us. If the latter gentlemen had their way, death, save at the hands of hangmen, Prohibition agents and other such legalized assassins, would be abolished altogether, and so the present differential in favor of the enlightened would disappear. I can't convince myself that that would work any good to the world. On the contrary, it seems to me that the current coddling of the half-witted should be stopped before it goes too far—if, indeed, it has not gone too far already. To that end nothing operates more cheaply and effectively than the prosperity of quacks. Every time a bottle of cancer specific goes through the mails *Homo americanus* is improved to that extent. And every time a chiropractor spits on his hands and proceeds to treat a gastric ulcer by stretching the backbone the same high end is achieved.

But chiropractic, of course, is not perfect. It has superb potentialities, but only too often they are not converted into concrete cadavers. The hygienists rescue many of its foreordained customers, and, turning them over to agents of the Medical Trust, maintained at the public expense, get them cured. Moreover, chiropractic itself is not certainly fatal: even an Iowan with diabetes may survive its embraces. Yet worse, I have a suspicion that it sometimes actually cures. For all I know (or any orthodox pathologist seems to know) it *may* be true that certain malaises are caused by the pressure of vagrom vertebræ upon the spinal nerves. And it *may* be true that a hearty ex-boilermaker, by a vigorous yanking and kneading, may be able to relieve that pressure. What is needed is a scientific inquiry into the matter, under rigid test conditions, by a committee of men learned in the architecture and plumbing of the body, and of a high and incorruptible sagacity. Let a thousand patients be selected, let a gang of selected chiropractors examine their backbones and determine what is the matter with them, and then let these diagnoses be checked up by the exact methods of scientific medicine. Then let the same chiropractors essay to cure the patients whose maladies have been determined. My guess is that the chiropractors' errors in diagnosis will run to at least 95% and that their failures in treatment will push 99%. But I am willing to be convinced.

Where is such a committee to be found? I undertake to nominate it at ten minutes' notice. The land swarms with men competent in anatomy and pathology, and yet not engaged as doctors. There are hundreds of roomy and well-heated hospitals, with endless clinical material. I offer to supply the committee with cigars and music during the test. I offer, further, to supply both the committee and the chiropractors with sound pre-war wet goods. I offer, finally, to give a bawdy banquet to the whole Medical Trust at the conclusion of the proceedings.

2

Criminology

The more I read the hand-books of the new criminology, the more I am convinced that it stands on a level with dogmatic theology, chiropractic and the New Thought—in brief, that it is mainly buncombe. That it has materially civilized punishment I do not, of course, deny; what I question is its doctrine as to the primary causes of crime. The average man, as every one knows, puts those causes in the domain of free will. The criminal, in his view, is simply a scoundrel who has deliberately chosen to break the law and injure his fellow-men. *Ergo*, he deserves to be punished swiftly and mercilessly. The new criminologists, in swinging away from that naïve view, have obviously gone too far in the other direction. They find themselves, in the end, embracing a determinism that is as childlike as the free will of the man in the street. Crime, as they depict it, becomes a sort of disease, either inherited or acquired by contagion, and as devoid of moral content or significance as smallpox. The criminal is no longer a black-hearted villain, to be put down by force, but a poor brother who has succumbed to the laws of Mendel and the swinish stupidity of society. The aim of punishment is not to make him sweat, but to dissuade and rehabilitate him. In every pickpocket there is a potential Good Man. All this, gradually gaining credit, has greatly ameliorated punishments. They have not only lost their old barbaric quality; they have also diminished quantitatively. Men do not sit in prison as long as they used to; the parole boards turn them out almost as fast as the cops shove them in. The result is a public discontent that must be manifest. Whenever a criminal of any eminence comes to trial there are loud bellows against any show of mercy to him, and demands that he be punished to the limit. One never hears complaints any more that the courts are too savage; one hears only complaints that they are too soft and sentimental.

I am a congenital disbeliever in laws, and have only the most formal respect for the juridic process and its learned protagonists; nevertheless, it seems to me that there is a certain reasonableness in this unhappiness. For what it indicates, basically, is simply the inability of the average man to grasp the determinism of the new criminologists. He cannot imagine an apparently voluntary act that is determined, or even materially conditioned, from without. He can think of crime only in terms of free will, and so thinking of it, he believes that it ought to be punished in the ancient Christian manner, *i.e.*, according to the damage flowing out of it, and not according to the temptations behind it. Certainly this is not an illogical ground to take. In all the other relations of life the average man sees free will accepted as axiomatic: he could not imagine a world in which it was denied. His religion is based squarely upon it: he knows, by the oath of his pastor, that his free acts can lift him to Heaven or cast him down to Hell. He works as a matter of free will, and is punished inevitably if he lags. His marriage, as he sees it, was a free will compact, and though he has some secret doubt, perhaps, that its issue came that way, he nevertheless orders his relations with his children on the same basis, and assumes it in judging them. In other words, he lives in a world in which free will is apparently omnipotent, and in which it is presumed even when there is no direct evidence for it. All his daily concerns are free will concerns. Well, what the criminologists ask him to do is to separate one special concern from the rest, and hand it over to determinism. They damn legislators for passing harsh laws, and judges and jailers for executing them—free will. They denounce society for "coercing" morons into crime—free will again. And then they argue that the criminals are no more than helpless victims of circumstance, like motes dancing along a sunbeam—determinism in its purest and sweetest form.

No wonder the plain man baulks! Suppose an analogous suspension of the usual rules were attempted in some other field. Suppose it were argued seriously that free will had nothing to do with, say, the execution of contracts. Suppose an employer who failed to pay his workmen on Saturday were excused on the ground that he was the helpless victim of an evil heredity or of the stupidity of society, and thus not to be blamed for dissipating his money on Ford parts, women, foreign missions, or drink? Suppose the workman who had got out a mechanic's lien against him and sought to levy on his assets were denounced as a cruel and medieval fellow, and at odds with human progress? Certainly there would be a horrible hullabaloo, and equally certainly it would be justified. For whatever the theoretical arguments for determinism—and I am prepared to go even further in granting them than the criminologists go—, it must be plain that the everyday affairs of the world are ordered on an assumption of free will, and that it is impossible, practically speaking, to get rid of it. Society itself, indeed, is grounded upon that assumption. Imagining it as determined is possible only to professional philosophers, whose other imaginings are surely not such as to give any authority to this one. The plain man simply gives up the effort as hopeless —and perhaps as also a bit anarchistic and un-Christian. So he is sniffish when the new criminologists begin to prattle their facile determinism, and when he observes it getting credit from the regular agents of the law he lets a loud whoop of protest. I do not believe he is naturally cruel and vindictive; on the contrary, he is very apt to be maudlinly sentimental. But sentiment is one thing, and what seems to him to be a palpably false philosophy is quite another. He no more favors letting criminals go on the ground that they can't help themselves than he favors giving money to foreign missions, or the Red Cross, or the Y.M.C.A. on the ground that it is his inescapable duty. In all of these cases he is willing to be persuaded, but in none of them is he willing to be dragooned.

Thus I fear that the criminologists of the new school only pile up trouble for themselves, and indirectly for their pets, when they attempt to revise so radically the immemorial human view of crime. If they kept quiet in the department of responsibility, they would be heard with far more attention and respect in the department of punishment, where they really have something apposite and useful to say. Their influence here, in fact, is already immense, and it works much good. Our prisons are no longer quite as sordid and demoralizing as they used to be. They are still bad enough, in all conscience, but they are not as bad as they were. Here there is room for yet more improvement, and it cries aloud to be made. The men to work out its details are the criminologists. They have studied the effects of the prevailing punishments, and know where those punishments succeed or fail. They are happily devoid of that proud ignorance which is one of the boasts of the average judge, and they lack the unpleasant zeal of district attorneys, jail wardens and other such professional blood-letters. They need only offer the proofs that this or that punishment is ineffective to see it abandoned for something better, or, at all events, less obviously bad. But when they begin to talk of criminals in terms of pathology, even of social pathology, they speak a language that the plain man cannot understand and doesn't want to hear. He believes that crime, in the overwhelming majority of cases, is a voluntary matter, and that it ought to pay its own way and bury its own dead. He is not bothered about curing criminals, or otherwise redeeming them. He is intent only upon punishing them, and the more swiftly and certainly that business is achieved the better he is satisfied. Every time it is delayed by theorizing about the criminal's heredity and environment, and the duty that society owes to him, the plain man breaks into indignation. Only too often that indignation has been wrecked upon criminology and the criminologists. More American States, of late, have gone back to capital punishment than have abandoned it. What set the tide to running that way was surely not mere blood-lust. It was simply a natural reaction against the doctrine that murder is mainly an accidental and unfortunate matter, and devoid of moral content, like slipping on an icy sidewalk or becoming the father of twins.

3

Eugenics

This great moral cause, like that of the criminologists, is much corrupted by blather. In none of the books of its master minds is there a clear definition of the superiority they talk about so copiously. At one time they seem to identify it with high intelligence, at another time with character, *i.e.*, moral stability, and at yet another time with mere fame, *i.e.*, luck.

Was Napoleon I a superior man, as I am privately inclined to believe, along with many of the eugenists? Then so was Aaron Burr, if in less measure. Was Paul of Tarsus? Then so was Brigham Young. Were the Gracchi? Then so were Karl Marx and William Jennings Bryan.

This matter of superiority, indeed, presents cruel and inerad-icable difficulties. If it is made to run with service to the human race, the eugenist is soon mired, for many men held to be highly useful are obviously second-rate, and leave third-rate progeny behind them, for example, General Grant. And if it is made to run with intellectual brilliance and originality the troubles that loom up are just as serious, for men of that rare quality are generally felt to be dangerous, and sometimes they undoubtedly are. The case of Friedrich Wilhelm Nietzsche is in point. I suppose that no rational person to-day, not even an uncured Liberty Loan orator or dollar-a-year man, would ar-gue seriously that Nietzsche was inferior. On the contrary, his extraordinary gifts are now unanimously admitted, save per-haps by the rev. clergy. But what of his value to the human race? And what of his eugenic fitness? It is not easy to answer these questions. Nietzsche, in fact, preached a gospel that to most human beings remains unbearable, and it will probably continue unbearable for centuries to come. Its adoption by Dr. Coolidge, by and with the advice and consent of the Senate, would plunge this Republic into dreadful woe. And Nietzsche himself was a chronic invalid who died insane—the sort of wreck who, had he lived into our time, would have been a cus-tomer of chiropractors. Worse, he suffered from a malady of a scandalous nature, and of evil effects upon the sufferer's off-spring. Was it good or bad luck for the worth, eugenically speaking, that he died a bachelor?

But their vagueness about the exact nature of superiority is not the only thing that corrupts the fine fury of the eugenists. Even more dismaying is their gratuitous assumption that all of the socially useful and laudable qualities (whatever they may be) are the exclusive possession of one class of men, and that the other classes lack them altogether. This is plainly not true. All that may be truthfully said of such qualities is that they ap-pear rather more frequently in one class than in another. But they are rare in all classes, and the difference in the frequency of their occurrence between this class and that one is not very great, and of little genuine importance. If all the biologists in the United States were hanged to-morrow (as has been proposed by the pastors and newspaper editors of Mississippi) and their children with them, we'd probably still have a sufficiency of biologists in the next generation. There might not be as many as we have to-day, but there would be enough. They would come out of the families of bricklayers and politicians, bootleggers and bond salesmen. Some of them, indeed, might even come out of the families of Mississippi editors and ecclesiastics. For the supply of such men, like the supply of synthetic gin, always tends to run with the demand. Whenever it is short, the demand almost automatically augments it. Every one knows that this is true on the lower levels. Before baseball was invented there were no Ty Cobbs and Babe Ruths; now they appear in an apparently endless series. Before the Wright brothers made their first flight there were no men skilled at aviation; now there are multitudes of highly competent experts. The eugenists forget that the same thing happens also on the higher levels. Whenever the world has stood in absolute need of a genius he has appeared. And though it is true that he has usually come out of the better half of humanity, it is also true that he has sometimes come out of the worse half. Beethoven was the grandson of a cook and the son of a drunkard, and Lincoln's forebears never lifted themselves above the level of village *prominenti*.

The fact is that the difference between the better sort of human beings and the lesser sort, biologically speaking, is very slight. There may be, at the very top, a small class of persons whose blood is decidedly superior and distinguished, and there may be, at the bottom, another class whose blood is almost wholly debased, but both are very small. The folks between are all pretty much alike. The baron has a great deal of peasant blood in him, and the peasant has some blood that is blue. The natural sinfulness of man is enough to make sure of that. No man in this world can ever be quite sure that he is the actual great-great-grandson of the great-great-grandfather whose memory he venerates. Thus, when the relatively superior and distinguished class ceases to be fecund (a phenomenon now visible everywhere in the world), natural selection comes to the rescue by selecting out and promoting individuals from the classes below. These individuals, in the main, are just as sound in blood as any one in the class they enter. Their sound blood has been concealed, perhaps for generations, but it has been there all the time. If Abraham Lincoln's ancestry were known with any certainty, it would probably be found to run back to manifestly able men. There are many more such hidden family-trees in the folk: the eugenists simply overlook them. They are also singularly blind to many familiar biological phenomena—for example, the appearance of mutations or sports. It is not likely that a commonplace family will produce a genius, but nevertheless it is by no means impossible: the thing has probably happened more than once. They forget, too, the influence of environment in human society. Mere environment, to be sure, cannot produce genius, but it can certainly help him enormously after he is born. If a potential Wagner were born to a Greek bootblack in New York City tomorrow, the chances of his coming to fruition and fame would be at least even. But if he were born to an Arab in the Libyan desert or to a Fundamentalist in Rhea county, Tennessee, the chances are that he would be a total loss.

The eugenists constantly make the false assumption that a healthy degree of human progress demands a large and steady supply of absolutely first-rate men. Here they succumb to the modern craze for mass production. Because a hundred policemen, or garbage men, or bootleggers are manifestly better than one they conclude absurdly that a hundred Beethovens would be better than one. But this is not true. The actual value of a genius often lies in his very singularity. If there had been a hundred Beethovens, the music of all of them would probably be very little known to-day, and so its civilizing effect would be appreciably less than it is. The number of first-rate men necessary to make a high civilization is really very small. If the United States could produce one Shakespeare or Newton or Bach or Michelangelo or Vesalius a century it would be doing better than any nation has ever done in history. Such culture as we have is due to a group of men so small that all of them alive at one time could be hauled in a single Pullman train. Once I went through "Who's Who in America," hunting the really first-rate men among its 27,000 names—that is, for the men who had really done something unique and difficult, and of unquestionable value to the human race. I found 200. The rest of the 27,000 were simply respectable blanks. Many of them (though certainly not all) were creditable members of society, but only the 200 had ever done anything useful that had not been done before.

An over-production of geniuses, indeed, would be very dangerous, for though they make for progress they also tend to disturb the peace. Imagine a country housing 100 head of Aristotles! It would be as unhappy as a city housing 100 head of Jesse Jameses. Even quasi-geniuses are a great burden upon society. There are, in the United States to-day, 1500 professional philosophers—that is, men who make their livings at the trade. The country would be far better off if all save two or three of them were driving taxicabs or serving with the Rum Fleet.

XI.

Life Under Bureaucracy

As the bureaucracy under which we all sweat and suffer gradually swells and proliferates in the Republic, life will become intolerable to every man save the one who has what is called influence, *i.e.*, the one who has access to the very privilege which the Fathers of the Republic hoped to abolish. It is, in fact, almost so already. The obscure and friendless man can exist unmolested in the United States only by being so obscure and friendless that the bureaucracy is quite unaware of him. The moment he emerges from complete anonymity its agents have at him with all the complex and insane laws and regulations that now crowd the statute-books, and unless he can find some more powerful person to aid him, either for cash in hand or in return for his vote, he may as well surrender himself at once to ruin and infamy. For if the job-holders don't fetch him with one law they will fetch him with another. Their one permanent purpose in life is to fetch him—by the heels if possible, and if not by the heels then at least by the ears.

Suppose, for example, he is one of the millions of Americans of foreign birth, duly naturalized but still unaccepted socially as a full-fledged citizen. He saves his money, and decides after awhile to make a visit to his birthplace, to show off his American watch and contemplate the tombs of his anthropoid ancestors. He must have, obviously, a passport, first to get out of the United States and then to get back. Well, procuring this passport is now so onerous and complicated a matter that to such a man, with no friendly 100% American to help him, it has become practically impossible. It takes him weeks, and in the end the chances are at least 10 to 1 that he will fail. Where does the blame lie, upon the laws or upon the bureaucracy? It lies upon the bureaucracy. The laws simply say that no man who is not actually a citizen shall have the passport. But the bureaucracy goes much further: it assumes that no man at all is a citizen. The moment he is heard of he is put down as an impostor, and thereafter the burden of proving that he is not is upon

him. As a practical matter, it is often impossible for him to furnish the proof. Long before the bureaucracy is satisfied, he is
worn out and in despair. Unless he can find some person of influence to help him he may as well give up before he begins.

It is the invariable habit of bureaucracies, at all times and
everywhere, to assume in this way that every citizen is a criminal. There one apparent purpose, pursued with a relentless and
furious diligence, is to convert the assumption into a fact.
They hunt endlessly for proofs, and, when proofs are lacking,
for mere suspicions. The moment they become aware of a definite citizen, John Doe, seeking what is his right under the law,
they begin searching feverishly for an excuse for withholding it
from him. A successful bureaucrat is simply one who is skilled
at such withholdings. A failure is one who gives Mr. Doe what
he is entitled to, without resistance and at once.

I have spoken of the poor hyphenate, the special mark and
victim of our American bureaucracy. But the 100% Nordic, in
his different way, suffers almost as cruelly. Consider, for example, his typical adventures with the bureaucrats of the Income
Tax Bureau. To begin with, they give him a blank to fill out
that not one man in a hundred, assuming that he has not had
long training as an accountant, can understand. Its very complexity is a triumph of bureaucracy. It is made unintelligible
deliberately, and by bureaucrats of the highest professional genius, expressly hired for the business. No ordinary man, filling
it out, can conceivably avoid errors. Well, the minute it is de-
posited in the bureaucratic machine the taxpayer is assumed
officially to be a criminal. His slightest slip is proof that he has
tried to swindle the government. And how do the bureaucrats
deal with him? By framing a definite accusation against him,
and giving him his day in court, as provided by Articles V and
VI of the Bill of Rights? Not at all. That would not be bureaucratic. They proceed by levying an additional (and often grossly
excessive) tax upon him, and demanding that he pay it forthwith. He is now wholly in their net. The charge against him is
no longer that he has deliberately falsified his return, which
would be difficult to prove, but simply that he has failed to pay
a tax lawfully levied, which is easy to prove. So he pays, and
thereafter, for five or six years, he struggles to get his money
back.

Not infrequently, it must be said, the bureaucrats finally give it to him. But only after a desperate resistance, made brilliant by innumerable demands for affidavits and endless conferences and hearings. All this hocus-pocus is of the very essence of the bureaucratic art and mystery. The bureaucrat, whatever his imbecilities otherwise, at least grasps clearly the central fact about government: he knows that it is the eternal enemy of the citizen. In his own eye he is an attorney employed to represent it in combats with citizens, and as a conscientious man he naturally tries to do the best he can for his client—legally if possible, but if not, then in any way feasible. His professional standing runs with his success. If he permits too many citizens to prevail against him, and so recover and preserve their rights, he loses caste, just as a surgeon loses caste when too many patients die upon the table, and his career is imperilled. The ideal bureaucrat is the one who beats the citizen every time.

Obviously, the realization of this ideal would make life almost impossible. We move steadily toward it, but so far we have not actually reached it. Many citizens, getting into the clutches of the bureaucracy, manage to escape. They achieve the business, commonly, by mustering up what is called influence. That is, they either demonstrate to the bureaucrats that they are themselves of such power and importance that oppressing them unduly would be dangerous, or they get the help of some other person of that sort. The fact explains the continued prosperity of political machines, despite the long effort to put them down. They offer even the humblest citizen an avenue of escape from the bureaucracy. In return for his vote they protect him. When the bureaucrats discover him and proceed to practice their art upon him, the machine brings pressure to bear upon their political superiors, and so hauls them off. This hauling off, as every one knows, is now the principal occupation of the inferior order of political hacks called Congressmen, and is fast becoming a crushing burden to them. In the early days of the Republic they spent their time at Washington (when not engaged in the bar-rooms and stews) debating the great problems of statecraft, often eloquently, and sometimes with what, on such modest levels of the human mind, passed for sense. But to-day, with the Federal laws enormously multiplied and the Federal bureaucracy glowing with professional skill and enterprise, they are forced to devote practically all of their energies to protecting their constituents. If a Congressman failed in that duty he would return home to find half of his constituents in jail and the rest fugitives from justice. So he has had to resign statecraft to a few leaders, mainly from remote and sparsely settled States. While they carry on the business of Congress he busies himself in the departments and bureaux, rescuing his customers from the clutches of the bureaucracy.

In this benign enterprise, alas, he fails far oftener than he succeeds. Only too often, indeed, his heart is not really in it, for as a professional feeder at the public crib he is something of a bureaucrat himself, and so his sympathies naturally run with the bureaucracy rather than with its victims. Here we come upon *esprit de corps*: there is a lot of it among the scoundrels who constitute the government of the United States: whatever their stupidities otherwise, they are at least bright enough to recognize the plain fact that they form a class separate from the general run of men, with interests opposed to those of the latter, and so they stand together resolutely whenever their common advantages are menaced. In a clash, before Congress, between the aspirations of the job-holders and the common weal, the aspirations of the job-holders nearly always prevail. And in a combat before the courts between a public official and a private citizen, the advantages of the public official are numerous and obvious. These advantages, rising beyond those lying naturally in friendly feeling and fellow interest, often show themselves, of late, in positive law. It was not by chance that Congress passed a statute providing that, when a Prohibition agent or other such chartered assassin is accused of murdering a citizen, the Federal district attorney of the district shall not prosecute him, but defend him. Here the job-holders of the legislative arm deliberately violated the ancient principle of equality before the law in order to give job-holders of the executive arm the full benefit of the natural prejudice in their favor among the district attorneys and judges of the judicial arm—appointees, as likely as not, of the same Anti-Saloon League which put them in their own jobs. In countless other ways the members of the prehensile oligarchy help one another to violate the common rights of the plain citizen. At

every session of Congress there is a legislative assault upon the
Bill of Rights for the benefit of some group or other of administrative bureaucrats, and save on very rare occasions the Federal courts always conjure up some sophistry to justify it. It
causes considerable surprise, indeed, when they fail to do so.
For whatever the adumbrations of theorists, the plain man is
well aware that the interests of the shifting but compact group
of self-seeking men constituting the so-called government of
the nation are opposed, in the main, to his own interests—in
brief, that the government, in its essence, is no more and no
less than a gigantic conspiracy against his well-being.

Thus democracy turns upon and devours itself. Launched
upon the world as a scheme for putting down privilege, it ends
by making privilege absolutely essential to a safe and peaceful
existence. The citizen who is too obscure to make a Congressman or some other such professional dealer in privilege want
to help him, and too weak to help himself—this citizen, under
our bureaucratic jurisprudence, now has no rights at all. He is,
indeed, no longer a citizen; he is a subject, and his lord is the
bureaucrat. He must do whatever he is ordered to do, or face
dire and devastating penalties. All of his natural daily acts
become converted into crimes. It is even a crime to-day, in certain situations, for him to criticize his oppressors. If, writhing
under their oppressions, he appeals to their official superiors,
he usually only makes his case worse, for one bureaucrat always
supports all other bureaucrats. The only man who escapes is
the man with a pull. The aim of every enlightened American is
to get that pull.

XII.

In the Rolling Mills

ALMOST the only thing I believe in with a childlike and un-
questioning faith, in this world of doubts and delusions,
is free speech; nevertheless, I find it increasingly difficult to
sympathize with the pedagogues who, ever and anon, are
heaved out of some fresh-water college for trying to exercise it.
Why? Mainly, perhaps, because I can't get rid of the suspicion
that nothing a pedagogue ever says, as pedagogue, is worth
hearing—that his avocation is as fatal to sense as that of an archbishop, a Federal judge, or one of the automata in Mr. Ford's
great squirrel-cage at Detroit. But also, no doubt, because I
am obsessed by the superstition that, assuming him miraculously to have sense, he is as much out of place in any ordinary
American college as an archbishop would be in a bordello.

What ails all these bogus martyrs is a false theory of education. They seem to believe that its aim is to fill the pupil's head
with a mass of provocative and conflicting ideas, to arouse
his curiosity to incandescence and inspire him to inquiry and
speculation—in the common phrase, to teach him how to think.
But this is surely nonsense. If education really had any such aim
its inevitable effect would be to reduce nine-tenths of its victims to insanity, and to convert most of the rest into anarchists.
What it seeks to do is something quite different—something,
in fact, almost the opposite. It is financed by the state and by
private philanthropists, not to make lunatics and anarchists,
but to make good citizens—in other words, to make citizens
who are as nearly like all other citizens as possible. Its ideal
product is not a boy or a girl full of novel ideas but one full of
lawful and correct ideas—not one who thinks, but one who
believes. If it actually graduated hordes of Platos and Nietz-
sches it would be closed by the Department of Justice, and
quite properly.

One of the most amusing things in life to a bachelor is the
horror that overcomes his married friends whenever one of
their children turns out to be intelligent. They feel instinctively

that the phenomenon offers a challenge to their parental dignity and authority, and when the child they suspect actually *is* intelligent it certainly does. For the first thing the youngster who has succumbed to the un-Christian vice of thinking attempts is a critical examination of its surroundings, and directly in the forefront of those surroundings stand the unfortunate composers of its being. The result, only too frequently, is turmoil and disaster at the domestic hearth. Children, as every one knows, are "ungrateful." So, argue judges and hangmen, are messieurs the condemned. Even the most intelligent agents and instruments of the Life Force are thus full of alarms when their progeny respond to Mendel's law: the very vigor and independence of judgment which they regard as their own most precious possession affrights them when it appears in their issue. I could tell some curious tales in point, but had better refrain. Suffice it to mention an old friend, extremely shrewd and realistic in all of his thinking, who was happily proud of his very intelligent daughter until, at the age of sixteen, she threatened to get a job in a shop if he sent her, as he proposed, to a finishing-school. Then he collapsed in horror, despite the plain fact that her ultimatum was an excellent proof of the intelligence that he was proud of. As man, he admired her differentiation from the mass. But as father he was made uneasy by her sharp departure from normalcy.

The great majority of American fathers, of course, have a great deal less fundamental sense than this one, who quickly recovered from his instinctive reaction, and ended, indeed, by boasting that his daughter had spurned the finishing-school at his advice. To this majority education can only mean the inculcation, by intensive torture, of all the superstitions and prejudices that they cherish themselves. When little Felix comes home to his patriotic and Christian home with the news that the Fathers of 1776 were a gang of smugglers and profiteers, and when his sister Flora follows with the news that Moses did not write his own obituary and that the baby, Gustave, was but recently indistinguishable from a tadpole, and later on from a nascent gorilla—when such subversive and astounding doctrines are brought home from the groves of learning there ensues inevitably a ringing of fire-bells, with a posse on the march against some poor pedagogue.

What I maintain is simply that the vigilantes are right and the pedagogue wrong. His error lies in assuming that taxpayers lay out their hard-earned money for the breeding of traitors and atheists; taxpayers actually lay out their money for the breeding of more taxpayers like themselves. And their natural desire that this program be followed strictly is supported by the overwhelming force of the state, which loses strength and authority in direct ratio as its citizens become heretics. What holds it up is not primarily brute force, as so many theorists argue; what holds it up is the fact that, on all really essential questions, the vast majority of its citizens think exactly alike—that there is never any general doubt of the fundamental communal superstitions. Once those superstitions are seriously challenged, the whole fabric of the state begins to crumble. The true function of the pedagogue is not to attack them, but to propagate them. His is a sort of priestly office. He is not paid to marshal doubts and weigh probabilities; he is paid to expound revelation. If he finds himself temperamentally unable to discharge that solemn and awful duty, then he should quit pedagogy and go into bootlegging or some other free craft. So long as he is publicly consecrated to the birch, he can no more depart from his text-book with seemliness than a Christian clergyman could depart from his sworn belief in witches.

Most of the current uproar in the colleges of the nation, I suspect, is due to a curse that I have often denounced in the past: the pestilential multiplication of Ph.D.'s. There was a time, before all the American universities began vomiting them forth by the thousand, when the whole annual produce of Ph.D.'s could be absorbed by the graduate-schools. In these graduate-schools, with all of the pupils of mature years and most of them already resolved to devote their lives to non-utilitarian and hence, by the national *mores*, subversive enterprises, it was safe enough to abandon the normal teaching process for a more or less free exchange of ideas. The teacher in such a school, having no authority to rattan his students, naturally had to submit to their cross-questioning criticism— sometimes, when they were intelligent, an embarrassing thing. In this atmosphere the Ph.D. could function unrestrained. Being compelled to suffer the doubts and even the derision of his students, he was free on his side to bombard them with all his vagaries, however unearthly and offensive. The result was not teaching, in any true sense, but a sort of learning in common. But when true yearly production of Ph.D.'s grew so large that the graduate-schools became glutted with them, and the profiteers who support all the higher institutions of learning began to yell "Enough!", many of them had to seek other situations. Some, as every one knows, took to the chautauquas. Others sat on public commissions, and drew up reports, or set up as executive secretaries or wowsers. Yet others began practice as experts in law-suits, *i.e.*, as professional perjurers. But great hordes remained, and these presently began to filter into the undergraduate-schools. In the old days the highest academic rank that a teacher in an undergraduate-school ever aspired to was that of M.A., but to-day most of them are Ph.D.'s, and an excess of Ph.D.'s, naturally of inferior quality, has emptied into the high-schools business colleges, correspondence schools and even grammar-schools.

It is these sick and wounded of the army of learning, I suspect, who are responsible for most of the academic Bolshevism that now fills the newspapers. Having been purged, by their superior education, of the fundamental communal superstitions —or, at all events, of a few of them—they get revenge upon the society that ill-uses them by inoculating the children of honest Rotarians with their own odd and often nonsensical heresies. These are the fellows who, at frequent intervals, commit *scandalum magnatum* by teaching that the American patriot infantry, at Bunker Hill, ran all the way down the hill, or that General Grant was a heavy lusher, or that the Bolsheviki have not really nationalized women, or that the world is older than the Bible says, or that the Nordic Blond, biologically, is no more than a bald chimpanzee. And these are the fellows who yell that they are undone when indignant trustees give them the gate.

It seems to me that those who protest against their thus getting the gate fall into the elemental error of assuming, only too often, that an American college is the exact equivalent of a European university. It is called a university, and so they accept it as one in fact. But it is really nothing of the kind. There has been but one genuine university in the United States in our time—the Johns Hopkins under Gilman—and it turned itself into a college with frantic haste the moment he died. The college student differs from a university student in a most important way: his formal education, when he matriculates, is not completed, but simply entering upon its last stage. That is to say, he has not yet taken in the whole of that body of correct and respectable ideas which all of us must somehow absorb before we are competent to think for ourselves—at all events, to any rational purpose and effect.

Only too often the fact is overlooked that even the most bold and talented of philosophers must suffer that stuffing before he is ready to go it alone. Aristotle, you may be sure, had the Greek alphabet rammed into him like any other Greek of his time, and studied the multiplication table, and learned the elements of Greek civics, and all that was then accepted about the nature of the Persians, the functions of the liver, and the aorist. Kant was grounded in Prussian history, the humoral pathology, and the Leibnitzian law of preëstablished harmony. Even Nietzsche had to master the grammar-book, the catechism and the Lutheran psalm-book, that he might be a good German and keep out of jail. Such training takes time, for children naturally resist it; it takes more time in America than elsewhere because our elementary-schools, in late years, devote themselves mainly to fol-de-rols borrowed from the Boy Scouts, Greenwich Village and Bernarr Macfadden. Thus the young American, when he enters college, is still only half-educated in the conventional sense. At least three of his four years are consumed in completing the lowly business of making him fit to vote, keep a check-book accurately, and understand what is in his newspaper. Every now and then some humorist subjects a class of freshmen to what is called a general information test. Four-fifths of them invariably turn out to be as ignorant as so many European schoolboys of ten or eleven.

Obviously, it is as imprudent to parade political heresies before such infants as it would be to lecture on obstetrics before girls of thirteen. When they are graduated at last, they are perhaps ripe for it, but when they are graduated they commonly depart the halls of learning for the bond business. The relatively few who remain seem to suffer no damage from such ideas as they encounter in the graduate-schools. At all events, there is never any complaint that they are being ruined, nor do they themselves complain that the notions of the salient anarchists are being withheld from them. Most of them, having no desire save to get their Ph.D.'s and settle down as pedagogues, are probably anæsthetic to whatever play of ideas goes on about them. A few, taking fire, afterward lecture scandalously in the prairie "universities" to which they are doomed, stir up the students to revolt against their colleagues, and so get themselves cashiered. But not many. Nor is the practical damage serious. There is always room enough for the minority of genuinely intelligent fellows in the graduate-schools whence they came. The spotlights of Babbitt do not bathe these schools, for his sons are not in them; thus they are quite free to monkey with ideas all they please, even with red-hot ones. What I have heard in my time from eminent ornaments of this higher faculty would make interesting news for both the Comstock Society and the Department of Justice. Antinomianism is rife among them, and seems to go unchallenged. So hands remain to carry on the torch.

I don't think the boy of lively mind is hurt much by going to college. If he encounters mainly jackasses, then he learns the useful lesson that this is a jackass world. The complaints come from fellows of small humor, which is to say, from fellows whose intelligence is like a glass of beer without foam. Nor, as I have hinted, am I greatly affected—certainly not to tears—by the grievance of the young professors. Do they complain bitterly that their superiors hobble the free play of their minds, and force them to teach doctrines that they don't believe in? Then examine, some day, the doctrines that they *do* believe in. You will find chiefly bilge—Liberalism and dish-water, the puerile heresies of the farm *bloc*, all the fly-blown fallacies of yesteryear. It is the dream of every such rambunctious Dr. Birch to crash the high gates of the *Atlantic Monthly* with a devilish essay entitled "A Plea for Necking." His goatishness passes with his youth. At forty he is lecturing docilely on the Lake School.

I am unable to discern any actual passion for the truth in such victims of the educational industrial system. What moves them more often, I suspect, is simply a desire to make a scandal and annoy their elders. The same martyr who argues that forbidding him to eulogize Lenin in class is an assault upon his sacred integrity—this same martyr is usually willing enough to teach that the late war was fought to save democracy, and that the United States played a chivalrous and honorable rôle in it. Is he heard against Fundamentalism to-day? Then why wasn't he heard against Prohibition eight or ten years ago—he or his predecessor? I don't cry him down; in his revolt, as in all revolts, there is something stimulating; he is at least not quite a clod. But his error, like that of his students, lies in mistaking the nature of the business he is engaged upon. It is a business that has very little, if anything, to do with the free play of ideas in this world. That goes on otherwhere, and on a different level. His business is to polish the rough casts turned out by an inept and humorous God, that they may be as smooth and uniform as possible, and rub one another as little as possible.

XIII.

Ambrose Bierce

T HE reputation of Ambrose Bierce, like that of Edgar Saltus, has always had an occult, artificial drug-store flavor. He has been hymned in a passionate, voluptuous, inordinate way by a small band of disciples, and he has been passed over altogether by the great majority of American critics, and no less by the great majority of American readers. Certainly it would be absurd to say that he is generally read, even by the *intelligentsia*. Most of his books, in fact, are out of print and almost unobtainable, and there is little evidence that his massive Collected Works, printed in twelve volumes between 1909 and 1912, have gone into anything even remotely approaching a wide circulation. I have a suspicion, indeed, that Bierce did a serious disservice to himself when he put those twelve volumes together. Already an old man at the time, he permitted his nostalgia for his lost youth to get the better of his critical faculty, never very powerful at best, and the result was a depressing assemblage of worn-out and fly-blown stuff, much of it quite unreadable. If he had boiled the collection down to four volumes, or even to six, it might have got him somewhere, but as it is, his good work is lost in a morass of bad and indifferent work. I doubt that any one save the Bierce fanatics aforesaid has ever plowed through the whole twelve volumes. They are filled with epigrams against frauds long dead and forgotten, and echoes of old and puerile newspaper controversies, and experiments in fiction that belong to a dark and expired age. But in the midst of all this blather there are some pearls—more accurately, there are two of them. One consists of the series of epigrams called "The Devil's Dictionary"; the other consists of the war stories, commonly called "Tales of Soldiers and Civilians." Among the latter are some of the best war stories ever written—things fully worthy to be ranged beside Zola's "L'Attaque du Moulin," Kipling's "The Taking of Lungtungpen," or Ludwig Thoma's "Ein Bayrischer Soldat." And among the former are some of the most gorgeous witticisms in the English language.

Bierce, I believe, was the first writer of fiction ever to treat war realistically. He antedated even Zola. It is common to say that he came out of the Civil War with a deep and abiding loathing of slaughter—that he wrote his war stories in disillusion, and as a sort of pacifist. But this is certainly not believed by any one who knew him, as I did in his last years. What he got out of his services in the field was a sentimental horror of it, but a cynical delight in it. It appeared to him as a sort of magnificent *reductio ad absurdum* of all romance. The world viewed war as something heroic, glorious, idealistic. Very well, he would show how sordid and filthy it was—how stupid, savage and degrading. But to say this is not to say that he disapproved it. On the contrary, he vastly enjoyed the chance its discussion gave him to set forth dramatically what he was always talking about and gloating over: the infinite imbecility of man. There was nothing of the milk of human kindness in old Ambrose; he did not get the nickname of Bitter Bierce for nothing. What delighted him most in this life was the spectacle of human cowardice and folly. He put man, intellectually, somewhere between the sheep and the horned cattle, and as a hero somewhere below the rats. His war stories, even when they deal with the heroic, do not depict soldiers as heroes; they depict them as bewildered fools, doing things without sense, submitting to torture and outrage without resistance, dying at last like hogs in Chicago, the former literary capital of the United States. So far in this life, indeed, I have encountered no more thorough-going cynic than Bierce was. His disbelief in man went even further than Mark Twain's; he was quite unable to imagine the heroic, in any ordinary sense. Nor, for that matter, the wise. Man to him, was the most stupid and ignoble of animals. But at the same time the most amusing. Out of the spectacle of life about him he got an unflagging and Gargantuan joy. The obscene farce of politics delighted him. He was an almost amorous connoisseur of theology and theologians. He howled with mirth whenever he thought of a professor, a doctor or a husband. His favorites among his contemporaries were such zanies as Bryan, Roosevelt and Hearst.

Another character that marked him, perhaps flowing out of this same cynicism, was his curious taste for the macabre. All of his stories show it. He delighted in hangings, autopsies, dissecting-rooms. Death to him was not something repulsive, but a sort of low comedy—the last act of a squalid and rib-rocking buffoonery. When, grown old and weary, he departed for Mexico, and there—if legend is to be believed—marched into the revolution then going on, and had himself shot, there was certainly nothing in the transaction to surprise his acquaintances. The whole thing was typically Biercian. He died happy, one may be sure, if his executioners made a botch of dispatching him—if there was a flash of the grotesque at the end. Once I enjoyed the curious experience of going to a funeral with him. His conversation to and from the crematory was superb —a long series of gruesome but highly amusing witticisms. He had tales to tell of crematories that had caught fire and singed the mourners, of dead bibuli whose mortal remains had exploded, of widows guarding the fires all night to make sure that their dead husbands did not escape. The gentleman whose carcass we were burning had been a literary critic. Bierce suggested that his ashes be molded into bullets and shot at publishers, that they be presented to the library of the New York Lodge of Elks, that they be mailed anonymously to Ella Wheeler Wilcox. Later on, when he heard that they had been buried in Iowa, he exploded in colossal mirth. The last time I saw him he predicted that the Christians out there would dig them up and throw them over the State line. On his own writing desk, he once told me, he kept the ashes of his son. I suggested idly that the ceremental urn must be a formidable ornament. "Urn hell!" he answered. "I keep them in a cigar-box!"

There is no adequate life of Bierce, and I doubt if any will ever be written. His daughter, with some asperity, has forbidden the publication of his letters, and shows little hospitality to volunteer biographers. One of his disciples, the late George Sterling, wrote about him with great insight and affection, and another, Herman George Scheffauer, has greatly extended his fame abroad, especially in Germany. But Sterling is dead and Scheffauer seems indisposed to do him in grand manner, and I know of no one else competent to do so. He liked mystification, and there are whole stretches of his long life that are un-accounted for. His end had mystery in it too. It is assumed that he was killed in Mexico, but no eyewitness has ever come forward, and so the fact, if it is a fact, remains hanging in the air.

Bierce followed Poe in most of his short stories, but it is only a platitude to say that he wrote much better than Poe. His English was less tight and artificial; he had a far firmer grasp upon character; he was less literary and more observant. Unluckily, his stories seem destined to go the way of Poe's. Their influence upon the modern American short story, at least upon its higher levels, is almost nil. When they are imi-tated at all, it is by the lowly hacks who manufacture thrillers for the cheap magazines. Even his chief disciples, Sterling and Scheffauer, did not follow him. Sterling became a poet whose glowing romanticism was at the opposite pole to Bierce's cold realism, and Scheffauer, interested passionately in experiment, and strongly influenced by German example, has departed completely from the classicism of the master. Meanwhile, it remains astonishing that his wit is so little remembered. In "The Devil's Dictionary" are some of the most devastating epigrams ever written. "Ah, that we could fall into women's arms without falling into their hands": it is hard to find a match for that in Oscar himself. I recall another: "Opportunity: a favorable occasion for grasping a disappointment." Another: "Once: enough." A third: "Husband: one who, having dined, is charged with the care of the plate." A fourth: "Our vocabu-lary is defective: we give the same name to woman's lack of temptation and man's lack of opportunity." A fifth: "Slang is the speech of him who robs the literary garbage cans on their way to the dump."

But I leave the rest to your own exploration—if you can find a copy of "The Devil's Dictionary." It was never printed in full, save in the ghastly Collected Works that I have men-tioned. A part of it, under the title of "The Cynic's Word-Book," was first published as a separate volume, but it is long out of print. The other first editions of Bierce are scarce, and begin to command high premiums. Three-fourths of his books were published by obscure publishers, some of them not too reputable. He spent his last quarter of a century in voluntary immolation on a sort of burning ghat, worshiped by his small band of zealots, but almost unnoticed by the rest of the human race. His life was a long sequence of bitter ironies. I believe that he enjoyed it.

XIV.

The Executive Secretary

SOME time ago, encountering an eminent bishop of my acquaintance, I found him suffering from a bad cold and what used to be called a fit of the vapors. The cause of his dual disorder soon became manifest. He was smarting under the slings and arrows of executive secretaries. By virtue of his lofty and transcendental office, he was naturally a man of wide influence in the land, and so they tried to enlist his interest in their multitudinous and often nefarious schemes. Every morning at 8 o'clock, just as he was rolling over for a last brief dream of Heaven, he was dragged to the telephone to hear their eloquent and lascivious night-letters, and there, on unlucky days, he stood for as much as half an hour, with his episcopal feet bare, and rage gradually mounting in his episcopal heart. Thus, on a cold morning, he had caught his cold, and thus he had acquired his bad humor.

This holy man, normally a most amiable fellow, told me that he believed the number of executive secretaries in the United States was increasing a the rate of at least a thousand a week. He said that he knew of 30,000 in the field of Christian and moral endeavor alone. There were, he told me, 8000 more engaged in running various pacifist societies, and more than 10,000 operating organizations for the detection and scotching of Bolsheviki. He estimated that the average number of dues-paying members behind each one did not run beyond half a dozen. Nine-tenths of them, he said, were supported by two or three well-heeled fanatics. These fanatics, mainly retired Babbitts and their wives, longed to make a noise in the world, and so escape oblivion. It was the essence of the executive secretary's art and mystery to show them how to do it. Chiefly it was done by discovering bugaboos and giving chase to them. But secondarily it was done by hauling poor ecclesiastics out of bed on frosty mornings, and making them listen to endless night-letters about the woes of the Armenians, the need of intensive missionary effort in Siam, the plot of

Moscow to set up soviets in Lowell, Mass., the high ideals of the Woodrow Wilson Foundation, and the absolute necessity of deeper waterways from the Lakes to the Atlantic.

The executive secretary is relatively new in the world. Like his colleague in well-paid good works, the Y.M.C.A. secretary, he has come into being since the Civil War. Compared to him, his predecessor of ante-bellum days was an amateur and an idiot. That predecessor had no comfortable office in a gaudy skyscraper, he got no lavish salary, and he had no juicy expense-account. On the contrary, he paid his own way, and, especially when he worked for Abolition, which was usually, he sometimes had to take a beating into the bargain. The executive secretary of to-day, as Perlmutter would say, is something else again. He belongs to the order of live wires. He speaks the language of up-and-coming men, and is not sparing with it at the sessions of Rotary and Kiwanis. In origin, not uncommonly, a shady and unsuccessful newspaper reporter or a press-agent out of a job, he quickly becomes, by virtue of his craft, a Man of Vision. The cause that he represents for cash in hand is not merely virtuous; it is, nine times out of ten, divinely inspired. If it fails, then civilization will also fail, and the heroic doings at Chateau Thierry and Hog Island will have been in vain.

It is a good job that he has—far better than legging it on the street for some gorilla of a city editor—far, far better than traversing the sticks ahead of a No. 4 company. There is no need to get up at 7 A.M. and there is no need to fume and strain after getting up. Once three or four—or maybe even only one or two—easy marks with sound bank accounts have been snared, the new "national"—or perhaps it is "international"—association is on its legs, and all that remains is to have brilliant stationary printed, put in an amiable and sightly stenographer, and begin deluging bishops, editors and the gullible generally with literature. The executive secretary, if he has any literary passion in him, may prepare this literature himself, but more often he employs experts to do it. Once a year he launches a drive. But it is only for publicity. The original suckers pay the freight. When they wear out the executive secretary starts a new "international" association.

Such sharks now swarm in every American city. The office-buildings are full of them. Their prosperity depends very largely upon the singular complaisance of the newspapers. The average American managing editor went through so dreadful a bath of propaganda during the late war, and was so thoroughly convinced that resisting it was a form of treason, that he is now almost unable to detect it from genuine news. Some time ago Mr. Stanley Walker, a New York journalist of sense and experience, examined a typical copy of one of the great New York dailies. He found that there were sixty-four items of local news in it—and that forty-two of them could be plainly traced to executive secretaries, and other such space-grabbers. The executive secretary, of course, does not have at his editors crudely. He seldom accompanies his item of "news" with any intimation that he is paid a good salary for planting it, and he discourages all inquires into the actual size, aims and personnel of his organization. Instead he commonly postures as the mere agent of men and women known to be earnest and altruistic philanthropists. These philanthropists are the suckers upon whom he feeds. They pay his salary, maintain his office, and keep up his respectability in newspaper offices. What do they get out of it themselves? In part, no doubt, an honest feeling that they are doing good: the executive secretary, in fact, has to convince them of it before he is in a position to tackle the newspapers at all. But in part, also, they enjoy the publicity— and maybe other usufructs too. In the United States, indeed, doing good has come to be, like patriotism, a favorite device of persons with something to sell. More than one great national organization for lifting up the fallen, especially in foreign lands, might be investigated to advantage. In such cases charity not infrequently gets its reward in the form of concessions.

Some time ago, sweating under this assault of executive secretaries, the editors of a great American newspaper hit upon a scheme of relief. It took the form of a questionnaire— something not seldom used, and to vast effect, by executive secretaries themselves. This questionnaire had a blank in which the executive secretary was asked to write his full name and address, and the amount of his annual salary. In other blanks there was room for putting down the total income and outgo of his association, with details of every item amounting to more than one per cent. of the whole, and for a full list of its contributors and employees, with the amount given by every one of the former contributing more than one per cent. and the salary received by every one of the latter getting more than one per cent. This simple questionnaire cut down the mail received from executive secretaries by at least one half. Many of them did not answer at all. Many others, answering, revealed the not surprising fact that their high-sounding national and international organizations were actually small clubs of a few men and women, and that they themselves consumed most of the revenues. It is a device that might be employed effectively by other American newspapers. When the executive secretaries return their answers by mail, which is usually the case, they are under pressure to answer truthfully, for answering otherwise is using the mails to obtain money by fraud, and many worthy men are jugged at Atlanta and Leavenworth for that offense.

I suggest this plan as a means of cutting down the present baleful activity of executive secretaries, but I am not so optimistic as to believe that it could conceivably dispose of them altogether. In the higher ranks of the profession are gentlemen so skillful that they no longer send out press-matter: they make actual news. To that aristocracy belong the adept executive secretaries who run such organizations as the Anti-Saloon League. These masters of the art do not beg for good-will in newspaper offices: they thrive upon ill-will quite as well as upon good-will. How are they to be got rid of? I am sure I don't know. In all probability the American people are doomed to suffer them forever, as they seem to be doomed to suffer Prohibition agents, revivalists, the radio and Congress.

XV.
Invitation to the Dance

W HAT this grand, gaudy, unapproachable country needs and lacks is an Ingersoll. It is, indeed, a wonder that the chautauquas do not spew one forth. Certainly there must be many a jitney Demosthenes on these lonely, dyspeptic circuits who tires mightily of the standard balderdash of his trade, and longs with a great longing to throw off the white chemise of Service and give the rustics a genuinely hot show. The old tricks begin to tire the steady customers, even in the heart of the Bible Belt. What made the rural Methodists of Iowa and South Carolina breathe hard and fast at the dawn of the century now only makes them shuffle their feet and yawn behind their hands. I have spies in all such horrible regions, and their reports all agree. The yokels no longer turn out to the last paralytic to gape at stereopticon pictures of the Holy Sepulchre and the Mount of Olives, or to see a genuine Hindu from Benares in his obscene native costume, or to listen to a sweating rhetorician flog "The Future of America." They sicken of the old stuff; more, they sicken of Service, Idealism, Vision. What ails them is that the village movie-parlor, the radio, the Ford sedan and the Ku Klux Klan have spoiled their primeval taste for simple, wholesome fare. They must have it hot now, or they don't want it at all. The master-minds of chautauqua try to meet the new demand, but cannot go all the way. They experiment gingerly with lectures on eugenics, the divorce evil, women in politics, and other such pornographic subjects, but that is not enough. They put on plays "direct from Broadway" —but have to omit the really tart ones. The horticulturists and their wives and issue pant for something more dreadful and shocking—something comparable, on the plane of ideas, to the tarring and feathering of the village fancy woman on the plane of manly sports. Their ears lie back and they hearken expectantly, and even somewhat impatiently. What they long for is a bomb.

My guess is that the one that would blow them highest, and

shake the most money out of them going up and coming down, is the big black bomb of Atheism. It has not been set off in the Federal Union, formally and with dramatic effect, since July 21, 1899, when Bob Ingersoll descended into Hell. Now it is loaded again, and ready to be fired, and the chautauquan who discovers it and fires it will be the luckiest mountebank heard of in these latitudes since Col. George B. M. Harvey thrust the halo on Woodrow's brow. For this favorite of fortune, unlike his fellows of the rustic big tops, will not have to drudge out all his days on the lonesome steppes, wrecking his stomach with fried beefsteak and saleratus biscuit and his limbs with travel on slow and bumpy trains. He will be able almost at once, like Ingersoll before him and the Rev. Billy Sunday in the last Golden Age, to horn into the big towns, or, at all events, into the towns, and there he will snore at ease of nights upon clean sheets, with his roll in his pantaloons pocket and a *Schluck* of genuine Scotch under his belt. The yokels, if they want to hear him, will have to come to Babylon in their Fords; he will be too busy and too prosperous to waste himself upon the cow-stable miasmas of the open spaces. Ingersoll, in one month, sometimes took in $50,000. It can be done again; it can be bettered. I believe that Dr. Jennings Bryan, if he had sold out God and gone over to Darwin and *Pongo pygmæus*, could have filled the largest hall in Nashville or Little Rock a month on end: he would have made the most profound sensation the country has known since the Breckenridge-Pollard case, nay, since Hannah and her amazing glands. And what Bryan could have done, any other chautauquan may now do, if not exactly in the same grand manner, then at least in a grand manner.

But this in a Christian country! *Soit!* But it was doubly a Christian country in the days of Bob the Hell-Cat. Bob faced a Babbittry that still went to church on Sunday as automatically as a Prohibition enforcement agent holds out his hand. No machinery for distracting it from that ancient practice had yet been invented. There was no baseball. There were no automobiles to take the whole family to green fields and wet roadhouses: the roads were too bad even for buggy-riding. There was no radio. There were no movies. There was no jazz. There were no Sunday comic supplements. There was no homebrewing. Moreover, a high tide of evangelistic passion was running: it was the day of Dwight L. Moody, of the Salvation Army, of prayer-meetings in the White House, of eager chapel-building on every suburban dump. Nevertheless, Bob hurled his challenge at the whole hierarchy of heaven, and within a few short years he had the Babbitts all agog, and after them the city proletariat, and then finally the yokels on the farms. He drew immense crowds; he became eminent; he planted seeds of infidelity that still sprout in Harvard and Yale. Thousands abandoned their accustomed places of worship to listen to his appalling heresies, and great numbers of them never went back. The evangelical churches, fifty years ago, were all prosperous and full of pious enterprise; the soul-snatching business was booming. Since then, despite the uproars that come from the Bible Belt, it has been declining steadily, in prosperity and in repute. The typical American ecclesiastic of 1880 was Henry Ward Beecher, a pet of Presidents and merchant princes. The typical American ecclesiastic of 1927 is the Rev. Dr. John Roach Straton, an inmate of the stable of Hearst.

In brief, the United States, despite its gallant resistance, has been swept along, to some extent at least, in the general current of human progress and increasing enlightenment. The proofs that it resists are only too often mistaken for proofs that it hasn't moved at all. For example, there is the matter of the Klan. Superficially, its appearance appears to indicate that whole areas of the Republic have gone over to Methodist voodooism with a bang, and that civilization has been barred out of them as effectively as the Bill of Rights is barred out of a Federal court. But actually all it indicates is that the remoter and more forlorn yokels have risen against their betters—and that their uprising is as hopeless as it is idiotic. Whenever the Klan wins, the fact is smeared all over the front pages of the great organs of intelligence: when it loses, which is at least three times as often, the news gets only a few lines. The truth is that the strength of the Klan, like the strength of the Anti-Saloon League, and that of the Methodist-Baptist bloc of moron churches, the pa of both of them, has always been greatly overestimated. Even in the most barbarous reaches of the South, where every village is bossed by a Baptist dervish, it met with vigorous challenge from the start, and there are not three Confederate States to-day in which, on a fair plebiscite, it could hope to prevail. The fact that huge hordes of Southern politicians jumped into night-shirts when it began is no proof that it was actually mighty; it is only proof that politicians are cowards and idiots. Of late all of them have been seeking to rid themselves of the tell-tale tar and feathers; they try to ride the very genuine wave of aversion and disgust as they tried to ride the illusory wave of popularity. As the Klan falls everywhere, the Anti-Saloon League tends to fall with it—and the evangelical churches are strapped tightly to both corpses.

This connection, when it was first denounced, was violently denied by the Baptist and Methodist ecclesiastics, but now every one knows that it was and is real. These ecclesiastics are responsible for the Anti-Saloon League and its swineries, and they are responsible no less for the Klan. In other words, they are responsible, directly and certainly, for all the turmoils and black hatreds that now rage in the bleak regions between the State roads—they are to blame for every witches' pot that now brews in the backwoods of the Union. They have sowed enmities that will last for years. They have divided neighbors, debauched local governments, and enormously multiplied lawlessness. They are responsible for more crime than even the wildest foes of the saloon ever laid to its discredit, and it is crime, in the main, that is infinitely more anti-social and dangerous. They have opposed every honest effort to compose the natural differences between man and man, and they have opposed every attempt to meet ignorance and prejudice with enlightenment. Alike in the name of God, they had advocated murder and they have murdered sense. Where they flourish no intelligent and well-disposed man is safe, and no sound and useful idea is safe. They have preached not only the bitter, savage morality of the Old Testament; they have also preached its childish contempt of obvious facts. Hordes of poor creatures have followed these appalling rogues and vagabonds of the cloth down their Gadarene hill: the result, in immense areas, is the conversion of Christianity into a machine for making civilized living impossible. It is wholly corrupt, rotten and abominable. It deserves no more respect than a pile of garbage.

What I contend is that hundreds of thousands of poor simpletons are beginning to be acutely aware of the fact—that they are not quite as stupid as they usually appear to be. In other words, I believe that they tire of the obscenity. One glances at such a State as Arkansas or such a town as Jackson, Miss., and sees only a swarm of bawling Methodists; only too easily one overlooks the fact that the bawling is far from unanimous. Logic is possible, in its rudiments, even to the *Simiidæ*. On the next step of the scale, in the suburbs, so to speak, of *Homo sapiens*, it flourishes intermittently and explosively. All that is needed to set it off is a suitable yell. The first chautauquan who looses such a yell against the True Faith will shake the Bible Belt like an earthquake, and, as they say, mop up. Half his work is already done for him. The True Faith, the only variety of the True Faith known to those hinds, is already under their rising distrust and suspicion. They look for the Ambassador of Christ, and they behold a Baptist elder in a mail-order suit, describing voluptuously the Harlot of Babylon. They yearn for consolation, and they are invited to a raid on bootleggers. Their souls reach out to the eternal mystery, and the evening's entertainment is the clubbing of a fancy woman. All they need is a leader. Christianity is sick all over this pious land, even in the South. The Christians have killed it. One blast upon a bugle horn, and the mob will be ready for the wake.

XVI.
Aubade

THE name of the man who first made a slave of fire, like the name of the original Franklin Pierce man, is unknown to historians: burrow and sweat as they will, their efforts to unearth it are always baffled. And no wonder! For isn't it easy to imagine how infamous that name must have been while it was still remembered, and how diligent and impassioned the endeavor to erase it from the tablets of the race? One pictures the indignation of the clergy when so vast an improvement upon their immemorial magic confronted them, and their herculean and unanimous struggle, first to put it down as unlawful and against God, and then to collar it for themselves. Bonfires were surely not unknown in the morning of the Pleistocene, for there were lightnings then as now, but the first one kindled by mortal hands must have shocked humanity. One pictures the news flashing from cave to cave and from tribe to tribe—out of Central Asia and then across the grasslands, and then around the feet of the glaciers into the gloomy, spook-haunted wilderness that is now Western Europe, and so across into Africa. Something new and dreadful was upon the human race, and by the time the *Ur*-Mississippians of the Neander Valley heard of it, you may be sure, the discoverer had sprouted horns and was in the pay of the Devil.

His fate at home, though his name is unknown, presents no difficulties to adepts at public psychology. The bad boys of the neighborhood, one may safely assume, got to the scene first of all and were delighted by the show, but upon their heels came the local pastor, and in two minutes he was bawling for the *Polizei*. The ensuing trial attracted such crowds that for weeks the saber-toothed tiger (*Machærodus neogæus*) and the woolly rhinoceros (*R. antiquitatus*) roamed the wilds unmolested, feasting upon colporteurs and wandering flint peddlers. The fellow stood confronted by his unspeakable and unparalleled felony, and could only beg for mercy. Publicly and without shame, he had performed a feat never performed by man before: *ergo*, it was as plain as day that he had engaged, anteriorly, in commerce with the powers of the air. So much, indeed, was elemental logic: even a lawyer could grasp it. But *what* powers? There the clergy certainly had something to say, and what they said must have been instantly damning. They were themselves the daily familiars of all reputable powers of the air, great and small. They knew precisely what could be done and what could not be done. Their professional skill and knowledge were admitted everywhere and by all. What they could not do was thus clearly irregular and disreputable: it issued out of an unlawful transaction with fiends. Any other theory would be laughable, and in plain contempt of court. One pictures the learned judge summing up, and one pictures the headsman spitting on his hands. That night there was a head on a pole in front of the episcopal cave of the ordinary of the diocese, and more than one ambitious cave hyena (*H. spelæa*) wore himself out trying to shin up.

But the secret did not pass with the criminal. He was dead, his relatives to the third degree were sold into slavery to the Chellean heathen down the river, and it was a capital offense, with preliminary tortures, to so much as mention his name. But in his last hours, one must bear in mind, he had a spiritual adviser, to hear his confession and give him absolution for his sorcery, and that spiritual adviser, it is reasonable to assume, had just as much natural curiosity as any other clergyman. So it is not hard to imagine that he wormed the trick out of the condemned, and later on, as in duty bound, conveyed it privately to his bishop. Nor is it hard to imagine its plans and specifications becoming generally known, *sotto voce*, to the adjacent clergy, nor some ingenious holy clerk, presently discovering that they could be carried out without bringing any fiends into the business. The lawful and laudable powers of the air, already sworn to the service of Holy Church, were quite as potent: a hint from the bishop was sufficient to set them to work. And so, if there is no flaw in my reasoning, the making of fire soon became one of the high privileges and prerogatives of the sacred office, forbidden to the laity upon penalty of the stone ax, and reserved in practice for high ceremonial uses and occasions. The ordination of a new rector, I suppose, was such an occasion. The consecration of a new cave was another. And among the uses were the laying of demons, the pursuit and scotching of dragons and other monsters, the abatement of floods and cyclones, the refutation of heresies, and the management of the sun, so that day always followed night and Spring came after Winter. I daresay fees were charged, for the clergy must live, but there was never any degradation of the new magic to sordid, secular uses. No one was allowed a fire to keep warm, and no one was allowed one to boil a bone.

It would be interesting to try to figure out, by the doctrine of probabilities, how long fire was thus reserved for sacramental purposes. The weather being, at this writing, too hot for mathematical exercises, I content myself with a guess, to wit, 10,000 years. It is probably over-moderate. The obvious usefulness of fire was certainly not enough to bring it into general use; it had to wait for the slow, tedious, extremely bloody growth of skepticism. No doubt there were heretics, even during the first two or three millennia, who set off piles of leaves far back in the woods, gingerly, cautiously and half expecting to be potted by thunderbolts. Perhaps there were even renegade clergymen who, unsettled in their faith by contemplation of *Pithecanthropus erectus* (the remote grandfather of the *P. biblicus* of our present Christian age), threw off the sacerdotal chemise, took to flight, and started forest fires. But the odds against such antinomians, for many centuries, must have been almost as heavy as the odds against a Unitarian in Tennessee to-day. They exited, but only as outlaws, with the ax waiting for them, and Hell beyond the ax. The unanimous sentiment of decent people was against them. It was plain to every one that a world in which they went unscotched would be a world resigned to sin and shame.

Nevertheless, they continued to exist, and what is worse, to increase gradually in numbers. Even when the regular force of police was augmented by bands of volunteer snouters, organized to search out unlawful fires in the deep woods and remote deserts, there were heretics who persisted in their contumacy, and even undertook to defend it with all the devices of sophistry. At intervals great crusades were launched against them, and they were rounded up and butchered by the hundred, and even by the thousand. The ordinary method of capital punishment prevailing in those times—to wit, decapitation with fif-

teen or twenty strokes of a stone ax—was found to be ineffective against such agents of the Devil, and so other and
more rigorous methods were devised—chief among them,
boiling to death in a huge pot set over a temple fire. More, the
ordinary criminal procedure had to be changed to facilitate
convictions, for the heretics were highly skilled at turning the
safeguards of the law to their baleful uses. First, it was provided that a man accused of making fire should be tried, not
before the judges who sat in common criminal cases, but
before judges especially nominated for the purpose by the
priests, or by the Anti-Fire League, an organization of citizens
pledged to law and order. Then it was provided that no such
prisoner should be permitted to consult counsel, or to enjoy
the privilege of bail, or to call witnesses in his behalf. Finally,
after all these half measures had failed, it was decided to abandon the whole sorry hocus-pocus of trial and judgment, and to
hand the accused over to the public executioner at once, without any frivolous inquiry into the degree of his guilt.

This device seemed to work very well for a time. It worked
very well, indeed, for nearly 5000 years. There were times during that long period when contraband fire-making seemed to
be practically extinct in the world. Children grew up who had
never seen a fire save in its proper place: a place of worship.
Come to maturity, they begat children equally innocent, and
so the thing went on for generations. But always, just as the
fire heresy seemed about to disappear from human memory,
some outlaw in the wilds revived it. These revivals sometimes
spread as rapidly as their own flames. One year there would be
complete peace everywhere and a spirit of obedience to the
law; the next year bonfires would suddenly sparkle in the hills,
and blasphemous whispers would go round. The heretics, at
such times, made great play at the young. They would lure
boys into the groves along the river-bottoms and teach them
how to roast chestnuts. They would send in spies disguised as
Chellean serving-maids to show little girls how much easier it
was to do the family washing with hot water than with cold.
The constituted authorities answered such defiances with vigorous campaigns of law enforcement. Fireleggers were taken
by the thousand, and put to death at great public ceremonials.
But always some escaped.

In the end (or, at all events, so I work it out by the device brought in by the new science of biometrics) enough escaped to make further proceedings against them dangerous and even impossible. No doubt it happened in what is now Southern France, in the region called the Dordogne. The fireleggers, taking to the hills, there organized a sort of outlaw state, and presently began passing laws of their own. The first of such laws, no doubt, converted fire-making from a crime into a patriotic act: it became the principal duty of every right-thinking citizen to keep a fire burning in front of his cave. Amendments soon followed. It became a felony to eat uncooked food, or to do the family washing in cold water. It became another to put out a fire, or to advocate putting it out, or to imagine putting it out.

Thus priests were barred from that outlaw state, and it became necessary to develop a new class of men skilled in public affairs, and privy to the desires of the gods. Nature responded with politicians. Anon these politicians became adept at all the arts that have distinguished them ever since. They invented new and more rigorous laws, they imposed taxes, they broke the fireleggers to military service. One day, having drilled a large army, they marched down into the plains, tackled the hosts of the orthodox, and overcame them. The next day the priests who had led these hosts were given a simple choice: either they could admit formally that fire-making for secular purposes was now lawful and even laudable, or they could submit to being burned alive upon their own sacramental pyres. Great numbers of them went heroically to the stake, firm in the hope of a glorious resurrection. The rest, retiring to their crypts and seeking divine guidance, emerged with the news that the gods were now in favor of universal fire-making. That night there was a cheerful blaze in front of every cave for miles around, and the priests themselves sat down to a hearty banquet of roast megatherium (*M. cuvieri*). Eight thousand years later a heretic who revived the primeval pagan habit of eating raw oysters was put to death for atheism.

XVII.
Appendix From Moronia

I
Note on Technic

HAVING made of late, after a longish hiatus, two separate attempts to sit through movie shows, I can only report that the so-called art of the film still eludes me. I was not chased out either time by the low intellectual content of the pictures on display. For one thing, I am anything but intellectual in my tastes, and for another thing the films I saw were not noticeably deficient in that direction. The ideas in them were simply the common and familiar ideas of the inferior nine-tenths of mankind. They were hollow and obvious, but they were not more hollow and obvious than the ideas one encounters in the theater every day, or in the ordinary run of popular novels, or, for that matter, in the discourses of the average American statesman or divine. Rotary, hearing worse once a week, still manages to preserve its idealism and digest carbohydrates.

What afflicts the movies is not unpalatable ideational content so much as an idiotic and irritating technic. The first moving-pictures, as I remember them thirty years ago, presented more or less continuous scenes. They were played like ordinary plays, and so one could follow them lazily and at ease. But the modern movie is no such organic whole; it is simply a maddening chaos of discrete fragments. The average scene, if the two shows I attempted were typical, cannot run for more than six or seven seconds. Many are far shorter, and very few are appreciably longer. The result is confusion horribly confounded. How can one work up any rational interest in a fable that changes its locale and its characters ten times a minute? Worse, this dizzy jumping about is plainly unnecessary: all it shows is the professional incompetence of the gilded pants-pressers, decayed actors and other such half-wits to whom the making of movies seems to be entrusted. Unable to imagine a sequence of coherent scenes, and unprovided with a sufficiency of performers capable of playing them if they were imagined, these preposterous mountebanks are reduced to the childish device of avoiding action altogether. Instead of it they present what is at bottom nothing but a poorly articulated series of meaningless postures and grimaces. One sees a ham cutting a face, and then one sees his lady co-star squeezing a tear—and so on, endlessly. These mummers cannot be said, in any true sense, to act at all. They merely strike attitudes—and are then whisked off. If, at the first attempt upon a scene, the right attitude is not struck, then all they have to do is to keep on trying until they strike it. On those terms a chimpanzee could play Hamlet, or even Juliet.

To most of the so-called actors engaged in the movies, I daresay, no other course would be possible. They are such obvious incompetents that they could no more play a rational scene, especially one involving any subtlety, than a cow could jump over the moon. They are engaged, not for their histrionic skill, but simply for their capacity to fill the heads of romantic virgins and neglected wives with the sort of sentiments that the Christian religion tries so hard to put down. It is, no doubt, a useful office, assuming that the human race must, should and will go on, but it has no more to do with acting, as an art, than being a Federal judge has with preserving the Constitution. The worst of it is that the occasional good actor, venturing into the movies, is brought down to the common level by the devices thus invented to conceal the incompetence of his inferiors. It is quite as impossible to present a plausible impersonation in a series of unrelated (and often meaningless) postures as it would be to make a sensible speech in a series of college yells. So the good actor, appearing in the films, appears to be almost as bad as the natural movie ham. One sees him only as one sees a row of telegraph poles, riding in a train. However skillful he may be, he is always cut off before, by any intelligible use of the device of his trade, he can make the fact evident.

In one of the pictures I saw lately a principal actor was George Bernard Shaw. The first scene showed him for fifteen or twenty seconds continuously, and it was at once plain that he had a great deal of histrionic skill—far more, indeed, than the average professional actor. He was seen engaged in a friendly argument with several other dramatists, among them Sir James M. Barrie and Sir Arthur Wing Pinero. Having admired all these notorious men for many years, and never having had the honor of meeting or even witnessing them, I naturally settled down with a grateful grunt to the pleasure of feasting my eyes upon them. But after that first scene all I saw of Shaw was a series of fifteen or twenty maddening flashes, none of them more than five seconds long. He would spring into view, leap upon Barrie or Pinero—and then disappear. Then he would spring back, his whiskers bristling—and disappear again. It was as maddening as the ring of the telephone.

There is, of course, a legitimate use for this off-again-on-again device in the movies: it may be used, at times, very effectively and even intelligently. The beautiful heroine, say, is powdering her nose, preparing to go out to her fatal dinner with her libidinous boss. Suddenly there flashes through her mind a prophylactic memory of the Sunday-school in her home town far away. An actress on the stage, with such a scene to play, faces serious technical difficulties: it is very hard for her— that is, it has been hard since Ibsen abolished the soliloquy —to convey the exact revolutions of her conscience to her audience. But the technic of the movies makes it very easy—in fact, so easy that it requires no skill at all. The director simply prepares a series of scenes showing what is going through the heroine's mind. There is the church on the hill, with the horde of unhappy children being driven into its basement by the town constable. There is the old maid teacher expounding the day's Golden Text, II Kings, 11, 23–24. There is a flash of the two she-bears "taring" the "forty and two" little children. There is the heroine, in ringlets, clapping her hands in dutiful Presbyterian glee. There is a flash of the Sunday-school superintendent, his bald head shining, warning the scholars against the sins of simony, barratry and adultery. There is the collection, with the bad boy putting in the suspenders' button. There is the flash showing him, years later, as a bank president.

All this is ingenious. More, it is humane, for it prevents the star trying to act, and so saves the spectators pain. But it is manifestly a poor substitute for acting on the occasions when acting is actually demanded by the plot—that is, on the occasions when there must be cumulative action, and not merely a series of postures. Such occasions give rise to what the old-time dramatic theorists called *scènes à faire*, which is to say, scenes of action, crucial scenes, necessary scenes. In the movies they are dismembered, and so spoiled. Try to imagine the balcony scene from "Romeo and Juliet" in a string of fifty flashes —first Romeo taking his station and spitting on his hands, then Juliet with her head as big as a hay-wagon, then the two locked in a greasy kiss, then the Nurse taking a drink of gin, then Romeo rolling his eyes, and so on. If you can imagine it, then you ought to be in Hollywood, dodging bullets and amassing wealth.

If I were in a constructive mood I'd probably propose reforms, but that mood, I regret to say, is not on me. In any case, I doubt that proposing reforms would do any good. For this idiotic movie technic, as I have shown, has its origin in the incompetence of the clowns who perform in the great majority of movies, and it would probably be impossible to displace them with competent actors, for the customers of the movie-parlors appear to love them, and even to admire them. It is hard to believe, but it is obviously so. A successful movie mime is probably the most admired human being ever seen in the world. He is admired more than Napoleon, Lincoln or Beethoven; more, even, than Coolidge. The effects of this adulation, upon the mime himself and especially upon his clients, ought to be given serious study by competent psychiatrists, if any can be found. For there is nothing more corrupting to the human psyche, I believe, than the mean admiration of mean things. It produces a double demoralization, intellectual and spiritual. Its victim becomes not only a jackass, but also a bounder. The movie-parlors, I suspect, are turning out such victims by the million: they will, in the long run, so debauch the American proletariat that it will begin to put Coolidge above Washington, and Peaches Browning above Coolidge.

Meanwhile, they are ruining the ancient and noble art of the dramatist—an art that has engaged the talents of some of the greatest men the world has ever seen. And they are, at the same time, ruining the lesser but by no means contemptible art of the actor. It is no advantage to a movie ham to be a competent actor; on the contrary, it is a handicap. If he tried to act, as acting has been understood since the days of Æschylus, his director would shut him off instanter: what is wanted is simply aphrodisiacal posturing. And if, by any chance, his director were drunk and let him run on, the vast majority of movie morons would probably rush out of the house, bawling that the film was dull and cheap, and that they had been swindled.

2
Interlude in the Socratic Manner

Having completed your æsthetic researches at Hollywood, what is your view of the film art now?

I made no researches at Hollywood, and was within the corporate bounds of the town, in fact, only on a few occasions, and then for only a few hours. I spent my time in Los Angeles, studying the Christian pathology of that great city. When not so engaged I mainly devoted myself to quiet guzzling with Joe Hergesheimer, Jim Quirk, Johnny Hemphill, Jim Tully, Walter Wanger and other such literati. For the rest, I visited friends in the adjacent deserts, some of them employed in the pictures and some not. They treated me with immense politeness. With murderers as thick in the town as evangelists, nothing would have been easier than to have had me killed, but they let me go.

Did any of them introduce you to the wild night-life of the town?

The wildest night-life I encountered was at Sister Aimée McPherson's tabernacle. I saw no wildness among the moviefolk. They seemed to me, in the main, to be very serious and even gloomy people. And no wonder, for they are worked like Pullman porters or magazine editors. When they are engaged in posturing for a film and have finished their day's labor they are far too tired for any recreation requiring stamina. I encountered but two authentic souses in three weeks. One was a cowboy and the other was an author. I heard of a lady getting tight at a party, but I was not present. The news was a sensation in the town. Such are the sorrows of poor mummers: their most banal peccadilloes are magnified into horrors. Regard the unfortunate Chaplin. If he were a lime and cement dealer his latest divorce case would not have got two lines in the newspapers. But, as it was, he was placarded all over the front pages because he had had a banal disagreement with one of his wives. The world hears of such wild, frenzied fellows as Tully, and puts them down as typical of Hollywood. But Tully is not an actor; he eats actors. I saw him devour half a dozen of them on the half-shell in an hour. He wears a No. 30 collar and has a colossal capacity for wine-bibbing; I had to call up my last reserves to keep up with him. But the typical actor is a slim and tender fellow. What would be a mere apéritif for Tully or me would put him under the table, yelling for his pastor.

So you caught no glimpses of immorality?

Immorality? Oh, my God! Hollywood, despite the smell of patchouli and rattle of revolver fire, seemed to me to be one of the most respectable towns in America. Even Baltimore can't beat it. The notion that actors are immoral fellows is a delusion that comes down to us from Puritan days, just as the delusion that rum is a viper will go down to posterity from our days. There is no truth in it. The typical actor, at least in America, is the most upright of men: he always marries the girl. How many actors are bachelors? Not one in a thousand. The divorce rate is high among them simply because the marriage rate is so high. An actor, encountering a worthy girl, leaps from the couch to the altar almost as fast as a Baptist leaps from the altar to the couch. It is his incurable sentimentality that fetches him: if he was not born a romantic he is not an actor. Worse, his profession supports his natural weakness. In plays and movies he always marries the girl in the end, and so it seems to him to be the decent thing to do it in his private life. Actors always copy the doings of the characters they impersonate: no Oscar was needed to point out that nature always imitates art. I heard, of course, a great deal of gossip in Los Angeles, but all save a trivial part of it was excessively romantic. Nearly every great female star, it appeared, was desperately in love, either with her husband or with some pretty and well-heeled fellow, usually not an actor. And every male star was mooning over some coy and lovely miss. I heard more sweet love stories in three weeks than I had heard in New York in the previous thirty years. The whole place stank of orange-blossoms. Is honest love conducive to vice? Then one may argue that it is conducive to delirium tremens to be a Presbyterian elder. One of the largest industries in Hollywood is that of the florists. Next comes that of the traffickers in wedding silver. One beautiful lady star told me that buying such presents cost her $11,000 last year.

But the tales go round. Is there no truth in them at all?

To the best of my knowledge and belief, none. They are believed because the great masses of the plain people, though they admire movie actors, also envy them, and hence hate them. It is the old human story. Why am I hated by theologians? It is because I am an almost unparalleled expert in all branches of theology. Whenever they tackle me, my superior knowledge and talent floor them. In precisely the same way I hate such fellows as the movie Salvini, Jack Gilbert. Gilbert is an amiable and tactful young man, and treats me with the politeness properly due to my years and learning. But I heard in Culver City that no less than two thousand head of women, many of them rich, were mashed on him. Well, I can recall but fifteen or twenty women who have ever showed any sign of being flustered by me, and not one of them, at a forced sale, would have realized $200. Hence I hate Gilbert, and would rejoice unaffectedly to see him taken in some scandal that would stagger humanity. If he is accused of anything less than murdering his wife and eight children I shall be disappointed.

Then why do you speak for Mr. Chaplin?

Simply because he is not a handsome dog, as Gilbert is. The people who hate him do so because he is rich. It is the thought that his trouble will bust him that gives them delight. But I have no desire for money and so his prosperity does not offend me. I always have too much money; it is easy to get in New York, provided one is not a professing Christian. Gilbert, I suppose, is rich too; he wears very natty clothes. But it is not his wealth that bothers me: it is those two thousand head of women.

So, failing researches, you continue ignorant of the film art?

Ignorant? What a question! How could any man remain ignorant of the movies after three weeks in Los Angeles? As well continue ignorant of laparotomy after three weeks in a hospital sun-parlor! No, I am full of information about them, some of it accurate, for I heard them talked day and night, and by people who actually knew something about them. There was but one refuge from that talk, and that was La McPherson's basilica. Moreover, I have hatched some ideas of my own.

As for example?

That the movie folks, in so far as they are sentient at all, are on the hooks of a distressing dilemma. They have built their business upon a foundation of morons, and now they are paying for it. They seem to be unable to make a presentable picture without pouring out tons of money, and when they have made it they must either sell it to immense audiences of half-wits, or go broke. There seems to be very little ingenuity and resourcefulness in them. They are apparently quite unable, despite their melodramatic announcements of salary cuts, to solve the problem of making movies cheaply, and yet intelligently, so that civilized persons may visit the movie-parlors without pain. But soon or late some one will have to solve it. Soon or late the movies will have to split into two halves. There will be movies for the present mob, and there will be movies for the relatively enlightened minority. The former will continue idiotic; the latter, if competent men to make them are unearthed, will show sense and beauty.

Have you caught the scent of any such men?

Not yet. There are some respectable craftsmen in Hollywood. (I judged them by their talk: I have not seen many of their actual pictures.) They tackle the problems of their business in a more or less sensible manner. They have learned a lot from the Germans. But I think it would be stretching a point to say that there are any artists among them—as yet. They are adept, but not inspired. The movies need a first-rate artist—a man of genuine competence and originality. If he is in Hollywood to-day, he is probably bootlegging, running a pants pressing parlor, or grinding a camera crank. The movie magnates see him in literary directions. They pin their faith to novelists and playwrights. I presume to believe that this is bad medicine. The fact that a man can write a competent novel is absolutely no reason for assuming that he can write a competent film. The two things are as unlike as Pilsner and coca-cola. Even a sound dramatist is not necessarily a competent scenario-writer. What the movies need is a school of authors who will forget all dialogue and description, and try to set forth their ideas in terms of pure motion. It can be done, and it will be done. The German, Dr. Murnau, showed the way in certain scenes of "The Last Laugh." But the American magnates continue to buy bad novels and worse plays, and then put over-worked hacks to the sorry job of translating them into movies. It is like hiring men to translate college yells into riddles. Æschylus himself would have been stumped by such a task.

When do you think the Shakespeare of the movies will appear? And where will he come from?

God knows. He may even be an American, as improbable as it may seem. One thing, only, I am sure of: he will not get much for his masterpieces. He will have to give them away, and the first manager who puts them on will lose money. The movies to-day are too rich to have any room for genuine artists. They produce a few passable craftsmen, but no artists. Can you imagine a Beethoven making $100,000 a year? If so, then you have a better imagination than Beethoven himself. No, the present movie folk, I fear, will never quite solve the problem, save by some act of God. They are too much under the heel of the East Side gorillas who own them. They think too much about money. They have allowed it to become too important to them, and believe they couldn't get along with-out it. This is an unfortunate delusion. Money is important to mountebanks, but not to artists. The first really great movie, when it comes at last, will probably cost less than $5000. A true artist is always a romantic. He doesn't ask what the job will pay; he asks if it will be interesting. In this way all the loveliest treasures of the human race have been fashioned—by careless and perhaps somewhat foolish men. The late Johann Sebastian Bach, compared to a movie star with nine auto-mobiles, was simply a damned fool. But I cherish the feeling that a scientific inquiry would also develop other differences between them.

Are you against the star system?

I am neither for it nor against it. A star is simply a performer who pleases the generality of morons better than the average. Certainly I see no reason why such a performer should not be paid a larger salary than the average. The objection to swollen salaries should come from the stars themselves—that is, assum-ing them to be artists. The system diverts them from their proper business of trying to produce charming and amusing movies, and converts them into bogus society folk. What could be more ridiculous? And pathetic? I go further: it is tragic. As I have said in another place, nothing is more tragic in this world than for otherwise worthy people to meanly admire and imitate mean things. One may have some respect for the movie lady who buys books and sets up as an intellectual, for it is a creditable thing to want to be (or even simply to want to appear) well-informed and intelligent. But I can see nothing worthy in wanting to be mistaken for the president of a bank. Artists should sniff at such dull drudges, not imitate them. The movies will leap ahead the day some star in Hollywood organizes a string quartette and begins to study Mozart.

3
Valentino

By one of the chances that relieve the dullness of life and make it instructive, I had the honor of dining with this celebrated gentleman in New York, a week or so before his fatal illness. I had never met him before, nor seen him on the screen; the meeting was at his instance, and, when it was proposed, vaguely puzzled me. But soon its purpose became clear enough. Valentino was in trouble, and wanted advice. More, he wanted advice from an elder and disinterested man, wholly removed from the movies and all their works. Something that I had written, falling under his eye, had given him the notion that I was a judicious fellow. So he requested one of his colleagues, a lady of the films, to ask me to dinner at her hotel.

The night being infernally warm, we stripped off our coats, and came to terms at once. I recall that he wore suspenders of extraordinary width and thickness—suspenders almost strong enough to hold up the pantaloons of Chief Justice Taft. On so slim a young man they seemed somehow absurd, especially on a hot Summer night. We perspired horribly for an hour, mopping our faces with our handkerchiefs, the table napkins, the corners of the table-cloth, and a couple of towels brought in by the humane waiter. Then there came a thunder-storm, and we began to breathe. The hostess, a woman as tactful as she is charming, disappeared mysteriously and left us to commune.

The trouble that was agitating Valentino turned out to be very simple. The ribald New York papers were full of it, and that was what was agitating him. Some time before, out in

Chicago, a wandering reporter had discovered, in the men's wash-room of a gaudy hotel, a slot-machine selling talcum-powder. That, of course, was not unusual, but the color of the talcum-powder was. It was pink. The news made the town giggle for a day, and inspired an editorial writer on the eminent Chicago *Tribune* to compose a hot weather editorial. In it he protested humorously against the effeminization of the American man, and laid it light-heartedly to the influence of Valentino and his sheik movies. Well, it so happened that Valentino, passing through Chicago that day on his way east from the Coast, ran full tilt into the editorial, and into a gang of reporters who wanted to know what he had to say about it. What he had to say was full of fire. Throwing off his 100% Americanism and reverting to the *mores* of his fatherland, he challenged the editorial writer to a duel, and, when no answer came, to a fist fight. His masculine honor, it appeared, had been outraged. To the hint that he was less than he, even to the extent of one half of one per cent., there could be no answer save a bath of blood.

Unluckily, all this took place in the United States, where the word honor, save when it is applied to the structural integrity of women, has only a comic significance. One hears of the honor of politicians, of bankers, of lawyers even of the honor of the United States itself. Everyone naturally laughs. So New York laughed at Valentino. More, it ascribed his high dudgeon to mere publicity-seeking: he seemed a vulgar movie ham seeking space. The poor fellow, thus doubly beset, rose to dudgeons higher still. His Italian mind was simply unequal to the situation. So he sought counsel from the neutral, aloof and aged. Unluckily, I could only name the disease, and confess frankly that there was no remedy—none, that is, known to any therapeutics within my ken. He should have passed over the gibe of the Chicago journalist, I suggested, with a lofty snort —perhaps, better still, with a counter gibe. He should have kept away from the reporters in New York. But now, alas, the mischief was done. He was both insulted and ridiculous, but there was nothing to do about it. I advised him to let the dreadful farce roll along to exhaustion. He protested that it was infamous. Infamous? Nothing, I argued, is infamous that is not true. A man still has his inner integrity. Can he still look

into the shaving-glass of a morning? Then he is still on his two
legs in this world, and ready even for the Devil. We sweated a
great deal, discussing these lofty matters. We seemed to get
nowhere.

Suddenly it dawned upon me—I was too dull or it was too
hot for me to see it sooner—that what we were talking about
was really not what we were talking about at all. I began to observe Valentino more closely. A curiously naïve and boyish
young fellow, certainly not much beyond thirty, and with a
disarming air of inexperience. To my eye, at least, not handsome, but nevertheless rather attractive. There was an obvious
fineness in him; even his clothes were not precisely those of his
horrible trade. He began talking of his home, his people, his
early youth. His words were simple and yet somehow very eloquent. I could still see the mime before me, but now and then,
briefly and darkly, there was a flash of something else. That
something else, I concluded, was what is commonly called, for
want of a better name, a gentleman. In brief, Valentino's
agony was the agony of a man of relatively civilized feelings
thrown into a situation of intolerable vulgarity, destructive
alike to his peace and to his dignity—nay, into a whole series of
such situations. It was not that trifling Chicago episode that
was riding him; it was the whole grotesque futility of his life.
Had he achieved, out of nothing, a vast and dizzy success?
Then that success was hollow as well as vast—a colossal and
preposterous nothing. Was he acclaimed by yelling multitudes?
Then every time the multitudes yelled he felt himself blushing
inside. The old story of Diego Valdez once more, but with a
new poignancy in it. Valdez, at all events, was High Admiral of
Spain. But Valentino, with his touch of fineness in him—he
had his commonness, too, but there was that touch of fineness
—Valentino was only the hero of the rabble. Imbeciles surrounded him in a dense herd. He was pursued by women—
but what women! (Consider the sordid comedy of his two
marriages—the brummagem, star-spangled passion that invaded his very death-bed!) The thing, at the start, must have
only bewildered him. But in those last days, unless I am a
worse psychologist than even the professors of psychology, it
was revolting him. Worse, it was making him afraid.

I incline to think that the inscrutable gods, in taking him off so soon and at a moment of fiery revolt, were very kind to him. Living, he would have tried inevitably to change his fame—if such it is to be called—into something closer to his heart's desire. That is to say, he would have gone the way of many another actor—the way of increasing pretension, of solemn artiness, of hollow hocus-pocus, deceptive only to himself. I believe he would have failed, for there was little sign of the genuine artist in him. He was essentially a highly respectable young man, which is the sort that never metamorphoses into an artist. But suppose he had succeeded? Then his tragedy, I believe, would have only become the more acrid and intolerable. For he would have discovered, after vast heavings and yearnings, that what he had come to was indistinguishable from what he had left. Was the fame of Beethoven any more caressing and splendid than the fame of Valentino? To you and me, of course, the question seems to answer itself. But what of Beethoven? He was heard upon the subject, *viva voce*, while he lived, and his answer survives, in all the freshness of its profane eloquence, in his music. Beethoven, too, knew what it meant to be applauded. Walking with Goethe, he heard something that was not unlike the murmur that reached Valentino through his hospital window. Beethoven walked away briskly. Valentino turned his face to the wall.

Here, after all, is the chiefest joke of the gods: that man must remain alone and lonely in this world, even with crowds surging about him. Does he crave approbation, with a sort of furious, instinctive lust? Then it is only to discover, when it comes, that it is somehow disconcerting—that its springs and motives offer an affront to his dignity. But do I sentimentalize the perhaps transparent story of a simple mummer? Then substitute Coolidge, or Mussolini, or any other poor devil that you can think of. Substitute Shakespeare, or Lincoln, or Goethe, or Beethoven, as I have. Sentimental or not, I confess that the predicament of poor Valentino touched me. It provided grist for my mill, but I couldn't quite enjoy it. Here was a young man who was living daily the dream of millions of other young men. Here was one who was catnip to women. Here was one who had wealth and fame. And here was one who was very unhappy.

CHRONOLOGY

NOTE ON THE TEXTS

NOTES

INDEX

Chronology

<table>
<tr><td>1880</td><td>Born Henry Louis Mencken on September 12, at what was then 380 West Lexington Street, Baltimore, Maryland, now 811 West Lexington Street; eldest child of August Mencken and Anna Abhau Mencken. (Grandfather Burkhardt Ludwig Mencken, born 1828 in Laas, Germany, landed in Baltimore, November 1848; was naturalized October 1852, and set up a tobacco business. Father, born June 16, 1854, established August Mencken & Bro. between 1873–75, managing it with his brother Henry, and building it into one of the most successful cigar manufacturers along the South Atlantic coast. An agnostic and a high-tariff Republican, August was a loyal member of the Masonic order, also part owner of the National Baseball Club of Washington, D.C. Mother, Anna Abhau, born June 11, 1858, was the daughter of Carl Heinrich Abhau from Hesse, Germany. August and Anna were married on November 11, 1879.)</td></tr>
<tr><td>1882</td><td>Brother, Charles Edward, born May 16.</td></tr>
<tr><td>1883</td><td>Family moves to 1524 Hollins Street, in a prosperous German-American neighborhood in West Baltimore, facing Union Square.</td></tr>
<tr><td>1886</td><td>Mencken enrolls at F. Knapp's Institute, a private school, in September. Sister Anna Gertrude born November 17.</td></tr>
<tr><td>1888</td><td>Begins piano lessons. Receives a self-inking printing press for Christmas.</td></tr>
<tr><td>1889</td><td>Brother, August, born February 18. Reads Mark Twain's Huckleberry Finn, which makes a huge impact on him. Family begins spending summers in Ellicott City, Howard County, west of Baltimore (1889–1892), and Mt. Washington (1892–1899), then a northwestern suburb.</td></tr>
<tr><td>1892</td><td>Mencken enters Baltimore Polytechnic Institute, a public high school, on September 5.</td></tr>
<tr><td>1893</td><td>Mencken keenly interested in chemistry, photography, journalism and literature. Visits the Enoch Pratt Free Library, reads four or five books a week, mostly English literature (including Dickens, Chaucer, Shakespeare, Herrick,</td></tr>
</table>

Pepys, Addison, Steele, Pope, Swift, Johnson, Boswell, Fielding, Smollett, Sterne, Arnold, Macaulay, George Eliot, Tennyson, Swinburne, Thackeray, Kipling). Mencken will later call the library "my school"; his brother August will recall that Mencken "read like an athlete." Fire engulfs August Mencken & Bro. Cigar factory, causing $25,000 worth of damage, December 2.

1895   Reads Stephen Crane's *The Red Badge of Courage*.

1896   Graduates at age 15 from the Baltimore Polytechnic Institute, with highest grade point average yet recorded, June 23. Publishes a poem ("Ode to the Pennant on the Centerfield Pole") anonymously in the Baltimore *American*, summer. Tells his father that he plans to become a newspaper reporter, but is strongly dissuaded. Starts full-time work as clerk and salesman at August Mencken & Bro.

1898   Subscribes to *The Criterion* (New York) and is influenced by the work of James Gibbons Huneker, Percival Pollard, Ambrose Bierce, Oscar Wilde, George Bernard Shaw, and Friedrich Nietzsche. Becomes an admirer of the prose style and ideas of Thomas Henry Huxley. Studies books on journalism; enrolls in a correspondence school, the Associated Newspaper Bureau School of Journalism in New York, and states his career goal is "to begin as a reporter & after that trust to hard work and luck for something better." Resolves to quit working at August Mencken & Bro.; his father asks him to postpone the decision for at least another year. In a moment of despair, Mencken contemplates suicide. August Mencken, Sr., collapses unconscious with acute kidney infection, December 31. (Mencken writes later: "I remember well how . . . I kept saying to myself that if my father died I'd be free at last . . . I had got along with him very well, but I detested business and was frantic to get into newspaper work.")

1899   Father dies on January 13 and is buried at Loudon Park Cemetery. Two weeks later Mencken visits the offices of the Baltimore *Herald* and asks for a job. First story published February 24. Hired at $7 a week, the youngest (and first) cub reporter on the *Herald* to get paid a salary, July 2. A poem addressed to Rudyard Kipling appears in December 1899 issue of *Bookman* magazine. Quits working part-time for his Uncle Henry at August Mencken & Bro. to devote himself to journalism, which he later calls "the maddest, gladdest, damnedest existence ever enjoyed by mortal youth."

1900   Reads Edward Kingsbury's editorials in the New York *Sun*, George Ade's *Fables in Slang*, the work of Émile Zola. Discovers Theodore Dreiser's *Sister Carrie*. Works twelve hours a day, seven days a week reporting for the *Herald*, writing short stories, poetry, and articles for out-of-town newspapers. Suffers from chronic bronchitis. Travels to Jamaica to recover, June. Gets third raise in salary, to $14 a week, August. Assigned to cover presidential election between William Jennings Bryan and William McKinley, November.

1901   Salary increased to $18 a week, February 1. Covers fire that devastated Jacksonville, Florida, in May. Becomes drama critic of the *Herald*, September, and editor of *Sunday Herald*, October (holds both positions until October 1903). Becomes an advocate of the work of playwrights Shaw and Ibsen.

1903   Becomes city editor of the *Morning Herald* in October 1903. Publication of *Ventures Into Verse*, a book of poetry modeled on Kipling. Begins subscribing to a service that provides clippings mentioning him or his books. (The clippings will fill more than 100 volumes during his lifetime.)

1904   Fire destroys more than 140 acres and 1,500 buildings in downtown Baltimore, February 7–8. The *Herald* is printed in Washington and Philadelphia and does not miss a single issue. Mencken attends the Republican National Convention in Chicago, June 19–24, and the Democratic National Convention in St. Louis, July 5–11. Made city editor of the Baltimore *Evening Herald*, August 25. Saturday Night Club established, a group of musicians who meet regularly, with Mencken at the piano.

1905   Promoted to managing editor of the *Herald*. Publication of *George Bernard Shaw: His Plays*, first book-length study of Shaw.

1906   The *Herald* ceases publication, June 17. Becomes editor of the Baltimore *Sunday Sun*, July 25. Makes sweeping changes in typography and content, introduces poetry, music criticism by John Philip Sousa; runs a twenty-four part report on the city's health concerns and serializes work by popular authors (such as George Ade's revised history of slang). Circulation climbs steadily.

1908   Publication of *The Philosophy of Friedrich Nietzsche*, first
        book in English on the philosopher. Meets Theodore
        Dreiser. First trip to Europe, March; he visits England
        and Germany. Meets George Jean Nathan, theater critic,
        in New York in May. Assumes additional duties as editor-
        ial writer for the *Sun* papers. Begins monthly book re-
        views for *The Smart Set*, November (to be continued until
        December 1923), and praises the work of James Branch
        Cabell, Twain, Joseph Conrad, and Dreiser among others.

1909   Works (in collaboration with Holger A. Koppel, Danish
        consul in Baltimore) on notes and introductions to a new
        edition of Ibsen's *A Doll's House* and *Little Eyolf*, to be
        published as part of *The Player's Ibsen*. The volumes are a
        commercial failure, and the series is discontinued.

1910   Baltimore *Evening Sun* established, April 18, with Mencken
        as an editor. Ghostwrites *What You Ought to Know About
        Your Baby* with Leonard Hirshberg. Publication of *The
        Gist of Nietzsche* and of *Men Versus the Man* (written with
        Robert Rives La Monte).

1911   Becomes close friends with Percival Pollard, American
        writer who widens Mencken's understanding of German
        culture. Begins "The Free Lance," a satirical daily column
        in the Baltimore *Evening Sun*, May 8, addressing issues of
        local public health, the plight of the city's African Ameri-
        cans, the women's movement, the American language,
        the pretensions of moralists, as well as several humorous
        pieces including the kernel of what would become his
        fictitious history of the bathtub. "Before it had gone on
        a year," he later notes, "I knew precisely where I was
        heading."

1912   Travels to Europe in April, visiting England, France,
        Switzerland, and Germany. Covers the Democratic Na-
        tional Convention in Baltimore, June 28. Publication of
        The Artist: A Drama Without Words.

1913   Meets publisher Alfred A. Knopf. Covers suffragist parade
        in Washington, D.C., March 3.

1914   Meets and becomes close friends with James Gibbons
        Huneker, influential American critic. Sails to Europe with
        George Jean Nathan and Willard Huntington Wright,
        April. Publication of *Europe After 8:15* with Nathan and
        Wright. First World War begins, July 28–August 4.
        Mencken and Nathan become co-editors of *The Smart*

Set, September. Publishes material from writers including F. Scott Fitzgerald, Edgar Lee Masters, Sherwood Anderson, Willa Cather, Ben Hecht, Eugene O'Neill, and Ezra Pound, as well as British and European writers such as Alexei Tolstoy, Anatole France, D. H. Lawrence, and James Joyce. The book reviews by Mencken, as well as the theater criticism by Nathan, attract wide attention.

1915   German sinking of the British liner *Lusitania* on May 7 increases anti-German sentiment in the United States. First issue of *Parisienne* magazine, edited anonymously with Nathan, is launched (last issue under their editorship will be October 1916). Mencken's pro-German stance become dominant in his increasingly controversial "Free Lance" column, as he scrutinizes the role of the press and examines stories of deliberate propaganda. "The Free Lance" ends abruptly, without explanation, on October 23.

1916   Dreiser's novel *The "Genius"* is suppressed when passages are deemed obscene by the New York Society for the Prevention of Vice. Mencken solicits the support of the Author's League of America for a petition in defense of the book (the novel remains out of circulation until 1922). Launches *Saucy Stories*, which (from August to October) he edits anonymously with Nathan. Publication of *A Book of Burlesques* and *A Little Book in C Major*. Resigns editorship at the *Sun*. Sails to England, December 28; travels to Germany to report on World War I.

1917   Germany commences unrestricted submarine warfare against neutral shipping on February 1. Mencken departs Germany to cover the Liberal revolt in Cuba against the U.S.-supported government of President García Menocal. Arrives in Havana, March 5, and returns to the U.S. on March 14. Stops writing for the *Sun* with publication of last dispatch, March 29. The United States declares war on Germany, April 6. Espionage Act goes into effect June 15. Writes for the New York *Evening Mail* from June 18 to July 8, 1918. Mencken meets James Weldon Johnson, begins to focus attention on African-American and cultural issues. "The Sahara of the Bozart," an indictment of Southern culture, published in the New York *Evening Mail*, November 13. "A Neglected Anniversary," Mencken's comic history of the bathtub, published in the New York *Evening Mail*, December 28. Publication of *A Book of Prefaces*, and of *Pistols for Two*, written with Nathan under the joint pseudonym "Owen Hatteras."

1918   The editor of the New York *Evening Mail*, Edward Rum-
            ley, is arrested July 8 over allegations that the paper re-
            ceived secret German government funding; control then
            passes to pro-war individuals and Mencken stops writing
            for it. (Mencken later reflects, "I stopped writing and
            believed I was done with newspaper work forever.") Ger-
            man language eliminated from Baltimore City Schools,
            July; anti-German feeling rampant. The Bureau of Inves-
            tigation (later the FBI) opens a case file on Mencken; his
            mail is opened and he is watched by agents. Mencken's
            Damn! A Book of Calumny is published by his close
            friend, Broadway producer Philip Goodman, who also
            publishes *In Defense of Women* (later editions published
            by Knopf beginning in 1919). Germany signs armistice,
            November 11.

1919   Publication of *The American Language* (first edition
            quickly sells out) and *Prejudices: First Series*, which also
            proves successful. With *Sun* publishers Paul Patterson and
            Harry Black, Mencken helps develop plan for expanded
            national coverage and an independent approach. Attorney
            General Mitchell Palmer orders mass arrests of radicals
            and foreigners. Mencken becomes increasingly frustrated
            by his work at *The Smart Set*, telling a friend: "We live,
            not in a literary age, but in a fiercely political age."

1920   Begins series of regular Monday columns in the Baltimore
            Evening Sun (they continue until January 31, 1938), regu-
            larly denouncing interference with free speech and calling
            for civil rights for all Americans. Reads manuscript of
            Main Street by Sinclair Lewis and encourages its publi-
            cation. With Nathan, launches *Black Mask*, a mystery mag-
            azine, April. Publication of *Prejudices: Second Series*.
            Publication of *Heliogabalus* and *The American Credo*,
            both written with Nathan. Publication of *The Anti-Christ*
            by Nietzsche, translated with an introduction by Mencken.

1921   Becomes contributing editor of *The Nation*, May (until
            December 1932). Covers the naval disarmament confer-
            ence in Washington, D.C. November-December. Publica-
            tion of the second edition of *The American Language*.

1922   Travels to England and Germany, August-October. Pub-
            lication of *Prejudices: Third Series*.

1923   On May 8, while lecturing at Baltimore's Goucher Col-
            lege, he meets Sara Powell Haardt (born March 1, 1898, in

Montgomery, Alabama), a fiction writer and member of the English faculty. Mencken solicits manuscripts from American writers for a new magazine focusing exclusively on American cultural and political themes, summer. Mencken and Nathan resign as co-editors of *The Smart Set*, December. Publication of the third edition of *The American Language*.

1924   First issue of *The American Mercury* is published in January with Mencken and Nathan as co-editors. Contributors will include Countee Cullen, James Weldon Johnson, W.E.B. Du Bois, Dorothy Parker, Sherwood Anderson, George Schuyler, as well as bricklayers, hoboes, bishops, senators, lawyers, American Indians, prisoners. Its layout, typeface, buoyant tone, and sections "Americana" (items culled from newspapers and magazines across the country) and "Profiles" (portraits written by well-known writers about well-known subjects) are widely imitated. Covers Republican National Convention in Cleveland, June 9–13, and Democratic National Convention in New York City, June 23–29. Writes columns for the Chicago *Tribune* (until January 29, 1928). Publication of *Prejudices: Fourth Series*.

1925   Tension between Nathan and Mencken increases, with Mencken insisting on more social and political commentary in *The American Mercury* and Nathan favoring an equal emphasis on literature. Nathan withdraws as co-editor of *The American Mercury* in July. Mencken travels to Dayton, Tennessee, in July to cover trial of John Scopes, high school teacher arrested for teaching theory of evolution in contravention of newly passed state law. Mother, Anna Abhau Mencken, dies 6 P.M. December 13 and is buried at Loudon Park Cemetery. Publication of *Americana 1925*. The first two books about Mencken are published (*H. L. Mencken* by Ernest Boyd and *The Man Mencken: A Biographical and Critical Survey* by Isaac Goldberg). Breaks friendship with Dreiser, because of a series of misunderstandings, among them Dreiser's seeming lack of sympathy concerning the death of Mencken's mother and Dreiser's callous treatment of women.

1926   Walter Lippmann calls Mencken "the most powerful personal influence on this whole generation of educated people." Through the influence of the New England Watch and Ward Society, the April issue of *The American Mercury* is banned in Boston because of Herbert

Asbury's short story, "Hatrack"; Mencken courts arrest by personally selling a copy to the Society's secretary; a judge declares the story not obscene and dismisses the complaint. Mencken tours the American South and arrives in California, October. Father's cigar factory, August Mencken & Bro., managed by uncle Henry, goes bankrupt. Publication of *Notes on Democracy*, *Prejudices: Fifth Series*, and *Americana, 1926*.

1927   Publication of *Prejudices: Sixth Series* and *Selected Prejudices*.

1928   Travels to Havana, Cuba, to cover Pan American Conference, January. Covers Republican National Convention, Kansas City, June 11–16, and Democratic National Convention, Houston, June 23–39. Travels with Al Smith on campaign tour, October 12–30. Publication of *Menckeniana: A Schimpflexicon*, a humorous collection of anti-Mencken invective that had appeared in newspapers and magazines across the country. Circulation of *The American Mercury* reaches its height of 84,000. Begins courting Sara Powell Haardt on a steadier basis.

1929   Sara Powell Haardt undergoes surgery for the removal of a tubercular kidney, July 6.

1930   Covers London Naval Conference, January–February. Announces secret engagement to Sara Powell Haardt to family members, April. Marries Sara Powell Haardt August 27 at St. Stephen the Martyr Church, Baltimore; they travel to Canada on their honeymoon. Moves to new residence, 704 Cathedral Street, Baltimore. Publication of *Treatise on the Gods*. Book sells well, but stirs controversy because of passage in which Mencken describes Jews as "plausibly the most unpleasant race ever heard of." (Passage is deleted in later editions.) In newspaper interview he denies he is an anti-Semite: "I don't like religious Jews. I don't like religious Catholics and Protestants." Begins writing a diary.

1931   Writes a series of controversial columns against lynching of Matthew Williams in Salisbury, Maryland, on December 4, causing a boycott of Baltimore businesses and the *Sun* papers by residents of the Eastern Shore. The *Nation* recognizes Mencken for "distinguished journalism in the face of personal danger," December.

1932   Mencken sails to the West Indies with Sara, January 9. Covers Republican National Convention in Chicago,

June 13–18, and Democratic National Convention in Chicago, June 26–July 2. Franklin D. Roosevelt elected President, November. Publication of *Making a President*. Continues suggesting authors and ideas for books to his publisher, Alfred Knopf; elected board member of Knopf, Inc.

1933   Mencken becomes increasingly critical of the New Deal, directing most of his criticism against the "quacks" of the Brain Trust rather than the President himself. Writes controversial columns against lynching of George Arnwood in Princess Anne on Maryland's Eastern Shore, October 18 (last lynching in Maryland). With Mencken's popularity at a low ebb, circulation of *The American Mercury* sinks to 28,329; Mencken resigns as editor with the December issue.

1934   Travels on a two-month cruise to the Mediterranean with Sara, January–March, and is fascinated by his visit to Jewish colonists in Palestine; his writing on the subject for the *Evening Sun* is privately printed in a book entitled *Eretz Israel*. Writes series of articles on American English for the New York *American*, July 9–May 20, 1935. Joins Board of Directors of the A. S. Abell Company, October 15. Resumes friendship with Theodore Dreiser. Speaks before the Gridiron Club in Washington, D.C., December 8; his address is mildly critical of the New Deal, but when it is Roosevelt's turn to speak, he turns Mencken's commentary on journalists against him by quoting a passage from *Prejudices: Sixth Series*. Publication of *Treatise on the Right and Wrong*. Last article for *The Nation*, December 12.

1935   Testifies in favor of the Costigan-Wagner Anti-Lynching Bill at Senate hearing, February 14. (Bill is later blocked by Senate filibuster.) Wife Sara Haardt Mencken dies of tubercular meningitis, May 31. Edits a compilation of her work, *Southern Album*; travels to England with his brother August, June 15.

1936   Returns to his family home at 1524 Hollins Street, which he calls "as much a part of me as my two hands." Publishes "Three Years of Dr. Roosevelt," a scathing attack on the President whom he compares to "a snake-oil vendor at a village carnival," in *The American Mercury*, March. *The New Yorker* publishes autobiographical essays, April. Covers Republican National Convention, Cleveland, June 8–13, and Democratic National Convention,

Philadelphia, June 22–28, as well as convention in support of the Townsend Plan (Cleveland, July 14–20) and Union Party convention organized by Father Charles Coughlin (Cleveland, August 13–18). Travels with Republican nominee Alf Landon on his campaign tour, August-October. Publication of the fourth edition of *The American Language*.

1937   Vacations in Daytona Beach, Florida, with his brother August, January. Publication of *The Sunpapers of Baltimore*, written with Frank R. Kent, Gerald W. Johnson, and Hamilton Owens. Publication of *The Charlatanry of the Learned*, edited by Mencken and translated from the Latin by Francis Litz; the book is a satirical attack on academic pretension, written by Mencken's ancestor, Leipzig scholar Johann Burkhard Mencke (1674–1732).

1938   Alarmed by what he sees as the Roosevelt administration's mastery at setting the agenda with the press, Mencken writes publisher Paul Patterson that "we confront a high development of government propaganda," and at Patterson's request becomes temporary editor of the Baltimore *Evening Sun*, January 24–May 9. Writes "Sunday Articles" for the Baltimore *Sun*, May 16–February 2, 1941. Appointed Chairman of the *Sunpapers'* committee to negotiate with the Newspaper Guild, summer. Travels to Germany, June–July; refrains from reporting on any of his observations. Writes column, "Help for the Jews," proposing the United States open its doors to German Jewish refugees fleeing Nazi persecution, November 27, 1938.

1939   Convinced that America's security would depend on America's abstention from European conflict, Mencken becomes increasingly isolationist. In a speech given before the American Society of Newspaper Editors, on April 20, Mencken reminds his audience of government censorship in 1917 and warns that war will once again pose a threat to freedom of the press. Suffers a minor stroke, "generalized arteriosclerosis," July 31. Hitler invades Poland, September 1. England declares war on Germany, September 3.

1940   Covers Republican National Convention in Philadelphia, June 22–29 and Democratic National Convention in Chicago, July 13–19. Travels with Wendell Wilkie on his campaign tour, August 16–November 3. Publication of *Happy Days: 1880–1892*, first of a series of memoirs. Death of best friend, Raymond Pearl, biometrician at the Johns Hopkins University School of Medicine.

1941   Resigns from the *Sun* papers, January 16, because of publishers' unease with his anti-Roosevelt and anti-war views. Begins writing memoir on his journalism career, "Thirty-Five Years of Newspaper Work" (published in 1994). Publication of *Newspaper Days: 1899–1906*. Travels to Havana, April. Helps several Jewish refugees find asylum in the United States; pleads their case in person to the United States State Department, August 26. Japanese attack on Pearl Harbor brings the United States into war, December 7.

1942   Begins writing memoir that focuses on his literary career, "My Life as Author and Editor"; works on it periodically until 1948 (published 1993). Publication of *A New Dictionary of Quotations*.

1943   Testifies in October on behalf of *Esquire* magazine, which had lost its mailing privileges on charges of obscenity. Publication of *Heathen Days: 1889–1906*.

1945   Publication of *The American Language: Supplement I*. The end of World War II officially declared September 2. In the aftermath of Allied bombing, which had appalled him, Mencken sends packages of food, shoes and other necessities to friends in Berlin, copies of his books to correspondents in Japan. Theodore Dreiser dies, December 28.

1946   Publication of *Christmas Story*, a satirical account of a holiday feast among the homeless of Baltimore, and how the organizers impose their Puritanical morality among the crowd.

1947   Buoyed by news of Truman's plans to help the economic recovery of Europe, March; argues for immediate economic rehabilitation of Germany. In August suffers a minor stroke but recovers after a few days. The autobiographical trilogy is published in one volume as *The Days of H. L. Mencken*. Interviewed by Edgar Kemler and William Manchester, who are separately writing biographies of Mencken.

1948   Vacations in Florida with brother August, February. Rejoins *Sun* staff to cover Republican Party Convention, June 19–22; covers Democratic National Convention, July 10–15, and Progressive Party Convention, July 23–26, all held in Philadelphia. Revival of interest in Mencken's life and work demonstrated by cover story in *Newsweek* magazine, April 5. Records an interview for the Library of Congress, June 30. Publication of *The American Language, Supplement II*. Last public appearance speaking before the American Philosophical Society, November 4. Writes series of articles for the *Sun*, August 1–November 9. Publication of last column, arguing against segregation, November 9. Suffers a massive stroke that prevents any further reading or writing for the remainder of his life, November 23. (In his remaining years he is cared for largely by his younger brother August.)

1949   Publication of *A Mencken Chrestomathy*, Mencken's selection from his writings. Spends remaining years helping his secretary organize his papers for posterity, well over 100,000 letters, as well as original manuscripts, memoirs, and books, dedicating the bulk of the collection to the Enoch Pratt Free Library, as well as to the New York Public Library and Dartmouth.

1950   Suffers heart attack, October 12. Members of the Saturday Night Club agree in December to disband permanently. Spends five months in hospital, before he is discharged in March, 1951.

1955   *Inherit the Wind*, play about the Scopes Trial by Jerome Lawrence and Robert E. Lee, featuring a character based on Mencken, opens in April. On Mencken's 75th birthday, Alistair Cooke's edition of *The Vintage Mencken* is published, selling out in two days. Secretary Rosalind Lohrfinck comes across an unpublished manuscript written by Mencken before his 1948 stroke (published posthumously the following year as *Minority Report: H. L. Mencken's Notebooks*).

1956   Dies in his sleep from a coronary occlusion, between 4 and 5 A.M. on January 29, leaving an estate valued at $300,000. Three-fourths of his estate is willed to the Enoch Pratt Free Library. He is cremated, and his ashes are interred at Loudon Park Cemetery, in West Baltimore, January 31.

Note on the Texts

This volume contains the complete texts of H. L. Mencken's *Prejudices: Fourth Series* (1924), *Prejudices: Fifth Series* (1926), and *Prejudices: Sixth Series* (1927). A Library of America companion volume, *Prejudices: The First, Second, and Third Series*, presents the complete contents of the three previous *Prejudices*, published in 1919, 1920, and 1922. The texts of the *Prejudices* have been taken from corrected later printings of the first editions of each collection, all published in New York by Alfred A. Knopf.

Mencken's relationship with Knopf was a congenial one, and he exercised an exceptional degree of control over the form in which his works appeared. He was also a careful proofreader of his own work, and encouraged Knopf (in a letter of March 24, 1921, noting some typographical errors in the first printing of *Prejudices: Second Series*), to "correct all such errors whenever the opportunity offers. Nothing looks worse than a dirty book. The English reviewers in particular, are very waspish about typographical errors." In the case of all of his *Prejudices*, Mencken's corrections to his proofs arrived too late to be incorporated into the first Knopf printings but were made in later printings. The present volume prints the texts of those printings that contain Mencken's final corrections: for *Prejudices: Fourth Series*, the third trade printing (issued in November 1924), for *Prejudices: Fifth Series*, the second trade printing (issued in December 1926), and for *Prejudices: Sixth Series*, the second state of a second limited printing (issued at an undetermined date, but soon after the October 1927 first printing, with Mencken's errata finally incorporated). All of Mencken's *Prejudices* contain material originally published in periodicals—including the Baltimore *Sun* papers, the *Smart Set*, and the *American Mercury*—and then extensively revised when he assembled his books. For a more detailed account of the periodical publication history of individual pieces in the *Prejudices*, see S. T. Joshi, *H. L. Mencken: An Annotated Bibliography* (Lanham, Maryland: Scarecrow Press, 2009).

This volume presents the texts of the printings and typescript chosen for inclusion, but it does not attempt to reproduce nontextual features of their typographic design. The texts are printed without change, except for the correction of typographical errors. Spelling, punctuation, and capitalization may be expressive features, and they are not altered, even when inconsistent or irregular. The following is a list of typographical errors corrected, cited by page and line number:

6.26, *non-sequiturs;* 31.40, beleagured; 33.9, *leit-motif*; 36.38, jucier; 70.33, themometer; 83.11, days; 105.7, statues; 143.22, that the; 150.27, Yoeman; 164.31, made a; 172.15, Brook; 174.32, Stationary; 184.26, *Ladies'*; 201.2, possesion; 212.17, Ashforth.; 219.33, as such; 227.27, T. T; 242.16, scioist; 247.36, white; 253.19, Browne, 257.5, Sinclair,; 260.28, extra-plaint; 275.29, Dr. Martin; 279.34, Apolliñaire's; 284.32, politics, 287.33, *legion*; 287.34, LL. D; 293.12, it it; 309. 6, Antonía,"; 309.6, "Hucklebery; 314.5, *Ladies'*; 314.33, Enforcemnt.; 323.9, venrated; 326.25, not they; 327.20, word; 332.39, resistence; 341.2, Gary,; 343.6, anthor; 391.7, spokesmen; 405.1, Scopes,; 417.1, 16; 418.17, Eric; 426.19, Calydon!"; 432.33, Cooglar,; 443.21, Poteet; 443.28, Sullen,; 445.23, reverence or; 359.10, Karlruhe; 468.8, months; 468.19, dietition; 492.33, ambulent; 494.31, treatment involved; 498.23, maudlingly.

Notes

In the notes below, the reference numbers denote page and line of this volume (the line count includes headings). No note is made for material included in standard desk-reference books. Quotations from Shakespeare are keyed to *The Riverside Shakespeare*, ed. G. Blakemore Evans (Boston: Houghton Mifflin, 1974). Biographical information beyond that included in the Chronology may be found in Marion Elizabeth Rodgers, *Mencken: The American Iconoclast* (Oxford, New York: Oxford University Press, 2005); Marion Elizabeth Rodgers, editor, *Mencken and Sara: A Life in Letters* (New York: McGraw-Hill, 1987); Marion Elizabeth Rodgers, editor, *The Impossible H. L. Mencken: A Selection of His Best Newspaper Stories* (New York: Anchor/Doubleday, 1991); Guy J. Forgue, editor, *Letters of H. L. Mencken* (New York: Knopf, 1961); Carl Bode, editor, *The New Mencken Letters* (New York: Dial Press, 1977); Thomas P. Riggio, editor, *Dreiser-Mencken Letters: The Correspondence of Theodore Dreiser and H. L. Mencken* (Philadelphia: University of Pennsylvania Press, 1986); Edward A. Martin, editor, *In Defense of Marion: The Love Letters of Marion Bloom and H. L. Mencken* (Athens: University of Georgia Press, 1996); Carl Bode, *Mencken* (Carbondale: Southern Illinois University Press, 1969); *Charles Scruggs, The Sage in Harlem: H. L. Mencken and the Black Writers of the 1920s* (Baltimore: Johns Hopkins University Press, 1984); Vincent Fitzpatrick, *H. L. Mencken* (Macon: Mercer University Press, 2004); Fred Hobson, *Mencken: A Life* (New York: Random House, 1994); William Manchester, *Disturber of the Peace: The Life of H. L. Mencken* (Amherst: University of Massachusetts Press, 1986); Terry Teachout, *The Skeptic: A Life of H. L. Mencken* (New York: HarperCollins, 2002); Charles A. Fecher, *Mencken: A Study of His Thought* (New York: Alfred A. Knopf, 1978); Richard J. Schrader, *H. L. Mencken: A Descriptive Bibliography* (Pittsburgh: University of Pittsburgh Press, 1998); and S. T. Joshi, *H. L. Mencken: An Annotated Bibliography* (Lanham, Maryland: Scarecrow Press, 2009).

PREJUDICES: FOURTH SERIES

3.4   William Crary Brownell]   American literary critic (1851–1928), author of *American Prose Masters* (1909), *Standards* (1917), *The Genius of Style* (1924), and other books.

3.7   *Gelehrte*]   Scholars.

3.12   George Creel]   American journalist and publicity director (1876–1953), chairman of the Committee of Public Information (1917–19), created by Woodrow Wilson as a propaganda organization to enlist support for American participation entry in World War I. Thousands of paintings, cartoons, speeches, posters, pamphlets, press releases, news stories, and movies were created, promoting the President's war message.

3.13   Newell Dwight Hillis]   Congregationalist clergyman (1858–1929), pastor of the Plymouth Congregational Church in Brooklyn, New York, from 1899 to 1924. He led a campaign against immorality in Broadway plays and subsequently wrote a number of books decrying alleged German atrocities in World War I.

3.14   James M. Beck]   James Montgomery Beck (1861–1936), lawyer, Solicitor General of the United States (1921–1925), and member of the U.S. House of Representatives (1927–1934); author of *War and Humanity* (1916).

3.14   A. Mitchell Palmer]   American statesman (1872–1936), U.S. attorney general, 1919–21. In November 1919 he initiated a series of raids directed against members of radical groups and others suspected of subversive activities; thousands were arrested, and ultimately 556 individuals were deported.

3.19   *os calcis*]   Heel bone.

4.26   *vibrissae*]   Thick hairs.

4.28   Doughty of Texas]   Walter Francis Doughty (1873–1931), Texas state superintendent of public instruction, 1913–19.

4.35   Beers, of Yale]   Henry Augustin Beers (1847–1926), professor of English literature at Yale, 1871–1926; author of studies of English romanticism.

4.38–39   Science and Health]   *Science and Health with Key to the Scriptures* (1875) by Mary Baker Eddy (1821–1910), founder of the Christian Science movement.

4.40   Marie C. Stopes]   Marie Carmichael Stopes (1880–1958), Scottish campaigner for women's rights and advocate of birth control. She was the author of *Married Love* (1918) and *Wise Parenthood* (1918).

5.4   Waldo Frank]   American novelist and critic (1889–1967), founder and editor of the short-lived but influential magazine *The Seven Arts* (1916–17). His critical and travel writings included *Our America* (1919), *Salvos* (1924), *Virgin Spain* (1926), and *South American Journey* (1943).

5.7   *S4N*]   Monthly magazine edited by Norman Fitts, published 1919–25; its contributors included Kenneth Burke, Waldo Frank, Hart Crane, E. E. Cummings, and others.

6.14   Brander Matthews]   American scholar and playwright (1852–1929), known for his studies of dramatic literature including *The Development of the*

Drama (1904), *Shakspere as a Playwright* (1913), *A Book About the Theater* (1916), and *Principles of Playmaking* (1919).

6.15   Sherman] Stuart P. Sherman (1881–1926), literary critic and professor at the University of Illinois (1907–24), author of *Americans* (1922) and *The Genius of America* (1923).

6.16   Erskine] John Erskine (1879–1951), English professor at Columbia University, 1909–37; author of both scholarly and popular works, including the bestseller *The Private Life of Helen of Troy* (1925).

6.16   Boynton] Percy Holmes Boynton (1875–1946), professor of English at the University of Chicago, author of *American Poetry* (1918), *Some Contemporary Americans* (1924), *The Challenge of Modern Criticism* (1931), and other works.

6.33   Ernest Boyd] Ernest Augustus Boyd (1887–1946), Irish-born critic, essayist, and translator from French and German. He settled permanently in the United States in 1920. His books included *Contemporary Drama of Ireland* (1917) and *Appreciations and Depreciations* (1918). He published a study of Mencken in 1925.

7.7   Donald G. Mitchell] Donald Grant Mitchell (1822–1908), American author popularly known as Ik Marvel. His books included *Reveries of a Bachelor* (1850) and *Dream Life* (1851).

7.8   N. P. Willis] Nathaniel Parker Willis (1806–1867), poet and journalist. Founded the *American Monthly* (1829–31) in Boston and later became a prolific reporter on social matters in the U.S. and abroad for the *New-York Mirror*. His journalism was collected in numerous volumes such as *Pencillings by the Way* (1835) and *Dashes at Life with a Free Pencil* (1845).

7.8   J. G. Holland] Josiah Gilbert Holland (1819–1881), journalist and poet, editor of *Scribner's Monthly* and author of *Timothy Titcomb's Letters to Young People, Single and Married* (1858), *The Marble Prophecy* (1872), and *The Puritan's Guest* (1881).

7.8   Charles Dudley Warner] Essayist, novelist, and popular lecturer (1829–1900), author of *My Summer in a Garden* (1871), *My Winter on the Nile* (1876), *Fashions in Literature* (1902), and other works; co-author with Mark Twain of *The Gilded Age* (1873).

7.8–9   Mrs. Sigourney] Lydia Huntley Sigourney (1791–1865), prolific poet and essayist known abroad as "the American Hemans"; her collections included *Moral Pieces in Prose and Verse* (1815), *Traits of the Aborigines* (1822), and *The Voice of Flowers* (1846).

7.9   the Sweet Singer of Michigan] Julia A. Moore (1847–1920), author of *The Sentimental Song Book* (1876) and *A Few Choice Word to the Public* (1878). Her poetry was widely mocked in the press for its maudlin and inept character; she was satirized by Mark Twain as Emmeline Grangerford in *Adventures of Huckleberry Finn* (1885) and alluded to in *Following the Equator* (1897).

7.18–19   Bayard Taylor]   Poet and travel writer (1825–1878), author of *Poems of the Orient* (1854), *Poems of Home and Travel* (1855), and such travel books as *Eldorado* (1850), *A Journey to Central Africa* (1854), and *Byways of Europe* (1869). His translation of *Faust* was published in two volumes, 1870–71.

7.31   Brandes]   Georg Morris Cohen Brandes (1872–1927), preeminent Danish critic and scholar of his time, a leading proponent of realism, and a prolific commentator on literature, politics, religion, and philosophy. He was the author of many books including *Main Currents in the Literature of the Nineteenth Century* (1872–75) and monographs on Kierkegaard, Ibsen, Nietzsche, and Goethe, among others.

8.9   Griswold]   Rufus Griswold (1815–1857), journalist, editor of literary anthologies including *The Poets and Poetry of America* (1842) and *The Female Poets of America* (1849). He quarreled with Edgar Allan Poe and, as Poe's literary executor, published a defamatory biography that had lingering influence.

8.19   Phelps of Yale]   William Lyon Phelps (1865–1943), literary scholar and professor of English at Yale, who became popular as lecturer and columnist. Author of *Essays on Modern Novelists* (1910), *The Advance of the English Novel* (1916), and other works.

8.22   Van Wyck Brooks' "The Ordeal of Mark Twain"]   Study (1920) by the critic and biographer (1886–1963).

8.29   Huneker]   James Gibbons Huneker (1857–1921), critic of literature, music, and art, a friend of Mencken. He was founder of the magazine *M'lle New York* and musical editor of the New York *Sun*. His many books include *Chopin: The Man and His Music* (1900), *Iconoclasts, a Book of Dramatists* (1905), *Egoists: A Book of Supermen* (1909), *Ivory Apes and Peacocks* (1915), the memoirs *Old Fogy* (1913) and *Steeplejack* (1920), and the novel *Painted Veils* (1920).

8.30–31   Henry van Dyke]   American clergyman, educator, and author (1852–1933), a prolific poet.

10.4   Madison Grant]   Anthropologist and eugenicist (1865–1937), a campaigner for immigration restriction and antimiscegenation laws. His 1916 book *The Passing of the Great Race* argued for the superiority of the "Nordic" race and called for the segregation of other ethnic groups.

10.4   Gertrude Atherton]   San Francisco-born novelist (1857–1948), author of *The Californians* (1898), *The Conqueror* (1902), *Rezánov* (1906), and *Black Oxen* (1923).

17.21   Omdurman]   An Anglo-Egyptian army commanded by Sir Herbert

Kitchener defeated the Mahdist forces in the Sudan at Omdurman on September 2, 1898, killing almost 10,000 Sudanese, while losing only 47 men.

17.21   Manila Bay] At the Battle of Manila Bay (May 1, 1898), the American squadron sank or disabled all ten of the Spanish ships it faced without suffering any damage itself.

18.1   Tannenberg] The Russian 2nd Army was almost completely destroyed by the Germans at the Battle of Tannenberg (August 26–31, 1914), with 50,000 men killed or wounded and 92,000 Russians taken prisoner.

18.5   Verdun] In 1916 the French successfully defended the town of Verdun against a series of German offensives that began on February 21 and lasted until mid-July. The battle continued until December 18, 1916, as the French regained some of the ground they had earlier lost. In the ten months of fighting, 162,000 French and 143,000 German soldiers were killed.

18.15   the Turks . . . in 1922] The Turks decisively defeated the Greek army in Anatolia in 1922.

21.35   Edgar Guest] British-born American poet (1881–1959) whose light and sentimental verse was immensely popular. His collections included *A Heap o' Livin'* (1916), *Just Folks* (1917), and *When Day Is Done* (1921).

21.35   Frank Crane] American Methodist clergyman (1861–1928) whose syndicated inspirational newspaper column appeared across the country from 1909–1928. His writings were collected in ten volumes in *Four-Minute Essays* (1919).

22.6   *Lumbricus terrestris*] Earthworm.

23.10–11   *Bos taurus*] Cow.

24.7–8   *Laborantem agricolam oportet primum de fructibus percipere*] "The husbandman that laboureth must be first partaker of the fruits": 2 Timothy 2:6.

24.10–11   Mesmers] Franz Anton Mesmer (1734–1815), Austrian physician who induced trance states in patients through the power of what he called "animal magnetism."

24.11   Grimaldis] Joseph Grimaldi (1778–1837), famous English clown.

28.8   E. W. Howe] Edgar Watson Howe (1853–1937), Indiana journalist, editor and owner of *E. W. Howe's Monthly* (1911–1937), and author of *The Story of a Country Town* (1883), a realistic treatment of life in the Midwest.

29.36   Volstead Act] The National Prohibition Act of 1919, also known as the Volstead Act after its sponsor, U.S. Representative Andrew John Volstead (1860–1947; R-Minn, 1903–1923).

30.10   Mann Act] The White-Slave Traffic Act of 1910 prohibited the transportation of females across state lines for "immoral purposes." It was named after its sponsor, James Robert Mann (1856–1922), Republican congressman from Illinois.

31.11   Comstock Act]   Law passed by Congress in 1873 which made it illegal to mail, transport, or deliver "obscene, lewd, or lascivious" information. It was named for Anthony Comstock (1844–1915), U.S. Postal Inspector who founded the New York Society for the Suppression of Vice.

32.13   *Eoanthropus*]   Dawn Man.

32.36   *Sus scrofa*]   Wild boar.

32.37   *Mephitis mephitis*]   Skunk.

33.10   Bleases]   Coleman Livingston Blease (1868–1942), governor of South Carolina (1911–15) and U.S. senator (1925–1931) known for his appeals to extreme populism and white supremacy.

36.20   Haeckel]   Ernst Heinrich Haeckel (1834–1919), German biologist and philosopher who published many works helping to popularize evolutionary theory. His books include *The Riddle of the Universe* (1901), *Artforms of Nature* (1904), and *The History of Creation* (1914). He was the author of the subsequently contested formulation that "ontogeny recapitulates phylogeny," summarized here by Mencken as "the history of the individual rehearses the history of the species."

36.36–37   Richard Mansfield]   Richard Mansfield (1854–1907), American actor, educated in England, who had his first major American success in the role of the brutal roué Baron Chevrial in A. M. Palmer's production *A Parisian Romance* (1883).

36.37   Schiller's play]   *Don Carlos* (1787), historical tragedy by Johann Christoph Friedrich von Schiller.

38.23–24   the Henty books]   Boy's historical adventure stories by the British novelist George Alfred Henty (1832–1902), including *Under Drake's Flag* (1883), *With Clive in India* (1884), and *With Wolfe in Canada* (1887).

45.5   *Biertisch*]   Beer table.

49.9   Espionage Act]   The Espionage Act, passed on June 15, 1917, included among its provisions severe penalties (up to $10,000 fine and twenty years' imprisonment) for persons found guilty of interfering with the draft or encouraging disloyalty to the United States. More than 1,500 persons were arrested for violating the act, including labor leader Eugene Debs and Socialist congressman Victor Berger, and several newspapers were barred from the mails, among them the *New York Call* and *Milwaukee Leader*.

50.5   Anti-Saloon League]   Organization, founded in Ohio in 1893, that played a major role in lobbying for Prohibition.

51.9   Liberty Loan]   One of a series of five bond issues floated by the U.S. Treasury Department that helped finance World War I.

51.22   the Chicago Socialist trials]   On September 5, 1917, a raid was conducted by federal authorities on the national headquarters of the American Socialist Party in Chicago. Among those indicted under the provisions of the Espionage Act was Victor L. Berger, a congressman from Wisconsin. On February 20, 1919, Berger and four other members of the party were sentenced to twenty years in prison; their conviction was overturned by the Supreme Court on January 31, 1921.

51.26   Burleson]   Albert S. Burleson (1863–1937), who served as U.S. postmaster general from 1913–21. During World War I he vigorously enforced the Espionage Act by attempting to bar radical and anti-war materials from the mails.

51.27   Hand, J.]   In July 1917 federal district judge Billings Learned Hand (1872–1961) ruled in New York that *The Masses* should not be barred from the mail under the Espionage Act.

51.27   Rose, J.]   John Carter Rose (1861–1927) was a federal district judge in Maryland, 1910–22, and a federal circuit judge, 1922–27.

52.22   judge who sentenced Debs]   David C. Westenhaver (1865–1928), U. S. Federal judge in Cleveland, Ohio sentenced Socialist labor leader Eugene V. Debs (1855–1926) to ten years in prison for violating the Espionage Act, on the basis of a speech Debs made on June 16, 1918, in Canton, Ohio, in opposition to World War I. His sentence was commuted by President Harding in 1921.

61.40   "Way Down East"]   Enormously successful play by Lottie Blair Parker, first produced by Florenz Ziegfeld in 1898.

61.40   Ben Hur]   Dramatization by William W. Young, first produced in 1899, of Lew Wallace's novel *Ben-Hur: A Tale of the Christ* (1880).

62.4   Char-Freitag music]   The Good Friday music in act 3, scene 1 of Richard Wagner's opera *Parsifal* (1882).

63.23   *Stammhalter*]   Ancestor.

67.11   *Cavia Cobaya*]   Guinea pig.

67.12–13   Hey-Rub-a-Dub-Dub]   Essay (1918) by Theodore Dreiser, submitted to Mencken at *The Smart Set* but rejected.

67.29–30   Helmuth von Moltke]   German field marshal (1800–1891), chief of staff of the Prussian army, 1857–87, during successful wars against Denmark (1864), Austria (1866), and France (1870–71).

67.35   Shonts, Yerkes, or Jim Fisk]   Theodore P. Shonts (1856–1919), chairman of the Second Isthmian Canal Commission (1905–19) and president of the Interborough Rapid Transit Co., New York City (1907–19); Charles E. Yerkes (1839–1905), financier, model for the protagonist of Dreiser's novels *The Financier* and *The Titan*; James Fisk (1834–1872), stock-market speculator.

69.32   I.W.W.]   Industrial Workers of the World, popularly known as "Wobblies," revolutionary international labor union founded in Chicago in 1905.

72.20   Babbitt]   Conformist, middle-class booster, from George F. Babbitt, the protagonist of Sinclair Lewis's 1922 novel *Babbitt*.

72.29   *Katzenjammer*]   Hangover.

73.7   Bishop Manning]   William Thomas Manning (1866–1949), Episcopal bishop of New York, 1921–46.

73.7   John Roach Straton]   American Baptist clergyman (1875–1929) who upheld fundamentalist and anti-evolutionist tenets in a series of debates with Charles Francis Potter, 1923–24, and published his remarks in *The Famous New York Fundamentalist Modernist Debates: The Orthodox Side* (1925). He led anti-Catholic opposition to the presidential candidacy of Al Smith.

77.4   Bela Kun]   Béla Kun, Hungarian revolutionary and politician (1886–1938), founder (1918) of the Hungarian Communist Party and leader (March–August 1919) of the short-lived Hungarian Soviet Republic. Kun fled to Soviet Russia in 1920 and became a prominent figure in the Comintern. He was arrested in June 1937 during the Great Purge and shot in August 1938.

80.15   Henry H. Rogers]   American financier and Standard Oil executive (1840–1909) who helped save Twain from financial ruin.

82.7   Harrison Anti-Narcotic Act]   The Harrison Anti-Narcotic Act of 1914 imposed registration and record-keeping requirements to control the distribution of opiates and cocaine.

82.26   Joaquin Miller]   Pseudonym of Cincinnatus Heine Miller (1837–1913), American poet and essayist, author of *Song of the Sierras* (1871).

84.2   *Totentanz*]   Dance of the Dead.

91.6   Hansa towns]   Refers to the Hanseatic League, a trade monopoly exercised by collusion between cities and guilds on Europe's northern coast.

92.21   Nick Carter and Old Sleuth]   Dime novel detective heroes. Nick Carter first appeared in *The Old Detective's Pupil* (1886) and was then featured in his own magazine, *Nick Carter Weekly*; many of his adventures were first-person narratives published under the pseudonym Nick Carter. Old Sleuth, created by Harlan Halsey, made his first appearance in *Fireside Companion* in 1872, and later was featured in *Old Sleuth Library*.

93.12–13   Ned Buntline]   Pseudonym of Edward Zane Carroll Judson (1823–1886), publisher and author of dime novels, among them those popularizing the exploits of "Buffalo Bill" Cody.

95.34   Anthony Comstock]   See note 31.11.

98.40   *Todsäufer*]   In *Happy Days* (1940), Mencken wrote: "A *Todsäufer* (literally, dead-drinker) was, and is a sort of brewer's customers' man. He is commonly called a collector, but his duties go far beyond collecting the bills owed to breweries by saloonkeepers. He is supposed to stand a general treat in the bar whenever he calls, to go to all weddings, birthday parties and funerals in the families of saloonkeepers, and to cultivate their wives and children with frequent presents . . . He is also one of the brewery's political agents, and must handle all the license difficulties of his clients."

99.13   Nicholas Murray Butler] American educator and diplomat (1862–1947), president of Columbia University, 1902–45, and president of the Carnegie Endowment for International Peace, 1925–45. He was active in various international peace conferences in the years preceding World War I.

103.9   *wie Gott im Frankreich*] *Leben wie Gott in Frankreich*: to live like a king.

106.12   Mr. Fall] Albert B. Fall (1861–1944), U.S. secretary of the interior, 1921–3. He resigned his office when it was disclosed that he had accepted bribes to transfer naval oil reserves (including the Teapot Dome reserve in Wyoming) to private oil operators in exchange for loans and without competitive bidding. Fall was convicted in 1929, and served a year in prison.

107.29   Denby, Secretary of the Navy] Edwin Denby (1870–1929), U. S. secretary of the navy, 1921–24), advised President Harding to transfer the administration of naval oil reserves (including those at Teapot Dome, Wyoming) to the Department of the Interior. Although not accused of corruption, Denby resigned on March 10, 1924.

108.3–4   Czolgosz] Leon Czolgosz (1873–1901), Detroit-born anarchist and assassin of President William McKinley.

109.40   Mr. Daugherty] Harry M. Daugherty (1860–1941), Republican party boss and U.S. attorney general under President Harding. He resigned in 1924 after coming under investigation for a kickback scheme, although he was eventually acquitted at trial.

116.2   *Veritas Odium Parit*] Truth begets hatred.

116.6   *et cognoscetis veritatem, et veritas liberabit vos*] And ye shall know the truth, and the truth shall make you free (John 8:32).

118.20   Lake Mohonk Conference] The Lake Mohonk Conference for International Arbitration, founded by Albert K. Smiley in 1895 to support the establishment of an international court. The annual conference took place in Lake Mohonk, New York from 1895 to 1916.

119.31–32   James Anthony Froude] English historian (1818–1894), author of *History of England from the Fall of Wolsey to the Defeat of the Spanish Armada* (1856–70), and biographer of Thomas Carlyle. His *The Knights Templars: Their Rise and Demise* was published in 1886.

120.5–6   *Schnorrer* and *Meshulachim*] Scroungers and charity collectors (sometimes perceived as fraudulent).

123.17   William McDougall] (1871–1938), professor of psychology at Harvard; he was interested in psychical research and eugenics, and diverged from orthodox Darwinian theory. He was the author of *The Group Mind* (1920).

133.15   Burns] William J. Burns (1861–1932), director of the Bureau of Investigation, 1921–24.

134.11   Stinnes] Hugo Stinnes (1870–1924), German industrialist and politician.

135.10–11   E. L. Godkin] Edwin Lawrence Godkin (1831–1902), founder and editor of *The Nation*.

135.11   Charles J. Bonaparte] Charles Joseph Bonaparte (1851–1921) served as Theodore Roosevelt's secretary of the navy (1905–1906) and U.S. attorney general (1906–09), in which capacity he founded the Bureau of Investigation.

136.26   Judge Gary] Elbert Henry Gary (1846–1927), president of U.S. Steel, 1901–27. Having served two terms as a county judge, 1884–92, he was commonly known as "Judge Gary."

141.37   "Atalanta in Calydon"] Verse drama (1865) by Algernon Charles Swinburne.

142.29–30   "Geschichten aus dem Wiener Wald"] *Tales from the Vienna Woods.*

146.20   Cosima Liszt-von Bülow] Cosima Wagner (1837–1930), daughter of Franz Liszt. Her first marriage to Hans von Bülow ended in divorce in 1869; she married Richard Wagner in 1870.

150.20   Admiral Gherardi] Rear Admiral Bancroft Gherardi (1832–1903).

150.23   Fighting Bob Evans] Robert Dunglison Evans (1846–1912), American naval officer.

150.23   Lillian Russell] American actress and singer (1861–1922), who became a star in the 1880s and retired from the stage in 1919.

150.25   Sampson-Schley controversy] The controversy involved credit for the American naval victory at the Battle of Santiago in July 1898; William T. Sampson was technically in command, but Commander Winfield S. Schley received popular credit for the victory.

150.29   Amos Rusie] Major League Baseball pitcher (1871–1942), known as the Hoosier Thunderbolt.

150.31   Admiral Sims] Rear Admiral William S. Sims (1858–1936).

151.27   Josephus Daniels] American journalist (1862–1948) and U. S. secretary of the navy, 1913–21.

153.14   Dwight L. Moody] American evangelist (1837–1899).

159.29   *Omnis homo mendax*] All men are liars.

168.1   Fergusson's "Capitol Hill,"] Novel (1923) by Harvey Fergusson (1890–1971), drawing on his experiences as a Washington reporter during the Taft and Wilson administrations.

168.12–13   Hamilton Wright Mabie] American essayist and lecturer (1846–1916), editor of the Christian magazine *The Outlook*; his books included *Books and Culture* (1896), *The Life of the Spirit* (1899), and *American Ideals, Character and Life* (1913).

168.18   Harriet Monroe] American poet (1860–1936), who founded *Poetry: A Magazine of Verse* in 1912, and edited it until her death. Contributors under her editorship included Ezra Pound, Wallace Stevens, Robert Frost, T. S. Eliot, Marianne Moore, Hart Crane, and many other major figures.

168.22   Augustus Thomas] Playwright (1857–1934) known for his use of American backgrounds in such plays as *Alabama* (1891), *In Mizzoura* (1893), *The Witching Hour* (1907), and *The Copperhead* (1918).

168.22–23   David Belasco] Playwright and theater producer (1853–1931), involved in more than a hundred Broadway productions. As a producer he was notable for technical advances in lighting and stage design. His plays included *Madame Butterfly* (1900) and *The Girl of the Golden West* (1905).

168.23   Clyde Fitch] Playwright (1865–1909) whose successes included *Barbara Frietchie* (1899), *The Climbers* (1901), and *Captain Jinks of the Horse Marines* (1901).

168.24   Hergesheimer] Joseph Hergesheimer (1880–1954), novelist whose many books, widely popular and in their time often critically acclaimed, included *The Three Black Pennys* (1917), *Java Head* (1919), and *Cytherea* (1922). He was a close friend of Mencken.

168.25   Cabell] James Branch Cabell (1878–1958), novelist whose works often explored a world of medieval fantasy. His books included *The Cream of the Jest* (1917), *Jurgen* (1919), which became a bestseller when it was denounced for obscenity, *Figures of Earth* (1921), and *The High Place* (1923).

168.28   Richard Harding Davis] Journalist and novelist (1864–1916). His novels included *Soldiers of Fortune* (1897); his war reporting was collected in many volumes including *Cuba in War Time* (1897), *The Cuban and Porto Rican Campaigns* (1898), *With Both Armies in South Africa* (1900), and *Notes of a War Correspondent* (1910).

168.28–29   Robert W. Chambers] Artist and bestselling author (1865–1933), best remembered for *The King in Yellow* (1895).

168.29   James Lane Allen] Novelist (1849–1925) best known for his local color stories set in Kentucky, including *A Kentucky Cardinal* (1894), *The Choir Invisible* (1897), and *The Mettle of the Pasture* (1903).

168.34   Paul Elmer More] Critic and philosopher (1864–1937) associated with the New Humanist movement. His *Shelburne Essays* were published in fourteen volumes (1904–36), and his other works included *Platonism* (1917), *The Religion of Plato* (1921), and *The Christ of the New Testament* (1924).

169.2   Hamlin Garland] Author (1860–1940) of fiction, memoirs, and poems, known for his realistic studies of farm life in Wisconsin. His early stories, collected in *Main-Travelled Roads* (1891) and *Boy Life on the Prairie* (1899), were followed by the autobiographies *A Son of the Middle Border* (1917) and *A Daughter of the Middle Border* (1921).

169.5   Mary Roberts Rinehart] Fiction writer and playwright (1876–1958), author of many mystery novels including *The Circular Staircase* (1908), *Where There's a Will* (1912), and *The Case of Jennie Brice* (1913). With Avery Hopwood she wrote the long-running mystery play *The Bat* (1920).

169.8   William Lyon Phelps] Literary scholar (1865–1943) and professor of English at Yale, who became popular as lecturer and columnist. Author of *Essays on Modern Novelists* (1910), *The Advance of the English Novel* (1916), and other works.

169.16   Edward E. Rose] Playwright (1862–1939) best known for his stage adaptations of popular novels, including *The Prisoner of Zenda* (1895), *David Harum* (1900), and *Richard Carvel* (1900).

169.27   Huneker] See note 8.29.

172.4   Winston Churchill] American novelist (1871–1947), author of historical novels including *Richard Carvel* (1899), *The Crisis* (1901), *The Crossing* (1904), and *Coniston* (1906).

172.4   Floyd Dell] Novelist and playwright (1887–1969), editor of *The Masses* (1914–17) and *The Liberator* (1918–24).

172.8   Charles W. Eliot] American academic (1834–1926) who began his long tenure as president of Harvard in 1869.

172.11   Fuller] Henry Blake Fuller (1857–1929), American novelist whose novels of Chicago included *The Cliff-Dwellers* (1893), *With the Procession* (1895), and *On the Stairs* (1918).

172.15   Otto Braun] The diaries, letters, and poems of Braun (1897–1918), a German soldier killed near Amiens in April 1918, were published in English in 1924.

175.34   Dunkards] Members of the German Baptist Brethren.

PREJUDICES: FIFTH SERIES

181.27   Volstead Act]   See note 29.36.

183.31   Postal Act . . . Comstock]   See note 31.11.

184.24   *Godey's Lady's Book*]   American monthly magazine, 1830–98, influential on taste and fashion. It was published in Philadelphia by Louis A. Godey, and edited from 1837 to 1877 by Sarah Josepha Hale.

184.36   John S. Sumner]   Sumner, a lawyer, succeeded Comstock as acting secretary of the Society for the Suppression of Vice in 1915.

185.2   "Three Weeks"]   Novel (1907) by Elinor Glyn (1864–1943), about an affair between a Balkan queen and an English aristocrat.

186.21–22   Sylvanus Stall]   Lutheran minister (1847–1915), author of books on sex such as *What A Young Boy Ought to Know* and *What a Young Woman Ought to Know*.

187.27   Jurgen]   Novel (1919) by James Branch Cabell, which became a bestseller when it was denounced for obscenity.

187.28   The 'Genius']   Novel (1915) by Theodore Dreiser; it was withdrawn from sale by the publisher after the New York Society for the Suppression of Vice declared it lewd and profane.

187.28   Mlle. de Maupin]   *Mademoiselle de Maupin*, novel (1835) by Théophile Gautier.

189.12   Anti-Saloon League]   See note 50.5.

190.29–30   Leopold-Loeb trial]   In 1924, Nathan Leopold (1904–1971) and Richard Loeb (1905–1936) were tried and convicted for the murder of Bobby Franks. Defense lawyer Clarence Darrow's summation asked that they be spared the death penalty; they each received a sentence of life imprisonment.

194.24   Venezuela episode]   In a note sent to the British government on July 20, 1895, Secretary of State Richard Olney stated that the dispute between Great Britain and Venezuela over the boundary of British Guyana fell under the Monroe Doctrine and should be settled by arbitration. After Lord Salisbury, the British prime minister and foreign secretary, rejected arbitration, President Cleveland sent a message to Congress on December 17 in which he proposed the creation of a commission to determine the boundary and warned that the United States would treat a British refusal to accept the new boundary as an act of aggression. The resulting crisis lessened when Joseph Chamberlain, the British colonial secretary, described a possible Anglo-American war as "an absurdity" on January 24, 1896. Britain and Venezuela agreed on February 2, 1897, to submit the dispute to arbitration, and a settlement was reached in 1899.

196.34–35   *Hexentanz*]   Witches' dance.

198.27–28   *durch componiert*] Through-composed.

199.12   Prof. Dr. Jadassohn] German composer and professor Salamon Jadassohn (1831–1902).

200.8–9   Benavente . . . Tagore] Jacinto Benavente y Martinez (1866–1954), Spanish dramatist (Nobel Prize, 1922); Verner von Heidenstam (1859–1940), Swedish poet (1916); Karl Adolph Gjellerup (1857–1919), Danish poet and novelist (1917); Rabindranath Tagore (1861–1941), Hindu poet (1913).

200.27   Hergesheimer] See note 168.24.

200.29–30   Lindley Murray] Scottish-American grammarian (1745–1826), author of grammar textbooks widely circulated in England and in the United States during the early 1800s.

203.1   La Belle Ettarre . . . Felix Kennaston] Characters in James Branch Cabell's *The Cream of the Jest* (1917).

205.5   Sam Slick] Humorous sketches collected in *The Clockmaker, or, The Sayings and Doings of Samuel Slick of Slickville* (1837) by Thomas Chandler Haliburton (1796–1865).

209.5   George H. Boker] George Henry Boker (1823–1890), poet and verse dramatist, author of *The Lessons of Life* (1848), *Poems of the War* (1864), and the play *Francesca da Rimini* (1855).

214.14   Peruna] Patent medicine marketed as a panacea by the Ohio physician Samuel Brubaker Hartman.

216.2   Mary Baker G. Eddy] See note 4.38–39.

216.2–3   Czolgosz] See note 108.3–4.

216.11   John W. Davis] Politician, lawyer, and diplomat (1873–1955), congressman from West Virginia (1911–13), solicitor general and ambassador to the United Kingdom under President Wilson, Democratic candidate for president in 1924.

216.14   Champ Clark] James Beauchamp Clark (1850–1921), U.S. congressman from Missouri who served as speaker of the house, 1911–19. He lost the Democratic presidential nomination in 1912 when William Jennings Bryan shifted his support to Woodrow Wilson.

217.27   Samuel Gompers] American union leader (1850–1924), founder of the American Federation of Labor.

217.35   Scopes case] John Scopes (1900–1970) was tried for violation of a recently passed Tennessee law against teaching the theory of evolution in tax-supported schools. The state's case was argued in court by William Jennings Bryan, while Scopes was represented by Clarence Darrow. Scopes was convicted and fined $100; the conviction was later reversed on technical grounds by the Tennessee supreme court.

224.24   Caliph Omar] In an account now regarded as apocryphal, Caliph Umar Ibn al-Khattab is said to have burned the Library of Alexandria in 640 on the grounds that if its contents agreed with the Koran they were superfluous and if they contradicted it they were heretical.

225.39   Ellis] Henry Havelock Ellis (1859–1939), English scientist and man of letters who studied the psychology and sociology of sex. His books included *The New Spirit* (1890), *Man and Woman* (1894), and the seven-volume *Studies in the Psychology of Sex* (1897–1928).

225.39   Moll] Albert Moll (1862–1939), German psychiatrist, a pioneer in the study of sexuality; author of *The Sexual Life of the Child* (1908).

227.23   Andy Gump] Protagonist of *The Gumps*, comic strip created by Sidney Smith in 1917.

228.17   Raffs] Joseph Joachim Raff (1822–1882), German-Swiss composer and pianist.

229.5   Korngolds] Erich Wolfgang Korngold (1897–1957), Austrian composer and conductor whose opera *Die Tote Stadt* premiered in 1920. Korngold later became an influential composer of Hollywood soundtracks.

229.21   Kulmbacher] German beer.

230.18–19   Bishop Manning] See note 73.7.

235.24   Graafian follicle] Fluid-filled cavity protecting the developing egg-cell in the ovary of a mammal.

237.31   *Veritas liberabit vos!*] The truth shall set you free (John 8:32).

242.6–7   Francis Asbury] Methodist Episcopal Bishop (1745–1816), a founder of the church in the United States, noted for the power of his preaching.

242.7   Jabez Bunting] English Wesleyan minister (1779–1858).

242.8   Robert Strawbridge] Irish immigrant who organized a Methodist church in Pipe Creek, Maryland, before the American Revolution.

242.15   *Blasmusik*] Brass music.

243.3   viewed from a tree] That is, seen from the viewpoint of Zacchaeus: a tax collector too short to see Jesus in the midst of a crowd, he climbed up a tree to do so (Luke 19:1–10).

244.5   Brisbane] Arthur Brisbane (1864–1936), influential editor and columnist for the Hearst newspapers.

244.5   Frank Crane] See note 21.35.

244.6   Mutt and Jeff] Daily comic strip created in 1907 by Bud Fisher (1885–1954).

244.24   Billy Sunday]   American evangelist (1862–1935), who gave up a career as a professional baseball player to become one of the most influential preachers of the early twentieth century.

247.29   Bossuet]   Jacques Bénigne Bossuet (1627–1704), bishop and renowned orator.

247.34   William Graham Sumner]   American economist, sociologist and educator (1840–1910), author of *Folkways* (1907). *The Forgotten Man and Other Essays* was published in 1919. The title essay opens: "The type and formula of most schemes of philanthropy or humanitarianism is this: A and B put their heads together to decide what C shall be made to do for D. The radical vice of all these schemes, from a sociological point of view, is that C is not allowed a voice in the matter, and his position, character, and interests, as well as the ultimate effects on society through C's interests, are entirely overlooked. I call C the Forgotten Man."

252.37   Robert Andrews Millikans]   Robert Andrews Millikan (1868–1953), experimental physicist, recipient of the 1923 Nobel Prize. He was a proponent of the need to reconcile science and religion.

253.24–25   John P. Altgeld]   German-born American politician (1847–1902), governor of Illinois, 1892–97. He was a leader of the Progressive movement and a supporter of workplace and labor reforms.

253.27   Raisuli]   Ahmed ibn-Muhammed Raisuli (1875?–1925), Berber insurgent who kidnapped several British and American citizens (including Ion Perdicaris and Walter Harris, correspondent for the London *Times*) in 1904. Theodore Roosevelt sent warships to Tangier and the slogan "Perdicaris Alive or Raisuli Dead" became a rallying cry for the Republican Party. Perdicaris was ultimately ransomed by the government of Morocco.

253.29   Wayne B. Wheeler]   Wayne Bidwell Wheeler (1869–1927), general counsel of the Anti-Saloon League of America (1915–1927).

253.29   McNamara Brothers]   James and John McNamara, members of the ironworkers union, were accused of bombing the offices of the anti-union *Los Angeles Times* in 1910, killing twenty-one employees. In 1911 James pled guilty to the newspaper bombing and was sentenced to life, while John received a sentence of 15 years after pleading guilty to the bombing of an iron works.

253.31   La Follette of 1917]   Wisconsin Senator Robert Marion La Follette (1855–1925) was an outspoken opponent of American entry into World War I, military conscription, and the Espionage Act.

254.1   Charlie Ross]   Charles Ross (born 1870) was abducted and held for ransom in Germantown, Pennsylvania, in 1874. Since he never was found, nor his remains recovered, rumors of sightings went on for years, and his name became a catchphrase.

254.5   *Gelehrte*]   See note 3.7.

254.29   Chicago anarchists]   In 1893 Governor John P. Altgeld pardoned
three of the eight defendants convicted of the Haymarket bombing of May 1,
1886. Four other defendants had already been executed, and one had committed suicide in his cell.

254.34   Pullman strike]   In 1894 President Cleveland sent 2,000 federal
troops to Chicago to put down a strike of Pullman railcar workers led by Eugene V. Debs. Thirteen strikers were killed, fifty-seven were wounded, and
Debs was imprisoned for defying a court injunction against the strike.

255.40   Dr. Crapsey]   Algernon Sidney Crapsey (1847–1927), Episcopal
clergyman from New York. He was convicted of heresy by an ecclesiastical
court in 1906 after delivering a lecture stressing the humanity of Jesus in a
fashion deemed contrary to literal Biblical interpretation.

256.26   *Stammvater*]   Ancestor.

257.35   Beers]   Henry A. Beers (1847–1926), an authority on English
romanticism.

257.36   Matthews]   See note 6.14.

259.35   Karl Ludwig]   Carl Friedrich Wilhelm Ludwig (1816–1895), German physiologist, a pioneer in cardiovascular research.

259.35   Jowett]   Benjamin Jowett (1817–1893), scholar and classicist,
Master of Balliol College at Oxford. His commentary on the epistles of St.
Paul (1855) stirred great controversy.

261.15   *Freiheitskrieg*]   War of liberation.

270.12–13   Dr. La Follette's vaporous schemes]   During the 1924 presidential campaign, Senator Robert M. La Follette, candidate for the Progressive Party, called for government ownership of railroads and utilities,
cheap credit for farmers, an end to imperialism in Latin America, and the out-
lawing of child labor.

272.29   Harris Dickson]   Lawyer and novelist (1868–1946), author of *The
Black Wolf's Breed* (1899) and *Lady Resolute* (1902).

273.11   John Sharp Williams]   Mississippi politician (1854–1932), U.S. senator, 1911–23.

274.12   Creel Press Bureau]   See note 3.12.

275.26   ORISON SWETT MARDEN]   American writer (1850–1924) associated with the New Thought movement, and author of self-help books
emphasizing the power of positive thinking in order to achieve success, including *The Secret of Achievement* (1898), *Cheerfulness as a Life Power* (1899),
and *The Hour of Opportunity* (1900).

275.29–30   Frank A. Munsey] American author and publisher (1854–1925), owner of the New York *Evening Sun* and *Evening Telegram*, *Munsey's Magazine*, and *Argosy All-Story Weekly*.

276.19   "Pushing to the Front"] *Pushing to the Front, or, Success Under Difficulties* was published in 1894.

276.31   James Oliver Curwood] Author of adventure stories (1878–1927), such as *The Courage of Captain Plum* (1908), *The Danger Trail* (1910), and *Back to God's Country* (1920).

277.10   Judge Elbert Gary] See note 136.26.

278.15   Matthew Josephson] American writer (1899–1978), author of *Zola and His Time* (1928) and other works; he edited the magazine *Secession* (1922–24), and was later a co-editor of *Broom*.

278.18–19   Ernest Boyd] See note 6.33.

278.23   *Broom*] Literary magazine established in Rome in 1921 by Harold Loeb and Alfred Kreymborg, and later edited in New York by Mathew Josephson, Slater Brown, and Malcolm Cowley. Its contributors included Sherwood Anderson, E. E. Cummings, William Carlos Williams, Conrad Aiken, and Jean Toomer.

278.23   *Little Review*] Literary quarterly, 1914–29, founded by Margaret Anderson and edited by her with Jane Heap. It was among the most influential magazines of its time, publishing W. B. Yeats, Ernest Hemingway, T. S. Eliot, Djuna Barnes, and Hart Crane. Its serialization of James Joyce's *Ulysses*, 1918–21, led to the editors being fined for obscenity.

278.25–26   Baroness Elsa von Freytag-Loringhoven] Poet and artist (1874–1927), born Elsa Hildegard Plötz in present-day Poland; she emigrated to the United States in 1910 and married the Baron von Freytag-Loringhoven in 1913. Her poems were published in *The Little Review* and other magazines; she became notorious for her outlandish appearance and extreme behavior. She returned to Europe in 1923 and died of asphyxiation in her Paris apartment three years later.

278.30–31   Paul Elmer More] See note 168.34.

278.33–34   Fred Lewis Pattee] Literary scholar (1863–1950), professor at Pennsylvania State College. His *History of American Literature Since 1870* appeared in 1915, followed by *The New American Literature, 1890–1930* (1930) and *The Feminine Fifties* (1940).

279.5   Eugène Sue] French novelist (1804–1857), author of long, serially published novels such as *The Mysteries of Paris* (1843) and *The Wandering Jew* (1845).

279.11   *Dial*] *The Dial*, major literary magazine of the 1920s, edited successively by Scofield Thayer and Marianne Moore; it published a wide range of international writers including D. H. Lawrence, T. S. Eliot, Ezra Pound, W. B. Yeats, Thomas Mann, and Sherwood Anderson.

279.30   Paul Morand] French writer and diplomat (1888–1976), author of fiction including *Open All Night* (1922) and *Closed All Night* (1923).

279.30   Harry Kemp] American poet and prose writer (1883–1960) who wrote about his travels as a hobo in *Tramping on Life* (1922) and other works.

279.31   André Salmon] French poet and art critic (1881–1969).

279.31   Maxwell Bodenheim] American poet and novelist (1893–1954).

281.19   Tupper] Martin Tupper (1810–1889) English author whose *Proverbial Philosophy* (1837), a collection of didactic and moral reflections, went through many editions in Great Britain and the United States.

285.5   Felicia Hemans] English poet (1793–1835) whose many volumes of verse included *The Forest Sanctuary* (1825) and *Songs of the Affections* (1830). She is best remembered for the poem "Casabianca."

285.5   Fanny Fern] Pseudonym of Sara Payson Willis (1811–1872), popular American writer of essays and children's books. Her books included *Fern Leaves from Fanny's Portfolio* (1853) and the novel *Ruth Hall* (1855).

286.30   *Aufklärung*] Enlightenment.

291.38   Edmund Clarence Stedman] Poet and critic (1833–1908). He edited *An American Anthology, 1787–1899* (1900), an influential survey of American poetry. He also co-edited, with Ellen M. Hutchinson, the eleven-volume *Library of American Literature 1880–1890* (1889–90) and, with George Woodberry, a ten-volume edition of Poe's works.

291.38   Richard Watson Gilder] Poet (1844–1909), editor of the *Century*, 1881–1909.

292.20   Max O'Rell] Pseudonym of Léon Paul Blouet (1848–1903), French writer best known for his travel books beginning with *John Bull and His Island* (1883).

292.20   Blasco Ibañez] Vicente Blasco-Ibáñez (1867–1928), Spanish novelist, author of *Blood and Sand* (1908) and *The Four Horsemen of the Apocalypse* (1916).

292.32–33   William C. Brownell] See note 3.4.

292.33   Augustus Thomas] See note 168.22.

292.33   Hamlin Garland] See note 169.2.

292.33–34   Owen Wister] Novelist (1860–1938), author of *The Virginian* (1902) as well as the memoir *Theodore Roosevelt: The Story of a Friendship* (1930).

292.34   Henry van Dyke]   See note 8.30–31.

293.12   Henry Sydnor Harrison]   Novelist (1880–1930), a frequent contributor to *Atlantic Monthly*. His works included *Queed* (1911), *V. V.'s Eyes* (1913), and *Angela's Business* (1915).

293.13   Clayton Hamilton]   Critic, playwright, and producer (1881–1946), who wrote theatrical criticism for various magazines including *Bookman* (1910–18), *Everybody's Magazine* (1911–13) and *Vogue* (1912–20).

293.15   Robert W. Chambers]   See note 168.28–29.

293.16   Herman Hagedorn]   American author (1882–1964) whose poetry was collected in *A Troop of the Guard* (1909), *Poems and Ballads* (1912), and other volumes. He was a close friend of Theodore Roosevelt, of whom he published a biography in 1918. He also published the novels *Faces in the Dawn* (1914) and *Barbara Picks a Husband* (1918).

293.25   Gerhart Hauptmann]   German playwright (1862–1946), author of *The Weavers* (1892), *The Beaver Coat* (1893), *The Sunken Bell* (1896), and many other works. He won the Nobel Prize for Literature in 1912.

293.27   A. Lawrence Lowell]   Abbott Lawrence Lowell (1856–1943), professor of government at Harvard (1900–1909) and president of Harvard (1909–1933).

293.28   Otto Kahn]   Investment banker and financier (1867–1934), a leading patron of the arts.

293.36   Nicholas Murray Butler]   See note 99.13.

294.2   Tex Rickard]   George Lewis Rickard (1871–1929), boxing promoter.

294.13   Frank Munsey]   See note 275.29–30.

294.15   Max Eastman]   Author and journalist (1883–1969), editor of *The Masses* (1913–1917) and *The Liberator* (1918–1922).

299.24–25   Terence V. Powderly]   American labor leader (1849–1924), head of the Knights of Labor, 1879–93.

300.21   William Wrigley, Jr.]   Industrialist (1861–1932), manufacturer of chewing gum and developer of Catalina Island off Los Angeles.

305.22–23   Alfred Kreymborg]   American poet (1883–1966), editor of the magazine *Others* (1917–20). His poetry was collected in *Mushrooms* (1916), *Scarlet and Mellow* (1926), and other volumes, and his autobiography *Troubador* appeared in 1925. He later edited numerous anthologies including *The American Caravan* (1927–36) and *Lyric America* (1930).

306.3–4   Potash . . . One-Eye Feigenbaum]   Characters from *Potash and Perlmutter* (1913) by Montague Glass; see note 309.34.

306.6   *Schnecken*]   Snails.

306.23–24   *Schön ist die Jugendzeit; sie kommt nicht mehr!*]   "Beautiful is youth; it will not return!": traditional German lyric.

309.6   Abraham Cahan]   Novelist and editor (1860–1951). He was the longtime editor of the *Jewish Daily Forward* and author of *Yekl: a Tale of the New York Ghetto* (1896) and *The Rise of David Levinsky* (1917).

309.34   Montague Glass]   English-born playwright and story writer (1877–1934), known for stories about Jewish businessmen dramatized as *Potash and Perlmutter* (1913), *Business Before Pleasure* (1917), and *His Honor Abe Potash* (1919).

310.15–16   Harvey Fergusson's "Capitol Hill"]   See note 168.1.

312.3   William Z. Foster]   Labor leader and politician (1881–1961). He organized the steelworkers' strike of 1919 and in 1921 joined the American Communist Party, serving as its general secretary, 1921–30, and chairman, 1945–56.

314.4   the Fox Sisters]   Three sisters from Hydeville, New York, who beginning in the late 1840s acquired a reputation for mediumistic abilities manifested through mysterious rappings. At the height of their celebrity they attracted support from many prominent figures, notably Horace Greeley. In 1888 Margaret Fox published a confession (later recanted) that the rappings had been faked.

314.5   Dr. Munyon]   James M. Munyon, manufacturer of patent medicines.

314.5   Godey of the *Lady's Book*]   See note 184.24.

314.5–6   Daniel Drew]   American financier, (1797–1879).

314.18–19   E. W. Howe's "The Story of a Country Town."]   See note 28.8.

315.6   Wayne B. Wheeler]   See note 253.29.

315.6   Billy Sunday]   See note 244.24.

323.3   Barrett Wendell]   American scholar (1855–1921), professor at Harvard and author of *A Literary History of America* (1900).

323.4   M. A. DeWolfe Howe]   Mark Anthony DeWolfe Howe (1864–1960), prolific author, biographer of John Jay Chapman, Oliver Wendell Holmes, and other New England figures; editor of *Youth's Companion* and *Atlantic Monthly*.

325.8   Sir Arthur Quiller-Couch]   English man of letters (1863–1944), sometimes known by the pen name "Q", author of many books including *On the Art of Reading* (1920).

325.39   Aldrich]   Thomas Bailey Aldrich (1836–1907), American poet, novelist, editor, author of *The Story of a Bad Boy* (1870).

325.39   Blaine]   James G. Blaine (1830–1893), American politician who served as congressman, senator, and secretary of state, and was a dominant figure in the Republican Party after the Civil War. He was defeated by Grover Cleveland in the 1884 presidential race.

327.11   Walter Prichard Eaton]   Drama critic (1878–1957), author of *The American Stage of Today* (1908) and *Plays and Players* (1916).

331.12   E. L. Godkin]   See note 135.10–11.

332.6   Villard]   Oswald Garrison Villard (1872–1949), journalist, editor and owner of *The Nation*, 1918–32.

335.6   Mr. Secretary Denby]   See note 107.29.

335.6–7   Falls and Dohenys]   Fall, see note 106.12; Edward L. Doheny (1856–1935), California oilman implicated in the Teapot Dome Scandal.

335.7   Mr. Secretary Wilbur]   Curtis Dwight Wilbur (1867–1954), U.S. secretary of the navy, 1924–29.

335.7–8   Josephus Daniels]   See note 151.27.

336.30   Cathcart case]   Vera, Countess of Cathcart, was denied entry into the United States in 1926 on grounds of adultery. (She had left her husband, the Earl of Cathcart, and taken up with the Earl of Craven.) A judge eventually ruled that she could stay in the United States; her play *Ashes of Love* had a brief run on Broadway in 1926.

339.22   John Roach Straton]   See note 73.7.

343.2   Edgar Saltus]   American writer (1855–1921), author of *The Philosophy of Disenchantment* (1885), *The Anatomy of Negation* (1886); novels including *Mr. Incoul's Misadventure* (1887), *The Truth about Tristrem Varick* (1888), *The Pace That Kills* (1889), *The Pomps of Satan* (1904), and *The Perfume of Eros* (1905); and works of popular history including *Mary Magdalen* (1891), *Imperial Purple* (1892), and *The Orgy* (1920, later retitled *Imperial Orgy*).

343.14   Percival Pollard]   Joseph Percival Pollard (1869–1911), German-born literary critic, a close friend of Mencken; he was educated in England and emigrated with his family to the United States in 1885. He was a frequent contributor to *The Criterion* (New York). His books included *Their Day in Court* (1909) and *Masks and Minstrels of New Germany* (1911).

346.6   Gertrude Atherton]   See note 10.4.

348.4   *Jack Ketch*]   Public executioner during the reign of Charles II.

351.37   Col. Goethals]   George Washington Goethals (1858–1928), chief engineer of the Panama Canal and governor of the Canal Zone until 1916; he was promoted to major general in 1915.

351.38   Col. Gorgas]   William Crawford Gorgas (1854–1920), U.S. Army surgeon general; as chief sanitary officer of the Panama Canal Commission (1904–1913), helped suppress yellow fever so that the canal could be completed.

352.19   Bleases]   See note 33.10.

352.19   Mayfields]   Earle Bradford Mayfield (1881–1964), U.S. senator, 1923–29.

352.19   Slemps]   Campbell Bascom Slemp (1870–1943), U.S. congressman from Virginia, 1907–22.

352.20   Peays]   Austin Peay (1876–1927), governor of Tennessee, 1923–27.

352.20   Vardamans]   James Kimble Vardaman (1861–1930), governor of Mississippi, 1904–8, and U.S. senator, 1913–19.

355.29   Hiram Johnson]   American politician (1866–1945), governor of California, 1911–17, and U.S. senator, 1917–45.

355.30   Williams Gibbs MacAdoo]   Lawyer and politician (1863–1941), secretary of the Treasury, 1913–18, and U.S. senator from California, 1933–38.

PREJUDICES: SIXTH SERIES

366.31   Johannes Müller]   German physiologist and comparative anatomist (1801–1858).

368.31   Heywood Broun]   American journalist (1888–1939), sportswriter, drama critic, and author of the syndicated column "It Seems to Me." He was the founder of the American Newspaper Guild.

368.33   Snyder trial]   Ruth Brown Snyder (1895–1928) was tried, convicted, and executed, along with her lover Henry Judd Gray, for the 1927 murder of her husband Albert Snyder.

370.1–2   news from China in the early part of 1927]   In March 1927 Chinese Nationalist troops in Nanjing attacked the British, American, and Japanese consulates, leading to the shelling of the city by British and American warships.

370.3   Miami hurricane of 1926]   A hurricane devastated Miami, Florida during September 17–18, 1926, killing 373 people.

372.29   Cyrus H. K. Curtis]   Cyrus Hermann Kotzschmar Curtis (1850–1933), American publisher, founder of the Curtis Publishing Co., publisher of *Ladies' Home Journal*, *The Country Gentleman*, and *The Saturday Evening Post.*

372.30   Frank A. Munsey]   See note 275.29–30.

372.33   Hearst papers] By the end of 1922, newspaper publisher William Randolph Hearst (1863–1951) was the owner of twenty daily papers and eleven Sunday papers in thirteen of the largest American cities. He also owned two wire services, King Features (the largest of the comic strip syndicates), six American magazines, a newsreel (Hearst Metronome News), and a motion picture production company. His chain of newspapers included the San Francisco *Examiner*, Boston *American*, New York *American*, New York *Mirror*, and the New York *Journal*.

372.34   Scripps-Howard newspapers] Newspaper chain founded as the E. W. Scripps Company by Edward Willis Scripps (1854–1926).

373.11   Brisbane] See note 244.5.

373.15   Cox] James Middleton Cox (1857–1957), newspaper publisher and politician. He served as Ohio congressman and governor of Ohio (1913–15, 1917–21), and was the Democratic presidential nominee in 1920, losing to Warren G. Harding. He published the *Dayton Daily News* and founded the newspaper company Cox Enterprises.

381.17   Lady Cathcart] See note 336.30.

382.6   Whitney case] Charlotte Anita Whitney (1867–1955), suffragist and radical political organizer, a member of the Communist Labor Party, was charged with criminal syndicalism in 1919 after working to establish the American Communist Party. Her conviction was upheld by the Supreme Court in 1927.

382.6   Kollontai case] In November 1926 Secretary of State William Kellogg denied an entry visa to Alexandra Kollontai (1872–1952), the new Soviet ambassador to Mexico, because of her involvement with "the International Communist subversive movement." (The United States did not establish diplomatic relations with the Soviet Union until 1933.)

384.33   Thackeray's Louis XIV] See "Meditations at Versailles," *The Paris Sketch Book* (1840).

386.17   Senator Wheeler] In 1924, an investigation led by Senator Burton K. Wheeler of Montana (1882–1975) into Attorney General Harry Daugherty's failure to prosecute government officials in the Teapot Dome Scandal led to Daugherty's resignation. One month later, a federal grand jury in Montana indicted Senator Wheeler on charges involving his private law practice. Wheeler called for a Senate investigation of the charges, claiming an attempt by the Justice Department to discredit him; he was finally acquitted of all charges.

386.19   O'Leary case] Jeremiah O'Leary, editor of *The Bull*, an Irish Nationalist newspaper opposed to American participation in what it called "England's war," was indicted in 1918 under the Espionage Act for allegedly receiving funds from the German government. He was acquitted in March 1919.

386.21   Fatty Arbuckle]   Roscoe Conkling "Fatty" Arbuckle (1887–1933), silent film comedian, was tried three times for manslaughter in the death of Virginia Rappe, whom he was accused of raping at a party he hosted in 1921. Although Arbuckle was eventually acquitted and received an apology from the jury for what they considered a gross injustice, his career was destroyed.

390.15–16   Professor Oppenheimer]   Franz Oppenheimer (1864–1943), German sociologist and political economist, author of *The State* (1914) and *The Idolatry of the State* (1927).

397.16   Penrose]   Senator Boise Penrose (1860–1921), Pennsylvania congressman 1897–1921, a champion of protective tariffs and pro-business legislation.

400.16   Rostand's "Chantecler."]   Play (1910) by French dramatist Edmond Rostand (1868–1918).

400.32   Edgar Albert Guest]   See note 21.35.

401.3   *Non in solo pane vivit homo.*]   Man does not live by bread alone (Matthew 4:4).

404.3   January 16, 1920]   The date when Prohibition went into effect.

405.1   "Only a Boy"]   Erotic story attributed to the poet Eugene Field (1850–1895).

414.37   Sylvanus Stall]   See note 186.21–22.

417.21–22   Upton Sinclair]   Novelist (1878–1968) who became famous with the publication of *The Jungle*, an exposé of conditions in the Chicago stockyards, in 1906. (It was originally serialized in the Socialist newspaper *The Appeal to Reason*.) His many other books included *The Metropolis* (1908), *King Coal* (1917), *Oil!* (1927), and *The Wet Parade* (1931).

417.28   Albert Abrams]   Self-proclaimed healer (1863–1924) who falsely claimed he had a medical degree from the University of Heidelberg and who marketed a machine called the Dynomizer which he asserted could diagnose any known disease. His defenders included Upton Sinclair and Arthur Conan Doyle. The American Medical Association mounted a successful campaign to debunk his claims.

417.39   A. Mitchell Palmer]   See note 3.14.

418.36   the Single Tax]   Economic theory propounded by Henry George (1839–1897) in *Progress and Poverty* (1879) and other works, advocating a tax on land. Hamlin Garland's novel *Jason Edwards: An Average Man* (1892) was written in support of the Single Tax.

419.10   Lucy Stone]   American suffragist (1818–1893).

424.1   Vachel Lindsay] American poet (1879–1931), author of *General William Booth Enters into Heaven* (1913), *The Congo* (1914), *The Chinese Nightingale* (1917), and other collections.

424.11–12   James Weldon Johnson] Writer and diplomat (1871–1938), editor of *The Book of American Negro Poetry* (1921) and *The Book of American Negro Spirituals* (1925), author of *The Autobiography of an Ex-Colored Man* (1912), *God's Trombones* (1927), *Black Manhattan* (1930), and other works, including "Lift Every Voice and Sing."

429.22   Billy Sunday] See note 244.24.

429.23   John Roach Straton] See note 73.7.

430.12   Adam-Zad] See Rudyard Kipling's "The Truce of the Bear" (1898), in which the bear represents Russia: "Make ye no truce with Adam-zad—the Bear that walks like a man!"

430.22   Peckniff, Chadband or Elmer Gantry] Pecksniff, villain who makes a show of piety in Dickens' *Martin Chuzzlewit* (1843–44); Chadband, pompous and hypocritical clergyman in Dickens' *Bleak House* (1852–53); Elmer Gantry, barnstorming evangelist who is the title character of Sinclair Lewis's 1927 novel.

430.25   Charles Gallaudet Trumbull] American writer (1872–1941), author of *Anthony Comstock, Fighter: Some Impressions of a Lifetime of Adventure in Conflict with the Powers of Evil* (1913).

431.10–11   Frances E. Willard] Educator (1839–1898) who campaigned for temperance and suffrage.

431.11   Daniel Drew] See note 314.5–6.

431.17   C.E.M. Joad] Cyril Edwin Mitchinson Joad (1891–1953), British philosopher and pacifist, author of *Common Sense Ethics* (1921), *Common Sense Theology* (1922), and *Guide to Modern Thought* (1933).

431.21   Filippo G. Bruno] Giordano Bruno (1548–1600), Dominican friar who was burned at the stake for heresy by the Roman Inquisition. His many works on philosophy, cosmology, and mnemonics included *The Art of Memory* (1582), *The Ash Wednesday Supper* (1584), and *On the Infinite Universe and Worlds* (1584).

431.22   *Se non è vero, è ben trovato.*] If it is not true, it is a good invention.

431.33   J. Gordon Coogler] James Gordon Coogler (1865–1901), South Carolina-born poet, whose *Purely Original Verse* was published in five editions between 1891 and 1897.

432.28–29   Charlie Schwab] Charles Schwab (1862–1939), steel industry magnate, chief executive of Bethlehem Steel, known for his lavish spending.

433.13   Hamilton Wright Mabie]   See note 168.12–13.

433.16–17   Gloria Swanson and Jack Gilbert]   Gloria Swanson (1889–1983), silent movie star whose films included *Male and Female* (1919), *Manhandled* (1924), and *Sadie Thompson* (1928); John Gilbert, silent movie star who appeared frequently with Greta Garbo, in such films as *Flesh and the Devil* (1926) and *A Woman of Affairs* (1928).

433.31–32   Aimée Semple McPherson]   Popular evangelist (1890–1944) who founded the International Church of the Foursquare Gospel in Los Angeles.

434.12–13   Montague Summers]   English scholar (1880–1948), author of *Jane Austen, An Appreciation* (1919). His later works on demonology and related matters would include *The Vampire, His Kith and Kin* (1928), *The Black Mass* (1936), and *A Popular History of Witchcraft* (1937).

434.20   Robert Andrews Millikan]   See note 252.37.

436.13–14   Bishop Manning]   See note 73.7.

436.16   William N. Guthrie]   Rector of St. Mark's-in-the-Bouwerie in New York.

436.32   Saorstát]   Free state (Irish).

438.20–21   George B. M. Harvey]   Journalist and publisher (1864–1928), editor of *The North American Review*, 1899–1926, and *Harper's Weekly*, 1901–13.

441.29   Mooney of Memphis]   Charles Joseph Patrick Mooney (1865–1926), managing editor (1908–1923), then owner (1923–1924) of the Memphis *Commercial Appeal*. He won the 1923 Pulitzer Prize for his relentless editorializing against the Ku Klux Klan.

441.31–32   Hall of Montgomery]   Grover Cleveland Hall (1888–1941), editor of the Montgomery (Alabama) *Advertiser*, who won the 1928 Pulitzer Prize for his editorials against racial intolerance

441.32   Wright of Columbia]   R. Charlton Wright, editor of the Columbia (South Carolina) *Record*.

441.32   Jaffe of Norfolk]   Louis I. Jaffe, editor of the Norfolk *Virginian-Pilot*, 1919–50.

441.33   Dabney of Richmond]   Virginius Dabney (1901–1995), editor of the Richmond *Times-Dispatch.*

441.37   Johnson of Greensboro]   Gerald White Johnson (1890–1980), journalist, editor, and novelist from North Carolina; Mencken enlisted him to write for the Baltimore *Evening Sun.*

441.38   Harris of Columbus, Ga.]   Julian LaRose Harris (1874–1963) and his wife Julia Collier Harris (1875–1967) were owners and editors of the

Columbus (Georgia) *Enquirer-Sun*. It won the 1926 Pulitzer Prize for public service (the first small city daily to be so recognized) for their stance against lynching, the Ku Klux Klan, and legislation banning the teaching of evolution in Georgia schools.

442.2 Frances Newman] Novelist (1883–1928), author of *The Gold-Fish Bowl* (1921), *The Hard-Boiled Virgin* (1926) and *Dead Lovers Are Faithful Lovers* (1928). At the time of her death Newman was suffering from severe and painful vision problems.

442.2 Nell Battle Lewis] Lawyer (1893–1956) and newspaper columnist for the Raleigh *News and Observer*.

442.2–3 Sara Haardt] Sara Powell Haardt (1898–1935), short story writer from Montgomery, Alabama, who married H. L. Mencken in 1930.

442.10 Emily Clark] Emily Tapscott Clark (1893–1953), Virginia-born writer, author of *Stuffed Peacocks* (1927), and founder and editor of the literary magazine *The Reviewer*.

442.11 Mrs. Julia Peterkin] Julia M. Peterkin (1880–1961), fiction writer who wrote about the Gullah region of her native South Carolina. Her novels included *Black April* (1927) and *Scarlet Sister Mary* (1928), for which she won the Pulitzer Prize.

442.11 T. S. Stribling] Tennessee-born writer (1881–1965), author of *Birthright* (1921) and winner of the 1933 Pulitzer Prize for *The Store*.

442.12 Clement Wood] Alabama-born poet and novelist (1888–1950), author of *The Glory Road* (1936).

442.12 J. W. Krutch] Joseph Wood Krutch (1893–1970), esssayist and critic, author of *Edgar Allan Poe: A Study in Genius* (1926), *The Modern Temper* (1929), *The Measure of Man* (1954), and *The Desert Year* (1952).

442.26 John R. Neal] Controversial law professor at the University of Tennessee, who was one of seven professors dismissed in 1923 for, among other reasons, liberal views on evolution.

442.37 Peay] See note 352.20.

443.3 Walter Hines Page] American journalist and diplomat (1855–1918), U. S. ambassador to Britain, 1913–18.

443.4 William E. Dodd] Historian (1869–1940), author of *Woodrow Wilson and His Work* (1920) and editor, with Ray Stannard Baker, of *The Public Papers of Woodrow Wilson* (1924–26).

443.5 John Spencer Bassett] Historian (1867–1928), author of *The Life of Andrew Jackson* (1911), *A Short History of the United States* (1913), and *Our War with Germany* (1919).

443.5   W. P. Trent]   Scholar (1862–1939), professor of English at Columbia University, author of *A History of American Literature, 1607–1865* (1903).

443.6   Ashby Jones]   Professor at Atlanta University.

443.11   Gerald W. Johnson]   See note 441.37.

443.12   Paul Y. Anderson]   Reporter (1893–1938) for the St. Louis *Post-Dispatch*; his investigative stories helped expose the Teapot Dome Scandal during the Harding administration.

443.19–20   W. L. Poteat]   William Louis Poteat (1856–1938), president of Wake Forest College in North Carolina (1905–1927), controversial for his acceptance of the theory of evolution.

443.20   John D. Wade]   Georgia-born literary critic (1892–1963), a participant in the Vanderbilt Agrarian movement along with John Crowe Ransom, Allen Tate, and Robert Penn Warren; he was the author of *Augustus Baldwin Longstreet: A Study of the Development of Culture in the South* (1924).

443.20   Paul Green]   North Carolina-born playwright (1894–1981), winner of 1927 Pulitzer prize for *In Abraham's Bosom*.

443.20   Howard W. Odum]   Sociologist (1884–1954), founder of the journal *Social Forces* at Chapel Hill, and author of several novels.

443.27   Clark Howell]   Journalist (1863–1936), editor in chief of the Atlanta *Journal Constitution*.

443.27   Douglas Freeman]   Douglas Southall Freeman (1886–1953), editor of the Richmond *News Leader*, 1915–49, and author of multivolume biographies of Robert E. Lee and George Washington.

443.28   Sullens, of Mississippi]   Frederick Sullens (1877–1957), editor of the Jackson (Mississippi) *Daily News* from 1904 on.

443.30–31   Bishop Candler]   Warren Akin Candler (1857–1941), bishop of the Methodist Episcopal Church, president of Emory University, and author of *The History of Sunday Schools* (1880).

446.19   Albert Jay Nock]   Social critic and political theorist (1873–1945), co-editor of *The Freeman*, 1920–24, and author of *The Myth of a Guilty Nation* (1922), *The Freeman Book* (1924), *Our Enemy, the State* (1935), and other works.

447.20   Alton B. Parker]   Lawyer and judge (1852–1926), Democratic presidential nominee in 1904.

447.20   Jimmie Cox]   See note 373.15.

447.21   W. G. McAdoo]   See note 355.30.

447.21   Cole Blease]   See note 33.10.

447.21   Ma and Pa Ferguson]   Miriam Amanda Wallace "Ma" Ferguson (1875–1961), first female governor of Texas, 1924–27 and 1933–35. The unusual number of pardons granted during her first term led to accusations of bribes and kickbacks. Her husband, James Edward "Pa" Ferguson (1871–1944), Texas governor 1915–17, was removed from office by impeachment.

447.21–22   John W. Davis]   See note 216.11.

447.22   Tom Taggart]   Thomas Taggart (1856–1929), Democratic national committeeman, 1904–16.

449.25   Howard A. Kelly]   Howard Atwood Kelly (1858–1925), professor of gynecology and obstetrics at Johns Hopkins and gynecological surgeon at Johns Hopkins Hospital. A strict religious fundamentalist, he kept a prayer book naming individuals whose souls he prayed for; topping the list was H. L. Mencken.

452.29   Paul Elmer More]   See note 168.34.

452.30   Bliss Perry]   Literary critic (1860–1954), teacher, and editor of the *Atlantic Monthly* (1899–1909).

452.32   Paul Shorey]   Classical scholar (1857–1934), author of *The Idea of Good in Plato's Republic* (1895).

452.33   Brander Matthews]   See note 6.14.

452.35   Henry van Dyke]   See note 8.30–31.

453.1   Robert Underwood Johnson]   Writer and diplomat (1853–1937), author of *The Winter Hour* (1891) and *Poems of War and Peace* (1916). He served as U.S. Ambassador to Italy, 1920–21.

453.3   William M. Sloane]   Educator and historian (1850–1928), author of *The French War and the Revolution* (1893) and *The Life of Napoleon Bonaparte* (1896).

453.5   William Crary Brownell]   See note 3.4.

453.30   *cabotin*]   Ham actor.

453.31   George Arliss]   English actor (1868–1946) whose stage career began in the 1880s. Among his best-known vehicles (later brought to the screen) were *Disraeli* and *The Green Goddess*.

453.32   Edith Wynne Matthison]   English actress (1875–1955) who appeared in New York in the early 1900s in *Everyman* and *As You Like It*.

463.22   Ziehrer]   Karl Michael Ziehrer (1843–1922), Austrian composer

463.23   Lincke]   Paul Lincke (1866–1946), German composer.

476.5   an article]   "A Neglected Anniversary."

476.10–11   *Stammvater*]   Ancestor.

478.9–10   Hans Vaihinger]   German philosopher (1852–1933), author of *The Philosophy of As If* (1911). He was a leading scholar of the work of Kant.

481.9   Mary Ware Dennett]   American pacifist (1872–1947) and advocate of birth control, who was indicted in 1928 under the Comstock Law for distributing her pamphlet "The Sex Side of Life."

485.34   John Roach Straton]   See note 73.7.

487.13–14   Felix Riesenberg's "East Side, West Side"]   Novel (1927) by engineer Felix Riesenberg (1879–1939).

487.30   John Paleologus]   Byzantine Emperor (1332–1391).

490.30   Andrew T. Still]   Physician (1828–1917), founder of the American School of Osteopathy in 1892.

491.1   Dr. Abrams]   See note 417.28.

491.7   Palmer]   Daniel David Palmer (1845–1913), founder of the Palmer School of Chiropractic (1897).

513.25   Bernarr Macfadden]   Publisher (1868–1955), a proponent of body-building and nutritional diets.

516.3–4   Edgar Saltus]   See note 343.3.

516.35   Ludwig Thoma]   Bavarian novelist, story writer, and playwright (1867–1921).

518.23–24   Ella Wheeler Wilcox]   American poet (1850–1919). Her poetry was collected in over twenty volumes including *Poems of Passion* (1883), *Poems of Pleasure* (1888), *Poems of Power* (1901), and *Poems of Sentiment* (1906). For some years she published a daily poem as a syndicated newspaper feature.

518.34–35   George Sterling]   American poet (1869–1926), leader of an artistic and literary circle in Carmel, California; a close friend of Mencken. His books included *A Wine of Wizardry* (1909), *The House of Orchids* (1911), and *The Caged Eagle* (1916).

518.36   Herman George Scheffauer]   San Francisco-born poet and playwright (1878–1927), an associate of Ambrose Bierce and George Sterling; his poetry collection *Looms of Life* was published in 1908. He moved to Germany in 1910 and committed suicide in 1927 after murdering his female secretary.

523.7   Stanley Walker]   Journalist (1898–1962), author of *The Night Club Era* (1933).

526.4   Bob Ingersoll]   Robert Greene Ingersoll (1833–1899), politician and orator, known as an advocate of agnosticism.

526.7–8   George B. M. Harvey]   See note 438.20–21.

527.2   Dwight L. Moody]   See note 153.14.

536.36   one of the pictures I saw lately]   *Masks and Faces* (1918), of which the New York *Herald Tribune* wrote: "Never before has such an aggregation of notables been seen on the screen."

538.33   Peaches Browning]   After a brief marriage, Manhattan teenager "Peaches" Browning, born Frances Belle Heenan (1910–1956), filed for divorce in January 1927 from her fifty-two-year-old husband, real-estate mogul Edward West Browning (1875–1934). The divorce proceedings brought to light his eccentric behavior and were widely publicized.

539.15–16   Joe Hergesheimer]   See note 168.24.

539.16   Jim Quirk]   James R. Quirk, publisher and editor of *Photoplay.*

539.16   Johnny Hemphill]   John Mickle Hemphill (1891–1951) practiced as an attorney in Philadelphia; ran as a "wet" Democratic candidate for governor in 1930. His first cousin Dorothy (née Hemphill) was married to Mencken's friend Joseph Hergesheimer, who dedicated *The Three Black Pennys* to John.

539.16   Jim Tully]   Hobo and writer (1891–1947), author of *Emmett Lawler* (1922) and *Beggars of Life* (1924); he was a frequent contributor to *The American Mercury.* He settled in California in 1912.

539.16–17   Walter Wanger]   Hollywood producer (1894–1968) who after serving in World War I began working for Jesse Lasky at Paramount, and went on to produce films ranging from *The Cocoanuts* (1929) to *Cleopatra* (1963).

542.40   The Last Laugh]   German silent film (1924), starring Emil Jannings and directed by Friedrich Wilhelm Murnau (1888–1931).

546.28   Diego Valdez]   See Rudyard Kipling, "The Song of Diego Valdez" (1902).

Index

THE LIBRARY OF AMERICA SERIES

The Library of America fosters appreciation and pride in America's literary heritage by publishing, and keeping permanently in print, authoritative editions of America's best and most significant writing. An independent nonprofit organization, it was founded in 1979 with seed money from the National Endowment for the Humanities and the Ford Foundation.

To subscribe to the series or to order individual copies,
please visit www.loa.org or call (800) 964.5778.

This book is set in 10 point Linotron Galliard,
a face designed for photocomposition by Matthew Carter
and based on the sixteenth-century face Granjon. The paper
is acid-free lightweight opaque and meets the requirements
for permanence of the American National Standards Institute.
The binding material is Brillianta, a woven rayon cloth made
by Van Heek-Scholco Textielfabrieken, Holland. Compo-
sition by Dedicated Business Services. Printing by
Malloy Incorporated. Binding by Dekker Book-
binding. Designed by Bruce Campbell.

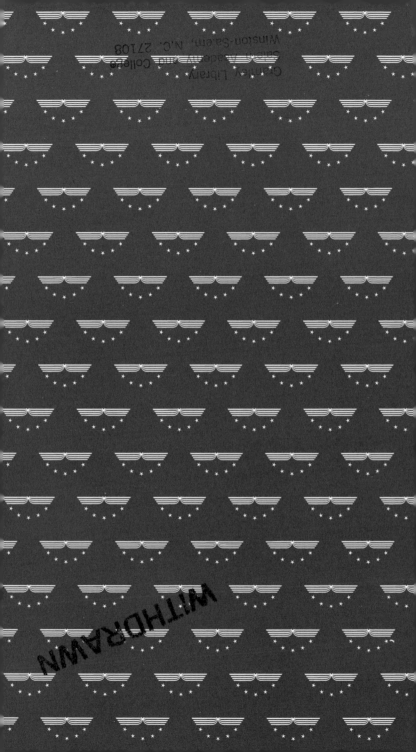